Statutory Authorities for Special Purposes

I0028291

ENGLISH LOCAL GOVERNMENT VOLUME 4

Statutory Authorities for Special Purposes

WITH A SUMMARY OF THE DEVELOPMENT OF LOCAL GOVERNMENT STRUCTURE

SIDNEY and BEATRICE WEBB

With a new Introduction by
B. KEITH-LUCAS

Routledge
Taylor & Francis Group

First published in 1922 by Longmans Green & Co.

This edition first published in 2018 by Routledge
2 Park Square, Milton Park, Abingdon, Oxon, OX14 4RN
and by Routledge
52 Vanderbilt Avenue, New York, NY 10017, USA

Routledge is an imprint of the Taylor & Francis Group, an informa business

© 1922 by Taylor and Francis

Publisher's Note
The publisher has gone to great lengths to ensure the quality of this reprint but points out that some imperfections in the original copies may be apparent.

Disclaimer
The publisher has made every effort to trace copyright holders and welcomes correspondence from those they have been unable to contact.
A Library of Congress record exists under ISBN: 42000428

ISBN 13: 978-0-367-14364-0 (hbk)
ISBN 13: 978-0-367-14365-7 (pbk)
ISBN 13: 978-0-429-03156-4 (ebk)

ENGLISH LOCAL GOVERNMENT

STATUTORY AUTHORITIES FOR
SPECIAL PURPOSES

ENGLISH LOCAL GOVERNMENT

A series of eleven volumes on the growth
and structure of English Local Government
by SIDNEY and BEATRICE WEBB

VOLUME 1   The Parish and the County.

VOLUMES 2 and 3   The Manor and the Borough.

VOLUME 4   Statutory Authorities for Special Purposes.
With a new introduction by B. KEITH-LUCAS
which is included in Volume 1. *The Parish and the County.*

VOLUME 5   The Story of the Kings Highway.
With a new introduction by G. J. PONSONBY.

VOLUME 6   English Prisons Under Local Government.
Including a long preface by G. B. Shaw.
With a new introduction by L. RADZINOWICZ.

VOLUME 7   English Poor Law History, Part 1.
The Old Poor Law.

VOLUMES 8 and 9   English Poor Law History.   Part 2.
The Last Hundred Years.   Volumes 1 and 2.

*VOLUME 10   English Poor Law Policy.
With a new introduction by W. A. ROBSON
which is included in Volume 7, *English Poor Law History, Part 1,
The Old Poor Law.*

*VOLUME 11   The History of Liquor Licensing in England.

*Volumes 10 and 11 were originally published separately, but are now
included to make the scope of the work more comprehensive.

Statutory Authorities for Special Purposes

WITH A SUMMARY OF THE DEVELOPMENT OF LOCAL GOVERNMENT STRUCTURE

SIDNEY and BEATRICE WEBB

With a new Introduction by
B. KEITH-LUCAS

*Senior Lecturer in Local Government
in the University of Oxford*

FRANK CASS AND CO. LTD.
1963

First published by Longmans Green & Co. in 1922

This edition published by FRANK CASS & Co., 10, Woburn Walk, London, W.C.1., by the kind permission of the Trustees of the Passfield Estate.

First published   1922
Reprinted   1963

Printed in Great Britain by
Thomas Nelson and Sons Ltd, Edinburgh

PREFACE

To most people, if not to all, the chief interest of this book will lie in the last two chapters, which analyse the development of English Local Government from the Revolution to the Municipal Corporations Act. This description of how the " Old Principles " were, between 1689 and 1835, gradually superseded by the " New Principles " summarises the contents, not merely of the present volume on *Statutory Authorities for Special Purposes*, but also of our two preceding works, *The Parish and the County* (1907), and *The Manor and the Borough* (1908). The three together complete our account of the structure of English Local Government.[1]

The Statutory Authorities for Special Purposes—the Commissioners of Sewers, the Incorporated Guardians of the Poor, the Turnpike Trusts and the Improvement Commissioners—have not previously been made the subject of historical study. We do not know whether our taste is peculiar, but we have found it interesting, and even exciting, to trace the origin and explore the development of the " Lords of the Level of Romney Marsh," and the other hitherto undescribed organisations for land drainage, which present, to the historian, some novel constitutional features. We have lingered willingly among the records of the " Corporations of the Poor," and the various other Boards of Guardians, Trustees or Directors, by which, from the end of the seventh century onwards, both rural and urban parishes repeatedly experimented in Poor Law adminis-

---

[1] We may refer also to our studies of particular functions of Local Government, such as *English Prisons under Local Government* (1922), *The Story of the King's Highway* (1913), *The History of Liquor Licensing in England* (1903), *The State and the Doctor* (1910), *The Prevention of Destitution* (1911 and 1920), *English Poor Law Policy* (1910), and *Grants in Aid* (1911 and 1920).

v

tration. The vast network of Turnpike Trusts, by which all England and Wales was once covered, seemed to us well to deserve some record. And we were interested to find, in the entirely unstudied archives of the hundreds of bodies of Commissioners for Paving, Cleaning, Lighting, Watching and Improving the streets of the various English towns—and not in the unreformed Municipal Corporations—the beginnings of the most important functions of our nineteenth century municipalities. But whether or not these annals of the less well-known parts of Local Government are found of popular interest, we enter a plea, not only for a more systematic preservation by Town and County Councils of the records of those who were their predecessors in local administration, but also for the more frequent study of these neglected sources by historians of the English people.

Much of the work of investigation of these records was done between 1899 and 1908; and we owe thanks, not only to their custodians, by whom we were always courteously received, but also to our helpers in what proved an extensive as well as a protracted task. Among those whose work is embodied in the present volume, we must mention Mr. F. H. Spencer, LL.D., author of *Municipal Origins*, now in the Ministry of Education; Mrs. Spencer, D.Sc. (Econ.); Miss M. Bulkley, B.Sc. (Econ.); and Miss Hadley, archivist to the London County Council. For criticisms and suggestions, none the less valuable because we have not always implicitly incorporated them, we thank especially Professor Graham Wallas and Mr. Harold Laski, of the London School of Economics and Political Science. To Miss Ivy Schmidt, now Mrs. Bolton, we are indebted for much laborious co-operation, and for the full index.

SIDNEY AND BEATRICE WEBB.

41 GROSVENOR ROAD, WESTMINSTER,
September 1922.

CONTENTS

CHAPTER I

CHAPTER II

CHAPTER III

CHAPTER IV

CHAPTER V

CHAPTER VI

INTRODUCTION

In our former volumes on English Local Government [1] we described the organisation and development, between 1689 and 1835, both of the Parish and the County, which professedly covered all England and Wales, and of the various types of Manor and Borough, which stood out as islands of franchises, immunities or exceptions to the common rule and jurisdiction. But these local governing bodies do not exhaust the list. There existed also, up and down the country, a number of other authorities, unconnected with the older bodies, which had been, in particular areas, for particular functions, by Royal Commission and Parliamentary enactment, superposed indifferently upon Parish and Manor, Borough and County. These, in a special sense statutory administrations, have now to be described. They fall, as we shall see, into four main classes, which have severally little or no connection with each other. We shall deal first with the archaic Courts of Sewers, which, over extensive areas of England, administered the sluices, the embankments and the drainage that alone made the land habitable. The second class comprises the peculiar bodies of Incorporated Guardians to whom was transferred, at the expense of the Parish, a large part of the administration of Poor Relief. We shall then describe the network of Turnpike Trusts, which, in the course of the eighteenth century, transformed our main roads. The last class is that of the Lighting, Watching, Paving, Cleansing, Street or Improvement Commissioners, in whom, from the middle of the

---

[1] *The Parish and the County*, 1907 ; *The Manor and the Borough*, 2 vols., 1908. We may refer also to other volumes of our work on English Local Government, dealing with separate functions, namely, *The Story of the King's Highway*, 1913 ; and *English Prisons under Local Government*, 1922 ; together with an incomplete sketch entitled *The History of Liquor Licensing in England*, 1903. A volume on the evolution of the Relief of the Poor and the Repression of Vagrancy is in preparation.

B

eighteenth century, the bulk of what we now call municipal government came gradually to be vested.

These Statutory Authorities, which have not hitherto engaged the attention of historians,[1] comprised, in the aggregate, something like eighteen hundred separate Local Governing Bodies. They were, accordingly, more than eight times as numerous as the Municipal Corporations, about which, because of the Parliamentary importance of many of them, so much has been said ; and thirty times as numerous as the Courts of Justices in Quarter Sessions that governed the Counties. The jurisdiction of these eighteen hundred Statutory Authorities extended, in the aggregate, over a much larger area, and over a considerably greater population, than the jurisdiction of all the Municipal Corporations put together ; and, as it may be suggested, affected much more closely the lives of the people. Even in respect of their pecuniary transactions, these Statutory Authorities hold an important place. By 1835 their aggregate annual receipts had risen to nearly three millions sterling, being (until the dramatic rise of the Poor Rate in the nineteenth century) not far short of the contemporary annual revenue of all the other Local Governing Authorities in the Kingdom put together. And if we measure our interest in past experiments in social organisation by the extent to which they have severally contributed to the Local Government of our own time, the Statutory Authorities, as we shall see, may claim our attention

---

[1] Reference to the various books dealing with these Statutory Authorities will be found at the beginnings of the following chapters.

It may be added that we do not deal with the bodies of Enclosure Commissions formed in pursuance of some four thousand separate Enclosure Acts. These Commissions, transient in their existence and in their functions, powerless to levy a tax on the public, and dealing only with individual property rights, cannot be deemed Local Governing Bodies. For the Enclosure Acts and the proceedings taken under them, see *An Enquiry into the Influence which Enclosures have had upon the Population of England*, by John Howlett, 1786 ; *The Case of Labourers in Husbandry Stated*, by David Davies, 1795 ; *Commons and Common Fields*, by T. E. Scrutton, 1887 ; *The Domesday of Inclosures, 1517–18*, by I. S. Leadam (*Royal Historical Society*, 1897); *Commons and Common Fields*, by G. Slater, 1907 ; *History of the English Agricultural Labourer*, by W. Hasbach, 1908 ; *The Disappearance of the Small Landowner*, by A. H. Johnson, 1909 ; *Commons, Forests and Footpaths*, by Viscount Eversley, 1910 ; *The Village Labourer, 1760–1832*, by J. L. and Barbara Hammond, 1911 ; *Common Land and Enclosures*, by Sir E. C. K. Gonner, 1912 ; *The Agrarian Problem in the Sixteenth Century*, by R. H. Tawney, 1912 ; *The Great Enclosures of Common Lands in Wales*, by I. Bowen, 1914 ; *English Field Systems*, by H. L. Gray, 1915 ; *Enclosure and Redistribution of Land*, by W. H. R. Curtler, 1920.

as the direct ancestors, more truly than the Municipal Corporation or the Manor, of a large part of the powers and functions, not only of our Borough Councils, as of our Urban and Rural District Councils, but also of the greatest of all our local governing authorities, the London County Council itself.

We can find no better general designation for these four classes of bodies established one by one to perform specifically prescribed functions—as we should now say, " *ad hoc* bodies "— than Statutory Authorities for Special Purposes. They differed essentially from the immemorial Parish, Manor and County, and even from the Manorial Borough and Municipal Corporation, which, in some cases, lawfully existed by prescription, in each of them taking its origin from some special legislative act, establishing, not a class of local governing bodies, but one particular Local Governing Authority to discharge one designated function, for one prescribed locality. Each of them enjoyed its powers and incurred its obligations, not by Common Law, but exclusively by virtue of that particular legislative act. It is true that, conformably to the general rule that there are, in Nature, no absolutely sharp lines of division between classes of any kind, we may detect a certain approximation between the Manorial Boroughs and Municipal Corporations, on the one hand, some of which were established by particular legislative acts, whether charter or statute, and, on the other, the Courts of Sewers, which were actually constituted by commission from the King, though from 1532 onwards, always under the authority of the Statute of Sewers ; and which (at least in the exceptional case of the Lords of the Level of Romney Marsh) could claim that some of their powers, obligations and procedure were rooted in immemorial custom, prescription and Common Law. But apart from this anomalous approximation of marginal instances, the Statutory Authorities for Special Purposes introduce us to a characteristic development of English Local Government in what is now known as the Local Act.

The Local Act, of which we find exceptional instances as early as the fourteenth century, but which is specially characteristic of the period from the Revolution to the Municipal Corporations Act with which we are concerned, is, we believe, in many of its features, peculiar to this country. It is, of course, not an enactment of the inhabitants, or of the governing body, of the

locality to which it refers, but an Act of Parliament, an enactment of the National Legislature itself. But unlike the better-
known Public General Acts of the National Legislature the
Local Act does not apply to the whole Kingdom, but only to
the district or governing body to which its terms relate. Thus,
in 1384, the Act 8 Richard II. authorises " pavage " in the
Borough of Southampton ; in 1488 the statute 4 Henry VII. c. 21
is entitled " An Act for the inhabitants of the Town of Southwold " ; in 1542, the Act 33 Henry VIII. c. 35 empowers the
Mayor and the Dean of Gloucester to provide a water supply ;
in 1647 an Ordinance of the Commonwealth establishes the
Corporation of the Poor of the City of London in order that
the indigent may be more effectually provided for. From the
beginning of the eighteenth century these Local Acts increased
steadily in number, and after the middle of that century they
were every year passed in crowds. And although what were
in effect Local Acts were known, as we have seen, before the
middle of the seventeenth century, and have been continuously
employed down to our own day, those of the particular century
and a half that we have here under review did, for the most
part, what was almost unknown before 1647 and came speedily
to an end after 1835, namely establish (or at least grant a renewed
term of existence to) particular local governing bodies for the
performance of local government functions. It is, in fact,
mainly as an instrument not merely conferring powers but
actually creating local government structure of a peculiar kind—
in Turnpike Trust or Incorporation of Guardians of the Poor,
Paving or Improvement Commission—that the Local Act finds
for us its greatest interest.[1]

The Local Act (along with " Private," " Personal " and other
statutes not classed as " Public General Acts ") is a Parliamentary

---

[1] For this reason we do not deal with the statutes, often called Private or
Personal, which merely affect the status of individuals, or their property
rights. Such Acts concerning individual cases of legitimacy, naturalisation,
marriage or divorce, the authorisation of private lotteries or the settlement of
estates, not to mention also the reallotment in severalty of lands held in common
(Enclosure Acts), were exceedingly numerous down to the beginning of the
nineteenth century, but have since become rare. On the other hand, statutes
incorporating companies for business enterprises, of which the New River
Company of 1617 was an exceptionally early example, became, in the eighteenth
and nineteenth centuries, down to the passing of the Companies Act of 1862,
exceedingly common for canals, railways, banks, waterworks, gasworks, etc.

statute enacted, like any other, by the King "by and with the advice and consent" of the House of Lords and House of Commons; and going through the same stages of first, second and third reading, committee and report in both Houses of Parliament. Originally, as it seems, it was dealt with in all respects as if it were what is now called a Public General Act. Gradually, however, the two Houses of Parliament evolved (but scarcely before the nineteenth century, and not effectively until after 1832) [1] additional safeguards and precautions in the concession of statutory authority to private individuals, local authorities or groups of persons.[2] Thus, special notice of the proposed

[1] How careless was the practice in the eighteenth century may be judged from the following example. In 1772 we learn from the Parliamentary Register that " Sir William Meredith moved, That it might be a general order, that no Bill, or clause in a Bill, making any offence capital, should be agreed to but in a Committee of the whole House. He observed that at present the facility of passing such clauses was shameful: that he was once passing a Committee room, when only one Member was holding a Committee, with a clerk's boy; he happened to hear something of hanging; he immediately had the curiosity to ask what was going forward in that small Committee that could merit such a punishment? He was answered that it was an Enclosing Bill, in which a great many poor people were concerned, who opposed the Bill; that they feared those people would obstruct the execution of the Act, and therefore this clause was to make it capital felony in any one who did so. This resolution was unanimously agreed to." (*Parliamentary Register*, Jan. 21, 1772; *The Village Labourer*, by J. L. and Barbara Hammond, 1911, p. 64.)

[2] For the gradual evolution of Parliamentary procedure in respect to statutes other than Public General Acts (whether "private," "local and personal," estate, divorce, nationalisation, enclosure, road, etc.) the student will consult the various Reports of Select Committees of the House of Commons on Private Bills (or Private Business) in 1810, 1821, 1824, 1825, 1831, 1837, 1838, 1841, 1846 and 1847; and the *Journals* of the House of Commons and House of Lords respectively, as cited in the undermentioned works. The ordinary enquirer will find sufficient information in the last named of them, which (although not indicated by the title) is an interesting and valuable monograph on the subject of Local Acts, deserving more attention than it has yet received.

The *Solicitor's Instructor in Parliament concerning Estate and Inclosure Bills*, by Charles Thomas Ellis, 1799; this extended and republished as *Practical Remarks and Precedents of Proceedings in Parliament relative to Bills for Inclosing and Draining Lands, making Turnpike Roads, etc.*, 1802 (and subsequent editions down to 1813); *The Manner of Proceeding upon Bills in the Commons*, by Sir George Bramwell, 1809; *Practical Instructions on the Passing of Private Bills through Both Houses of Parliament*, by a Parliamentary Agent, 1827; *Proceedings in Private Bills*, by Thomas M. Sherwood, 1829–1831; *On Passing Private Bills*, by John Halcomb, 1836; *The Practice of the Court of Referees on Private Bills in Parliament*, by Frederick Clifford and A. G. Rickards, 2 vols.; *Cases decided during the Sessions* [from 1867 onwards] *by the Court of Referees on Private Bills in Parliament*, by the same; and *The History of Private Bill Legislation*, by Frederick Clifford, 2 vols. 1885; *Parliamentary Costs*, by E. Wheeler, 1881; *Private Bill Legislation and Provisional Orders*, by L. Macassey,

legislation had to be given to all persons whose interests would
be affected by it, and the service of such notice had to be formally
proved before the Bill was allowed to proceed. Fees had to be
paid to various officials of each House. A whole code of precedents became established, which had to be followed under penalty
of grave risk of the Bill failing to become law. From 1800
(when a salary was assigned to the office), if not, indeed, from
1778 or earlier,[1] the Chairman of Committees of the House of
Lords gradually assumed authority, for the protection of the
public interest, to scrutinise closely the provisions of each Bill,
prior to its formal introduction into either House ; and the
veto of the " Lords' Chairman " upon any novel encroachment
on public interests or private rights—meaning that this trusted
representative would advise the House summarily to throw out
any Bill which contained anything to which he had formally
objected—seriously limited the demands of promoters of this
legislation. And when all these preliminaries had been gone
through, every Bill not classed as " Public "—whether " Private,"
" Personal " or " Local "—had to run the gauntlet of special
consideration by a committee of each House in succession,
before which, in public session, witnesses had to prove the
necessity and desirability of granting the proposed statutory
powers, and other witnesses could demonstrate the inconvenience
or the undesirability of such a course. Before these Parliamentary committees all the parties could be, and from 1832
onwards, almost invariably were, represented by learned counsel,
who not only examined and cross-examined the witnesses, but
also addressed the tribunal in support of the evidence of their
respective clients. The final stage in this evolution of procedure
was reached in the decision of both Houses of Parliament, not
arrived at until the third decade of the nineteenth century,
to appoint their " Private Bill Committees " in all cases

1887 ; *Standing Orders of the Lords and Commons relative to Private Bills*, by J.
Bigg, 1889 ; *Private Bill Procedure*, by C. Dodd and H. W. W. Wilberforce, 1898 ;
The Practice of Private Bills, by G. J. Wheeler, 1900 ; together with such general
works as *A Treatise on the Law, Privileges, Proceedings and Usage of Parliament*,
by Sir T. Erskine May, 1906 ; *Legislative Methods and Forms*, by Sir C. P.
Ilbert, 1901 ; and *Recht und Technik des englischen Parliamentarismus*, by Josef
Redlich, 1905, translated as *The Procedure of the House of Commons*, 1908 ;
the whole examined and summarised, as regards Local Acts, in *Municipal
Origins*, by F. H. Spencer, 1911.
    [1] *Municipal Origins*, by F. H. Spencer, 1911, pp. 325-329.

from among members without pecuniary interest in or local
association with the projects of the promoters of the Bills ;[1]
and to adopt, as the guiding principle for the action of these
committees, the assumption that they should act strictly as
judicial tribunals, eliminating all personal predilection and
party bias.

These Local Acts constituted, during the century and a half
with which we are here dealing, actually the greater part, so far
as bulk is concerned, of the legislative output of Parliament.
" If any contemplative person," says Mr. Spencer, " will go to
one of our great libraries and stand for a moment before the
ponderous mass of volumes containing the Acts of our Parliament from the beginnings of its history until to-day, he will
notice a curious phenomenon. He will observe that the space
occupied by legislation for the century from about 1745 to 1845
is immensely greater than that needed for any other century of
our Parliamentary history. As might be expected, a single
volume will contain the legislation of a whole reign, or sometimes several reigns, from the time of the Plantagenets almost
until the departure of the Stuarts. From about 1700 onwards,
however, the bulk of the annual output increases, until a year's
legislative work begins to fill a stout volume ; and as soon as we
get beyond the middle of the eighteenth century two, three or even
four volumes begin to be required. . . . The greater part of the
tremendous bulk of legislation of this period consisted . . . of
. . . Local Acts."[2] Even omitting the four thousand Enclosure
Acts, and all the " Private " and " Personal " legislation, the
statutes specifically establishing or continuing one or other of
the eighteen hundred Local Authorities described in the present
volume, or altering their powers or obligations, must number in
the aggregate something like ten thousand. This enormous
array of legislation has, so far, scarcely been explored, or even

---

[1] Even as late as 1825 it was the practice, as reported by the House of
Commons Committee of that year, for each Bill to be " committed to the
member who is charged with its management, and such other members as he
may choose to name in the House, and the members serving for a particular
County (usually the County immediately connected with the object of the
Bill, and the adjoining Counties) ; and consequently it has been practically
found that the members to whom Bills have been committed have been generally those who have been most interested in the result." (Quoted in *The Village
Labourer*, by J. L. and Barbara Hammond, 1911, pp. 45-46.)

[2] *Municipal Origins*, by F. H. Spencer, 1911, p. 1.

surveyed by historians,[1] whether what they were writing about
was the evolution of law, of local government, of public administration, of manners and morals, or of Parliament itself. We
were ourselves daunted by the portentous magnitude and the
repulsive aridity of the mass of sources that stood before us.
But it was plain that the history of English Local Government
was not to be understood without an analysis of the statutes
upon which it so largely depended, even if they were styled
Local Acts ; and great and wearisome as was the work, it yielded
much of interest and value.

What adds to the difficulty of consulting these Local Acts
of the eighteenth century is the great length and pedantically

---

[1] Thus Fitzjames Stephen, writing a learned history of English criminal
law, could content himself with the following reference to the masses of Parliamentary statutes which created innumerable novel crimes, substituted for the
Manorial Courts the authority of the Justices of the Peace, and practically
revolutionised criminal procedure for the bulk of offences by introducing
summary jurisdiction. "At a time *which I am not able to give with precision*,"
wrote this historian of 1853, "but which from expressions in the Report of the
Municipal Corporations Commission I think must have been in the latter part
of the last century, it became customary to pass Local Improvement Acts by
which the management of matters connected with the police of towns was
usually vested in a body of Trustees or Commissioners distinct from the
Corporation itself. There were great differences in the manner in which these
powers were allotted." (*History of the Criminal Law of England*, by Sir J.
Fitzjames Stephen, 1853, vol. i. pp. 195-196.) Other historians have been
equally neglectful. W. E. H. Lecky wrote his eight volumes on the eighteenth
century with scarcely a reference to these Local Acts. Spencer Walpole, who
seems to have compiled his *History of England from the Conclusion of the Great
War in 1815* almost exclusively from a file of the *Times* and a set of the Blue-
books, devotes only three pages out of his five volumes to Private Bill legislation
(vol. iv. pp. 15-18). Sir George Nicholls, for his *History of the English Poor Law*,
1854, quotes abundantly from every Public General Act that comes anywhere
near poor relief, but absolutely ignores all the enactments that were not classed
as Public General Acts, even when they dealt explicitly with poor relief itself.
    How illogical is this ignoring of Local Acts may be seen from the fact that
the classification of Acts of Parliament has varied from time to time. Thus,
prior to 1702 "Turnpike Acts" were "public"; from 1702 to 1720 they were
"private"; from 1720 to 1753 they were printed and bound with the ordinary
Public General Acts; from 1753 to 1790 they were bound separately, and are
described as "Public Acts not printed in the collection," or more succinctly,
as "Road Acts," whilst from 1798 to 1868 they were included among "Acts
Local and Personal." From 1798 to 1868 all the statutes were divided among
three classes, namely, (1) Public General Acts, (2) Local and Personal Acts
declared public and to be judicially noticed; and (3) Private and Personal
Acts. Since 1868 the three divisions have been (1) Public General Acts;
(2) Local Acts, and (3) Private Acts. (House of Commons *Journals*, vol. lii.
p. 413; *History of Private Bill Legislation*, by F. Clifford, 1887–89, vol. i. p. 269;
Legislative Methods and Forms, by Sir C. P. Ilbert, 1901, pp. 26-27; *Municipal
Origins*, by F. H. Spencer, 1911, pp 45-46; *The Story of the King's Highway*,
by S. and B. Webb, 1913, p. 148.)

involved phraseology of their clauses. This was due to the necessity of repeating and re-enacting in each statute all the general provisions as to the procedure for acquiring land and other matters of common form, which are now embodied for general application in the Lands Clauses Acts, and other statutes of like character. In the typical Local Act of the eighteenth century all this essentially " common form " had to be set out in the cumbrous and elaborate phraseology of the legal draughtsman of the time. Only sparingly and occasionally could the eighteenth-century Parliament, deprived of the assistance of the Ministers (who remained absolutely indifferent to the requirements and the troubles of Local Government), bring itself to enact any general statute giving powers to all Parish officers, to all Turn-pike Trusts, to all Municipal Corporations, or to all County authorities to carry out their respective functions. Accordingly, the successive changes in structure and function, the gradual alteration in the idea of what the various kinds of local governing bodies should be and do, the evolution in the very conception of government itself, have to be traced in the variations, from one decade to another, in the contents of the thousands of Local Acts, whilst the results of these variations may be verified in the archives revealing the development of the various Local Authorities themselves.

In the following chapters we shall describe, first, the ancient Courts of Sewers, with their archaic and partly traditional organisation of juries and presentments ; next the Incorporated Guardians of the Poor ; then the growing multitude of Turnpike Trusts ; and finally the bodies of Paving, Cleansing, Lighting, Watching, Street or Improvement Commissioners, and their work in the crowded urban districts. And we shall find, not only that the life-histories of these eighteen hundred Statutory Authorities for Special Purposes afford us a new vision of what the life of the people of England in the eighteenth century actually was, but also that the evolution of structure and func-tion of these little-studied Local Authorities led to results im-portant in subsequent developments. These Local Authorities it was, far more than the Parish, the Borough and the County, that brought in the paid professional staffs of voluntarily serving officials out of which has sprung our modern municipal Civil Service. It was among these Statutory Authorities for Special

Purposes that first developed the essentially English system of administration by committees of representatives of the electorate of ratepayers, directing and controlling the staff of professional officers. It is in the long succession of Local Acts establishing or continuing these Statutory Authorities that we watch the earlier stages of that creation of new misdemeanours and that multiplication of merely police offences, together with the almost limitless extension of summary jurisdiction, which has become so characteristic of modern civilisation. And above all, it is in these Local Acts, and particularly in the practice of the latest of the four classes of Local Authorities for Special Purposes which they set up, namely the Street Commissioners, that we find the direct lineal ancestors, alike of the multiplicity of functions relating to sanitation, police and all the amenities of urban life now characterising our municipalities, and of the rates, or ever-growing municipal taxes which, whilst grumbling, we nevertheless willingly contribute in return for the literally inestimable services rendered.[1]

[1] This vast and chaotic mass of legislation remained almost unnoticed by contemporary jurists and reformers. It is remarkable how little it engaged the attention, to name three very different observers, either of Jeremy Bentham, or of William Cobbett or of Francis Place. Sir Samuel Romilly's attention was called to the savage punishments authorised by some of the Local Acts ; and his intervention led to the passing of Public General Acts in 1814–16 (54 George III. c. 170 ; 56 George III. c. 129 ;) repealing such clauses wherever they occurred. But nothing was done to restrain the authority over the helpless poor carelessly given by many of these statutes. When, in the middle of the nineteenth century, Toulmin Smith was vainly striving to re-establish what he fondly imagined to be the " self-determination " of the ancient Parish or Manor, and the inviolable supremacy of the Common Law, it was the Local Acts (which he chose to consider a quite recent innovation) that excited his greatest animadversion. " There is," he wrote in 1852, " one form which modern law-making takes which needs reform. It is a form at once probably the most burdensome of any to members of Parliament, and one of the most pernicious in itself ; while it is a wholly illegitimate field of Parliamentary labour. It is the system of Local Acts. . . . There are a mass of Local Acts which never ought to come near Parliament at all. All Borough Acts, and others of that class, come under this head. . . . Under cover of these Local Acts, infringements are made upon the constitutional rights and liberties of freemen which are truly astounding ; and that without any possibility of redress. Wide powers of summary jurisdiction are often given in direct opposition to the spirit and principles of the Common Law. . . . A man in the pursuit of his lawful calling or in the course of needful self-protection, finds the all-essential rights which he enjoys at Common Law, and which no charter of the Crown can invade, nor even his own consent take away, cut from under him by some hidden section of a Local Act of Parliament he never heard of." *Local Self-Government*, by J. Toulmin Smith, 1852, pp. 147-150 ; see also *Minute on Public Health Legislation prepared at the Request of Sir William Molesworth*, by the same, 1853 ; and *Local Self-Government Unmystified*, by the same, 1857, p. 92.}

With the present volume we complete our account of the structure of English Local Government from 1689 to 1835. It seems, accordingly, convenient to close the volume with an analysis of the ideas and conceptions, or as we may say, the principles, in which this structure was rooted at the beginning of the period, and the manner in which they were affected by the social evolution of this century and a half. The period, as it is unnecessary to remind the reader, was one of exceptional change. At the close of the seventeenth century, although the old order was already in an advanced stage of decay, England was still predominantly an agricultural community, with the greater part of the land in common fields, cultivated by small working farmers closely bound together by social ties and family relationships with the cottagers, the bulk of them having certain property rights or customary privileges as tenants of the manor, copyholders or freeholders, or at least enjoying rights of common. In the urban centres, even in the ports and the then rapidly growing Metropolis, the greater part of the manufacturing industry and the internal trading was still carried on by small master-craftsmen, each employing only a few journeymen and apprentices who lived in the families of their employers, and often married their masters' daughters ; or by independent handicraftsmen who directly served their own customers. By the beginning of the nineteenth century the economic organisation of society had almost entirely changed. The landowners had come to let the soil on commercial contracts for steadily increasing rents to farmers who could invest, in what became essentially a business enterprise, capitals of from a few hundred to some thousands of pounds each. The men, women and children, who worked on the land and constituted at that time four-fifths of the entire population of the rural parishes, had, by the operation of the enclosures, the absorption of the little copyholds and freeholds, and the disappearance of the manorial system, for the most part, lost whatever property rights they had possessed, and had sunk to be merely a wage-earning proletariate, to be ultimately deeply pauperised by the " parish pay." In the rapidly developing urban districts, in the mining areas, in the growing ports, in the greatly swollen Metropolis and even in the relatively stagnant county towns, the growth of the new machine industries, the vast capitalist enterprises in mining, in shipping, and in commerce as well as in manufactures, and the enormous development of both internal and international trade had brought the town populations to a like " cash nexus " between a constantly shifting body of capitalist employers, many of them amassing great fortunes, taking on and dismissing, according to the fluctuations of speculative demand, armies of unorganised manual workers whom they knew only as the "hands" to whom they paid an inadequate and inconstant wage.

Such an economic revolution, coincident with the gradual emergence of the idea of political Democracy, and with the spread of Nonconformity in religion, could not fail to make its mark on the local institutions. In the present volume, taken in conjunction with those on *The Parish and the County*, and *The Manor and the Borough*, we have sought to describe the myriad changes in the structure of Local Government that did, in fact, occur between 1689 and 1835. What remains to be done, and what the reader will find attempted in the last two chapters of the present volume, is to analyse and summarise what we may call the intellectual features that these myriad and apparently disconnected changes had in common. We shall seek to show how it was that an unorganised congeries of very varied Local Authorities—rooted mainly in immemorial local custom and the Common Law ; arising out of an ancient vocational organisation of society ; dependent on the universal obligation to serve in turn gratuitously in the various public offices ; with authority confined to the owners of property, meaning originally property in land—developed into another congeries of no less varied Local Authorities ; deriving their power mainly from constantly amended Parliamentary statutes ; increasingly getting their functions performed by hired labourers and profitmaking contractors ; and progressively shedding the remnants of vocational organisation in favour of control by the " consumers " of the services, as property owners or rate-payers —the resulting chaos leading, finally, in the Poor Law Amendment Act of 1834 and the Municipal Corporations Act of 1835, to the initiation of what has, in the course of another century, proved to be a systematic reorganisation of Local Government on the basis of a universal Democracy.

CHAPTER I

THE COURT OF SEWERS

IT is difficult, in the twentieth century, to form any adequate conception of the extent to which the England of the Middle Ages, or even down to the end of the seventeenth century, was made up, to use the picturesque words of " the famous and learned Robert Callis," himself a Lincolnshire Sewer Commissioner, of " huge, great and vast fens and marishes." [1]

---

[1] No satisfactory account of the work and proceedings of the various Courts of Sewers has been written. The student will consult the well-known *Reading of the Famous and Learned Robert Callis, Esquire, upon the Statute of Sewers,* first published in 1647, the latest edition being that of 1824 ; also *The Learned Reading of John Herne . . . concerning Commissioners of Sewers,* 1659 ; and *The Laws of Sewers, or the Office and Authority of Commissioners of Sewers,* 1726 and 1732. *The Justice of the Peace,* by Theodore Barlow, 1745, gives (pp. 484-494) a clear account of what was then taken as law on the subject ; whilst *The Law of Waters and Sewers,* by Humphry W. Woolrych, 1830, conveniently supplies a later picture. The present law is most easily consulted in *The Law of Land Drainage and Sewers,* by G. G. Kennedy and J. S. Saunders, 1884 ; *The Land Drainage Act of 1861,* by T. Thring, 1862 ; or *The Land Drainage Act,* 1861, by R. B. Grantham, 1865. *The Laws and Customs of Romney Marsh* have been many times printed, the last separate edition being that of 1840. For the early history, the great storehouse of materials is *The History of Imbanking and Draining of Divers Fens and Marshes,* by (Sir) William Dugdale, 1652, reprinted 1772, together with the works subsequently cited in connection with the Fenland, the Bedford Level, Romney Marsh, and Lincolnshire respectively. A useful collection of documents is given in *Public Works in Mediaeval Law,* by C. T. Flower (Selden Society, 1915). Some idea of the engineering problems involved may be gained from such books as that *On the Drainage of Lands, Towns and Buildings,* by G. D. Dempsey, 1890 and 1894 ; *The Drainage of Fens and Lowlands,* by W. H. Wheeler, 1888 ; *History of the Fens of South Lincolnshire,* by W. H. Wheeler, 1894, with a useful bibliography ; *Fens and Floods of Mid Lincolnshire,* by J. S. Padley, 1882 ; or the papers in the *Proceedings of the Institute of Civil Engineers.* The best brief accounts are those in *The Lives of the Engineers,* by Samuel Smiles, 1861, vol. i. part i., and *Descriptive and Statistical Account of the British Empire,* by J. R. MacCulloch chap. i. sec. 4. We have, however, been able to draw our information mostly from the MS. minutes of the Com-

In the eastern counties, what is now the great level plain
of the Fenland was, every flood-time, for literally hundreds of
square miles, one broad waste of water, and of water, as Defoe
says, "the colour of brewed ale ";[1] in some parts deep pools
and river channels, elsewhere merely beds of waving rushes, bog
myrtle and flowering grasses, the home of innumerable wildfowl,
and, in autumn, of flocks of starlings, which, when disturbed,
rose in thick clouds.   Here and there, on a patch of higher land,
would be a hamlet clustering round the church, or the hall of
the squire, whilst, when the day happened to be free from fog,[2]
the towers and spires of Ely and Peterborough, Boston and Lynn,
Whittlesey and Croyland caught the eye for miles.   But besides
these larger patches, where for a few acres there existed " winter
lands," the whole district was studded with islets, having only a
few square yards above the flood-time water level, each with its
little homestead among the willows and poplars, its tiny field
behind the banks, and its pasturage on the " summerlands " of
green grass flat, and of browner peat where the fen lay deeper ;
with here and there the darker velvet green of alders amid wind-
ing streams and shining meres, and rich sedge-grass so slightly
uncovered by the summer droughts that, as noticed by a lady
traveller in 1695, the " many swans' nests on little hillocks of
earth in the wet ground " looked " as if swimming " amid the
broods of cygnets.[3]   This " vast morass," as Camden calls it,
where, to use the words of Dugdale, " there is no element good,
the air being for the most part cloudy, gross and full of rotten
harrs ;   the water putrid and muddy, yea, full of loathsome
vermin ;   and the fire noisome by the stink of smoky hassocks,"

---

missioners of Sewers for Somerset, East Kent, Greenwich, Surrey and Kent,
Poplar, St. Katherine's, Tower Hamlets, Holborn and Finsbury and West-
minster ; together with those of the Governors of the Bedford Level (North
Level), and those of the unique " Lords of the Level " of Romney Marsh.

   [1] A Tour through the Whole Island of Great Britain, by Daniel Defoe, vol. iii.
p. 28 of 1748 edition.

   [2] The " fogs and stagnant air " of the Fens, mentioned by Dugdale as
prevalent, were execrated by Defoe, who tells us that, early in the eighteenth
century, the whole district was, in autumn, " generally . . . covered with
fogs, so that when the downs and higher grounds of the adjacent country
glistered with the beams of the sun, the Isle of Ely seemed wrapped up
in mist and darkness, so that nothing could be discerned but now and then
the cupola of Ely Minster " (ibid. vol. i. p. 91, vol. iii. pp. 19-28, of edition
of 1748).

   [3] Through England with a Side Saddle in the Reign of William and Mary,
being the Diary of Celia Fiennes, edited by the Hon. Mrs. Griffiths, 1888, p. 131.

afforded " overmuch harbour to a rude and almost barbarous sort of lazy and beggarly people." [1] On the other side of England, many miles of Somersetshire, in the broad flats through which the Parrott and the Axe wandered sluggishly to the sea, presented an almost similar aspect. In Kent and Sussex the well-known Romney Marsh, a hundred square miles of green flat, intersected by dykes of stagnant water, had been gradually abandoned by the sea, and " inned " by successive embankments of Roman or Saxon times. Here the marshmen of the seventeenth century, like those of the

[1] *History of Imbanking and Draining*, by Sir William Dugdale, 1652, p. 171 of edition of 1772. " Hassocks " seems to have been a fen word for the uppermost tufts of grass, which had to be removed before the land could be cultivated. A distinguished traveller through the Fens in 1833 notices the perpetual smell of burning dried " wreck " and weeds (*Memoirs of Dr. Thomas Chalmers*, by W. Hanna, 1851, vol. ii. p. 411). A more disagreeable stench constantly pervaded the Fenland. " Upon the walls of the ordinary people's houses," noticed a lady in 1695, " the cowdung [is] plastered up to dry in cakes, which they use for firing ; 'tis a very offensive fuel, but the common people use little else " (*Through England on a Side Saddle in the Reign of William and Mary . . . Diary of Celia Fiennes*, edited by Hon. Mrs. Griffiths, 1888, p. 132). " The natives dry the cowdung for firing in the winter, so 'tis kept in heaps about the fields, as is also the dung of their yards, so when you walk the stink is inconceivable " (Mrs. Harris to her son, afterwards Lord Malmesbury, 19th June 1763 ; in *A Series of Letters of the First Earl of Malmesbury*, 1870, vol. i. p. 91). Of Louth (Lincolnshire) in 1795, it was said (in *The State of the Poor*, by Sir F. M. Eden, vol. ii. p. 394) " it is hoped that the introduction of coal will induce the inhabitants to desist from their ancient practice, not yet entirely disused, of using the dung of their cattle for fuel." The custom, which is, of course, common throughout most of Asia, still existed in 1830, though such a fuel had, it was admitted, " a strong disagreeable smell in burning " (*History of the Drainage of the Great Level of the Fens*, by Samuel Wells, 1830, vol. i. p. 790).

Even for the rich the life of the Fens had many drawbacks. " All the summer long," writes a traveller about 1690, " there are continually such swarms of stinging gnats and other troublesome flies throughout all these quarters that a stranger can find but a very unhospitable lodging and reception " (*Three Years' Travels in England, Scotland and Wales*, by Rev. James Brome, 1700, p. 143). Here is a description of Cottenham in Cambridgeshire, in the leafy June of 1763 : " The country about here is the most disagreeable I ever saw. . . . The parsonage . . . is surrounded by fens, and you are teased beyond expression by the gnats. When we got here, about nine on Saturday, the Dean's butler came to your father with a pair of leathern stockings to draw on so as to protect his legs, which in hot weather is dreadful. Besides this the beds have a machine covered with a silk net which lets down after you are in bed and covers you all over. Without this, there could be no sleeping ; for notwithstanding all these precautions we were most miserably stung. There are fourteen hundred cows kept in the parish of Cottenham, which feed on the fens in the summer. The water is in this dry season up to their bellies. . . . Mr. Harris took a ride to survey these fens, and he says nothing can be so detestable. He talked with the natives, who told him that, during the winter, the water was constantly above their ankles in their houses " (*A Series of Letters of the First Earl of Malmesbury*, 1870, vol. i. p. 91).

Middle Ages, found their very existence dependent on their watchful maintenance of the great wall, fourteen miles long, that protected their sheep and their homesteads from the winter storms. The whole estuary of the Thames, from the Mole to the Medway, from Millbank in Westminster to the Maplin Sands, had its broad marsh lands, habitable only by the maintenance of interminable stretches of river wall and the construction of innumerable dykes and sluices, many of them of unknown antiquity. In the interior of England nearly every county had its hundreds or its thousands of acres of " moss " or swamp, along the valley bottoms or on the boggy uplands. To render these acres serviceable involved the construction and maintenance of miles of " ditches, gutters, gates and sewers." [1] Moreover, at many points along the low-lying coasts, there went on a perpetual struggle between " the power of man's hand " and " the swallowing and devouring surges of the seas and waters." The salt marsh, gradually uncovered by a receding sea, had to be protected against storms and exceptional tides. Elsewhere, fields and homesteads—even flourishing ports like Dunwich and Ravenspur—had to be defended, sometimes in vain, against the advancing ocean. The " great fresh rivers and streams " Callis tells us,[2] had also to have " their passages made clear and that their walls, banks and other defences be repaired, kept and maintained, whereby the fair, delightful, pleasant, and fruitful meadows and pasture grounds which lie in the greatest abundance upon or near the rivers, brooks and streams, may be preserved from the inundation of fresh waters, which many times annoy them."

The bulk of this work of reclamation, from the time when most of England formed practically one continuous forest and swamp and moorland moss, down to the Enclosure Acts of the eighteenth and nineteenth centuries, was doubtless the result of individual enterprise, great or small. Here the great lord embanked from the floods the meadows at the foot of his castle ; there the toiling cottager laboriously built up his plot of garden-ground against the marsh. But when each man had raised his bank, or built the bit of river wall that protected his own land, he was often still liable to be flooded out by a high tide or a spring freshet, owing to the neglect of his neighbour to keep the bank

---

[1] 23 Henry VIII. c. 5 (1532).
[2] *The Reading of . . . Robert Callis upon the Statute of Sewers*, 1647.

in repair, or to the want of uniformity in their defences against the common enemy. A small breach at any one point might, any winter, flood not the land of the negligent owner alone but the whole of the neighbouring lowlands. Individual enterprise brought, moreover, its own additions to the perils of the waters in the multitude of "fishgarths, milldams, locks, hebbing wears, hecks, floodgates and other like annoyances," which served as hindrances "to navigation, or stops whereby the abundant waters cannot have their free passage to the sea."[1] To cope with these difficulties we see, first the primitive forms of communal co-operation for land drainage—as yet scarcely investigated and deserving further study—and then, as these were found lacking in authority, amid the growing centralisation of the judicial power, the establishment of Courts of Sewers, wielding the might of the King.

The Origin of the Court of Sewers

We know nothing of the collective regulation of the sewers and banks of British, Roman, Anglo-Saxon or Norman times. From the provision in Magna Carta[2] forbidding assessments to maintain embankments except where customary, we may infer the existence, and even the increase, of some local organisation of such services. In thirteenth- and fourteenth-century documents we get glimpses, as for instance in the marshes of Kent and Sussex, of an interesting form of local self-government, sometimes avowedly based on the agreement of those concerned, sometimes asserting a compulsory authority exercised "time out of mind." Thus, in 1250, as we learn from a contemporary document, it could be asserted that it had, from time immemorial, been the custom in Romney Marsh for the Twenty-Four Jurats, chosen by the land-owners of the marsh, to watch over the sea wall and watercourses, compelling each owner to maintain in repair a certain length of wall and of "watergangs." These Jurats had a Bailiff, who summoned their meetings and enforced, by distraint on recalcitrant owners, the payment of damages assessed by the Jurats for any neglect of duty. There seem to have been also one or more collectors and an "Expenditor," in case the owners preferred, in any particular work, to have the repairs executed as a

---

[1] 23 Henry VIII. c. 5 (1532).
[2] Sec. 23 ; see Stubbs' *Select Charters*, p. 300.

C

collective service out of a primitive "acre rate." But these
ancient local distraints and assessments were sometimes resisted
by powerful landowners. At Romney this resistance went so
far that "the walls and watergangs lay waste and ruinated, by
reason whereof the inundations of the sea and other waters overflow a great part thereof, to the great detriment of our Lord the
King and the men of the same Marsh." Whereupon the King
gave a special charter to the Four and Twenty "Lawful Men,"
forbidding the Sheriff of the County to interfere with their distraints. When this proved inefficacious, six years later, he sent
down Sir Henry de Bathe, one of the principal judges, to determine
the differences and record the customs of Romney Marsh. For
the next two hundred years we read, in the pages of Dugdale, of
a succession of visits of specially commissioned King's Justices,
to adjudicate, with the aid of a Jury of indifferent men, summoned
by the Sheriff of the County, in disputes between the Twenty-
Four Jurats of the Marsh on the one hand, attended by their
Bailiff, Expenditor, collectors and the commonalty, and this or
that powerful landowner having fields within the Marsh, who had
defied their ordinances and assessments.[1] The same kind of
local organisation for the protection and drainage of land was
imitated in other marshes in Kent and Sussex, where previously
there had been "no certain law of the said marsh ordained or used
before that time, but at the will of those lords who had lands
within the same"; and "wherein the Marsh Law" was henceforth to be "established and used."[2] Much the same organisation seems also to have existed in some other marshy districts,
notably, as we shall describe, in Somersetshire, and along the
banks of the Thames; and to have persisted, in spite of the imposition of a newer constitution, down to the nineteenth century,
possibly even to the present day.

Meanwhile, in all the low-lying parts of England, the need for
some organisation of the works of embanking and land drainage
had led monarch after monarch, on the emergency of some flood
or inroad of the sea, or because of the importunity of some
particular suitor, to issue temporary Commissions, appointing

---

[1] *History of Imbanking and Draining*, by Sir William Dugdale, 1652, pp.
16-35 of edition of 1772; *History of Romney Marsh*, by W. Holloway, 1849;
The Cinque Ports, by Montagu Burrows, 1889; *The Manor and the Borough*,
by S. and B. Webb, 1908, vol. i. pp. 372-380.

[2] *History of Imbanking and Draining*, by Sir William Dugdale, pp. 25, 95.

Justices to survey and enquire, by Juries, into the needs of different districts; to discover what particular persons were liable, according to ancient custom, to execute repairs or to contribute to the common charges; and to settle the innumerable disputes that arose. We are not concerned to unravel, from the archives themselves or from the involved account given by Dugdale, all the complications and diversities of these casual judicial authorities — sometimes the King's Assize Judges, listening to the presentments of the ordinary Hundred Juries, and trying indictments on traverse by the common Petty Juries; sometimes special " Justices of Sewers," issuing precepts to the Sheriff to call " Juries of Sewers," composed of indifferent persons, who found particular landowners liable for works of repair; sometimes, again, standing Sewers Juries, like the Twenty-Four sworn men of Romney Marsh; apparently permanent bodies of representatives of the local owners whose presentments to the King's Justices, if traversed, were tried before a Jury of indifferent persons summoned by the Sheriff. These local organisations and customs, spasmodically interfered with and controlled by casual Justices depending only on the fiat of the King, with their uncertainties of law and diversities of procedure, were partly fortified and partly superseded by a series of Parliamentary enactments [1] culminating in the celebrated Statute of Sewers of 1532, which definitely established the authority of the King's Commissions of Sewers, and of the Courts of Sewers held by them; and formulated " for all parts within this Realm," a fixed constitution and procedure for what now became practically permanent local governing bodies.[2]

[1] 6 Henry VI. c. 5 (1427); 8 Henry VI. c. 3 (1429); 18 Henry VI. c. 10 (1439); 23 Henry VI. c. 9 (1499); 12 Edward IV. c. 6 (1472); 4 Henry VII. c. 1 (1488); 6 Henry VIII. c. 10 (1514). The Public Record Office contains masses of records relating to the proceedings of these Courts of Sewers in the fourteenth and fifteenth centuries. See *Public Works in Mediaeval Law*, by C. T. Flower (Selden Society, 1915), p. xxvii; and the fuller "Note on the Constitution and Records of Commissions of Sewers," by H. G. Richardson, in Report of Royal Commission on Public Records, vol. ii. part ii. pp. 98-100.

[2] 23 Henry VIII. c. 5 (1532). It is needless to remind the student that the King's right to issue a Commission of Sewers in no way depended on these statutes. The very learned *Nouvelle Nature Brevium* of Sir Anthony Fitzherbert, in editions from 1534 to 1794, is authority for the issue of writs to Justices of Sewers, irrespective of statute law, touching " sea-walls, ditches, gutters, sewers, arches, banks, wears and trenches " (*Local Self-Government*, by J. Toulmin Smith, 1851, p. 342). The records show that " the King in

The Legal Framework of the Court of Sewers

Under the great Statute of Sewers of 1532, as slightly amended in subsequent years,[1] the body of persons to whom the King issued his Commission to govern the sewers of a particular district resembled in many respects the Justices of the Peace of the county. Like the Justices of the Peace, the Commissioners of Sewers had, unless they were barristers, to possess a qualification in freehold land,[2] though provision was made from the first for allowing Commissioners free of any corporate Borough to qualify merely by the possession of personalty. They had, like the Justices of the Peace, to take elaborate oaths, under a similar

Chancery issued a continuous series of Commissions of Inquiry during the three centuries preceding the Statute of 23 Henry VIII., which created a machinery which soon led to a quasi-permanent Commission of Sewers " (*Public Works in Mediaeval Law*, by C. T. Flower (Selden Society, 1915), p. xxvii). " The Kings of England " granted Commissions of Sewers " for the surveying and repairing sea banks, walls, etc., long before any statute was enacted in Parliament for it " (*The Law of Sewers*, 1732). " All statutes of sewers," had said a lawyer, lecturing in 1638, " are made in aid of the ancient prerogative of the King " (*The Learned Reading of John Herne . . . concerning Commissioners of Sewers*, 1659). It may be added that the Bishop of Durham issued a Commission of Sewers in 1353, on his own authority (*History and Antiquities of the Parish of Hemingbrough, Yorkshire*, 1886) ; and the Bishop of Ely, though never actually in a position of so much independence, issued many such Commissions (MS. records of Ely diocese ; see 12th Report of Historical MSS. Commission for 1889 (Appendix, part ix.) ; *Ely Episcopal Records*, 1891). The palatine earls and other potentates exercising quasi-royal authority within their respective territories, apparently did the same. "The interest of the Duchy of Lancaster in the Fens on account of the Soke of Bolingbroke was so great that in 1549 an elaborate code of Fen laws was drawn up at a Duchy Court, and was maintained from time to time until the later systematic enclosure of the Fens " (*Public Works in Mediaeval Law*, by C. T. Flower, Selden Society, 1915, p. 282; see also *infra*, p. 55). The Duchy of Lancaster issued a Commission of its own to the Westminster Commissioners of Sewers, so as to enable them to exercise jurisdiction over the Precinct of the Savoy (Report of House of Commons Committee on Sewers in the Metropolis, 1823, p. 38). Many others are among the Duchy records in the Public Record Office, for marshlands on the Duchy's estates in different parts of the country. See *The Parish and the County*, book ii. chap. i. Appendix, " On some Anomalous County Jurisdictions, including the Counties Palatine," pp. 310-318.

[1] 25 Henry VIII. c. 10 (1534) ; 3 & 4 Edward VI. c. 8 (1549) ; 13 Elizabeth, c. 9 (1571) ; 7 Anne, c. 10 (1709) ; House of Lords Journals, 25th March, 8th and 11th April, 1709. The " Laws and Ordinances of the Sewers," 1602–1831, among the Chancery Petty Bag records, in the Public Record Office, relating chiefly to the Bedford Level, deserve to be further studied.

[2] Of " 40 marks " annual value. By 13 Eliz. c. 9 (1571) the qualification (for farmers) is stated as " forty pounds sterling." By 3 & 4 William IV. c. 22 (1833) it was raised to £100 a year freehold, or £200 a year leasehold, within the county. Unlike the Justice of the Peace, the Commissioner of Sewers had expressly to be " resident within the county " (25 Henry VIII. c. 10, 1534).

" dedimus potestatem." Each Commission, too, specified some of them as being what was termed " of the quorum." [1] They had allowed to them, like the Justices, their four shillings a day, with two shillings for their Clerk. More significant to the constitutional student is the fact that, like the Justices of the Peace, they combined in themselves, judicial, executive and even legislative powers,[2] all exercised under the forms of a Court of justice. On the other hand, the authority of the Commissioners of Sewers, unlike that of the Justices of the Peace, was limited alike in time and in extent. In both cases the Commission came automatically to an end on the demise of the Crown, and might be earlier terminated by writ of supersedeas. But each Commission of Sewers purported to be a strictly temporary one, enduring at first only for three years in each case, though this term was afterwards made ten years.[3] And their jurisdiction was at all times confined to matters concerning land drainage and embankments, or, as the statute expresses it, to the " walls, streams, ditches, banks, gutters, sewers, gates, calcies, bridges, trenches, mills, mill-dams, floodgates, ponds, locks, hebbingwears, and other impediments, lets and annoyances . . . in the rivers, streams and other floods " [4] within the defined area. Thus the Courts of Sewers differed fundamentally from the Parish, the County, the Lord's Court or the Municipal Corporation that we have described in the preceding

[1] See *The Parish and the County*, pp. 302-303.

[2] *Digest of the Statutes relating to the Metropolitan Commission of Sewers*, 1847, p. 76. The oath that continued to the last to be administered in the Metropolis distinctly expresses the legislative as well as the judicial function. " Ye shall swear that you to your cunning, wit and power shall truly and indifferently execute the authority to you given by this Commission of Sewers, without any favor, affection, corruption, dread or malice, to be borne to any kind or manner of persons ; and as the case shall require, ye shall consent and endeavour yourself, for your part, to the best of your knowledge and power, to the making of such wholesome, just, equal and indifferent laws and ordinances as shall be made and devised by the most discreet and indifferent of your fellows, being in commission with you, for the due redress, reformation and amendment of all and every such things as are contained and specified in the said commission ; and the same laws and ordinances, to your cunning wit and power, cause to be put in due execution, without favor, meed, dread, malice or affection, as God you help and all saints " (23 Henry VIII. c. 5, 1532 ; Report of House of Commons Committee on Sewers in the Metropolis, 1823, p. 4).

[3] 13 Eliz. c. 9 (1571). A minor point of difference was that the quorum of the Sewer Commissioners was fixed by statute at six, three of whom had to be among those named in the Commission as of the quorum.

[4] 23 Henry VIII. c. 23 (1532).

volumes, all of which dealt generally with all the affairs of their particular localities. The Courts of Sewers belonged essentially to the class of " ad hoc " bodies, created for some special function, which became, as we shall see, a characteristic feature of the local government of the eighteenth and early nineteenth centuries.

The Commissioners or " Justices " of Sewers were empowered to hold, when and where they chose, within the area prescribed by their Commission, the so-called Court of Sewers ; [1] a Court of Record, to which the Sheriff was required on their precept to return Juries of "honest and lawful " men. This Court determined, by the verdict of the Jury, both the obligations of particular persons to do or abstain from doing certain things, and the extent to which they had failed to fulfil such obligations. If the offence was wilful, and done " vi et armis," it was punishable by fine or imprisonment at the Commissioners' discretion.[2] Mere neglect or default in any person, under obligation " by frontage, tenure, custom or covenant," or merely by ownership of the bank, to maintain any work, led to his amercement by the Jury in the amount of the damage. Upon this verdict the Commissioners gave judgment, which they enforced through their own officers by distraint. Any fines that they imposed as punishments were " estreated " into the Court of Exchequer, there to be enforced by the Sheriff as debts due to the Crown.

The Commissioners of Sewers were, however, more than a judicial authority. They were authorised and required by their Commission, as well as by the statutes,[3] " to survey the said walls, streams, ditches, banks, gutters, sewers, gates, .calcies, bridges, trenches, mills, milldams, floodgates, ponds, locks, hebbing wears and other impediments, lets and annoyances " ; to cause them " to be made, corrected, repaired, amended, put down or reformed as the case shall require," according to their own " wisdoms and discretions " ; to appoint their own " Keepers, Bailiffs, Surveyors, Collectors, Expenditors and other ministers and officers " ; to impress into their service as many " carts, horses, oxen, beasts and other instruments," and

[1] *The Reading of . . . Robert Callis,* etc., pp. 195-198 of edition of 1824.
[2] It should be said that we do not find Courts of Sewers in the eighteenth century actually imprisoning any one ; though they would occasionally threaten to do so for contempt of court.
[3] 23 Henry VIII. c. 5 (1532).

also as many "workmen and labourers" as they deemed necessary; and to appropriate compulsorily as much "timber and other necessaries" as they required. For, beyond the usual works of maintenance, if the violence of waters was exceptionally great," says the learned Callis, "either by breaking in of the sea in an extraordinary manner, or by a sudden flood or inundation of fresh waters after rain . . . no man is amerciable therefor." [1] In that case, the Jury had to apportion the estimated cost of the work among all those whose lands benefited. Meanwhile the Commissioners, as a merely administrative body, were empowered to execute "according to their wisdoms and discretions" the needful works.

The authority of the Commissioners had even its legislative side. They were expressly empowered "to make and ordain statutes, ordinances and provisions from time to time, as the case shall require, for the safeguard, conservation, redress, correction and reformation of the premises," either "after the

[1] *The Reading of . . . Robert Callis*, p. 211 of 1824 edition. It was always a matter of doubt whether the Courts of Sewers could, even on presentment of a Jury, in the greatest emergency, decide to construct an entirely new work, by a rate upon the owners of the land benefited. Sir Edward Coke decided, in the great case concerning the Isle of Ely, that no such power to rate for new works was given by the Commission. Callis, on the other hand, argued that in reason they must have such a power, and that the Statute of Sewers might be interpreted as implying it, the terms "to make new" being extended to "new making," as well as to renewing, the defences (p. 119). This view had, in fact, been held by Chief Justice Popham, and was implicitly taken by the Privy Council in 1615, when it refused to restrain certain Commissioners of Sewers who had made new banks, drains and sluices about the Isle of Ely. (The order is given in full in *The Law of Sewers*, 1726, pp. 36-41.) As a matter of fact, the Commissioners (except under special statutes) usually restricted themselves to what could, by a wide interpretation, be deemed the renewal of old works, unless they secured the unanimous consent of the owners rated. Even in Westminster in 1832 and 1845, Sewers Rates were levied only "for upholding, maintaining and improving existing lines of sewers"—not for building new lines of sewers, and eminent counsel advised that "the general powers do not extend to making new sewers" (*Substance of an Opinion delivered at a Court of Sewers for the City and Liberty of Westminster*, by T. L. Donaldson, 1835, pp. 12-13 ; House of Commons Return No. 686 of 1847, p. 19). On the other hand, the Tower Hamlets Commissioners held, in 1834, that they had power under the Statute of Sewers to make entirely new sewers by a special district rate—a claim which was upheld in the Court of Chancery in a case in 1822 (Report and Evidence of Select Committee on Metropolitan Sewers, 1834, p. 65 of Appendix D ; see also *The Law of Land Drainage and Sewers*, by G. G. Kennedy and J. S. Saunders, 1884, p. 60). Explicit authority to make new works was given in the Sewers Act of 1833 (3 & 4 William IV. c. 22, sec. 19), subject to the consent of the owners and occupiers of three-fourths in value of the lands to be charged ; but this statute was made not to apply to the Middlesex Commissions (sec. 61) which Parliament did not trust.

laws and customs of Romney Marsh," [1] or "otherwise by any ways and means" according to their own "wisdoms and discretions." The Commissioners were expressly empowered to compel obedience to their commands and regulations, either "by distress, fines and amerciaments" or by such other "punishments, ways and means" as seemed expedient to them. Finally, by a remarkable provision, the "laws and ordinances" so made by the Commissioners, which would otherwise have expired on the termination of their authority, might be made permanently binding on all men, by being "ingrossed on parchment and certified under the seals of the said Commissioners into the King's Court of Chancery, and then the King's Royal Assent be had to the same." [2] Forty years later this peculiar use of the Royal Assent was dispensed with, and the "laws, ordinances and constitutions" of the Commissioners, on the mere authority of the seals of any six of them, were made permanently binding (until expressly abrogated by other Commissioners) even after the term of the Commission had expired, or had been summarily brought to an end by writ of supersedeas.[3] Truly, the Parliaments of Henry the Eighth and Elizabeth weighed out powers to the King's Commissioners with no niggard hand! [4]

Thus, the Court of Sewers was, in structure and formal procedure, closely analogous to the Court of Quarter Sessions in its dealings with such matters of civil administration as the county bridges. But in the "laws and customs of Romney Marsh," to which the great Statute of Sewers makes pointed reference, there survived, as the student will have noticed, in the

---

[1] The Laws and Customs of Romney Marsh, thus made the authoritative model for all Commissioners of Sewers, were accordingly many times reprinted, often as an appendix to any legal treatise on the law of sewers.

[2] 23 Henry VIII. c. 5 (1532).

[3] 13 Eliz. c. 9 (1571).

[4] Throughout all their proceedings the somewhat mysterious powers of the Commissioners of Sewers added to their authority. As a Court of Record, they could fine and imprison without limit. Any kind of "contempt" of their authority, any disobedience of their decrees, and even any dissuading "persons assessed" not to pay the rate or obey the law, was summarily punishable. They could issue their own distress warrants, and their officers could thereupon distrain for all fines or amerciaments due (including Sewers Rates). They could appoint any local resident as one of their subordinate officers, and enforce service by fines. They could fine their own officers for breach of duty. When they abandoned the acre rate for a rate in the pound, they could make their own valuation and assessment of property, though in practice they latterly accepted that of the Poor Rate (*The Local Taxes of the United Kingdom*, by Danby P. Fry, 1846).

Four and Twenty Jurats representing the landowners of the
Marsh, something very like the "Gentlemen of the Four and
Twenty," who governed the little community of Braintree in
Essex, or a typical Northumberland parish.[1] Moreover, the
Court of Sewers had a good deal of the spirit which animated the
Court Leet. To the eminent Justice who in 1258 enquired into
the customs of Romney Marsh, local government meant primarily,
not the collective administration of services by a select body,
but the decisions of a judicial Court, empowered to compel each
man to abstain from committing nuisances and to fulfil his
own particular obligations to the community. With this com-
mingling of ideas, it is not unnatural that we should find it
difficult to discover what exactly was the sphere and function of
the Jury in the Court of Sewers. In the course of our preceding
volumes we have described (apart from the procedure in civil
suits between parties) four different types of Jury. The Court
Leet Jury was a Jury of neighbours, who acted on their own
view and knowledge, and who presented offenders, found them
guilty and declared their amercements. The members of the
Hundred Jury, on the other hand, as they appeared at the Court
of Quarter Sessions, acting on their own view and knowledge,
only determined facts and presented offenders. The Grand Jury
at Quarter Sessions or at the Assizes did no more, but its members
combined with their own view and knowledge the advantage of
hearing witnesses in support of the complaint. The presentments of the Grand Jury were, equally with those of the Hundred
Jury,[2] of no effect or avail unless they were, at somebody's risk
and expense, formulated into definite indictments, which could
be "traversed" by the defendants. Finally we have the
Traverse Jury (or "Felon's Jury" or simply "Petty Jury"),
composed, not of neighbours, but of indifferent persons from the
body of the County; acting, not on their own view and know-

---

[1] See *The Parish and the County*, 1907, book i. chap. v. pp. 173-246; *The
Manor and the Borough*, 1908, pp. 156, 172, etc. "It is abundantly clear that,
at least in a considerable number of districts, Commissioners found the local
community already organised for the purpose of defending the marshland; in
some districts the Commissioners set up a form of local administration on the
lines of that already existing in other places; in either case it was upon the
local community that the continuous duty, year in year out, of protecting and
draining the marshes devolved." ("Note on the Constitution and Records of
Commissions of Sewers," by H. A. Richardson, in Report of Royal Commission on Public Records, vol. ii. part ii. pp. 98-100.)

[2] And, we may add, those of the Coroner's Jury.

ledge, but exclusively on the evidence produced in Court; not presenting offenders or otherwise initiating any proceedings, but confining themselves strictly to the trial of an issue placed before them; and finding only a verdict of fact, without presuming to assess the punishment or pronounce the sentence. To which of these types did the Jury of the Court of Sewers legally belong? We might imagine from the words of the Statute of Sewers that the Jury was one of indifferent persons, to be summoned by the Sheriff of the County for each case, or at any rate for each session of the Court; whose duty was to confine themselves, like the members of the Traverse Jury, to returning a verdict of fact, on the evidence produced before them. Yet the Jury which formed part of the Court of Sewers had also, it seems clear, the duty of presenting offenders and initiating proceedings; and had, moreover, to find, not only the individuals " through whose default the said hurts and damages have happened "; but also " who hath or holdeth any land or tenements or common of pasture or profit of fishing, or hath or may have any hurt, loss or disadvantage by any manner of means in the said places "; a duty which could best be discharged by such a standing committee of resident neighbours as we know to have existed in Romney Marsh, and as we find, in fact, continuing, under the name and style of the Jury, in connection with some Courts of Sewers. Whether the presentments of such a standing Sewers Jury were, like those of the Grand Jury and Hundred Juries at the Court of Quarter Sessions, legally liable to be traversed by the person presented,[1] and whether such person could, in that event, claim to " put himself on his country," and have the issue tried by a Traverse Jury of indifferent persons chosen from the body of the County—whether, on the contrary, the Sewers Jury, like the Court Leet Jury, had ever been legally empowered (to use the words of the Bedford Level Act of 1663) " to inquire of, present and try "[2]—that is, discover the default, present the

---

[1] In the nineteenth century the Jury of Sewers was so described by lawyers, admittedly in contradiction of the practice. Its presentment, said the Clerk to the Tower Hamlets Court in 1823, " may be traversed and in that case we must issue a new precept to the Sheriff to impanel twenty-four persons from the body of the County." But it was admitted that, in all the centuries of experience of the Tower Hamlets Court, there had never been a traverse; nor within living memory, at any rate, in that of Holborn and Finsbury (Report of House of Commons Committee on Sewers in the Metropolis, 1823, pp. 9, 15).

[2] 15 Chas. II. c. 13, sec. 5.

offender, find him guilty and assess the fine, as certainly often
happened—remains to us, after much study of Callis and other
authorities, in comparison with what we know to have been the
practice, more than ever doubtful.[1]

The Corporation of the Bedford Level

We shall presently describe the evolution, between 1689 and
1835, of the local authorities formed under the statutes and Commissions of Sewers. We may believe that the extensive powers
and authorities wielded by them during the sixteenth and seventeenth centuries sufficed to provide the local government necessary
for the maintenance of the numerous embankments and walls,
sewers and dykes that had already been constructed in the low-
lying lands of Surrey and Kent, Middlesex and Essex, Somersetshire and Gloucestershire and generally along many of the sea-
coasts of the kingdom. But the great district of the Fenland [2]

---

[1] On one occasion Lord Ellenborough reprobated the practice of Courts of
Sewers having a standing Jury (Dore *v.* Gray, 2 T.R. ; Report of House of
Commons Committee on Sewers in the Metropolis, 1823, p. 9) ; see report of
a meeting of the Tower Hamlets Court of Sewers in 1828, where a ratepayer
argued the point, *Times*, 16th February 1828. The changes in practice in the
East Kent Court of Sewers are instructive on this point. It was held in a
Somersetshire case that a presentment by a standing Jury, consisting of local
landowners, and serving normally for life, was not valid, though such a Jury
was according to ancient custom in that Court of Sewers. The presentment
was held to be so far void as even not to be properly traversable, the traverse
being tried by a Jury of indifferent persons. It was held that the presenting
Jury must itself hear evidence in court (R. *v.* Commissioners of Sewers for
Somerset, in *Reports of Cases*, etc., by Sir E. H. East, vol. vii. p. 71). This case
of 1823 evidently caused much perturbation, and upset old customs. The
Sewers Act of 1833 (3 & 4 William IV. c. 22, sec. 11) decided the matter by
prescribing elaborately (sec. 11) that the Jury of the Court of Sewers should be
empanelled by the Sheriff from " substantial and indifferent persons . . .
qualified and usually summoned to serve on Grand Juries," who were, like the
Grand Jury, to hear witnesses, and to invite complaints by public notice ;
upon which they were to make their presentments, which could (as is clear
from sec. 46) be traversed, when the issue had presumably to be tried by a
Traverse Jury. But even then the Act carefully preserved the right of
Courts of Sewers to continue any " ancient custom or usage " in the way of
enquiry and presentment by Jury (sec. 17).
The different kinds of Juries deserve further examination by historians.
See the many references in *The Parish and the County*, 1907, index, pp. 625-627 ;
and *The Manor and the Borough*, 1908, index, pp. 803-805.
[2] For the strangely interesting life and history of the Fenland, see (in
addition to the works cited at p. 13) *The Fenland Past and Present*, by S. H.
Miller and S. B. Skertchley, 1878, and *Fenland Notes and Queries*, from 1889
onward. We append a list of the principal books containing information on
the subject. For mediaeval times, see *Victoria County History of Lincolnshire*,

presented a different problem. This area of thirteen hundred square miles, the largest plain of Britain, extending from Lincoln on the North to Newmarket on the South, from Stamford on the West to King's Lynn on the East, and comprising a great part of the Counties of Lincolnshire, Norfolk, Suffolk, Cambridgeshire, Northamptonshire and Huntingdonshire, was, at the end of the sixteenth century, probably at its worst. To the enterprising statesmen of Elizabeth and James the First it seemed intolerable that so large a portion of the kingdom should remain little more than "vast spreadings of water"; forming, during three-quarters of each year, an almost continuous level of "drowned lands," infested with malarious vapours and clouds of insects; good for nothing but fish and wildfowl; its half-submerged islets and bordering lands inhabited by an enfeebled and brutalised amphibious race of "breedlings" or "fen slodgers";

---

vol. ii., article on "Social and Economic History," by W. O. Massingbird, and the authorities there cited, especially *Court Rolls of the Manor of Ingoldmells*, 1902, and *History of the Parish of Ormsby*, by W. O. Massingbird, 1899. For the seventeenth, eighteenth and nineteenth centuries, see *History of the Great Level of the Fens*, by Sir Jonas Moore, 1685; *History of the Ancient and Present State of the Navigation of King's Lynn*, by T. Badeslade, 1725; *An Essay on Drainage, more particularly with regard to the North Division of the . . . Bedford Level*, 1729; *Reasons offered to the Proprietors . . . in the North Level against . . . any New Tax*, by G. Maxwell, 1788 (and over a hundred other pamphlets in B.M. vols. 8775 bb. 1, 816 m. 8, 725 g. 34, etc.); *An Historical Account of the Great Level of the Fens*, by William Elstobb, 1793; *General View of the Agriculture of the County of Hunts*, by George Maxwell, 1793; *A Collection of Laws . . . of the Bedford Level Corporation*, by C. N. Cole, 1761 and 1803; *Historical Account of the Ancient Town of Wisbech*, by W. Watson, 1827, pp. 1-84; *History of the Drainage of the Great Level of the Fens called Bedford Level*, by Samuel Wells, 1828-1830; *Regulations and Orders . . . of the Bedford Level Corporation*, by Samuel Wells, 1840; Sir J. Rennie's address to the Institute of Civil Engineers, in its *Proceedings*, 1846, vol. v. pp. 43-50; papers by R. B. Grantham in the same, 1860, vol. xix. pp. 65-75, 91-98; *Fen Sketches*, by J. A. Clarke, 1852; "The Fens," in *Prose Idylls*, by Rev. C. Kingsley, 1873; *Reminiscences of Fen and Mere*, by J. M. Heathcote, 1876; *Fenland*, by L. Gibbs, 1888; *The Story of a Great Agricultural Estate*, by the Duke of Bedford, 1897. The Ely Cathedral Library appears to contain 60 works on the Fenland between 1745 and 1810 (see list in *Fenland Notes and Queries*, vol. iii. pp. 28-29). In the realm of fiction, see *Hereward the Wake*, by Rev. C. Kingsley, 1866; *Dick o' the Fens*, by G. M. Fenn, 1888; *Cheap Jack Zita*, by S. Baring-Gould, 1893; *A Daughter of the Fen*, by J. T. Bealby, 1893; *The Camp of Refuge*, by C. Macfarlane, edited by G. L. Gomme, 1897; and *The MS. in a Red Box*, anon., 1903.

The Public Record Office has a volume of "Laws and Ordinances of the Sewers," 1602-1831, among the Chancery Petty Bag Records; a series of "Bedford Level Decrees," 1663-1683, and other records relating to the Fenland; and the Ely MS. archives contain many more (*Ely Diocesan Records*, 1891).

half fishermen and fowlers and half "commoners," keeping geese and cutting reeds in the "summerlands" of the fen. Tradition had it that in past centuries the Fenland had been forest and meadow, defended against the waters by the skill and industry of the religious houses, to whom much of it had belonged.[1] It was plain that neglect of the old works of drainage, and the silting up of the river estuaries, were at least partly responsible for the evil state to which the district had been reduced. Yet experience showed that all the powers of Commissioners of Sewers, of whom the area had had many, were inadequate to the task of reclamation. Meanwhile, the example of the Dutch Netherlands, where an even greater area had been won from the waters, inspired the statesmen of the time to new expedients. It was an age of "adventurers," encouraged by monopolies and grants. Under the patronage, first of King James and then of King Charles, successive bodies of "undertakers" were authorised to attempt the reclamation of the "surrounded" or "drowned" lands of the Fens, and were stimulated by the grant in fee simple of a large share of them. Over these enterprises we see the King, the local Commissioners of Sewers, the Lords ·of Manors and the commoners becoming involved, during the first half of the seventeenth century, in a complicated tangle of bargains and agreements concerning principally the central "Great Level" of the Fens, concluded with different groups of undertakers, whose successive engineering failures, interspersed with rebellions of the Fenmen,[2] the breaking

---

[1] It seems clear that the monks had been famous embankers and drainers; see *Ely Diocesan Records*, 1891; *The Ramsey Cartulary* (Rolls Series), 1884-1893; and *Economic Conditions of the Manors of Ramsey Abbey*, by N. Neilson, 1899. "There is a tradition that this district [the Great Level of the Fens] was overflown by the sea in the year A.D. 368, and it is beyond doubt that constant effort was needed and is still needed to keep back the incursions of the sea and to prevent the district from becoming waterlogged in winter and insanitary in summer. With this object the Romans built great dykes, such as Carsdyke and Fossedyke; and actuated as they always were to plant their settlements where abundance of hard work would purify the celibate life, the religious orders made the low-lying parts of Lincolnshire their special province. Bardney, Barlings, Spalding, Kirkstead, Torksey, Crowland, Semperingham, and many other abbeys and priories continued the work of draining this difficult district" (*Public Works in Mediaeval Law*, by C. T. Flower (Selden Society, 1915), Introduction, p. xxvii).

[2] A great majority of the inhabitants of the Fens were "utterly hostile to a general drainage of the Great Level. . . . The proceedings of the Commissioners of Sewers, basking in and flourishing under the sunbeams of royalty, were exceedingly arbitrary" (*History of the Drainage of the Great Level of the*

down of the newly established works and the bankruptcy of the contractors,[1] ended at last in the patriotic Earl of Bedford taking up the work for the good of the country. In 1663, after various earlier attempts, he and his fellow-adventurers were incorporated by Act of Parliament [2] into a new governing authority, the " Corporation of the Governors, Bailiffs and Commonalty of the Company of Conservators of the Great Level of the Fens " ; a Company which combined, with the ordinary powers of Commissioners of Sewers, those of a group of owners in severalty of 95,000 acres of " Adventurers' Lands," subject to onerous common responsibilities for maintaining the drainage of the whole 307,000 acres of the central Level of the Fenland, henceforth known as the Bedford Level. We cannot here relate the long and complicated story of the reclamation of the " Great Level " by the engineers whom the Earl and his fellow-adventurers employed ; of the prolonged struggle between the wild and lawless life of the fenmen, and the utilitarian but public-spirited aims of the local landlords ; of the gigantic engineering experiments, started with little science and less method, abandoned from lack of funds, hotly discussed and criticised at meetings of county magnates, begun anew on fresh plans, and only finally completed in our own day. Down to the early years of the nineteenth century, various parts of the Great Level were repeatedly " drowned " by exceptional floods.[3] Since that date, as was prematurely observed eighty years ago, an " alteration has taken place which may appear the effect of magic. . . . A forlorn waste has been converted into pleasant and fertile pastures. . . . Drainage, embankment, engines and enclosures have given stability to the soil . . . as well as salubrity to the air. . . . Where sedge and rushes [grew] but a few years since

---

Fens called Bedford Level, by Samuel Wells, vol. i. p. 105 ; see the *Calendar of State Papers Domestic,* especially for 1653–1656 ; and *History of England,* by S. R. Gardiner, vol. i.).

[1] For further details as to these " undertakers " for reclaiming " surrounded " lands in different parts of England, especially characteristic of the period 1600–1650, see the *History of Imbanking and Draining,* by Sir William Dugdale, 1652 ; *Lives of the Engineers,* by Samuel Smiles, 1861, vol. i. part i.

[2] 15 Charles II. c. 13 (1663).

[3] Such drownings have now ceased, though there was an exceptional temporary inundation in 1862 (see *The Story of a Great Agricultural Estate,* by the Duke of Bedford, 1897, pp. 38-48 ; *Reminiscences of Fen and Mere,* by J. M. Heathcote, 1876, pp. 97-98) ; and much land was under water for months in the exceptional rainfall of 1912.

we now have fields of waving oats and even wheat."[1] To-day, though only because steam-power and centrifugal pumps have replaced both the old windmills and the older horse-mills that were brought to the aid of drainage by gravitation,[2] the Fenland has at last been made permanently dry, and though much of its ancient charm has fled, "the long lines of pollards with an occasional windmill, stretching along the horizon as in a Dutch landscape ; the wide extended flats of dark peaty soil intersected by dykes and drains, with here and there a green tract covered with sleek cattle, have an air of vastness, and even grandeur which is sometimes very striking."[3] The anomalous Corporation of the Bedford Level, under which, with the multitudinous Local Boards, Trusts and Commissions, executing hundreds of separate Acts of Parliament, most of the work has been done, still continues in vigorous existence.[4] But its constitution has remained

[1] Report of Poor Law Commissioners on the Sanitary Condition of the Labouring Classes, 1842, p. 80.
[2] *History of the Drainage of the Great Level of the Fens*, by S. Wells, 1830, vol. i. p. 426 ; *The Drainage of Fens and Low Lands*, by W. H. Wheeler, 1888. Windmills did not become numerous until after 1726 ; steam engines not for a century afterwards ; and centrifugal pumps not until after the middle of the nineteenth century (the *Victoria County History of Lincolnshire*, vol. ii. p. 351, says not until 1867).
[3] *Lives of the Engineers*, by Samuel Smiles, 1861, vol. ii. part vii. p. 169.
[4] The Corporation of the Bedford Level, established by 15 Charles II. c. 13 (1663), consists of a Governor, six Bailiffs, twenty Conservators, who form "the Board" or governing body, and the commonalty, made up of the registered owners of the 95,000 acres of "Adventurers' Lands." All such owners can attend the public meetings of the Corporation, but only those possessing 100 acres or more can vote for the officers or the members of the governing body, who (together with the Surveyor-General, the Register, the Receiver and Expenditor-General, an Auditor, the Serjeant-at-Mace, four Superintendents and numerous sluice-keepers) are elected annually, at a meeting held, until 1809, at the "Fen Office" in London, but since that date at Ely. The Conservators and the Bailiffs and Governor must be chosen from owners of 200 and 400 acres respectively of Adventurers' Lands. The Governor has always been the Earl (or Duke) of Bedford for the time being. The Corporation, as such, owns none of the land, except its embankments and other works, with the score or so of public-houses, the cottages, and the other erections upon these embankments. Its corporate revenue (apart from the rents of these houses and the privilege of fishing, and the tolls levied on traffic along the banks and channels) is derived from taxation of the owners of the 95,000 acres of Adventurers' Lands. These have, since the Act of 20 Charles II. (1668), been divided into eleven grades, paying from 4d. to 3s. 8d. per acre for each single "tax." One or more such taxes are annually levied by the Board. Payment can be enforced by distraint, or by sale by auction of the land in default. In former years much was so forfeited, 20,000 acres being sometimes on the "arrear roll." The method of sale was peculiar, the amount due being stated, and offers being invited from those willing to pay the exact sum in return for a certain acreage, the lowest bid in area being accepted, and that

absolutely unique ;[1] and though it (and with it the Fenland generally) amply deserves a constitutional historian of its own, its story has little or no significance in the general course of English Local Government. In particular, as it was not primarily a Court of Sewers, as it has made practically no use of its powers as such a Court, and as the innumerable statutory bodies working under it, or alongside of it in the rest of the Fenland,[2] were themselves not Courts of Sewers, it can claim no further place in the present chapter.

---

acreage being alone transferred. Its corporate expenditure is incurred in the maintenance and repair of the various works under its charge throughout the whole 307,000 acres of the Level. The different parts of the Level have also separate organisations and taxations of their own ; partly due to the division into the North, Middle, and South Levels, and the respective districts of each, for which the Corporation keeps distinct accounts and levies differential taxes, expended by local committees ; partly due to the formation of District Boards, Commissions and Trusts under innumerable Acts of Parliament, for the special improvement of particular parts of the Level, or particular river channels, under which taxes are levied on all the owners of the districts, and spent by the different local governing bodies. So numerous were the Local Acts that Parliament passed a Standing Order requiring special notice to be given to the Corporation of the Bedford Level in each case (House of Commons Journals, 17th March 1813). It may be added that the members of the governing body of the Corporation were, by the Act of 1663, constituted Commissioners of Sewers in and for the entire Level, as well as for the works executed outside it. The latter provision was taken advantage of in 1816 and 1822, in order to enable the Corporation to take land compulsorily outside the Level, in order to get puddling clay. A Jury was summoned by the Serjeant-at-Mace, and a Court of Sewers held. Such a court was thenceforth regularly held as a matter of form. A glimpse of the organisation and procedure of the Corporation in 1822 is afforded by the *Autobiographic Recollections of George Pryme*, 1870, pp. 144-148. Apart from the works cited *ante*, p. 28, we know of no statistical or other exact account of the complicated local government set up by all this machinery ; or of its state at the present day. By permission of Mr. Rowland Prothero (now Lord Ernle), we have looked through the MS. Minutes of the North Level Commissioners, under an Act of 1754, from that date down to 1818, and we find them no different from those of Improvement Commissioners of the ordinary type, which we subsequently describe.

[1] In the reign of Charles II. a Bill is said to have passed the House of Lords, but to have been rejected by the House of Commons, for establishing, for Hatfield Chase in Lincolnshire, a Corporation exactly like that of the Bedford Level (*History and Topography of the Isle of Axholme*, by Rev. W. B. Stonehouse, 1839, p. 103).

[2] It is said of South Lincolnshire alone that " upwards of a hundred and sixty Acts have been passed relating to the drainage, reclamation and enclosure " of this part of the Fenland (*History of the Fens of South Lincolnshire*, by W. H. Wheeler, 1894, preface). There were, for instance, " seventeen sets of Commissioners or other authorities having jurisdiction over the Witham between Grantham and the Sea " (*The Rainfall, Water Supply and Drainage of Lincolnshire*, by W. H. Wheeler, 1879, pp. 17, 26).

Romney Marsh

Turning from the unique Corporation of the Bedford Level to the Courts of Sewers in rural districts, we are confronted with the remarkable jurisdiction of the Lords of the Level of Romney Marsh.[1] We have already described the emerging into history in the thirteenth century of the ancient local organisation for the management of the sluices and embankments of this part of the Kentish coast. Without attempting to trace its career for the next four centuries, we find it in 1689 in full operation as a Court of Sewers, existing by prescription fortified by ancient decrees and charters, without any Commission from the Crown under the Statute of Sewers. This organisation has continued, with the very minimum of alteration, down to the present day—an immobility and persistence which is in itself remarkable. We can therefore combine in a single description both its condition in 1689 and its slight development down to 1835.

The government of Romney Marsh remains, as it has apparently been from the earliest historic times, in the hands of the principal landed proprietors. The " Lords of the Level," as they have always been called, consist of the owners for the time being of

[1] For " the Lords of the Level of Romney Marsh "—to be distinguished from the entirely distinct Chartered Corporation of the Bailiff, Jurats and Commonalty of Romney Marsh, a Municipal Corporation which we have incidentally described in *The Manor and the Borough*, 1908, vol. ii. pp. 262, 281, 298, 299, 325, 327, 329, 333, 361, 367, 492, 791—we have had the privilege of access to the MS. archives from 1602 onward, preserved in the fine Elizabethan hall of the Lords, behind their great embankment at Dymchurch. We have found no adequate printed description of their organisation or functions. Beyond the great work of Sir William Dugdale, and the so-called *History of Romney Marsh*, by William Holloway, 1849, pp. 174-175, which contains singularly little on this point, we can only refer the student to the often reprinted *Laws and Customs of Romney Marsh*, dating from the thirteenth century, of which the last separate edition seems to have been that of 1840 ; and to such incidental references as are contained in papers in the *Proceedings of the Institute of Civil Engineers*, especially " An Account of the Dymchurch Wall " by James Elliot, jun. (vol. vi. pp. 466-484, 1847), and another by Green and Borthwick (vol. vii. pp. 194-196, 1848) ; *The Report of . . . British Archaeological Association . . . meeting at Canterbury*, 1844 ; the *Report of the Royal Commission on Tidal Harbours*, 1845 ; the *Report on Excavations at Lymne*, by Charles Roach Smith, 1852 ; the papers by Thomas Lewin and W. H. Black on " The Portus Lemanis of the Romans," in *Archaeologia*, vol. xl. pp. 361, 380 ; the various papers in vol. xiii. of *Archaeologia Cantiana*, 1880 ; *History of the Weald of Kent*, by Robert Furley, 1871-1874 ; *The Cinque Ports*, by Montagu Burrows, 1888 ; and *A Quiet Corner of England*, by Basil Champneys, 1875.

D

twenty-three particular estates in the Marsh,[1] together with the Bailiff for the time being of the chartered Municipal Corporation into which the commonalty of the Marsh had, in 1461, been formed. The Lords have the right of nominating deputies to represent them; and we find, as a matter of fact, in 1689 and 1835 as in 1922, most of them using this privilege. Once a year, in Whit week,[2] the Lords or their deputies met, as a "General Lath" or "Grand Lath," to appoint the officers of the Level, to decide upon the "scot" or general Marsh Rate to be levied, and to order any considerable works of repair. At other meetings, often held monthly and known as Special Laths, or Petty Laths, the current routine business was despatched and any urgent matter required for the welfare of "the Country," as the Level seems often to have been called. The officers of the Level were an Expenditor,—originally, perhaps, one of the Lords, but by 1689 a salaried executive officer[3] in whom some engineering knowledge came gradually to be expected—two Surveyors, taken in turn from among the Lords or deputies themselves; the Bailiff of the Marsh, who was also the head of the Municipal Corporation of the Commonalty; an Expenditor of the Waterings, who apparently disbursed the proceeds of the separate differential "scots" levied upon the sixteen different districts into which the Marsh was divided; and the Common Clerk, who wrote the letters and recorded the proceedings of the Lords.[4] The Bailiff of the Marsh, annually appointed, as we have mentioned, by the twenty-three Lords of the Level, but nevertheless entitled to sit and vote as one of them, was the common head of two distinct organisations, both subordinate to the Lords of the Level. Under the Charter of 1461 he was the head of the Corporation of the Bailiff, Jurats and Commonalty of Romney Marsh, renewing itself by co-option, which exercised over the whole area the magisterial and other functions of a Municipal Corporation, and

[1] No documentary warrant, by Charter or statute, can be produced for this hereditary descent of a local governing authority—a unique instance, so far as we know, in the Britain of the twentieth century, of government by tenure, resting merely on prescription.

[2] "The Lords, Bailiffs, Jurats and other officers of Romney Marsh . . . keep . . . a General Court called the Lath every Whitsun week, for the dispatch of all affairs which depend hereon " (*Travels over England, Scotland and Wales*, by Rev. James Brome, 1700, p. 268).

[3] Already in 1670 he was paid £20 a year for "extraordinary services" (MS. Minutes, Lords of Romney Marsh, 1670).

[4] *Ibid. passim.*

which has already been described by us as such.[1] But the
Bailiff had under him also the Jurats of the Level—sometimes
designated Jurats of the Walls, or even Jurats of the Marsh—
who might by tradition be twenty-four in number, but who seem
usually not to have exceeded half a dozen. These were appointed
for life by the Lords of the Level from time to time ; and they
were not necessarily, or even usually, the same as the Jurats of
the Municipal Corporation of Romney Marsh. These Jurats of
the Level were chosen from among the principal tenant farmers
of the Marsh, and their function was to serve, under the Bailiff,
as local advisers and superintendents.[2] They acted as a Jury
when any land was required, either for the enlargement of the
defences, or " to be carted," as the phrase ran, for strengthening
the great sea-wall.[3] There was, moreover, yet another subordinate organisation of the Marsh, by its immemorial division
into sixteen " Waterings," each under the Expenditor of Waterings, having its own " Quilor," or collector appointed for life
at the General Lath ; sometimes its own Expenditor, levying
and expending, under the general authority of the Lords of the
Level, a separate Watering Scot, or differential rate ; and
apparently also its own subordinate officers, who could be
ordered, as in 1670, to " brush " the common sewers of their
Watering at least once a year.[4]

[1] This peculiar Municipal Corporation (as to which see *The Manor and the
Borough*, pp. 272, 281, 298, 309, 325, 327, 329, 333, 361, 367, 492, 721) still
(1922) continues to exist in its unreformed state, its members annually electing,
from among its twenty-four Jurats, four of them to act as Justices of the Peace.
These, with the Aldermen of the City of London, the Mayors of Boroughs
and the Chairmen of the Urban District Councils, are (1922) probably the
only popularly elected magistrates in England. The Corporation of Romney
Marsh was omitted from the Municipal Corporations Act of 1835, and was
specially excepted from the operation of that of 1883.

[2] Thus, in 1611, the Bailiff and Jurats are instructed " to be assisting to
the Expenditor to look after the workmen " ; being allowed eighteen pence
each day employed (MS. Minutes, Lords of Romney Marsh, 1611).

[3] " It is ordered that a survey be taken by the Bailiff and Jurats on the
land of Mr. B. in the occupation of T. A., and now fenced off to the Country ;
and to report the quantity, quality and value of the said lands at the next
General Lath ; and that the same be discharged and discontinued from paying
any further scots for the future from this present Lath " (*ibid.* 1707). " Ordered
that the Bailiff and Jurats do before the next monthly meeting survey the lands
of the said A. B. where the Country shall have occasion to set a wall, and at
the said monthly meeting to report the quantity and quality and value of the
said lands " (*ibid.* 1707).

[4] *Ibid.* 1670. The officers of the Waterings had to be in attendance at
every Lath. " It is ordered that the Surveyors do give to the Marsh six days
notice of every monthly account, and that they forthwith give notice to the

Under this somewhat complicated organisation—which remained, notwithstanding its elaboration, essentially of the most primitive type — the proprietors, tenant farmers and wage labourers of Romney Marsh seem to have jogged along in peace with the very minimum of history. Most of the Lords habitually left it to their agents or stewards to attend the Laths, and to serve in turn as Surveyors. The two Surveyors, usually appointed in alphabetical order, indiscriminately from among Lords or deputies, acted for their year of service as a sort of executive committee, with whom the Common Clerk or the Expenditor would confer. The Expenditor carried out all the works. The Bailiff and his four or six Jurats served as a kind of Standing Jury, either reporting " on their own view and knowledge " minor repairs that were required, or superintending the different works : occasionally, as we have seen, assessing the compensation due to particular owners and occupiers. We do not find that the vague authority of the Lath to levy " scots " ; to appropriate the " Marsh thorns " ; [1] to occupy particular lands for new defences, sluices or roads ; or to order the valuable top soil of other lands, as the phrase ran, " to be carted " to the wall, was ever disputed.[2]

Sergeant, and the Sergeant give four days notice to the Bailiff, Jurats and Quilors of the several Waterings, that they may give their attendance at the said account ; and that the said Quilors give in their said accounts at every monthly meeting " (MS. Minutes, Lords of Romney Marsh, 1689). There was sometimes also an " Expenditor of the Outlands," and we hear of a Woodreeve, a Sergeant of the Walls, and other officers.

[1] This relates to the stunted whitethorn trees which once existed on the Marsh. Down to the middle of the eighteenth century timber was extensively used in strengthening the sea-wall ; and the Lords of the Level enforced a right of felling, for the use of " the Country," such trees as were needed. With this view, all clumps of trees on the Marsh—called " bush "—were held sacred and reserved, the owner having no power to destroy them for his own purposes. When a " bush " was deemed unsuitable, or not likely to be required, it might be " discharged," and thus placed fully within the power of the landowner. Hence we read, in the first volume of the existing minutes (1602–1671), many entries such as " Mr. A.'s bush discharged " ; " all bushes to be discharged which shall be reported not worth keeping " ; and " all bushes to be surveyed after the fellings [to see] if felled according to order." The owners were paid so much a load for these " Marsh thorns " (ibid. 1602–1671). All such " bush " had, we learn, disappeared from the Marsh by 1700. (" Account of the Dymchurch Wall," by James Elliott, jun., in Proceedings of Institute of Civil Engineers, 1847, vol. vi. pp. 466-484.)

[2] Arrears sometimes accumulated, chiefly through the neglect of the Bailiff, who delayed to enforce payment " by the usual return of a Bill of Wains, according to the Laws and Customs of Romney Marsh " (MS. Minutes, Lords of Romney Marsh, 1820).

The thousand years of warfare with the waves, by which alone the Marsh had been won, had evidently produced an abiding sense of the need for a strong government.[1] Along with this goes perhaps the fact that the compensation which " the Country " made to the individual was assessed on a liberal scale. If he had to cede his thorns to repair the wall, he secured a good market for every load. If his land was taken, both he and his tenant farmer got generous terms.[2] Even if it was merely the surface of two or three acres that was " carted " to the wall, he might be paid " twenty years' purchase at the rate of twenty-two shillings per acre per annum," whilst his tenants would receive compensation in addition " for the damage in their herbage and grass." [3] The cost of the works, as of the current administration, was defrayed by substantial rates or scots levied according to acreage, either uniformly throughout the Marsh, or upon one or more Waterings, and collected from the tenant farmers. These rates sometimes ran up to six or seven shillings per acre, but it was customary for the landlords to allow their tenants to deduct from their rents any exceptional levies. Such allowances have always been recommended by the Lath ; [4] and it has long been the practice of the owners voluntarily to allow the tenants any excess in the rate over half-a-crown per acre. At the very end of our survey, it was suggested by the Expenditor of Waterings, in 1833, that the differential " Watering Scots " might be done away with, and merged in the general scot levied on all alike [5] —a suggestion that was presently adopted.

[1] Only once do we find the authority of the Lords seriously questioned, and that was subsequent to 1835. In 1854 some discontented persons obtained a Mandamus against them, ordering them to show cause why they did not appoint the full number of 24 Jurats of the Marsh. The Lords resisted, claiming full discretion, and the case came to trial at the Assizes in July 1856. No decision was arrived at, as it was agreed by the parties to state a special case for the Court of King's Bench ; and before this was done the claimants abandoned the case (MS. Minutes, Lords of Romney Marsh, 1854–1856).

[2] In 1732 an owner was paid thirty years' purchase at thirty shillings per acre per annum, for land taken for the wall (ibid. 17th May 1732).

[3] Ibid. 1707.

[4] " At this Lath," we read in 1706, " it is declared that (considering the expensive and extraordinary scots to be raised for the defence of this Level) it is very reasonable that the landlords and owners of land in this Level do allow proportionate part of the scots paid by their tenants, forasmuch as their inheritance is in danger " (ibid. 1706).

[5] Ibid. 23rd May 1833. These differential rates had begun to be complained of. In 1829 the Lath imposed (1) a general " scot " of sixpence per acre ; (2) an additional sixpence " on the Wall " ; (3) half-a-crown " on Willop and

We need not follow the chequered engineering experiences of the Lords of the Level ; the successive stages by which their Expenditor became an expert civil engineer, commanding a permanent staff of skilled workmen ; [1] the calling in of the great Rennie in 1803 to organise their defences on a scientific basis ; the multiplication and elaboration of their sewers and sluices ; and the gradual transformation of their great dam, from a shingle bank strengthened by a long perpendicular earthwork, " armed " by a facing of brushwood, held down by oak stakes and lathes,[2] into the present massive front of stone and concrete, guarded by projecting steps and breakwaters.[3] More interesting may be the glimpse that we catch, in 1804, of the visit of " the Chancellor of the Exchequer and Lord Warden of the Cinque Ports " (William Pitt), accompanied by three Generals, to arrange for the instant flooding of the whole Marsh in the expected event of the French landing. Four of the Lords of the Level were got together to meet the Great Commoner, and these took upon themselves to order the Common Clerk, if he received the word from the General in command, to direct the Expenditor instantly to open the sluices and admit the sea— a patriotic order confirmed nine days later at a Special Lath.[4]

It is one of the minor paradoxes of English Local Government that the Lords of the Level of Romney Marsh, whose reorganisation in 1258 by Sir Henry de Bathe became a starting-point for subsequent reorganisations of local Courts of Sewers all over

---

Horne's Waterings " ; and (4) one and fivepence " on the Waterings sewing at Clobsdon." The occupiers of Willop and Horne's Waterings protested that this charge ought to be met by a general scot ; and the Lath adopted their view (MS. Minutes, Lords of Romney Marsh, May, July and August, 1829).

[1] In 1814 the Lords put the office up to auction, inviting by advertisement " tenders for the place of Expenditor . . . from persons undertaking the management of the Walls and Sewers " (ibid. 1814).

[2] See paper by Green and Borthwick in Proceedings of Institute of Civil Engineers, 1848, vol. vii. pp. 194-196.

[3] In 1706 much of the Marsh was under water, and the defences had to be strengthened. Between 1766 and 1806 great timber groins were constructed to prevent the shingle shifting. Not until 1803 was any professional engineer consulted ; and then about £50,000 was spent on Rennie's advice, in transforming the Wall from a perpendicular to a sloping dam. Stone did not begin to be used until 1825, and the present systematic walling of stone and concrete was begun in 1837 on the advice of Walker (" An Account of the Dymchurch Wall," by James Elliott, jun., in Proceedings of the Institute of Civil Engineers, 1847, vol. vi. pp. 466-484).

[4] MS. Minutes, Lords of Romney Marsh, 5th September 1804 ; see footnote on p. 106.

the country; whose "Laws and Customs" were specifically adopted as the model for all other Courts, and were eventually made the basis of the celebrated Statute of Sewers, should never themselves have come under that statute, or been included in any Commission of Sewers from the Lord Chancellor. The Lords of the Level continue to-day (1922), as they were in 1689–1835, an ancient relic of pre-statutory local government, which we have had perforce to describe as a Court of Sewers—indeed, as the very arch-type of all Courts of Sewers—but which nevertheless is not, and never has been, as other Courts of Sewers are.

Somersetshire

We return to our description of the constitutional evolution of the ordinary Courts of Sewers acting under periodically renewed Commissions from the Crown. Exactly how many Commissions of Sewers were in force at each period between 1689 and 1835 is not now to be discovered, though we gather that it never exceeded a hundred.[1] They were, we infer, occasionally initiated during the eighteenth century among the Justices in Quarter Sessions, who directed the Clerk of the Peace to petition for a Commission of Sewers for a particular district, where some authoritative intervention was required; when the Justices ordered him to pay the fees out of the county fund.[2] Excluding the authorities of the Fenland, and those which we shall presently describe as acting for the Metropolitan area, the proceedings of these Courts of Sewers do not appear to have been either important or exciting. Their organisation appears

[1] The number is given as 80 in the *First Report of the Royal Commission on the Health of Large Towns*, 1845. A list of 42 will be found in the *Report of the Poor Law Commissioners on Local Taxation*, 1844, which is there stated to comprise all the commissions then in force (p. 71). But this includes only two or three of the Fenland authorities. The 42 Courts had 5809 members, varying from 16 (Fobbing in Essex) and 18 (Narberth and Tenby), up to 290 for Nottingham District, and no fewer than 593 for Somersetshire. We note the statement, without verifying it, that these rural commissions of sewers present striking resemblances to the "associations polderiennes" or (the very word used for a district and rating unit in Romney Marsh) "wateringen" existing in Belgium (*Le Gouvernement Local de l'Angleterre*, by Maurice Vauthier, 1895, p. 342).

[2] So in Suffolk in 1745 for the Hundreds of Blything, Wangford, Mutford and Lothingland (MS. Minutes, Quarter Sessions, Suffolk, 7th October 1745); and in Cambridgeshire in 1795 for 30 parishes about Trumpington and Grantchester (MS. Minutes, Quarter Sessions, Cambridgeshire, 16th January and 13th February 1795).

to have been of the most primitive character.[1]   It is, however,
fair to warn the student that this is the most obscure corner in
the whole of English Local Government.   We know of no
detailed description of the actual working of these Courts in
the rural districts,[2] and only in two cases have we been able
to consult their manuscript records.   What seems interesting,
from such scanty information as we possess, is the unexpected
part that, during the eighteenth century, we find played by the
Jury.

To take, for instance, the county of Somerset, which had
many square miles of marsh, including the ancient " Isle of
Avalon " and the historic Athelney, to be protected from floods.[3]

[1] " In the rural districts the men appointed as surveyors by the local Commissioners [of Sewers] are very little better than common labourers. . . . They
are commonly a sort of foreman of the labourers, called ditchcasters " (*Poor
Law Commissioners' General Report on the Sanitary Condition of the Labouring
Population*, 1842, p. 316).

[2] Brief and unilluminating accounts of such rural Commissions may occasionally be found in local histories : see, for instance, that of the Tendring
Hundred Level (Essex) in *Tendring Hundred in the Olden Time*, by J. Yellowby
Watson, 1878, p. 70 ; and those of the two separate " Levels " of Gloucestershire, in *New History of Gloucestershire*, by S. Rudder, 1779, p. 26.   A paper
on the Commissioners for the Lewes Levels by Sir Henry Ellis will be found
in *Sussex Archaeological Collections*, vol. x., 1858, pp. 95-99, giving documents of
1421-1538 only.   More information as to their working may be gained from
occasional cases, such as R. *v.* Commissioners of Sewers for Essex, 1820, in
Reports of Cases, etc., by J. Dowling and A. Ryland, vol. ii., 1823, pp. 700-706 ;
or from the very infrequent controversial pamphlets.

An " Order of the Court of Sewers for Berks and Oxon," held at Abingdon,
26th May 1681, is given in *House of Lords Manuscripts*, vol. i. (N.S.), 1900,
pp. 547-548.   Some Municipal Corporations (among which we may mention
Norwich, Southampton and Oxford) got established Courts of Sewers to help
them to deal with their river conservancy and navigation ; and we have been
able to consult the records of these Courts, which often became practically committees of the Corporation, among the municipal archives (see *The Manor and
the Borough*, 1908, pp. 556, 577, etc.).

[3] For the Somerset Courts of Sewers, we have been able to consult the MS.
Minutes from 1789 to 1835 ; see also the incidental references and descriptions
in *The History of Imbanking and Draining*, by Sir William Dugdale, 1652,
pp. 104-110 of edition of 1772 ; *General View of the Agriculture of the County
of Somerset*, by John Billingsley, 1794, pp. 123-126, 2nd edition, 1798, pp. 166-
198 ; *Observations on the Great Marshes and Turbaries of . . . Somerset*, by
Rev. W. Phelps, 1835; " An Historical Account of the Marshlands of Somerset,"
by Richard Locke, in *Bath and West of England Agricultural Society's Letters
and Papers*, vol. viii. pp. 259-284 ; *Report of the Poor Law Commissioners on
the Sanitary Condition of the Labouring Population*, 1842, pp. 86-87 ; *Lives of
the Engineers*, by S. Smiles, 1861, vol. i. p. 15 ; *A General Account of West
Somerset*, by Edward Jeboult, 1873, pp. 85-86 ; *The Seaboard of Mendip*, by
F. A. Knight, 1902 ; *History of a Part of West Somerset*, by Sir C. E. H. Chadwick Healey, 1901 ; and *Victoria County History of Somerset*, vol. ii. chapter
on " Social and Economic History," by Gladys Bradford.   Something may be

Here, as in the Fenland, the "drownings" were "caused, not so much by high tides from the sea, as by the banks of the main rivers not being sufficiently strong or elevated, and from the bridges not being capacious enough to carry the immense body of water brought down from the neighbouring hills and country higher up, which, in heavy rains, sometimes takes place so rapidly as to completely overflow the banks in twenty-four hours." But, in addition to the inundations due to this cause, or to the "casual or accidental giving way of the banks of the rivers," minor floodings were sometimes caused, we are told, "by interested persons for the purpose of warding off the mischief from themselves by throwing it on their neighbours."[1] The casual interventions of the King's Justices to settle the disputes that arose as to drainage seem to have been succeeded, long before the end of the seventeenth century,[2] by a single and virtually permanent Commission of Sewers for the whole county, which included, as we gather, practically all the important landowners. But it is significant that we do not find this body, as might have been expected from the tenor of its Commission, holding a single Court of Sewers, using a Jury of indifferent persons summoned by the Sheriff[3] to try issues of fact, issuing its decrees by its own officers, executing the works decided on by its own ordinances, and levying its Sewers Rate upon the whole of the marsh lands within its jurisdiction. On the contrary, we see, right down to the nineteenth century, the daily administration of the banks and sluices of the Somerset marshes performed—as we imagine, quite extra-legally—by a couple of thousand of the marsh-dwelling commonalty, divided into about a hundred separate bodies called Juries. Each marsh had, in

gathered from the important case, R. v. Commissioners of Sewers for Somerset, in *Reports of Cases*, etc., by Sir E. H. East, vol. vii. p. 71; the Sedgemoor and other Inclosure Acts; the "Drainage Awards" for the Axe and the Brue, and for Congresbury, 1806, 1810 and 1826, in *Seventh Report of Hist. MSS. Commission*; and from various papers in the *Transactions of the Somerset Archaeological and Natural History Society*, from 1849 onwards.

[1] *Report of the Poor Law Commissioners on the Sanitary Condition of the Labouring Population*, 1842, p. 86.

[2] Commissions of Sewers for different parts of Somerset have been traced from 1304 (*A General Account of West Somerset*, by E. Jeboult, 1873, p. 85).

[3] So little had the High Sheriff to do with constituting or attending the Somerset Courts of Sewers as a county official that we find him, on one occasion, presiding over the Court as a Commissioner during his year of office as Sheriff (MS. Minutes, Court of Sewers, Somerset, Bridgwater, 18th March 1801).

fact, its own Standing Jury, composed, not of indifferent persons summoned by the Sheriff from the body of the county, but of the occupiers of the lands and tenements actually concerned impanelled by the Foremen of the Juries themselves ; serving apparently in rotation or on the nomination of the other jury-men ; [1] presided over by a Foreman on whom great responsibility was cast, and who was compelled to act continuously for at least ten years,[2] making their own regular perambulations of their respective marshes to scrutinise all the banks and walls, " clys " and " rhines," gates and sluices ; formulating their decisions in " presentments " on their own view and knowledge ; amercing individuals for neglect to fulfil their customary obligations ; deciding whether the necessary repairs fell to the charge of particular landholders or should be paid for by a " Moor Rate " on the marsh as a whole ; and, through their Foremen, both collecting and expending the rate so assessed.[3]

It is impossible not to see in these Standing Juries the sur-viving remnants of some primitive organisation, under which

---

[1] " Chedzoy Jury, W. H. and J. E. to be discharged next Sessions on pro-viding two men to be sworn in their stead (MS. Minutes, Sewer Commissioners, Somerset, Bridgwater, 11th June 1790). " Any two jurymen . . . are allowed to exchange places on their respective Juries on application to the Court " (*ibid.* Langport, 29th September 1790). " Whereas," runs a decree of the Langport Court in 1790, " several improper persons are compelled to serve, and others are drawn to attend the duty of sewers at a great distance from their homes ; a number of Juries are composed of 23 persons, while others have scarce enough to perform their duty properly ; and a quick succession takes place in some Juries, the persons thereon sometimes serving no more than two years, while others are compelled to serve twenty years, it is hereby ordered that . . . the Clerk issue no summons for a juror or jurors till he or they shall be presented to this Court as proper persons to serve on Juries at the Sessions of Sewers ; and the Foremen of all and every Jury are ordered to make a list of persons so to be presented at the following sessions " (*ibid.* Langport, 29th September 1790).

[2] " Ashcote Jury, Mr. J. M. Foreman, to go out of the Jury next Sessions " (*ibid.* Bridgwater, 11th June 1790). " That no person who shall have been discharged as Foreman of a Jury of Sewers shall at any future time be subject to be called upon to serve on a Jury but as Foreman ; and that no Foreman shall be discharged under service of ten years, unless sufficient cause shall be shown to the contrary " (*ibid.* Langport, 1st June 1803).

[3] " A rate granted at fourpence per acre for the repair of the clys, bridge and rhines within the parish of Weston Zoyland, and Mr. T. H. and Mr. T. are appointed Collectors ; sum raised £35 : 15 : 5 " (*ibid.* Bridgwater, 8th May 1789). " A rate was granted at ten shillings per leaze on 74 leazes for re-pairing Ham Wall : sum raised £37 " (*ibid.* Bridgwater, 11th June 1790). " Upon the petition of the Foreman and Jurors . . . it is ordered that a rate be granted on the proprietors of lands in the Salt Marsh at threepence in the pound for repairing and amending certain walls, old clys and other works " *ibid.* Bridgwater, 8th October 1790).

the peasant owners or occupiers of each marsh looked after their little defences. In the nineteenth century—perhaps because of the animadversions of the Judges, who could not understand how there came to be a Standing Jury of neighbours instead of a Jury of indifferent persons summoned by the Sheriff from the body of the County; or perhaps in direct consequence of the 1833 Act—we see these ancient Juries fading away, and being replaced in their administrative functions, after 1833, by Dyke-reeves acting under the instructions of the Commissioners themselves.[1]

As we have already mentioned, the Somerset marshes came very early to enjoy, instead of the occasional intervention of specially commissioned Justices of Sewers, the superintendence of a virtually permanent body of the principal landowners. It is interesting to see that, as the Court of Sewers for the County of Somerset, this body itself assumed an extra-legal form, possibly in conformity with ancient local custom. The Commissioners, instead of holding one Court, divided themselves habitually into four groups, according to the locality of their lands, each district having its own Court, distinct from the rest of the county. Each Court had the superintendence of the two or three dozen Juries of its neighbourhood.[2] The scanty minutes of what were virtually four, and presently five, separate Courts, which sat respectively at Bridgwater, Axbridge, Langport, Glastonbury and Wells, with occasional adjournments to smaller places, show how formal or spasmodic was the intervention which the half a dozen Commissioners who deigned to attend the annual or six-monthly Court of their district exercised in the administration of its drainage works. A large proportion of the decrees of the Courts relate, indeed, not to the works, but to the Juries—fining

[1] MS. Minutes, Court of Sewers, Somerset, 1833-1834; R. v. Commissioners of Sewers for Somerset, in *Reports of Cases*, etc., by Sir E. H. East, vol. vii. p. 71; *Observations on the Great Marshes and Turbaries of . . . Somerset*, by Rev. W. Phelps, 1835, pp. 6-8.

[2] These Courts even multiplied themselves by fission. In 1827, in response to petitions from several of the Juries, the Court held at Wells came to the conclusion that " the holding of a Session at Glastonbury twice a year, as well as Wells, would tend greatly to the expediting the public business and be a great convenience to several of the Juries, who are obliged to take a long journey to Wells." Accordingly, 16 of the Juries are ordered henceforth to attend at Glastonbury only, the Commissioners similarly divide themselves in their attendance as their propinquity dictates, and what to all intents and purposes is a separate Court is thenceforth constituted (MS. Minutes, Court of Sewers, Somerset, Wells, 8th August 1827).

persons who refuse the onerous office, or fail to put in an appearance ;[1] discharging those who are unfit for service or who undertake to provide a substitute ; transferring particular banks and
sluices from the purview of one Jury to that of another ; auditing
the accounts of the Foremen as Collectors and Expenditors, and
so on. Beyond this general work of supervising the action of
the Juries, the chief function of the Somerset Courts seems to
have been that of formally confirming and legalising the various
small " Moor Rates " imposed for the works ordered by the
several Juries ; and that of arbitrating between the Juries and
particular owners or occupiers on whom the duty of repair had
been cast. On complaint from one or other party, the Court
would depute some of its members to hold a special " view,"[2]
and on report made to the next Court would pronounce a final
decree. In an exceptional case we see a Court requiring or
permitting a joint meeting of all the Juries within its Division
(which may, however, have been only a meeting of their Foremen), to " present that from the imperfect drainage . . . through
the whole of the said Division the same is continually flooded . . .
and . . . that it appears necessary that some new drains should
be made." The Court thereupon points out that such works
would necessitate an Act of Parliament, for which the Commissioners decide to apply.[3] But so little did the Commissioners
deal with executive business that the minutes hardly ever show
them as entering into contracts either for works or supplies. It
is clear that each Expenditor bought his own supplies and hired
his own labour. When, however, unusually important works
were specified in any Jury presentment, as, for instance, the
rebuilding of a sea-wall, it is occasionally suggested in the latter
years that the advice of a competent engineer should be obtained ;
and then we see the Commissioners employing such an officer,
discussing his report, and apparently ordering the work, at the
expense, be it noted, of the landholders of the particular marsh,
who in one case are expressly requested " to advance necessary
sums of money," to be adjusted when the rate on all those

---

[1] " H. J. F. of Taunton, silversmith, fined £5 for not attending his Foreman
and Jury on their view. Absolutely having been duly summoned. Estreated "
(MS. Minutes, Court of Sewers, Bridgwater, 7th October 1791). Generally, the
fines were remitted, on the juror attending, subject to his paying a small fee for
his discharge.
[2] *Ibid.* Bridgwater, 8th May 1789.   [3] *Ibid.* Langport, 4th June 1800.

interested has been levied.[1] When extensive new works were required for the drainage of the River Axe district, the Court of Sewers exercising jurisdiction over that district sanctioned an Act of Parliament being obtained. But that Act conferred the necessary powers on a separate body of Commissioners, who carried out the work, brought their business to a close within the ten years allowed to them by the Act, and then handed the district back to the Court of Sewers to be administered for the future under its ordinary powers.[2]

East Kent

The owners and occupiers of lands in East Kent [3] had an easier, if a more varied problem to deal with than those of Somerset.

[1] MS. Minutes, Court of Sewers, Bridgwater, 22nd January and 6th February 1799. In another case, where a proprietor had himself repaired Huntspill sea-wall, he compelled the Commissioners by mandamus to levy a rate for his reimbursement, after they had formally refused to do so, on all the proprietors of lands within that particular Level (*ibid.* Bridgwater, 11th January and 28th September 1802, 10th and 27th June 1803).

[2] *Ibid.* Axbridge, 20th November 1800, 26th January, 11th February, 18th March, 18th May, 6th and 20th January, and 20th October 1801, 1st October 1811. River Axe Drainage Act, 1802 ; *Observations on the Great Marshes and Turbaries of . . . Somerset*, by Rev. W. Phelps, 1835, p. 13 ; *The Seaboard of Mendip*, by F. A. Knight, 1902, pp. 350-351. This precedent was not always followed. The Brue Drainage Act of 1801 (41 George III. c. 72) seems to have been administered by the Commissioners who acted in the Mid-land Division of the County, meeting at Wells ; but their proceedings under it seem, from the exiguous MS. Minutes, 1801–1880, to have been unimportant, involving only one meeting a year. The Sedgemoor Drainage Act (10 & 11 William III. c. 26 (1699) was similarly administered by those for the Western Division, meeting at Bridgwater. Sedgemoor was enclosed under Act of 1791 (31 George III. c. 91). There is now a Drainage Board under the Acts of 1865 and 1877 (28 & 29 Vic. c. 23, and 40 & 41 Vic. c. 36).

[3] We know the Commissioners of Sewers for East Kent practically only through their MS. Minutes, which we have read from 1681 to 1829. There were other Courts in Kent, some of them mentioned as existing in 1290 in Sir William Dugdale's *History of Imbanking and Draining*, edition of 1772, p. 37. Some correspondence of 1747–1759 as to various Courts of Sewers in Kent is catalogued in the *Archives of All Souls College*, by C. Trice Martin, 1877, pp. 226-227 ; whilst incidental references to these Courts will be found in the House of Lords *Journals* for 16th May 1776, and in such works as *Collections for a History of Sandwich*, by W. Boys, 1792, p. 724, and *History of Romney Marsh*, by W. Holloway, 1849. We have not fathomed the relations between these several Courts of Sewers, including that mentioned in the old pamphlets about the Rother Levels in South-West Kent, entitled *A Remonstrance of some Decrees and other Proceedings of the Commissioners of Sewers*, 1659 ; *An Objection made against the Abatement of the Scots of those lands, formerly deep drowned lands and now called summer lands*, 1650 ; and *The Animadverter Animadverted*, 1663—all by Sir Nathaniel Powell, Bart. Nor do we know what relations, if any, they had with the Lords of the Level of Romney Marsh.

Here and there along the coast, from Whitstable to Deal, we read of the occasional inroads of the sea. More troublesome than these winter storms seem to have been the sluggish streams of the Stour and its tributaries, which were always getting choked with weeds, and causing, at every rainy season, floodings of the adjacent lands. Even in the ancient " County Corporate " of the City of Canterbury, the houses along the river were in such continual peril of inundation that we find their owners specially charged at a double rate for the maintenance of the river banks.[1] And in this County, more than in any other, we hear of the misdeeds of the millers, who will not open their sluices so as to let down the water which is " drowning " the lands above them ; or who do not stop the weeds from passing down the stream to the annoyance of those below them.[2] To remedy all these evils, we find existing in 1689, a single body of Commissioners, over one hundred in number, whose jurisdiction apparently extended from Whitstable on the north, right away to Wye on the south-west, and covered all the eastern portion of the County of Kent, including the City of Canterbury, and, at Sandwich, even a small part of the territory of the Liberty of the Cinque Ports.

The hundred or more Commissioners of Sewers for East Kent, unlike those for the County of Somerset, exhibit no sign of multiplication by fission. We see them meeting, ten or twenty in number, always as a single Court, regularly at Canterbury in " General Sessions " ; at first in the Archbishop's Palace, and afterwards at the municipal Guildhall, three times a year ; and in " Special Sessions " occasionally at the principal taverns of the city. As in Somerset, there are Standing Juries, who were, for a long time, not summoned by the Sheriff " from the body of the County," but served practically for life, appointed by the

[1] MS. Minutes, Commissioners of Sewers of East Kent, 8th June 1710. This fell into abeyance in 1732, when the inhabitants opposed the tax ; and the Court let it drop. In 1828 the question was again raised, and the Corporation agreed to do the necessary work, if the Commissioners would contribute something (ibid. 22nd May, and 2nd and 4th June 1828).

[2] As to opening the sluices, ibid. 24th April 1707 ; as to the weeds, ibid. 1st May 1690, 3rd June 1708. " Upon complaint made to this Court of the several millers of . . . in suffering the weeds to pass through their several mills, whereby it becomes very prejudicial to the valleys below, it is ordered that the said several millers do cause the said weeds to be drawn out before they do pass through their respective mills, upon penalty of forty shillings, etc." (ibid. 1st May 1690).

Court " during the Court's pleasure " one by one, as vacancies occurred by death or otherwise ; and periodically resworn in a body, at the session at which the new Commission was read.[1] These Standing Juries, evidently composed of local farmers, went about in twos and threes, " viewing " streams and sluices, and making presentments to the Court.[2] We may suspect them of being, like other similar Sewers Juries, older than the Commissioners to whom they came to be subordinate, but of this, in East Kent, we have no actual evidence. At the end of the seventeenth century we find existing one such " Jury of the General Valleys," whatever these may have been, and between twenty and thirty other Juries for particular " Valleys," as the local districts or " levels " seem to have been called.

It is interesting to notice that one juryman from each Jury, and only one, was required or allowed to be in attendance at the sessions of the Court,[3] a fact which reminds us of the representation by the " Chief Pledge " of the other members of his tithing.[4] Presently, in 1713, some one raises the question as to the status of these Juries ; and when the Commissioners take counsel's opinion, they are advised to get the Sheriff to summon the Juries. From 1713, accordingly, the Sheriff of the County of Kent has to be requested every decade, when a new Commission is obtained, by means of a special journey of the Clerk which costs thirty shillings, to go through the form of summoning a Jury from the body of the County. He does this for a guinea fee ;[5] and the Sheriff of the City of Canterbury does the same for the Jury for that " County Corporate." But it is a matter of form only. The old jurymen are nominated to the Sheriff, as each Commission comes to the end of its term, for him to summon the same person to serve for another decade.[6] The Juries thus remain Standing Juries, not of " indifferent persons " charged to return a verdict on a particular case, but permanently composed of the very

[1] MS. Minutes, Commissioners of Sewers of East Kent, 12th October 1699, 13th October 1715, 31st May 1716, 20th June 1717.
[2] Usually only signed by two Jurymen (*ibid.* 24th April 1718).
[3] *Ibid.* 27th April 1693. There was, it should be explained, an allowance for dinner. The Expenditor designated the Juryman who was to appear, and the duty was not to be imposed on a man more than once in a twelvemonth.
[4] *The Manor and the Borough*, pp. 22, 23.
[5] MS. Minutes, Commissioners of Sewers, East Kent, 15th October 1713, 6th October 1739.
[6] *Ibid.* 28th April 1715, 8th April 1725, 8th October 1757, 8th April 1758.

persons whose lands and interests are concerned; really local bodies of subordinate administrators.[1]

There was evidently an extensive and well-understood series of obligations on particular lands, probably of immemorial usage, to keep in good order the portions of the sluices, walls and embankments on the several holdings, and to "repair their several defects."[2] Sometimes the owners and occupiers themselves were ordered to restore particular embankments and sea-walls, each apparently being responsible for the portion on his own land.[3] We see the Municipal Corporation of Sandwich held responsible for keeping in repair the walls and embankments within that Borough; and the Mayor and Jurats are hauled over the coals by the Commissioners for also neglecting to cleanse the stream by "coffining."[4] But the main instruments for executing works were the Expenditors. The Court appointed, not only a Bailiff and "General Expenditor," as well as a Clerk to the Commissioners, but also an Expenditor for each of the Valleys; choosing apparently from among two names submitted every second year by the jurymen of each Valley at the Easter session of the Court.[5] It was the Expenditors, who seem to have been paid about thirty shillings a year each, who were blamed for "not looking after the sluice and for not cleansing . . . the stream."[6] It was usually the Expenditors who were ordered to execute works—to cleanse away "the foulness of Blackwell Dyke"; to "cause the weeds of the Little River to be drawn out betwixt this and Midsummer next"; to drag the Great Stour

[1] In 1738 counsel's opinion was again taken, the advice being that there should be a Jury of at least 24 persons summoned by the Sheriff, for continuous service during the whole decade; and that their presentments should be made by at least twelve of them (MS. Minutes, Commissioners of Sewers, East Kent, 7th October 1738). This advice was acted upon until 1823, when the decision in R. v. Commissioners of Sewers for the County of Somerset upset the practice (*ibid.* 14th June 1823; 22nd May 1828). The "views" and presentments of the Juries, with the attendances of the Expenditors, and their dining together, and the engrossing of the "inquisitions" became expensive—in one case running up to £178 : 5 : 4 (*ibid.* 6th October 1759).

[2] *Ibid.* 29th April 1693, 24th April 1707, 15th October 1719. The occupiers in one case are ordered to "make up the Lowes on each side of the Barreways " (*ibid.* 23rd May 1695).

[3] "Upon complaint, this day made . . . for the not repairing of a certain wall in Hackling's Land . . . which if not speedily done will endanger the overflowing of several lands there . . . ordered that the owners or occupiers . . . do sufficiently amend the said wall," etc. (*ibid.* 11th June 1691).

[4] *Ibid.* 12th October 1699, 28th April and 11th June 1750.

[5] *Ibid.* 1st May 1701.   [6] *Ibid.* 7th April 1692.

with an iron harrow to prevent the accumulation of weeds ; [1] to erect a new penstock in a sewer ; [2] to repair immediately any breaches in the sea-wall, even to the extent of advancing " fifty or sixty pounds towards the said work " ; [3] to " lay a gut " or " set down a new sluice " ; [4] or to clear away the weeds in the " Canterbury River " [5] The accounts of all the Expenditors were annually allowed by the Court. The Court granted to the Expenditors, and thereby imposed on the owners and occupiers, not only an annual general " scot " or rate, usually at sixpence or a shilling per acre, but also special or extra " scots," and, in addition, local " scots " or " half scots " of from twopence to two shillings per acre, on particular " valleys " or districts.[6] We find the Court deciding, in 1689, that of these " scots " the occupiers shall pay two-thirds and the landowners one-third.[7] Occasionally two-thirds of the expense would be charged on the occupiers of particular lands, and one-third put to " the general charge of the Valley."[8]

We gather from the records that the Commissioners and the jurymen jogged along year after year, all on the best of terms with themselves and the rest of the owners and occupiers, taking their fees, levying their scots, and amicably dining together, with the very minimum of compulsion, on the basis of common consent. The Court occasionally legislated for the common good in the form of prohibiting novel nuisances.[9]

It was usual to obtain the consent of the landowners and farmers concerned before ordering any new works. In 1775, however, an unusual emergency arose. An expert surveyor from the Bedford Level was called in to advise how to remedy the steadily worsening condition of the Stour Valley, which was

---

[1] MS. Minutes, Commissioners of Sewers, East Kent, 1st May 1690.
[2] *Ibid.* 19th June 1690.   [3] *Ibid.* 13th December 1690.
[4] *Ibid.* 23rd April 1691, 19th April and 7th June 1694.
[5] *Ibid.* 12th October 1693, " Ordered that none are to empty tubs or houses of office into Canterbury River upon penalty of forty shillings " (*ibid.* 11th October 1694, 11th June 1696).
[6] " A scot of fifteen pence per acre on the lands single scotted, and half a crown on the lands double-scotted, to T. S., Expenditor, by special order " (*ibid.* 30th October 1690). These occasional impositions were transformed, in 1827, into a regular annual tax, for the general expenses of the Court, of twopence per acre and twopence in the pound on the rent (*ibid.* 31st May 1827).
[7] *Ibid.* 30th October 1689.   [8] *Ibid.* 26th May 1692, 6th June 1757.
[9] " Ordered that if any person shall water any flax in any heading, dike, sewer or stream, he shall for every such offence forfeit the sum of five pounds " (*ibid.* 15th October 1713).

E

getting annually more water-logged. The expert recommended "a new cut," for which statutory authority was required.[1] There was (as usual with river drainage works) vehement argument for and against "the new cut"; but in the end it is resolved upon.[2] Accordingly, in 1776, the Commissioners, having obtained general consent from the landowners, fortified themselves by a Local Act, passed "after a very strong and tedious opposition from the inhabitants of Sandwich"; upon which they borrowed £2400, with which to pay the costs of the Act, and to execute the necessary works of improvement of the River Stour.[3] The operation seems to have been a somewhat primitive one. The "Expenditor of the General Valleys" was authorised to take on as many men as he required for the work, at 1s. 9d. each per day; the day's work, it is interesting to note, was expressly ordered to be eight hours; and the "proper person to superintend" was to get 2s. 6d. per day.[4] How "the new cut" acted we know not, but there are for over fifty years no more complaints.

We need not follow the Commissioners further in their harmonious proceedings. The only point of interest is the report by a committee of themselves in 1823, evidently acting on legal advice, that there was now reason to believe, from the recent decision against the Somerset Court of Sewers, that the very "foundation and proceedings" of their Jury system were illegal, and accordingly that the whole action of the Court was, strictly speaking, null and void. It was deemed necessary to give up the immemorial Standing Jury, and to ask the Sheriff to summon a Jury each time that a presentment was required, or at any rate, one for each session of the Court. The Jury so sworn had henceforth to decide, not upon their own view and knowledge, but solely upon the evidence of witnesses in open Court. There could no longer be a separate Jury for each Valley; and the same formal procedure had to be followed by the Jury even for the granting of a "scot."[5] The "constant service of the antique

[1] MS. Minutes, Commissioners of Sewers, East Kent, 29th April and 25th May 1775.
[2] Ibid. 26th August, 28th September and 26th October 1775.
[3] Ibid. 8th February and 3rd June 1776. [4] Ibid. 5th July 1776.
[5] Ibid. 25th October 1823, and 22nd January 1825. A separate Jury had to be summoned by the Lord Warden of the Cinque Ports for the area within his jurisdiction, as well as one by the Sheriff of the City of Canterbury for that city.

world," which the Courts of Sewers had continued so long, was now passing away. Once scrutinised by critical eyes, there was revealed much in the procedure—as we suspect, of immemorial antiquity—for which no warrant could be found in the comparatively modern Statutes of Sewers or King's Commissions. In East Kent, however, the work itself was now passing from the Commissioners' hands. A joint stock company, empowered to levy tolls on the navigation, took up the task of rehandling the whole course of the Stour and improving Sandwich Harbour. The Commissioners strongly opposed the Bill, but came at last to terms, on protective clauses being inserted.[1] The Act was passed in 1825, and we leave the Court of Sewers at this date steadily dwindling in importance.

Lincolnshire

How far there existed in other Counties any primitive communal organisation for land drainage such as that we have described in Romney Marsh and Somerset, and to what extent any such organisation continued in existence under the practically permanent Courts of Sewers established from the fifteenth and sixteenth centuries onward, we have but the scantiest information. In the great County of Lincoln, with fens and marshes needing protection on almost every side of it, we find existing in the eighteenth century, after many specially commissioned Justices of Sewers for the disputes of particular localities, a single Commission of Sewers for the county as a whole,[2] which

---

[1] MS. Minutes, Commissioners of Sewers, East Kent, 1st and 8th May and 11th December 1824, 8th January and 19th March 1825.

[2] For the Lincolnshire Court of Sewers we have to rely entirely on the material afforded by secondary sources such as *The History of Imbanking and Draining*, by Sir William Dugdale, 1652, edition of 1772 ; *General View of the Agriculture of the County of Lincoln*, by Arthur Young, 1799 ; *The Rainfall, Water Supply and Drainage of Lincolnshire*, by W. H. Wheeler, 1879 ; *History of the Fens of South Lincolnshire*, by W. H. Wheeler, 1894 and 1896 ; *Fens and Floods of Mid-Lincolnshire*, by J. S. Padley, 1882 ; *History and Antiquities of Boston*, by P. Thompson, 1856 ; *History and Antiquities of the Isle of Axholme*, by Rev. W. B. Stonehouse, 1839 ; *History and Topography of the Deanery of Doncaster*, by J. Hunter, 1828–1832 ; *History of the County of Lincoln*, by T. Allen, 1834 ; *Lives of the Engineers*, by Samuel Smiles, 1861 ; *Victoria County History of Lincolnshire* ; *Memorials of Old Lincolnshire*, by E. M. Sympson, 1910 ; *Glossary of Words, etc. . . . East Lincolnshire*, by J. Good, 1911 ; *Highways and Byeways in Lincolnshire*, by W. F. Rawnsley, 1914 ; and others mentioned in *Bibliotheca Lincolniensis*, by A. R. Corus, 1904 ; and such pamphlets as *South Holland Drainage Acts of Parliament*, 1846 ; *Proceedings of the Committee*

has continued down to the present day, though from its jurisdiction the areas administered under Local Acts by special
bodies have always been regarded as excluded, either implicitly
or by express provision in their Acts.[1] But, as in Somersetshire, the Lincolnshire Court of Sewers has, time out of mind,
taken what we must call an extra-legal form. We see the
Commissioners dividing themselves into groups, according to the
locality of their properties, and holding regularly several separate
Courts, at Boston, Spalding and other places, each exercising
jurisdiction only over a particular district, comprising one or
more Wapentakes or Hundreds, and each attended, in practice,
only by its own set of Commissioners.[2] Judging simply from the
legal documents, it might be assumed that these Courts of Sewers,
with the assistance of a Jury summoned by the Sheriff of the
County, did the whole of the work. We gather, however, that
there were during the eighteenth century, as at the present day,
many local Juries, with diverse local customs, though how
far these resembled the Standing Juries of Somersetshire, or
the Juries for particular " Valleys " in East Kent, we have
not ascertained.[3] More prominent in Lincolnshire — perhaps
specially characteristic of that county—were the Dykereeves,
evidently ancient officers of the Parish or Manor, upon whom,
during the eighteenth and nineteenth centuries, fell the daily
work of administration of the banks and sluices. Of these local

Appointed to confer with the lessees of the Fossdyke Navigation, etc., 1827;
*Statement of the Proceedings . . . to promote the Improvement of the . . . Drain-
age of the Lowlands . . . bordering upon the Louth Navigation,* 1830, etc. *Public
Works in Mediaeval Law,* by C. T. Flower, Selden Society, 1915, contains
(pp. 218-316) 98 pages of ancient records relating to the maintenance of sewers,
bridges and roads in South Lincolnshire.

[1] *History of the Fens of South Lincolnshire,* by W. H. Wheeler, 1896, p. 56.

[2] " The members have the right of attending and voting at any of the Courts,
a privilege which is sometimes taken advantage of on important occasions, or
when the appointment of a clerk or other officer is made. As a rule, however,
the members confine their attendances to the Court which has jurisdiction
over the neighbourhood in which they reside " (*ibid.* p. 56).

[3] We read of " a Dykereeve's Inquest," near Spalding, in 1571, when the
Foreman of the Jury delivered a memorable verdict " setting out the various
sewers and banks maintainable by the parishes, and . . . that the sea bank
. . . ought to be amended by the landholders by ' acre silver,' and that the
inhabitants for their passage thereon should make common ' menework ' " (or
compulsory day labour) (*ibid.* p. 103). " A couple of centuries later, in the
Kirton and Skirbeck Wapentakes a Riding Jury used annually to make an
inspection of the seabanks and works of drainage, and report to the Court as
to any defects. They were allowed 10/- per day for horse hire and expenses in
their Wapentake, and 14/- if they attended out of it " (*ibid.* p. 48).

officers, and of the local customs that they enforced, we hear
incidentally already in the thirteenth century. In 1297, as
Dugdale records, "upon a suit concerning the repair of the
ditches and sewers of Waynflete the jurors found that the custom
of that town was such that the ditches there ought to be cleansed
once a year . . . and that every inhabitant thereof, having
lands there, ought to be assessed and taxed according to the
quantity of his lands, to contribute to the charge of such cleansing
and scouring of them. And . . . that the money . . . ought,
according to the said custom, to be levied and collected by certain
of the inhabitants of the said town called Dykereeves, and not
by any others."[1] "As often as the sewers there made for the
draining of their lands did want repair," as appears from another
record, "they ought to be viewed by the commonalty of that
place ; and . . . thereupon every person having lands and
tenements there ought to be assessed for the repair of those
sewers according to the proportion of his said lands."[2] In the
thirteenth and fourteenth centuries, it is clear, such obligations
of the landholders of each little community were enforced in the
Lord's Court. "Such was the custom," we are told, "in that
town of North Waynflete that certain of the inhabitants thereof
were assigned to view the marsh ditches, therein, every year on

[1] *History of Imbanking and Draining*, by Sir William Dugdale, 1652, p. 154
of edition of 1772. Edmund Oldfield, in his *Account of Wainfleet and the
Wapentake of Candleshoe*, 1829, "quotes from Dugdale's work on embankments
an account of a . . . suit . . . in which the defendant set out the custom
prevalent in North Wainfleet as to the repair of the sewers, which was to be
regulated by the view and assessment of the commonalty, and that it was also
the custom to view the marsh-ditches yearly on the feast of St. Andrew, and to
present defaults to the Court of the Earl of Lincoln, who could impose a fine
of sixteen pence " (*Public Works in Mediaeval Law*, by C. T. Flower, Selden
Society, 1915, p. 287).

[2] *History of Imbanking and Draining*, by Sir William Dugdale, 1652,
p. 155. We may perhaps identify with the Dykereeves the "two lawful
persons " assigned to levy the Marsh Rate for Kentish marshes in a Commission of 1290. They are specially mentioned by name in various Commissions of the thirteenth and fourteenth centuries preserved in Sir William
Dugdale's *History of Imbanking and Draining*, for places in Kent (p. 37),
Norfolk (pp. 275, 290), and Cambridgeshire (pp. 316, 344) ; whilst in Essex we
hear of Wallreeves as manorial officers. In 1824 we find the Somerset Court
of Sewers apparently adopting the same officers for certain parishes. "At
this sessions " certain "Standing Juries were discharged, and Dykereeves
appointed and sworn to inspect, oversee and take care of the several works
heretofore within the view of such Juries (MS. Minutes, Sewer Commissioners,
Somerset, Bridgwater, 8th October 1824). We have found in East Kent no
trace of Dykereeves, or of any other parochial or manorial officers connected
with the sewers.

the Feast Day of St. Andrew, and to present the defaults which
they should find in them at the next Court of Henry de Lacy,
Earl of Lincoln, then Lord of that town ; and that every tenant
of that Lordship who ought to make any repairs thereto be
amerced in 16d. at the said Court." [1]   Such scanty information as
we possess of the actual administration in the eighteenth century
of the Lincolnshire works of local drainage points to the continuance, practically unchanged, of these thirteenth-century
customs.   Though by the wording of the Commission and of the
Statute of Sewers it was for the Commissioners to appoint all the
officers, and assess all the rates, "the ordinary course of proceeding in this district," we are told, "is for each parish to
appoint two officers called Dykereeves to lay and collect the
necessary rates and maintain the banks and sewers ; and these
appointments, and all that relates to them, are subject to the
approval of the Court." [2]   Whether this approval of the Commissioners was more than a form we have not ascertained.   What
is clear is that the inhabitants in Vestry assembled not only
appointed the Dykereeves, but also controlled their expenditure.
"The Dykereeves," we learn, "present their accounts to the
Vestry of the parish at Easter." [3]

[1] For information as to Wainfleet, see *History of the Fens of South Lincolnshire*,
by W. H. Wheeler, 1896, pp. 76, 77.   In Marshland in Norfolk we hear, in 1337,
of "the penalty of Bylaw, which is for every perch sixpence," for those who
neglect to repair the banks on the days assigned by the Dykereeves.   "All the
tenants and commoners in Watlington should meet twice in the year, and hold
the customs of Marshland" (*History of Imbanking and Draining*, by Sir William
Dugdale, 1652, p. 290 of edition of 1772).   In many other places the obligation
to keep in repair a definite piece of river wall or length of sewer, usually that
abutting on or traversing the land held, was enforced on the tenants of a Manor
by the ordinary procedure of the Court Leet ; see, for instance, a Lincolnshire
case of 1410 in *History of the Parish of Ormsby*, by W. O. Massingbird, 1899,
p. 275 ; *Growth of the Manor*, by P. Vinogradoff, 1905, p. 269.   We are told, in
1324, of the origin of such a custom in the marsh of Stepney or Poplar.   It was
found by an inquisition of 18 Edward II. that a previous Lord of the Manor had
demised over one hundred acres of reclaimed land to tenants, each under the
obligation to maintain his own bit of river wall.   Two Wallreeves were annually
appointed at the Manorial Court, whose duty was to warn the tenants to repair,
and to present defaults.   No rate was levied until 1401, when the Court of
King's Bench held that every tenant in the marsh was liable, in addition to his
individual obligation, to contribute towards the works rendered necessary by a
great inroad of the tide (*History of Imbanking and Draining*, by Sir William
Dugdale, 1652, p. 69 of edition of 1772).
[2] *History of the Fens of South Lincolnshire*, by W. H. Wheeler, 1896, p. 48.
[3] *Ibid.* p. 48.   During the greater part of the eighteenth century—in some
places right down to the nineteenth century—where the marshes remained
unenclosed, and unallotted in severalty, their use as common pasture neces-

The Lincolnshire sewers were divided into two classes, possibly according to their antiquity : those which were maintained by the frontagers or other owners, and those which were a charge on the " Dykereeves' Rate " or " acreshot," assessed according to the " acrebook " of the parish.[1] We infer that, as in Somersetshire, the function of the Courts of Sewers in Lincolnshire was principally the exercise of a general superintendence over some such local communal organisation [2] as Juries and Dykereeves ; to maintain it in efficiency by compelling service ; to arbitrate between it and recalcitrant owners or occupiers, and to confer legal authority upon its ordainments and amercements, in substitution for the Manorial Courts.[3]

sarily led to communal regulation. Most of this was parochial or manorial. " Before being sent into the common fen, the live stock were collected at certain defined places and marked, and again, on being taken off in the autumn they were brought to the same place to be claimed by their owners. Thus in Pinchbeck the stock was collected at the Market Cross and a due called Hoven was paid. Bailiffs were appointed to look after the stock. On the marshes in South Holland a ' Marsh Reeve ' was also appointed, and a ' Marsh Shepherd,' their wages being paid by a rate of 1s. 6d. for each horse and neat beast, and 3d. for each sheep grazed on the common " (*History of the Fens of South Lincolnshire,* by W. H. Wheeler, 1896, p. 38, and Appendix I. p. 30). These appointments were continued to be made by the Vestry until the enclosure in 1793 (p. 122). There was necessarily a great deal of " intercommoning," and the Council of the Duchy of Lancaster, as lords of most of the district, drew up an elaborate code of 72 articles, which was settled at the Great Inquest of the Soke of Bolingbroke in 1549, and confirmed in 1573. This Fen Code, relating to the marking and commoning of cattle, the taking of fish, fowl, eggs, turf and fodder, the dates on which reeds might be cut, etc., remained in force until, in our own day, the last of the common lands were enclosed and allotted in severalty. See *History and Antiquities of Boston,* by P. Thompson, 1856, pp. 642-644 ; *History of the Fens of South Lincolnshire,* by W. H. Wheeler, 1896, pp. 36-38 ; *Public Works in Mediaeval Law,* by C. T. Flower (Selden Society, 1915), p. 282.

[1] *History of the Fens of South Lincolnshire,* by W. H. Wheeler, 1896, pp. 61, 141. At Fishtoft, for instance, " acrebooks " were made in 1662, 1709 and 1733 (*History and Antiquities of Boston,* by P. Thompson, 1856, p. 493). For " acreshot " see *History of Imbanking and Draining,* by Sir William Dugdale, p. 348 of edition of 1772.

[2] It is perhaps of some importance in this connection to note that the Lincolnshire Fenland " has never been dominated by any large territorial owners " (*History of the Fens of South Lincolnshire,* by W. H. Wheeler, 1896, p. 421). " In the Fen parishes," in 1799, " half " the land belonged to small peasant freeholders (*General View of the Agriculture of the County of Lincoln,* by Arthur Young, 1799).

[3] Occasionally (as at Frampton in 1754) the Court would order lands lying in one parish, but draining into another, to pay the Dykereeves' Rate to the latter parish, instead of to their own (*History of the Fens of South Lincolnshire,* by W. H. Wheeler, 1896, pp. 69, 82). We notice a persistent tendency for the charge of maintaining particular works to be transferred, by order of the Court, from particular owners to the Dykereeves' Rate (for instance, see *ibid.* p. 73).

When any works of magnitude were undertaken, a surveyor was apparently employed by the Court and charged as part of the cost of the work, which was levied by the Court as a Sewers Rate. In 1810, when an exceptionally high tide flooded the whole of one great " level " the Court of Sewers sitting at Boston, acting on the opinion of eminent counsel, "spread the charge over the whole level of the Wapentakes of Skirbeck and Kirton," and in that case the Court proceeded strictly according to the Statute of Sewers, not calling upon the Dykereeves or the standing local Juries, but getting the Sheriff of the county to summon a Jury of indifferent persons for each Wapentake, by whom " the extent of land liable, and the proportion in which the money required should be paid " were judicially assessed, at rates per acre varying from 1s. 2d. to 10s.[1] For the most part the cost of repairs and works were, throughout the eighteenth century, borne by particular owners or frontagers, and only the minor expenses of cleaning the ditches, maintaining the sluices and keeping down the vermin were paid by the Dykereeves out of the " acreshot." Occasionally, with the consent of the local Vestries and usually of all parties concerned, we see the Court accepting and endorsing a presentment, by which an exceptional work is made a charge over the whole parish, and the Dykereeves are ordered to collect Sewers Rate accordingly, sometimes at differential rates for lands more or less benefited.[2] " For the general expenses of the Court," which were, throughout the eighteenth century, inconsiderable, the Court made an order " on the Dykereeves of the several parishes," in some customary proportion.[3]

We may add here that the rural Courts of Sewers, together with the Lords of the Level of Romney Marsh and the Corporation of the Bedford Level, and unlike the Courts of Sewers of the Metropolitan area, about to be described, continue in existence down to the present day (1922). No revolution like that of the Municipal Corporations Act of 1835, or the Poor Law Amendment Act of 1834, has swept them away ; nor have they, like

[1] *History of the Fens of South Lincolnshire*, by W. H. Wheeler, 1896, pp. 49, 62-66. The Court sat on the Sunday following the catastrophe (*Boston Gazette*, 13th November 1810).

[2] *History of the Fens of South Lincolnshire*, by W. H. Wheeler, 1896, p. 50. In 1715, on presentment by a Jury, the Court directed a new outfall sluice to be made into the Welland (*ibid.* p. 84).

[3] *Ibid.* p. 48.

the Turnpike Trustees or the Improvement Commissioners, been absorbed by newer authorities.[1]

Metropolitan Courts of Sewers

For one long stretch of marsh and low-lying lands—as it happens the most important district of all—we are fortunate enough to have had access to nearly complete records for the last three centuries. The 118 square miles along the banks of the Thames, which are now under the jurisdiction of the London County Council, were formerly divided among eight separate Courts of Sewers, the minutes of the proceedings of which exist, in some cases, from 1569.[2] It fortunately happens that these

[1] At the present time, we understand that Commissions of Sewers are issued by the Crown on the advice of the Board of Agriculture and Fisheries, which has succeeded to the Enclosure Commissioners. The procedure is that a petition is presented to the Board, and, after approval, it is communicated to the Home Office. The Home Secretary, with the approval of the Crown, then instructs the Clerk of the Crown to prepare a warrant for the issue of Letters Patent under the Land Drainage Act of 1861. Once appointed, the Commissioners of Sewers are not subject to the control of any Government Department, except that they have to obtain the sanction of the Board of Agriculture for raising loans, the compulsory acquisition of land and the commutation of any liabilities. They have, however, to forward their accounts to the Local Government Board (now Ministry of Health). The Crown, acting through the Home Secretary, could probably supersede or suppress any Commission of Sewers by writ of supersedeas in accordance with the Statute of Sewers of 1532; and it was, in fact, in this way that (as mentioned below) the Metropolitan Commissions of Sewers were brought to an end. In effect, however, a Commission of Sewers can, in its ordinary administration, be controlled by proceedings upon the motion of private individuals in the High Court of Justice, which would act by certiorari and mandamus, prohibition and injunction, as with other public officers or bodies (see " Notes on the Constitution and Records of Commissioners of Sewers," by H. G. Richardson, in *Report of Royal Commission on Public Records*, vol. ii. part ii. pp. 98-100).

[2] These records, amounting to "about 4250 separate volumes, sheets or rolls," extending from 1569 to 1855, are now preserved by the London County Council, which at one time intended to publish some of the earlier volumes and should certainly do so. One volume only appears to have been published, entitled *Court Minutes of the Surrey and Kent Sewer Commission*, London County Council, 1909, vol. i. Minutes, 1569-1579, 352 pp. Apart from this full material, sources of information for the Metropolitan Commissions of Sewers are exceptionally few. The student will consult the Acts, and also the *Digest of the Statutes relating to the Metropolitan Commission of Sewers*; *The Law of Waters and of Sewers*, by Humphrey W. Woolrych, 1830; the reports and evidence of the House of Commons Committees of 1823 and 1834; the House of Commons Returns of 1831 and 1847 (No. 686); the first report and evidence of the Metropolitan Sanitary Commission, 1847; a valuable paper " On the Main Drainage of London," by (Sir) J. W. Bazalgette, in *Proceedings of the Institute of Civil Engineers*, vol. xxiv., 1865; with the incidental references in the *Poor*

eight Courts of Sewers include, as we believe, representatives of every type presented by these authorities outside the Fenland. The long succession of marshes that once stretched from the Mole to the Medway exhibit, in fact, the most diverse conditions, and have had the most varied history. The Commissioners of Sewers who acted for these miles of riparian marshland had to deal with the storms of the sea and exceptional tides ; they had also to cope with the morasses created by stagnant accumulations of the rain-water from the uplands ; they had in many places to administer the earthen embankments and sluices of wholly uninhabited marshes ; and in others the sewers of densely crowded streets of houses and the walls and camp-shedding of river landing-places and commercial wharves.

Greenwich

We begin with the Commissioners of Sewers for the marshes extending on the Kentish bank of the Thames from the mouth of the Ravensbourne (including the site of the ancient village of Greenwich) down to as far as the Borough of Gravesend. In the constitution and procedure of the rulers of these marshes we find surviving, right down to Victorian times, much of the ancient organisation of Romney Marsh. " Before the 23rd of Henry the Eighth," we are told, " the government of this Level was entirely in the owners of the land, who acted under the ancient customs of the town of Greenwich." [1] We gather that the owners of the marsh elected a body of Jurats, a Bailiff, and one or more Collectors, whilst the larger proprietors were deputed

---

Law Commissioners' Report on the Sanitary Condition of the Labouring Population, 1842 ; *Old Southwark*, by W. Rendle, 1878 ; *English Sanitary Institutions*, by Sir John Simon, 1890 ; *History of Private Bill Legislation*, by F. Clifford, 1887 ; *The Sanitary Evolution of London*, by H. Jephson, 1907 ; and *Municipal Origins*, by F. H. Spencer, 1911, pp. 242-263. A few local pamphlets and other sources will be found mentioned in connection with the several Commissions. We do not include among Courts of Sewers the so-called Commissioners of Sewers for the City of London, established under various Statutes, which was, down to 1897, annually appointed by the Common Council. This body did not act under the Statutes of Sewers and had no judicial authority ; it was, in fact, virtually a Committee of the Corporation of the City of London, and has already been described as such (*The Manor and the Borough*, 1908, pp. 577-646) ; whilst it exercised the usual powers of a body of Improvement or Street Commissioners, including drainage (see *The Manor and the Borough*, 1908, p. 577, and *post*, pp. 347-348).

[1] MS. Minutes, Sewer Commissioners, Greenwich, 24th March 1744.

in rotation to serve the office of Expenditor.[1] We need not
attempt to unravel the changes brought about by the issue of
successive Commissions of Sewers in the sixteenth and seventeenth centuries, except to notice that even after the issue of
these Commissions the landowners of the marsh continued, as
we are expressly informed, to assess " the wallscot themselves
and acted by the virtue of their local customs " ; and that in
1624 the jurisdiction of the Commissioners of Sewers of East
Greenwich, with whom we are now concerned, was limited to
the portion of the marsh that lay between the Ravensbourne
and the Lombard Wall.[2] In 1689, when we take up the story,
the Commissioners were the leading landed proprietors of the
neighbourhood, who, once a year, met ceremoniously as a Court
of Sewers, with all the forms and paraphernalia of a judicial
tribunal. If we were to judge by the wording of the Commission
itself, or by that of the Statute of Sewers under which the Court
acted, we should infer that the whole work was done, and the
whole power wielded, by the Commissioners themselves. But
the records make it clear that the ancient organisation had never
ceased to exist, and we find it, with only the slightest of changes,
continuing to function under the aegis of the relatively modern
Court of Sewers.[3] The practical work was done by the Jurats,
now called the Jury ; and by the Expenditor, combining in
himself, since 1657, the powers and duties of the three ancient
offices of " Bailiff, Collector and Expenditor." [4] In the volumes

[1] See the incidental references to these Thames marshes in the *History of
Imbanking and Draining*, by Sir William Dugdale, 1652, pp. 59-65 of edition
of 1772.

[2] MS. Minutes, Sewer Commissioners, Greenwich, 27th March 1744.

[3] Even the oath taken by the Expenditor continued, down to 1738, to run
in the archaic form, alluding to the " wallscot " as being assessed by the owners
of the marsh, instead of by the Commissioners of Sewers (*ibid.* 24th March
1744). It is significant that, as late as 1690, the summons to this Court was
issued by the " Bailiff, Collector and Expenditor . . . by virtue of his office
and according to the ancient custom, and by the consent of their Majesties'
Commissioners of Sewers " ; that it is not called a Court but " the General
Lathe " ; and that it is not summoned to try pleas or offenders, but " . . . to
do and perform what shall be thought fit for the weal and good of the said
Marshes " (*ibid.* 4th September 1690). The ancient " books, rolls and other
papers relating to the Marshes " were, in 1696, not in the custody of the Commissioners but in the " church chest," whence they were then reclaimed (*ibid.*
20th November 1696).

[4] *Ibid.* 6th January 1698. Not until 1699 was this officer appointed by
any " warrant, commission or some such like instrument as is the custom
amongst Commissioners . . . in other Levels " (*ibid.* 2nd October 1699).

of manuscript minutes in which the proceedings have been, since 1625, elaborately recorded, the daily working of this constitution may easily be followed down to 1835, at which point we leave the story. The Expenditor remains throughout nominally unpaid, the office devolving in turn upon the principal land-owners of the Marsh, whether these are men or women, adults or minors, residents or absentees, individuals or corporations.[1] But the office was habitually served by the appointment of a paid deputy, at a salary of no more than £4 a year,[2] whose main business was to collect from the fifty or sixty freeholders of the marsh the amount per acre assessed by the Jury on their respect-ive holdings—making, if need be, distraint on any goods belong-ing to them or any of their tenants [3]—and to pay, after a certifi-cate of completion by the Jury, for the work that had been ordered to be done. But in the eighteenth and nineteenth, as in the thirteenth and fourteenth centuries, it was the body of jurats or jurors that constituted the mainspring of the whole machinery. They were now returned by the High Sheriff of the County at the opening of each new Commission, instead of holding office by election or in virtue of their tenure of certain lands or Manors ; and they served, not for life, but continuously for at least ten years. They were, however, always composed not of indifferent persons from the body of the county, but of forty-eight of the peasant freeholders and tenant farmers of lands within the Marsh, and we gather that many of them acted decade after decade ; whilst their Foreman, whose presence was necessary to give validity to their proceedings, in one instance at any rate filled that office for a whole generation. In any emergency the Foreman could himself call together the Jury— perhaps he always did so—and we see him collecting some of

---

[1] So strict was the rotation, and so compulsory the service, that we find the Board of Ordnance (MS. Minutes, Sewer Commissioners, Greenwich, 26th November 1708) and the Commissioners of Customs required to accept the office when it fell to the turn of the lands held by their departments ; and when in 1704, the obligation came to some land which had come to be possessed by Queen Anne herself (having been seized for a debt to the Crown), no exception was made in her favour (*ibid.* 28th September 1704). This compulsion to serve the office of Expenditor was not peculiar to the Greenwich Court of Sewers. But we find it determined in Chamber's case (Andrew 335) and in the Vicar of Dartford's case in 1739, that the incumbent of a parish was not liable to serve in respect of his benefice (*Report of Adjudged Cases*, by Sir John Strange, 3rd edition, 1795, vol. ii. p. 1107 ; and the other authorities there cited).

[2] MS. Minutes, Sewer Commissioners, Greenwich, 20th November 1695.

[3] *Ibid.* 6th January 1698.

the members to aid him with their counsel. Twice a year, in spring and autumn, the whole body gathered at daybreak at some appointed place, whence the members dispersed in separate detachments, attended by the Wallreeve and the Sluice-keepers, to walk the whole length of the embankments and river walls, in order to scrutinise their soundness, and the amount of nettles and brambles by which they were overgrown. We see them, in the grey morning mists characteristic of the Thames estuary, following up the sluices and dykes that extended for miles towards the higher lands, in order to discover which needed scouring or repairing. Towards the afternoon they assemble at one of the taverns of the village of Greenwich, to discuss over their dinner " the due execution of last year's ordainments, as also what is necessary to be done for the weal and good of the Level for the year next ensuing." [1] At this convivial meeting, under the presidency of the Foreman, they decided the number and tenor of their presentments ; whether these were to be " public " or " private " ; and in the latter case, upon which owners lay the obligation to execute the necessary works ; the date before which such repairs must be completed, and the fine to be levied by the Court in case of default. Where the presentment was " public," that is when no particular owner could, according to custom, be saddled with the necessary work, the Jury proceeded to define precisely what was to be done,[2] together with the estimated cost, to be formally levied as " wallscot "— the lawyers would have said by the Court of Sewers when next it should be held, but to the jurymen it seemed as if they levied it themselves, at the customary differential rates between " single " and " double " lands, exactly as their predecessors had done for three or four centuries.[3] Their presentments—

[1] Charge to Jury, MS. Minutes, Sewer Commissioners, Greenwich, 27th October 1694.

[2] Imprimis we do ordain 8 rods to be filled up against the " Great Meadow ; charge 8s. ; we ordain the top of Bendiss sluice to be opened and the defects thereof to be repaired and amended ; charge thereof £5 ; we ordain 4 rods to be timbered there ; charge £5 ; . . . we also ordain 5000 bavins, ethers and stakes against the Pits, £3 ; 100 tons of chalk to be laid against Mr. Snap's land, £8 : 15s. ; . . . we ordain 100 load of gravel to be laid in the marsh land ; charge £7 : 10s. ; we ordain the wall to be strewed with reeds ; charge £1 " (*ibid.* 4th September 1690).

[3] In 1690–1693 the average total expenditure per annum was about £200 ; and the " wallscot " was ten shillings per acre on " Land Marsh " and five shillings per acre on " Combe Marsh." In 1726, when the expenditure was £650, an extra

called in fact, " ordainments "—were usually obeyed and the works done, long before the next Court of Sewers was held, at which they could be formally recorded. Once in a generation we find them spending some days, or even weeks, in making, on the model of such " tax-books or other ancient precedents " [1] as they could obtain, an elaborate new " assessment " of the marsh, which here meant not a valuation, but, as in Lincolnshire, an " acrebook " ; a detailed record and map of the exact acreage, ownership and occupancy of each of the four or five hundred separate holdings. For all this work the members of the Jury received no pay, beyond an allowance for the customary dinner. Throughout the whole period it is this convivial dinner that binds the Jury together into an efficiently working body ; and the Commissioners themselves, whom we find occasionally grumbling at " the great or rather uncontrollable expense which the Jury put this Commission into for their eating and drinking," [2] are inclined, on the whole, to take a generous view of the entertainment. Amid the high prices of 1811, the jurymen successfully plead for a larger sum. They had already got the allowance up successively from 1s. 6d. to 4s. per head, but now found even this insufficient. " We, the Jury of Sewers for the said Level," so runs their presentment to the Court, " beg leave to represent that owing to the increased charge for every necessary of life, the allowance now made by the Court of four shillings to each of the jurymen per day on account of expenses is very inadequate to the expenses unavoidably incurred, as the charge for a bare plain dinner alone exceeds the allowance, without considering anything for wine or other liquors usually drunk upon such occasions, so that every juryman, besides giving up his time to the benefit of the Level is, on every day of duty, put to a considerable private cost." The Commissioners thereupon graciously allowed eight shillings " for every day of walk or attendance on

---

levy of twenty shillings per acre had to be made. The levy was announced immediately after service one Sunday at the Chapel of the Royal Hospital, Greenwich (MS. Minutes, Sewer Commissioners, Greenwich, 27th August 1716). On the opposite side of the Thames, in the Marshes of the Isle of Dogs the rate annually levied during the eighteenth century was never less than four shillings and sometimes as much as eight shillings and sixpence per acre (*ibid.* Poplar, 1690-1835).

[1] *Ibid.* Greenwich, 7th November 1695 ; 24th March and 20th October 1744, 19th October 1745 and 5th April 1746.

[2] *Ibid.* 2nd June 1729.

the Court." [1] Later on, in a fit of economy, the Court cut down the number of the Jury to fifteen, allowing them each ten shillings a day.[2] But the jurymen resented this diminution of their company. " The Foreman of the Jury represented that under the arrangement made by the Court in May last he found great difficulty in assembling a Jury, as the division thereby created rendered them generally uncomfortable by breaking up the society they had been accustomed to from the commencement of the Commission ; and he thereupon submitted the propriety of summoning the whole of the Jury in future, with an allowance for expenses to such an expense as the Court should think itself warranted in granting." The Commissioners acceded to this request and permitted the whole Jury to be summoned, but restricted the total allowance to £10 per day.[3] The minor paid officers—the Sluice-keepers, the Wall-reeve,[4] and the Mole-catcher (whose salaries remained each at forty shillings a year throughout the whole century and a half), as well as the gangs of casual labourers who were from time to time employed— worked under the joint superintendence of the Foreman of the Jury and the Expenditor. But it is clear that in the eighteenth and nineteenth centuries it was the Foreman of the Jury, without whose presence the Jury could not proceed to business, who had the effective responsibility for action in any emergency. What sort of service it was that he rendered may be seen by the following example that we take from the minutes. " Whereas on Friday last, 13th November, there happened a very high tide between 3 and 4 P.M., which, with the extraordinary winds attending it, occasioned a great slip in the wall against Sir Edward Betenson's two acres ; which the Wall-reeve, perceiving,

---

[1] MS. Minutes, Sewer Commissioners, Greenwich, 30th May 1811 ; see also 13th April 1793.

[2] *Ibid.* 29th May 1824. The Commissioners had apparently attempted to make a similar reduction in the number of jurymen in 1699, but no notice was taken of their order (*ibid.* 1699).

[3] *Ibid.* 14th October 1824. We see similar attempts to limit the cost of the jurymen's dinner in the Isle of Dogs and Tower Hamlets Courts (*ibid.* Poplar, 7th April 1669, 5th May 1702 ; *ibid.* Tower Hamlets, 7th October 1709). Latterly, the jurymen for the Isle of Dogs, still governing a thinly inhabited tract of marsh land, received a pound for each day's attendance and served about four days a year (Report and Evidence of House of Commons Committee on the Sewers of the Metropolis, 1834).

[4] In the Isle of Dogs, the corresponding officer was called the Marsh Bailiff (MS. Minutes, Sewer Commissioners, Poplar).

immediately repaired to the Foreman of the Jury, and acquainted him thereof. Whereupon the said Foreman immediately sent a messenger to the Expenditor to inform him also of the same, but to prevent any ill consequence that might happen till the return of that messenger, the said Foreman desired the Wall-reeve to proceed in what was necessary to be done for securing any further hurt that might happen by any delay whatever ; and upon the return of the said messenger, the Foreman received a letter from the Expenditor that he was ill and not able to come out, and desired the Foreman would take such care he could of it, but the Wall-reeve being at work by such directions as the Foreman had before given him with six men which he had got together, they worked upon the same all that night and till after high-water next morning tide." The Wall-reeve and Foreman imagined that their hasty action would suffice, but three days later strong winds and a high tide brought the work down again. The Wall-reeve, who had been keeping watch continuously, reported at once to the Foreman, who hastily got together what jurors he could to survey the breach. The jurors viewed the damaged wall, and ordered repairs to be instantly executed to the value of £33.[1] It is noteworthy that though the Jury doubtless consisted, from generation to generation, of nearly the same persons, we do not find that they excited any jealousy among their fellow denizens of the Marsh, nor do we discover that their presentments were ever disputed or hostilely received. Individual owners, nervous about the stability of the embankment, were willing to pay the expenses of special views by the Jury ; and as the village of Greenwich increased in population, we find groups of respectable householders using the Sewers Jury to get remedied the common urban nuisances for which there might otherwise have been no redress.[2] The same confidence was shown by the Commissioners and the inhabitants in the Foreman of the Jury. It was he who sometimes bought, as opportunities presented themselves, the loads of earth or chalk with which the embankments were repaired. It was, as a rule, upon him that fell the responsibility of devising the works of repair to be executed. We find in 1827 a special expression of

[1] MS. Minutes, Sewer Commissioners, Greenwich, 17th November 1741.
[2] In 1761, three of the jurymen were carpenters ; and the Commissioners gave them the carpentering work to do, each having six months of it in rotation (*ibid.* 18th October 1761).

the thanks of the Court to the then Foreman, for "the ability, skill and assiduity exercised for a long series of years . . . in superintending the works of the level, and particularly the late new embankment," as well as for "the constant promptitude evinced by him as immediate occasions have arisen from high tides and other emergencies (thereby protecting the property of the landowners from injury and devastation)." As an exceptional mark of esteem and acknowledgment the Commissioners thereupon voted fifty guineas to this aged and long-serving officer, which he laid out in a piece of plate.[1]

It is, indeed, not easy to discover what function was fulfilled in the Greenwich marshes by the Commissioners themselves. Whatever they may have been at the outset, they became, it is clear, a body renewing itself virtually by co-option.[2] Though the total number on the Commission was fifty or sixty, including several peers and ecclesiastical dignitaries,[3] the usual attendance was confined to fewer than a dozen of the resident gentry ; and these intimate friends and neighbours used their "wages" to provide themselves with a dinner on every Court day.[4] The Court of Sewers—which they solemnly held once, and latterly

[1] MS. Minutes, Sewer Commissioners, Greenwich, 12th April and 18th October 1827.

[2] As each term of ten years came near its expiration the Clerk was told to "take care to get a new Commission of Sewers against the sitting of the next general court, and to insert therein such other gentlemen to be Commissioners (with them already so nominated and appointed) as shall be directed him by the present Commissioners or any of them " (*ibid.* 29th September 1692).

[3] See, for instance, the list in *ibid.* 1712. In 1810 it had grown to 98, but only 45 had qualified within the first year (*ibid.* 9th November 1810, 13th April 1811). The Poplar Commissioners were 49 in number in 1689, 114 in 1757, but only 66 in 1800. Of these between one-third and one-half usually qualified (*ibid.* Poplar, 1689, 1757, 1800). Those for the Tower Hamlets in 1714 were 129, of whom 58 qualified ; in 1725, 195, of whom 70 qualified ; in 1737, 150, of whom 81 qualified ; in 1821, 140, of whom 88 qualified ; and in 1831, 173, of whom 107 qualified (*ibid.* Tower Hamlets, 1714, 1725, 1737, 1821, 1831). The Westminster Commission of 1837 (the last) included 240 persons.

[4] This dinner was, we believe, taken in lieu of the 4s. a day allowed by statute which (as in the case of the Justices of the Peace) was, as we have seen (*The Parish and the County*, 1907, pp. 305, 409, 413, 423, 428), latterly seldom drawn in cash. The Tower Hamlets Commissioners, after dining together for many years, decided in 1779, " that in future the Commissioners attending the whole business of the Commission do receive 4s. apiece pursuant to Act of Parliament, and that no dinners in future be provided " (MS. Minutes, Sewer Commissioners, Tower Hamlets, 16th December 1779). This evidently did not continue. In 1822 they are again dining together, and direct that " no other wines be ordered than port, sherry, Lisbon or Bucellas " (*ibid.* 15th May and 17th July 1822).

F

twice, a year, at which all " owners, tenants and jurats " of the
Marsh were required to " answer to their names " [1]—seems to
have done little more than receive the presentments made by the
Jury since the last Court, to record them as decrees of the Court,
and formally to levy the sums recommended by the Jury. We
find no trace of any dispute or divergence of interest between
the Commissioners and the Jury. The Court occasionally made
byelaws, doubtless on the recommendation of the Jury, for the
future regulation of the Marsh : as to the date after which reeds
might be cut; [2] as to the prohibition of particular nuisances, and
as to the use of the river wall and embankment as a wharf or
landing-place, especially for the landing of manure from London. [3]
The Commissioners themselves directed some of the more important contracts to be entered into for chalk and other materials
needed by the Jury ; [4] but they did not mind making use of one
of the jurymen who mentioned that he was going to Maidstone
in the following week, and would be able to arrange for a supply
of stone. [5] In 1826, when they were building a new river wall,
they gladly adopted the suggestion of the Foreman of the Jury
that he should get earth, as opportunity offered, by " merely
giving some beer to the bargemen " bringing down the stuff ex-
cavated from the dock and other works about London. [6] They
permitted the building of a wooden bridge over the Ravensbourne
by a particular landowner, for his private use only. [7] It was the
Court, too, which gave permission for the erection of windmills
or other buildings on the banks ; [8] and it was in its name that
the Clerk made any communications to outside authorities and
dignitaries. The Court appointed its own " Clerk of Sewers," a
local solicitor remunerated by small fees and perquisites, with
whom the Commissioners were perpetually having difficulties ; [9]

[1] See " methodus tenendi curiam de Sewers," on the last page of vol. ii. of
MS. Minutes, Sewer Commissioners, Greenwich. " This being a Court of
Record, three proclamations must be made," is a memorandum in the MS.
Minutes, Sewer Commissioners, Poplar, 1802.

[2] *Ibid.* Greenwich, 10th December 1702, 28th September 1704.

[3] *Ibid.* 10th December 1702, 8th May and 18th September 1703, 28th
September 1704.

[4] *Ibid.* 4th April 1761, 26th May 1775.

[5] *Ibid.* 21st April and 2nd June 1781.   [6] *Ibid.* 12th October 1826.

[7] *Ibid.* 31st July 1729.   [8] *Ibid.* 6th January 1698.

[9] Not till 1795 was the salary made £21 a year (*ibid.* 10th October 1795).
But the salaries paid to the Clerks, Bailiffs, Wall-reeves and Surveyors of the
Courts of Sewers were not the whole of their authorised remuneration. There

and they filled vacancies in the minor offices of Sluice-keeper, Wall-reeve and Mole-catcher. But we see no attempt on their part to develop any executive staff other than that of the Standing Jury. Down to 1729, indeed, they do not seem even to have appointed committees, except on rare occasions, and then they only made use of this administrative device for obtaining further information and for audit. Their principal pre - occupation seems, in fact, to have been with the accounts of the money raised and expended under the direction of the Jury. They had constant difficulties with the Expenditor for the time being, who could not be got to render accounts, and who was perpetually trying to throw on the Commission the payment of his deputy.[1] Once, at least, they had to get the Sheriff to pursue a recalcitrant Deputy Expenditor, arrest him, and bring him up in custody.[2] Once only in the course of the century and a half do we find the Commissioners really troubling their heads about the means of protecting the Marsh from the waters ; [3] and then, in the need that became manifest about 1825—whether owing to the long-continued dredging for ballast near the embankment,[4] or to the

---

were customary fees payable by individuals for every act performed for their benefit, including every order, permit, respite, discharge or view. Tables of these authorised fees were occasionally fixed by the Court (*e.g.* MS. Minutes, Sewer Commissioners, Surrey and Kent, 27th March 1700). Fees were abolished in Holborn and Finsbury by the Act of 1814 ; and in the Tower Hamlets, by Sir Daniel Williams' reforms of 1821 (Report of House of Commons Committee on Sewers in the Metropolis, 1823, pp. 5, 25) ; but they survived elsewhere.

[1] In this he was at last successful. The salary of £4 a year was raised in 1809 to £10 (MS. Minutes, Sewer Commissioners, Greenwich, 14th October 1809).

[2] *Ibid.* 29th November 1729, 8th February and 28th March 1730. The women owners were, we grieve to record, particularly troublesome. In 1699 the Court had to meet no fewer than seven times, partly because Dame Margaret Boreman (whose name is preserved in the parish by her charitable endowments) would not pay her " marsh tax " (*ibid.* 6th January 1698, 22nd February 1699) ; partly because Mrs. Gransdell, the Expenditor for the previous year, would not render any accounts (*ibid.* 2nd October, 9th and 28th November and 7th December 1699), whereupon she was eventually fined £4 (leviable by distraint by the Sheriff), and threatened with a further fine of £40. It is pathetically noted that " Mr. Day, one of the Commissioners, did concur in the same order, but desired he might be excused from signing the same, the Expenditrix being his daughter " (*ibid.* 7th December 1699).

[3] In 1699 it was specially provided that the Commissioners should " have notice given them by a written ticket when the Jury walk that they may (if they please) walk with them and inspect the condition of the Level " (*ibid.* 10th January 1699).

[4] *Ibid.* 16th June 1711, 19th May 1715, 14th August 1716. We see similar complaints of the ballast lighters " digging ballast near the walls," in the MS. Minutes of the Sewer Commissioners, Poplar, 7th August 1727, 13th October

wash of the new steamboats [1]—for a new sea-wall to be " built further inland," they were wise enough to call in both Rennie and Telford ; to take the advice of these engineers ; and to arrange among themselves and their fellow-proprietors for the cession of the necessary land and the raising of the requisite funds by a special rate of fifty shillings per acre—all by the unanimous consent of all concerned—in order to avoid the expensive luxury of an Act of Parliament.[2] The Commissioners of Sewers for East Greenwich were, indeed, for all the legal phraseology of their Royal Commission, not so much a judicial tribunal superseding the primitive organisation of the denizens of the Marsh, as a standing committee of the principal among these, tacitly permitting the ancient customs to continue, and exercising as a Court little more than an occasional friendly superintendence over the work done by the Jury of their less wealthy tenants and neighbours, to whose proceedings they lent the requisite legal authority.[3]

Westminster

It is characteristic of the extreme flexibility of English Local Government between 1689 and 1835, and of the anarchic diversity resulting from its complete local autonomy, that identical legal instruments, under the same statute, should have produced two such utterly different governing bodies as the Courts of Sewers for Greenwich and Westminster [4] respectively. This diversity

---

1736, 10th December 1737, etc. ; and as early as 1575 the Jury for East Surrey presents various " ballast men and their servants for that they dig ballast and gravel within fifty feet of the Thames wall át Rotherhithe . . . which is like to be a great decay both to the banks and walls " (MS. Minutes, Sewer Commissioners, Surrey and Kent, 14th February 1575).

[1] " We present that owing to the constant action of the wave caused by steamboats upon the banks and walls of the river . . . the foreland has been washed away within a few years to the extent of 47 feet in depth on an average " (ibid. Greenwich, 11th April 1833).

[2] Ibid. 13th and 29th October and 22nd December 1825, 5th, 11th and 23rd January, 9th February, 12th October 1826, 10th April 1828, 7th May 1829.

[3] From 1690, for at least sixty or seventy years, the Commissioners evidently owned " reed lands," which they let to various tenants who cut the reeds. In 1745 these lands were marked on the map then made, and in 1755 the Commissioners paid tithe, Poor Rate and Highway Rate upon them. After 1800 there is no trace of these lands—the reeds had perhaps become valueless—and when in 1834 a committee attempted to trace them it came to the conclusion that the Commissioners had never any legal ownership in them, and that lapse of time had made it hopeless to discover them (ibid.).

[4] For this body, see its MS. Minutes, 1659–1847, and voluminous printed papers (now with the London County Council) ; Statutes relating to the Sewers

was, of course, partly due to the difference between both the work and the environment of the two bodies. Instead of a uniform stretch of marsh-land, sparsely inhabited by man or beast, the Commissioners who were, just before the Restoration, appointed to govern the drainage of Westminster and its western environs, found themselves in charge of a district extraordinarily heterogeneous in its character—on one side, houses densely packed in narrow streets and alleys, crowding up against the Royal palaces and parks, Parliament and the Courts of Justice, the Abbey and its foul " sanctuary " precincts, hemmed in by the wharves and landing-places of the Strand and the morass of Mill-bank; on the other side, low-lying fields extending indefinitely to the westward, submerged at every high tide, where the little towns of Chelsea and Kensington stretched out their scattered houses towards the rural villages of Fulham and Hammersmith. The whole territory was, in fact, either already built on or in process of becoming so. We may well believe that, by the time that the King and his Court had returned to Whitehall, the need had become patent and urgent for instant action, both to remove the accumulated nuisances of the older parts of the City and Liberties and to prevent the growth of even worse conditions in the streets of mean houses that were arising all around.

We note at once that the Commission for Westminster was issued, not to the principal owners of the land, but to a group of official dignitaries—great officers of the King's household,

---

within Westminster and part of Middlesex, editions of 1796 and 1813 ; *An Historical Account of the Subways in the British Metropolis,* by J. Williams, 1828 ; Home Office Domestic State Papers in Public Record Office, Misc. 1831, pp. 20-24 ; *The Vestryman,* 26th July 1834 ; *Substance of an Opinion delivered at a Court of Sewers for the City and Liberty of Westminster,* by T. L. Donaldson, Chairman, 1835 ; House of Commons Committee Reports and Evidence on Metropolitan Sewers, 1823 and 1834 ; *An Historical and Topographical Description of Chelsea,* by Thomas Faulkner, 1829 ; *The Local Government of the Metropolis* (Anon.), 1835 ; " The Sewage of the City of Westminster," by John E. Jones, a brief abstract only, in *Proceedings of Institute of Civil Engineers,* vol. i. 1839, pp. 63-65 ; *A Charge delivered to a Jury summoned to make a Presentment on the District of the Western Division of the Westminster Sewers,* by the Chairman, T. L. Donaldson, 1841 ; *A Short Address to the Representative Vestries under Sir John Hobhouse's Vestry Act,* by John Leslie, 1845 ; House of Commons Return, No. 686 of 1847 ; First Report and Evidence of Metropolitan Sanitary Commission, 1847 ; *Selections from the General, Local and Personal Statutes relative to Sewers within the Jurisdiction of the Commissions for the City and Liberty of Westminster,* etc., 1847. For the general local government of Westminster, and the works relating to it, see *The Manor and the Borough,* 1908, chap. iv. pp. 212-241.

trusted courtiers of experience alike in war and in council, and judges of the Courts at Westminster, together with some useful underlings of the Ministry, of whom the most active was the contemporary " Court Justice," charged with the local adminis- tration of the police.[1] This group of officials established, from the first, a form of government the exact opposite of that of the rural Courts of Sewers that we have been describing. In the detailed minutes of their proceedings, we see them meeting from the outset every week, themselves doing all the business, and getting through it with the high-handed despatch characteristic of men versed in great affairs, if not also with that disregard of legal technicalities which seems to mark in administration the lawyer outside his own domain. At these Saturday or Thursday afternoon meetings—sometimes held actually in the Courts of Chancery or King's Bench [2]—the Westminster Court of Sewers appointed salaried executive officers ; received their reports ; called for special surveys by outside experts ; ordered sewers to be new-bottomed, drains to be enlarged, ditches to be scoured, and sluices to be repaired ; commanded owners and occupiers to be assessed, rates to be levied and goods to be distrained ; all, apparently, without troubling itself much with the paraphernalia

[1] Among the principal landowners of Westminster, in the seventeenth as in the nineteenth century, were—not to mention the Grosvenors, whose Belgravian fields were not yet generally of building value,—the great families of the Russells, Cecils, Howards and Percies, together with the ecclesiastical dignitaries. None of these seem to have been represented among the active Commissioners of Sewers, though the Dean and Chapter, at any rate, were presumably formally named in the Commission. The members most frequent in attendance in- cluded the veteran Earl of Craven, the Earl of Newport, Sir Charles Berkeley, Treasurer of the King's Household, Sir William Playter, Bart., Sir John Denham, Knight of the Bath, " Surveyor of His Majesty's Works," General Sir William Pulteney, Sir Charles Harbord, Sir Hugh Cartwright, Sir George Barker, Sir Richard Everard, Sir John Baker and Sir Edmondbury Godfrey, whose contemporary work as Court Justice we have already described (The Parish and the County, 1907, pp. 236, 338). He acted as Treasurer, and was apparently the most active Commissioner. In the Minutes for 12th October 1678, it is noted in the margin, " Sir Edmondbury Godfrey missing to-day "— an entry reminding us of the sensation caused by his unexplained murder (Who Killed Sir Edmund Bury Godfrey ?, by Alfred Marks, 1905).
[2] It used to be an " office tradition that formerly the business of the Com- mission was transacted in the Court of Queen's Bench, that the Chief Justice occupied the chair, a few Commissioners only surrounding him " (Minutes of Evidence to First Report of Metropolitan Sanitary Commission, 1846, p. 38). The MS. Minutes show the Commissioners to have sat " in the Court of King's Bench, Westminster Hall " on 20th June 1662, and many other days at this period. On 1st August 1662, they met " in the Chancery Court in Westminster Hall." No chairman is named.

of a Court of Justice or necessarily waiting for the dilatory expedient of a presenting Jury.[1]   Nor do the Commissioners content themselves with issuing orders to their little staff of executive officers.   Between the weekly meetings, one or two of the members undertake themselves to view a broken drain or noisome ditch, or to survey, as a whole, the drainage of a particular street. Another of them, the ever-busy Sir Edmondbury Godfrey, himself acts as Treasurer and Accountant, receiving the money from all the parochial rate collectors, and paying the numerous small bills.[2]   Presently, Sir Christopher Wren, appointed a Commissioner but too busy rebuilding churches after the Great Fire to attend every week, is specially summoned to be present, and is set to solve a particular problem.[3]   In 1667, the whole administration is reorganised by a committee of nine Commissioners, under Sir John Denham, " His Majesty's Surveyor," with the result that the Court becomes even more of an executive and less of a judicial authority than before.[4]   A permanent chairman is appointed with a Standing Committee of accounts.   Both the revenue and the expenditure of the Commission, heretofore professedly divided among the innumerable separate works done, are apparently to a great extent consolidated, and a regular expenditure is budgeted for, including a large item for " emergencies."   It is, in fact, impossible not to see, in the archives of this Commission during its opening years, the records, not of a judicial Court, but of an active executive authority, impelled—probably under Royal mandate—by a determination to get the Westminster land drainage into something like order.   Nor were the Commissioners forgetful, in their zeal for efficiency, of the need of securing the co-operation and consent of the inhabitants at

[1] The officers appear to have included a Clerk, a Cryer, a " Bailiff of the Sewers," and several " sworn surveyors " (MS. Minutes, Sewer Commissioners, Westminster, 15th August 1662).   But others are gradually added.   It is for instance " ordered that Mr. A. P. be appointed to look after the cleansing of the new Sewers and to have £20 yearly for his salary " (*ibid.* 22nd August 1662).

[2] It is ordered that a fine of 10s. be imposed on the nine collectors appointed for the new sewer at Charing Cross, " who were legally summoned to attend Mr. Godfrey, Treasurer, for the perfecting of their accounts, and failed " (*ibid.* 29th August 1662).

[3] *Ibid.* 13th April and 16th November 1678, 29th January and 17th June 1680.   Wren's proposal for a new sewer in Westminster is referred to in the paper by (Sir) J. W. Bazalgette, " On the Main Drainage of London," in *Proceedings of the Institute of Civil Engineers*, vol. xxiv., 1865, p. 281.

[4] MS. Minutes, Sewer Commissioners, Westminster, 17th August 1667.

large. They leave each parish to assess and collect all the sums that they levy upon its inhabitants ; though they peremptorily require this service to be regularly performed, by Assessors and Collectors whom the parish officers—sometimes the Surveyors of Highways, sometimes the Constable and Churchwardens—have to present for their approval.[1] These Assessors and Collectors, who received apparently no remuneration, had to account to the Treasurer of the Court, and were liable to be fined for any neglect of their duty. At every weekly meeting the Commissioners were open to receive any complaints from individuals or groups of individuals,[2] and they even ordered that, whenever any work was done in any parish, a committee of the inhabitants was to join with the Commissioners in signing the orders for the expenditure of the rate.

What is remarkable is the small part that the Jury plays in this " Court " of Sewers. The entries in the minutes relating to Juries are few and far between. Every two years the Sheriff is called upon to empanel two new Juries, one for the City of Westminster and the other for the remaining part of Middlesex

[1] MS. Minutes, Sewer Commissioners, Westminster, 20th and 27th April, 4th and 18th May 1667. A nearly contemporary record in a neighbouring Court of Sewers gives us the whole procedure. On receipt of a complaint or a petition for a work of repair, the Commissioners ordered the Jury to view and had an estimate of the probable expense of the work prepared by the Surveyor. A notice was then sent to the Churchwardens and Constable of the parish to return the names of fit persons to assess the necessary sum. When the names were furnished the Commissioners signed a warrant authorising these persons, eight in number, to assess the amount. When they returned the " book of rates " so made, they gave in the names of two persons fit and able to serve as Collectors. These persons were thereupon empowered by the Commissioners to collect the rates (*ibid.* Tower Hamlets, 12th October and 2nd November 1703).

[2] " Upon a petition exhibited to this Court by several inhabitants of the Great Ambrey, complaining of the great nuisance and annoyance they suffer by means of a branch of the sewer issuing and running into the Thames sluice sewer ; ordered that a view thereof be taken by any three of the Commissioners, who are to meet on Saturday, 21st June, to take the view and to report their opinion on the next Court day " (*ibid.* Westminster, 16th June 1662). They report that it is a serious nuisance and recommend, as " the only way to remove the annoyance," that steps be taken " to stop up the said ditch, the street to be levelled and paved . . . with a channel to run in the middle thereof " (*ibid.* 20th June 1662). This is decided on, and the Court orders " that an assessment be brought into this Court equally laid and imposed upon the several . . . inhabitants concerned, that is to say, upon all such who have any gutter, drain, sink or spout running into the same, . . . and that Sir Hugh Cartwright, one of the Commissioners of this Court, be waited on by the inhabitants and desired to see the said work done accordingly " (*ibid.* 11th July 1662).

that lay within the jurisdiction of the Commissioners.[1] These Juries are now and again directed to view particular sewers and drains which had been complained of as offensive, and to report who was in default.[2] Occasionally an inhabitant is fined for non-attendance or discharged for some good reason. It is apparently their business spontaneously to present anything that is wrong with the sewers. We have even cases in which the Jury is reproached for not making presentments, and given a month's grace to discover some nuisances.[3] In one case, on the other hand, the Jury is ordered not to present any nuisances in a certain place, as the Commissioners have it in mind to deal otherwise with the district. Only very occasionally do we find any one being " amerced " by the Jury, and the fine estreated into the Court of Exchequer.[4] For the first ten years of the Commission, we see the Jury ousted from its task of assessing the persons who are liable to pay the cost of the several works, this work being done by the Parish Assessors. In no case has the Jury anything to do with the execution of any work, and it is not even called upon to certify that it has been completed. In short, the Jury of Sewers of the Westminster Court was, from the beginning, utterly unlike the Standing Juries of Sewers of the Court Leet type, which governed the marshes of Greenwich and Somersetshire and may be traced in East Kent and Lincolnshire. It resembled rather the Hundred Jury which during these very years was presenting nuisances to the Courts of Quarter Sessions of Essex, Dorset and Devon.[5] This resemblance is strengthened by the fact that, from the outset, the Westminster Commissioners permitted the presentments of their Jury of Sewers to be traversed by defendants as a matter of course, on a recognisance in the sum

[1] MS. Minutes, Sewer Commissioners, Westminster, 6th July 1667. Neither Westminster nor the Tower Hamlets, though otherwise important " Liberties," were out of the jurisdiction of the Sheriffs of London and Middlesex (as to whom see *The Parish and the County*, 1907, pp. 288, 312; and *The Manor and the Borough*, 1908, pp. 670-673). On the other hand, for the Court of Sewers of St. Katharine, near the Tower of London, the persons to serve on the Juries were returned by the High Bailiff of the Liberty of the Hospital and Precinct of St. Katharine (MS. Minutes, Sewer Commissioners, St. Katharine). For the Tower Hamlets Court, however, the duty was performed by the Sheriffs of London and Middlesex.
[2] *Ibid*. Westminster, 18th May and 27th July 1667.
[3] *Ibid*. 11th October 1662.
[4] See a case, *ibid*. 11th October 1662.
[5] *The Parish and the County*, 1907, pp. 456-480.

of 40s. being entered into ; and they arranged for a trial of these traverses at a subsequent sessions of the court, we presume by a separate " Traverse Jury."[1] Like the Hundred Jury itself, the Jury of Sewers was, in Westminster, an insignificant part of the judicial machinery ;—in short, a mere " Annoyance Jury " only spasmodically made use of and persisting only as an atrophied traditional remnant.

The high-handed efficiency and extra-legal methods of the Commissioners whom Charles the Second had appointed did not go wholly undisputed. The Statute of Sewers enabled the Court to charge the cost of particular works on the owners of lands benefited, but it gave no authority to tax the community at large for such general expenses of a permanent establishment as were not met by the usual fees of office. Hence we see the West-minster Commissioners casting about for some source of general revenue. In 1667 they applied for a " privy seal " which should authorise them to retain for the purposes of the Commission the fines and forfeitures which they were required to estreat unto the Court of Exchequer,[2] a request to which the Court of Exchequer (or the contemporary Treasury officials) seem to have demurred. The Commissioners take upon themselves, on their own authority, to make a general sewers rate of a penny in the pound " upon all houses, lands, tenements and hereditaments " throughout the whole jurisdiction, on an assessment of not less than one half the rack rent, leaseholders being authorised to deduct the amount from their rents.[3] The general penny rate was, from the outset, intended as an annual impost to meet the cost of the general works and standing charges, and it was re-peated in the same form in the following year.[4] But this led to revolt. The Parishes more than two miles distant from the City of London denied the Commissioners' jurisdiction ;[5] whilst these and others also raised the question whether the Commissioners could lawfully levy any money except for particular purposes, from the particular persons declared liable, by formal present-ment of a Jury of Sewers. The Assessors appointed for the

---

[1] MS. Minutes, Sewer Commissioners, Westminster, 19th January 1667.
[2] *Ibid.* 17th August 1667.
[3] *Ibid.* 17th August 1667.   [4] *Ibid.* 22nd August 1668.
[5] The Statute of Sewers, 3 James I. c. 14 (1605), had expressly given juris-diction over streams, whether tidal or not, within two miles of the City of London.

Parish of Kensington refused to collect the general Sewers Rate, and were eventually upheld in their refusal by the King's Judges.[1] It is probably owing to this legal decision that we find the Commissioners now nominally calling in for rating purposes, instead of the Parish Assessors, its own Jury of Sewers, and levying its rates on long lists of persons—including, we believe, the owners of all the lands and houses within the district—in the form of presentments by that Jury. The use of this judicial form did not, in fact, prevent the continued levy of a general rate " for emergencies," at least on all the Parishes within the ancient City of Westminster, and in 1690 the Commissioners got a clause inserted in the London and Westminster Paving Act of that year,[2] definitely extending the authority of the various Metropolitan Commissions of Sewers to all the Parishes within the Bills of Mortality, together with the " town of Kensington."

After the Revolution we note a rapid deterioration both in the social status and in the initiative and efficiency of the Court. The great personages gradually withdraw themselves from regular attendance. The names of noblemen and civil and ecclesiastical dignitaries are duly enrolled in every new Commission issued, decade after decade, by the successive Lord Chancellors right down to 1837, but from the latter part of the seventeenth century it seems to have been the custom for these to have been supplemented by batches of new names of humbler folk, which were, in fact, suggested on the occasion of each new Commission, by the more active members of the expiring body.[3] Thus, whilst the total number of Commissioners increased, the actual attendance became restricted to a score or so of the smaller folk, who thus came, in effect, to recruit themselves by

---

[1] MS. Minutes, Sewer Commissioners, Westminster, 26th September, 31st October 1668, 27th November, 11th and 18th December 1669, 22nd January, 19th February, 5th and 12th March, 18th June 1670.

[2] 2 William and Mary, session 2, cap. 8, sec. 14; see *post*, pp. 239-240.

[3] This is described in detail in the " Statement of Proceedings usually adopted upon Applications for the Renewal of Commissions," printed for the Westminster Sewer Commissioners in 1837, and included in House of Commons Return, No. 686, of 1847. In 1837, when the Commissioners applied as usual for a new Commission, submitting the names of all the surviving existing Commissioners, Lord Cottenham, then Lord Chancellor, took the unprecedented course of asking which of the Commissioners had ever attended ; struck off most of those who had not even qualified, and added some reformers, notably John Leslie, a local master tailor, through whose pertinacity the maladministration was eventually exposed (*ibid.*).

co-option. The formal organisation of the Court remained unaltered, but we see certain significant changes occur in procedure, in the character of the work done, and in the methods of administration. Whether or not by reason of some legal decision, for three-quarters of a century no extended or expensive new sewers are undertaken. The Commissioners confine themselves to clearing the existing sewers, repairing the iron gates by which their orifices were protected, and peremptorily ordering the removal of the "houses of office" which were everywhere being stealthily connected with the underground channels. The employment of outside experts to survey the drainage of a particular district as a whole is silently abandoned. Committees of inhabitants to help the Court with their local supervision are no longer summoned. Parish Assessors and Collectors are dispensed with. The Jury retires into the background, almost ceasing even to present nuisances, and finds its function limited to a formal adoption of presentments as to the owners, occupiers and rental value of lists of tenements drawn up by the Clerk. There are no Standing Committees. The Court itself, except for a somewhat fuller attendance at the formal opening of each new Commission, becomes a shifting dozen or so of unknown persons, varying from meeting to meeting according to chance or to the "interest" which this or that member has in particular properties. For the most part the actual administration devolves upon little committees of the Commissioners, the members resident in each locality being supposed themselves to view and report nuisances, and to supervise any works undertaken. The one or two ill-paid "sworn surveyors" are reinforced, and partly superseded, by a set of master workmen, or incipient contractors —a bricklayer, a digger, a pavior—who are formally appointed to undertake all the work of the Commission, supplying the labour at standing prices. We see signs of repeated petty jobbery, against which the superior folk who attend the opening meetings of each new Commission spasmodically struggle. Now and again a special committee of investigation discovers continued frauds in the use of the Commissioners' material by the "workman in trust." It becomes necessary to pass resolutions prohibiting Commissioners from acting as such "workmen" under the Court: resolutions which are apparently soon forgotten. Yet with all this, down to about 1760 our vision of the Court, taken as a whole, is that of a naïve and candid Authority ; muddling through its internal and external difficulties in fairly straightforward fashion ; accurately recording its doings in its records, including its own delinquencies ; and maintaining the extremely low level of efficiency at which alone it aimed, without malversations more serious than a constant mean jobbery. Presently a new development becomes apparent. In the last quarter of the eighteenth century we are conscious of the same sort of change in the Westminster Commission of Sewers as we have described in the Middlesex Quarter Sessions.[1] In both cases there is on the surface a new kind of efficiency and an increased breadth of view. The Court of Sewers now meets regularly every month or six weeks by public notice. It is presided over by a standing chairman, elected for a year. It is, from 1776 onwards, served by standing Committees on Accounts, Works and Rates respectively, which are annually appointed.[2] The staff of permanent officials is increased, and the scale of salaries is raised. The demand for an improvement in the amenity of the streets, which led, in 1760–1780, to the establishment of Paving Commissioners, and the repaving of the whole of the West End of London with flat stones for the side-walks and squared granite blocks for the roadways, was, we may believe, not without its effect on the Westminster Commissioners of Sewers. The Paving Acts required them to make good their iron grates in each street as it was repaved, and a special officer was appointed to attend to this work.[3] New sewers were undertaken for the benefit of the new houses about Park Lane, and on the Western side of the Green Park.[4] On the issue of a new Commission in 1769 the Court attempted to take the Western parts of its district [5] seriously in hand, and appointed a separate set of officers to cope with the work. But it was baffled in this ambition by renewed resistance on the part of the outlying Parishes, a recalcitrant owner at Hammersmith successfully repelling, in the Court of King's Bench, its claim to exercise any

[1] *The Parish and the County*, 1907.
[2] MS. Minutes, Sewer Commissioners, Westminster, 14th June 1776.
[3] *Ibid.* 5th July 1765.
[4] *Ibid.* 13th October 1769.
[5] Defined as Chelsea, Kensington, Hammersmith, Chiswick, Ealing, Acton, Brentford, Hanwell, Isleworth, Twickenham, Teddington and Hampton (*ibid.* 25th February 1769).

jurisdiction beyond Chelsea and Kensington.[1] Even in the
densely peopled part of its district the Court of Sewers evidently
lagged behind the energetic Paving Commissioners—not even
troubling to communicate with them as to their intention to
tear up the pavement for sewer repairs [2]—and in 1773 a proposal
was made by the latter that, for greater convenience of street
administration, the two bodies should, by a new Paving Act,
be completely amalgamated.[3] This proposal was indignantly
rejected by the little knot of active Commissioners running the
Court of Sewers, whom we see jealously guarding their own
powers against encroachment.[4] Meanwhile the volume of
business was steadily increasing, and the financial transactions,
which were always met out of the current rates, amounted, in
the aggregate, to large sums. The collection of the general
Sewers Rate, and of the special rates levied for particular
benefits,[5] is now in the hands of permanent collectors appointed
by the Court. The Jury practically disappears, except as a mere
formality. The little master-workmen at " standing prices "
are replaced by capitalist contractors, who are assumed to tender
for the whole work of each year at competitive rates. The
administration is now done behind the closed doors of the standing committees, whose reports (which were, of course, not
printed), are always adopted by the Court, the so-called open
sessions of which are merely formal. Unfortunately neither
these reports nor the decisions of the Court upon them are
reproduced in the minutes, which become decorous, and even
elaborate in their formality, but at the same time unenlightening.
Judging not only from these formal minutes, but also from what
is revealed in the course of Parliamentary enquiries in 1823 and

[1] MS. Minutes, Sewer Commissioners, Westminster, 2nd February, 20th
July, 26th November 1770. An attempt to remedy this lack of jurisdiction
by a Local Act failed (see House of Commons Journals, 21st December 1770,
22nd January 1771).
[2] Ibid. 30th August 1776.   [3] Ibid. 3rd and 17th December 1773.
[4] Ibid. 7th February 1783, 15th May 1789.
[5] In 1776 we see the tendency to defray everything from a uniform
general Sewers Rate in the order " that all persons who receive benefit from
the sewers by means of a communication either above or under ground are to
pay the whole of the rate assessed as being equally benefited " (ibid. 29th
November 1776). It is of some interest to find the surveyor reporting in 1790,
" that he examined the premises of Jeremiah Bentham, Esq., who appealed
by letter . . . and that they do not receive any benefit from the sewer.
Ordered that he be excused paying the rate assessed on him " (ibid. 26th
November 1790).

1834 respectively, and in the hostile criticism that gradually made itself heard, it seems to us that the outward show of vigour and efficiency which marks the Westminster Commission from 1760 onward, was not accompanied by any improvement in administrative purity. What happened was that the character of the corruption changed. The naïve and petty jobbery of the earlier years of the eighteenth century was replaced by collusion between some of the Commissioners and the contractors, who were allowed to go on charging the same prices year after year, without competitive tendering.[1] The organisation of the Court, even after a century of development, was, in fact, not strong enough to stand the strain of the enormous increase of business that poured in upon it towards the end of the century, when the fields of Pimlico and Paddington, Marylebone and St. Pancras were being rapidly covered with houses, and when every speculative builder was seeking to connect his new erections with the public sewers.

If we attempt to visualise the Westminster Commission of Sewers as it was in the nineteenth century, we shall realise how far it had departed both from the legal framework of a Court of Sewers, as set forth in the statute of 1532 and in its own Commission, and from the practical administration of the little group of courtiers and officials whom we saw, in the early days of the Restoration, despatching business in the Court of King's Bench. By 1800 the Westminster Commission seems to have included nominally about two hundred members, among them being some

---

[1] We see one of the Commissioners named Holland bringing in his son as a contractor for making the new sewers, at first as the lowest of five tenderers for brickwork and digging (MS. Minutes, Sewer Commissioners, Westminster, 13th October 1769) ; then, when a carpentering job has been tendered for, the father, as a Commissioner, suggests that his son would do it for less (*ibid.* 24th November 1769) ; presently, when the father is again present, the general digging work is given to the son, in spite of the protest of the person already appointed (*ibid.* 2nd November 1770) ; the same thing happens with the general bricklaying work (*ibid.* 30th October and 11th December 1772), by which time it appears that all sorts of extra allowances and privileges are accorded to him over other contractors ; seven years later we find him regularly installed as the general contractor for digging, bricklaying, carpenters' and smiths' work for a term of years (*ibid.* 14th January 1780) ; and this contract is periodically renewed at the same prices without other tenders being invited (*ibid.* 4th October 1782). Twenty years later he and another man have the whole of the work between them, and their prices are repeatedly increased at their request, without any tendering (*ibid.* 26th August 1803, 31st May 1805, 15th December 1809). At last they relinquish the business, which a new pair of contractors monopolise for another generation (*ibid.* 2nd March 1810).

fifty peers and privy councillors, many of the landowners of the district, great and small, and a miscellaneous collection of ecclesiastical dignitaries, members of Parliament, private gentlemen, architects, surveyors and builders, all purporting to be qualified by the ownership of freehold property. Meetings were held at the Westminster Guildhall about eight times a year—presently at the Sewers Office nearly every week—nominally "in Open Court," but no provision was made for admitting the public, and no spectator seems ever to have attended. Every ten years, at the first meeting of a new Commission, there would be a gathering of some size, when two or three of the dignitaries might be present. But half the persons included in the Commission never took the trouble to qualify for the office by attending even once to take the oath, and not more than thirty or forty attended more than a few times throughout the whole decade. Six Commissioners formed a quorum, and the usual attendance seems to have varied from that number up to a score. A Jury was still empanelled by the Sheriff from time to time, but its presentments had become mere formalities, and the jurymen were such as attended only to oblige the Commissioners or for the sake of the fees.[1] From the very beginning of the century,[2] we see the Commission falling more and more into the hands of

---

[1] When they wanted a Jury, the Commissioners themselves suggested to the Sheriff which jurymen to summon, and they took care to include tradesmen supplying the Commission and other subservient persons (Evidence to First Report of Metropolitan Sanitary Commission, 1847, p. 39). But the Jury had, even in 1823, long since ceased to " view," and did nothing but formally make the assessments in the office (Report of House of Commons Committee on Sewers in the Metropolis, 1823, p. 35).

[2] In 1807 the Commission for the first time succeeded in getting an Act of Parliament of its own, definitely declaring the district subject to its rule (47 George III. sess. 1, c. 7). This was to include Westminster, St. Giles-in-the-Fields, St. George's, Bloomsbury, St. Pancras, Marylebone, Hampstead, Paddington, Kensington, Chelsea, and even part of Willesden, but nothing beyond the brook which bounded Chelsea on the west. It was, however, claimed that the Act left untouched the jurisdiction over the tidal or navigable waters of Middlesex west of that brook (Report of House of Commons Committee on Sewers, 1834, p. 1). The Act also authorised the Commissioners to require notice of the making of any new sewer by a private person, and even gave them express power " to order and direct the making of any new vaults, sewers, drains and water-courses," though (as was afterwards contended) not to pay for them at the expense of the general rate. Another Act in 1812 enabled them to buy a house for a public Sewers Office, at which their meetings were subsequently held ; and gave them power to take copies of the Poor Rate assessment for use as the basis of their own rate (52 George III. c. 48 ; House of Commons Journals, 20th January and 20th April 1812).

one George Saunders, an architect and surveyor in active local
practice, who was chairman continuously from 1808 to 1835.
Under his rule every kind of regularity and order seems to have
disappeared. From the Court itself, which now met nearly
every week, every trace of judicial procedure had vanished.[1]
Any person desiring to connect his drain with the sewer, or
attending to make any complaint, found himself before an
arbitrary gentleman seated at the head of a long table, assiduously
waited on by the clerk and the surveyor, with half a dozen other
Commissioners coming and going, or sitting at the table engaged
in desultory conversation. This was the Authority which was
supposed to manage the drainage of nearly the whole of West
London, and which contrived to spend on an average thirty
thousand pounds a year on its work. There was no systematic
survey, no use of the printing press, no careful consideration or
examination of the reports of professional officers, not even any
fixed agenda, the chairman being left to bring on any item when
and where he thought fit.[2] The whole of the work was, in fact,
done by the chairman and three or four other Commissioners of
the humbler sort who chose to attend with some regularity.[3]

[1] Reports of House of Commons Committees on the Sewers of the Metropolis,
1823 and 1834 ; the numerous MS. and printed papers now in possession of
the London County Council ; *The Local Government of the Metropolis*, Anon.,
1835 ; *The Vestryman* for 26th July 1834 ; and *A Short Address to the Representative Vestries under Sir John Hobhouse's Vestry Act*, by John Leslie, 1845.
Leslie was himself a Commissioner, and gives us vivid pictures, both of the
procedure of the Court and of its negligence.

[2] Report of the House of Commons Committee on the Sewers of the Metropolis, 1834, pp. 130, 134.

[3] How shifting was the composition of successive Courts may be shown by
one example. The House of Commons Return, No. 686 of 1847, gives the
attendances at three successive meetings in May and June 1822, when (as was
alleged) a gross job was perpetrated. The attendances at these meetings,
besides the chairman, was 17, 13, 13. But only four Commissioners attended
all three meetings (pp. 14-15). At three other meetings in 1826, when gross
partiality to a particular contractor was shown, the attendances were 19, 15,
11. But only two Commissioners were present at all three meetings (pp. 16-17).
Commissioners, in fact, attended only when they were interested in a particular
case. It was significantly computed a few years later that the attendances of
the Commissioners who were architects or agents for estates, or past or present
building speculators, amounted to 47 per cent of the total attendances. The
Commissioners were not paid, the allowance of four shillings a day made by
23 Henry VIII. having long before ceased to be drawn in cash. But at Westminster as elsewhere it was customary for the active Commissioners to dine at
the expense of the rates, "and on dinner days," we are told in 1847, "the
attendances are more numerous," and mainly of the professional men and
builders (Evidence to First Report of Metropolitan Sanitary Commission, 1847,
p. 36).

G

When we add that most of the property owners had their estate agents on the Commission to look after their interests ; that the chairman himself was one of these, and was, moreover, professionally interested in many of the houses affected ; that some, if not all the other members, of the little group were directly interested in local building speculations; that there was absolutely no publicity ; that costly works were sometimes decided on without notice, on mere oral statements by the chairman and officers ; that there was no public advertisement for tenders, and no professional or independent or even public audit of the accounts —it will readily be understood how easily jobs were perpetrated and how extravagantly the ratepayers' money was spent. Apart from the favouritism shown to particular landowners and particular builders, in providing their estates with access to the public sewers on easy terms, there was, it need hardly be said, corruption in the execution of the work. For the first forty years of the nineteenth century the Westminster Commission, as can now plainly be seen, was in the hands of a couple of families of contractors to whom—just as to their fortunate predecessors during the previous thirty years—practically all the contracts for sewer work were given, without publicity, without competitive tendering, and without any sort of check upon the prices charged. The salaried surveyor to the Commission was himself secretly engaged as a builder within the area which he had to supervise ; and when this fact became known to the Commissioners by his becoming a bankrupt, it did not prevent their reappointing him, after a brief interval, to his responsible office.[1] Under these circumstances it need hardly be said that the quality of the sewer work executed was as unsatisfactory as the price charged for it. Many years afterwards heavy damages were recovered from one of these contractors on its being discovered that he had, during these years, deliberately omitted rings of brickwork from the sewer arches.[2] There is, indeed, reason to think that the Westminster Commission was run by the same corrupt clique of Justices of the Peace as we have described contemporaneously dominating the Middlesex Quarter Sessions. The Mainwarings and the Mercerons were prominent members. The profitable

---

[1] MS. Minutes, Sewer Commissioners, Westminster, 7th July 1826 and 30th September 1830.

[2] The case occurred in 1846 (Westminster Commissioners of Sewers v. George Bird) ; see the archives of London County Council.

current account of the Commission was, in 1806, suddenly transferred to the bank of William Mainwaring, then Chairman of
Quarter Sessions, though no reason is given for taking it away
from Drummond's bank, where it had been for nearly a century.[1]
But though we do not know how to apportion among particular
persons the disgrace of the corrupt inefficiency of the Commission
in these years, their record is, indeed, a bad one. It was, perhaps,
not altogether their fault, seeing that the Statute of Sewers had
not contemplated the construction of new works, that, at the
beginning of the nineteenth century, many of the streets in Westminster had absolutely no sewers of any kind, or that thousands of
houses were still unconnected with such sewers as existed. But
what is inexcusable is that the Commissioners should have gone
on for generations without any accurate plan of their sewers,
or any systematic scheme for dealing with their district ; that
they should have suffered such sewers as existed to get into a
terrible state of disrepair ; [2] that, even after their Act of 1807
had given them power to compel new sewers to be made by the
landowners at their unfettered discretion, they should have
neglected to use this power to any but the smallest extent ; [3]
that, in spite of the professional knowledge at their command,
they should have clung desperately to the oldest and worst shapes
and sizes of sewers, and should have allowed their contractors to
construct them of faulty material in the cheapest and worst
possible way ; that they should have been grossly partial in their

[1] MS. Minutes, Sewer Commissioners, Westminster, 16th May 1806. After
the failure of Mainwaring's Bank in 1814, when the Westminster Court of
Sewers, with others, lost heavily, the account was restored to Drummond's
(Report of House of Commons Committee on the Sewers of the Metropolis,
1823, pp. 8, 36 ; *ibid.* 1834, p. 5).

[2] In 1791 a "lottery inspector" writes to the surveyor that "yesterday
while I was searching a house in Orange Court . . . where I was informed a
private lottery was carrying on, I discovered a large hole cut through the
brickwork in the cellar into the sewer, seemingly for the purpose of escape
. . enabling the offenders to avoid my pursuing them " (MS. Minutes, Sewer
Commissioners, Westminster, 20th September 1791).

[3] We never find them compelling owners or builders to make sewers ;
though they issue notices insisting on being informed whenever a sewer is
about to be made, and they demur to its being made at too great a depth for their
convenience. Their only remedy for the building on low-lying land—destined
hereafter to be a cause of great public expense and private inconvenience—
was to " give notice that whenever the lower floors or pavements of buildings
shall have been laid so low as not to admit of their being drained with a proper
current, they will not allow any sewers, or drains into sewers, to be made for
the service of such buildings " (*Morning Advertiser*, 3rd March 1818).

benefits to the lands of particular owners and in their dealings with particular builders ;[1] and, finally, that they should have made no effort to prevent the poorer streets and alleys of their district getting into the awful sanitary state to which attention was called by the ravages of cholera in 1832 and 1848.[2]

Other Metropolitan Courts of Sewers

The two Courts of Sewers of Greenwich and Westminster, remaining in their different ways essentially unchanged in constitution for the whole century and a half, may be taken as the two leading types from which the half a dozen other Courts of Sewers of the Metropolitan area more or less diverge in one direction or another. So long as a district remained essentially rural, its Court of Sewers approximated to the Greenwich type. Wherever it becomes urban in character, its Court of Sewers developed the constitutional features of that of Westminster. The dykes and sluices of the great stretch of Surrey Marshes

[1] As examples of the constant complaints about the inequality and careless partiality of the assessments to the sewers rates, see MS. Vestry Minutes, Marylebone, 7th March 1807. By 1834 the complaints were getting voiced in the Court itself. At an excited meeting in that year, when some newly appointed Commissioners attended, one of them said that " immense sums of money had been levied for sewers rate, and it was a well-known fact that a certain Commissioner possessing property at Notting Hill, and another at College Street, Westminster, could have new sewers erected without the slightest difficulty, and that the pickaxe had been set to work to create damage, merely as an apology for rebuilding." The Chairman (Saunders) refused to submit a resolution in favour of a certain new sewer, alleging that its construction would be illegal (*The Vestryman*, 26th July 1834).

[2] A fearful description of the accumulation of filth in the poor parts of Westminster was given to the Home Secretary in 1831 (Domestic State Papers in Public Record Office, Misc., 1831, pp. 20-24). Even of the wealthy district of Marylebone it could be said in 1848 that " the sewers were put in piecemeal as the streets were formed, without system, and irrespective of the requirements of adjoining streets and surrounding districts. Their bottoms are flat and wide ; the levels are very irregular ; many of the sewers have little or no fall whatever, while a few have a considerable fall, and the bottoms of others run up and down, forming a series of ridges and hollows. Hence in general they retain most of the soil drainage of the parish, instead of affording the means of conveying it away as fast as it is produced. . . . Depth and regularity of fall were not taken into account. The efficiency of the system was never thought of. So long as a sewer was put down in front of the houses into which it was possible to carry a drain that was deemed sufficient ; and is likely to continue to be so until a combined authority be strictly exercised over all speculative building operations " (Report of Mr. John Phillips, Surveyor to the Metropolitan Sewers Commission, on the Report of the Vestry of St. Marylebone on the Sanitary Condition of the Parish, 1st March 1848). And see *Sanitary Evolution of London*, by H. Jephson, 1907.

from Wandsworth to Deptford Creek, which, except for the Borough of Southwark and a few scattered groups of houses, were at the end of the seventeenth century only sparsely inhabited ; and the great river wall surrounding the practically uninhabited Isle of Dogs, were, at the Revolution, administered almost wholly by Standing Juries, made up of the local occupiers of farms. On the other hand, the Tower Hamlets, and Holborn and Finsbury, districts already covered with suburban streets, were governed, like Westminster, by Courts of Sewers, in which the principal part was played by the Commissioners themselves.[1] Moreover, as the whole area governed by these Courts of Sewers became (with the exception of the marshes below Greenwich) more densely populated, we find them all slipping more or less into the habits of the Westminster Court—reaching, too, at one period or another, much the same depth of inefficiency, if not of corruption. This development from administration by judicial process, through the presentments of Standing Juries of neighbours in Open Court, to administration by executive orders of a little clique of Commissioners working through secret committees and salaried servants, without publishing reports or enjoying public discussion, can be discerned even in the records of the Commissions of Poplar, St. Katharine and the Tower Hamlets.[2]

[1] See *The Law of Waters and of Sewers*, by Humphrey W. Woolrych, 1830 ; *Municipal Origins*, by F. H. Spencer, 1911, pp. 242-263.

[2] The MS. Minutes of the Tower Hamlets Commissioners of Sewers exist from 1702 ; those of the Commissioners of Sewers " for the Hospital and Precinct of St. Katharine " (adjoining the Tower of London) only from 1782, though this little Commission is mentioned from at least 1720 ; and those of the Poplar Commissioners for the " limits between Limehouse and Blackwall in the parish of Stepney . . . commonly called Stebunheath Marsh or Poplar Marsh," from 1629. These Minutes, now in the custody of the London County Council, afford a rich mine of information. The Blackwall and Poplar and Stebunheath Marsh Commissioners continued to deal with marshes, and retained the characteristics of the Greenwich Court of Sewers. The Tower Hamlets Commissioners, who met at the " Whitechapel Court House," seem to have been slack and inefficient (except for the making of one great new sewer), but not obviously corrupt. It is interesting to note that their procedure and organisation were remodelled after 1820, by Sir Daniel Williams, on the lines of the Holborn and Finsbury Commission. The St. Katharine's Commissioners, of whom the " Master of the Chapter " was ex-officio chairman, dealt only with a small area (the old precinct of St. Katharine's Hospital), and found themselves, after 1824, without work, owing to the practical absorption of their district by the St. Katharine's Dock. There seems but little information as to these Commissions, outside the Minutes and the Parliamentary Papers of 1823, 1834 and 1847. See, however, the House of Commons Journals, 23rd February 1797, for two petitions from the Tower Hamlets Commissioners ; the evidence of Peeke, Surveyor to the Tower Hamlets Commission, in Report of Select Committee

But these Commissions dealt with relatively small populations, which, down to 1835, exhibited no such tremendous increase as was seen to the West and the South. They show, accordingly, only slight changes in constitution and procedure, interesting chiefly as illustrations and supplementary examples of the more marked developments elsewhere. We shall, therefore, not trouble the reader with our elaborate notes of these Courts, but confine ourselves to brief accounts of the course of development of the Commissioners of Sewers of Holborn and Finsbury on the one hand, and of those of Surrey and Kent on the other.

Holborn and Finsbury

What sort of authority it was that, during the seventeenth century, looked after the drainage of the fenny districts North of the City walls, periodically inundated as these were by the rainstorms from the Hampstead and Highgate Hills, we have no information. The Minutes of the Court of Sewers " held for the limits of the Holborn and Finsbury Divisions of the County of Middlesex " exist only from 1716,[1] when the Court had been long in existence, and when most of its district had already become urban in character. During the whole of the eighteenth century the constitution and procedure of this Court, though approximating on the whole to those of the Westminster Court, embodied some interesting remnants of the earlier type. Like the Westminster

on the State of Large Towns, 1840 ; the *Report of the Committee (of the Tower Hamlets Commissioners) on some of the Statements in the . . . Report of the Poor Law Commissioners on the Sanitary Condition of the Labouring Population*, 1843 ; and a stray report in *Times*, 16th February 1828.

It should perhaps be mentioned here that the Act providing for the building of Regent Street under the Office of Woods and Forests (53 George III. c. 121) in 1813 contained clauses establishing a separate Commission of Sewers for the new district. The Regent's Park and Regent Street Commission appears to have consisted of about fifty persons representing principally various Government departments (Report of House of Commons Committee on the Sewers of the Metropolis, 1834, p. 128 ; the Crown Estate Paving Act, 1824, 5 George IV. c. 100).

[1] Beyond these minutes, and *A Collection of the Public Statutes relating to Sewers and the Local Acts for Holborn and Finsbury Divisions, Middlesex*, 1830, we know this Court of Sewers only from the Parliamentary Papers of 1823, 1831, 1834 and 1847, and the somewhat frequent references to its later work, and to its energetic surveyor, John Roe, in the writings of Sir Edwin Chadwick. See, for instance, *Report of the Poor Law Commissioners on the Sanitary Condition of the Labouring Population*, 1843.

Commissioners of the eighteenth century, those of Holborn and
Finsbury were not important landowners, nor yet Court officials,
but men of unknown names and (as we soon discover) parsi-
monious ideas. As in Westminster, they had supplied themselves with one or two ill-paid officers, but they relied mainly
on the little master-workmen whom they appointed for Holborn
and Finsbury respectively—local bricklayers, paviors, carpenters
and smiths. They were even behind the Westminster Commissioners in that they could not bring themselves, until 1775,[1] to
incur the expense of a surveyor, preferring to exact from their
leading bricklayer, without remuneration, such plans and surveys
of the work to be done by himself or his fellow-craftsmen, or of the
position of the existing sewers, as were absolutely indispensable.[2]
As at Westminster, the locally resident Commissioners themselves
ordered the various works, saw to their execution, sent the workmen's bills to their colleague, the Treasurer,[3] by whom they were
paid, the necessary rates—levied separately for each Common
Sewer equally upon all those who benefited by it [4]—being collected by little officials of the Court itself. But unlike the Westminster Commissioners, those of Holborn and Finsbury by no
means did the whole of the government. Their Court met only
four times a year, and its proceedings maintain, throughout the
century, a distinctly judicial character. The Commissioners did
little or nothing on their own initiative ; they merely listened to

[1] They had some sort of a surveyor in 1720, but when he died, they resolved
to make shift with the bricklayer (MS. Minutes, Sewer Commissioners, Holborn
and Finsbury, 4th May 1720, 28th October 1728), and then with the " Summoner
to the Court " (*ibid.* 18th July 1729). They appointed a surveyor at £30 a
year in 1775 (*ibid.* 3rd January 1775).

[2] These bricklayers, who were paid for their brickwork at per rod, were
required " to do the business of a surveyor to the Court without any gratuity
or reward whatsoever, and that they do not presume to charge more for their
prices and rates . . . than they do to private gentlemen " (*ibid.* 26th January
1728). For the result on the bricklayers' bills, see *ibid.* 18th July 1729.

[3] In 1756 the Clerk was appointed Treasurer, the " bricklayer to the Court "
and one of the Commissioners serving as his sureties (*ibid.* 15th April 1756).
Not until 1792 did the Court have a banker, when Child & Co. were appointed
(*ibid.* 23rd February 1792). The Tower Hamlets Commissioners did not
employ a banker till 1759, when they opened an account with Sir Charles Asgill
& Co. (*ibid.* Tower Hamlets, 8th March 1759).

[4] In 1718 " persons who have cesspools in their respective yards and
gardens " give trouble " by pretending they were not liable to pay the full
tax to any common sewer, but half the said tax." The Court decides that " all
such persons that are liable to be taxed but to one common sewer and no
more, shall be charged with the full tax to the said common sewer " (*ibid.*
Holborn and Finsbury, 21st October 1718).

complaints by inhabitants and to the long detailed presentments of their two Juries, relating to all sorts of nuisances.[1] These Juries were, down to 1778, an important and very effective part of the organisation. Returned originally by the Sheriff of the County, they served continuously for five or seven years—until, in fact, they were discharged by the Court at their own request.[2] Every quarter they made a complete inspection of their respective districts, apparently as systematic as that made by the Standing Jury of Greenwich, not only presenting nuisances, but recommending what works, new as well as old, should be undertaken ; and determining by whom the cost should be borne. Unlike the two local Juries of Westminster, those of Holborn and Finsbury do not seem ever to have had their presentments traversed ; and we even see them used, not infrequently, for the purpose of enquiring, like a Traverse Jury, " into the truth of the premises," when individuals complained of the annoyances committed by other persons, or disputed the assessments imposed by the Commissioners. On the other hand, differing from the Juries of Sewers of Greenwich and Somerset, those of Holborn and Finsbury took no part in the execution of any works or in the administration of any sluices or gates. At the close of each Court, when they had made their presentments, their function was at an end until their next periodical survey. They seem, in fact, to have been a cross between the merely presenting Jury of the Hundred composed of local neighbours, and the Traverse Jury of indifferent persons summoned to try indictments.

[1] These nuisances comprised not only foul ditches, filthy drains and obstructed sewers, but also " houses of office," pigsties, and slaughterhouses. In 1719 the jury presented a group of persons in " Hog Island," Gray's Inn Lane, for keeping large numbers of pigs, to the defiling and obstructing of the sewers. On failing to remove their pigs, they were fined £5 each, duly estreated into the Court of Exchequer (MS. Minutes, Sewer Commissioners, Holborn and Finsbury, 1st May 1719). One Jeremy Jummins of Shoreditch kept " between two and three hundred hogs," whereby the common sewer was " filled up with dirt, dung and soil occasioned by the said hogs." He was fined £20 (ibid. 21st October 1719). As a contemporaneous example we may cite that, in the Tower Hamlets Court of Sewers, we have the Jury, in 1706, ordered to go to Spitalfields " and return such nuisances as they shall find, and that the surveyor attend the same time, and that the Jury present the houses of office, and also view of the intended sewers in Church Lane be annoyed by the hog-house in Whitechapel Field, thereby adjoining " (ibid. Tower Hamlets, 8th May 1706).

[2] " Ordered that the old Juries be discharged . . . according to the prayer of their petition, they having done good service for the Court between six and seven years last past " (ibid. Holborn and Finsbury, 19th October 1753).

In the last quarter of the eighteenth century we see the constitution and procedure of this Court of Sewers undergoing rapid changes. In 1778 the Commissioners, who were always at issue with the Corporation of the City of London (through whose sewers all their drainage had to pass on its way to the Thames), took advantage of the Bill which the Corporation promoted for the benefit of its own estates in Finsbury to secure a great increase of their own powers.[1] The Commissioners were for the first time expressly empowered to build new sewers, at any rate where any trace of an old sewer existed, and to raise a general pound rate on all occupiers or owners, both without the intervention of a Jury. These powers had reference, it is true, only to the Finsbury Division, but there was nothing to prevent the funds raised in Finsbury being used for the general expenses of the Commission. From this date the Commissioners felt relieved from any necessity for summoning a Jury for Finsbury, whilst that for Holborn rapidly became a merely formal adjunct of the quarterly Court, signing the presentments put before them by the clerk, and (in pursuance of the precedent set by the 1778 Act for Finsbury) finding liable to pay the Sewers Rate indiscriminately all the occupiers or owners within the district.[2] Along with this

[1] The Corporation was lessee for 99 years of " the prebendal estate of Halliwell and Finsbury," which was being laid out for building, and sought power to make new sewers (by the City Commissioners of Sewers) at its own expense, subject to the payment by the Holborn and Finsbury Commissioners of Sewers of a contribution of £150 a year. It was professedly to enable the Commissioners to raise that sum that they were given power to levy a general rate, with other incidental powers. See 18 George III. c. 66 (1778); MS. Minutes, Commissioners of Sewers, Holborn and Finsbury, 2nd April and 2nd May 1777 ; and (for the quarrels and fights with the Corporation workmen) 16th April and 9th July 1778.

[2] No rate was, however, collected in respect of hereditaments on the high ground towards Hampstead, on the plea, upheld in a case taken to the Court of King's Bench in 1814, that these lands received no benefit, and were not protected against any damage by the sewers (Report of House of Commons Committee on the Sewers of the Metropolis, 1834, p. 12). The Commission restricted itself, moreover, to such parts of the Holborn and Finsbury Divisions as were within two miles of the City of London (*ibid.* pp. 12, 158). The judges seem to have always felt unable to construe the various Acts of Parliament, by which the different Metropolitan Sewer Commissions sought to define their jurisdiction, as giving any power of taxation beyond the limits implied by the old law of sewers—that is, beyond the area that actually received benefit or avoided injury by some pre-existing sewer. The high grounds of Surrey got exemption from the imposts of the Surrey and Kent Commissioners. Nor was it the high grounds only that claimed exemption. The Tower Hamlets Commission purported to include Hackney, but the Court could seldom get its rates paid there, both because much of it was beyond two miles from the City

shrinking up of the Jury, we see the Commissioners themselves developing in the course of the next two decades an exclusively executive organisation. The casual committees of local Commissioners are replaced in 1795 by a single standing committee elected at the opening of each new Commission for the whole ten years. This standing (or as it is sometimes termed " select ") committee quickly became the real governing authority. It met and adjourned whenever it thought fit, engaged officers, decided on new sewers, entered into contracts, assessed rates, supervised work and paid the workmen's bills—transacted, in fact, the whole business of the Commission, merely reporting its acts for ratification to its own members when, with one or two more Commissioners, they assembled at Hicks Hall each quarter as a formal Court of Sewers. These reports (which, unlike those of Westminster, are entered in full in the minute books) are interesting to the technical student in the detailed examples they present of the contemporary problems of drainage, but they yield little information as to the character and administrative procedure of this all-powerful executive. From other sources we learn that the eight or ten members met frequently at the Crown Tavern in Clerkenwell, and spent about £500 a year on their entertainments ; that their total disbursements amounted to many thousands of pounds a year ; that they published no record of their proceedings, and did not even print a statement of accounts ; and that they entered into contracts for extensive works without advertisement or competitive tendering. To this we may add that even the formal minutes reveal a suspicious identity between the surnames of Commissioners, contractors and officials.[1] When in 1812 a Standing Committee of Accounts was appointed, which might have served as a check on their proceedings, we see this manned exclusively

---

of London, and because it drained into the Lea, and not into the sewers leading to the Thames. A sturdy resistance by the inhabitants began in 1788, which led to interminable litigation, that seems to have gone on spasmodically from 1800 to 1835 (MS. Minutes, Sewer Commissioners, Tower Hamlets, 3rd and 22nd July, 28th August 1788, 5th March, 19th May, 15th September 1824, 28th November 1827).

[1] In 1774 a vacancy in the office of Clerk and Treasurer was filled by the appointment of one of the Commissioners (ibid. Holborn and Finsbury, 7th April 1774). In 1775, when at last the Court appoints a Surveyor, he has the same surname as one of the active Commissioners (ibid. 3rd January 1775).

by members of the General Purposes Committee. It remains to be said that this all-powerful little group included the principal members of the corrupt clique of Justices of the Peace who were, in the same years, dominating the Middlesex Quarter Sessions, and several other local governing bodies in the Metropolitan area. From 1795 to 1808 the Chairman of the Court was the sanctimonious banker, William Mainwaring, who was Chairman of Quarter Sessions. From 1800 the Chairman of the Standing Committee was his chief henchman, Colonel (afterwards Sir) Daniel Williams, then newly appointed one of the new stipendiary magistrates, who followed Mainwaring in the chairmanship of the Court, whilst retaining his chairmanship of the Standing Committee. During these years the most regular attender of its meetings was their friend, Joseph Merceron, the notorious " boss " of the parish of Bethnal Green, whom we find invariably present from 1795 onward, when accounts are to be audited, privileges granted or contracts made. The Holborn and Finsbury Commissioners of Sewers were, in fact, travelling fast in the same direction as the Westminster body. Fortunately they were pulled up by a catastrophe. In 1812 Mainwaring got himself elected as Treasurer, and, repeating what he had already done in the Tower Hamlets and Westminster, immediately transferred the large current balance kept by the Commissioners from Child's Bank to his own, which was already on the very brink of bankruptcy. Within a couple of years the Commissioners found themselves short of several thousands of pounds which he was unable to pay ; [1] and were compelled to levy a " double rate " on their district. A great uproar arose, and an effective agitation, headed by Serjeant Wilde, afterwards Lord Truro, and John Wilks, a leading Finsbury resident. The various Parish Vestries insisted on the promotion of a Bill to reform the practice and procedure of the Commissioners, and, in spite of the vigorous protests of the latter, this Bill became law in 1814. [2] The main interest of the reformers who obtained the Act was to provide against corrupt dealings. All work over £50 in value was to be executed by

[1] Report of House of Commons Committee on the Sewers of the Metropolis, 1834, p. 17.

[2] 54 George III. c. 219 ; Hansard, 10th May 1814 ; House of Commons Journals, 19th November 1813 and 10th May 1814 ; MS. Minutes, Holborn and Finsbury Sewers Commissioners, 29th July 1814 ; Report of House of Commons Committee on the Sewers of the Metropolis, 1823, p. 25.

contract, entered into after public advertisement ; the accounts were to be published and communicated to the Parishes concerned ; all fees of office were abolished ; any Commissioner personally interested in any case was to withdraw during its consideration ; and the dinner expenses of the Commissioners were limited to £450 per annum. But the Act is, perhaps, of wider interest, as marking the final step in the transition from the old procedure of the Court of Sewers to that of a modern administrative body. The powers of rating given in the 1778 Act were extended to the whole area under the Commissioners. The antiquated system of Jury presentments was definitely abandoned and all power of deciding what works should be undertaken and who should be taxed was expressly vested in the Commissioners, subject to appeal to Quarter Sessions. And though no authority to construct new sewers, when no pretence at a sewer had previously existed, was expressly given, the wording was so wide, and the Commissioners put so liberal a construction on this wording, that new sewers were, in fact, constructed under this Act wherever they were deemed necessary.

The changes in the legal procedure and powers of the Holborn and Finsbury Commissioners appear to have resulted in a remarkable rise in their standards of administrative efficiency and integrity. The formal structure remained almost unchanged, many of the 150 or so persons named in the Commission never troubling to qualify, still less to attend.[1] The working constitution was only slightly modified. Instead of one standing committee, there are henceforth nominally two — the Commissioners for General Purposes and the Commissioners for Audit and Assessment. But this change was only nominal, as the two committees were composed of practically the same members, and had a common chairman, who was also chairman of the Court. What was revolutionised was the administrative procedure. The Bank of England became the Treasurer, and full publicity was given to the accounts, which were printed and circulated not only to the Commissioners, but also to the local Vestries. An elaborate code of standing orders was adopted, and apparently adhered to. A staff of four salaried surveyors and inspectors was definitely ordered to keep an exact account,

---

[1] About half of them would, however, qualify, which was above the average. We do not gather that more than a score or so ever attended.

and to maintain a minute supervision of all the work executed. All contracts were entered into " in Open Court," after public advertisement ; and the express statutory prohibition of Commissioners or officers being in any way concerned in them seems to have been obeyed. It is only fair to the memory of Sir Daniel Williams, whom we have reported as in suspicious company, to record that these internal reforms seem to have been carried out by him ; that a few years later he reorganised the Tower Hamlets Court of Sewers on almost identical lines ; [1] that he remained down to 1830 chairman of the Court, and of both its committees, being until 1828 at least the responsible person for what was done ; and that we discover nothing during these years that is otherwise than creditable to him. Finally, we have to note that the Commission was fortunate enough to secure, about 1820, first as inspector and then as surveyor, the services of John Roe, a man of exceptional inventiveness and ability, who made a real study of the problems of drainage, and who set himself, between 1825 and 1835, to transform the shapes and sizes of the Holborn and Finsbury sewers, in accordance with his own discoveries, getting the Commissioners in 1829–1835 to adjust the levels, build new sewers, contribute up to a third of the cost of new sewers made by others, and systematically arch over the remaining open drains.[2] Thus, we leave the Holborn and Finsbury Court of Sewers in 1835 in vigorous activity ; praised by such reformers as Edwin Chadwick ; and cited to contemporary Parliamentary Committees as the pattern local governing body in the Metropolis—though it is not clear to us whether this position was due to its own excellence or merely to the contrast that it presented to the nadir of inefficiency and corruption into which other Courts of Sewers, notably that of Surrey and Kent, had meanwhile sunk.

Surrey and Kent

The Commissioners of Sewers for Surrey and Kent had under their jurisdiction the whole of the low-lying marshland on the southern shore of the Thames, between the River Ravensbourne

---

[1] MS. Minutes, Sewer Commissioners, Tower Hamlets, 1820–1830 ; Report of House of Commons Committee on the Sewers of the Metropolis, 1823.

[2] *Ibid.* Holborn and Finsbury, 23rd April 1830 ; 25th October 1833 ; Report of House of Commons Committee of 1834, pp. 13-14, 17.

in Kent and the Ember Branch of the River Mole in Surrey. We are not concerned here to enquire how it was that this particular area, extending into two Counties, and comprising numerous Manors and Parishes, came to be governed as a single unit.[1] Nor need we do more than call attention to the fact that, when the earliest minutes begin in 1569, they show us a body of Commissioners, made up apparently of the principal resident proprietors of land, superintending and controlling what seem to be the remnants of older local organisations for the maintenance of sluices and stretches of river wall. There were, as in Somerset, standing bodies of "Jurats"[2] for different localities, with bailiffs and collectors ; all sworn to perform the duties of their offices ; all unpaid and compulsorily serving. The periodical meetings of the Commissioners, held with all formality as a Court of Record, and attended, it appears, by the Under Sheriff for Surrey,[3] served practically only to give ratification and legal validity to the presentments of the Juries, and opportunities for appeal.

In 1689, when we take up the story, little had yet been changed. The district — but for the steadily increasing "Borough" of Southwark and the slowly growing hamlets and villages that dotted the levels from Deptford to Molesey—was still essentially common and marsh. The "Court of Sewers" was still composed of the principal landowners,[4] under whose superintendence three or four Standing Juries, in as many

---

[1] In the earliest minutes the jurisdiction of the Court is stated as "from the Ravensbourne in the County of Kent to the Church of Putney in the County of Surrey" (MS. Minutes, Sewer Commissioners, Surrey and Kent, 3rd January 1569). One volume, *Court Minutes of the Surrey and Kent Sewer Commission*, 1569–1579, has been published by the London County Council (1909, 352 pp.). Beyond the MS. Minutes, which extend over nearly three centuries, we have no sources of information for this Court of Sewers other than the Parliamentary papers of 1823, 1831, 1834 and 1847 ; a pamphlet entitled *Reports relating to Sewage with reference to Observations of the Poor Law Commissioners*, printed by order of the Court (of Sewers for Surrey and Kent), 1843 ; and incidental references in the works already cited, especially *Old Southwark*, by W. Rendle, 1878, which gives various extracts from the Minutes.

[2] So called, for instance, in MS. Minutes, Sewer Commissioners, Surrey and Kent, 11th December 1573.

[3] MS. Minutes, Sewer Commissioners, Surrey and Kent, 9th January 1691.

[4] The new Commission issued on the accession of William and Mary comprised 56 persons, of whom 43 were of the quorum. They included one earl, five baronets, ten knights, 27 "esquires" and 13 "gentlemen" (MS. Minutes, Sewer Commissioners, Surrey and Kent, 29th August 1689). Among them were John Evelyn and his eldest son, of Deptford and Wotton (*ibid.* 9th June

different districts,[1] were periodically viewing all the ditches, sluices and embankments, presenting defects, amercing defaulters, and through their respective Foremen, not infrequently superintending the sluice-keepers and supervising the execution of the work done by the various " Scavelmen." [2] We watch these jurymen, who served for about four years each, individually bringing " their several and respective presentments " to their Foreman, three days at least before the Court Day, in order that he may prepare them and combine them with his own, for their joint signature.[3] We see the several Juries assessing the particular lands benefited by each specific work, and also levying a general rate on a particular marsh or a particular " level " for works performed for its own common advantage. These rates were payable to special local Expenditors.[4] But the Commissioners were already taking some matters into their own hands. They would periodically of their own authority order the levy of a " General Tax " on all the lands and houses throughout the whole district of the Commission, directing " that the several Juries do against the next Court bring in lists of all the owners and occupiers . . . within their respective limits." [5] This General Tax was paid to their own " Expenditor-General."

1691 ; " To Greenwich being put into the new Commission of Sewers," is an entry of 1685 in *Diary and Correspondence of John Evelyn*, 1862, vol. ii. p. 255) ; and as we incidentally learn elsewhere, Elias Ashmole, the antiquary (*Memoirs of the Life of Elias Ashmole*, edited by Charles Burman, 1717, pp. 53, 76).

[1] Apparently the extension of the district of this Court of Sewers into two Counties made necessary two panels of jurymen, returned by the Sheriffs of Kent and Surrey respectively. The Surrey panel was, time out of mind, in two parts, one for the Eastern and the other for the Western division of the marshes within that county. Between 1695 and 1698 a fourth Jury seems to have formed for " the Level of Earl Sluice."

[2] Scavelmen were men employed to " cast " or cleanse the ditches.

[3] MS. Minutes, Sewer Commissioners, Surrey and Kent, 20th March 1694.

[4] In 1701 Isaac Loader of Deptford, a local freeholder, is appointed " Expenditor of the Level of Church Marsh," and also to take charge of the Church Marsh Sluice (*ibid.* 23rd May 1701).

[5] " Ordered that all the Commissioners in this Commission be summoned to the next Court of Sewers in order to lay a tax upon all the levels within the limits of this Commission " (*ibid.* 9th September 1691, also 24th September 1708). This " General Tax " was disputed between 1703 and 1712, especially by the parish of Christchurch, but precedents back to Elizabeth's reign were produced, and the tax was maintained and enforced by distress of double the amount due, at so much per acre on land, and so much in the pound on the annual value of messuages and tenements (*ibid.* 3rd March, 16th and 23rd September, and 26th November 1703, 6th March and 28th September 1704, 27th September 1711, and 12th October 1712).

who was a member of the Court. They had, in their own employment, besides the staff of Sluice-keepers, Wall-reeves and "Scavelmen," a Clerk, two Bailiffs and Cryers, and various collectors. In case of any serious breach in the river wall, or an important sluice, the Commissioners sent their Committee to view the damage and contract for its immediate repair. On complaint of any presentment of a Jury, they would depute some of their number to join with the Jury in a new view;[1] or, less frequently, they would permit the complainant to traverse the presentment, and have it tried by a specially summoned Jury.[2] Moreover, the Jury for the Western District, or Wandsworth, as it was called, was habitually so dilatory in its action, and so partial in its presentments, that the Commissioners were coming more and more to supersede it, by the executive proceedings of their own members and their own local officers. Yet, for a whole generation after the Revolution, the large landowners who constituted the Court seemed always anxious to stimulate the initiative, maintain the vitality and secure the co-operation of the local Juries of their tenants, and to continue their reputation as an open Court of Justice, in which any one could obtain redress against partiality or remedy for misunderstanding.[3] During the first half of the eighteenth century, we note a gradual change in the working constitution. The local Juries increase in number, but sink in importance; any parish that presses for a Jury of its own is apparently allowed to have one, until, eventually, there are about a dozen separate Juries. Their presentments become perfunctory and superfluous. Their chief function comes to be that of assessing the owners and occupiers liable to pay the general and special rates, level by

[1] Upon information of a defective sluice in 1690, four named Commissioners are deputed " to meet to-morrow morning at nine of the clock at Mr. Cave's at the Bunch of Grapes, near the said sluice and from there to take a view of the said sluice with six or more of the East Jury of Sewers " (MS. Minutes, Sewer Commissioners, Surrey and Kent, 21st January 1690).

[2] We gather that the Traverse Jury, unlike the ordinary Jury of Sewers, received the customary common juryman's fee for each day's attendance. Persons presented took advantage of the privilege of traversing, by getting their cases removed by certiorari to the Court of King's Bench, when neither party troubled to take further proceedings. The Court, therefore, engaged an attorney to take the necessary steps (*ibid.* 9th June 1691 and 8th April 1692).

[3] In 1704 it is " ordered that no motion be made whereby anything is granted by this Court to any particular person (other than a view), unless whilst the Jury are present, and therefore that the same be done before dinner " (*ibid.* 19th December 1704).

level, and eventually parish by parish.[1] The number of Commissioners meanwhile increases, and we become aware of a
certain jostling of the smaller folk to obtain the privilege of
acting as Commissioners. The noblemen, baronets and knights
cease to attend the meetings, and presently cease even to qualify
by taking the oaths. The open Court of Sewers held periodically
with the paraphernalia of a Court of Justice, is supplemented,
if not practically superseded, by numerous adjournments,
" Special Courts," " Audit Courts," and committee meetings,
held at various taverns in different parts of the district, at which
the attendance of the Jury is dispensed with, and at which all
sorts of business may be transacted.[2] When a particular individual wants a " view," this is now made by a small committee
of the Commissioners without any members of the Jury. Even
general inspections are so made.[3] Gradually the characteristic
feature of " assessment according to benefit " is abandoned ;
particular works are done at the common expense ; from 1758
onwards even the levels cease to have their own rates ; and
everything becomes chargeable to the General Tax, levied by
order of the Court itself, collected by a single collector over the
whole area and received and disbursed by the Expenditor-
General.[4] Coincidently with these changes of procedure, there
are unmistakable signs of the petty jobbery usual at the period :
the Chairman himself supplies chalk to the Court ; [5] another
active Commissioner fills the post of " carpenter in chief to the
Court " ; [6] persons amerced by the Jury for defaults frequently
qualify as Commissioners at the next meeting of the Court, when
they invariably have their amercements discharged ; [7] persons

---

[1] For a short time they were even paid a percentage on the amount of their
assessments ; being, in 1757, expressly " allowed after the rate of 4d. in the
pound on the gross amount of such rate for their expenses " (MS. Minutes,
Sewer Commissioners, Surrey and Kent, 22nd September 1757).
[2] Already in 1704 we see an " Audit Court " taking executive action in an
emergency. " The Foreman of the Eastern Jury reporting that the flap of
Duffield Sluice being blown off, and the Level in danger of drowning, he went
down upon the information of the sluice-keeper at 12 o'clock at night and
secured the same for that time ; but being still in great danger, ordered that
the Foreman direct the further securing of the same and employ proper workmen ; the Expenditor to disburse the money and the Clerk to charge upon
Duffield Sluice account " (*ibid*. 2nd February 1704).
[3] *Ibid*. 11th October 1715.   [4] *Ibid*. 22nd June 1758.
[5] *Ibid*. 7th January and 3rd February 1740.
[6] *Ibid*. 27th May and 18th June 1747.
[7] *Ibid*. 19th January 1749 and 19th July 1750.

H

who are not Commissioners, but who commit nuisances annoying
tenants of Commissioners, are so severely and partially dealt with
that they get redress from the Court of King's Bench;[1] whilst
we see other Commissioners obtaining from complacent colleagues
special views of this or that bank or sewer, the repair of which
they get cast upon the general rate of the level.[2] Whenever one
of the little paid offices falls vacant, there is an unseemly scramble
to appoint a successor before the other Commissioners, who do
not happen to be present, can even become aware of the opportunity of serving their own friends.[3] It would, indeed, be
hardly an exaggeration to say that, between 1727 and 1771,
the minutes themselves reveal that appointments, contracts,
exemptions and privileges are habitually influenced by the
presence at the meeting of some interested party. But, down
to 1771 at any rate, all these mean dealings amounted to very
small sums, and were of little concern to the public at large.
From the standpoint of the common good the most serious
indictment against the Commissioners during this period is the
short-sighted parsimony in the expenditure of rates, and dislike
for regulation, which was permitting the ditches to become foul
by unrestricted houses of office ; clusters of squalid cottages to
be run up destitute of any drains whatsoever ; and whole areas to
be infested by unregulated tan-yards and slaughter-houses, and the
keeping of hundreds of swine ; whilst streets and streets of miserable houses were being built actually below the level of the river.
    By 1771, however, the pressure of new buildings and the

    [1] MS. Minutes, Sewer Commissioners, Surrey and Kent, 9th June and
11th August 1763.
    [2] Ibid. 25th September 1707. In this the Surrey and Kent Commissioners
surreptitiously anticipated, by more than a century, a general movement. In
the Isle of Dogs the whole of the repairs, works and maintenance " requisite
for the protection of the level " were, by common agreement, in 1828, thrown
upon the general rate, and " the repair of works by reason of tenure " was
abolished (ibid. Poplar, 22nd March 1828). During the nineteenth century
all such sewers rates were, throughout the Metropolis, increasingly thrown
on the tenant, by the landlord's conditions of occupancy. And, in 1899,
without any provision for adjustment of rent or other compensation, Parliament, incidentally, and without notice or discussion, transferred the burden
from the landlord to the occupier, even where, by the agreement of tenancy,
the landlord had hitherto paid the rate (London Government Act, 1899, 62 &
63 Vic. c. 14, sec. 10)—a curiously arbitrary interference with existing contracts which may one day be cited as a precedent !
    [3] MS. Minutes, Sewer Commissioners, Surrey and Kent, 4th September 1771,
20th March 1778. For late cases of the same scrambling, see ibid. 20th December
1804 and 27th October 1808.

terrible character of the nuisances that were being produced, forced the Commissioners into greater activity over a small part of their immense district. An Act of Parliament obtained for the Borough of Southwark, which established a body of Street Commissioners, incidentally gave power to the Surrey and Kent Commissioners of Sewers to make new sewers, and to levy a uniform rate, without the intervention of a Jury.[1] From this time forward we see a rapid development of executive structure and function. A standing committee is appointed, four surveyors are engaged and contracts for new works are entered into.[2] A public office is opened for the transaction of the rapidly growing work, which was increased, not only by the increasing demands of builders for permission to connect with the sewers, but also by the undertaking, in 1793, by the Commissioners themselves of the cleansing and scouring of their own sewers.[3] The peculiar feature is the growth in importance, in all this development, of the office of Expenditor-General. The Commissioner who fills this unpaid post gradually becomes the chief executive officer of the Court. He not only received and expended all the income, now amounting to several thousands of pounds, and advanced money at four per cent when the revenue was behindhand ; but he ordered works, supervised their execution by direct employment of labour, and was apparently regarded as the person responsible for the proper maintenance of all banks and sluices.[4] By the time we come to the

[1] 11 George III. c. 17 (1771). The Commissioners of Sewers had to content themselves until 1809 with this power, though they sought in 1787 to get a Local Act of their own, which the opposition of the Vestries prevented (MS. Minutes, Sewer Commissioners, Surrey and Kent, 23rd May 1787 ; MS. Vestry Minutes, Deptford, Kent, 1788).

[2] MS. Minutes, Sewer Commissioners, Surrey and Kent, 13th June 1771. It did not seem objectionable to the Court that its surveyors should, for repair work, have a standing general authority to employ such local tradesmen as they thought fit (*ibid.* 30th May 1823).

[3] *Ibid.* 7th March 1793.

[4] In 1771, possibly in consequence of some legal decision, the Juries were directed to omit from their assessments all " high ground on an ascent," as this could not derive any benefit, or be protected from any injury, from the sewers (*ibid.* 13th June 1771). In practice the Court, in the eighteenth and nineteenth centuries, restricted its area of jurisdiction for all purposes to the low-lying marsh lands at about the Thames level (Report of House of Commons Committee on the Sewers of the Metropolis, 1834, p. 90). In the sixteenth century there was no such limitation of the Court's jurisdiction, at any rate as regards its regulative and judicial functions. In 1573, for instance, the inhabitants of Streatham were amerced for not scouring a sewer, and even the inhabitants of Croydon for not repairing a local bridge (MS. Minutes, Sewer Commissioners, Surrey and Kent, 11th December 1573).

nineteenth century, the work was increasing by leaps and bounds. The whole low-lying area between the river bank and the rising ground of Brixton was being rapidly covered with houses.   In the years 1809, 1810 and 1813, the flooding of the low-lying houses was felt to be so intolerable that a conference representing no fewer than sixteen of the Parish Vestries pressed the Commissioners to undertake the systematic construction of main sewers, at the expense of a common rate.   The Commissioners thereupon obtained power to borrow up to £100,000, execute the works and levy a shilling rate.[1]   With the advent of these new powers the last remnant of a judicial character departs from the Commissioners.   All pretence at holding an open Court of Record is abandoned.   The Juries cease to be summoned, their presentments being replaced by reports of the different surveyors appointed by the Commissioners, which retain the old name.[2] There is appointed, perhaps in imitation of the Holborn and Finsbury Commission, a Standing Committee for General Purposes, on whom complete executive power is cast.[3]   But all the real power and authority is now concentrated in the Expenditor-General, who actually combines with this post those of Chairman of the Court, Chairman of the General Purposes Committee and Chairman of all other Committees.[4]   He orders the works.   It is expressly provided that he may sue and be sued on behalf of the Court,[5] and we find him presented for defects in the sewers.   It becomes plain that corruption on a large scale sets in.   Particular landowners and particular builders on the Commission get made what drains they need.   The work is done by contract without publicity, without tendering and without any real check on prices or on quality.   No sort of regulation is enforced as to the provision of drainage for houses, new or old.   Moreover, when

---

[1] 49 George III. c. 183 (1809); 50 George III. c. 144 (1810); and 53 George III. c. 79 (1813); as to which see House of Lords *Journals*, 12th June 1809; House of Commons *Journals*, 9th December 1812 and 21st May 1813; and MS. Minutes, Sewer Commissioners, Surrey and Kent, 13th July, 3rd and 22nd August, 21st September and 20th December 1809, 22nd February, 26th April, 21st June and 5th July 1810.   These Acts applied only to the Eastern part of the Commissioners' district, from Deptford to Clapham inclusive.

[2] After 1811, the Commissioners ceased to give the formal instructions to the Under-Sheriff to return jurors.   Juries were, however, summoned in exceptional cases in 1824 and 1830 (MS. Minutes, Sewer Commissioners, Surrey and Kent, 16th November 1824, 8th November 1830).

[3] *Ibid.* 6th May 1813.

[4] *Ibid.* 25th August 1820.   [5] 49 George III. c. 183, sec. 59.

any particular site was ready to be built upon, the landowner
or speculative builder would offer to construct the necessary
sewers at his own expense, provided that the Commissioners would
make him a grant ; and the Commissioners, at a hole and corner
meeting, without notice, without previous report, without expert
examination, without system or rule, would make him a grant
of public money to improve his own building estate, of whatever
amount might please the all-powerful Chairman or the particular
knot of Commissioners who happened to be present.[1] Exactly
the same course was followed in voting compensation to persons
who alleged that they had suffered by the Commissioners' action
—compensation to persons who had fallen into sewer excavations,
or for damage caused by the falling in of sewers ; compensation
to tradesmen because the road was blocked by sewer works; compensation for injury caused by floods.[2] The funds necessary for
this profligate expenditure were borrowed by the Commissioners
from their officers, from their friends, and from themselves individually, at such rates of interest or upon such annuity payments
as they were pleased to allow to each other.[3] Under these circumstances it is not surprising to find that, by 1825, the Surrey and
Kent Commissioners—in this respect unique among Courts of
Sewers—had piled up a debt of £33,691, by 1833 one of £67,722,
and by 1834 one of no less than £81,722 ;[4] and that they were
levying at the latter date a revenue of more than £12,000 a year ;
whilst still leaving the crowded slums of Southwark, the squalid
cottages of Walworth Common, the mean streets of Lambeth
and the vile purlieus of Vauxhall without any effective system
of underground drainage whatsoever. "In all that thickly
peopled area," it was said in 1832, "the channels and ditches

[1] Report of House of Commons Committee on the Sewers of the
Metropolis, 1834, p. 96. "I found," reports a zealous member of Parliament in 1834, "that this Court was composed of a number of gentlemen
sitting at a long table and gossiping . . . instead of attending to business.
. . . The only person who really took the matter into consideration was the
Surveyor " (*ibid.*).
[2] MS. Minutes, Sewer Commissioners, Surrey and Kent, 24th July 1806.
[3] *Ibid.* 5th August 1813, 23rd December 1814, 13th October 1815, etc.
The rule was to borrow two-thirds of the cost of new works, charging the
balance to the current rate (Report of House of Commons Committee on the
Sewers of the Metropolis, 1834, p. 93).
[4] MS. Minutes, Sewer Commissioners, Surrey and Kent, end of volume for
1818–1825 ; 25th January 1833 ; Report of House of Commons Committee
on the Sewers of the Metropolis, 1834, pp. 87, 92.

for carrying off the water remain in their natural state, overflowing with filth and impurity." [1]

The Court of Sewers in 1835

At this point we have to break off the story of the Commissioners of Sewers, though in their case the years 1832–1835 do not constitute any particular era, of reform or otherwise. The reader of the preceding pages—remembering perhaps fierce outbreaks of revolt and agitations for reform that we have described with regard to the Close Vestries and the Municipal Corporations—will ask why no corresponding movement arose against the Commissioners of Sewers.

It must, in the first place, be remembered that the vast majority of the Courts of Sewers—practically all those outside the Metropolitan area—excited, in 1835, no animadversion ; their very existence being, indeed, then as now, unknown to any one not immediately concerned with the drainage of the particular lands. To no one in 1835 did they seem a class, or to belong to Local Government at all. The works and the levies of each of them had become matters of routine, consented to by every one aware of them. The service was, in fact, in each case, still in the hands of those who paid for it, who could thus spend as much or as little on it as seemed to suit their interests. But in the Metropolitan area, where the eight Courts of Sewers (exclusive of the City of London) were, by 1835, expending nearly £100,000 a year,[2] and where, as we have seen, glaring abuses were rife, we are ourselves somewhat surprised that there should, in these years, have been so little protest against the proceedings of such " arbitrary, irresponsible and unconstitutional " bodies, violating, as was said, " the fundamental principles of our law that a man shall not be taxed without the consent of himself or his representatives." [3] There were, indeed, many obvious resemblances between the Commissioners of Sewers and the Justices of the Peace, about whom exactly the same constitutional objections could be made, and who were, in these very

---

[1] *The Extraordinary Black Book*, 1832 edition, p. 670.

[2] See the figures given for five of these Courts, in *Local Government in the Metropolis*, 1835, p. 19.

[3] Evidence of a witness, in Report of House of Commons Committee on the Sewers of the Metropolis, 1834, pp. 83-84.

years, being stripped of some of their powers.[1] Both, in form appointed by the Crown, had become, in effect, close bodies, homogeneous in class, renewing themselves by co-option. Under the pressure of new duties, both had practically given up administration by judicial process, thereby losing the popular element implied by the use of the Jury and the transaction of business "in Open Court." In both cases the machinery of a Court of Justice had been replaced by standing administrative committees, meeting behind closed doors, unchecked by public reports or open discussions, and acting through salaried officials. And to complete the resemblance, both constitutions had broken down in the Metropolitan area, which had, as regards both the Commission of the Peace and the Commission of Sewers, become the happy hunting-ground of similar, if not identical, gangs of self-seeking building speculators, architects, surveyors and others who could make a profit out of them, whilst the agents of the great estates, keen only on getting for their owners the maximum benefit from the sewers and on contributing as little as possible to their cost, had every motive for not making themselves objectionable to the other Commissioners by resenting their minor partialities and corrupt bargains.[2]

To whatever cause we may attribute it, there was, in 1835, as yet no general feeling and no public agitation for the reform of the Commissioners of Sewers. Various Bills had been from time to time introduced for enlarging their powers ; and a Committee of the House of Commons was appointed in 1823, which heard the evidence only of representatives of the Commissioners them-

---

[1] As to the feeling against the Justices of the Peace, and " why the Justices survived," see *The Parish and the County*, 1907, Book ii. chap. vi. pp. 556-607.

[2] Even a superficial comparison of the lists reveals many persons serving on several of the Metropolitan Commissions. Local propinquity may explain the fact that a great many of the Commissioners for Poplar and St. Katharine's were also Commissioners for the Tower Hamlets. But we fear that the presence of the Mainwarings and the Mercerons on the Commissions for Westminster, Holborn and Finsbury and Tower Hamlets, if not also on others, was more equivocal ; whilst it is, to say the least of it, suspicious to find so many persons interested in building estates, like the Rhodes family, and so many architects and estate agents, like the Donaldsons and Cockerells, on several Commissions. We have already referred to the simultaneous Chairmanship of Sir Daniel Williams in both the Tower Hamlets and the Holborn and Finsbury Commissions. The clerks and surveyors of one body were often themselves members of others. Other persons on several Commissions whose interests we do not know were George Byng, M.P., and Luke Thomas Flood. Lists of the above-named Commissions (but not of that of Surrey and Kent) are printed in the reports of the House of Commons Committees of 1823 and 1834.

selves, and had not time to make any recommendations.[1] In 1833 a general Bill promoted by the friends of the Commissioners actually became law, which did not in any way reform the administration of the peccant Courts of Sewers in the Metropolis, and by which many of the archaic formalities of these Courts throughout the country were dispensed with, whilst their powers of direct administration, and of assessment and enforcement of rates, were greatly increased. No opposition seems to have been made to conferring these new powers on the Surrey and Kent Commissioners, any more than on those for Greenwich, though, significantly enough, we do find the various Middlesex Commissioners expressly excluded from its scope.[2] In the following year a strong House of Commons Committee for the first time dragged to light the ineptitudes and malpractices of the Westminster Commissioners, and with them those of the Surrey and Kent, and other Metropolitan Courts of Sewers. Even then the Committee could not see its way even to suggest disturbing the existing Courts as the sewer authorities, though it did propose that the Commissioners should for the future cease to be appointed, in form, by the Crown ; which the Committee saw to mean, in practice, a close body co-opting its successors. The only alternative that could be found was, as vacancies occurred, to let the Vestries of the several parishes in rotation appoint members in proportion to their respective populations and rentals.[3] The reputation of the Metropolitan Vestries, open or close, was, however, at that moment so bad that this proposal evoked no enthusiasm. The importance to the health of a city of a complete system of underground drainage was, in spite of the cholera of 1831–1832, still undiscovered. The Members of Parliament, like the reformers outside, were, moreover, staggered by the magnitude of the engineering problem presented by the drainage of so huge an area as London, and bewildered by the technicalities and conflicting opinions of the budding experts on the sizes and shapes of drains, the respective values of gulley-holes, grates and traps,

[1] Report of House of Commons Committee on the Sewers of the Metropolis, No. 542 of 1823.
[2] 3 & 4 William IV. c. 22 (1833). There were, however, separate Local Acts for the Westminster Commission in 1834 (4 & 5 William IV. c. 96) and 1847 (10 & 11 Vic. c. 70).
[3] Report of House of Commons Committee on the Sewers of the Metropolis, No. 584 of 1834.

and the mysteries of hydraulics, whilst they were terrified at the newly discovered insinuating ways and explosive vagaries of sewer gas. It must be remembered, in extenuation of this helplessness—and indeed, in partial excuse for the inefficiency of the Sewer Commissioners—that what was being required of them was, not the work of land drainage for which they had been established, but an entirely new service demanding for its efficient performance both a science and a technique not then in existence. In addition to keeping out the high tides and facilitating by open ditches the flow of the storm water from the hills, the Commissioners of Sewers, in the course of a century and a half, had found themselves tacitly required to transport by underground channels, not only the rapid flow of surface water from many miles of paved streets, but, what was still more unprecedented, the whole excreta of a densely populated city.[1] In other parts of England other Local Authorities were beginning to grapple with the same problem, if on a smaller scale. Close Corporations like that of Liverpool, Street Commissioners elected by rate-payers as at Leeds and Manchester, special bodies recruited by co-option as at Plymouth were at work, in no case making much headway in their course. In the Metropolitan area the problem was not only intensified by its magnitude, but was seemingly all the more insoluble because of the inability of any particular parish or district to manage its drainage by itself. No authority could be expected to make a good job of London main drainage so long as it was divided among half-a-dozen separate bodies, differing among themselves about the sizes, shapes and levels of the sewers and maintaining altogether different standards of efficiency. It is therefore not so surprising as it at first sight appears that even to the reformers of the Close Vestries and Municipal Corporations it was impossible to get up any enthusiasm over

---

[1] The connection of " houses of office " with the sewers continued in London to be nominally forbidden and spasmodically prevented, down to about 1811. The assumption long continued that none but liquid matter should pass from the cesspools into the sewers. The change of policy came with the general adoption, between 1800 and 1840, of water-closets, in all but the poorer houses of the Metropolis. It was only in these years that the word " sewer " obtained its present malodorous meaning. "A Sewer," had said the old authorities, " is a fresh Water Trench or little River, encompass'd with Banks on both sides " (*The Laws of Sewers or the Office and Authority of Commissioners of Sewers*, 1726, pp. 25, 26 ; also Tomlins' *Law Dictionary*, 1820, and *Municipal Origins*, by F. H. Spencer, 1911, pp. 242-263. For the history, see *Water Closets, a Historical, Mechanical and Sanitary Treatise*, by Glenn Brown, 1884).

a proposal to change the constitution of particular Courts of
Sewers. Ten years later public feeling became almost suddenly
intense, and we see the Metropolitan Courts of Sewers, sunk
still deeper into inefficiency — we fear, with partiality and
corruption added—summarily swept away in 1848 by a brand-
new Commission of Sewers for the whole Metropolis ; we watch
this gentlemanly but futile body of Crown nominees, constantly
changing in constitution and membership, driven hither and
thither by the rival projects for dealing with the Metropolitan
sewage,[1] and in 1855 abruptly superseded by the indirectly elected
Metropolitan Board of Works ; itself destined, in another generation, to be condemned for corruption, and replaced, in 1889, by
the directly elected London County Council. It is one more
example of the complicated evolution of English Local Government that we should have to recognise, as the ancestors of the
largest, the most democratic in form and the most powerful of the
world's great city governments, both the little knot of Court
officials who after the Restoration met in Westminster Hall,
and the groups of peasant farmers who, in the grey morning mists,
had, time out of mind, walked the marshes of Wandsworth and
Greenwich.

[1] " Within nine years after its formation, the Metropolitan Commission of
Sewers was six times superseded, and six new and differently constituted Commissions were successively appointed " (" On the Main Drainage of London,"
by (Sir) J. W. Bazalgette, in *Proceedings of the Institute of Civil Engineers*,
vol. xxiv., 1865, p. 284. See *Sanitary Evolution of London*, by H. Jephson,
1907 ; *Municipal Origins*, by F. H. Spencer, 1911).

We may add here a belated reference to an incident described on p. 38.
A few days before William Pitt hurried to Romney Marsh in 1804 to arrange
for its instant flooding on the French invasion, Sir John Moore, then at Sand-
gate, close by, was writing in the following terms to Creevey : " We understand that Government have positive information that we are to be invaded,
and I am told that Pitt believes it. The experience of the last twelve months
has taught me to place little confidence in the information or belief of Ministers,
and as the undertaking seems to me so arduous, and offering so little prospect
of success, I cannot persuade myself that Bonaparte will be mad enough to
attempt it. He will continue to threaten, by which means alone he can do
us harm. The invasion would, I am confident, end in our glory and in his
disgrace " (General Sir John Moore, August 27, 1804, in *The Creevey Papers*,
1904, vol. i. p. 29).

CHAPTER II

THE seventeenth century saw the inauguration of a new series of Local Authorities, established in particular places by separate Acts of Parliament for a specific purpose, namely, the local administration of the Poor Law. These Local Authorities, which came to number in all about 125, bore slightly differing titles (such as Guardians, Trustees, Governors, Directors or Corporation of the Poor); but we may include them all under the common designation of Incorporated Guardians of the Poor. Local governing bodies of this kind, deliberately formed for permanence, exercising new powers under their own Local Acts, having their own officers and their own revenues, and forming thus distinct corporations, require a chapter to themselves—the more so as they exhibit, both in their legal constitutions and in their working procedure, peculiar characteristics of their own, and mark an important stage in the development of English Local Government. But their study presents difficulties. The Courts of Sewers, which we have already described, like the Turnpike Trusts with which we shall subsequently deal, were bodies unconnected with the then existing Local Government structure ; assumed to be temporary in character ; thrust by Parliament in between the Parish and the County, and capable therefore of being easily studied as separate entities. On the other hand we find the new bodies of Incorporated Guardians of the Poor invariably structurally connected with existing Local Government authorities. They were, in most cases, practically autonomous federations of parish authorities, urban or rural ; in a few instances they were little more than statutory committees of the Municipal Corporation ; in others again, mere outgrowths of the Close or Open Vestry of a single parish. Further, unlike the Court of Sewers and the Turnpike Trust, the Incorporated Guardians were not merely endowed with newly devised powers ; they always had transferred to them some of the powers and obligations that had previously belonged to the Parish ; and, occasionally, some of those of the County. Their story, moreover, much more than that of the Court of Sewers, or that of the Turnpike Trust, is inextricably interwoven with the history of the function to which they were devoted.[1] It is impossible to give any clear vision of the origin of the Incorporated Guardians of the Poor, of their legal constitutions and actual working, or of the success and failure of their organisation, without trenching upon an important episode in the history of the Relief of Destitution, namely, the attempt to establish self-supporting institutions for the employment of the able-bodied poor, the industrial education of children and the correction of idle and disorderly persons. We hope, in a

[1] " We would further remark that the nature and extent of a Local Act for the relief of the poor appear to be often misunderstood. It is not infrequently assumed that the existence of a Local Act places a parish under a separate system of law with respect to the relief of the poor. This assumption, however, is thoroughly erroneous, and is repugnant to the entire spirit and effect of the local legislation of this country. Like other Local Acts, a Local Act for the relief of the poor presupposes the general law on the subject, and only modifies or adds to it in certain specified particulars. The legal presumption is that the general law prevails everywhere ; and this presumption can only be repelled by the existence of a provision in a Special Act clearly derogating from the general law with respect to the district. Thus the general law of rating, settlement, removal and the like prevails over the whole country ; but Local Acts have established varieties in the constitution of the body which administers relief, the mode of its appointment, the authorities by which the rate is collected, and other such matters. A Local Act, therefore, is not (as the expressions used on the subject sometimes seem to imply) an entire poor-law code for a certain district ; but it is merely a fragment of legislation, modifying and supplying the general law in a few specified heads, for the most part relating to the mode of its administration. Thus the local poor-law legislation for Leeds consists only of a clause in an Act for lighting and cleansing, which directs that, in the Borough of Leeds, the number of Overseers of the Poor appointed under the 43 Elizabeth shall not be limited to four, as under that statute. In like manner the Local Act for Salisbury only vests the management of the united parishes in a body of Churchwardens and Overseers appointed for the several parishes according to the 43 Elizabeth. A scale might be formed, commencing with such simple and meagre provisions as these, and rising to the more complex and elaborate legislation of Marylebone, in which latter parish there are several Local Acts in force, regulating the poor-law administration. Even, however, where the local legislation is most voluminous it is a mere fragment as compared with the mass of the general poor-law statutes which affect the parish " (Ninth Annual Report of Poor Law Commissioners, 1843, p. 22).

future volume on English Local Government in relation to Poverty and Vagrancy, to describe these interesting experiments as part of the history of the Poor Law. In the present chapter we can do no more than allude to them in so far as they bear on the origin, the varieties of constitution, and the success and failure of the bodies of Incorporated Guardians themselves.

The 125 Incorporated Guardians of the Poor were established not by any general statute, but by separate Acts of Parliament—numbering, with amending statutes, over two hundred—which, because they were classed as Local Acts, have been almost ignored by historians.[1] These statutes extend over nearly two centuries, beginning with the Commonwealth Ordinance of 1647, for establishing the " Corporation of the Poor of the City of London," and ending with Acts of 1831–1833 reorganising the Unions of city parishes in Birmingham, Leicester, Norwich and Gloucester.

The new Local Authorities thus established tried, as we shall see, a whole series of experiments in dealing with the destitute, from which much was gradually learnt. Their experience in workhouse management was the means by which the idea of " setting the poor to work," as a possible way of providing their own maintenance, was finally disposed of. Moreover, their constitutional structure was found, as one of the Poor Law reformers of 1834 remarked, to embody " principles of organisation which, with some modifications, may be made both beneficially and generally applicable."[2] It was from these statutory Poor Law Authorities that was derived the machinery of administration by committees, for unions of parishes, through salaried officials, with the workhouse in the background, out of which was constructed the Poor Law reform of 1834. Indeed, it is scarcely too much to say that their peculiar " principle of combining an elective controlling power with a paid executive "[3]

---

[1] They are, for instance, not dealt with in the voluminous *History of the English Poor Law*, by Sir George Nicholls. Practically the only study of these Local Acts relating to the Poor Law is that of Mr. F. H. Spencer in his *Municipal Origins*, 1911 (chap. vii. pp. 281-308) ; but the Second, Ninth and Tenth Annual Reports of the Poor Law Commissioners, 1836, 1843 and 1844, incidentally afford much information.

[2] Captain Chapman's report on Statutory Poor Law Authorities in Appendix A of First Report of the Poor Law Inquiry Commissioners, 1834, pp. 522-523.

[3] *Ibid.*

has become the dominant feature of the constitutional structure of English as distinguished from American and from Continental forms of Local Government.

We shall find that these Incorporated Guardians of the Poor, varied as they were in constitutional structure and in the organisation of their activities, fall into four classes, which we designate respectively the Union of Urban Parishes, the Union of Rural Parishes, the Vestry Executive and the Reorganised Vestry.

The Union of Urban Parishes

We take, as the type-specimen of the Unions of Urban Parishes, not the first to be established, with regard to the actual working of which little is known, and which does not appear to have been influential as an example ; [1] but the most

---

[1] The first statutory authority of this kind was the Corporation of the Poor of the City of London, established by Parliament in 1647, under a president and governors, for " the constant relief and employment of the poor and the punishment of vagrants and other disorderly persons in the City of London." This body set up a workhouse in which orphan children were maintained, gave out materials to be worked on at home, and even sent some able-bodied men to sea in fishing smacks captured from the Dutch and granted to the Corporation for this purpose (*The Early History of English Poor Relief*, by E. M. Leonard, 1900, pp. 272-273 ; and the authorities there quoted). This premier Poor Law authority, of which the records could probably be found among the City archives, seems to deserve a monograph. Some description of its constitution and work is given in old editions of Shaw's *Parish Law*. The Ordinance of 1647 was confirmed in 1662 by the Act, 13 & 14 Charles II. c. 12 (made perpetual by 12 Anne, St. 1, c. 18, in 1714), which defined the constitution of the Corporation to be the Lord Mayor and Aldermen and fifty-two other citizens chosen by the Common Council ; and which enabled like Corporations of the Poor to be established in the City of Westminster, on the nomination of the Lord Chancellor, and for other parishes within the Bills of Mortality on the nomination of the County Justices (*A Practical Treatise on the Laws, Customs, Usages and Regulations of the City and Port of London*, by Alexander Pulling, first edition, 1842, third edition, 1854, pp. 242-243). We are not aware that any such Corporations were formed, either in Westminster or elsewhere, under this statute. It could even be said officially in 1843 that " no Corporation was formed under this Act of Parliament until the year 1698, and no steps were taken for hiring a workhouse in the City of London until the following year " (Ninth Annual Report of Poor Law Commissioners, 1843, p. 94). This, however, was plainly incorrect, as " reports of the Governors of the Corporation were published in 1655 " (*History of English Philanthropy*, by B. Kirkman Gray, 1905, pp. 72-74). The Corporation of the Poor of the City of London continued in existence, and its workhouses to be used, throughout the eighteenth century ; but this did not prevent various City parishes from obtaining their own Local Acts and, in some cases, establishing their own workhouses. Thus, St. Botolph, Aldgate, did so in 1765, by 6 George III. c. 64 ; St. Botolph, Bishopsgate, in 1795, by 35 George III. c. 61 ; and St. Bride's, Fleet Street,

noteworthy and most widely imitated of them all, the Corporation of the Poor of the City of Bristol, established by the Act, 7 and 8 William III. c. 32, in what was then the second city of the kingdom. It had its origin, we may say, in a combination of reason and philanthropy curiously analogous to nineteenth-century movements. A century of experience of the Elizabethan Poor Law had revealed serious evils in its practical administration, especially in the crowded cities. The Overseers had found it difficult and troublesome to " set the poor to work." They had been directed by the Act of 1601 to provide a sufficient stork of flax, hemp, wool, thread, iron and other necessary stuff for the poor to work on, the assumption being, apparently, that these materials should be given out to destitute persons to be worked up into valuable commodities in their own homes. At any rate the Overseers were given no powers of acquiring land, or of borrowing money to build or purchase premises ; and they had no express authority to establish and maintain a workhouse, even if the premises were provided. How far the directions of the Elizabethan statute with regard to the provision of material were ever acted upon we do not know. There is evidence of considerable but not ubiquitous activity for the first three decades of the seventeenth century, under the influence of the Privy Council, the Assize Judges and the Justices of the Peace.[1] But this organised supervision from the centre came to an end. It is plain that by the middle of the seventeenth century, after the dislocations of the Civil War, the Overseers had fallen into

---

in 1799, by 39 George III. c. 4, and 7 George IV. session 1, c. 14.   What happened to the administration of the Corporation of the Poor, and what were its relations to the City parishes, we have not ascertained.   We gather that it was dissolved, and its workhouse was sold, by authority of the Acts 5 George IV. c. 83, and 10 George IV. c. 43, in the decade preceding the passing of the Poor Law Amendment Act, 1834.   On the passing of that Act it was remarked that none of the ninety-six parishes within the City walls possessed a workhouse either singly or in combination.   These parishes were formed into the City of London Union in 1837, whilst the twelve others were divided between two other new Unions, the East and West London respectively, in 1838 (Third and Fourth Annual Reports of Poor Law Commissioners ;   Pulling's *Practical Treatise*, etc., 1842, pp. 248-249).

[1] See the *Calendars of State Papers, Domestic State Papers*, and *Privy Council Registers* for the first half of the seventeenth century ; the contemporary municipal records (such as those of the City of London, Shrewsbury, Plymouth, Norwich, St. Albans, Windsor) ; *Quarter Sessions from Elizabeth to Anne*, by A. H. Hamilton, 1889 ; *The Country Justice*, by Michael Dalton, 1655 ; *The Early History of English Poor Relief*, by E. M. Leonard, 1900.

the habit of distributing what we should now term out-relief to all whom they considered destitute.[1] The resulting rise in the rates,[2] if not the other evils that ensued, was sufficient to attract the attention both of philanthropists and of statesmen. No less a person than John Locke, then newly appointed one of the Commissioners of the Board of Trade, drew up in 1697 an elaborate report in which he attributed "the multiplying of the poor and the increase of the tax for their maintenance" to the relaxation "of discipline and corruption of manners."[3] It seemed, he said, nowadays to be taken for granted by Overseers that "every one must have meat, drink, clothing and firing," the result being that "so much goes out of the stock of the kingdom whether they (the recipients) work or no." The dominant idea of the reformers of the time was "the setting of the poor to work"; and this was inculcated by William III. in several successive speeches from the throne.[4] These speeches, like others nearer to our own time, failed to get embodied in any general legislation. Meanwhile a merchant of Bristol, John Cary, seriously concerned at the growing demoralisation of the poor, had written a powerful pamphlet, and called meetings of the inhabitants; finally inducing the Mayor and Aldermen of the city and other principal inhabitants to apply to Parliament for a Local Act. The reasons for the application, as is stated in the preamble, were that "it is found by experience that the

---

[1] "It is rare to see any provision of a stock in any parish for the relief of the poor" (*A Discourse touching provision for the Poor*, by Sir Matthew Hale; published in 1683 after his death, but written probably before 1660); see *History of the Poor Law*, by R. Burn, 1764; *History of the English Poor Law*, by Sir George Nicholls, 1854, vol. i. pp. 287-290.

[2] "Thus in a pamphlet entitled *Bread for the Poor*, printed at Exeter in 1698, quoted by Mr. Ruggles and attributed to Mr. Dunning, it is stated that the charge of maintaining the poor in some parishes in Devonshire had, within sixty years, advanced from forty shillings to forty pounds a year; in others twice that sum, and most wheres double within twenty years, and like to double again in a short time" (*History of the English Poor Law*, by Sir George Nicholls, 1854, vol. i. p. 329).

[3] *Report of the Board of Trade to the Lords Justices in the year 1697 respecting the Relief and Employment of the Poor, drawn up by Mr. John Locke, one of the original Commissioners of that Board*, 1787, p. 110; see *State of the Poor*, by Sir F. M. Eden, 1797, vol. i. pp. 244-245; *Pauperism and Poor Laws*, by Robert Pashley, 1852, pp. 235-236; *History of the English Poor Law*, by Sir George Nicholls, 1854, vol. i. p. 352.

[4] *History and Proceedings of the House of Commons, 1660-1743*, by Richard Chandler, 1742-1744; *State of the Poor*, by Sir F. M. Eden, 1797, vol. i. p. 247; *History of the English Poor Law*, by Sir George Nicholls, 1854, vol. i. p. 351.

poor in the City of Bristol do daily multiply, and idleness and debauchery amongst the meaner sort doth greatly increase, for want of workhouses to set them to work, and a sufficient authority to compel them thereto, as well to the charge of the inhabitants and grief of the charitable and honest citizens of the said city, as the great distress of the poor themselves for which sufficient redress hath not yet been provided." An attempt in 1681 to cope with the situation by getting a contractor to employ the poor at spinning yarn at piecework wages had brought no lasting improvement.[1] Cary's proposals, which were destined to be copied up and down the kingdom for a whole century, were summarised as follows :

1. That a spacious workhouse be erected at a general charge, large enough for the poor to be employed therein ; and also for room for such as, being unable to work, are to be relieved by charity.

2. That the rules of the house may force all persons to work that are able, and encourage manufacturers to furnish them with materials to work upon.

3. That persons not able to maintain their children may put them into this workhouse or hospital at what ages they will, so that these children may be bred up to labour, principles of virtue implanted in them at an early age, and laziness be discouraged.

4. That the ancient shall be provided for according to their wants.

5. That the rates of the city being united into one common fund, the magistrates will be freed from the daily trouble which they have about settlement of the poor, the parish officers will be eased, the poor's stock will not be spent in law, but they will be provided for without being sent from parish to parish, and their children will be settled in a way serviceable to the public good, and not be bred up in all manner of vice as they now are.

6. That the governor be empowered to force all poor people to work who do not betake themselves to some lawful employment elsewhere, but spend their time lazily and idly.

7. That the governor have power to settle out the young people at such ages as may be thought fit, the boys to navigation

[1] *Some Proposals for the Employment of the Poor*, by Thomas Firmin, 1681 ; *The State of the Poor*, by Sir F. M. Eden, 1697, vol. ii. p. 184.

I

and the maids in service ; and to bind them apprentices for a certain number of years ; that this will prevent children from being starved by the poverty of their parents and the neglect of parish officers, which is now a great loss to the nation, inasmuch as every person would by his labour add to the wealth of the public.

Parliament passed the Bill on the 18th January 1696, and allowed the City of Bristol to try its experiment. The Act took the whole management and relief of the poor out of the hands of the Overseers of the nineteen crowded city parishes, and established a new " Corporation of the Poor " for the whole city, consisting of the Mayor and Aldermen of the city and the Churchwardens of the parishes, together with four persons elected by a public meeting of the inhabitants of each ward.[1] The Corporation of the Poor of the City of Bristol was—if we leave aside the immemorial traditional usages of the Corporations of London, Norwich, and a few other ancient municipal bodies [2]—

[1] The principal source for the history of this celebrated " Corporation of the Poor of the City of Bristol " must always be its own well-kept and voluminous MS. Minutes, which we have found of great use ; see also the Acts, 7 & 8 William III. c. 32 ; 12 Anne, st. 2, c. 15 ; 4 George I. c. 3 ; 18 George II. c. 30 ; 31 George II. c. 56 ; 3 George IV. c. 24 ; 1 William IV. c. 4 ; An Account of the Proceedings of the Corporation of the Poor of Bristol, by John Cary, 1700 ; The State of the Poor, by Sir F. M. Eden, 1797, vol. ii. pp. 182-203, vol. i. pp. 275-278 ; Transactions of the Corporation of the Poor in the City of Bristol during a period of 126 years, by James Johnson (Bristol, 1826); An Address to the Inhabitants of Bristol on the subject of the Poor Rates, by James Johnson (Bristol, 1820) ; Observations on the Bill about to be introduced into Parliament by the Corporation of the City and the Poor, by Thomas Stocking (Bristol, 1822); Letters, essays, etc., illustrative of the Municipal History of Bristol, and of the trade of its port, written and collected by a burgess (Bristol, 1836) ; Appendix A to First Report of Poor Law Inquiry Commissioners, 1834 (Chapman's Report), p. 510 ; Ninth Annual Report of Poor Law Commissioners, 1843, pp. 138-181.

[2] The Manor and the Borough, by S. and B. Webb, 1907. It will be remembered that the Corporation of the Poor of the City of London was to consist of the Lord Mayor and Aldermen ex officio, with 52 other citizens nominated by the Common Council. The elective element was thus indirectly chosen. Of the Bristol body, we may say that its manuscript minutes show it to have been, from the outset, a dignified and well-organised body, presided over by a " governor " who habitually continued in office for a term of years ; acting under well-framed standing orders ; working through a permanent executive of fifteen members, who were divided into four or five standing committees ; and served by a relatively large staff of salaried officials, including latterly even an " investigator " to detect impostors. " The services of the Guardians," writes the able governor in 1820, " are gratuitous. No member of the Corporation of the Poor can even supply the Hospital with goods ; nor does the whole body of Guardians put the City to any, the most trifling expense ; for when upon Committees, etc., any refreshment is wanted, it is sent for to a neighbouring inn and paid by the respective individuals " (Address

the first local governing body directed by Parliamentary statute
to be based mainly upon popular election in all the wards of a
great city.

The Bristol Workhouse quickly became widely known as a
promising experiment ; and within the next fifteen years thirteen
towns—Crediton (1698), Tiverton (1698), Exeter (1698), Hereford
(1698), Colchester (1698), Hull (1698), Shaftesbury (1698), King's
Lynn (1700), Sudbury (1700), Gloucester (1702), Worcester (1704),
Plymouth (1708), and Norwich (1712)—successfully applied to
Parliament for Local Acts which superseded the authority of
the Overseers and incorporated a body of "Guardians of the
Poor," to act for the whole city. The idea underlying all these
Acts was the desirability of organising the labour of the unemployed, with the double object of maintaining them without
disorder and of increasing the national wealth. It was impossible to do this without providing a large and costly workhouse,
for which no powers were given by the general law, and which
could hardly be established separately in each of the small and
densely crowded parishes of an old walled town. Incidentally
the union of these parishes brought the great advantage of avoid-
ing much of the complication of the law as to settlement, and of
equalising the poor rate throughout the city.

The sanguine projects of so organising the labour of the poor
as to produce at least the cost of their maintenance were soon
proved to be delusive. At Bristol, for instance, the plan of
employing the poor at wages in the workhouse was quickly
discovered to involve not less, but greater expense per head than
their maintenance by doles of outdoor relief.[1] But the new workhouses were incidentally found of use in providing an alternative
to the indiscriminate distribution of money by the Overseers.

---

to the Inhabitants of Bristol on the subject of the Poor Rates, by James Johnson,
1820, p. 7). St. Peter's Hospital, as the Bristol Workhouse was styled, was
incidentally referred to in 1835 by an Assistant Poor Law Commissioner as
" one of the most cleanly and well regulated establishments in England "
(Mr. Mott's Report in First Annual Report of the Poor Law Commissioners,
1835, p. 177). There was even a "whole-time" medical officer (Ninth Annual
Report of Poor Law Commissioners, 1843, p. 161).

[1] When it was abandoned, the plan of farming out the poor to a contractor
was reverted to. "A malt and corn dealer . . . was to bear all the costs and
take all the profits of the sack-making business carried on by the city poor.
He was to give each worker a small gratuity as he thought fit. . . . Thus the
scheme initiated by Cary in the hope of raising wages was used to depress
them " (*History of English Philanthropy*, by B. Kirkman Gray, 1905, p. 212).

These early reformers had, in fact, accidentally stumbled on the discovery of the " workhouse test." It became possible to offer maintenance to the able-bodied applicant in a form that he did not like, with the result that the demand for relief immediately fell off, to the great saving of the ratepayers. And so in 1723, Sir Edward Knatchbull induced the House of Commons to pass a general Act enabling the officers of separate parishes to hire premises and maintain them as workhouses for the poor. Within a decade over a hundred workhouses were set up by parishes under this Act. The demand for Local Acts establishing new bodies of Incorporated Guardians of the Poor was for a time checked. But the general Act of 1723 merely enabled the Churchwardens and Overseers of particular parishes to hire or purchase premises for a workhouse ; and gave no power to parishes to combine for the purpose. Accordingly, we find presently beginning again the demand for Local Acts incorporating a body of Guardians for a union of parishes. Such new statutory authorities were established at Canterbury (1727), Bury St. Edmunds (1748), Chichester (1753), Chester (1762), Salisbury (1770), Oxford (1771),[1] Southampton (1773), and Maidstone (1780).

We make no attempt to describe the results of the experiments in " setting the poor to work " by the Incorporated Guardians of Bristol and the score of towns which followed its example in the first eighty years of the eighteenth century.[2] Some of them quickly abandoned the experiment. Others discontinued it and resumed it at a later date, when the memory of the earlier failure had been lost. It will be more convenient

---

[1] As to the Incorporated Guardians of Oxford, see *Oxford in the Eighteenth Century*, by J. R. Green and G. Roberson (vol. xli. of Oxford Historical Society Publications, 1901, p. 318). Coventry (1801) and Lincoln (1812) were belated imitators, probably influenced by the Shrewsbury House of Industry, if not also by the Suffolk and Norfolk Hundreds about to be described.

[2] Besides those of the Corporation of the Poor of the City of Bristol, we have been able to consult the MS. Minutes of the corresponding bodies at Norwich, Plymouth and Gloucester ; which are, however (unlike Bristol and Shrewsbury), not illuminated by any considerable pamphlet literature, or the records of contemporary controversy. See, however, *Report of the Special Provisional Committee appointed by the Court of Guardians in the City of Norwich, with an account of the savings which have been produced by the late regulations in the diet of the Workhouse*, etc., by Edward Rigby (Norwich, 1788). Later information is supplied by Sir F. M. Eden in his *State of the Poor*, 1797 ; and in the Ninth and Tenth Annual Reports of the Poor Law Commissioners, 1843 and 1844.

to see what happened in the subsequent case of Shrewsbury, which was widely and persistently advertised throughout the kingdom.[1] In 1783, some of the principal inhabitants of what was still the Metropolis of the Welsh Border, tired of the maladministration of the Overseers and Vestries of the six little parishes crowded within the walls and liberties of that ancient city, obtained a Local Act for the incorporation of a body of Guardians of the Poor, with power to borrow £10,000 for the erection of a House of Industry. The Guardians consisted of all owners of freehold or copyhold property within the city worth £30 a year, and all inhabitant occupiers rated at £15 a year. This body itself appointed the Clerk, Treasurer, Governor, Steward, Matron and Chaplain, but also elected twelve Directors of the Poor in whom the whole administration was vested. They were fortunate in finding ready to hand premises admirably suited for their objects, on a magnificent site at a high cliff in a bend of the Severn, adjacent to the city. This building had been erected in 1759–1765 at a cost of £14,000 by the Foundling Hospital of London for the accommodation of children drafted from its principal establishment, but had been disused in 1774 on such provincial homes being discontinued. The Shrewsbury

---

[1] The Shrewsbury House of Industry was greatly " boomed " about 1791–1800 by its enthusiastic promoter, Isaac Wood. We have not seen the MS. Minutes, which possibly still exist : but abundant information is afforded by the Acts 24 George III. c. 15 (1784), and 7 George IV. c. 141 (1826) ; *Directions for the Conduct of the Overseers of the Poor for the Six United Parishes in the Town and Liberties of Shrewsbury*, 1800 ; *Some Account of the Shrewsbury House of Industry*, by Isaac Wood, 1791, which ran through five editions ; *An Introduction to the Fifth Edition of Some Account*, etc., by the same, 1800 ; *Observations on the Accounts of the Shrewsbury House of Industry*, by the same, 1799 ; *Letter to Sir William Pulteney, Bart.*, by the same, 1797 ; *General Observations on the Year's Account of the Shrewsbury House of Industry*, by the same, 1800 ; *An Address to the Parochial Committees at Bath . . . for the establishment of a House of Industry*, by J. (really Isaac) Wood, 1798 ; *An Address to the Poor . . . within the Town of Shrewsbury . . . delivered at the House of Industry*, by Rev. Thomas Stedman, 1786 ; *Appendix to some Account of the Shrewsbury House of Industry, containing a correspondence with the Rev. J. Howlett*, 1791 ; *The State of the Poor*, by Sir F. M. Eden, 1797, vol. ii. pp. 622-643 ; *Annals of Agriculture*, vol. xxxv., 1800, pp. 157-163, 608-621 ; *General View of the Agriculture of Shropshire*, by Joseph Plymley, 1803, p. 131 ; *Some Account of . . . Shrewsbury*, by Hugh Owen, 1808, pp. 333-346 ; *General View of the Agriculture of North Wales*, by Walter Davies, 1813, p. 434 ; *Aris's Birmingham Gazette*, 15th November 1824 ; *Report of the Committee appointed to collect information and documents as to the inexpediency of repealing the . . . Shrewsbury Incorporated House of Industry Act*, 1824 ; First Report of Poor Law Inquiry Commissioners, 1834, Appendix A, Lewis's Report, p. 659 ; Ninth Annual Report of Poor Law Commissioners, 1843.

Guardians purchased this building (which had been used by the Government during the American war for the confinement of prisoners of war) for £5500, and rapidly equipped it for its new purpose. The House of Industry which they established, with its farm, its corn-mill and its woollen manufactory, had the good fortune to enlist the devotion of Isaac Wood, an indefatigable local citizen, who evidently lavished upon its administration an incessant personal attention. His enthusiastic descriptions of its success were widely circulated, and did much to revive the faith in the profitable employment of the poor.[1]

The object of the Shrewsbury Directors was, primarily and avowedly, " to furnish employment for the poor and compel them to earn their own support," which had " been found impracticable in parish workhouses, under the direction and management of those officers who are annually chosen and annually removed. . . . Nor could the still more important object of training up the children of the poor to habits of industry and virtue be here obtained. In these workhouses, as well as in their private dwellings, they are incorporated with the abandoned and depraved."[2] For ten years the experiment had no small measure of success. The erection of a well-planned institution, administered by a standing committee and salaried officers, evidently brought about a great improvement in the condition of the paupers, whilst diminishing the Poor Rates by one-third.[3]

---

[1] The example of Shrewsbury was in 1791-1792 followed by five neighbouring districts of rural character, viz. Oswestry district (31 George III. c. 24, 1791) ; Ellesmere and other parishes (31 George III. c. 78, 1791) ; Whitchurch (32 George III. c. 85, 1792) ; Atcham and other parishes (32 George III. c. 95, 1792) ; Montgomery and Pool district of Montgomeryshire and Shropshire (32 George III. c. 96, 1792, 36 George III. c. 38, 1796, and 6 George IV. c. 123, 1825 ; House of Industry at Forden). As to these Shropshire experiments in rural districts, which in various respects resemble those of the Suffolk and Norfolk Hundreds to be described subsequently, and which deserve a local monograph, see the references given as to the Shrewsbury House of Industry. Two parishes at Bath also started a House of Industry ; see the printed broadsheet of *Rules, Orders and Regulations for . . . the House of Industry as agreed upon by the . . . Vestries of the Parishes of St. Peter and Paul and St. James,* 1800. An attempt was made at Sheffield in 1791 to establish a House of Industry on the Shrewsbury model ; see *The Substance of Mr. Ward's Speech at the Town Hall in Sheffield . . . at a meeting . . . to give assent or dissent to the Bill for the proposed new workhouse* (Sheffield, 1791) ; *Municipal Origins,* by F. H. Spencer, 1911, pp. 39-40.

[2] *Some Account of the Shrewsbury House of Industry,* by Isaac Wood, 1791, p. 4.

[3] *Ibid.* p. 13. The out-relief, including " nurses' pay," went down from £834 in 1784-1785 to £322 in 1789-1790 ; whilst the sums recovered from fathers

Between two and three hundred men, women and children were
brought into the House of Industry. Systematic arrangements
were made for bathing and medically examining them on admission ; and for the treatment in a separate infirmary of such
of them as were sick.[1] Most of them were set to work at preparing,
spinning and weaving wool, whilst " at the same time working
rooms or shops were set apart for the shoemakers, tailors, carpenters, etc., where those paupers who had been brought up to
these occupations were immediately employed, the most intelligent and trusty being appointed to cut out the work and
superintend the rest." [2]   But the Shrewsbury Directors never
contemplated refusing all outdoor relief. What they believed, as
Wood later expressed it, was that " Indiscriminate allowances
and indiscriminate confinement to a Poor House are equally
absurd and injurious. . . . We discriminate. This is the grand
hinge upon which every plan of parochial reform ought to turn." [3]
" To compel all claimants to come into the House," he explained,
" never made any part of their plan, and is an idea that has never
been acted upon in any period of their practice. In cases of real
distress the poor are more liberally relieved at their own dwellings
than they ever were before this establishment took place. Nevertheless, by the proper examination of each respective case before
a weekly board of respectable Directors, and the regular modes of
enquiry instituted by the byelaws of the House, such a check has
been given to fraud and imposition that the amount of the Poor
Rate is one third less than when the House was opened in 1784. . . .
Such a result could never have been obtained without employment had been provided for the poor in the House of Industry. . . .
At the same time our experience has demonstrated, and it is a fact
of the utmost moment, that it is not necessary to furnish the
employment for the great body of the poor at large ; it is sufficient
that you have it to offer to such applicants as allege the want of

of illegitimate children or from other parishes rose from £142 in 1784–1785 to
£286 in 1789–1790 (*Appendix to Some Account of the Shrewsbury House of Industry,
containing a correspondence with the Rev. J. Howlett*, 1791, p. 106). Yet where
occasional relief was needed it was liberally given (*Letter to Sir William Pulteney, Bart.*, by Isaac Wood, 1797, p. 39).
   [1] *Some Account of the Shrewsbury House of Industry*, by I. Wood, 1791,
p. 39.
   [2] *Ibid.* p. 21.
   [3] *An Introduction to the Fifth Edition of Some Account of the Shrewsbury
House of Industry*, by Isaac Wood, 1800, p. xxxix.

work in justification of their demands upon the parochial fund. . . .
Out of 7000 poor we have never had occasion, at one and the same
time, to furnish employment for half seven hundred." [1]   At first
all was done according to rule. Every case was strictly enquired
into. The payment of rent was peremptorily stopped. Those
who pleaded sickness were visited and examined by the doctor.
Gifts of clothing were discontinued. All constant doles were
stopped, relief being only given to tide over temporary emergencies. And where destitution was plainly caused by a large
family of young children, the Directors preferred to take some of
the children into the House of Industry, rather than relieve the
family by a dole.[2]   Such a system, it is clear, depended for any
success on a strict and continuous policy. After Wood's death—
which took place in 1801 from fever caught whilst inspecting the
House—the results were less successful. Within a few years we
note a complete revulsion of feeling in Shrewsbury itself.[3]   The
once belauded House of Industry is seen to be a centre of
demoralisation rather than of reform.[4]   In 1824–1826 we have
a successful agitation for the dissolution of the Incorporation,
and a reversion to parish management. "It is curious to find,"

[1] Isaac Wood, in *Annals of Agriculture*, vol. xxxv., 1800, p. 158 ; he had
expressed the same view in 1791 (*Some Account of the Shrewsbury House of
Industry*, by Isaac Wood, 1791, pp. 5-7).

[2] *Ibid.* pp. 14-19.

[3] In 1803 the Shrewsbury institution could still be referred to as "un-
rivalled" (*General View of the Agriculture of Shropshire*, by Joseph Plymley,
1803, p. 131). But by 1808 we learn that public opinion in the town had
"experienced a great revolution " ; and the system inaugurated by Wood has
been given up (*Some Account of . . . Shrewsbury*, Anon., 1808, p. 553).

[4] Within a very few years Sir F. M. Eden could report of the Ellesmere
House of Industry that "notwithstanding the promised advantages of this
institution, it is said that the incorporated parishes are, in general, heartily
sorry that they ever engaged in the erection " (*State of the Poor*, by Sir F. M.
Eden, 1797, vol. ii. pp. 619-620). Here is a description of the Houses of Industry
at Oswestry and Ellesmere in 1834. Their industries, it was remarked, are
"worked by the able-bodied inmates in such a feeble and languid manner that
the occupation is anything but calculated to preserve, much less generate, habits
of industry. . . . With the exception that their dormitories are separate, men,
women and children associate as they please. . . . Women of notoriously bad
characters are admitted and permitted to communicate freely with the other
female inmates. . . . Children of both sexes, from the sad examples of conversation they daily see and hear, are exposed to the pollution of vice at the
very dawn of life. . . . Such an indiscriminate mixture of persons of all ages,
sexes and characters, it is almost needless to remark, is a system ill calculated
to promote the comfort or improvement of paupers who are aggregated together
in Houses of Industry " (First Report of Poor Law Inquiry Commissioners,
1834, Appendix A, Lewis's Report, p. 660).

reports the Assistant Poor Law Commissioner of 1842, " that the Act . . . which was anxiously watched over in its infancy, and matured into vigour under the eye of its enthusiastic parent, was doomed to live through not half a century ; and that almost before the generation in which it had sprung up had passed away we find it avowed [by the Shrewsbury Committee of 1824] that the objects stated in the preamble had never been attained, and that the mere recital of them in the present day was sufficient to expose their absurdity." [1]

The Union of Rural Parishes

The desirability of combining for the administration of poor relief was even more obvious in the case of thinly inhabited rural parishes, each containing an average of only a few dozen or a few score families, than in that of crowded urban communities. The results of the general Act of 1723, which authorised the establishment of workhouses by one or more parishes, had, after the first flush of apparent success, not been such as to lead to its adoption in rural districts, where the defects of management under parish officers, or the horrors of the farming system, soon outweighed the advantages of the workhouse itself. In the country parishes, at any rate, something more efficient than parochial management was required. Yet not for more than sixty years was the example of Bristol followed in any rural area.

John Cary had pointed out that the only way to get workhouses in the country districts was to incorporate a larger area than the parish. The difficulty was to decide upon this larger area, and upon the constitution of the governing body. Cary's suggestion was that all the Justices of the Peace and all the freeholders of each County should be constituted the Poor Law authority for the entire County.[2] John Locke had proposed the

[1] Ninth Annual Report of Poor Law Commissioners, 1843, p. 281. The magnificently placed site of the House of Industry, affording one of the finest views in Europe, together with the substantial building overlooking the Severn, eventually became the property of Shrewsbury School, which was transferred to the premises of the old workhouse, suitably converted for its new uses, in 1882.

[2] *Essay towards Regulating the Trade and Employing the Poor of this Kingdom*, by John Cary, 1700 ; *The State of the Poor*, by Sir F. M. Eden, 1797, vol. i. pp. 253-257. Ruggles, himself a Suffolk Magistrate, thought that Cary's plan " may probably have given the hint to those gentlemen who applied to Parliament . . . for the Act for . . . Colneis and Carlford " (*History of the Poor*, by Thomas Ruggles, 1794, vol. i. p. 177).

establishment of workhouses in the several Hundreds of each County.[1] Both these suggestions were, between 1750 and 1755, more than once embodied in general Bills, which failed to become law.[2] The Bill for the establishment of " general County work-houses " struck the average country gentleman as " a huge un-wieldy scheme, attended with such an amazing certain expense, and liable to so many reasonable objections that the Parliament rejected it. Then it was proposed to have County workhouses to take in children only. But this, though it considerably reduced the other proposal, was subject to very many of the same objections which attended that, and therefore this likewise was rejected." [3] William Hay's project for a workhouse in each Hundred seemed more feasible, but the Hundred varied enormously in size and character in different Counties, and no member succeeded in pro-ducing a scheme that commended itself to the County repre-sentatives generally.[4] At last, in 1756, the energy and per-sistence of the gentlemen of two small Hundreds in the South of Suffolk, headed by Admiral Vernon, the victor of Portobello, resulted in the passing of a Local Act, which set up, for these two Hundreds of Carlford and Colneis, a new local governing body, empowered to erect a workhouse, and practically to take over, from the officers of the 28 parishes concerned, the whole adminis-tration of the Poor Law.[5]

---

[1] *Report of the Board of Trade to the Lords Justices in the year 1697 respecting the Relief and Employment of the Poor* (reprinted, 1787).

[2] The chief advocate in the House of Commons was the zealous William Hay, M.P., who, as early as 1735, actually got passed a series of resolutions for the division of each County into suitable areas, each to have a workhouse, under twelve Guardians. On the revival of interest, Hay published his plan as *Remarks on the Laws relating to the poor, with Proposals for their better Relief and Employment*, 1751. This was commented on in *Observations on the Defects of the Poor Laws*, by Rev. T. Alcock, 1752. Alcock agreed that there should be a single workhouse for the whole Hundred, but thought that the Overseers and clergyman of each parish should manage it for a year, in rotation ! There were also pamphlets by the Earl of Hillsborough (1753), Henry Fielding (1753) and William Bailey (1758), as well as a Select Committee of the House of Commons in 1759, all advocating workhouses for extensive combinations of parishes (see Sir Francis Eden's *State of the Poor*, 1794, vol. i.).

[3] Rev. R. Canning, in *The Christian's Magazine*, vol. iii., 1763, p. 28.

[4] It is characteristic of Sir George Nicholls that, deriving his information almost exclusively from the collection of Public General Statutes, he should declare that " nothing further was done " (*History of the English Poor Law*, by Sir George Nicholls, 1854, vol. ii. p. 55) ; entirely omitting the episode now to be described ; and, indeed, scarcely mentioning any of the constitutional experiments described in this chapter.

[5] 29 George II. c. 79 (1756). In the promotion of this Act, Admiral Vernon

The objects of the promoters of this Act are well set out in a nearly contemporaneous document. " We propose to incorporate," says this writer, in order " to administer proper comfort and assistance to the sick, infirm and aged, introduce sobriety and virtue among them, and in an especial manner, to render their children useful to society by acquainting them with their duty towards God and man, whence many are saved from untimely end, and all of them enabled to acquire an honest livelihood, and so not remain any longer a burden and reproach to our county. We incorporate too, to ease the respective parishes in their rates, a grievance very loudly and very commonly complained of by all sorts of occupiers; and also to feed and clothe the objects of their care with that plenty and decency that their wants and situation can reasonably require. . . . Our design, too, is to invite gentlemen to attend to the state and conduct of the poor— a concern which, however weighty and important in itself, it must be confessed, is not, nor is it likely it ever will be, regarded by them in the separate parishes, seeing that but very few owners of any fashion live where their estates are situated, and whenever it happens that they do reside there, the indelicacy and rudeness of parish meetings oblige them never to come into such assemblies." [1] With such high hopes we see some fifty of the squires and clergy of these South Suffolk parishes meeting, in June 1756, at an Ipswich tavern. One of them, the Rev. R. Canning, advances twenty pounds towards the initial expenses.[2] Admiral Vernon, whom they make chairman, gives a site on Nacton Heath on which to build the workhouse, and lends £1000 at 3½ per cent towards its erection.[3] For a couple of years we watch the little group of reformers planning their new institution, carefully

---

and the Rev. R. Canning had the assistance of Sir Richard Lloyd, a leading lawyer of the time (*Observations on the Poor Laws*, by R. Potter, 1775, p. 33); and himself interested in Poor Law reform.

[1] *A Letter to J. W., Esquire, relating to Mr. G——y's Pamphlet upon the Poor Laws, with some reflections in favour of the House of Industry at Nacton, in the County of Suffolk, and on the Utility of such designs*, 1756, 24 pp. No copy of this is known to us, but voluminous extracts from it are given in a letter signed XX in the *Ipswich Journal*, 23rd July and 10th September 1825. The inscription on the House of Industry at Melton was as follows : " Erected in the year 1768 for the Instruction of Youth, the Encouragement of Industry, the Relief of Want, the Support of Age and the comfort of Infirmity and Pain " (MS. Minutes, Incorporated Guardians, Loes and Wilford, 1768).

[2] *Ibid.* Colneis and Carlford, 25th June 1756.

[3] *Ibid.* 28th June and 29th December 1756.

ordering the various items of furniture and equipment, and deciding all the details of its organisation.[1] By March 1758, the " Nacton House of Industry " is completed according to the best science of the time ; and we see transferred to it [2] the paupers, male and female, young and old, well and sick, who had previously been lodging in the dilapidated village poor-houses, or eking out by begging and pilfering their weekly doles of out-relief. In the Nacton House of Industry they were apparently well provided for and kindly treated, but set to work at weaving cornsacks out of hemp,[3] making cordage of various sorts, especially ploughlines, and spinning wool for the weavers of Norwich.[4] " This institution," it was said, " puts an end to the usual custom of pecuniary payments to the poor, which are generally abused by them, and, as generally, given without discretion. . . . Many children are rendered useful who otherwise would have figured nowhere but in a landscape of Gainsborough's, the spawn of gipsies, lying upon a sunny bank half naked, with their bundles of stolen wood by their sides—a daily task which those who pretend to have the care of them never fail to exact." [5]   " By means of the Act," wrote one enthusiast in 1764, " the poor in these Hundreds are much better maintained, are happier in themselves, and more useful to the public than in any other part of the kingdom ; and by the account which has been published, it appears that this scheme will considerably lessen the present expense, for, from Easter 1758 to Michaelmas 1762, notwithstanding some very extraordinary expenses attending the first institution of it in these Hundreds, a saving has been already made of above £2000 ; and in a few years the debt contracted for its first institution will be cleared, and the rates will not be above half of what they are at present." [6]   So successful did the

[1] MS. Minutes, Incorporated Guardians, Colneis and Carlford, 1757–1758.
[2] *Ibid.* 20th and 23rd March 1758.
[3] *Ibid.* 26th June 1758.
[4] *History of the Poor*, by Thomas Ruggles, 1794.   Other industrial occupations carried on in these Houses of Industry (besides the cultivation of their few acres) were the making of linen clothes, shoes and stockings for their own use ; spinning worsted yarn ; making fishing nets ; handknitting, and the weaving of coarse woollen cloth.
[5] *A Letter to J. W., Esquire, relating to G——y's Pamphlet upon the Poor Laws, with some reflections in favour of the House of Industry at Nacton*, by XX, 1766 ; see *Ipswich Journal*, 10th September 1825.
[6] *Definitions and Axioms relating to Charity, Charitable Institutions and the Poor Laws*, by Samuel Cooper, 1764.

experiment appear, both in the reduction of the Poor Rate and the better maintenance of the poor, that in 1763–1764 no fewer than seven other Hundreds or pairs of Hundreds, of Suffolk and Norfolk, obtained Local Acts of a similar kind,[1] to be followed, a few years later, by half-a-dozen more ;[2] so that, by 1785, over the greater part of the area of these two large Counties the administration of the Poor Law had been withdrawn from the parish officers and vested in fourteen new bodies of Incorporated Guardians of the Poor.[3]

[1] These were the Hundreds of Blything (4 George III. c. 56 ; House of Industry at Bulcamp) ; Bosmere and Clayton (4 George III. c. 57 ; House of Industry at Barham) ; Lodden and Clavering (4 George III. c. 90 ; House of Industry at Heckingham) ; Loes and Wilford (5 George III. c. 97 ; House of Industry at Melton) ; Mutford and Lothingland (5 George III. c. 89 ; House of Industry at Oulton) ; Samford (4 George III. c. 59 ; House of Industry at Tattingstone) ; and Wangford (4 George III. c. 91 ; House of Industry at Shipmeadow).

The statistical returns presented to the House of Commons in 1776 include 8 of these " Hundred Houses," which had each cost from £4000 to £12,000 to build, and contained each from 150 to 350 inmates, who were employed in spinning, weaving, and knitting hemp and wool into sacking, twine, cloth and stockings ; making fishing nets, and farming the land. Some of the labour was let out to farmers. Most of the Houses kept a tailor, a shoemaker and a " mantuamaker " at wages (Second Report of House of Commons Committee, 21st May 1776).

[2] East and West Flegg (15 George III. c. 13) ; Mitford and Launditch (15 George III. c. 59 ; House of Industry at Gressinghall) ; Forehoe (16 George III. c. 9 ; House of Industry at Forehoe) ; Cosford and Polsted (19 George III. c. 30 ; House of Industry at Semer) ; Hartismere, Hoxne and Thredling (19 George III. c. 30) ; Stow (18 George III. c. 35 ; House of Industry at One-House) ; and Tunstead and Happing (25 George III. c. 27 ; House of Industry at Smallburgh). There was a belated incorporation of nine Norfolk parishes (Buxton, Everingham, etc.) in 1806, by 46 George III. c. 44 ; and another in 1816, when by 56 George III. c. 66, a number of parishes (Shardlow, Milne, etc.) in Derbyshire, Leicestershire and Nottinghamshire were similarly combined. Neither of these we have explored. More directly imitative may have been the five Unions of Shropshire parishes, arising in 1791–1792 from the early success of the Shrewsbury House of Industry, which we have already described.

[3] These Suffolk and Norfolk Incorporated Guardians were frequently made the subject of particular references and brief descriptions, though we have found nothing in the nature of a monograph on the subject. We have had access to the MS. Minutes of those of Colneis and Carlford, Loes and Wilford, and Samford. Besides the minutes, the chief sources of information are the various Acts ; the House of Commons Returns as to Poor Laws, 1776 ; the numerous sets of " Rules and Orders " and other printed documents, and the reports of sundry local committees of investigation hereafter cited. Various printed documents of these Incorporations are accidentally preserved in the British Museum, volumes 10351 i. 10 and 10351 i. 24. Much may be gathered from the files of the *Ipswich Journal,* especially between 1815 and 1830. The chief description of the Houses of Industry at different dates are those in *The Farmer's Tour Through the East of England,* by Arthur Young, 1771, vol. ii.

These "Incorporations" of Guardians of the Poor were, with insignificant variation, all constituted upon a practically identical plan. All the Justices of the Peace resident within the district, or sometimes within five miles of it; all the owners of freeholds worth £30 or £60 a year and upwards ; all the Rectors or Vicars of the respective parishes ; sometimes all their curates also ; and all the leaseholders of lands or tenements worth £60, or £100, or £120 a year and upwards, were constituted " Guardians of the Poor." [1] This indeterminate and unwieldy body, which was directed to meet quarterly, became the ultimate governing authority. At its first meeting it was required to appoint twenty-four from among its own number to be " Directors of the Poor," serving for life, and also to elect a President of the Incorporation. There had also to be chosen, out of the Guardians, sometimes by the whole meeting, sometimes by the Directors only, twenty-four or thirty-six " Acting Guardians," one-half or one-third of whom retired annually. It was in the hands of these two bodies of Directors and Acting Guardians that the whole executive authority, and practically the entire government, of the Incor-

---

pp. 178-190 ; *Observations on the Poor Laws*, by R. Potter, 1775, pp. 33-49 ; *A dialogue in two conversations . . . in answer to Observations on the Poor Laws*, by Thomas Mendham, 1775 ; *Thoughts on the Construction and Polity of Prisons*, by Rev. John Jebb, 1786, pp. 11 ; *History of the Poor*, by Thomas Ruggles, 1794, vol. ii. (this account was reproduced as appendix to *General View of the Agriculture of Suffolk*, by Arthur Young, 1794) ; *Charitable Institutions and the Poor Laws*, 1763 ; a pamphlet entitled *Definitions and Axioms relative to Charity, Charitable Institutions and the Poor Laws*, 1764, by Samuel Cooper, of which we have found no copy, but which is described by Sir Francis Eden and quoted in the Ninth Annual Report of the Poor Law Commissioners, 1843 ; *The Insufficiency of the Causes to which the increase of our Poor and of the Poor's Rates have been commonly ascribed, the True One stated, with an Inquiry into the Mortality of Country Houses of Industry*, etc., by Rev. J. Howlett, 1788 ; *The State of the Poor*, by Sir F. M. Eden, 1797, vol. ii. ; *History of the Poor*, by Thomas Ruggles, 1794 ; *General View of the Agriculture of Norfolk*, by Arthur Young, 1804 ; *Letters on the Kind and Economic Management of the Poor, chiefly as regards Incorporated Poor Houses*, by Edward Moon, 1825. See also the Report of the Poor Law Inquiry Commissioners, 1834, Appendix A, Stuart's Report, p. 355, and pp. 187-198, 203-294 ; and the First and Second Annual Reports of the Poor Law Commissioners, 1835 and 1836, the latter containing a valuable " Report on the administration of the Poor Law Amendment Act in Suffolk and Norfolk," by James Phillips Kay ; the Ninth Annual Report, 1843 ; together with *The Christian's Magazine*, 1762-1763, vol. ii. pp. 524, 578, vol. iii. p. 24 ; and *The Annals of Agriculture*, especially about 1800.

[1] Women freeholders or leaseholders were not excluded, but they were required to vote by proxy. At the first meeting five Guardians " delivered proxies from the women undermentioned " (MS. Minutes, Incorporated Guardians, Colneis and Carlford, 25th June 1756).

poration was legally placed. The exact relation between these two executive bodies, and the precise distribution of duties between them, varied slightly in the different Local Acts. The general principle seems to have been that the Directors were to appoint the Treasurer, the Clerk and other chief officers, and to decide from time to time such large issues of financial policy as borrowing money, acquiring land, and erecting workhouses ; whilst the Acting Guardians were to undertake the routine duties of workhouse management. But in many of the Acts it is the Directors and Acting Guardians together who are authorised to perform most of the duties that are recited, and we do not find it easy to make out the line of demarcation. Between them they were always authorised to borrow a substantial capital sum, to erect and maintain a workhouse ; to receive in it such poor persons as the parishes chose to send to them ; to set the inmates to work ; to make byelaws for their government, and to punish the refractory ; to bind children apprentices to any person legally liable to take them within the district ; apparently to relieve the destitute in any other way they thought fit ;[1] and to levy the cost upon all the parishes within the district, in proportion to the average Poor Rates paid by each during the seven years preceding the Act, which were not to be exceeded.

The relation in which these Incorporations stood to the authorities of the County and the Parish was one of some intricacy and obscurity. The Local Acts, under which they were established, did not professedly relieve the Justices of the Peace from their responsibility for the supervision of the Poor Law administration ; and did not in any way exempt the new Directors and Guardians of the Poor from magisterial control. They were even expressly required to submit their accounts for allowance at each Quarter Sessions, when an opportunity was afforded for any person to make objection to their proceedings, and for the

---

[1] They were even given powers of compulsorily placing within the House of Industry persons who were not paupers. The Incorporated Guardians of Colneis and Carlford petition the House of Commons in 1763, " That they conceive it would very much tend to the better government of the said poor if your petitioners were authorised to apprehend any idle, lazy or disorderly persons found within the Hundred begging or refusing to work, and to carry them to some Justice of the Peace ; and if such Justice was authorised to commit such offenders to the House of Industry, there to be dealt with according to law under the direction of the said Justice of the Peace " (MS. Minutes, Incorporated Guardians, Colneis and Carlford, 3rd October 1763). The desired power was given in the Local Act, 4 George III. c. 58.

Court to give such orders as it thought fit. It is, however, easy to see that, as with all the new Authorities established under Local Acts, this subjection of the Suffolk and Norfolk Incorporations to the Justices was entirely illusory. Their very creation was taken to imply, and was probably intended to imply, that they were themselves to exercise whatever discretion had previously been exercised in Poor Law administration by the Single or the Double Justice, or in Petty or Special Sessions. We see this supersession of the Justices forcibly described by a fervent admirer of the new system. " When you are incorporated," he declares to the parishes, " the Directors and Guardians are judges of the measure of relief. When you are disincorporated it will be fixed by the Justices. And do you really believe that these gentlemen are better judges of the real wants of the poor, than a committee of the House, composed of a mixture of gentlemen and men of business ? Or do you suppose that smaller allowances will be made in the Sessions Hall at Woodbridge, than in the committee-room of the House of Industry. . . . The pauper makes his complaint to the Overseer and the Overseer takes it to the Committee. If the complaint is unreasonable or experimental . . . the Committee refuses relief, and there is an end of the business ; the pauper grumbles perhaps, but submits, because he knows there is no remedy. Not so in an un-incorporated parish. The pauper who is refused relief to-day comes again to-morrow ; frequently with abusive language ; not infrequently with threats. However often repulsed, he returns again to the charge ; drags the Overseer to half the Justices in the County, and at last by importunity and worrying obtains an allowance that he ill-deserves, and which is given rather to purchase quiet and forbearance than because it is wanted." [1]

This quasi-judicial authority of the Directors and Acting Guardians of the new Incorporations comes out in their relations with the parish authorities. The Directors and Acting Guardians took over from the Overseers the whole administration of Poor Law relief ; but the Local Acts in no way relieved the parishioners from their statutory obligation to serve as Overseers, and in no way exempted the Overseers from any of their duties or obligations. What happened was that the parish officer acquired, in

[1] *Ipswich Journal*, 22nd May 1825.

place of the Justices of the Peace, a new set of masters, from whom he received peremptory orders. He had to attend the meetings of the Directors and Acting Guardians whenever required ; to produce lists of the poor in his parish, lists of children, lists of persons liable to take apprentices, and any other information required.[1] Whenever it was desired that outdoor relief should be given in any case, the parish officers had to attend the " Weekly Meeting " of the committee and support the application.[2] The parish officers might even be required to attend regularly at the House of Industry every week as a matter of course, the journey probably sacrificing nearly a whole day of their time.[3] All the outdoor relief that the Directors and Acting Guardians allowed in particular cases was paid weekly under their orders by the Overseers ; [4] and this had to be done, as one order directs, " in specie personally by themselves." [5] Any failure to discharge these duties, or to obey any of the directions of the Directors and Acting Guardians, might be visited by the penalty of a fine, inflicted not by the Justices but by the Directors and Acting Guardians themselves.[6] In case any parish failed to pay its quota, the Directors and Acting Guardians could themselves inflict a fine on the Overseer.[7] The

[1] MS. Minutes, Incorporated Guardians, Colneis and Carlford, 30th March 1778. " That the Churchwardens within the several parishes do make lists of the number of poor with their families . . . and do attend the committee . . . with such lists in order that the committee may judge of the necessitous poor, and give them such relief as their present necessary occasions may require " (MS. Minutes, Incorporated Guardians, Samford, 14th July 1795).

[2] *Ibid.* Loes and Wilford, 1st April 1811. " That no pauper shall be relieved by a weekly committee or quarterly meeting unless accompanied by the Churchwarden or Overseer of the Parish where they live" (*Byelaws, Rules, Orders and Instruction for the Better Government and Support of the Poor in the Hundred of Bosmere and Claydon in Suffolk*, 1813, p. 20).

[3] " Ordered that the Overseers . . . do regularly attend at the Poor House every Wednesday. . . . In case of their non-attendance . . . they will be subject to the penalty under the 44 section of the last Act " (MS. Minutes, Incorporated Guardians, Samford, 1st October 1799).

[4] " Ordered that Mary B. and her son Thomas B. of Bradfield, an idiot, and she old and infirm, be allowed 2/6 a week to be paid by the Overseer until further orders " (*ibid.* Loes and Wilford, 18th July 1768).

[5] *Ibid.* Samford, 25th June 1833.

[6] Two Overseers were summoned to appear before the Directors and Guardians in 1768 and fined a shilling each " for neglect of duty " (*ibid.* Loes and Wilford, 26th December 1768). Two more in 1778 were fined half a guinea each (*ibid.* 29th June 1778).

[7] In 1762 we see an Overseer, who had not paid the contribution due from his parish, after repeated formalities, summarily sentenced by the Directors and Acting Guardians themselves, to pay a fine of forty shillings (MS. Minutes,

K

Suffolk and Norfolk Incorporations were thus, in effect, a combination of the Justices and the parish officers, exercising many of the supervising and judicial functions of the one, and most of the administrative duties of the other ; forcibly interpolated between the two ; and yet nominally leaving unimpaired the legal powers and obligations of both of them.

Let us now enquire how the elaborate statutory constitutions of these bodies of Incorporated Guardians actually worked in practice. To the first rulers of these incorporations their organisation seemed devised upon the most perfect principles of administration. " To guard against frauds and jobs," reports the most enthusiastic of their founders, " all considerable contracts are made at the quarterly meetings, in the most public manner. No money is paid by the Treasurer but by order of a quarterly meeting, or by warrant under the hands of the Directors and Acting Guardians, in a quarterly meeting, or in a weekly committee assembled. And at these general quarterly meetings, all the vouchers of the preceding quarter are stated and settled, and the vouchers examined and compared with them. And forasmuch as many persons pay to the rates, who are not concerned in the management of the poor, these accounts, so stated and signed by the members of the general quarterly meetings, are referred to His Majesty's Court of Quarter Sessions, there to be finally allowed and confirmed.[1] And here if any man can suggest fraud or mismanagement before such final allowance and confirmation, he may be heard. What better care could be taken to prevent jobs ? "[2] " A committee room," as another enthusiast tells us, " spacious, commodious and pleasantly situated, is set apart for the weekly meetings of the Directors and Guardians. . . . They consist of the principal gentry, clergy and tenantry in the County. They visit in rotation, each taking

---

Incorporated Guardians, Colneis and Carlford, 27th December 1762). The penalty on parish officers neglecting to raise and pass over the assessments due was raised from £5 to £50 by the Blything Act of 1793 (33 George III. c. 126).

[1] So entirely was Quarter Sessions still regarded as a Court that this submission of accounts had apparently to be made by counsel, no one else being allowed to appear on behalf of the Incorporation ; and the Directors and Acting Guardians of the Colneis and Carlford Hundreds complained that the solicitor's and counsel's fees, at five guineas each time, had cost them £73 in five years.

[2] Rev. R. Canning, in *The Christian's Magazine*, 1763, vol. iii. pp. 29, 30.

a month.   Two Directors from the gentry, three Acting Guardians
from the yeomanry, with the Clerk, form the weekly meeting.
The governor of the House attends to answer enquiries and
complaints.   He brings up his report of the material events of
the preceding week.   All business respecting the economy of
the House and current expenses is then settled.   The stores and
provisions are inspected, the apothecary who attends for a yearly
stipend, is examined with respect to the sick.   In this whole
affair no person complains of the fatigue of attendance, but
rather takes pleasure in the discharge of so useful an employment." ¹   It was, in fact, assumed that the compulsory incorporation of all the substantial gentry and the leading tenantry
of the district as Guardians would ensure the exercise of a constant
oversight, by those on whom fell the main burden of the rates,
over the administration carried on at their joint expense.   When
it was objected to the Incorporation that no one would take the
trouble to look after them, their sanguine promoters rejoined as
a conclusive answer that, " As the attendance is so easy, we may
reasonably expect that it will be complied with, especially as
it will always be the interest of the persons whose attendance is
wanted that this affair should succeed well." ²   It is needless to
say that the great bulk of the squires and clergy neglected, from
the outset, to attend even the quarterly meetings, or to pay any
attention to the House of Industry.   There was, indeed, nothing
for the Guardians—as distinguished from the Directors and
Acting Guardians—to do at their meetings, after they had once
elected the President, the other officers, and the two executive
bodies.³   Even at the first meeting of a new Incorporation only

¹ *Thoughts on the Construction and Polity of Prisons*, by Rev. John Jebb,
1786, p. 11.   He had resigned a Suffolk living in 1775, and thus probably wrote
from memory of the early years of the Houses of Industry.
² Rev. R. Canning, in *The Christian's Magazine*, 1763, vol. iii. p. 29.
³ In some of the Acts the apprenticing of children and the letting out of
the poor for hire was apparently reserved to the Guardians as a whole (Mitford
and Launditch Act of 1775 ; Blything Act of 1793 ; also the letting out of the
poor to work in harvest time, in the East and West Flegg Act of 1775).   The
process in 1797 is described for us by Sir F. M. Eden.   The boys and girls at
14 are " drafted out to the parishes to which they belong.   If a person to
whose lot a child falls should refuse to take him or her for a year (which is the
stated term) he forfeits 20s., which goes to the master who accepts his allot-
ment ; if he should likewise refuse, he also forfeits the same sum, which is
then paid to the third person on his accepting the child ; when the year is
expired, the child is again put by lot to another master, in case his old master
does not wish to keep him, and he is not able to provide for himself " (*The*

a few score persons would deign to put in an appearance ; and these had perforce to elect themselves as the 24 Directors and the 24 or 36 Acting Guardians that the Act required.[1] The two executive bodies were, therefore, in effect, self-elected, renewing themselves on the occurrence of vacancies by simple co-option. Vacancies remained, however, long unfilled, owing to the difficulty of finding persons willing even to promise to serve.[2]

Though no such distinction is expressed in the Acts, both the intention and the practice seems to have been for the Directors to be chosen from among the clergy and gentry, and the Acting Guardians from among such substantial farmers and tradesmen as possessed the statutory qualification.[3]   The Directors assumed as their sphere the decision of important matters, such as the erection of a building or the borrowing of money, whilst the current administration of relief, and the daily management of the House of Industry was left principally to the Acting Guardians, though Parliament had striven to secure that some, at least, of the Directors should also be present.   What happened in practice was that the separate meetings of the two bodies were dropped, as was that of the Guardians at large.   Only one kind of meeting was held, both quarterly and annually, this being attended indiscriminately by Directors and Acting Guardians, at which formal resolutions were passed, and various kinds of relief were administered.   For the actual management of the House of Industry the Directors and Acting Guardians divided themselves up into small committees of about five, each being supposed to attend to the management for one month, and to be absolved

---

State of the Poor, by Sir F. M. Eden, 1797, vol. ii. p. 455).   The Colneis and Carlford amending Act of 1763 transferred all the powers of the Guardians to the Directors and Acting Guardians.

[1] At the first meetings of the new Incorporations, the following attendances were recorded : 50 (MS. Minutes, Incorporated Guardians, Colneis and Carlford); 31 (*ibid.* Loes and Wilford, 1st July 1765).

[2] " Notwithstanding the Act of incorporation requires all vacancies to be filled at each quarterly meeting after they respectively happen, there are at this time three, two of them of about a year's standing, and the third of more than two years and a half " (*Report of the Committee appointed to inquire into the Actual State of the House of Industry at Melton*, 1791, p. 13).

[3] In the Loes and Wilford Incorporation in 1825–1826, out of the 24 Directors 11 were clergymen and 3 esquires ; whilst the Acting Guardians were all styled " Mr." (*List of the Directors and Acting Guardians in the Hundreds of Loes and Wilford, with their months of attendance at the House of Industry for the years 1825–1826*).

from meetings all the rest of the year.[1] In actual practice we
find, in case after case, most of the Directors and Acting Guardians
not attending meetings of any sort, and hardly any of them ever
going to the House of Industry; the whole management being
left, practically for years together, in the hands of the paid
officials. It was in vain that the Act of Parliament prescribed
penalties for non-attendance, and that resolutions were passed
threatening to put the penalties in force. In the Loes and
Wilford Incorporation, when the grave financial position had
led, in 1791, to a committee of enquiry, it was reported that
within the preceding ten years there had been forty-five meetings
at which there had been no quorum; that the prescribed weekly
committees had not been held; and that in no one case had any
Director or Acting Guardian obeyed the byelaw which required
each of them individually to visit the House at least once in the
course of the particular month assigned to him.[2] Within five
years after the reorganisation that followed this investigation,
the system had again broken down. The Directors and Acting
Guardians then tried the experiment of dividing themselves,
not by months in the year, but into nine continuous subject-
committees; for religion and morality, industry, maintenance,
clothing, medicines, building and repairs, finance, law and
apprenticeship respectively; each being instructed to meet at
least once a quarter as a minimum.[3] We gather that this proved
no more successful than the preceding arrangement. When the
meetings were called at the House of Industry no members
whatever attended.[4] When they were held in the more comfortable surroundings of the White Hart Tavern at Wickham Market
the record was not much better.[5] In some Incorporations the
device was invented of permitting the Acting Guardians to
appoint deputies to attend in their stead; with the result, as
might be imagined, that the privilege was " scandalously "
abused; " the person chosen to discharge " the delegated office
being often " so far from equal to its duties that he could not
sign his name to the accounts he admitted, nor read even what

[1] Rev. R. Canning, in *The Christian's Magazine*, 1763, vol. iii. p. 29.
[2] *Report of the Committee appointed to inquire into the Actual State of the
House of Industry at Melton*, 1791, p. 13.
[3] MS. Minutes, Incorporated Guardians, Loes and Wilford, 2nd July 1796.
[4] *Ibid.* 5th July (as regards three meetings), and 11th October 1798.
[5] *Ibid.* 11th April 1805; 6th January 1806 (2 present).

he allowed."[1] In despair of securing a better attendance for any length of time the more active and zealous Directors and Acting Guardians of these Incorporations put their trust in the formulation of elaborate " Rules and Orders." " When general laws are once established," fondly remark the compilers of one such code, " the public is in no danger of losing at any future time any of the advantages which a former zeal had promised, or a past vigilance had procured. For should that zeal here-after abate, or that vigilance relax, the institution by means of its General Rules, remains like a machine, which, having its springs of motion within itself, will, with but an ordinary atten-tion, and only common application, go on to perform without interruption its accustomed functions, and to produce without variation its usual benefits. Nothing therefore can be more unjust than the common objection to Houses of Industry and similar institutions that, however well they may be administered at first, they will at length fall into neglect. For do but establish General Rules and the objection is at once obviated."[2]

The Suffolk and Norfolk Houses of Industry were thus practi-cally handed over, sooner or later, to the management of the officers, under such " Rules and Orders " as the zeal and wisdom of the squires and clergy had provided. These officers consisted, as a rule, of a Clerk to the Incorporation, usually a local attorney, paid a small salary[3] for the formal business of the Annual Meeting and the preparation of the necessary documents ; a Treasurer, one of the Directors or Acting Guardians, who kept the current balances for his own profit, but sometimes received also a small stipend.[4] More important than these, who seem seldom or never to have visited the institution itself, was the Steward or Master or Governor of the House of Industry, who ran the whole establishment, managed its few acres of land, directed its little manufactures, governed the pauper inmates,

[1] *Report of the Committee appointed to inquire into the Actual State of the House of Industry at Melton*, 1791, p. 13.

[2] *Rules and Orders for . . . the Directors and Acting Guardians of the Poor of the Hundreds of Loes and Wilford.*

[3] Ten guineas a year (MS. Minutes, Incorporated Guardians, Loes and Wilford, 1st July 1765) ; twenty pounds a year (*ibid.* Loes and Wilford, 27th June 1768) ; thirty pounds a year (*An Account of the Proceedings of the Special Committee . . . to enquire into the Expenditure in the House of Industry at Heckingham*, 1793).

[4] Six guineas a year (MS. Minutes, Incorporated Guardians, Loes and Wilford, 1st July 1765) ; twenty pounds a year (*ibid.* 14th October 1802).

and was evidently the mainspring of the administration. For this responsible position the Guardians seem nearly always to have allowed a salary of £40 a year with board and lodging,[1] sometimes with a trifling bonus on the amount of wool spun, or other production of the paupers[2] . . . a remuneration which did not permit them to find anybody of greater administrative ability than a bankrupt farmer, a village shopkeeper or a promoted servant or labourer. The Governor was assisted by a Chaplain, at £25 a year, who was for this sum to "read prayers daily and preach one part of the day every Sunday, catechise the children once a week every Wednesday, christen the children, visit the sick and bury the dead."[3] There were also usually several doctors appointed, at from £21 to £40 a year, one to physic the inmates of the House, and the others to look after the outdoor poor in particular districts.[4] Presently the larger Houses have also a Matron, a Schoolmaster, and a Schoolmistress.[5] The reader will be prepared to learn that the officers so appointed and left practically uninspected to manage their several institutions were seldom found satisfactory for any length of time. Notwithstanding all the elaborate rules, it was impossible to prevent the Governor of the House from embezzling the material, the stores and the cash.[6] The quantity of food consumed could not be made to bear any constant relation to the number of inmates, and was always going up.[7]

[1] MS. Minutes, Incorporated Guardians, Colneis and Carlford, 22nd November 1757 ; *ibid.* Loes and Wilford, 27th June 1768 ; *ibid.* Loddon and Clavering (*An Account of the Proceedings of the Special Committee . . . to enquire into the Expenditure in the House of Industry at Heckingham,* 1793).

[2] At the Tattingstone House of Industry the Guardians presented the Governor annually with a " gratuity " of £50, together with £10 for his daughter, who taught the knitting school, in lieu of salary (MS. Minutes, Incorporated Guardians, Samford, 26th March 1833, 1st April 1834).

[3] *Ibid.* Côlneis and Carlford, 2nd October 1758 ; elsewhere it was £35 (*ibid.* Loes and Wilford, 27th June 1768) or £30 (*An Account of the Proceedings of the Special Committee . . . to enquire into the Expenditure in the House of Industry at Heckingham,* 1793).

[4] MS. Minutes, Incorporated Guardians, Samford, 26th June 1780. Presently this Incorporation tried the experiment of having one Resident Doctor to do all the work, giving his whole time for a salary of £85 a year, with board and lodging (*ibid.* 5th July 1791). The Loddon and Clavering Guardians gave as much as £105 (*An Account of the Proceedings of the Special Committee . . . to enquire into the Expenditure in the House of Industry at Heckingham,* 1793).

[5] MS. Minutes, Incorporated Guardians, Loes and Wilford, 11th April 1811.

[6] *Ibid.* 29th June 1789.

[7] In one Incorporation it was found that the aggregate weight of food per head had risen by 33 per cent in fifteen years (*An Account of the Proceedings*

There were, however, apart from mere shortcomings of management, two developments in the working of these institutions which, in their unforeseen effects, must, in any case, have gone far to destroy whatever chance they may have had of successful administration. The Directors and Acting Guardians could not refrain, in spite of their rigid theories, from granting practically indiscriminate outdoor relief. Before the first House of Industry had been open a year, we see the grant of weekly doles beginning, at first to " a bedridden man," then to widows, and presently to families of good character. There was at first some discrimination between those who were forced to enter the House of Industry and those who were not. During the famine years between 1795 and 1800, relief was given indiscriminately to all the labourers, "head money " being often paid for each child where there were more than one in the family.[1] In the final stages of these Incorporations there came to be more outdoor relief than indoor maintenance. For the ten years 1800–1810, the figures in the Loes and Wilford Hundreds were £20,208 outdoor and £32,477 indoor ; in 1810–1820, £51,908 and £37,466 ; and in 1820–1824, £23,917 and £15,037 respectively.[2]

This result was partly caused by the change in the method of apportioning the expenses of the Incorporation among the constituent parishes, which was gradually adopted between 1801 and 1820. The original intention had been to relieve each parish of the administration of its own Poor Law, charging it exactly what it has previously paid as Poor Rate, and undertaking not to exceed that sum. When the new Houses of Industry had paid off their capital debt, it was contemplated that the charge upon the parishes should be rateably reduced. In the Blything Incorporation a reduction of one-eighth was actually made from 1780 on-

of the Special Committee . . . to enquire into the Expenditure in the House of Industry at Heckingham, 1793). The Governor's explanation was that " he was obliged to give the paupers more food than they wanted, or could eat, to preserve order in the House " (ibid. p. 2).

[1] " That there be a general relief to the poor families in each parish in the following ratio, viz. a family with 2 children, 6d. each ; with 3 children, 8d. each ; with 4 children, 9d. each. No children above the age of 12 years to be allowed " (MS. Minutes, Incorporated Guardians, Samford, 19th January 1796).

[2] Report of the Committee appointed . . . to investigate the Receipts and Expenditure for the Support of the Poor, 1825. A stirring protest was made in 1823 against the outdoor relief of the Blything Incorporation by Rev. Richard Whateley ; see his broadside of that date.

wards, the whole debt of £12,000 having been discharged.[1] The Cosford Hundred, too, is reported by 1800 to have reduced its debt of £8000 to £180, and to have reduced its Poor Rate by three-eighths.[2] Generally speaking, however, the parishes continued to pay the same Poor Rates as they had previously done ; and sometimes these were even increased.[3] In the course of a few years the numbers of paupers belonging to the several parishes inevitably underwent changes, whilst the parishes continued to contribute in a fixed ratio. This led to complaints from those parishes which found themselves paying in a higher ratio than that of their current pauperism. To satisfy these complaints, and arrange what seemed a fairer basis of contribution, it was provided by various amending Acts, first that the parishes should contribute according to a new triennial or decennial average ; [4] and eventually that each parish should bear the cost of the out-relief of its own poor, and should contribute to the cost of the House of Industry in strict proportion to the number of inmates that it sent thither. This change in system had a disastrous consequence. The amending Acts, in fact, unwittingly " offered a direct premium for keeping paupers out of the House." [5] As the expense per head in the House of Industry was high, each parish saw its way to save money by giving small doles of outdoor relief, rather than augment its numbers in the House. Finally, the quondam " House of Industry " became for the parishes, only a sort of co-operative hospital for the sick, an orphan asylum for the deserted children, and a place to which the Overseers could send any able-bodied poor to whom they did not choose to allow the weekly dole.

For a generation, however, it was apparently still possible to believe in the success of these Incorporations. We see them

---

[1] *History of the Poor*, by Thomas Ruggles, 1794.

[2] *An Introduction to the Fifth Edition of Some Account of the Shrewsbury House of Industry*, by Isaac Wood, 1800, p. lviii.

[3] In the Stow Incorporation they were increased by one quarter for three years by common consent (*ibid.*). The Colneis and Carlford Act of 1790 authorised a maximum of double the former rate.

[4] Mitford and Launditch Act of 1801 (41 George III. c. 63) ; Loes and Wilford Act of 1810 (50 George III. c. 119) ; Blything Act of 1820 (1 George IV. c. 6) ; First Report of Poor Law Inquiry Commissioners, 1834, Appendix C, pp. 187, 264 ; *General View of the Agriculture of Norfolk*, by A. Young, 1804, pp. 494-496.

[5] First Report of Poor Law Inquiry Commissioners, 1834, Appendix C, p. 194.

repeatedly belauded by Poor Law reformers; and even imitated in various localities. Of these imitations we have already described the most important, the Shrewsbury House of Industry. Of the others we need describe only that established in the Isle of Wight.

The Isle of Wight, with its few thousand inhabitants scattered among 30 parishes, all within a walk, and none containing any considerable town, formed, it would seem, an obviously convenient unit of administration. The County Justices of the Island, as we have elsewhere described,[1] effected an extra-legal separation between themselves and their colleagues on the mainland of the County ; held their own Quarter Sessions, and made their own County Rate, virtually as if the Island were a distinct shire. Yet so strong was the influence of the immemorial division into parishes that, not until 1770, do we find on the Island any common action as to Poor Law ; [2] and not for forty years afterwards any common action as to road maintenance.[3]

The thirty Island parishes, having an average population during the first three quarters of the eighteenth century of a few score families, were plainly incapable of organising separately any sort of Poor Law institution (though Newport had some sort of workhouse in 1732) ; and their Poor Law administration had evidently remained of the most primitive rural type. In 1770, when the Suffolk and Norfolk Houses of Industry were still in the first flush of reputed success, the principal gentry and clergy of the Island met and decided to promote a bill to enable them to follow so promising an example. Under the Local Act of that session an Incorporation was formed exactly on the model of those of the Suffolk Hundreds. Eighty acres of Parkhurst Forest were acquired from the Crown, and

<hr />

[1] *The Parish and the County*, by S. and B. Webb, 1907,. p. 429.

[2] For the Incorporated Guardians of the Poor of the Isle of Wight, see the Acts 11 George III. c. 43 (1771), and 16 George III. c. 53 (1776) ; *General View of the Agriculture of the County of Hants*, by Abraham and William Driver, 1794 (containing a special section on the Isle of Wight by Rev. R. Warner) ; a long description in *The State of the Poor*, by Sir F. M. Eden, 1797, vol. ii. pp. 233-266 ; Report of House of Commons Committee on Poor Laws, 1817 (Sewell's evidence) ; First Report of Poor Law Inquiry Commissioners, 1834, Appendix A, Pringle's Report, p. 305 ; *The Isle of Wight System of Roads, and System of Guardians of the Poor, not a Model, but a Warning to the Legislature*, 1845.

[3] In 1813 the Isle of Wight Turnpike Trust was formed, by 53 George III. c. 92 ; and did not come to an end until superseded by the County Council instituted for the Island under the Local Government Act of 1888 (*The Story of the King's Highway*, by S. and B. Webb, 1913, p. 236).

a spacious House of Industry was erected to accommodate no fewer than 700 paupers, who were employed in agriculture, making corn sacks, weaving linsey woolsey, knitting stockings, embroidery and lacemaking. Notwithstanding a lengthy description by Sir F. M. Eden, we know little of the actual working of this constitution. The House of Industry long continued to enjoy a reputation for moderate success, though the industrial enterprises yielded a very doubtful profit, and the Poor Rates were apparently not reduced. We hear, at any rate, of no desire to revert to parochial management.[1]

There is something pathetic in the dismal uniformity of the stories of the actual working of the carefully organised administrations of all these bodies of Incorporated Guardians of the Suffolk type. The substitution of the enlightened and public-spirited squires and incumbents for the selfish and ignorant parish officers, and the organisation of the labour of the paupers in a House of Industry, were everywhere going to reduce the Poor Rates, and at the same time to afford a better provision for the children, the sick and the aged. And there is reason to believe that, for a few years in each case, the new bodies not only made better institutional provision for the aged, the sick and the infirm, but also effected some considerable reduction of actual pauperism. As the parishes had to contribute rateably to the common charge, whether or not they made use of the new institution, they promptly disburdened themselves of all their poor, directing them all to go to the House of Industry, and refusing all outdoor relief.[2] So drastically was the reform effected in Suffolk during the first few years that the common people rose in revolt ; and we hope, in a future volume on Poverty and Crime, to describe the picturesque little Suffolk rebellion of 1765, when a formidable mob, armed with cudgels and scythes, perambulated the County for a week, demolishing the new workhouses and compelling Directors and Acting Guardians to sign written promises to desist

---

[1] Another union of rural parishes was established in Sussex in 1812 (West-firle, etc., Act).

[2] The efficacy of this "test" in reducing the number of paupers was everywhere seen. Its drawbacks were not at first noticed. "This was an important point gained," says a writer of 1813, "but many were unable to maintain themselves, and unhappily were too refractory to accept of their maintenance in the House. These necessarily commenced itinerant beggars, and got a miserable livelihood by wandering through the neighbouring parishes" (*General View of the Agriculture of North Wales*, by Walter Davies, 1813, p. 433).

from erecting such places in which to imprison the poor—demanding, on the contrary, " that the poor should be maintained as usual ; that they should range at liberty and be their own masters." [1]   When this miniature rebellion had been put down by a troop of dragoons, the erection of the Houses of Industry was continued, and the poor were swept into them. The new buildings were, relatively to anything that had previously existed in the separate parishes, spacious and well planned. [2] The arrangements were carefully considered and humanely designed. [3]   In their provision for the education of the children and for the medical attendance and nursing of the sick [4] they seemed to con-

[1] *A Letter to J. W., Esq., relating to Mr. G——y's Pamphlet upon the Poor Laws, etc.*, by XX, 1766.

[2] " I generally found," said an Assistant Poor Law Commissioner in 1835, " the House of Industry a substantially built and sometimes a handsome structure. The Stow Hundred House had so palatial a character that I was tempted to enquire whether any peculiar concurrence of circumstances had occasioned the erection of an edifice, the appearance of which seemed to me so little in unison with the wants of the houseless and necessitous poor. . . . My enquiry soon elicited information that the character of the structure had been usually attributed to the circumstance that it was situated in the immediate vicinity of the country-seats of the Directors, who were naturally inclined to adorn rather than disfigure the landscape. The future subject of chagrin had not been anticipated: the Hundred House eclipsed some of the neighbouring mansions ! " (Second Annual Report of the Poor Law Commissioners, 1836, p. 155).

[3] In the Suffolk Houses of Industry it was said, in 1775, " of the aged no labour is required ; their silver cord is loosed, and their golden bowl broken ; the evening of their days is here made comfortable ; they are rescued from want, and consigned to respect and tranquillity ; to them the doors are always open, and whenever inclination and the weather tempts them abroad and their strength permits, all proper indulgence is allowed ; or in the House they have the liberty of decent rooms, where they form their little parties of conversation, sit around the fire, and tell their tales of ancient times.   Every married couple has a bed and a room distinct and appropriated to themselves, which they have the liberty to lock up if they please, to retire to it when they please, undisturbed, unintruded upon by others ; and their children, if young, are lodged in the same or the adjoining apartments, under the immediate care of their parents. And indeed, these decent lodgings for the married constitute one of the most striking beauties and conveniences of each House " (*Observations on the Poor Laws*, by R. Potter, 1775, p. 41).

[4] " Infirmaries are provided at a proper distance, that the disease may not be communicated to others. . . . At Bulcamp there is also an Airing House to receive them for a time after their recovery, that no remains of the disease may annoy others ; a caution worthy of imitation " (*Observations on the Poor Laws*, by R. Potter, 1775, p. 39).   Nevertheless, there was a terrible " putrid fever " at the Bulcamp House in 1781 (*History of the Poor Laws*, by Thomas Ruggles, 1794, vol. ii. p. 266).   " Ordered that seven handbarrows be provided for the more safe and easy conveyance of persons to the House of Industry with broken limbs " (MS. Minutes, Incorporated Guardians, Colneis and Carlford, 31st January 1760).

stitute an advance on anything that had hitherto been done for
the rural poor. "The poor came to us," says the worthy
originator of the first of these Incorporations, "in a most miserable and filthy condition ; they were clothed in rags, and some
of them, the children especially, almost literally naked. We
expected and were prepared for this, so that to prevent the introduction of vermin, before they were admitted they were shaved
and cleansed thoroughly by washing in warm water, and then all
new clothed throughout from head to foot." [1] It was impossible,
as a later critic observed, to refuse approval to "institutions that
forced cleanliness upon those who are dirty, and wholesome food
upon those of depraved appetites." [2] Yet, within a very few years
in each case we see the eulogistic descriptions of the first period
succeeded by grave complaints.[3] The cost of maintenance
rises ; the industrial enterprises invariably become unprofitable ;
the Houses of Industry are decimated by epidemics, and plainly
have an excessive death-rate; they even become places of horrible
demoralisation and disorder. A critic of 1813 observes that
"In whatever light these institutions are viewed . . . there is
scarcely anything to be perceived but degeneracy and ultimate
disappointment. Persons of judgment and deliberate reflection,
who once thought favourably of them, now produce reasons for
their apostasy . . . both in point of expense, and the morals
of the poor youth brought up there ; as well as the unnatural
state the old and infirm are confined to, among strangers who
cannot be supposed capable of much sympathy. Experience
also teaches us that the children brought up in such places, when
grown up are fit only for a manufactory . . . not for outdoor
employments, except, indeed, the men become soldiers (such as
they be) and the females . . . often have recourse to prostitu-

---

[1] Rev. R. Canning, in *The Christian's Magazine*, vol. iii. 1763, p. 30.
[2] *General View of the Agriculture of Shropshire*, by Joseph Plymley, 1803,
p. 131.
[3] For the complaints against the Houses of Industry of Suffolk and Norfolk,
and the management of the Incorporated Guardians, see *The Report of the Committee appointed to inquire into the Actual State of the House of Industry at
Melton*, 1791 ; *An Account of the Proceedings of the Special Committee . . . to
enquire into the Expenditure in the House of Industry at Heckingham*, 1793 ;
*Report of the Committee . . . Loes and Wilford . . . to investigate the Receipts
and Expenditure, etc.*, 1825 ; *Ipswich Journal*, 22nd October 1825 ; First Report
of Poor Law Inquiry Commissioners, 1834, Appendix C, pp. 187-198, 203-204 ;
First, Second and Ninth Annual Reports of Poor Law Commissioners, 1835,
1836 and 1843.

tion." [1] Presently the constituent parishes, not finding their
Poor Rates reduced, and gradually discovering both the un-
profitableness of the enterprise and the demoralisation of the
inmates, themselves revolt against the system ; eagerly revert
to the grant of doles, and strive to reassume the management of
their own poor. In case after case, they obtain new Local Acts ;
sometimes according new powers and removing restrictions found
to be inconvenient ; sometimes fundamentally changing the
constitution, sweeping away the gentry and clergy, and replacing
them by a board elected by the parish Vestries ; [2] sometimes,
again, dissolving the Incorporation, selling or demolishing the
workhouse, and reverting to the parochial administration of the
Poor Law.[3] Already in 1813 it could be confidently predicted
that " These elegant structures will become deserted fabrics." [4]
For this uniform failure, there were, as the student will have seen,
abundant causes in the nature of the legal constitutions with which
these Incorporated Guardians were equipped, and in the absence
both of any continuous administration by devoted amateurs and
of any class of salaried officials competent for such a task. But it
would be to miss the most important results of their experience
if we did not here mention, what we hope hereafter to demonstrate in a subsequent volume on Poverty and Vagrancy, that the
principal object of all of them—that of so organising the labour
of the paupers as to make them a self-supporting community—
was, from the outset, a wholly impracticable one. Though this
golden dream did not finally fade out of the imagination, even of
competent Poor Law experts, until the reign of Victoria—though
it still periodically captivates the unwary—it was, we think, the

[1] *General View of the Agriculture of North Wales*, by Walter Davies, 1813,
p. 434. " The twenty-five parishes incorporated " [in the Samford Hundred],
we are told in 1797, " are almost unanimous in wishing to have the Incorporation dissolved ; as they think they can maintain their poor at less expense,
and with more comfort, at home ; but this measure is strenuously resisted
by a neighbouring gentleman " (*The State of the Poor*, by Sir F. M. Eden, 1797,
vol. ii. p. 692).

[2] As in the case of Forehoe (3 & 4 William IV. c. 107, 1833).

[3] As in the cases of Cosford and Polsted (47 George III. sess. 2, c. 73, 1807) ;
Loes and Wilford (7 George IV. c. 1, 1826) ; and Shrewsbury (7 George IV. c.
141, 1826).

[4] It is characteristic of the time that the writer remarks that " it is to
be regretted they were not erected on some powerful streams, that in case
they failed of their primary object, they might be converted into woollen or
cloth manufactories " (*General View of the Agriculture of North Wales*, by
Walter Davies, 1813, p. 433).

experience of the Incorporated Guardians of the Suffolk and
Norfolk Hundreds, together with that of the Shrewsbury House
of Industry and the Bristol Hospital of St. Peter, that actually
caused it to be abandoned by all competent Poor Law students.
The factors at Norwich, through whom the woollen yarn was
disposed of, were, to say the least of it, neither zealous nor
scrupulously honest.[1]   At House after House the various manufacturing industries that were tried had eventually to be given up,
owing to the impossibility of so buying and selling, and so organising the labour, as to make a profit.   The Houses of Industry
became then mere places to which the sick and impotent poor
were driven, and to which resorted such dissolute and worthless
persons as found the lax promiscuity not unpleasant.[2]   " It has
. . . been long a practice," said the Loes and Wilford Committee in 1791, " to receive into your House at the approach of
winter a number of lazy, notorious and abandoned prostitutes
who, tainted with the foulest of diseases, resort thither for cure ;
and when the summer advances then quit their retreat . . . often
leaving as a pledge an unaffiliated child : and this, all, with impunity.   Nay, instead of being kept apart, and fed on the
meanest viands, and compelled to a severe species of toil, the most
profligate of them are permitted in habits of familiar intercourse,
and even to board and to bed, not only with each other, but with
others of better character, and especially the young." [3]   Nor did
their character improve.   " Everybody concerned," wrote a
correspondent of the *Ipswich Journal* in 1825, " knows that this

---

[1] *Report of the Committee appointed to inquire into the Actual State of the
House of Industry at Melton*, 1791.

[2] It was at this stage that the Suffolk Houses of Industry were scathingly
described by Crabbe ; see *The Borough*, 1808 (Letter XVIII., " The Poor and
their Dwellings "). In footnotes to this eloquent poem, in the collected edition
of his *Works* (by his son, 1810), it is said, of systems of Poor Relief, " Of one
method only I venture to give my sentiments—that of collecting the poor of
a Hundred into one building. This admission of a vast number of persons,
of all ages and both sexes, of very different inclinations, habits and capacities,
into a society, must, at a first view, I conceive, be looked upon as a cause of
both vice and misery ; nor does anything which I have heard or read invalidate
the opinion : happily the method is not a prevailing one, as these Houses are
I believe still confined to that part of the kingdom where they originated
(p. 242). . . . These odious Houses of Industry seem, thank God, to exist only
in Suffolk, near the first founder's residence (one proof they are not very beneficial), in which the poor of a whole Hundred are collected in one building—
well fed and clothed I grant—but imprisoned for life " (p. 234).

[3] *Report of the Committee appointed to inquire into the Actual State of the
House of Industry at Melton*, 1791, p. 10.

House has been made use of as a kind of second-hand prison for all the incorrigible, pilfering rogues and vagabonds among the men, and all the worthless strumpets and vilest among women— in short the very scum of the Hundreds." [1]

The Vestry Executive

We need not dwell at any great length upon the remaining types of Incorporated Guardians of the Poor. Where the parish was large and populous, there seemed no need for union with other parishes ; but the lack of adequate authority to buy and build and manage an extensive institution, and the vagueness of the powers of the parish officers, sometimes led to the creation of a statutory executive, nevertheless retaining some connection with the " inhabitants in Vestry assembled."   Thus, the growing parish of Manchester, which had tried to get a statutory Corporation of the Poor in 1731, but had failed through sectarian jealousies,[2] obtained an Act in 1790, by which the Churchwardens and Overseers for the time being were themselves created a corporate body, expressly empowered to borrow money, and to maintain the workhouse, whilst remaining individually in the old relation to the Vestry.

We may note a few other examples of this creation of a statutory body to serve as an executive for the Parish Vestry.[3] In the important parish of Birmingham an exceptionally democratic Local Act of 1783 (23 George III. c. 54) established a body of 108 " fit and substantial persons " as Guardians of the Poor, to be elected every three years by all the ten-pound ratepayers.   Power to appoint Assistant Overseers and to pay them by poundage had to be obtained by a second Act in 1806 (46 George III. c. 44).   Additional powers were given by another Local Act in 1831 (1 & 2 William IV. c. 67) ; but it is significant that the franchise was then raised from a £10 to a £12 rating occupancy, whilst the qualification for a Guardian was fixed at

[1] *Ipswich Journal*, 12th March 1825.
[2] *History of the County Palatine of Lancaster*, by Edward Baines, 1836, vol. ii. pp. 293, 306 ; *Municipal Origins*, by F. H. Spencer, 1911, p. 14.
[3] See the Act 30 George III. c. 81 ; *Municipal Origins*, by F. H. Spencer, 1911, 17, 305 ; *A Report of the Committee of the Associated Leypayers of the Township of Manchester*, 1794 ; and other local sources cited in *The Parish and the County*, by S. and B. Webb, 1907.

occupancy of a £20 tenement. This last Act is interesting chiefly as giving the first statutory authority for the establishment of a creche, as a means not so much of educating the children as of preventing juvenile crime ; and perhaps also of facilitating the industrial employment of women by manufacturers eager for cheaper labour. The Guardians were empowered to rent rooms for the reception of any children of the " poor of the parish," whose parents were willing to place them during working hours in the Guardians' care, for employment in such manner as the Guardians might decide under the supervision of a salaried caretaker.[1] Unfortunately, as we learn in 1843, this interesting experiment was never put in operation.

But it was in the densely populated parishes of the Metropolitan area that we find the largest number of statutory bodies formed, virtually, as executives for the ancient Vestry. In the eighty years between 1750 and 1830 there were established more than fifty such bodies, usually for single parishes, large or small ; but occasionally (as in the case of St. Nicholas and St. Paul, Deptford) for combinations of adjacent parishes. The Churchwardens and Overseers are nearly always ex-officio members, and frequently also the Rector or Vicar, together with a prescribed number of " substantial and discreet persons," elected by the inhabitants in Vestry assembled, or by the Close Vestry itself. The variety of these constitutions in detail is, however, almost endless ;[2] and there is noticeable a tendency to replace

---

[1] *Municipal Origins*, by F. H. Spencer, 1911, pp. 295-296. The preamble of the Act (1 & 2 William IV. c. 67) is worth quotation : " And whereas many persons in the said town of Birmingham, who receive parochial relief, would be enabled to provide for their families by their industry if their children under seven years of age could be taken care of during the hours of labour, and it would greatly tend to diminish crime and the number of juvenile offenders and pauperism if such children were placed during such period in some room or place for their protection ; and whereas it would be beneficial if the Guardians had authority to apply for the purposes aforesaid a portion of the relief which such persons would otherwise receive for their children." For the contemporary evolution of local government in Birmingham, see *The Manor and the Borough*, by S. and B. Webb, 1908, pp. 157-160.

[2] See the analysis given in *Municipal Origins*, by F. H. Spencer, 1911, pp. 116-126, and Ninth Annual Report of Poor Law Commissioners, 1843, pp. 230-251.
Among the bodies thus established may be mentioned the Guardians (or Trustees, or Governors and Directors) of the Poor of East Greenwich (26 George II. c. 100 ; 9 George IV. c. 43) ; Christchurch (26 George II. c. 98 ; 37 George III. c. 79) ; St. Nicholas and St. Paul, Deptford (27 George II. c. 38) ; St. Luke's (30 George II. c. 42) ; Bermondsey (31 George II. c. 45 ; 31 George III.

L

the elective element by persons named in the Act, renewable by co-option. Their statutory functions were more nearly identical. They were empowered to acquire or erect a workhouse, and to provide within for the poor, either by employment or otherwise ; to teach or apprentice the children ; to apprehend vagrants, beggars, wandering persons or deserted children, and to send them to the workhouse ; to call upon the Vestry to levy rates for all the expenses, and in default, to levy the necessary rate directly upon the inhabitants.[1]

The Reorganised Vestry

In a small number of cases, nearly all in the Metropolitan area, we find the Parish Vestry itself superseded, either at once, or by a subsequent Act, by transformation into a new statutory body, on which the desired additional powers are conferred. We have, in our book on *The Parish and the County*, sufficiently described the evolution of these parish constitutions. In some

---

c. 19) ; St. James, Westminster (2 George III. c. 58) ; St. Matthew, Bethnal Green (3 George III. c. 40) ; St. Mary, Whitechapel (3 George III. c. 53) ; St. Andrew, Holborn, and St. George the Martyr (6 George III. c. 100 ; 6 George IV. c. 175) ; St. Botolph, Aldgate (6 George III. c. 64) ; Liberty of Saffron Hill, Hatton Garden, and Ely Rents (10 George III. c. 80) ; St. Martin's in the Fields (10 George III. c. 75) ; St. Botolph, Bishopsgate (12 George III. c. 79) ; St. Sepulchre (12 George III. c. 68) ; Old Artillery Ground (14 George III. c. 30) ; St. Saviour's, Southwark (14 George III. c. 75) ; St. Leonard, Shoreditch (14 George III. c. 29 ; 53 George III. c. 112) ; St. Giles in the Fields and St. George, Bloomsbury (14 George III. c. 108) ; St. Marylebone (15 George III. c. 21) ; St. Mary, Islington (17 George III. c. 5) ; St. James and St. John, Clerkenwell (15 George III. c. 23) ; Mile End (20 George III. c. 66 ; 53 George III. c. 37) ; St. John, Wapping (22 George III. c. 35 ; 23 George III. c. 32 ; 59 George III. c. 15) ; St. John, Southwark (26 George III. c. 114) ; St. George's, Hanover Square (29 George III. c. 75) ; Hampstead (39 & 40 George III. c. 35) ; St. Pancras (44 George III. c. 47 ; 45 George III. c. 99) ; Woolwich (47 George III. c. 3) ; St. George's in the East (46 George III. c. 46) ; Ratcliffe (50 George III. c. 83) ; St. John, Hackney (50 George III. c. 190) ; Poplar (53 George III. c. 84) ; Liberty of the Rolls (50 George III. c. 84) ; Paddington (5 George IV. c. 126) ; Lewisham (54 George III. c. 43) ; St. Bride's, Fleet Street (7 George IV. c. 114).

[1] The Metropolitan statutory Poor Law bodies have been even less studied than those of provincial cities or rural Hundreds. They are usually quite ignored by the parish historians. We have been able to consult the MS. Minutes of those of Paddington, St. Pancras, Islington, Marylebone, Woolwich and various parishes in the City of London ; see the index references in *The Parish and the County* and *The Manor and the Borough*, by S. and B. Webb. Much useful information is afforded by *Municipal Origins*, by F. H. Spencer, 1911.

cases—as at Woolwich in 1807,[1] at Chelsea in 1821, at Islington and Paddington in 1825, and at Kensington in 1826—we have the transformation of the Open Vestry, which might be attended by all the adult inhabitants, into a more or less representative body, of which at least a substantial portion was annually elected by the more substantial householders. In a few instances, as we have described in Marylebone in 1768 and St. Pancras in 1819,[2] we see the peremptory supersession of the Open Vestry by a body of persons designated in the Act, and renewing themselves by co-option.

The Experience and the Outcome of the Incorporated Guardians

The long drawn-out experiments in the establishment of incorporated bodies for Poor Law administration—extending as they do over a century and three-quarters, and relating to both rural and urban conditions in all parts of the country—make up a confused medley which it is difficult to analyse or to classify. With regard to constitutional structure, we have to note that, whilst invariably including in their membership a strong ex-officio element, the new Poor Law bodies introduced what was then a novel feature, in that they nearly always depended, to some extent at least, upon popular choice, either by nomination by the Vestry, or by actual election by the inhabitants, with or without a definite qualification for the franchise. In this respect they differed essentially in form from the Court of Sewers that we described in our last chapter, and even from the Turnpike Trusts and the Improvement Commissions, which stand, on the whole, subsequently to them in date, and will be described in the chapters that follow. The relief of the poor, at that time wholly defrayed from the proceeds of the local rates, was apparently regarded, even by the Parliaments of the period, as rightly involving at any rate some degree of democratic control.

To pass from the constitution of these statutory Poor Law bodies to their working—that is, to the practical effect for good or evil of all this organisation—we must confess to having neither the information nor the time needful for any accurate estimate

[1] As to this, see the graphic vision of "parish politics" given in *Municipal Origins*, by F. H. Spencer, 1911, pp. 22-32.
[2] *The Parish and the County*, by S. and B. Webb, 1907; for Marylebone, see also *Municipal Origins*, by F. H. Spencer, 1911, pp. 15-19.

of the total result ; and this, in any case, would be more appro-
priately dealt with in connection with the history of Poor Law
administration in general.   But from such evidence as we have
been able to study, we have formed a few general impressions,
which may here be given, as to the peculiar advantages and
disadvantages of these statutory Poor Law authorities, as compared with the ordinary parish government of the time.   The
statutory authorities had, in general, the advantage of substituting for annually changing, and often unwilling individual
administrators, a continuously existing and deliberately selected
council, acting through salaried officials.   Hence we watch, in
the Incorporated Guardians, the initiation of something like
Poor Law policy ; always crudely empirical and usually ill-
adapted to attain its end, but superior, by the mere fact of being
a policy, to the variable and haphazard action of individual
Overseers.   It was, perhaps, an accident that all the Incorporated
Guardians made the workhouse an essential part of Poor Law
administration.   They wanted the workhouse for an impracticable end, namely to organise profitably the labour of the paupers.
Incidentally, however, they introduced what was at the time
the only practicable " test " of the genuineness of able-bodied
destitution—the " offer of the House," [1] with the usual result
of greatly diminishing pauperism in the earlier years of their
existence.   This advantage they usually lost after a short time,
owing to their failure to recognise the device which they began
by unconsciously adopting.   A more equivocal expedient, at
any rate under the unscientific administration of the period,
was the institutional treatment of the children,[2] the infirm and
the aged.   Finally, it must be remembered that more than a
third of the statutory Poor Law authorities had the undoubted
advantage of combining a number of small or thinly populated

    [1] " It is probable that at the passing of Sir Edward Knatchbull's Act in
1722, the actual effects of the Local Acts had suggested sounder views as to
the specific utility of workhouse management, for . . . workhouses were . . .
used, with the greatest effect, strictly as tests of destitution. . . . The effect
of these workhouses in reducing the poor rates in many of the parishes appears
to have been immediate, and the reduction varied from 25 to 65 per cent on
the previous expenditure " (Mr. Twistleton's Report on Local Acts, in Ninth
Annual Report of the Poor Law Commissioners, 1843, pp. 96-97).
    [2] The Bristol Corporation of the Poor started by collecting over two hundred
children in their workhouse (Transactions of the Corporation of the Poor in the
City of Bristol during a period of 126 years, by James Johnson (Bristol, 1826),
p. 21).

parishes into a union large enough to escape the greater part of the difficulties presented by the Law of Settlement, as well as to admit of some sort of classification of paupers, and the employment of permanent salaried officials.[1] On the other hand, it was a grave drawback that these statutory Poor Law authorities escaped all outside control. Such authoritative criticism, audit and control as were elsewhere given to the Overseers by Petty Sessions, individual Justices of the Peace and the Open Vestry were, to all intents and purposes, non-existent for the statutory body ; and there was, as yet, no central authority to take their place. This independence was the more dangerous in that the Incorporated Guardians sat always in secret, published no accounts or regular reports and were subject to no outside inspection.[2] They were moreover endowed, by the careless apathy of Parliament, with extensive powers of apprehending, detaining, controlling and punishing, entirely at their own discretion and without appeal, not only the inmates of their institutions, but also such " idlers and vagrants " as they chose to arrest. These unpleasant characteristics were seen at their worst in those cases in which the statutory authority was entirely independent of popular election. The greatest failures of all

---

[1] In Bristol, and most of the city Incorporations formed upon its model, there was the further advantage of a common system of assessment and rate collection for the whole city. " The whole city," writes the enthusiastic annalist of the Bristol Corporation of the Poor, " became, after 1696, as one parish, and one law officer did the business in which nineteen had been employed before. Another great advantage arose in having one general rate or assessment made upon the whole city, and not on each parish separately, the magistrates having the power to apportion out the sum required for each year's service of the poor, amongst the different parishes according to their ability to pay it " (*Transactions of the Corporation of the Poor in the City of Bristol during a period of 126 years*, by James Johnson, p. 7). Stress had been laid on this advantage in John Locke's report of 1697, " that in all cities and towns corporate the poor's rate be not levied by distinct parishes but by one equal tax throughout the whole corporation " (*Report of the Board of Trade to the Lord Justices in the year 1697*, reprint of 1787, p. 112).

[2] The Plymouth Incorporated Guardians expressly refused, in 1813, a request that the Mayor should be empowered to inspect their " ill-arranged mass of buildings in the centre of the town." ";That this Court, after due consideration, cannot consistently accede to the proposition that a clause be inserted in the bill, or that the bill be so altered and amended to allow the Chief Magistrate or other acting magistrate of the Borough free admission into the House of Correction within the workhouse and to visit all the prisoners confined therein " (MS. Minutes, Incorporated Guardians of Plymouth, 28th April 1813) ; Ninth Annual Report of Poor Law Commissioners, 1843, pp. 83-123 ; *The State of the Poor*, by Sir F. M. Eden, 1797, vol. i. p. 257.

were the Suffolk and Norfolk Unions where the governing council was nominally composed of the whole body of wealthy residents. We do not pretend to be able to balance these advantages and disadvantages. Perhaps more important than any of them was the fact that these statutory bodies made experiments, which, unlike the casual expedients of the annually changing Overseer, were systematically recorded and could be subsequently investigated. Their experience in workhouse management was the means by which the idea of obtaining profit, or even maintenance, by " setting the poor " to work, was finally disposed of. Even more important in the evolution of English Local Government was the fact, to which we have already referred, that it was the statutory Poor Law authorities that—in contrast with the County Justices, the Manorial Courts, the Municipal Corporations and the Parish Vestries of the time, and also with the Courts of Sewers described in the preceding chapter—based their administration on appointed and permanently serving salaried officers, who were merely directed and supervised by committees of the governing body. In their " principle of combining an elective controlling power with a paid executive," [1] or as we should nowadays say, in their organisation of a primitive Civil Service under administrative committees, they stood in marked contrast both with the practice of previous English Local Authorities (and also with that of the contemporary New England townships), and they may almost be said to have originated the typical constitutional machinery of the English Local Government of to-day.

With the passing of the Poor Law Amendment Act of 1834 and the adoption of a policy of national uniformity in Poor Law administration, we may for the present leave the Incorporated Guardians.[2] The 1834 Act contemplated the prompt dissolution of these special bodies, and the merging of their areas in the new Unions to be formed. The Poor Law Commissioners were expressly empowered to issue their rules, orders and regulations

[1] First Report of Poor Law Inquiry Commissioners, 1834, Appendix A, Chapman's Report, pp. 522-523.

[2] Their subsequent history is to be traced, apart from their own voluminous MS. records, usually in the possession of the existing Board of Guardians for the locality, in the successive Annual Reports of the Poor Law Commissioners (especially the Ninth and Tenth); of the Poor Law Board (especially the Twentieth), and of the Local Government Board. See also *History of the English Poor Law*, by Thomas Mackay, 1899, pp. 331-340.

to all Unions and parishes under Local Acts; to change the areas of the Unions to which these Acts applied; to alter the method of election of their governing bodies, and even to dissolve any Union formed under Local Act. But in order to avoid opposition to the passing of the Bill from the Incorporated Guardians, who might have claimed to be heard by counsel, and who could have fomented considerable opposition, the power to alter the method of election was made subject to the consent of a majority of the local ratepayers and property owners, whilst the power to dissolve the Unions was made dependent on the prior consent of two-thirds of the Guardians themselves. Without power to dissolve, the Poor Law Commissioners were afraid peremptorily to command. The result was to delay for half a century the complete uniformity of Poor Law administration at which the Somerset House administrators persistently aimed. In 1843 the Poor Law Commissioners directed their Assistant Commissioners to make a special enquiry into the administration of all the Poor Law bodies claiming to exist under Local Acts, the results of which were published in the Ninth and Tenth Annual Reports of the Commissioners. In 1844, by 7 & 8 Victoria c. 101, the requirement that two-thirds of the Guardians must approve before the Incorporation could be dissolved was dispensed with as regards parishes of less than 20,000 population; and the smaller bodies were successively dissolved and their parishes absorbed into the new Unions. The Incorporated Guardians in the Metropolis and the large towns, dealing with populations exceeding 20,000, could still stand out, and they long continued to do so. Nearly a quarter of a century later, those in the London area were brought into line in 1867 by the operation of the Metropolitan Poor Act, 1867 (30 Victoria c. 6); which, with its establishment of a Common Poor Fund, permitted the Poor Law Board to assimilate all the Metropolitan parishes to a uniform system. Only very slowly and gradually were the remainder of the larger Local Act Incorporations, by successive slight acts of administrative pressure and encroachment by the Local Government Board, assimilated to the ordinary Unions created by administrative order, and brought into line with the rest of the Poor Law administration of the country.

CHAPTER III

THE TURNPIKE TRUSTS

AMONG all the Statutory Authorities, as we have called them—
the Local Governing Bodies established for particular places by
Special Acts of Parliament or Royal Commissions—the most
numerous were the Turnpike Trusts. Of Courts of Sewers in
England and Wales there may have been, at one time or another
during the eighteenth century, a hundred or so. Of Incorporated Guardians of the Poor we have particulars of about 125.
Of separate bodies of Police or Improvement Commissioners, large
or small, presently to be described, nearly three hundred may be
enumerated. But of Turnpike Trusts, from the beginning of the
eighteenth century, steadily increasing in number throughout a
century and a quarter, there came to be, by 1835, over 1100
simultaneously in existence ; or twice as many as all the other
kinds of Statutory Authorities put together. The Turnpike
Trusts were, in the first quarter of the nineteenth century, about
five times as numerous as the Municipal Corporations, and nearly
twenty times as numerous as the Courts of Quarter Sessions that
governed the Counties.[1] Only the immemorially ubiquitous
Parish and Manor, for which no statutory or other formal origin
can be assigned, exceeded them in number. In the records of
English Local Government of the eighteenth century, these Turnpike Trusts—which eventually levied an annual revenue of more
than one and a half millions sterling, accumulated a debt of seven
millions, and administered twenty-three thousand miles of road
—cut no mean figure. But their principal importance lies not in
their constitution but in their function. They are of interest
chiefly for the part they played, during a period of a century and

The Parish and the County, 1907 ; *The Manor and the Borough*, 1908.

a half, in the evolution of the immemorial public service of road maintenance. Their legal constitutions, for whatever place or in whatever decade they were established, were of one uniform pattern ; and the type showed little capacity for diversity of administrative procedure or extra-legal developments. The origin of these bodies ; their complicated relations to the Parish, to the County and to the whole community of road users ; and the intervention in their affairs, between 1800 and 1835, not only of Parliament but also of two government departments, all present features of interest to the student of the constitutional development of English Local Government as a whole.[1]

We need not repeat the account given elsewhere [2] of the

---

[1] Of the Turnpike Trusts no systematic history—apart from chap. vii. of our *Story of the King's Highway*, 1913, pp. 115-150, and vol. i. of *The Development of Transportation in Modern England*, by W. T. Jackman, 1916, pp. 61-283—has been written, and the student needing more detail than is supplied in these two books can only be referred to such general references and descriptions as are to be found in the *History of Private Bill Legislation*, by F. Clifford, 1885–1887, vol. ii. chap. vii. ; *A Treatise on Roads*, by Sir Henry Parnell, afterwards Lord Congleton, 1st edition, 1833, 2nd edition, 1838 ; *Life of Thomas Telford, Civil Engineer, Written by Himself*, edited by John Rickman, 1838 ; *Voyages dans la Grande Bretagne*, by Baron Charles Dupin, 1824, troisième partie, " Force Commerciale," vol. i. p. 33 ; *Descriptive and Statistical Account of the British Empire*, by J. R. M'Culloch, 1846, vol. ii. chap. v. sec. 3 ; and to the almost innumerable Parliamentary Reports on Highways and Turnpikes throughout the eighteenth and nineteenth centuries. A good vision of the working of a Turnpike Trust is afforded by the two Reports of a Select Committee on various Metropolitan Turnpikes, one printed at length in the House of Commons Journals for 1763 (vol. xxix. pp. 645-664), the other presented in 1765 ; in the brief account of the " Whetstone Turnpike Trust, 1754-1863," in *Middlesex and Hertfordshire Notes and Queries*, vol. iv. pp. 91-94 ; in *A Turnpike Key, or an Account of the Proceedings of the Exeter Turnpike Trustees*, 1753-1884, by W. Buckingham, 1885 ; and in the interesting volume entitled *Minutes of the Epping and Ongar Highway Trust*, 1769–1870, by Benjamin Winstone, 1891. Much incidental information of all sorts is afforded in the excellent manual, *Digests of the General Highway and Turnpike Laws*, by John Scott, 1778. *Rebecca and her Daughters*, by Henry Tobit Evans (Cardiff, 1910), supplies detailed information of the most notorious of Turnpike riots. The MS. Minutes of the eleven hundred Turnpike Trusts, where they are preserved at all, are mostly hidden away in solicitors' offices, but they are occasionally to be found among municipal or county archives. County Councils would be well advised to invite the local solicitors to place these records in safety at the County Hall. We have had access to the MS. Minutes of the Oldham Turnpike Trust, 1806–1880 ; the Dursley and Berkeley Turnpike Trust, 1779–1874, and a few others ; but we have found most information in the (literally) tens of thousands of bills, petitions, reports of committees and proceedings in Parliament relating to roads during the past two centuries, and in the innumerable references to the roads in the books and pamphlets cited in our *Story of the King's Highway* and in the present chapter. A fuller list will be found in the *Bibliography of Roadmaking and Roads in the United Kingdom*, by Dorothy Ballen, 1914.   [2] *The Story of the King's Highway*, 1913, chaps. i.-iv.

manner in which the English highways were constructed and maintained prior to the seventeenth century. At the accession of Queen Elizabeth, when English highways were perhaps at their worst, and even during most of the ensuing century, it is hardly an exaggeration to state, there was, from one end of England and Wales to the other, no such thing as a road in the modern meaning of the term. To the citizen of to-day the " King's Highway " appears as an endless strip of land, with definite boundaries, permanently and exclusively appropriated to the purpose of passage, and having a surface artificially prepared for its peculiar function. To the citizen of the twelfth, the fifteenth or even the eighteenth century, the " King's Highway " was a more abstract conception. It was not a strip of land, or any corporeal thing, but a legal and customary right—as the lawyers said, " a perpetual right of passage in the Sovereign for himself and his subjects over another's land." [1] What existed was, in fact, nothing but a right of way, from village to village, along a certain customary course, which, if much frequented, became a beaten track. And we must add to this understanding of the immemorial highways that they were used, by the inhabitants of the locality, almost exclusively for foot traffic, of man or beast. That the ways must in winter be impassable for wheeled traffic was habitually taken for granted. This primitive conception of locomotive needs lasted, in remote corners of England, right down to the end of the eighteenth

[1] See, for instance, Rolle's *Abridgement*, title " Chimin," p. 392, where it is laid down that " the King has nothing but a perpetual right of passage for himself and his people " ; or *The Law Relating to Highways*, by W. C. and A. Glen, 1897. Thus, to this day, " the right of the public in a highway is an easement of passage only—a right of passing and repassing. In the language of pleading, a party can only justify passing along, not being in, a highway " (*Pratt and Mackenzie's Law of Highways*, by William W. Mackenzie, 16th edition, 1911, p. 2). Hence it has been expressly held that there is no right to use a highway for racing, or for a public meeting (*ibid.*) ; nor may a man stand still on the road to shoot pheasants flying over it (R. v. Pratt, 1855, 4 E. and B. 860). He may not even walk up and down so as maliciously to interfere with others' rights (Harrison v. Duke of Rutland, 1893, 1 Q.B. 142)—see *The Common Law of England*, by Blake Odgers, 1911, vol. i. pp. 7-10. It is only inferentially that it has quite recently been suggested that a passenger along a highway may lawfully stop to rest on it for a short time, or to take a sketch (per A. L. Smith, L.J. in Hickman v. Matsey, 1900, 1 Q.B. 756). Any other use of a highway is a trespass.

But in legal definitions, as in common parlance, the term highway is now used to denote the land as well as the easement. " The term highway in its widest sense comprises *all portions of land* over which every subject of the Crown may lawfully pass " (*Pratt and Mackenzie's Law of Highways*, by W. W. Mackenzie, 16th edition, 1911, p. 1).

century. In Cumberland, we are told, "in the Spring of the year the Surveyor used to call on the people to go with him to open the tracks over the common, from which the old tumble-wheel carts of the country had been excluded during the winter ; for, in 1792, the principal part of the corn was conveyed to market on the backs of horses." [1] The ideal of road maintenance which the old-fashioned Englishman set before himself was, in fact, no more than " removing every kind of impediment that incommodes or molests the traveller, such as want of proper drains, overhanging trees and hedges, timber-logs, etc." ; in short, everything " that prevents the roads from growing better of themselves." [2] It was the obligation to maintain a highway of this kind— that is, a free passage from village to village—that had been, at common law, and by the statute of 1555,[3] cast upon the Parish ; and it was this obligation that was assumed to be fulfilled, down to 1835, by the system of six days forced " Statute Labour," to be rendered by all householders, under the superintendence of one of them, compulsorily serving his year as Surveyor of Highways ; the whole under the authority of the Justices of the Peace. If the Parish failed to fulfil this obligation of road maintenance, it could, as we have described in *The Story of the King's Highway*, be indicted and fined in the Courts of Justice. It was a comparatively late development when the Parish was allowed, with the sanction of Quarter Sessions, to levy a limited Highway Rate, in those cases in which the " Statute Labour " had proved to be insufficient to keep up the free passage. [4]

[1] Speech by W. Blamire, *Cumberland Pacquet*, 2nd February 1830.
[2] *A General Plan of Parochial Police*, by W. M. Godschall, 1787, p. 60.
[3] 2 & 3 Philip and Mary c. 8, 1555.
[4] So far as we are aware, the earliest rates levied by Parishes or Counties for road maintenance occurred under the Commonwealth (see our *Story of the King's Highway*, 1913, pp. 20-23, 25 ; *A Proposal for Maintaining and Repairing the Highways*, by E. Littleton, 1692, p. 10 ; *Three Centuries of Derbyshire Annals*, by J. C. Cox, 1890, vol. ii. p. 227 ; *The Interregnum*, by F. C. Inderwick, 1891, p. 107). Such rates, as we have described, were authorised temporarily by statutes of 1662 and 1670 (13 & 14 Car. II. c. 6, and 22 Car. II. c. 12) ; and we find them, though very exceptionally, actually levied (*e.g.* MS. Churchwardens' Accounts, St. Mary's, Reading, Berkshire, 22nd May 1670, 24th April and 15th September 1671, 31st March 1673, 12th April 1680) ; in one case, even as early as 1663, when the Manorial Court of Spittal and Tweedmouth mentions " the assessment that was gathered for repairing the highways " (see *The Manor and the Borough*, by S. and B. Webb, 1908, vol. i. p. 95). But not until after 1691 (3 William and Mary, c. 12) do they become frequent ; and not until 1835 could they be levied by the Parish, as a matter of course, without the special sanction of the Justices in each case.

During the seventeenth, and still more during the eighteenth century, we see constantly increasing what was practically a new use of the roads, namely the through traffic of wheeled vehicles of every kind. The soft tracks, with which the local agriculturists had contented themselves, proved quite insufficient to bear the waggons, carts, post-chaises and coaches by which they were now coming to be thronged. In 1694—to trouble the reader with only one quotation—" the highways . . . were grown so foundrous (as the law terms it) and so extremely bad, that the owners and occupiers of lands in most places have been necessitated to suffer their fences to lie down, and to permit people to travel over their enclosed ground . . . by reason of the impassableness of the highways."[1] Meanwhile, the parishes through which the main thoroughfares of the nation passed, were complaining that, owing to this new use of the King's Highway, it had " become so ruinous and almost impassable that the ordinary course appointed by all former laws and statutes of this realm is not sufficient for the effectual repairing of the same." [2] To cope with this difficulty, one locality after another petitioned Parliament to permit the taxation of the users of the road. We find the suggestion in Littleton's pamphlet of 1692. " Every person," it was urged, as came to be taken for granted for the ensuing century and a half,[3] " ought to contribute to the repair of roads in proportion to the use they make of, or the convenience that they derive from them." Moreover, the increasing traffic called, in some places, actually for new roads, or for the re-making of bits of road. Neither the Parish, nor any other authority, had power to make a new road ; a power which could be given only by special statute, for which the principal inhabitants of this or that locality would petition. From the Restoration onwards,

[1] *A Guide to Surveyors of the Highways*, by G. Meriton, 1694. Already in 1610 we hear of " great hurt and spoil of fences and grounds, with riding and going over the corn, and such like, by shifting and seeking the best way diversely " (*A Profitable Work to this Whole Kingdom concerning the Mending of the Highways*, by Thomas Procter, 1610). It had long before been held by the judges that if the beaten track became foundrous the King's subjects might diverge from it, in their right of passage, even to the extent of " going upon the corn " (*A Treatise of the Pleas of the Crown*, by W. Hawkins, edited by T. Leach, 1795, vol. i. p. 153).

[2] 15 Car. II. c. 1, 1663.

[3] *A Proposal for Maintaining and Repairing the Highways*, by E. Littleton, 1692, p. 11 ; *An Inquiry into the Means of Preserving the Public Roads*, by Rev. Henry Homer, 1765, p. 18.

successive Parliaments, falling back on certain mediaeval precedents,[1] acceded to these requests. Hence the turnpike [2] and its toll.

The power of taking toll of passengers, and expending its proceeds on the maintenance of the road, was, however, first granted, not to special bodies established for the purpose, but to the Justices of the Peace in Quarter Sessions.

In 1656, the Vestry of the little parish of Radwell, in Hertfordshire, petitioned Quarter Sessions for help with its roads. In vain had the inhabitants tried to keep them in order ; these highways still " stand in much need of repair, which they are no ways able to perform (though the whole revenue of the parish should be employed), the Great North Road lying for two miles together in the said parish, and the nature of the soil being such as the winter devours whatsoever they are able to lay on in the summer, and the parish is so small that it hath in it all but two teams." In 1663, perhaps as a tardy outcome of this petition, it was represented to Parliament by the Justices of the Counties of Hertford, Cambridge and Huntingdon that " the ancient highway and post road leading from London to York, and so into Scotland . . . by reason of the great and many loads which are weekly drawn in waggons " to Ware (whence there was water carriage to London),

[1] Road tolls seem to have been unknown in England in 1650, as they had been for a century or more, except where a municipal corporation charged a Through Toll, or other *octroi*, and possibly in the case of a few private franchises as to bridges. Various isolated precedents for their levy by royal licence on particular stretches of road can be found in the records of the thirteenth and fourteenth centuries. Authority seems to have been given in 1267 to levy a toll in a Gloucestershire manor ; " capiat in feod unum dener, le quilibet caracte transeunte per manerie qua de Thormerton et Littleton " ; see Index of the Patent Rolls, Henry VII., and *Notes and Queries*, 27th December 1851. " In 1346 a toll for pavage was levied by the City authorities on vehicles passing from St. Giles in the Fields to Temple Bar " (*History of Private Bill Legislation*, by F. Clifford, 1885–1887, vol. i. pp. 4-5, vol. ii. pp. 3-8).

[2] The name " turnpike " was given from the adoption of " horizontal tapering bars of iron or wood suspended upon a rigid perpendicular pillar, around which, as an axis, they revolved. They corresponded," says an author of 1845, " with those modern cross wickets or sidegates, which may be seen in the vicinity of certain towns, with this difference that, until the dues or toll was paid, these pikes or styles could not be made to turn either to right or left " (*Road Reform*, by William Pagan, 1st edition, 1845, 3rd edition, 1857, p. 1). " A turnpike road," said a learned judge in 1840, " means a road having toll-gates or bars on it, which were originally called ' turns.' . . . The distinctive mark of a turnpike road is the right of turning back any one who refuses to pay toll " (Lord Abinger, C.B., in Northam Bridge Co. *v.* London and Southampton Railway Co., 1840, 6 M. & W. 428). " Pike " came popularly to be used for the toll-bar or toll-gate ; and also for the toll itself.

and " the great trade of barley and malt . . . is become so ruinous
and almost impassable that the ordinary course appointed by all
former laws and statutes of this realm is not sufficient for the
effectual repairing of the same." On this petition Parliament
fell back on various ancient precedents, and authorised, by a
special statute, each of these three Quarter Sessions to erect gates
and levy tolls at Wadesmill (Herts), Caxton (Cambridgeshire)
and Stilton (Huntingdonshire) respectively, for the next eleven
years, and to devote this revenue to specially repairing the parts
of the Great North Road within their respective jurisdictions.[1]
Only one of these three gates was successful. That at Stilton excited so much local opposition that it was never erected. That
at Caxton was put up, but was so easily evaded that practically
nothing was collected. The third, at Wadesmill, was thus the
first effective toll-gate in England. For over thirty years it seems
to have remained unique. A generation later, when the state of
the roads was exciting much attention, Parliament gave similar
powers by special statutes, in respect of other pieces of road, to the
Justices of Essex, Norfolk, Surrey, Gloucestershire, Somerset,
Cheshire, Bedfordshire, Wilts, Hampshire and Kent ; sometimes
to the Justices of a particular Division of the County in special
Highway Sessions, sometimes to a certain number of Justices
representing different Counties, but more usually to the Justices
of the whole County in Quarter Sessions assembled.[2] For fifteen

[1] 15 Car. II. c. 1 (1663) renewed by 26 Car. II. (1674), 4 & 5 William and
Mary (1692), and again by 6 Anne (1707), as to which see House of Commons
Journals, 8th, 21st, 27th January and 6th March 1707. The 1663 Act is
described in the *Story of the King's Highway*, pp. 115, 148 ; *History of Commerce*,
by A. Anderson, vol. v. p. 44 ; *A Treatise on Roads*, by Sir Henry Parnell,
afterwards Lord Congleton, 1833, p. 17 ; *History of Private Bill Legislation*, by
F. Clifford, 1885–1887, vol. ii. pp. 12-14 ; in " The Old North Road," by J. H.
Hinde, in *Archaeologia Aeliana*, part ix., 1858, pp. 237-255 ; *Notes from the
Hertfordshire County Records*, p. 6 ; and *Byegone Hertfordshire*, by W. Andrews,
1898, p. 264. But most of these Acts have remained unnoticed, and the whole
episode deserves further study.

[2] The Harwich road, Essex (7 & 8 William III. c. 9, 1695, containing the
first statutory mention of the word " Turnpike ") ; the Wymondham and
Attleborough road, Norfolk (7 & 8 William III. c. 26, 1695 ; renewed by 7 Anne
c. 4, 1708, 12 George I. c. 22, 1729, and 20 George II; c. 16, 1746) ; the Reigate
and Crawley road, Surrey (8 & 9 William III. c. 15, 1697) ; the Birdlip and
Gloucester road, Gloucestershire (9 & 10 William III. c. 18, 1698, renewed by
9 George I. c. 31, 1723, and 16 George II. c. 21, 1742) ; the Minehead roads,
Somerset (12 & 13 William III. c. 9, 1701) ; the Woodford road, Essex (1 Anne
s. 2. c. 10, see House of Commons Journals, 19th November 1702, renewed by
10 George I. c. 9, 1723, and 17 George II. c. 9, 1743) ; the Barnhill to Hatton
Heath road, Cheshire (4 & 5 Anne c. 9, 1705) ; the Hockley and Woburn road,

years it looked as if the maintenance of the high roads was to become a function of the County Justices, either in Quarter Sessions or in special Highway Sessions. Suddenly the course of legislation changes. After 1711, so far as we have been able to ascertain, Parliament no longer resorted to the County Justices for its new road authorities. In 1706,[1] in the case of the highway between Fornhill in Bedfordshire and Stony Stratford in Buckinghamshire ; in 1709, in the case of the Sevenoaks and Woodsgate Road ; and again in 1710, for certain highways leading from Hertfordshire into Huntingdonshire, forming part of the Great North Road, we have the creation of new statutory bodies, consisting of so many named persons, not necessarily or exclusively Justices of the Peace, who were empowered to levy tolls and to fill vacancies by co-option. These Acts appear to have been the first of what proved to be a long series of statutes creating special bodies of Turnpike Trustees, which came, eventually, to exist in every county of England and Wales, administering all the more important highways, and raising and spending an annual revenue exceeding that collected by any other kind of Local Authority of the period.

These Turnpike Trusts, established or renewed by, literally, thousands of separate Acts of Parliament,[2] were given almost

---

Bedfordshire (5 Anne c. 10, see House of Commons Journals, 22nd February 1707) ; the Sheppard's Shord and Devizes road (5 Anne c. 26, see House of Commons Journals, 13th, 26th and 31st March 1707) ; the Bath roads (6 Anne c. 1, 1707, renewed by 7 George I. c. 19, 1721) ; the Portsmouth road (9 Anne c. 8, 1710) ; the Gravesend and Rochester road (10 Anne c. 34, 1711). Almost the only mention of these Acts, and then only of one or two of them, down to our *Story of the King's Highway*, 1913, pp. 115, 148, and *The Development of Transportation in Modern England*, by W. T. Jackman, 1916, is that in the *History of Private Bill Legislation*, by F. Clifford, 1885–1887, vol. ii. pp. 15-16.

[1] 5 Anne (1706), not printed, but mentioned in House of Commons Journals, 3rd and 27th March 1707, 15th and 24th February 1710, and in preamble of 3 George I. c. 15 (1716); 8 Anne c. 15 (1709); renewed by 11 George I. c. 15 (1725), 9 Anne c. 7 (1710), of which we may quote the quaint preamble : " Whereas by the happy union of this kingdom the great post road from London to North Britain is become much more frequented than the same formerly hath been, and a great part of that road . . . is become very ruinous, insomuch as without very great hazard and danger members coming up to Parliament and other persons cannot pass that way . . . for remedy whereof, etc."

[2] The arrangement of the statute law is so defective that it is difficult to state with certainty what Acts were passed. Down to 1702 turnpike statutes were " public," and printed in ordinary form ; from 1702 to 1720 they were all classified as " private " and were not always printed, so that our information may be incomplete ; from 1720 to 1753 they were printed and bound

identical constitutions and functions. The Trustees were always empowered to construct and maintain a specified piece of road, to which their powers were especially confined, and to levy tolls on that piece of road upon certain kinds of traffic. The powers were invariably given only for a limited term of years, usually twenty-one ; but every Trust, in due course, applied for a new Act containing its existence for another term, so that they became virtually permanent Local Authorities, entirely unconnected with either County or Parish, Manor or Borough.

The Turnpike Trusts were distinguished from the Municipal Corporations on the one hand, and from the Incorporated Guardians and Improvement Commissioners on the other, by the uniformity and rigidity of the constitutional structure which Parliament imposed upon them. In all the thousands of Turnpike Trusts established or renewed between 1710 and 1864 [1] the governing body consisted of a number of persons named in the Act as Trustees, who were supposed to be qualified by the possession of a definite amount of property, and who were reinforced occasionally by a certain ex-officio element, such as the Mayor of a neighbouring Municipal Corporation,[2] or even occasionally the Mayor, Aldermen and Recorder of an important Borough through which the road passed.[3]

After 1820 it becomes usual in the Acts to add, as ex-officio members, all the Justices of the Peace for the particular County or Division. In all cases the Trustees were permitted, but were not required, to fill vacancies arising in their membership by the co-option of duly qualified persons. All such bodies had their

with the ordinary public general statutes ; from 1753 to 1798 they were bound separately, and are described as " Public Acts not printed in the collection," or, more succinctly, as " Road Acts " ; whilst from 1798 to 1868 they were included among " Acts Local and Personal." After 1868 there are three divisions, viz. Public General Acts, Local Acts and Private Acts (see House of Commons Journals, vol. lii. p. 413 ; *History of Private Bill Legislation*, by F. Clifford, 1887–1889, vol. i. p. 269 ; *Legislative Methods and Forms*, by Sir C. P. Ilbert, 1901, pp. 26-27 ; *Municipal Origins*, by F. H. Spencer, 1911, pp. 46-48).

[1] This applies to all Turnpike Trusts formed after 1710. In the few earlier Acts, as we have mentioned, the new powers were usually entrusted to all the Justices of the County, or of one of its Divisions, or (as in the exceptional Act of 1707 for the road from Bath to Kingsdown Hill, 6 Anne c. 1) to selected Justices, representing three Counties and the City of Bath respectively.

[2] As at St. Albans (1 George I. c. 12, 1714).

[3] As at York (23 George II. c. 38, 1750) ; and Durham (50 George III. c. 3, 1810) ; or the Mayor and Aldermen only, as at Launceston (33 George III. c. 59, 1760).

jurisdiction confined to the one subject of road maintenance,[1] and geographically limited to a particular stretch of road, defined in the Act itself. In no case that we have found were the Turnpike Trustees entitled to levy a rate, or even to claim a share of the various Highway Rates made by the Justices in particular parishes. This incapacity to levy a rate distinguishes the Turnpike Trust, along with the Manorial Courts, from all other local governing bodies. Another marked feature of the Turnpike Trusts which they share with the Courts of Sewers, but which distinguishes them from the Incorporated Guardians and the Police or Improvement Commissioners, as well as from the Manorial Courts, was the provision for their automatic extinction at a certain date. The earlier Acts confined the existence of the Turnpike Trusts which they created to varying periods such as eleven, fifteen or twenty years.[2]

From 1702 onwards the term was uniformly twenty-one years, at which they all remained till 1833, when it was enlarged to thirty-one years. As a matter of fact, as in the analogous case of the Commissioners of Sewers, every Trust applied for and obtained successive extensions of its term, so as to become virtually a permanent body. It was perhaps for this reason that the Courts of Quarter Sessions made no demur to the establishment of these new authorities, on which the Justices individually found themselves placed.[3]

[1] Very occasionally indeed a Turnpike Act may contain a clause giving power to pave, light and cleanse certain streets ; but in such cases the special power is always given to some authority other than Turnpike Trustees of the ordinary type (*e.g.* in 6 Anne, c. 1, 1708, to the Mayor, Recorder and Justices of the City of Bath in conjunction with County Justices). The only instance that we have found of a Turnpike Trust having statutory power to watch and light is that of the Shoreditch to Enfield Trust (1790). Conversely, we find occasionally a body of Police or Improvement Commissioners obtaining power to construct or maintain roads in an urban area, or to exercise over their roads some of the powers of Turnpike Trusts (see, for instance, the Beverley Act, 13 George I. c. 4 ; the Leeds Act, 49 George III. c. 122 ; the Sudbury Act, 6 George IV. c. 70 ; the Yeovil Act, 11 George IV. c. 116 ; the Exeter Act, 2 & 3 William IV. c. 106 ; *Municipal Origins*, by F. H. Spencer, 1911, p. 274).

[2] Thus the earliest Act of 15 Charles II. c. 1, prescribed 11 years ; one of 4 & 5 William and Mary, 15 years ; one of 8 & 9 William III. c. 15, 20 years ; and one of 1 Anne, sess. 2. c. 10, 21 years.

[3] Where, as frequently happened, the road lay in more than one County, there was an additional reason for constituting a special body. The earlier Acts entrusting the powers to Quarter Sessions had broken down in such cases. A Committee of the House of Commons in 1714 found the Great North Road from Royston in Cambridgeshire to Waternewton in Huntingdonshire very bad, " notwithstanding that three turnpikes had been erected on the said road "

M

For the first half of the eighteenth century, in fact, every one took it for granted that the Turnpike Trust, with the toll that it levied, was only a temporary device, designed to cope with the exceptionally ruinous state into which a bit of road had fallen. It was not foreseen that this assumed temporary nature of the new body would be practically inconsistent with its power to borrow money without limit on the security of its income from tolls, which it was able formally to mortgage to the lender, though it could, of course, give legal security only for the un-expired portion of the term which Parliament had granted.

The powers of these separate bodies of Turnpike Trustees, conferred upon them as they were in the first instance by these separate local Acts, varied indefinitely in detail, but showed in the course of the eighteenth century certain general lines of development. The main purpose of these Acts was, as regards the particular piece of road dealt with, to bring additional revenues and additional powers to the reinforcement of the general highway law. The body of Trustees, who were, so to speak, "incorporated" by a Turnpike Act, were entrusted with the exclusive management of the designated piece of road, and authorised to engage officers and servants, and to purchase material and plant for its amendment and maintenance. They were empowered to erect "toll-houses," "tollbars," "turn-pikes," "crates" or "gates" on any part of the road under their jurisdiction, and to exact, as a condition of passage, a toll on all vehicles, horsemen and cattle passing through.[1] This novel

since June 1710. It appeared "that upon the first erecting of the toll gates on that road some of the most ruinous parts thereof were tolerably repaired, but that the Commissioners appointed to put the Act in execution seldom met though obliged to it four times at least in the year ; they being not able to constitute a board without three Commissioners of the County of Cambridge and three of the County of Huntingdon, which was found difficult to assemble ; that this discontinuance of meetings caused a stop to be put to the working on the said road " (Report of House of Commons Committee on Management of money collected for repairing highways ; see House of Commons Journals, 15th April 1714).

[1] The usual toll was from one to six pence. Thus, whilst a horse was charged a penny, every stage coach, hackney coach, carriage, waggon or cart was charged sixpence, every score of sheep a penny, every score of calves or hogs twopence, and every score of cattle sixpence (8 & 9 William III. c. 15, Reigate and Crawley Turnpike Act, 1697). Double tolls were usually charged on Sundays. A later specimen makes the toll on a carriage drawn by six or more horses one shilling, by four sixpence, by two or three threepence, by one three halfpence ; a one-horse cart or waggon paid a penny ; a two-horse ditto,

impost differed radically from the ancient due, custom or toll which some manorial or corporate authorities levied under royal grant, in that it was strictly limited in duration, minutely specified in amount, and legally applicable to a given public service. Thus, as we have already stated, all Turnpike Acts were temporary only, the usual period of their validity being twenty-one years, after which, it was fondly assumed, the special need for extra-ordinary repairs would have passed away, and the road might be maintained free of toll by the ordinary highway revenue. For over half a century it was even enacted, in most of the Turnpike Acts, that if the roads were sufficiently repaired, and all debts paid, before the end of the term, the Justices should order the toll-gates to be removed, and bring the tolls to an end.[1] The number and position of the toll-gates was usually left to the discretion of the Trustees. But every Turnpike Act specified the maximum toll that might be levied on vehicles, horsemen or cattle (usually doubled on Sundays), and many of the Acts included provisions against the exaction of repeated tolls on the same day,[2] or in respect of passage along the same stretch of road, whilst others contained elaborate exemptions in favour

---

three halfpence ; a horse, mule or ass, a halfpenny ; a drove of meat cattle, fivepence a score ; a drove of calves, hogs, sheep or lambs, twopence halfpenny a score (11 George II. c. 33, Loughborough and Derby Turnpike Act, 1737).

We do not find in England the ordinary French provision for exacting double tolls at the entrance to the Metropolis, or any place at which the King or Queen is staying (see, for instance, *Liste générale des postes de France dressée par ordre de . . . Comte Dargenson*, 1751).

[1] For power to bring the Turnpike Trust prematurely to an end, see, for instance, 15 Car. II. c. 1 (1663), 8 & 9 William III. c. 15 (1697). A similar power is given to Quarter Sessions in many Turnpike Acts down to the middle of the eighteenth century ; but we have not noticed it in any later Act.

[2] The regulations as to tickets were varied. A ticket was given on each payment of toll, and this freed the payer from any further payment for the same animal or vehicle during the same day, according to the terms of the particular Local Act and the orders of the particular Trustees, either at that gate, or at that gate or some others, or at all gates on a particular section of road, or at all the gates of the Trust. The " day " usually ended at midnight (sometimes at midnight in summer and 10 P.M. in winter ; see 3 George I. c. 4, Hampstead and Highgate Turnpike Act, 1716). A more complicated arrange-ment prevailed on the Kensington road, where it was expressly ordained " that for all droves of cattle passing through the turnpike gates, the tickets that shall be delivered on Saturday shall be in force till Monday noon following ; and the tickets that shall be delivered for droves of cattle every other day besides Saturday shall be in force till the day following at noon " (House of Commons Committee on the Management and Application of money collected during the last eleven years for repairing any particular highway ; see House of Commons Journals, 19th April 1763, vol. xxix. p. 646).

of persons who used only minute portions of the road (as, for
instance, in crossing from one field to another), or who were
engaged in particular occupations, or, in some cases, who owned,
occupied or inhabited particular premises.[1] It was always the
intention of Parliament that the payers of the toll should get
quid pro quo in useful improvements. The tolls were, in some
cases, not to be levied until Quarter Sessions had bound some
" able and sufficient persons " in sureties to put the road in
sufficient repair within five years.[2] In most of the early Acts
it is expressly provided that the Justices in Quarter Sessions may
appoint fit persons to " survey the highways and enquire of the
toll, and in case of misapplication . . . they are to certify the
same to the Judges of Assize."

From the standpoint of modern administration, there were,
however, glaring shortcomings in the provisions of these Acts,
which, as we shall see, went far to frustrate the good intentions
of Parliament. The equitable incidence of the toll was undermined by clauses enabling the Trustees to grant preferential
rates to particular individuals or classes. There was no limit
to the amount of borrowed capital for which the Trustees could
mortgage the tolls, so that the mere interest on the mortgage
debt might easily absorb the whole revenue destined for current
repairs. Each generation of Trustees succeeded in obtaining a
greater measure of freedom from legal limitation or executive
supervision in the expenditure of their income : they could spend
what they pleased, borrow what they pleased and manage the
business as they pleased. They might, at their option, have
their own official establishment of collectors and surveyors, or
farm out both toll collection and road repair for lump sums.

[1] Thus, an Act of 1746 contained a section exempting " the owners, occupiers
and inhabitants of Coley House, and of the farm adjoining thereunto . . .
their several workmen, servants and agents . . . with horses, cattle, coaches,
carts and carriages " (20 George II. c. 6, Reading and Puntfield Turnpike Act,
1746).

[2] For the provision making the levying of the tolls contingent on sureties
for the repair of the road, see 9 & 10 William III. c. 18 (1698). In an early
Bedfordshire Act it was provided that " No turnpike is to be erected nor toll
demanded . . . nor shall the said causey, without the consent of the lord
. . . of the . . . manor . . . be laid open for . . . carriages, until sufficient
security be given by able and sufficient persons to the Justices of the Peace
. . . that the said way . . . shall within three years be sufficiently repaired
and amended " (5 Anne, c. 10, Hockley and Woburn Turnpike Act, 1706).
The Justices' power to investigate the state of the road and the amount of the
toll was given generally in 9 George I. c. 11 (1722).

And whilst the control given in the early Acts to the County Justices over turnpike roads, and over the Trustees who managed them, was, in the middle of the eighteenth century, gradually removed, no new provisions were inserted requiring the Trustees to account for their receipts and expenditure to any public authority. Not less important were the powers gradually conceded to these new authorities to alter, at their own discretion, the means of communication between one place and another. In the course of half a century they not only accumulated, in their successive statutes, all the powers of the Justices under the General Highway Acts but even added new ones. They could buy land compulsorily in order to widen narrow ways and improve gradients. They could erect bars against bye-lanes, close up ancient highways, divert others at their pleasure and compel every one to travel by the new road they had constructed. In this way an ancient hamlet might find itself suddenly deprived of a public road, in order that the journey from one town to another might be shortened or straightened, or even so that a particular mansion or farmhouse might be favoured with easy access to the market town.

It is characteristic of the slovenly ways of the eighteenth-century Parliament, and of the incapacity of the early Hanoverian administrations, in all that concerned internal affairs that the new bodies of Turnpike Trustees, exercising special powers over small areas, were intruded into the complicated hierarchy of English Local Government without any consideration of what should be their relations to the older organisations of the Parish and the County.[1] For the grant to the Turnpike Trust of power to tax the users of the road was never intended by Parliament to exempt the parishes through which the road passed from their obligation of maintaining it, or to excuse any person from the performance of Statute Labour or Team Duty. It seems to have been assumed at the beginning that the modicum of repair to be rendered by the Parish Surveyors of Highways and the unpaid Statute Labour and Team Duty of the inhabitants would have

---

[1] The state of the highway organisation of the Parish in the middle of the eighteenth century may be well seen in the excellent work by John Shapleigh, entitled *Highways : a Treatise showing the Hardships and Inconveniences of Presenting or Indicting Parishes and Towns, etc., for not repairing the Highways*, 1749. Compare the earlier pamphlet by an anonymous Justice, *For Mending the Roads of England*, by J.P., 1715.

been completed before the special Surveyors appointed to lay out
the proceeds of the new revenue came on the scene. These
Surveyors were authorised to require the performance of such
additional labour as they thought necessary, "for which the said
Surveyors," declared Parliament, " shall pay unto such labourers
and to the owners of such teams, carts and wains according to the
usual rate of the country." [1] Presently the situation is simpli-
fied. The power to exact extra labour compulsorily is dropped,
and whatever additional service is required has to be hired in the
open market. On the other hand, in all that concerned the maintenance of the special length of road—the " turnpike road "—
the Surveyor appointed by the new road authority is gradually
invested with nearly all the powers of the Parish Surveyor of
Highways appointed from among the inhabitants. He is
authorised summarily to suppress nuisances, and enabled to take
compulsorily without compensation from the common or wastes,
within the parish or without, or out of any river or brook, whatever " gravel, chalk, sand or stones " are needed for the mending
of his road ; and to resort for this purpose also to private grounds,
on payment merely of the actual damage done.[2] More important

[1] So by the Act of 15 Car. II. c. 1 (1663) ; but no one was to be compellable
to travel above three, four or five miles from home, nor to work more than
two days in any one week, nor on any day in seed-time, hay-time or corn harvest
(7 & 8 William III. c. 9, 1695 ; so also 7 & 8 William III. c. 26, 1695). The
power of the Surveyor to require this extra labour is given without limit in
9 & 10 William III. c. 18 (1698).   In the Kent County records in 1729 we
read that " it is ordered by this Court that it be referred to Thomas Marsh, Esq.,
one of His Majesty's Justices of the Peace for this County, and the rest of the
Justices of the Division wherein Longport lies, to settle and set the price of
labourers employed in and about the repairing, surveying and looking after
Boughton highways, in this County, on the London road," the amount so set
to be paid by the County Treasurer (MS. Minutes, Quarter Sessions, East Kent,
10th October 1729).
[2] As regards these powers, see, for instance, the nuisance and obstruction
clauses in 7 George II. c. 13 (1733); 1 George II. c. 33 (1727) ; 17 George II.
c. 29 (1743) ; and especially the very comprehensive powers given in 20
George III. c. 71 (1780). As regards powers over private property, see, for
instance, 15 Car. II. c. 1 (Great North Road Turnpike Act, 1663) ; 7 & 8
William III. c. 9 (London and Harwich Turnpike Act, 1695) ; 6 Anne, c. 1
(Bath and Kingsdown Hill Turnpike Act, 1708).   Subsequently, private interests are better safeguarded. The Surveyor has to pay reasonable rates for
the material so taken from private land (6 George I. c. 25, Stevenage and
Biggleswade Turnpike Act, 1720) ; later on, express notice must be given to
the owner, and specific order made by Justices, after hearing objections (39 & 40
George III. c. 3, Leicester and Hinckley Turnpike Act, 1800).   The 1663 Act
had required pits from which materials were dug to be filled up and levelled,
" or else railed about . . . so as that the same may not be deemed dangerous

still, from 1714 onwards, he is given express power to require the performance under his own direction of a specific proportion of the ordinary Statute Labour and Team Duty of the parishioners. The proportion of the six days Statute Labour to which the turnpike road was entitled was sometimes specified in the Act at two, three or four days ; or was left to be fixed by the Turnpike Trustees or their Surveyor, with an appeal, in case of difference, to the Justices in Petty or Special Sessions. Gradually the apportionment comes normally to be settled by two Justices, on the application of the Parish Surveyor of Highways. Sometimes the Justices were empowered to allot particular parishioners, as many as they thought fit, to labour on the turnpike road ; or otherwise to settle what proportion of the whole six days due from all the inhabitants should be so directed.[1] From 1716 onward the Turnpike Surveyor was, in many cases, even given power to agree with the parish for an annual amount to be raised by the Parish Surveyor by a rate, and to be paid in a lump sum to the Turnpike Surveyor, in lieu of this specific share of the Statute Labour.[2] Hence the new turnpike authority found itself in

---

or prejudicial to man or beast " (15 Car. II. c. 1) ; an obligation not made usual until the Public General Act of 1753 (26 George II. c. 28), which required any holes or pits made in commons or wastes for this purpose to be fenced ; and specific clauses to this effect again appear in many subsequent Turnpike Acts, " so that " these pits " may not be dangerous to passengers or cattle " (see 10 George III. c. 54, Norwich and Block Hill Turnpike Act, 1770).

[1] The relations between the Parish Surveyor and the Turnpike Surveyor thus became complicated. The Parish Surveyor of Highways was to deliver a list of persons liable ; the Turnpike Surveyor was to give him notice of the time and place for them to come ; he was then to summon all persons liable ; and they were to put in three days' work on the turnpike road ; see 1 George I. sess. 2, c. 25 (Tyburn and Uxbridge Turnpike Act, 1714, for what is now the Bayswater Road, Notting Hill and Uxbridge Road) ; see also the detailed clause in 13 George II. c. 9 (Hockliffe and Stony Stratford Turnpike Act, 1739). As late as 1800 there was an appeal by a Parish Surveyor of Highways against a conviction by Petty Sessions for not having summoned, in response to a demand from the Turnpike Surveyor, certain inhabitants " to perform their statute work upon part of the said road " (MS. Minutes, Quarter Sessions, Lancashire, 15th July 1800).

For cases in which the Justices were left to fix the number of days' labour to be given to the turnpike road or by whom it should be given, see 7 George I. c. 18 (Highgate and Barnet Turnpike Act, 1720) ; 16 George II. c. 21 (Birdlip and Gloucester Turnpike Act, 1742) ; 13 George II. c. 9 (Hockliffe and Stony Stratford Turnpike Act, 1739) ; 17 George II. c. 9 (Harlow and Stump Cross Turnpike Act, 1743).

[2] For power to require a money composition, see 3 George I. c. 4 (Highgate and Hampstead Turnpike Act, 1716) ; 4 George I. c. 4 (London and East Grinstead Turnpike Act, 1717) ; 4 George I. c. 5 (Southwark and East Green-

possession of a money income derived, not only from its own tolls, but also from the parish rates on occupiers. This income from rates was, however, at no time anything but a lump sum composition of the Statute Labour and Team Duty. In no case that we have found were the Turnpike Trustees entitled themselves to levy a rate upon the owners or occupiers of property, or upon the inhabitants as such.

Meanwhile nothing was done to relieve the Parish from the risk of indictment and fine for the non-fulfilment of its obligation to maintain all the highways within its area, including therefore the turnpike road. With the rise in the standard of road maintenance that occurred in the course of the eighteenth century, there came a corresponding change in the opinion of Assize Judges, Justices of the Peace and Juries as to what constituted a

wich Turnpike Act, 1717); and many subsequent Acts. In 19 George II. c. 19 (Liverpool and Prescot Turnpike Act, 1745), the power to raise the composition money by rate is expressly given to the Parish Surveyor of Highways. These compositions naturally ed to embittered negotiations between the Parish and the Trust. Hackney, for instance, was made to pay £100 a year towards the Kingsland Road Turnpike Trust, and this arrangement was embodied in 12 Anne, st. 1, c. 1 (1714). In 1741–1744 payment was, on some pretext, withheld by the parish, and to compel the parish officers to collect the necessary rate required a special Act (17 George II. c. 41, 1743), which changed the composition for the future to 200 days' work of eight hours, by teams of three good horses, able to carry 24 bushels each load, each to be attended by two able men. Twenty-three years later, the Vestry Minutes show the parties to be again at issue. " The parishioners present were acquainted that the Trustees of the Kingsland Turnpike Road were making an application to Parliament to enlarge the term and powers of the Acts relating to that Trust, and that by the said Acts the Parish of Hackney are to do yearly 200 days' statute work with teams on that road, or pay to the Trust the sum of £100 in lieu thereof, and that by an Act of the last session of Parliament relating to the public highways, and the determination of His Majesty's Justices of the Peace in consequence of it, every person liable to do statute work with a team might compound for the same for 4s. 6d. a day instead of the former penalty of 10s. ; and that if the said Trustees should obtain a clause in the said intended Act for this Parish to pay the Trust £100 per annum in lieu of statute work, it would be a net loss to the Parish, as the Parish must by composition lose 5s. 6d. in every ten shillings." The Vestry thereupon appointed a committee to watch the Bill (MS. Vestry Minutes, Hackney (Middlesex), 12th December 1767). Twelve years later the Vestry opposes another Bill of the same Trust, because it was proposed to fix the rate of composition for the parish contribution of statute labour at too high a figure (ibid. 23rd March 1789). The sum of £100 seems to have been a favourite one for the annual composition of a large parish. The Surveyor of Highways of the Township of Manchester had, down to 1812, for many years paid to the Trustees of the Oldham Turnpike Roads a lump sum of £100 a year by agreement in " lieu of statute labour and liability, by indictment or otherwise " (MS. Minutes, Oldham Turnpike Trust, 29th August 1806, 11th September 1812).

state of good repair ; and Parishes found themselves fined for highways in no worse condition than would, in the seventeenth century, have been regarded as quite adequate to all legitimate needs. Thus, when a Parish had to endure an inefficient or impecunious Turnpike Trust, it was placed in an impracticable position. It had lost all control over the repair of the turnpike road, without having liberated itself from any of its responsibilities. " As the law now stands," wrote Sir J. C. Hippisley in 1808 to the President of the Board of Agriculture, " if any part of a turnpike road be out of repair, remedy is given by presentment or indictment of the parish, in which such road is situate, subjecting the Parish to great expense and inconvenience, although the nuisance be wholly imputable to the Trustees of the turnpike." [1]

This injustice moved even the Yorkshire antiquary Whitaker to an outburst of indignation amid his genealogies and Church annals. " It is a great iniquity," he writes in 1816, " as well as absurdity that parishes and townships should be indictable or presentable for the neglect or passive defaults of others over whom they have no control, while they are condemned to be passive in the introduction of expensive and burdensome roads through their respective districts, and at the same time actively responsible for all the consequences occasioned by the fraud or negligence of strangers.[2]

The relation of the Turnpike Trust to the Rulers of the County was less ambiguous than that to the parishes through which its road passed ; but owing to the constant slight changes in the law, difficult to express with accuracy. For the first half of the eighteenth century, Parliament seems to have regarded the Turnpike Trusts as bodies to be superintended and controlled by the Court of Quarter Sessions. Right down to 1835, indeed, Quarter Sessions continued to be the tribunal of arbitration between the Trusts and the various parishes with which they had dealings, determining which parishes were liable to contribute Statute Labour, and in what proportion, and how the Statute Labour was to be distributed between the turnpike road and the other highways

---

[1] Sir J. C. Hippisley, Bart., M.P., to Sir John Sinclair, 4th April 1808 ; in Second Report of House of Commons Committee on Highways, Appendix A, p. 136.

[2] *Loidis and Elmete,* by T. D. Whitaker, 1816, p. 82.

of each parish. Quarter Sessions could require the Trust to
erect "weighing engines."[1] If the Trustees chose to allow more
than the statutory maximum number of horses to be used on
steep hills, their order was subject to the confirmation of Quarter
Sessions;[2] if they put up any toll-gates not authorised by their
Act, the Justices in Quarter Sessions were summarily to order
the Sheriff to remove them.[3] But from about the middle of the
eighteenth century, we see the Turnpike Trusts shaking themselves gradually free from any control by the Rulers of the
County over their administration, or over the expenditure of
their funds. Their powers are from decade to decade constantly increased. They are authorised to exact additional
tolls for heavy weights, to erect weighing machines, to seize
horses in excess of the lawful number, to charge double rates
for narrow wheels and altogether to exempt from toll the broadest
wheels. It was by successive statutory provisions of this kind,
obtained first by one Turnpike Trust and then by another,
increasing at each renewal of the term, rather than by any
deliberate policy of Parliament, that the Trusts and their
officers obtained, as the century wore on, such far-reaching and
uncontrolled powers. What is remarkable is the long-continued
failure of the House of Commons, unaided by any intervention
of the Cabinet or any Government Department, to view the
problem as a whole.

Across this mass of Local Acts, each applicable only to a few
miles of road, there came, between 1727 and 1766, half a score
of general statutes for the "more effectual preservation" of
the turnpike roads.[4] Two of the earliest of these were directed

---

[1] 13 George III. c. 84, sec. 7.
[2] *Ibid.* sec. 18.   [3] *Ibid.* sec. 51.
[4] The general statutes relating to turnpike roads, prior to the consolidating
Acts of 1766 and 1773, were 1 George II. c. 19 (1727); 5 George II. c. 33
(1731); 8 George II. c. 20 (1734); 14 George II. c. 42 (1740); 21 George II.
c. 28 (1747); 24 George II. c. 43 (1750); 26 George II. c. 30 (1753); 28 George II.
c. 17 (1755); 30 George II. c. 27 (1757); 30 George II. c. 43 (1757). The
Act imposing the penalty of death for destruction of turnpike property was
that of 1734. These statutes, together with the consolidating Acts of 1766
and 1773, were made the subject of an able and instructive commentary by
John Scott, in his *Digests of the General Highway and Turnpike Laws*, 1778,
from which the quotations in the text are taken (pp. 277, 265 and 259); see
also *Observations on the General Highway and Turnpike Acts passed in the
Seventh Year of His Present Majesty*, by Thomas Butterworth Bayley, 1773.
Among other manuals we may cite *The Laws respecting Highways and Turnpike
Roads*, by James Barry Bird, 1801. The 1773 Act, together with fifteen sub-

against the " ill-designing and disorderly persons [who] associated
themselves together both by day and night, and cut down,
pulled down, burnt and otherwise destroyed several turnpike
gates and houses "—the alarming frequency of this offence
between 1726 and 1734 inducing an eighteenth-century legislature
to raise the sentence, from three months hard labour and a public
whipping, to death without benefit of clergy. But the County
Justices and Turnpike Trustees who swarmed on the benches of
the House of Commons discovered more insidious enemies of
their turnpikes than mere rioters ; and from 1741 onward we see
them passing Act after Act to protect their roads against the
wear and tear of heavy weights and narrow wheels. These Acts
gave all bodies of Turnpike Trustees power to erect weighing
machines, to exact prohibitive tolls for extraordinary weights, to
seize horses in excess of the lawful number, to charge double
rates for narrow wheels, and altogether to exempt the broadest
wheels from their tolls. To quote the words of an able com-
mentator, the users of wheeled vehicles were to be " in some
instances compelled to obedience, like slaves, by severe penalties ;
and in others enticed to it like children with a sugar plum." Unfortunately for all concerned these amateur " Act-constructors,"
as John Scott terms them, were as unskilful as they were irresolute.
" Sometimes one is at a loss to conceive the end at which they
were aiming," continues Scott ; " and sometimes when their
end is obvious one can find no reason for their choice of the
means that are designed to accomplish it." " If the Parliament
would but fix on any one reasonable plan," the farmers remarked
to Scott, " and keep to it, let it be what it might, they should be
satisfied ; but that such perpetual alterations as they had for
some time experienced, were inconvenient beyond expression,
for they never knew what they had to do for two years together."
At the conclusion of peace in 1763, after the Seven Years' War,

sequent statutes of 1774 (4), 1776 (2), 1777, 1778 (2), 1781, 1785, 1812, 1813,
1815 and 1817, were repealed and re-enacted by 3 George IV. c. 126 (1822) ;
see *The General Turnpike Road Act*, by Joseph Bateman, 1822 ; *A Supplement
to the General Turnpike Road Act of 3 George IV. c. 126*, by the same, 1823 ;
and *A Second Supplement*, by the same, 1827 ; *The Law of Turnpikes*, by
William Cobbett, junior, 1824 ; *The General Turnpike Act*, by William Knight
Dehany, 1823 ; *The Law relating to Highways, Turnpike Roads, Public Bridges
and Navigable Rivers*, by John Egremont, vol. i. only, 1830 ; and, as to the
muddle, *An Argument for more of the Division of Labour in Civil Life in this
Country*, by William Wickens, 1829, pp. 67-73.

the chaos of statutes had become so intolerable that a public-spirited knot of local government reformers, headed by the well-known Thomas Gilbert, set themselves to consolidate the whole of the general law relating to turnpikes—an arduous and complicated enterprise which, after an unsatisfactory essay in 1766 (7 George III. c. 40), eventuated in the comprehensive General Turnpike Act of 1773 (13 George III. c. 84).

This Act, which was made to apply to all turnpike roads, existing or thereafter constructed, was, like the legislation which it superseded, framed rather in the interest of the Turnpike Trustees and the mortgagees of their tolls than in that of the users of the roads or the public at large. It was, indeed, in the main, merely a consolidating Act. In so far as it altered the powers of Turnpike Trustees, it strengthened their control over their own officials, and enlarged the authority of these officials over the community. To strengthen the position of the Trusts—possibly with a view to improving their credit as borrowers—it included the old clauses requiring a high property qualification for Trustees, and disqualifying publicans from serving as officials, whilst incorporating new provisions formalising their procedure, and making it incumbent on them, whenever they leased the tolls, to lease them to the highest bidder. But the obvious defects in the Local Acts that we have already pointed out were not remedied. No provision was made to prevent malversation or extravagance by the Turnpike Trustees ; there was required no audit of their accounts ; no check was imposed on the amount of their borrowings, or the rate of interest to be paid ; and no curb was placed on their uncontrolled power to divert, alter or close the ancient highways at their will. The bulk of this wordy, complicated and badly arranged statute consisted, in fact, in a mere stringing together of the existing clauses relating to wheeled vehicles—prohibitions, exemptions, special tolls, fines and forfeitures, one piled on top of another until, as John Scott heard " a very respectable and intelligent gentleman now in the House [of Commons] observe, . . . the Trustees would have enough to do if they were bound to reconcile all the contradictions of the Act and make sense of its nonsense." It was this statute that, with only trifling modifications, remained the basis of turnpike administration right down to 1822, when it was superseded by another hardly less complicated.

The optimistic assumption of Parliament that the turnpike and its toll would be but a temporary device to meet an exceptionally ruinous state of a particular bit of road was, we need hardly say, everywhere falsified. Whenever the term for which Parliament had granted a toll drew near to expiry, the particular turnpike authority invariably petitioned for a renewal of its Act. The power to take toll, it was alleged, had " been of great benefit to all carriages and persons travelling those roads ; the said roads are not fully repaired, nor all the moneys borrowed by virtue of the said Act paid " ; " sometimes the deep and long commons over which the roads went were so impassable " as to require the construction of a causeway or other new work. After a while the application for renewal becomes so much a matter of course that no special reason is alleged for it, and the new bill " for enlarging and continuing " the powers of each Turnpike Trust appears automatically as the term comes to an end. And these renewal bills generally included new powers, either in the form of a schedule of augmented tolls, or by extension to additional lengths of roads, or through the concession of more drastic means of enforcing payment. In the first half of the century, these steadily extending powers of taxation did not fail to arouse complaints from those who had hitherto used the roads free from toll. As the number of turnpike bills increases, the applications to the House of Commons are met by counter-petitions from groups of users alleging, as in the case of the fishermen of Hastings, that the proposed tolls will " discourage them from following their employment," and will " impoverish the greatest part of the inhabitants," or, as in the case of inhabitants of Gloucestershire, declaring that the highways remain, in spite of the toll, " in a ruinous and almost impassable condition," so that they see no benefit in a renewal of the impost.[1] The third decade of the century, which is noted as a period of expansion and active experiment in the administration of the Poor Law, was marked also by a rapid multiplication of Turnpike Trusts. Between 1720 and 1730 no fewer than 71 new Trusts were established, the total mileage under toll being thereby more than trebled. This great extension of taxation on the users of the

[1] The quotations from petitions for and against Turnpike Bills are from the House of Commons Journals (8th January 1707, 24th January 1709, 20th December 1709, and 3rd February 1710).

roads did not fail to arouse resistance, especially in districts where small holdings or cottage manufacturers prevailed. Serious riots broke out in Somerset, Gloucestershire and Herefordshire in 1726, and continued spasmodically for a whole decade, in the course of which turnpikes were destroyed, and the pike-keepers ill-treated. " Great numbers of riotous and rebellious persons," we read, in 1732, "armed with firearms and other dangerous weapons have . . . frequently assembled themselves together in the night-time, and marched in formidable bodies into that City [Hereford] and pulled down and destroyed the turnpikes erected on the roads leading thereto, and the houses of the said turnpike keepers . . . after they had plundered the same, and fired their guns into the windows of several other dwelling houses and in the public streets . . . threatened and declared that they would not only destroy the turnpikes but would murder the keepers thereof, and all such Trustees who should presume to act under the Act of Parliament ; and at the public market place . . . have given notice in a most audacious manner that if the magistrates or any other persons should interrupt or oppose them, they would set the said City on fire." Similar riots broke out at Bristol in 1749, in which turnpikes were tumultuously demolished. The rioters were " armed with rusty swords, pitchforks, axes, guns, pistols, clubs, etc., and called themselves Sack a Lents. . . . They ranged themselves in the main street before the George Inn, by beat of drum, huzzas and a hunting horn, three drums attending them. Here they drank freely, with much noise, and then broke the windows of one Mr. Durbin, Tithingman of the Hundred who had, by order of the [Turnpike] Commissioners, carried persons concerned in destroying the turnpikes before two Justices, by whom they were committed to Newgate." After the disorder had lasted a fort-night, the rioters were dispersed by the arrival of the soldiers. A few years later there were turnpike riots at Leeds, in which the military had to fire on the rioters, with some loss of life.[1]

[1] For the successful turnpike riots at Kingswood in 1727, see the letter from the Mayor of Bristol, 28th June 1727, in Home Office archives in Public Record Office (Calendar of State Papers, Domestic), and Oldmixon's *History of England*, 1735, p. 804 ; for those at Hereford, see *Read's Weekly Journal*, 25th November 1732, and House of Commons Journals, 2nd and 28th March 1732 ; for an armed attack on the turnpike at Cainscross, near Stroud, on 9th July 1733, see Home Office archives in Public Record Office (Calendar of

About the middle of the century, in spite of the annually increasing mileage of road subjected to toll, and the automatic renewal and extension of the powers of the various bodies of Turnpike Trustees, opposition, either by petition or riot, dies away, and Turnpike Acts multiply fast.[1] After the Peace of 1748 a perfect mania seems to set in, and the number of new Trusts rises suddenly from about three a year to nearly twenty a year. Between 1748 and 1770 the number of separate Trusts in existence rose from about 160 to about 530, whilst the mileage subject to toll was quadrupled. When we remember the eighteenth century impatience of new taxation and hatred of restraints on personal freedom, this acquiescence in the extension, all over England, of an entirely new impost, is, we think, a matter for surprise. We attribute it less to a conviction in the payers of the toll that they were actually getting *quid pro quo*, than to certain common features in the constitution and working of the

---

State Papers, Domestic, vol. 32, No. 64) ; compare also the account of those at Ledbury in 1735 in petition of Ledbury Turnpike Trustees (*ibid.*), and in *Daily Gazetteer* for 8th October and 9th December 1735, given in *The Law of Highways*, by W. C. Glen, 1865, pp. 53-55. A letter to the Duke of Chandos, 8th January 1737, describes the forcible demolition of the turnpike at Wilton by an armed band disguised by white smocks over their clothes (Home Office archives in Public Record Office ; Calendar of State Papers, Domestic, vol. 40, No. 1). For the riots at Bristol in 1734 and 1749, see *Annals of Bristol in the Eighteenth Century*, by J. Latimer, p. 157, and *Gentleman's Magazine*, August 1749, p. 276 ; for that at Leeds in 1753, *Loidis and Elmete*, by T. D. Whitaker, 1816, p. 77.

[1] From the earliest three Turnpike Trusts of 1706–1710, the number rose at first slowly. The third decade of the eighteenth century—noted also, as we shall hereafter show, for great developments in Poor Law administration— saw no fewer than 71 new Trusts established, the mileage being trebled. By 1748 the number had grown to 160. After the Peace of Aix-la-Chapelle—still more after the conclusion of the Seven Years' War in 1763—when the nation advanced rapidly in all sorts of internal improvement, Turnpike Trusts multiplied on all sides, the number rising, between 1748 and 1770, to 530, and the mileage being quadrupled. The remainder of the century saw a steady increase, the number and mileage again doubling in thirty years ; reaching, in 1838, 1116, having 22,000 miles of road. As each Trust had to get a new Act every fifteen or twenty-one years, the number of Turnpike Acts reached more than three times these figures. Between 1760 and 1774 they were passed at the rate of thirty a year ; between 1785 and 1809 at the rate of forty a year. By 1838 no fewer than 3800 separate Turnpike Acts had been put on the statute book (*History of Private Bill Legislation*, by F. Clifford, 1885–1887, vol. ii. p. 18, etc. ; Report of Royal Commission on Roads, 1840 ; Report of House of Commons Committee on Turnpike Trusts, 1839 ; *Journal of the Royal Statistical Society*, 1839). In *The Development of Transportation in Modern England*, by W. T. Jackman, 1916, p. 743, a table is given showing the Road Acts passed in 1701–1750, 1751–1770, 1771–1790, 1791–1810, and 1811–1830 respectively.

various Turnpike Trusts themselves. It must, in the first place, be remembered that the tolls were never levied on foot passengers, and were thus unfelt by the labouring poor. The projectors of each new Turnpike Trust were so anxious to secure local support that they included among their proposed Trustees every one of local influence or authority—noblemen, clergy, squires, farmers and even traders—a constitution of the governing body which, at whatever cost of efficiency, at any rate went far to secure assent. But it was not merely the principal inhabitants who were placated. The new source of road revenue promised to relieve the parishioners of their ancient Statute Labour. The little farmers and cottagers looked forward to the cost of repairs being henceforth met out of the tolls to be paid by the carriage folk and the London carriers. "As soon as a turnpike Act is obtained," it was said in 1754,[1] " all the parishes through which the road passes consider the Act as a benefit ticket, and an exemption from their usual expenses, and elude the payment of their just quota towards the reparation of the road, by compounding with the Trustees for a less sum, or by doing their Statute Labour in a fraudulent manner ; and in both these cases they are generally favoured by the neighbouring Justices and gentlemen, for the ease of their own estates." Hence the very defects in structure and function of the Turnpike Trusts served to prevent resistance to the new impost which they levied.

From the standpoint of a national system of road communication, the Turnpike Trusts had, from first to last, many grave defects. Foreign critics complained that, instead of the main routes of through traffic, from one end of the kingdom to another, being systematically dealt with, the abandonment of the subject by the English Parliament to a local initiative and local public spirit resulted, at best, in a strange patchwork. Whether or not a particular bit of road remained in the ruinous and impassable condition implied by parish management depended, not on the needs of the users, or the national importance of this particular link, but on the degree of enlightened self-interest or public spirit of the squires, farmers, and traders in its immediate neighbourhood.[2] If, during the eighteenth century, any one had

---

[1] *Gentleman's Magazine*, September 1754, p. 395.
[2] "The system," said a writer of 1834, "is radically bad, being based on principles in the highest degree objectionable chiefly as respects the manage-

taken the trouble to make a turnpike map of England, this would have shown, not a system of radiating arteries of communication, but scattered cases of turnpike administration, unconnected with each other ; appearing at first as mere dots on the map, then gradually increasing in number and size so as to form continuous lines ; and only by the end of the century becoming, as John Holt somewhat optimistically declared in 1794, " so multiplied and extended as to form almost an universal plan of communication through the kingdom." [1] It took, in fact, practically a whole century of disconnected effort before even such national arteries of communication as the Great North Road from London to Edinburgh, the Irish road from London to Holyhead, or the Great Western Road from London to Exeter came, for the whole of their lengths, under the administration of Turnpike Trusts. The travellers from Glasgow to London in 1739 found " no turnpike road till they came to Grantham, within 110 miles of London." A foreign visitor in 1752, travelling on the Great Western Road, declares that " after the first 47 miles from London, you never set eye on a turnpike for 220 miles. . . . What fine roads," he exclaims satirically, " from London to Land's End, or even to Exeter, Plymouth or Falmouth ; you have such roads as the lazy Italians have fruits, namely, what God left them after the Flood." [2] And yet, as another traveller observes, " there may be a profusion of too many turnpikes round a single city, half of which carried on

ment and superintendence of roads. There is in fact no general system of management or superintendence. The system is much the same as if we were in a great town to put the management of each street under the sole direction and control of a selection of persons located in each street, irresponsible to the general body and naturally careful of their own private local interests alone, without regard to the general interests of the township, or any portion other than that in which they saw and felt a direct personal interest " (*A Treatise on Internal Intercourse and Communication in Civilized States and Particularly in Great Britain*, by Thomas Grahame, 1834, p. 19).

[1] This optimistic statement of John Holt is in his *General View of the Agriculture of Lancashire*, 1794. It was quoted in Second Report of House of Commons Committee on Highways, 1808, Appendix 7A, p. 183.

[2] For the condition of the Glasgow to London road in 1739, see Dr. Bannatyne's scrapbook, quoted from in Cleland's *Statistical Account of Glasgow*; *Penny Magazine*, 16th March 1833 ; Place MSS. 27828-10. For the foreigner's account of the road from London to Land's End, see *Gentleman's Magazine*, November 1752. Two years later, another correspondent stated that, out of the 172 miles to Exeter, there are " no turnpikes more than 40 miles from London, except . . . people go round by Bath or Wells " (*ibid.* August 1754).

N

in a straight line would have proved a national rather than a
private good." [1] For even in those districts in which Turnpike
Trusts had been established, there was no security, or even
likelihood, that the most frequented, the most direct and the
easiest right of way would be selected for improvement. The
Commissioners employed by the Board of Agriculture in 1794
are continually remarking on the "malignant degree of in-
genuity . . . displayed in sending them [*i.e.* the turnpike roads]
up hills," or "over such a dreary, dangerous and hilly common." [2]
The motives for this inconsiderate choice of routes were varied
and diverse. The old pack-horse track, which went up hill and
down dale wherever the surface was good enough, was often
converted into a carriage road without regard for the fact that
its gradients made it a quite unsuitable route for wheeled traffic.
The first waggon highways were, moreover, as a House of
Commons Committee was informed in 1806, sometimes deliberately "carried up steep ascents to gain the open country and
avoid the valleys, because the roads through the latter could not
easily be made passable in the wet seasons of the year." [3] More
sinister motives were found in the "partiality" and "selfishness" of individual landowners, who sought, it was complained
in the *Gentleman's Magazine* in August 1754, "to make turnpikes
avenues, more or less, to this or that country seat." "If the
great man," it was said in 1794, "who generally takes the lead
in laying out the turnpike road has no immediate interest himself,
he has often a friend to oblige, or an enemy to mortify, by sending
the road up hill to save the land of one, or through the middle of
a meadow to hurt the other. A tippling house on the top of a hill,
or a favourite piece of land at the bottom, compels the husband-
man at this day, in many parts of this kingdom, to keep one-third
more cattle in his team than there would otherwise have been

[1] *Gentleman's Magazine*, August 1752.
[2] For the opinion of the Commissioners employed by the Board of Agriculture in 1794, see, for instance, *General View of the Agriculture of Hereford*,
by John Clark, 1794, p. 51 ; *General View of the Agriculture of Northumberland*,
by John Bailey and George Culley, 1794, p. 56 ; *General View of the Agriculture
of Durham*, by John Granger, 1794, p. 26. "Had . . . plans and sections,"
sums up Thomas Butterworth Bayley, "been sent with the petitions for Turnpike Acts during the last 40 or 20 years, Parliament would not have sanctioned
the enormous waste of public money in carrying on the schemes of ignorant
projectors or interested individuals."
[3] Second Report from the House of Commons Committee on Broad Wheel
Acts, 1806, p. 12.

occasion for." [1] Even as late as 1828, when the efficacy of public opinion had enormously increased, we see no less a personage than Sir Robert Peel, the elder, not scrupling to attempt to divert the new turnpike road between London and Liverpool out of its way, in order that it might pass close to his own residence and cotton-mills, to the ruin of the town of Tamworth—an attempt frustrated by counter-petitions from Tamworth and, most potent of all, an able letter to the *Times*.[2] Nor was it always powerful individuals who perverted the action of Turnpike Trustees. The whole of the inhabitants of particular towns frequently asserted their separate interests to the detriment of a national service. " Local interest," said John Scott in 1778, " often produces strange distortions. A few years ago a new turnpike road was made from St. Alban's to Reading . . . designed to open an easy communication between the East and West of England, and had the straight line been preserved, would have been many miles nearer than the way through London. It was, however, found necessary to make a zigzag line by Watford, Amersham, High Wycombe and Marlow, solely to oblige the inhabitants of those towns, by which means the difference between the two roads is rendered inconsiderable." [3] In other cases the reverse would happen, and a powerful corporation would try to prevent the new impost being levied on its own inhabitants. " The town of Liverpool," it was reported, " is a great enemy to turnpikes : there are only three toll-gates within eight miles of it, none within four." The result was that the road revenue was so much lessened that the Turnpike Trustees found themselves unable to keep any part of the roads in good repair. " Most of the great towns " of Lancashire, it was said in 1794, " have had sufficient interest to place the toll-bars at some miles distance from them " ; and this, it was alleged, was

[1] *General View of the Agriculture of Hereford*, by John Clark, 1794, p. 53.
[2] As to the Tamworth case, see *Times* of 31st May and 16th June 1828, which explains that " It so happens . . . that the residence of Sir Robert Peel is distant from Tamworth about 2 miles and immediately adjacent to his cotton and spinning factories at Fazeley, a village almost exclusively Sir Robert's own property, with a population consisting of his artizans. Under these circumstances Sir Robert has been using his powerful interest to exclude Tamworth in order to bring the road through Fazeley, and the proposed line is now changed accordingly, by which Tamworth will be entirely ruined."
[3] *Digests of the General Highway and Turnpike Laws*, by John Scott, 1778, p. 317.

" almost the sole cause of the wretched condition of the turnpike roads " in that county as late as 1808.[1]

The narrow limits of each Trust, and the pecuniary interests involved, not only militated against the wisest choice of a route, but also obstructed the further increase of lines of communication. " Instead of Turnpike Acts being obtained for particular roads," wrote an able critic of road administration, in 1765,[2] " they ought to have been made general throughout counties. As things are at present conducted, the Commissioners of particular roads, in order to enhance their revenues, generally take the liberty of blocking up the principal avenues of every other road which falls into or leads across theirs . . . so that, in fact, every Act which passes for the repair of a road, with the usual extensive powers to Commissioners to erect gates, is an Act also to prevent any of the roads leading into or across it, be they ever so bad, from receiving the same remedy." The Turnpike Trustees went, however, further in their obstructiveness. Towards the latter part of the eighteenth century, when the several oases of turnpike administration were impinging on each other, the Trustees of every existing Trust, in conjunction often with their mortgagees or other creditors, were quick to petition Parliament against any proposals for new turnpike roads which threatened to compete with their line of route. Thus, in 1780, when a new road was projected from Horsley to Dudbridge in Gloucestershire, the Trustees of the Gloucester and Stroud Turnpike complained loudly to the House of Commons that this new road would " open up a communication of road from Gloucester to Dudbridge, and through the parishes of Standish and Stonehouse, by which

[1] The exempted areas of Lancashire are described in the *General View of the Agriculture of Lancashire*, by John Holt, 1794, and in the Second Report of House of Commons Committee on Highways, 1808, Appendix A, p. 182. Another case may be cited from Yorkshire. When in 1802 the trustees of a certain twenty miles of the Great North Road in the North Riding got their Act, the inhabitants of the two little villages of Thirsk and Yarm, which formed the terminal points, secured clauses inserted forbidding the erection of toll-gates within four miles of each place. The result was that all local traffic was able to use eight out of the twenty miles free of toll, and cunning travellers managed even to get free of the toll on the other twelve, by using slightly longer parallel bye-lanes (*Statement concerning the Thirsk and Yarm Road*, by the Committee of Trustees, etc., Stockton, 1823). See also the pamphlets for and against the establishment of a Turnpike Trust for the road between Keighley and Kendal, in the British Museum volume, 213, i. 2.

[2] *An Inquiry into the Means of Preserving and Improving the Public Roads*, by Rev. Henry Homer, 1765, pp. 21-22.

means," it was said, the traveller from Gloucester to Bath would be able to go more quickly and easily, " as by the intended road several steep hills would be avoided." If the bill passes, they ask that their own tolls may be increased. The Trustees of the Cirencester and Stroud Turnpike go further, and demand the entire rejection of the project.[1] So, in the same year, the Trustees of Newcastle-under-Lyme and Macclesfield Turnpike petition vehemently against a projected extension of the territory of the Macclesfield and Buxton Trust, as the proposed improvement of certain branch roads " will materially interfere with the petitioners' trust, as they will be a means of lessening the tolls." In the very middle of the eighteenth century there seems to have been a pitched battle in Parliament—reminding us of similar railway struggles a century later—as to the direction to be taken by the main line of road from London to the North-Western Counties. We see Sheffield and Derby petitioning in favour of rival projects, via Leicester and via Bedford respectively, and enlisting, each of them, the support of wayside parishes. Out of many similar petitions we quote the following in 1800. The Trustees of the Maidenhead and Reading Turnpike, having under their charge part of the Great Western Road, strongly oppose a projected new turnpike road from New Windsor to Longford in Middlesex, because it would make the road from London by that way considerably shorter, which might tempt the traveller to avoid Maidenhead altogether. If we remember that the Trustees, mortgagees and creditors of an existing turnpike road would certainly include the county members, the resident Justices of the Peace, the local landowners, and the more substantial farmers of the neighbourhood, we shall be able to estimate how effective was the obstruction to the Parliamentary sanction, or even to the initiation, of a shorter or easier line of communication than that to which the inhabitants were accustomed.

---

[1] For the petitions against the new Horsley to Dudbridge road, see House of Commons Journals, 25th and 28th January 1780. A new road, admittedly advantageous, might even be opposed by a rival trader. In 1760 there was a petition presented against a new Turnpike Bill by an individual Derbyshire coalowner on the plea that the new road would " give such advantage to the proprietors of the collieries " near it as to be detrimental to his trade (House of Commons Journals, 22nd February 1760). For the petition against the Macclesfield and Buxton Turnpike Trust Bill, see *ibid.* 21st February 1780. For the struggles between the rival roads between London and the North, see *ibid.* January and February 1750. For that in protection of Maidenhead, see *ibid.* 9th June 1800.

We may here notice the somewhat analogous development of toll bridges. The privilege of levying bridge toll, or " pontage," had been conceded by the King in special cases, notably during the thirteenth and fourteenth centuries, by way of indemnity for erecting particular bridges ; but such a grant was, we understand, always limited in duration to three, five or eight years. Except for such cases, the bridges that existed seem to have been free from toll. In Lancashire in 1621, and again in Essex in 1746, we hear of attempts by neighbouring landowners to exact tolls, which are repressed by Quarter Sessions. In the eighteenth century, however, under the influence of the imperative demand for better means of communication, and of the new idea that the actual users of the highways should be made to bear the expense of their maintenance, we see erected, from 1725 onward, a whole series of new toll bridges, corresponding with the new turnpike tolls. Such a levy of tolls required statutory authority, which was granted by Local Act, sometimes (as in the cases of the City of London, Bristol, Norwich, Windsor and other corporate towns) to the Municipal Corporation ; sometimes (as in the cases of Westminster and Putney Bridges, Preston Bridge, Deritend Bridge at Birmingham and Bishopwearmouth Bridge at Sunderland) to public bodies of Commissioners incorporated for the purpose ; and sometimes (as in the cases of the bridges at Walton on Thames, Hampton Court and several of those within the Metropolis) to individual landowners or groups of speculators. These Corporations, Commissioners or Companies differed from the Turnpike Trusts in securing powers unlimited in duration, and in levying tolls on pedestrians. They seem to have resembled the Turnpike Trusts in the general inefficiency of their administration, in the frequent farming of their tolls, in the complications and extortions of the imposts that they levied on vehicular and animal traffic, and in the delays to which, in London at any rate, the congestion at their toll-gates eventually gave rise.[1]

[1] As to bridges, see chap. vi. of *The Story of the King's Highway*, pp. 85-112. For cases of the grant of " pontage " during the fourteenth century, see the references to the Parliament Rolls in *History of Private Bill Legislation*, by F. Clifford, 1887, vol. i. pp. 25-35. It was in 1621 that the Lancashire Quarter Sessions was seeking to suppress the exaction of tolls on County Bridges. " The Justices here present are of opinion that if any toll or stellage be taken for the carriage over Crosford Bridge or any other bridge repaired by the common charge of the County the same is extortion, and ought not to be taken

When we consider the administration of the various Turnpike
Trusts of the eighteenth century, from the narrower standpoint
of the repair and construction of particular bits of road, we find
ourselves in the midst of the haphazard and anarchic diversities
characteristic of an age lacking alike in technological and administrative science. The County Justices in Quarter Sessions, who,
as we have seen, controlled the earliest of the turnpike roads,
sometimes appointed an officer at a small fee to lay out the proceeds of the toll as he thought fit; or, in other cases, contented
themselves with ordering the Treasurer of the moneys arising
from particular turnpikes to pay lump sums to the Parish Surveyors of Highways " after the said Surveyors have made it
appear . . . that the inhabitants of the said parish have done
their full six days work, pursuant to the statute, of teams and
labourers, and have expended a sixpenny rate in repairing their
highways." Occasionally Quarter Sessions would request the
Justices to " view the roads in their several Divisions and to

---

or paid, and that the takers thereof shall be dealt with withall by indictment
of extortion *quo warranto* or otherwise as the law will warrant, yet nevertheless
all bridges shall be repaired by the charge of Counties and Hundreds as formerly
they have been accustomed " (*Manchester Sessions Notes of Proceedings*, 1616–
1623, edited by Ernest Axon, 1901, p. 142). More than a century later, the
Essex Quarter Sessions had expressly to require the " owners of any bridge
or bridges built over any river or stream running across any highways . . .
immediately (to) take or cause to be taken the chain or chains from off the
same " (MS. Minutes, Quarter Sessions, Essex, 15th July 1746).

Among the Local Acts authorising toll bridges to be built by Municipal
Corporations may be mentioned those of Norwich (1726), Windsor (1735),
London (1756, 1758, 1762, 1767, etc.), Maidenhead (1772). Special bodies of
commissioners were incorporated by Local Acts for the purpose of building
and maintaining Westminster Bridge (1741, 1744, 1745); Putney Bridge
(1725); Preston Bridge (1750); Deritend Bridge at Birmingham (1788, 1792,
1813 and 1822; see *Old and New Birmingham*, by R. K. Dent, pp. 421-422;
A Century of Birmingham Life, by J. A. Langford, pp. 68-71); Bishopwearmouth Bridge at Sunderland (1792, 1814). Sometimes bodies of Police or
Improvement Commissioners received such powers, as for the bridge over the
Thames at Windsor (9 George I. c. 15); and for that over the Severn at Evesham
(5 George IV. c. 67). To these must be added the Local Acts obtained by
landowners or private speculators, such as those for bridges at Walton-on-
Thames (20 George II. c. 22, 1746) and Hampton Court (23 George II. c. 37,
1749), and those relating to the various toll bridges built by joint-stock companies in the Metropolis (Report of House of Commons Committees on Metropolitan Bridges, 1854, 1876, 1877 and 1881). The most valuable toll bridge,
still existing as private property, is probably that of Lord St. Levan, con-
necting Plymouth with Devonport, and yielding a revenue of many thousands
a year. As long ago as 1800 the tolls were rented from year to year at the
" immense sum of £2500 " (*The Plymouth Dock Guide*, 1800, p. 28; *A View of
Plymouth Dock*, 1812, p. 53).

cause the Surveyor to measure such parts of the roads as are out of repair, and to report at the next Quarter Sessions." [1] But we do not gather that, for the first half of the century at any rate, Quarter Sessions, where it was responsible for a turnpike road, gave any directions, either to its own officer or to the parish Surveyors of Highways, as to the way in which the work was to be done. Some of the early bodies of Turnpike Trustees seem to have shown rather more activity, if less discretion, than the County Justices. The active Trustees, often, as we gather, the farmers and tradesmen of the neighbourhood, added petty jobbery and a foolish officiousness to their ignorance. Nor were the proceedings made any better by the intervention of the ordinary eighteenth-century squire. " We may blame," says a graphic but inelegant critic in the *Gentleman's Magazine* for August 1754, " the ignorance and obstinacy of John Trot, and reflect on Tom Buttertub, the grocer, the booby Trustee of the next parish ; of course the profile of the road is injudiciously constructed. . . . John Trot is not so much the object of contempt for being an incorrigible blockhead, as Squire Satskull and Sir John Shallow are, for their pride, avarice, insolence, ignorance, petulancy and meanness. . . . This meanness in our gentry brings it about that a tenant shall be employed in repairing the road upon his own terms, and the more he cheats the [turn]pike, the better he will be able to pay his rent. The squire likes his proposals, and the rest of the Commissioners acquiesce, being either farmers or tradesmen. . . . We cannot justly wonder that turnpike roads should be in such bad condition as they are, when we find such meanness amongst those who ought to be examples of public spirit and virtue." " At the first erection of turnpikes," reports another critic in the same journal for September 1754, " the road-makers *ex professo*, who perhaps

---

[1] The examples of the Justices' action are taken from the minutes of Quarter Sessions, Essex, 1704–1775. In 1704 "it is ordered that Mr. L. and Mr. E. A. of Coxford in this County are hereby appointed Surveyors for the road lying between Kelvedon and Strennaway, commonly called Domsey Road, for one whole year, and . . . that all the moneys now in the hands of . . . (the) Receivers of the toll at the turnpike be by them paid unto the said Surveyors and by them . . . to be employed and laid out in repairing Domsey Road " (MS. Minutes, Quarter Sessions, Essex, 25th April 1704). For 15 Orders for payments to as many parishes, see MS. Minutes, Quarter Sessions, Essex, 5th October 1725. For the order to the Justices to view the roads in their Divisions, *ibid.* 15th January 1722.

were yeomen-like farmers and gentlemen's bailiffs, made a very poor figure in their undertaking ; witness, amongst others, that great road from London to Bath ; it errs and blunders in all the forms ; its strata of materials were never worth a straw ; its surface was never made cycloidal ; it hath neither good side ditches, nor footpaths for walkers ; no outlets were made for water that stagnates in the body of the road ; it was never sufficiently widened, nor were the hedges ever cleared—of course it is the worst public road in Europe, considering what vast sums have been collected from it." Other Turnpike Trusts shifted the whole work and responsibility to their Treasurer, a gentleman whose custody of the turnpike moneys brought him a small profit, and who was therefore considered as remunerated for his trouble.

We may note here the slowness and reluctance with which the Turnpike Trustees, even more than other Local Authorities of the eighteenth century, appointed any salaried officers or even made use of the growing banking facilities. The Treasurer was, almost invariably, one of the Trustees themselves, usually a country gentleman, without any special knowledge of business, or any great proficiency in bookkeeping. The Treasurer had to get in the money either from the " pikemen," as they collected it ; and, naturally, it was found easier to employ a contractor, or toll-farmer, who could be required to pay over by regular instalments the price that he had promised to pay for his privilege. The Treasurer seems habitually to have mixed these sums of a few hundreds up to a few thousands of pounds with his own cash ; and to have paid out such expenditure on behalf of the Trust as had been authorised, or as he himself decided. Efficient audit there was none ; but periodically, after long delay, the Treasurer would produce accounts to his brother-Trustees— sometimes only on the occasion of a change of Treasurer—when the balance in hand might be transferred. In the meantime it was thought quite in order that the Treasurer should make for himself whatever profit he could, by thrifty investment of the floating balance. We may understand the reluctance of the Trustees, in their corporate capacity, to entrust their funds to the private bankers of the period. It is less easy to appreciate the simplicity with which they allowed their Treasurer to play with these public moneys for his own advantage. Under such circumstances it was almost inevitable that many bodies of Turnpike Trustees, especially in the latter half of the century, should fall back on the common administrative expedient of the period, that of "farming," which we have already described.

With such primitive views of administration, we can understand how many of the earlier Turnpike Trusts hardly conduced to the actual improvement of the roads.   Thus, Robert Phillips, in his dissertation of 1737 to the Royal Society,[1] "concerning the present state of the high roads of England," complains that the "turnpike roads, instead of being mended, have been made bad by art . . . so that all the money that has been laid out in such roads . . . has been rather of prejudice than service." The people who have had the care of the roads, he explains, have heaped loamy gravel on them, deep hard-baked ruts have been formed, which are constantly filled with water. "If the turnpikes were taken down," he sums up, "and the roads not touched for seven years, they would be a great deal better than they are now." These haphazard methods of road maintenance continued to prevail in the smaller and more remote Turnpike Trusts right into the nineteenth century.   From about 1750, however, we watch the larger and more important Trusts—those administered by active and intelligent Justices or by the principal inhabitants of populous districts—enlisting in their service permanent salaried officials who proceeded to experiment in road construction and repair, without engineering knowledge, it is true, but at any rate according to some deliberate policy, which was consistently followed.   The result was an amazing variety of shapes and surfaces, each for a time believed in by its inventor.[2]   The "road laid wavy," or "trenched road," with a

[1] *Dissertation concerning the Present State of the High Roads of England, especially those near London*, by Robert Phillips, 1737, pp. 3, 4, 15.

[2] As to the fantastic shapes of roads, see *Digests of the General Highway and Turnpike Laws*, by John Scott, 1778, p. 322.   "Some roads in England . . . are laid wavy, or rising and falling, and men attend . . . after rain, to let out the water with their spades " (*Gentleman's Magazine*, May 1749, p. 218).   " In level countries, where the roads are cut, these waves are absolutely necessary. . . . The first waving of the roads was begun in Whitechapel on the Essex Road," or else in Leicestershire.   " The waves were then short and high, and soon were found so excessively inconvenient to the travellers, both on foot and horseback and in carriages, that they were discarded. . . . The Hackney road . . . followed the waving method, but made the ascents and descents longer " (*ibid.* November 1759).

" The angle in the pantile roof road," observes Scott, " is often so great as to endanger overturning on the least collision of carriages, and always enough

" continuation of little hills and valleys " ; the " angular road sloping like a pantile roof from one hand to the other " ; the " concave road," or " hollow way," into which a stream was periodically turned to clean its surface ; the built-up " horizontal road," flanked by deep ditches, sometimes a " causeway from 20 to 30 feet wide, nearly horizontal on the top, with precipices on each side of four or five feet perpendicular depth,"—could all be seen within a day's journey of the Metropolis. Regarded in the light of the modern art of road construction, all these fantastic forms and surfaces were grotesquely inconvenient and wasteful. But we may well believe that they were all of them improvements on the deep holes and inevitable ruts which resulted from the careless dumping of clay, dirt and rubbish by the little road-farmer or the ignorant workman who carried out the orders of the local Trustee. And the constant observation and comparison of these deliberately shaped roads seems to have produced, by the end of the century, something like a consensus of opinion, among the more intelligent Trustees and Surveyors, in favour of a moderately convex surface, artificially constructed of small pebbles and gravel—an immeasurable improvement on both the " natural " surface and the heaped-up dirt which it superseded.[1]

---

to occasion anxiety to the timorous passenger " (*Digests of the General Highway and Turnpike Laws*, by John Scott, 1778, p. 320). For the concave road or hollow way, see *Dissertation concerning the State of the High Roads of England*, by R. Phillips, 1737, p. 15. This is, we imagine, the " washway " referred to in the *Inquiry into the Means of Preserving and Improving the Public Roads*, by Rev. Henry Homer, 1765, p. 30. In such a road, " instead of the water being thrown off, it is here made the repairing agent, by being conducted from the sides to the centre, and from thence to the lowest part of the road, where a side outlet is made for it ; in its course the water washes the whole surface, carries off the mud, and leaves the road firm and clean " (C. M. Ward to Sir John Sinclair in Report from House of Commons Committee on Broad Wheels and Turnpike Roads, 1809). The wilful obstruction of any " water which, by order of the Trustees or their Surveyor, shall be reserved to run or be let in upon any part of the said road " was often made punishable by fine and imprisonment (see, for instance, 17 George III. c. 20).

For the best opinion on road-making in 1778, see the admirable Appendix " On the Construction and Preservation of Roads," in the *Digests of the General Highway and Turnpike Laws*, by John Scott, 1778, pp. 313-352.

[1] It may be here noted that it is to the turnpike roads that we owe the general establishment of milestones, which (if we ignore those which were placed by the Romans on their roads) date from about 1720. At first they were put up voluntarily on a few roads. " At every mile from Grantham to Stangate," says Defoe, " are stones set up by Mr. Boulton which he designed to have carried on to London for the general benefit " (*Tour through the whole*

But the richer and larger turnpike authorities did more than merely improve the surface of the roads. Here and there we find them widening and straightening the narrow and crooked bits of their thoroughfares ; bridging the numerous " water-splashes " through which generations of travellers had passed ; improving gradients by cutting through the hilltops and raising the valley bottoms ; and, in the latter half of the century, constructing entirely new roads from place to place. Thus, as early as 1708, we find an order made at the Hertfordshire Quarter Sessions " for the widening by eight yards, of the highway from Ware to Wadesmill . . . for the length of 25 poles, and for a jury to be empanelled to assess reasonable compensation not exceeding 25 years purchase." [1]　In Essex, in 1725, the parish of Chelmsford petitioned Quarter Sessions " to grant them some supply towards the charges of purchasing and pulling down the old houses in a row called Middle Row, and lay the ground into the highway for enlarging thereof, it being but nine feet wide." It was thereupon ordered by Quarter Sessions " that the sum of £50, more and besides the sum of £100 given them last Sessions, be given to the Churchwardens, Overseers and Surveyors of the said Parish for the time being, after they have purchased and

---

Island of Great Britain, by Daniel Defoe, vol. iii. p. 28, edition of 1748).　From about 1744 most Turnpike Acts contain a clause (see, for instance, 17 George II. c. 4, Chatham and Canterbury Turnpike Act, 1744) requiring the Trustees to measure their road and set up stones or posts stating the distance.　In 1766 this requirement (including also those of direction posts at crossways and " graduated posts or stones " where the road was subject to " deep or dangerous floods ") was made universal by 7 George III. c. 40, sec. 30 (the General Turnpike Act, 1766), re-enacted by 13 George III. c. 84, sec. 41 (the General Turnpike Act, 1773).　The " milestones " were sometimes wooden posts ; those of the Epping and Ongar Turnpike Trust in 1787 were to be of oak, 5 feet high and 11 inches wide ; angular, with letters and figures on each side denoting the distance from Epping and Chelmsford respectively (*Minutes of the Epping and Ongar Highway Trust,* 1769–1870, by B. Winstone, 1891, p. 138).

The signpost is earlier than the milestone.　Paul Hentzner, the German traveller, was directed by a signpost in Kent in 1598 (*Itinerarium Germaniae, Galliae, Angliae, Italiae,* by Paul Hentzner, 1612).　In 1695 we read of Lancashire, " they have one good thing the most parts of this County . . . that at all cross ways there are posts with hands pointing to each road with the names of the great town or market towns that it leads to " (*Through England on a Side-Saddle . . . Diary of Celia Fiennes,* edited by the Hon. Mrs. Griffiths, 1888, p. 157).　As early as 1697 the Justices in Special Highway Sessions were authorised to require Surveyors of Highways to put up a " direction stone or post " at " cross highways " (8 & 9 William III. c. 16).

[1] *Notes from the Hertfordshire County Records,* p. 39 ; and MS. Minutes, Quarter Sessions, Essex, 5th October 1725 ; and *Gentleman's Magazine,* May 1753.

pulled down all the said houses and made a highway there."
But, as might have been expected, it was the Turnpike Trusts
in the distinctly urban districts that were most energetic in this
work of road improvement. The Trustees of the main road from
London into Kent had, about the middle of the century, " widened
several places in the road to Dartford, being," says the *Gentleman's
Magazine* for May 1753, " perhaps the first who began to widen
and make the roads straight." They " likewise widened and
mended some narrow and bad ways from Lewisham to Bromley
and Beckenham . . . and added a new bridge." Presently, as
we learn, the local Turnpike Trustees widened the road " going
off of Clapham Common to Mitcham." " The gentleman of
Camberwell " did the same for " a very bad hollow way leading
by the Fox & Goose near that town." In country districts this
most necessary work of widening and straightening the roads
was often obstructed by the selfishness of landowners. " If,"
it was said in the same journal in September 1754, " there be
necessity of a small strip of land to make a road more commodious sometimes it is peremptorily refused ; and if you
would obtain it legally it would cost twenty times as much as it
is worth. If to obtain a short cut, or avoid a morass, you want
to pass through a field, you are generally refused, and put to
three times as much expense as the thing is worth." But the
greatest obstacle to improvement was found in the lack of
administrative ability among the Turnpike Trustees themselves.
It practically never occurred to such Trustees to get a professional
survey made of the road to be improved ; they never saw the
importance of getting competent advice as to the engineering
problems to be solved ; and when they did have some person
in their employment who was called a Surveyor, they failed to
realise that it would not do to let him at the same time act as
contractor for the execution of the work which he was required
to supervise.

The most defective side of turnpike administration was that
of finance. There was, to begin with, in nearly all Turnpike
Trusts, the usual eighteenth-century jobbery [1] in the purchase

[1] It seems to have been quite usual for a Turnpike Trust, in spite of an
express prohibition by Parliament, to give orders for materials or work to
individual Trustees. Thus, when a House of Commons Committee looked into
the accounts of the Kensington Turnpike Trust for 1764, it was found that
an incredible number of loads of gravel were entered as put on three-quarters

of materials, in the connivance at bad work by contractors,
and in the appointment of the officials of the Trust itself. In
these respects, however, so far as our information goes, there is
no reason to suppose that the Turnpike Trustees were either
better or worse than contemporary local authorities generally.
It was in the method of raising their resources that the Trusts
were most open to criticism. Their relation with the compulsory Statute Labour, to be rendered by the parishes through
which the road passed, was, with the uncertainty as to the amount
that they could exact and the method of obtaining it, in the
highest degree unsatisfactory. But the special source of revenue
of Turnpike Trustees was, of course, the toll, the collection of
which led to endless evasions, inequalities and favouritisms of
all kinds, arbitrary exactions, and systematic petty embezzle-
ments. We need not here dwell on the various devices by which
the legislature and the Trustees tried to protect themselves
against the ingenuities of those seeking to avoid the tolls—the
vigilant closing up of bye-lanes or side roads, and the perpetual
shifting or multiplication of the gates in order to counteract
the inveterate desire to go round ; together with the long array
of penalties on such dodges as taking off the supernumerary
horses, or lightening the load where going through the turnpike
gate, dashing through without payment, or fraudulently pretending to come under one or other of the categories of exemption.[1]

of a mile of road (Piccadilly) between Clarges Street and Knightsbridge ; and
further enquiry revealed that the gravel was supplied by one of the Trustees.
All the carpenter's work of the same Trust was contracted for by the partner
of another Trustee (Report of House of Commons Committee appointed to
enquire into the application of money collected within the last twelve years,
by virtue of any Act of Parliament, for repairing any particular highway, 1765 ;
see House of Commons Journals, vol. xxix.). Adam Smith had, it will be
remembered, the meanest opinion of the financial management of Turnpike
Trustees. " The money levied is more than double of what is necessary for
executing, in the completest manner, the work, which is often executed in a
very slovenly manner, and sometimes not at all " (Wealth of Nations, 1776).
John Scott, who knew them at first hand, remarks that " the Surveyors of
turnpike roads . . . are frequently decayed farmers or tradesmen, recommended by some friend or relation to an office they are absolutely unqualified
to execute." . . . [Some] " Trustees . . . are most earnest to provide a maintenance for their poor favourites by recommending them to offices they are
unfit for " (Digests of the General Highway and Turnpike Laws, by John Scott,
1778, pp. 255, 350).
    [1] Evasion by taking off supplementary horses before coming to the turn-
pike gate was specifically forbidden by 24 George II. (1750). There is a reference to this practice in Gentleman's Magazine, September 1752. Lightening

What made the incidence of the tolls specially inequitable, and
created a permanent sense of injustice, was the multiplicity
of exemptions and abatements that were allowed to favoured
trades or individuals. There were, to begin with, any number
of exemptions in favour of agriculture ; ploughs and implements
of husbandry of every kind, carts carrying manure, cattle going
to pasture, waggons bringing home the harvest were all privileged
to pass and repass free of toll, however much they wore out the
road.[1] Sometimes other local industries would be specially
favoured ; round Evesham, in Warwickshire, the flour-millers
were secured freedom of access for their customers and for the
materials needed for the repairs of their mills ; in Berkshire, in
a vain attempt to resuscitate a decaying local manufacture, it
was stipulated that " any cart or horse carrying or bringing
back any cloth, drugget, serge or other woollen manufacture,

---

the load in the same way was prohibited by 13 George III. c. 84, sec. 10
(General Turnpike Act, 1773). " Returning by way of frolic," relates Sir
Nathaniel Wraxall, " very late at night, on horseback, to Wimbledon from
Addiscombe, the seat of Mr. Jenkinson, near Croydon, where the party had
dined, Lord Thurlow the Chancellor, Pitt and Dundas found the turnpike gate
situate between Tooting and Streatham thrown open. Being elevated above
their usual prudence, and having no servant near them, they passed through
the gate at a brisk pace, without stopping to pay the toll, regardless of the
remonstrances and threats of the turnpike man, who running after them discharged the contents of his blunderbuss at their backs. Happily he did no
injury."

[1] The exemption found most serious to the Turnpike Trustees seems to
have been that in favour of manure carts, perhaps because of the fact that,
with the increasing use of town manure (which Arthur Young found still unusual in most parts of England), this exemption became greatly stretched.
" It would undoubtedly be a real hardship on a farmer," said Scott already
in 1778, " to pay toll for bringing dung a few poles' length from his own yard
to his own fields . . . but the matter is quite dissimilar when old rags, chalk,
lime, bones, etc., are carried, in heavy loads, ten, twelve and perhaps twenty
miles, and at once reap the benefit of the road and contribute to damage it "
(*Digests of the General Highway and Turnpike Laws*, by John Scott,1778, p. 276).
It was just these " narrow wheeled waggons carrying muck from Norwich "
that were complained of in 1808 as perpetually cutting up that turnpike road.
" The damage which this never-ceasing wear and tear does to the road," it
was said, " is much greater than arises from all the other traffic upon it put
together " (*Second Report of House of Commons Committee on Highways*, 1808).
Attempts were made to get also exempted carts and waggons going empty
to town in order to bring back manure ; see the report of the meeting of
" gentlemen, farmers, gardeners, and landowners " held in London, *Morning
Advertizer*, 4th April 1810. This was conceded by Parliament under complicated restrictions. The toll was to be paid, and a special " manure ticket "
given in exchange, on production of which on the return journey with manure,
the money was to be repaid by the toll-collector (52 George III. c. 145, 53
George III. c. 82).

to or from any fulling mill," should be free from toll.[1]　The
conveyance of coal was specially favoured in some districts,
and that of " peat, peat ashes, or turf " in others.　A particular
town would insist on the exemption of " carriages carrying hay
or straw to be used within the said borough."　More general
was the exemption—specially useful because most tolls were
doubled on Sundays—of local residents riding or driving to and
from church, or attending a funeral.[2]　Most Acts forbade the
taking of toll on the days of Parliamentary elections in the
district, the borough and county elections being sometimes
both particularly specified.　Post-horses carrying mails, waggons
transporting the baggage of soldiers on the march, and carts
used for the passing of vagrants were almost universally
exempted.[3]　What was, however, more invidious was the special

[1] Special exemptions in the interests of particular trades included the
following : (a) flour-milling : exempted from toll were " all persons who shall
carry any grist to be ground for their own private use, and all horses (called
the load horses) employed by any miller to carry grist belonging to any private
family to or from the mill," as well as " horses and carriages " used to carry
materials for " building and repairing mills," 17 George II. c. 13 (Evesham
Turnpike Act, 1743) ; (b) cloth making : 20 George II. c. 6 (Reading and Puntfield Turnpike Act, 1746) ; (c) coal-carrying : 24 George II. c. 11 (Lancaster
and Richmond Turnpike Act, 1750) ; (d) peat-carrying : 20 George II. c. 6,
1746 ; (e) hay and straw carrying : 17 George II. c. 13 (Evesham Turnpike
Act, 1743).

[2] The invariable provision as to doubled tolls on Sundays did not satisfy
the Sabbatarians, and it was frequently urged that there should be " a great
additional toll at each turnpike gate," on carriages passing through on Sunday;
see for such a recommendation in 1800, *Anecdotes of the Life of Richard Watson,
Bishop of Llandaff*, by his son, Richard Watson, 1817, p. 342.

[3] As to exemption on election days, see, for instance, 24 George II. c. 29
(Ludlow Turnpike Act, 1750). We append a specimen exemption clause : " No
toll shall be taken for any person . . . carrying any quantity of materials for
repairing the said road ; or for carrying dung, mould, soil or compost of any
kind for manuring lands or gardens ; nor for carrying hay or corn in the straw
being the product of . . . the said townships . . . to be laid up in the houses,
etc., of the . . . inhabitants . . . nor shall toll be taken for any ploughs or
other instruments of husbandry . . . nor for any person residing in the townships . . . passing . . . to and from church . . . or who shall attend the
funeral of any persons who shall die or be buried in either of the said townships ;
or for post-horses carrying the mail or packet ; or for any cattle going to or
from water or pasture ; nor for the horses of soldiers on the march or carriages
attending them ; or for horses, carts or waggons travelling with vagrants sent
by legal passes " (24 George II. c. 13, Stretford and Hulme Turnpike Act,
1750).　As regards soldiers, " in early Turnpike Acts, as for instance local
statutes passed in Charles II.'s and later reigns, the army upon its march
was exempted from the tolls thereby imposed.　In 1778 the General Turnpike
Act (18 George III. c. 63) contained the first general exception in favour of
the Army, which in the year 1799 was inserted in the Mutiny Act " (*Military
Forces of the Crown*, by C. M. Clode, 1869, vol. i. p. 214).　The exemption in

privilege of exemption which influential inhabitants were sometimes able to secure, for themselves, their families, their workmen, their servants, and their agents, and for those of all successive
owners and occupiers of their premises, as the price of abstaining
from Parliamentary opposition.[1] These specific Parliamentary
exemptions by no means exhausted the list of favours. The
Trustees were authorised, both by general statutes and by their
own Local Act, to compound for the tolls ; and this power was
very generally exercised, not only in the case of regular and
frequent users of the road, but also in favour of the inhabitants
of particular parishes, and even of individual Trustees themselves. In the records of the Epping and Ongar Trust, as we
have already mentioned, we find, between 1769 and 1789, from
a score to fifty compounders, paying from 5s. 3d. to 21s. each a
year, for exemption from all tolls on themselves, their horses,
their carriages, their families and their servants. But the
exemptions and compositions accounted only for a small part of
the Trustees' loss of revenue. The men whom they appointed
as toll-collectors—turnpike gate-keepers, or " pikemen," as they
were called—were mere labourers, paid a wage of ten or twelve
shillings a week, often unable to read or write, and usually
incapable of keeping accounts. It was found necessary in 1763
elaborately to forbid them to absent themselves from their
posts during their periods of duty, and to require them to remain
until they were actually relieved.[2] The varying rates of charge,

---

favour of the Post Office had a similar history. Practically all Turnpike Acts
contained clauses exempting the mails, but some mentioned only post-horses,
others also carriages carrying mails. A General Act of 1785 made the broader
exemption universal (25 George III. c. 57).

[1] In lieu of erecting a new turnpike gate at a certain point, the Trustees
of the Lincoln and Peterborough Road were authorised to agree with the
inhabitants of fifteen specified parishes for an annual payment of not more
than £40 each, in lieu of toll ; so long as this sum is paid, the gate is not to
be erected (39 & 40 George III. c. 70, Lincoln and Peterborough Turnpike
Act, 1800).

In 1764 the " compositions " received by the Kensington Turnpike Trust
amounted to £326, or 8 per cent of the total receipts from toll; and those of
the Marylebone Turnpike Trust to £308, or 13 per cent (Report of House of
Commons Committee to enquire into the application of money, etc., 1765).

For the Epping and Ongar case, see *Minutes of the Epping and Ongar Highway Trust, 1769-1870*, by Benjamin Winstone, 1891, pp. 103-104, 137-138, 154.

[2] For the prohibition of " pikemen " to leave their posts, see Report of
House of Commons Committee on the management and application of money
collected during the last eleven years for repairing any particular highway ;
House of Commons Journals, 19th April 1763, vol. xxix. p. 646.

O

the exemptions and compositions, the validity of tickets for return journeys or other gates, and many other complications of the toll made it impossible to devise any effective check on their receipts. It was notorious that they habitually kept back part of each day's collection for themselves. Hence, from the very first, many Trusts resorted to the plan of " farming," leasing each gate with its power of exacting toll for a definite sum per annum.[1] At first the gates were let by private contract by the personal negotiations of the Justices of the Peace or Turnpike Trustees themselves, to any one who would make himself responsible for a lump sum,—sometimes to a publican, a little tradesman, or even a labourer. Presently it became customary, and Parliament made it compulsory, to resort, for the letting of the tolls, to public auction and to accept the highest bidder as lessee. As the mileage of turnpike roads increased, there grew up a whole class of professional toll-farmers, often men of large capital, farming tolls amounting to many tens of thousands a year, and employing under them small armies of professional " pikemen." Old prints and descriptions enable us to visualise these men, whom Dickens loved to describe, and who have long since disappeared from among us. " A pikeman . . . wore a tall black glazed hat and corderoy breeches, with white stockings. But the most distinctive part of his costume was his white linen apron." [2] Both masters and men quickly became notorious for every kind of sharp practice, illicit collusion and embezzlement. At the periodical auctions at which the tolls were let, Parliament had

[1] In 1709, the turnpike on the " Mountnessing road . . . with its profits and tolls " was let by the Essex justices to a man for £400 per annum ; and in 1710 the lease was renewed to the same tenant at the same rent for three years (MS. Minutes, Quarter Sessions, Essex, 12th July 1709, 11th July 1710).

" Ordered . . . that it be referred to the Justices of the Peace of Chelmsford Division or to any two of them at their Petty Sessions . . . to treat with the present tenants of the profits of the Turnpike arising at Mountnessing or with any other person for the letting the same for a term of years, and that they endeavour to procure the best rent and tenants that can be got for the same, and do make report thereof at the next General Quarter Sessions " (*ibid.* 7th October 1718).

The West Kent Justices in Quarter Sessions let the " profits and tolls " of the turnpike at Chalk in 1747 to the local alehousekeeper for £260 a year, and in 1750 to " James Pearson of Chalk, Labourer," for £300 for a year (*ibid.* West Kent, 6th June 1747, and 11th January 1750). In 1773 alehousekeepers were prohibited from being either Turnpike Trustees, or surveyors or toll-collectors ; but they might become toll-farmers, if they employed others as collectors (13 George III. c. 84, sec. 46, General Turnpike Act, 1773).

[2] *The Exeter Road,* by C. G. Harper, 1899, p. 4.

been careful, in 1773,[1] to specify with minuteness that elaborate public notice was to be given, that the highest bidder was to be accepted, and that " to prevent fraud or undue preference in letting the said tolls, the Trustees must provide a glass, with so much sand in it as will run from one end to the other in one minute ; which glass, at the time of letting the tolls, must be set upon a table and immediately after every bidding the glass must be turned, and as soon as the sand is run out, it must be turned again, and so for three times unless some other bidding intervene." Sometimes the Trustees would announce a definite reserve price as the lowest that they would accept. But what probably neither Parliament nor the Trustees contemplated, and what they certainly did not succeed in preventing, was the series of elaborate combinations and private " knock-outs " among the toll-farmers, which often prevented the full value of the tolls being obtained.[2] " The tolls," it was said in 1809, " are annually

---

[1] The statutory requirement of a minute-glass at toll auctions is in 13 George III. c. 84, sec. 31. For specimen advertisements of such lettings, see that of the Trustees of the Shrewsbury roads, *Shrewsbury Chronicle*, 20th February 1773 ; that of the Trustees of the Whetstone Turnpike, *Morning Advertizer*, 25th January 1806 ; the Trustees of the Marylebone Turnpike, for two newly-erected " weighing engines or bridges," *ibid.* 19th May 1806 ; the Trustees of the Old Street Road Turnpike, *ibid.* 22nd March 1810 ; the Trustees of the Surrey New Roads, and those of the Old District of Brentford (including weighing engine), *ibid.* 13th February 1818. The toll auctions were frequently made scenes of convivial festivity, in order to attract possible bidders. In one case, in 1814, £10 was granted for a dinner to those who attended the auction (*Minutes of the Epping and Ongar Highway Trust, 1769–1870*, by Benjamin Winstone, 1891, p. 172). A graphic description of a letting of tolls in the early part of the nineteenth century is given in *Records of Old Times*, by J. K. Fowler, 1898, chap. ii., which is largely reproduced in *The Development of Transportation in England*, by W. T. Jackman, 1916, vol. i. App. 4, pp. 681-683, where other particulars are given. The sums involved were sometimes very large. One gate on the Brighton road was said to take £2400 a year in tolls. Tongue, of Manchester, was said to be responsible for the collection of over £50,000 a year in tolls (*Records of Old Times*, by J. K. Fowler, 1898, p. 20). But the Napoleon of toll-farmers was Levy, who was reported to have contracted at one time for as much as half a million a year, being a third of the aggregate toll revenue of the Kingdom ; as well as for £300,000 a year post-horse duty (*Highways and Horses*, by Athol Maudslay, 1888, pp. 84-85 ; *Old Coaching Days*, by Stanley Harris, 1882, p. 188). The tolls of the Whetstone Turnpike Trust, for 8 miles in Middlesex of the London and Holyhead road, were let by auction in 1831 for no less than £7530 per annum (*Middlesex and Hertfordshire Notes and Queries*, vol. iv. pp. 91-94). At this time there were daily on the road to Barnet " 18 mails and 176 other coaches, besides road waggons, postchaises and other vehicles " (*The Holyhead Road*, by C. G. Harper, 1902, vol. i. p. 27).

[2] It was definitely said in 1833, upon evidence given by the Macadams, father and son, and others, that " combinations have been . . . successfully

farmed or let to individuals by auction, according to the last
year's produce. This the farmers keep as secret as possible, and
the amount can only be inferred from the increase of the terms
he proffers for the ensuing year. It is then his interest to make
the tolls as productive as possible ; but the gate-keepers he must
employ are more exposed to temptation, and over them exists
less control, than perhaps occurs in any other condition of men
in society. The only check their masters have upon them is by
reserving, upon detached days in the year, the tolls themselves,
and averaging by the produce the annual receipts, by changing
their stations almost daily, and by arbitrarily discharging them
if their returns do not reach the estimated amount. This becomes equally well-known to the gatekeeper, and he withholds
all beyond that amount. Instead of preventing, by information,
the violations of the laws limiting the number of passengers,
they are paid by the coachman to connive at the abuse ; and
the nature of their office renders them ready and constant
channels for the circulation of base coin." [1]

To the student of public administration, it is interesting to
see how the imperfection of the financial machinery destroyed
the whole efficacy of many of the Parliamentary devices for
preserving the roads. When the simple prohibition of narrow
wheels, heavy loads and excessive teams had been proved to be

---

organized to defeat the provisions of the said Act . . . with regard to the
letting of tolls " (Second Report of House of Lords Committee on Turnpike
Trusts, 1833). A graphic account of them, and of the so-called " Whispering
Gallery " of conspirators, is given in *Records of Old Times*, by J. K. Fowler,
1898, pp. 18-20. One such combination or " knock-out " we see in the case
of the letting of the Epping and Ongar Turnpike tolls in 1801, when the two
pretended rivals in the auction-room afterwards come forward jointly to take
up the contract which had been knocked down to one of them for £1055. The
Trustees " suspected that there had been underhand proceedings . . . collusion
between those bidding for the tolls." This was eventually admitted by the
parties, who agreed to an increase in the price to £1201, at which a lease was
granted to them (*Minutes of the Epping and Ongar Highway Trust, 1769–1870*,
by Benjamin Winstone, 1891, pp. 162-164). See also *Road Reform*, by William
Pagan, 1845, and our *Story of the King's Highway*, 1913.

[1] The quotation as to fraud by pikemen is from a letter of C. M. Ward to
Sir John Sinclair ; see Report of House of Commons Committee on Broad
Wheels and Turnpike Roads, 1809, Appendix A. There are frequent complaints
as to the arbitrary exactions of the " pikemen " from inexperienced or timid
travellers ; see letter to *Times*, 18th June 1824. The lessee of the Epping and
Ongar tolls in 1816 was found persistently " taking more tolls on coaches,
postchaises, etc., than he was entitled to." Criminal proceedings against him
were begun, but subsequently compromised (*Minutes of the Epping and Ongar
Highway Trust, 1769–1870*, by Benjamin Winstone, 1891, pp. 173-174).

ineffective,[1] the country gentlemen who drafted the various highway and turnpike statutes fondly thought to achieve their end by imposing extra rates of toll for every narrow-wheeled vehicle however loaded, and for every hundredweight of loading on any vehicle, over and above a legally specified amount, varying according to a complicated scale depending on the kind of vehicle, the breadth of its wheels, the distance between them, and even the season of the year. For this purpose Turnpike

---

[1] We cannot here enter upon the elaborate contrivances for regulating the shape, size and arrangement of wheels, so as to injure a soft road as little as possible, which lasted for more than half a century. See *A Treatise upon Wheel Carriages*, by Daniel Bourn, 1763 ; *Observations on the Structure and Draught of Wheel Carriages. an Inquiry into the Means of Preserving and Improving the Public Roads*, by J. Jacob, 1773 ; *Some Brief Remarks upon Mr. Jacob's Treatise on Wheel Carriages*, by Daniel Bourn, 1773 ; *Remarks on the Comparative Advantages of Wheel Carriages of Different Structure and Draught*, by Robert Anstice, 1790 ; *Observations on the Effects which Carriage Wheels with rims of different shapes have on the Roads*, by Alexander Cumming, 1797 ; *A Supplement to the Observations on the contrary effects of Cylindrical and Conical Carriage Wheels*, by the same, 1809 ; *A Treatise on Wheels and Springs for Carriages*, by Davies Gilbert, M.P., F.R.S. ; *An Essay on the Construction of Roads and Carriages*, by R. L. Edgeworth, 1817 ; *Cursory Remarks on Wheeled Carriages*, by John Cook ; and *An Essay on the Construction of Wheel Carriages as they affect both the roads and the horses*, by Joseph Storrs Fry, 1820. The subject engaged most of the attention of the House of Commons Committee on the Preservation of Roads, etc., which published nine reports between 1806 and 1811. For the whole subject see our *Story of the King's Highway*, 1913.

One inventor went so far as to supersede wheels altogether, replacing them by two or four broad iron rollers, which it was supposed would level the ruts, clear away the mud and cement the gravel. See *A Treatise upon Wheel Carriages*, 1763, and *Some Brief Remarks upon Mr. Jacob's Treatise on Wheel Carriages*, 1773, both by Daniel Bourn ; and *Digests of the General Highway and Turnpike Laws*, by John Scott, 1778, pp. 269-270.

Apart from the difficulty of getting the law enforced, the provisions as to width of wheels were largely nullified by the exception always made in favour of carts used in and about husbandry and manuring of land (see, for instance, 5 George I. c. 6, 1718), and by the use of " dishing " or " conical " wheels, with " tapering rims," by which the " tread " was reduced. " We have lately seen," writes a practical critic in 1773, " the broad wheels of waggons which, by Act of Parliament, should press a surface of nine inches, in reality bear only on one of about three ; some of them by means of bevelling the edges and raising the middle of the periphery ; and others by bevelling the whole periphery and having the inner edge considerably higher than the other " (*Observations on the Structure and Draught of Wheel Carriages*, by J. Jacob, 1773, p. 89). It may be said, in excuse of these regulations, that the heavy waggons were demonstrably so destroying the soft roads of the time as to cause the cost of their repair to become an intolerable burden. Certain Warwickshire roads in 1765 were actually costing £84, and even £121, per mile per annum (*Inquiry into the Means of Preserving and Improving the Public Roads*, by Henry Homer, 1765, p. 78) ; or more than double the average cost of the far superior turnpike roads of 1815.

Trustees were, from 1741 onwards, authorised, and might by
Quarter Sessions be required, to erect "a crane, machine or
weighing engine" to weigh the loads—not the convenient modern
weighbridge, which had not then been invented, but a huge and
complicated structure, rising high over the road, and actually
lifting the vehicle and its contents from the ground.[1] One such
machine may still be seen *in situ* at Woodbridge, Suffolk, and a
weird and incomprehensible structure it is. Its erection was
costly, and the expense of keeping men to work it was still
greater. It was never very accurate, and was always getting
out of order. "It is a very common case," it was said in 1796,
"that a load will pass at one engine, when the same load at
another will be subject to an increased toll." It was, moreover,
hugely inconvenient to the users of the road, especially as it
was practically impossible to be always sure that a load was
under a given weight. There was thus every inducement to
evasion and neglect ; and the Trusts soon found that, apart
from the ordinary charges, the weighing machine did not yield
enough in extra tolls to pay for the necessary attendance and
upkeep. On the other hand, the toll-farmer was willing to give
a considerable additional price for the tolls if he was permitted
to rent also the weighing machine. The Trustees, in fact, were
in a dilemma.[2] "If," it was acutely pointed out to a House

[1] The provision as to a weighing machine is in 14 George II. c. 42 (1740) ;
the power was often specifically repeated in Turnpike Acts ; see, for instance,
20 George II. c. 7, Essex Turnpike Act, 1746 ; it was afterwards embodied in
the General Turnpike Acts, 7 George III. c. 40, sec. 1, and 13 George III. c. 84,
sec. 1. For the uncertainty of such weighings, see Report of House of Commons
Committee on the General Turnpike Acts, 1796, p. 749. "The persons concerned in the trade of market gardeners never are able to know the weight of
their articles, for sometimes it happens from a shower of rain a loading of
2 tons 5 cwt. will be increased three or four hundredweights."
[2] As to the dilemmas presented by the weighing machine, see *The Case
and Reasons for Disusing Weighing Machines on the Turnpike Roads*, 1774 ;
*Observations on Stage-Waggons, Stage-Coaches, Turnpike Roads, Tollbars, Weigh-
ing Machines, etc.*, by William Deacon, 1807 ; and the letters from C. M. Ward
and F. Dickins to Sir John Sinclair, in Report of House of Commons Committee on Broad Wheels and Turnpike Roads, 1809, Appendix A. The Clerk
to the Trustees of the Stamford Hill roads said that he was satisfied that the
lessees of the weighing machines suffered "carriages to pass through upon a
certain weekly sum without weighing them," though he could not prove it.
This led to the recommendation : "that . . . as weighing engines are intended to
prevent excessive weights, and not to increase the revenue of the turnpikes, the
trustees of roads should be restrained from leasing or otherwise letting the same"
(Report of House of Commons Committee on the General Turnpike Acts, 1796).
    It was perhaps in consequence of this dilemma that these costly weighing

of Commons Committee in 1808, "the engine continues in the hands of the Trust, its purpose is completely defeated by the corrupt connivance of the keeper employed; not only may he allow overweight to pass for a small reward, but he may share profits with the driver carrying extra weight unknown to his employer, and thus both the Trust and the master carrier will be defrauded. If the weighing machine is let by the year for a certain sum, nearly equal to its supposed receipts, to an individual whose own interest will keep him vigilant, that very interest will lead him to compound with the carriers of overweight; indeed composition is the only way by which he can repay himself for the rent of the engine. Were he to be rigid in the exaction of every penalty he would put a stop to overweights and to his own profits together. If, in a word, the weighing engine constituted an effectual check to overweighted carriages, the penalties exacted would amount to a very trifling sum.

---

engines were sometimes left, like one at Hammersmith in 1800, "for many years disused and suffered to fall into decay" (*Report of a Committee of the Hammersmith and Brentford Turnpike*, 1800, p. 7). Already in 1796 the Trustees of the Surrey Turnpike had removed their engine seven or eight years before (Report of House of Commons Committee on the General Turnpike Acts, 1796). A Committee in 1833 recommended the total "abolition of the use of weighing engines" (Second Report of House of Lords Committee on Turnpike Trusts, 1833).

Among other heavy vehicles objected to came, in the latter part of the century, the heavily laden stage coaches, which were exempt from subjection to the weighing engines. An Act of 1788 restricted them to six outside passengers, in addition to two on the box by the driver (28 George III. c. 57). A more stringent measure in 1790, known as "Gammon's Act," attempted to reduce this to four and one respectively, or fewer if under three horses, and did its best to prevent drivers allowing more by imposing a toll of five shillings on every passenger in excess (30 George III. c. 36). But, as with the excess tolls for overweight, it was soon found that the pikemen "notoriously compound with the drivers of coaches," and the practice continued unabated (*Report of Committee of Hammersmith and Brentford Turnpikes*, 1800, pp. 18, 33). "Mr. Gammon's Act," it was pointed out in 1794, "is now openly set at defiance, and sometimes 20 persons are to be found at the outside of a stage coach on the roof which by law is limited to six" (*Times*, 19th April 1794). "The salutary regulations provided by these Acts," reported a Committee of 1806, "have been by a variety of contrivances most grossly evaded, insomuch that instead of 6 (the number limited by the original Act) 20 passengers and more are often carried on the outside of stage coaches" with results not only "extremely destructive" to the roads, but also dangerous, as "scarce a week passes without some of these carriages breaking down" (First Report from House of Commons Committee on Broad Wheels and Turnpike Roads, 1806). A further Act was then passed, facilitating the enforcement of the preceding ones (46 George III. c. 136). See *The Danger of Travelling on Stage Coaches and a Remedy Proposed*, by Rev. W. Milton, 1810, and *Brief Considerations on the Present State of the Police of the Metropolis*, by L. B. Allen, 1821.

But they are let or farmed out for considerable sums, which completely proves that, instead of operating as a prevention, they only become an additional toll for extra load." Assuming that, on the soft surface of the period, it was desirable to discourage the conveyance of heavy weights, especially on narrow wheels in winter, it is impossible to avoid the conclusion, drawn by an able critic, in 1808, that, as actually worked, the whole system of extra tolls and weighing machines was " injurious to the roads instead of tending to their preservation, because being rented, the renters compound with the owners of waggons to receive double tolls going and returning, on permission to carry any weight. The immense rents given for weighing machines could not be raised by any other means."

The most serious of all the financial defects of the Turnpike Trusts was, however, the deficit into which many of the bodies of Trustees fell. The new revenue of tolls seemed, at first, to promise inexhaustible annual resources, which Parliament allowed to be mortgaged without check or limit. Already by 1773, the effect of reckless finance had made itself apparent in many Trusts. "At the first erection of turnpikes," wrote Thomas Butterworth Bayley, " the people imagine the roads are to be made and kept in repair by the very charm of the word turnpike, and not being obliged to continue their statute work with so much attention as formerly, depend entirely on the tolls, and fall into a state of negligence and indifference till at length the first materials are worn out, and then the tolls being mortgaged to the height, the whole burden of renewing and supporting the roads again is laid upon them with the additional tax of the tolls." [1] By the end of the century the mortgaging of tolls had

---

[1] *Observations on the General Highway and Turnpike Acts,* by Thomas Butterworth Bayley, 1773, p. 52. " Cases may be found," said the House of Commons Committee, " where persons taking the management are rather disposed to maintain establishments beneficial to themselves, than to relieve . . . the public burdens " (Second Report of House of Commons Committee on Highways, 1808). " There is not a gentleman in the Kingdom," writes one who was himself a squire, " who cannot bear testimony tò the lax manner in which the duties of turnpike road commissioners are discharged, to the total absence of all personal responsibility . . . and to the general improvidence of the expenditure " (*A Letter to the Right Hon. C. B. Bathurst, M.P., on the subject of the Poor Laws,* by Richard Blakemore, 1819, p. 32).

See also *Observations on the Formation, State and Condition of Turnpike Roads and other Highways, with Suggestions for their Permanent Improvement on Scientific Principles,* by A. H. Chambers, 1820.

been carried to a great height, and many Trusts made default
in the payment of interest on their bond debt. Between 1830
and 1838 no fewer than 84 separate Trusts were thus in default.
Sir James Macadam stated in 1839 that he knew of some Trusts
which had paid no interest for over sixty years. " In some
instances," reported the House of Commons Committee in 1808,
" they have contracted debts bearing an interest nearly equal to
the amount of their tolls, and when those have been increased
fresh debts are incurred ; so that the contributions levied on
individuals using the road become directed to purposes wholly
different from their repair." In some instances the road was
seized by the mortgagees, who levied the tolls for the payment of
their own claims. In many other cases the arrears of interest
were habitually added to the bonded debt, which came, in consequence, eventually to exceed seven millions sterling for the
whole kingdom—a considerable part of which was never repaid.[1]

With the whole or the greater part of the tolls thus alienated
for payment of interest on past indebtedness—sometimes even
with the mortgagees in possession, taking the whole money
revenue for their arrears of interest and heavy legal expenses—
the expenditure on the repair of the road was naturally reduced
to a minimum, and it may well be that, in many cases, the last
state of such turnpike roads was worse than the first. Arthur
Young, in his travels about England, clearly implies that the
great majority of the turnpike roads were far better than the
parish highways, but occasionally he comes across one in Wales,
in Lancashire or in Suffolk which he cannot believe to be a turnpike, so vile is its condition of disrepair. It was, indeed, as was
subsequently perceived, a " great defect in the system of turnpike
laws " that there was an utter lack of " provision to compel each
Trust to account before some competent tribunal. Road Commissioners," said the *Edinburgh Review* in October 1819, " are the
only persons entrusted by Parliament to levy a large revenue
from the public without being required to account in any way
for what they receive. A still greater defect is the want of any

---

[1] *Analysis of the Defective State of Turnpike Roads and Turnpike Securities,
with Suggestions for their Improvement,* by Francis Phillips, 1834 ; House of
Commons Committees on Turnpikes, 1833, 1836, 1838 ; Royal Commission on
Roads, 1840; *History of Private Bill Legislation,* by F. Clifford, 1885–1887, vol.
ii. p. 18 ; *The Development of Transportation in Modern England,* by W. T.
Jackman, 1916, pp. 612-613.

proper remedy when a set of Commissioners abuse their trust. They may suffer their road to become a perfect ruin ; they may embezzle funds and commit every sort of malpractice, and yet go on levying tolls, keeping possession of the road and defying all complaints." There was, in fact, no practical method of bringing a defaulting, hopelessly incompetent or dishonest Turnpike Trust to book. Subject to no official superintendence or central control, under no inspection, rendering no accounts, it could use or neglect its powers as it chose. A Turnpike Trust could not even be indicted for letting its roads become impassable. The only legal remedy was the presentment or indictment of the parish or township within which the road lay.[1] The creation of a special statutory Trust had left unimpaired the liability of the parish to maintain " the good passage " on all parts of the King's Highway, whether or not some other persons had received a statutory right to exact tolls from those who travelled on it. Spasmodically the law would be put in force. Some public-spirited Justice of the Peace would formally present an exception-ally neglected bit of turnpike road, or the parish would find itself indicted at the suit of some aggrieved user of the road, with the result of a fine, a special highway rate, a momentary spurt of activity in enforcing Statute Labour, and an early reversion to

---

[1] When the Post Office wanted to extend its mail coach service from Shrewsbury to Holyhead, and found the turnpike road actually unsafe, the Postmaster-General began by sending letters to the Treasurers of the several Turnpike Trusts on the route, asking them to effect improvements. This producing no result, he had 21 parishes indicted, and thus compelled them to do some repairs, though they proved insufficient to bring the road up to the requirements of a fast mail coach route (Second Report of House of Commons Committee on the Holyhead Road, 1810 ; *Her Majesty's Mails*, by W. Lewins, 1864, p. 142).

The provision as to apportioning the fine and costs is in 13 George III. c. 84, sec. 33, General Turnpike Act, 1773. " As the law now stands," wrote Sir J. C. Hippisley to Sir John Sinclair in 1808, " if any part of a turnpike road be out of repair, remedy is given by presentment or indictment of the parish in which such road is situate, subjecting the parish to great expense and inconvenience, although the nuisance be wholly imputable to the trustees of the turnpike. . . . It is true that . . . Quarter Sessions may apportion fines and costs between the Parish and Turnpike Trust, yet this power can afford very inadequate relief or compensation in many cases, where the parishes have been harassed by prosecutions for nuisances for which they have in no respect been equitably responsible ; for their parish officers, travelling thirty or forty miles to the Quarter Sessions ; for loss of time, etc."

(Sir J. C. Hippisley, Bart., M.P., to Sir John Sinclair, 4th April 1808 ; Second Report of House of Commons Committee on Highways, 1808, Appendix A, p. 136.)

the former neglect. It is true that, from 1773 onward, the Court could apportion the fine and costs between the parish and the Trust, but only "in case it shall appear to the Court from the circumstances of the Turnpike debts and revenues that the same may be paid without endangering the security of the creditors who have advanced money upon the credit of the tolls "; and the parish, in practice, never got reimbursed the expense to which it was put. So flagrantly unjust was it to punish the local parishioners, who had nothing to do with the administration of the Turnpike Trust, for the default or neglect of a separate authority, which still went on exacting its tolls, that this procedure of presentment and indictment was, in practice, even less effective for turnpike roads than for parish highways. The injustice was so glaring that public opinion was arrayed against any such presentment of parishes, and in 1809 it was definitely discouraged by a Committee of the House of Commons.[1]

The foregoing description of the theory and practice of turnpike administration, and our analysis of its defects, might lead the student to assume that all the effort and money lavished by the eighteenth-century Turnpike Trusts resulted in no net advantage to the community. This would be a false conclusion. The parish highway often consisted, as we have described in our *Story of the King's Highway*, of a mere horse track across a miry common, or a watery hollow lane twisting between high banks and overhanging hedges. So deep and narrow were these ways that "the stag, the hounds and the huntsmen," Edgeworth tells us,[2] "have been known to leap over a loaded waggon in a hollow way without any obstruction from the vehicle." Such a highway was practically impassable for wheeled vehicles, and sometimes even for horsemen, for half the year. With the coming of the Industrial Revolution, with a rapidly increasing population, with manufactures ready to leap from the ground, with unprecedented opportunities for home and foreign trade, improvement of communication between different parts of the kingdom became,

---

[1] " That it is the opinion of this Committee that, in the case of any presentment or indictment of any highway being a turnpike road, the said presentment or indictment should be preferred against the treasurer of such Trust, instead of the parish through which such roads run " (Report of House of Commons Committee on Broad Wheels and Turnpike Roads, 1809).

[2] *An Essay on the Construction of Roads*, by R. L. Edgeworth, 2nd edition, 1817.

from the standpoint of material prosperity, the most urgent of national requirements. To-day, the railway and the tramway, the telegraph and the telephone, have largely superseded roads as the arteries of national circulation. But, barring a few lengths of canal in the making, and a few miles of navigable river estuaries, it was, throughout the eighteenth century, on the King's Highway alone that depended the manufacturer and the wholesale dealer, the hawker and the shopkeeper, the farmer, the postal contractor, the lawyer, the government official, the traveller, the miner, the craftsman and the farm servant, for the transport of themselves, and the distribution of their products and their purchases, their services and their ideas. Hence, to open up even some of the ways between the Metropolis and the rest of the country, between the ports and the landward counties, between the food-producing districts and the new manufacturing centres, was worth almost any money cost, however vexatiously it might be raised or however wastefully it might be spent. And all contemporary evidence indicates that, what with surface-making and embanking, widening and straightening, levelling and bridging, the mileage of usable roads was, by the eighteenth-century Turnpike Trusts, very greatly extended.[1] The frequent complaints of the local

[1] " The Commissioners of the road from Whitechapel into Essex very well understand and perform their office. . . . Justice ought to be done also to the Commissioners of the Turnpikes leading into Kent over Shooters Hill, who endeavour to make the road straight, by cutting off all angles, and widening it " (Gentleman's Magazine, May 1749). Speaking generally of the roads in England, a writer declares in 1754 that " amendments made of late years . . . have been very considerable. . . . The turnpike now forming Truro to Falmouth, on the West, and to Grampound on the East, I look upon as a very masterly and complete piece of workmanship ; and indeed, it must be acknowledged that the new turnpikes are better than the old. Thus, the Taunton Turnpikes are better than the Bath or Bristol ; the Exeter better than either ; and the Truro in a fair way to exceed them all " (ibid. October 1754). The dithyrambic quotation is from An Enquiry into the Means of Preserving and Improving the Public Roads, by Henry Homer, 1765, p. 8.

    We may quote a few of these statements of the surveyors employed by the Board of Agriculture in 1794. Of Kent we read that " the turnpike roads, and those most frequented, are kept in tolerably good order ; but the bye-roads of West Kent are frequently impassable for postchaises " (General View of the Agriculture of Kent, by J. Boyes, 1796, p. 90). Of Westmoreland it is said that " the great roads leading through the county are kept in excellent repair by the sums collected at the turnpike gates " (General View of the Agriculture of Westmoreland, by A. Pringle, 1794, p. 37). The Nottinghamshire reporter testifies that " the roads of this country are of late years much improved, many parishes having learnt from the example of the turnpikes to form them properly, and have them executed under an understanding surveyor " (General

absence of turnpikes indicate in themselves how completely the new system had commended itself to the ordinary traveller. Before the middle of the century particular roads are marked out for praise. Between 1750 and 1770, when the number of Turnpike Trusts was actually trebled, the contemporary self-complacency over the new roads rises to dithyrambic heights. "There never was a more astonishing revolution accomplished in the internal system of any country," declares an able and quite trustworthy writer in 1767, "than has been within the compass of a few years in that of England. The carriage of grain, coals, merchandise, etc., is in general conducted with little more than half the number of horses with which it formerly was. Journeys of business are performed with more than double expedition. . . . *Everything wears the face of dispatch* . . . and the hinge which has guided all these movements and upon which they turn is the reformation which has been made in our public roads." Thirty years later, when the standard of efficiency in roads had greatly risen, the reports by the critical surveyors of the Board of Agriculture are more grudging. But with the exception of Wales, they everywhere report a substantial improvement and development, by the agency of the Turnpike Trusts, of the means of communication within each county And we have the significant fact that the most eminent observers of, and participators in, the local government of the latter half of the century—Sir Henry Hawkins, Dr. Richard Burn, John Scott, and Arthur Young—all expressly assert, or at least unequivocally imply, the expediency of the Turnpike Trust and its toll. Our own conclusions coincide with this verdict. The intense jealousy of any increase of the national executive government, and the abhorrence of new local rates would have made impracticable any project for a centralised road administration, or for raising the necessary income by direct assessment. "If rates on land had been resorted to," said Sir Henry Parnell, "the measure would inevitably have failed, because the land-

---

View of the Agriculture of Nottingham, by R. Lowe, 1794, p. 53). Of Northumberland it is said that "the turnpike roads are most in good order, but badly designed" (*General View of the Agriculture of Northumberland*, by J. Bailey and G. Culley, 1794, p. 56). As to Lancashire, where manufactures had so enormously increased, and turnpikes were almost universal, we are told that "Great exertions have been of late years at very considerable expense to improve the roads, the effects of which are very apparent" (*General View of the Agriculture of Lancashire*, by John Holt, 1794, p. 64).

owners would, beyond all doubt, have preferred bad roads and
low rates to good ones and high rates ; in point of fact, very
indifferent roads would have answered all their local purposes.
If the roads had been vested in the hands of government, it may
safely be said that this plan would also have failed, for government would never have been able to obtain the consent of Parliament to vote upwards of a million and a half a year for those
roads only which now are turnpike roads.   It is therefore to the
turnpike system of management that England is indebted to her
superiority over other countries with respect to roads. . . .
Nothing but leaving the management of the roads to those
people who live in their neighbourhood would ever have induced
the people of England to pay, as they now do, a road revenue,
arising from turnpike tolls, to the amount of £1,500,000 a year ;
for, though tolls are in every respect fair and proper for maintaining a road ; and although Government by employing scientific
engineers, might have expended the produce of them with
greater skill than country gentlemen ; the hostility to pay
them, if they had been wholly at the disposal of government,
would no doubt have prevented the making of useful roads so
universally over the whole country as they have been made under
the established system." [1]   The Turnpike Trust and its toll was,
in short, the only way open.   Without the local initiative and
local support fostered by the thousand separate Trusts ; without
the emulation and mutual instruction which their several experiments promoted ; without the large revenues which the toll
drew from the multitudinous but politically helpless road users,
no considerable improvement in the highways of England would
have taken place for, at any rate, the first three-quarters of the
eighteenth century, and very little would have been achieved
before the passing of the Reform Bill.[2]

[1] *A Treatise on Roads*, by Sir Henry Parnell, afterwards Lord Congleton,
1833, pp. 263-264, 288-289.
[2] As late as 1824 the English Turnpike system was a subject of envy to a
French traveller.   Baron Dupin, who had long been impressed with the English
administration (see his *Mémoires sur la marine et les ponts et chaussées de
France et Angleterre*, 1818), observes that " In France, during the Revolution,
the government wished to establish turnpikes on our main roads, as in England ;
and as in England the people at first rose in revolt against the system.   But
the Directory had not sufficient firmness for maintaining this useful innovation,
which ought now to be taken up again, and energetically enforced " (*Voyages
dans la Grand Bretagne*, Troisième Partie, Force Commerciale, by Baron Charles
Dupin, 1824, vol. i. p. 33).   We may here conveniently give some statistical

Passing from the legal constitution and powers of the Turnpike Trust, we may get from the descriptions of contemporaries
some glimpses of the body as it actually existed. In order to
avoid local opposition, those who were promoting a Turnpike
Bill made a point of including as Trustees every one of influence
in the neighbourhood—not merely the squires and parsons and
their agents or bailiffs, but also the principal tenant-farmers
and shopkeepers. " The practice," said Sir Henry Parnell,
" is to make almost every opulent farmer or tradesman a trustee,
residing in the vicinity of a road, as well as all the nobility and
persons of large landed property ; so that a Trust seldom consists
of fewer than 100 persons, even if the length of the road to be
maintained by them does not exceed a few miles." [1] Of these

conception of the height reached in England and Wales by this system. In
1838 the 22,000 miles of turnpike road, representing about one-fifth of the
total highway mileage of the kingdom, were under 1116 Trusts, employing 3555
treasurers, clerks and surveyors (besides some 20,000 toll-collectors, etc.) and
levied £1,458,000 at their 7796 toll-gates and side bars, spending in all about
£51 a year on each mile of road, and having over £7,000,000 of debt (*Journal
of the Royal Statistical Society*, January 1839).

For a vision of the stage-coach organisation at its best, see such books as
Coaching, with Anecdotes of the Road, by Lord William Lennox, 1876 ; *Annals
of the Road, or Notes on Mail and Stage Coaching in Great Britain*, by Nimrod
(Captain H. E. Malet), 1876 ; *Old Coaching Days*, 1882 ; and *The Coaching
Age*, 1885, by Stanley Harris ; *Brighton and its Coaches*, by W. C. A. Blew,
1894 ; *Forty Years at the Post Office*, 1895, and *On the Track of the Mail Coach*,
1895, both by F. E. Baines ; *Coaching Days and Coaching Ways*, by W. O.
Tristram, 1901 ; and *Stagecoach and Mail in Days of Yore*, by C. G. Harper,
1903. " A passenger could coach from Portsmouth to Holyhead, from Barn-
staple to Berwick, with changes and stoppages it is true, but by a continuous
mailcoach road, without passing through London. The country resounded with
the blast of the horn and the rattle of pole-chains " (*Forty Years at the Post
Office*, by F. E. Baines, 1895, pp. 37-38). There was eventually coaching
communication, with changes, from Falmouth to Thurso. Birmingham was,
in effect, the centre of the system, at which most coach lines crossed.

It may be added that the stage-coaches, rendered possible only by the
turnpike roads, carried inside passengers at from 2½d. to 4d. per mile, and
outside passengers at from 2d. to 3d. per mile. The new railways adopted fares
only slightly lower than these rates, being about 3d. per mile first class, 2d.
second class, and a penny to three halfpence third class. But they carried
passengers at about 24 miles per hour, or two or three times the speed of the
coaches (*The Development of Transportation in Modern England*, by W. T.
Jackman, 1916, p. 605). The rate at which the coaches travelled, which, in
1750, had been only five or six miles per hour and 50 to 70 miles in a day, had
risen by 1830 to 9, 10 and even 12 or 13 miles per hour, for 185 miles (to
Manchester), 259 miles (to Holyhead), and even 400 miles (to Edinburgh) at
a stretch, taking 19, 27 and 45½ hours respectively (*ibid.* pp. 684-700).

[1] *A Treatise on Roads*, by Sir H. Parnell, 1833, pp. 268-269 ; there were
" a prodigious number of Commissioners, frequently from one hundred to two
hundred, for the care of 10 or 15 miles of road " (*Edinburgh Review*, October
1819).

two or three hundred persons, all belonging to the ten or twelve square miles directly served by the road, the numerical majority were, in social status and education, little above the persons who usually served the parish offices, and it was into their hands that the meetings usually fell. Some of the Justices of the Peace and clergymen who were on an important Turnpike Trust in Middlesex and Essex petitioned Parliament in 1740 about this very point. " There are many persons appointed " to their Trust, they explain, " who have very little or no freehold in either of the said Counties, and consequently are not so much concerned for the same as the petitioners ; yet the said persons, being many in number, and dwelling for the most part in or near the parish of Whitechapel, where the meetings are held during the six winter months . . . by reason of their vicinity are frequently more in number than the gentlemen whose freeholds lie at a greater distance in Essex, from whence it happens that the affairs of the said turnpike are chiefly influenced and governed by them, who do sometimes carry questions by surprise, particularly at a late meeting where they did, in a most extraordinary and unjustifiable manner at an unreasonable time of the day, without giving any notice, take upon themselves to discharge one of the principal officers of the said Trust, without any charge or accusation against him, or giving him any opportunity to make his defence, though the said officer was at that very time absent with their privity and consent." [1] The inevitable tendency that the numerical majority of the active Commissioners should make, not only the time and place, but also the tone and manners of the meetings such as was most congenial to them, cannot have failed to discourage the attendance of the greater folk. The filling up of vacancies by co-option worked, as we have shown in our work on *The Parish and the County*, in the cases of the Close Vestries and the County Justices, and we may now add also, in that of the Commissioners of Sewers,

---

[1] House of Commons Journals, 16th January 1740. In this case the gentry appeared to have persisted in their struggle, with the result that this Trust earns, in 1749, the praise of the *Gentleman's Magazine*. " The Commissioners of the road from Whitechapel into Essex," it was said, " very well understand and perform their office " (*Gentleman's Magazine*, May 1749). They were the first to adopt what seemed then an improvement in road construction, viz. " the waving method," or laying out the road in short " waves," alternately rising and falling, so as to let the water run off (*ibid.* November 1759).

towards an homogeneity of membership, which—especially in
the Metropolitan area—almost inevitably tended downwards.[1]

Unlike the Incorporated Guardians the majority of the Turnpike Trusts do not appear to have developed, right down to the
end of their being, any system of administration by executive
committees and salaried staffs. The whole body of one or two
hundred Trustees would be summoned—we gather, merely by
public advertisement and notices affixed to the turnpike gates—to
meetings held at the principal inn of the market-town ; and the
number and character of those who actually attended varied
enormously, according to the district, and also according to the
occasion. In the absence of an organised and responsible
executive, and even of authoritative standing orders, the gather-
ings often went anything but smoothly. " The whole time of
these meetings," says an Edinburgh Reviewer of 1819, " is
occupied in tumultuous and unprofitable discussions, and in
resolving on things at one meeting which run a good chance of
being reversed at the next ; so that the well-informed and
civilized Commissioners become very soon disgusted with the
disorderly uproar, or the want of sense, temper or honesty of
some of their companions ; and that the management finally
falls into the hands of a few, busy, bustling persons of low condition, who attend the meetings with no idea of performing a
public duty, but for the purpose of turning their powers, by some
device or other, to the profit of themselves or of their friends and
relations." [2] At first, the meetings were often held, to suit the
ease and convivial desires of the majority, late in the afternoon,
which prevented many persons of the best class from attending.
This was partly stopped by a section of the General Turnpike Act
of 1773, which required all such meetings to begin between 10 A.M.
and 2 P.M.[3] Even then it was complained that " Such meetings
continue sitting in many parts of the Kingdom to a very late
hour, and in some instances, commence at a late hour in the

---

[1] In the Kensington Turnpike Trust in 1763 the custom as to filling vacancies
was as follows. Two vacancies were always left unfilled, in case of some
special need for the appointment of a particular person. The others were
filled on the nomination of single Trustees, each nominating for a vacancy in
turn, as their names stood in alphabetical order ; subject, however, as a matter
of form, to the nominee in each case receiving the approval of a ballot of the
Trustees present (*House of Commons Journals*, vol. xxix. p. 650, 19th April
1763).
[2] *Edinburgh Review*, October 1819.   [3] 13 George III. c. 84, sec. 56.

afternoon, to the great inconvenience of those trustees and others who attend from a distance." [1] Where the meeting was less of a convivial occasion, it was often found impossible to induce any one to come, especially during the winter months. In the Epping and Ongar Turnpike Trust, no meeting of five Trustees could be obtained between September 1780 and May 1781.[2] The Turnpike Trust responsible for the important road between Manchester and Oldham held four successive meetings in the half year between August 1806 and March 1807 without being able to get a quorum.[3] " I have known," writes Dr. Burn in 1764, " a turnpike meeting advertised from three weeks to three weeks, and never a competent number of trustees attended for a year together." [4] It was, in fact, usually impossible to persuade the country gentlemen and clergymen, who might have been expected to supply the best element on the Trusts, to devote any zeal or public spirit, or to give any continuous attention, to the monotonous details of road repair. John Scott, the ablest Turnpike Trustee of his time, complains bitterly of this neglect among the Hertfordshire gentry. " If," he says, " the Trustees will not meet above two or three times a year, and then not in a sufficient number to transact the affairs of their Trusts, or in case their meetings are more frequent and better attended, if those who attend will engage in common conversation instead of attending to the business of the day (consulting on the state of their roads and considering how to remedy defects or produce improvements) it is easy to tell what must be the consequence. An adoption of that absurd maxim that everybody's business is nobody's business, the parsimony of private life carried into public affairs, an habitual retention of money which can be of no service to the retainers, an acquiescent disposition fearful of offending this man or the other man ; and an interested disposition watching every opportunity of serving self or a relation or a tenant or a descendant, are all, more or less, operative to the destruction of the roads of the nation." [5]

[1] Sir J. C. Hippisley, Bart., M.P., to the Chairman of the Board of Agriculture, in Second Report of House of Commons Committee on Highways, 1808, Appendix, p. 136.

[2] *Minutes of the Epping and Ongar Highway Trust*, 1769–1870, by B. Winstone, 1891, p. 122.

[3] MS. Minutes, Manchester and Oldham Turnpike Trust, 1806–1807.

[4] *History of the Poor Laws*, by Richard Burn, 1764.

[5] *Digests of the General Highway and Turnpike Laws*, by John Scott, 1778.

It was characteristic of Turnpike Trustees, to an even greater degree than other Local Authorities of the period, that they saw no necessity for incurring the expense of a qualified salaried staff. The clerk—often called " Law Clerk " [1]—was habitually a small local attorney, paid principally for the legal business, and concerning himself not at all with the executive work. The nearest approach to a salaried officer was the person called the " Surveyor "—frequently only a superior labourer, a little master craftsman, or an ex-butler or valet jobbed in by some leading Trustee. " The Surveyors of turnpike roads," we are told in 1778, " are frequently decayed farmers or tradesmen, recommended by some friend or relation to an office they are absolutely unqualified to execute." [2] During the eighteenth century the Surveyor was often engaged only when a particular piece of work had to be done, but by the nineteenth century he had usually become a permanent officer at a low wage, eked out by the profits of contracting with the Trust for the execution of the very work that he had to superintend. " The art of taking levels," we are told, " was at first above the capacity " of the persons who acted as Surveyors to Turnpike Trusts ; their " contracted ideas extended no further than to the surface of the land which was the scene of their operations. To them it would have appeared a chimerical undertaking to have attempted to execute any plan for reducing ground to a regular descent where it was to be effected by raising valleys and sinking hills." [3] What the best of the eighteenth-century road administrators aimed at getting was an honest and diligent manager of labour, and (when a new piece of work had to be done) a trustworthy contractor. Only very occasionally—as in the extraordinary case of the blind fiddler, John Metcalfe (1717–1810), who made many of the Lancashire and Yorkshire roads between 1760 and 1790 [4]—did the con-

[1] For instance, in MS. Minutes, Manchester and Oldham Turnpike Trust, 2nd July 1806.
[2] *Digests of the General Highway and Turnpike Laws*, by John Scott, 1778, p. 255.
[3] *An Inquiry into the Means of Preserving the Public Roads*, by Rev. Henry Homer, 1765.
[4] *Life of John Metcalfe, commonly called Blind Jack of Knaresborough*, by himself, 1795 ; *Lives of the Engineers*, by Samuel Smiles, 1861, vol. i. ; *Three Lectures on Roads and Roadmakers*, by H. A. Glass, 1864 ; *Old Yorkshire*, by William Smith, 1883, pp. 170-174 ; *Roadmaking and Maintenance*, by Thomas Aiken, 1900, p. 11 ; *Story of the King's Highway*, by S. and B. Webb, 1913, p. 154.

tractor display any genius for road engineering. Even John
Scott was capable of saying that, when the Trustees are reasonably educated, "and will condescend to give their attendance, . . .
the best Surveyor they can employ will be an honest industrious
labourer, who has docility enough to understand and dexterity
enough to perform their orders." [1] Down to at least 1820 the
great majority of Turnpike Trustees refused to believe that the
office could not be efficiently filled by any person whatsoever.
"Every ignorant peasant," declares a professional writer of 1818,
"considers himself competent to lay out and execute roads in all
directions." [2] "I found at Epsom," said the younger Macadam
in 1819, "a person as Surveyor who had been an underwriter
at Lloyd's Coffee House, at a salary, as I am informed of £60 per
annum ; and who was permitted to keep the carts and horses
and do the cartage for the Trust. At Reading I found an elderly
gentleman as the Surveyor, who was also one of the Commissioners, at a salary of twenty or thirty pounds per annum. I
found at Cheshunt three Surveyors the Trust being divided into
three districts. One of the Surveyors was an infirm old man,
another a carpenter, and another a coal merchant. I found on
the Wade's Mill Trust three Surveyors also, . . . one . . . was a
very old man, another a publican at Buckland, and the other a
baker at Backway, with a salary of fourteen shillings a week each.
I found on the Royston road a publican as Surveyor there; and
I found at Huntingdon a bedridden old man who had not been
out of the house for several months." [3] It is only fair to say,
in justice to the Trustees, that the eighteenth-century roads had
not the advantage even of such engineering skill as then existed,
as road-making was regarded as beneath the dignity of a civil
engineer ; and right down to the nineteenth century "this profession," says Sir Henry Parnell, "has been too commonly
deemed by Turnpike Trustees as something rather to be avoided
than as useful and necessary to be called to their assistance."
The ordinary run of Turnpike Trustees may not unreasonably
have objected, in fact, to a trained professional civil engineer or

---

[1] *Digests of the General Highway and Turnpike Laws*, by John Scott, 1778,
p. 255.

[2] *Practical Directions for Laying Out and Making Roads*, by James Clarke,
1818, p. 1.

[3] Evidence of James Macadam (son), in Report of House of Commons
Committee on the State of the Highways, 1819.

surveyor, who would in the eighteenth century have made a parade of "mathematics and mechanics and all that sort of thing" to very little practical purpose. Such persons, it was said in 1778, "are often very great men, and assume consequential airs for doing little matters." [1]

This indisposition, or want of capacity, to organise an efficient executive, served by a professional staff, led—especially during the eighteenth century—to the adoption of equivocal methods of administration, which were open to grave abuse. In many districts the whole administration fell into the hands of the Treasurer, who, as we learn in 1778, was "generally one of the most opulent and intelligent of the Trustees, and . . . chairman of their meetings." [2] The office carried with it no salary, but as the Treasurer had at his disposal the monies received from tolls, practically during his own pleasure, and with the minimum of audit, it was often one of considerable advantage ; and we find the Treasurer in many places assuming a position of authority equivalent to that of the Expenditor General of some of the contemporary Courts of Sewers described in our first chapter. Thus, of the important County of Surrey we are told, in 1794, that "for several years past the turnpike roads have been under the direction of Treasurers who are Trustees of the roads, and are appointed by the Trust at large, at a meeting held for that purpose. A knowledge of the fundamental principles of making roads is not deemed at all necessary to the erection of such Treasurers, but they are generally some respectable gentlemen in business, if near town, and whither perhaps they go every day. Each appoints some inferior tradesman of the district in which he lives to be the Surveyor, and who may be a carpenter, a bricklayer or any other profession as it may happen, so that without a particle of knowledge on the maintenance and principles of roads on either side, is the expenditure of hundreds of pounds committed to the day labourers, who are for the most part old and decrepid, and who being generally left to themselves take every advantage ; and as the Surveyor does not know how much should be done, he is easily imposed upon by the men ; and as the money does not come out of his pocket it is not very material

[1] *A Treatise on Roads*, by Sir Henry Parnell, 1833, p. 291 ; *Digests of the General Highway and Turnpike Laws*, by John Scott, 1778, p. 255.
[2] *Ibid.* p. 254.

for him to give himself much trouble about it. Thus, from the want of experience in the Surveyor, and the want of leisure in the Treasurer, these roads, which, from their proximity to the gravel on all sides, might, under a proper system, be kept sound and in a good condition all the year round, are found to be daily diminishing, and the public will, ere a few years longer, find it expedient to take some steps to remedy so great a defect." [1]

Careless and indolent Turnpike Trustees hit on even a worse administrative device than leaving the business entirely in the hands of an unpaid and unprofessional Treasurer. We see them putting the whole work of the Trust out by contract to the speculator who offered the most advantageous terms. The practice of farming the revenue of the Trust—the letting by auction of the toll-gates and weighing machines to a " piker " or toll-farmer, who paid a lump sum for the privilege of levying the toll—quickly became universal, though the Trustees might occasionally find themselves driven to take the collection into their own hands for a short term, when for some reason they had failed to agree with a contractor. This practice of farming the tolls led, as we have shown in our *Story of the King's Highway*, to many frauds and exactions. But it enabled the Trusts to dispense with the organisation of their own collecting staff, and considering the surpassing difficulty of checking the collection of tolls at many different gates at great distances apart, there was, under eighteenth-century conditions, something to be said for the practice. But many Turnpike Trusts applied the favourite contemporary device of contracting for the execution of their service as well as for the collection of their revenues. Some local tradesman or tenant farmer would undertake, for a lump sum, to keep the whole stretch of road in repair. The contemporary writers agree that this device proved no more satisfactory in the maintenance of roads than in the maintenance of workhouses or prisons. It was merely to " a desire in Trustees to be exonerated from trouble," that John Scott ascribed " that most pernicious practice of farming roads, which, like farming the poor, is the disgrace of our country. The Trustees, when once a road is farmed, have nothing to do but meet once a year to eat venison and pay the farmer his annuity ; the farmer has

---

[1] *General View of the Agriculture of Surrey*, by W. J. and Jacob Malcolm, 1794, pp. 62-63.

nothing to do but to do as little work and pocket as much money as he possibly can; he has other fish to fry, other matters to mind, than road-mending. Encroachment after encroachment takes place; the hedges and trees grow till they meet overhead; the landholders are excused from their Statute Duty, and the water and the narrow-wheeled vehicles complete the business. At length, perhaps, the universal complaint of travellers, or menaces of indictment, rouse the Trustees for a moment; a meeting is called; the farmer sent for and reprimanded, and a few loads of gravel buried among the mud serve to keep the way barely passable. . . . These practices of farming roads and farming the poor ought to be prohibited by law." [1]

The foregoing description may be taken to represent the working constitution of the numerical majority of the thousand Turnpike Trusts right down to 1835. But many of the more important and wealthier Trusts—such, for instance, as those administering busy lengths of road near the Metropolis or other populous centres, and taking several thousand pounds a year in tolls—were, by the nineteenth century, driven, in one way or another, to develop a more efficient executive. There is fortunately accessible to the general reader a complete account of the internal administration of one such Turnpike Trust—that of the roads about Epping and Ongar in Essex [2]—which, in its good and bad features alike, is, we think, fairly typical of the larger Turnpike Trusts of the reign of George the Third. The road between Harlow and Woodford—the principal thoroughfare in that part of Essex—had been one of those placed under the care of the local Justices of the Peace at the latter part of the seventeenth century, and for three-quarters of a century tolls were levied, special surveyors appointed and the roads repaired under their authority. In 1768, we know not for what reason, the

[1] *Digests of the General Highway and Turnpike Laws*, by John Scott, 1778, p. 345.

[2] *Minutes of the Epping and Ongar Highway Trust, 1769–1870, a Contribution to Local History*, by Benjamin Winstone, privately printed, 1891; 1 William and Mary (1690); 1 Anne, s. 2, c. 10 (1702); *House of Commons Journals*, 19th November 1702; 10 George I. c. 9 (1723); 17 George II. c. 9 (1744); 9 George III. (1768); 30 George III. (1790); 51 George III. (1811); 3 George IV. c. 44 (1822); 6 William IV. (1836).

Another Trust of which a printed record is available is that of the roads about Exeter; see *A Turnpike Key, or an Account of the Proceedings of the Exeter Turnpike Trustees, 1753–1784*, by W. Buckingham, 1885.

powers were, by a new Local Act, transferred to a body of some three hundred Commissioners or Trustees, whose names—carelessly recited in the Act in approximately alphabetical order—appear to include, besides all the local Justices of the Peace, practically all the clergy and resident gentry, and, we imagine, also all the more substantial professional men, yeomen, tenant farmers and tradesmen of the district—in fact, everybody who was judged worth a thousand pounds, which was then the qualification.[1] At the first meeting after the obtaining of the Act about fifty Trustees attended ;[2] one baronet, five " esquires," five clergymen, and the remainder designated in the minute-book either by the humbler prefix of " Mr.," or by Christian and surname only, without any prefix whatever—a fact which we translate to mean that the majority were farmers, tradespeople and others considered by the clerk as being below the gentry. The Lord of the Manor was appointed Treasurer,[3] and we find him serving in this capacity for a whole generation. The local firm of attorneys were appointed " joint clerks," at a guinea per meeting, with ten shillings for their expenses. A Surveyor was retained at a yearly fee of £25. For the next thirty years we see the whole body of Trustees summoned to frequent meetings —sometimes one a fortnight—where the little knot, who alone habitually attend, struggle with all the business of arranging where the toll-gates are to be placed, appointing their own toll-gatherers (at seven shillings a week !),[4] or letting the tolls to the highest bidder, suppressing such nuisances as hogs roaming on the roads, ordering repairs, or putting the maintenance of the road out to contract for one or more years. For a whole generation there is no committee of management, and the executive authority is wielded by the Treasurer, sometimes accompanied by a Trustee living in the neighbourhood. One of the constant difficulties was the loss of revenue by exemptions and compositions. Between 1769 and 1789 there seem to have been always from a score to as many as fifty " compounders," who paid from 5s. 3d. to 21s. each a year, for exemption from all tolls on them-

---

[1] The list includes one peer, one Knight of the Bath, eight baronets, several Knights and " Honourables," about forty clergymen, and half a dozen doctors of medicine.

[2] *Minutes of the Epping and Ongar Highway Trust, 1769–1870*, by B. Winstone, 1891, p. 93.

[3] *Ibid.* pp. 94-95. [4] *Ibid.* p. 152.

selves, their horses, their carriages, their families and their servants. The Treasurer himself set the example by getting all his extensive establishment freed for a guinea a year.[1] The Surveyor, who had his residence in the neighbourhood, and appears to have carried on some sort of contractor's business, assumed, until 1775, that all his " waggons, carts, and carriages " were exempted by virtue of his office.[2] Not until 1789 do the Trustees seem to have realised how seriously their revenue was being curtailed by these nominal compositions, and they then resolved " that it will be very beneficial to the Trust not to permit any persons to compound for their tolls in future." [3] The list of compositions thereupon disappears from the minutes. But this self-denying ordinance was vehemently objected to by some of the Trustees ; and the Treasurer himself, who profited more than any one else by commuting, insisted on the resolution being rescinded. Within a year he carried his point, subject only to the composition rates being doubled ; and the list of compounders reappears in the minutes.[4] During these first thirty years, the active Trustees, evidently a little knot of local residents, displayed a continuous small activity in widening the road, levelling steep ascents and making better connections from point to point. Sometimes they put the work out to contract ; sometimes they did it themselves by direct employment, both systems proving equally unsatisfactory. What was constant was their reliance on the surveys and reports of individual members of their own body,[5] supplemented by no better advice than they could get from the person whom they called their Surveyor, and who was only distinguished by the stipend of £25 a year from being what we should now regard as a humble sort of contractor. Very frequently he undertook to carry out the specific improvement required for a lump sum. At other times the Trustees gave him thirty shillings a week for superintending

[1] *Minutes of the Epping and Ongar Highway Trust, 1769–1870*, by B. Winstone, 1891, p. 103.
[2] *Ibid.* pp. 106-107.　　　　　　　　[3] *Ibid.* p. 154.
[4] *Ibid.* pp. 154-156. We learn that, in 1764, the " compositions " of the Marylebone, Islington and Kensington Turnpike Trusts made up nearly 7 per cent of the revenue (Report of House of Commons Committee on the Application of Money . . . for repairing particular roads, 1765).

[5] As late as 1806, on so important a road as that between Manchester and Oldham, we see the Turnpike Trustees appointing their own members, by twos, " Surveyors and Superintendents " of definite portions of the road (MS. Minutes, Manchester and Oldham Turnpike Trust, 2nd July 1806).

the labourers whom they themselves paid. When the work was undertaken for a lump sum, it happens more than once that it is subsequently complained of as badly done or left altogether unfinished. When the Trustees had their own labourers under such superintendence, the work invariably proved to cost enormously more than had been anticipated. These administrative failures led, first to repeated changes of Surveyor, and presently, after the exhaustion of the original impetus, to an abandonment of the task in despair, practically no important improvements being undertaken for a whole generation. At length in 1830, when the Trustees nerved themselves to renewed activity, they began by engaging Macadam as consulting surveyor,[1] whose reputation as a roadmender was then at its height; and we may leave them in his hands, at last making a scientific survey of their whole road, borrowing £22,000 on the security of the tolls,[2] expending this sum freely on improvements under his skilful guidance, and apparently making a good job of the business.

It would be unfair to imply that the Epping and Ongar Turnpike Trust represented the high-water mark of turnpike administration. We have, by chance, an elaborate printed report, for instance, of a committee of the Hammersmith and Brentford Turnpike Trust in the year 1800 ; a document which reveals no small amount of administrative organisation, an experienced staff, and upright and thoughtful Trustees. This Trust let its tolls, with due precautions against fraud, for a large annual sum, the Trustees devoting all their attention to the maintenance and improvement of their highway, which, as the first stage out of London on the main Great Western Road, was, at that date, one of the busiest thoroughfares in the world, along which, it was said later, a fully laden stage-coach passed every six minutes day and night, throughout the year.[3] We gather that the Trustees not only met regularly as a body, but also appointed an Administrative Committee, which inspected every inch of the road. Their meetings were always attended, not by their Law Clerk, but also by their Surveyor, from whom they

---

[1] *Minutes of the Epping and Ongar Highway Trust*, by B. Winstone, 1891, p. 199.   [2] *Ibid.* pp. 200, 202.

[3] In 1834 there were on this road 115 lines of coaches, doing over 800 journeys per week each way (*The Development of Transportation in Modern England*, by W. T. Jackman, 1916, vol. ii. p. 609 ; *The Exeter Road*, by C. G. Harper, 1899 ; *The Bath Road*, by the same, 1899).

received detailed reports. They executed their own repairs, keeping a permanent staff of labourers, and buying their materials by competitive tendering after public advertisement. In 1800 we find them proposing to straighten the road at a certain dangerous corner, by acquiring houses for demolition; to fill up a part which is below the general level; to cart away the road scrapings from those parts which do not need raising; and to contract the side-walks where the roadway is unduly narrow. We see them even deliberating on an experimental handing over of a certain length of road to a professional roadmaker, in order to let him try a new system; the Committee suggesting an arrangement " with some person or persons scientifically acquainted with, and practically experienced in, the formation and management of turnpike roads. Without hastily abandoning the present system," they suggest that " a trial might be made by the mile on certain parts of the road. Thus the Board might be enabled to form a correct opinion of the expediency of this mode, and of the ability of any such contractor or contractors as might be engaged to make the experiment, and thus your Surveyor might be improved in theory and in practice and a desirable emulation be excited." [1]

The best example of enlightened administration on the part of a Turnpike Trust is, however, that presented for the first twenty years of the nineteenth century by the Trustees of the roads of the Bristol District, which, with no less than 148 miles of much frequented thoroughfares, had, since 1799, become the largest single road authority in the kingdom. This important Turnpike Trust had the good fortune to include among its members John Loudon Macadam, to whose career as Justice of the Peace and Turnpike Trustee we have, in *The Parish and the County*, already alluded. We have, in our *Story of the King's Highway*, described Macadam's remarkable career as a road administrator,[2] and discussed the celebrated new technique to which he gave his name. Here we have to notice the readiness

---

[1] *Report of Committee of Trustees of the Hammersmith and Brentford Turnpikes*, 1800, p. 17.

[2] No more detailed account of John Loudon Macadam (1756–1836) exists than the notices in the *Imperial Dictionary of Biography* and the *National Dictionary of Biography*; and we have therefore specified in our *Story of the King's Highway*, both the chief events of his life, and some of the materials for the biography which is his due (pp. 135, 176, 184–185, etc.).

with which his colleagues on the Bristol District Turnpike Trust welcomed the experience that he had gained in Ayrshire and on his travels ; and the ease with which he was able to organise an efficient executive under that large and unwieldy Trust. In 1810 he communicated his ideas to the Board of Agriculture, which, under the enlightened leadership of Sir John Sinclair and Arthur Young, was then energetically striving for a general improvement of the roads. Macadam's proposals were in this way brought to the notice of various Parliamentary Committees, and extensively advertised throughout the kingdom. In 1815 his fellow Trustees begged him to take over the entire management of their roads, and he became their surveyor at a salary of £400 a year, which was then considered an extraordinary sum for the office. His fame now spread far and wide, and it is, we think, to the credit of the Turnpike Trusts that his services were so eagerly competed for. He quickly became a general consulting surveyor to many of the more important Trusts, and, by 1819, was acting, with the assistance of his son, as salaried surveyor to no fewer than " 34 different bodies of Commissioners," having simultaneously " 328 miles under repair " according to his system, and another 300 miles under survey with a view to his advising upon it.[1] We need not here pursue the story of the improvements brought about by Macadam. What concerns us is to emphasise the fact that the credit of recognising and promoting his genius for road repair is to be shared between the Bristol District Turnpike Trustees and the then Board of Agriculture, whilst the rapid acceptance and application of his plans, once they were announced, must be counted as merit to the hundreds of Turnpike Trusts, including practically all those of any importance, by whom he was, between 1815 and his death in 1836, so eagerly consulted.

The Commissioners of the Holyhead Road

It was not so much the imperfection of the administration of the Turnpike Trusts, or the financial insolvency into which so many of them had fallen, as their incapacity to provide the main lines of national inter-communication, that led to the intervention of the Government, in a way that came near to superseding them

[1] Report of House of Commons Committee on Highways, 1819.

altogether by a national system of road administration. From the very beginning of the nineteenth century the Postmaster-General had found himself driven by the increasing postal traffic, at a time when all mails were road-borne, to press for the improvement of the main arteries of communication. We see him writing to different Turnpike Trusts, sending his "riding surveyors" to inspect the various routes, and even indicting the parishes where the Trusts had failed to provide good roads. Especially in the valleys of North Wales did these efforts prove ineffectual, and between Shrewsbury and Holyhead the road continued so bad as to make it in some places positively unsafe to use a mail-coach. At last, spurred on by the Irish Members of Parliament as well as by the Post Office, the Government agreed to propose a vote of £20,000 towards the improvement of the Holyhead road, as an enterprise transcending the capacity of any of the existing Trusts. Thomas Telford, whom we have elsewhere described building bridges for the Shropshire Quarter Sessions, had been, since 1803, making roads in Scotland for the Commissioners of Highland Roads, and in 1815 he was set to work on the Holyhead road, under the direction of a special body of ten Commissioners established by Act of Parliament.[1] These Commissioners included no fewer than three Ministers of the Crown, but the principal part was played and the work done by an able and energetic Irish baronet, Sir Henry Parnell, who for twenty years devoted most of his energy to the task.[2]

In the annual reports of the Holyhead Road Commissioners we see Parnell and Telford maintaining, between 1817 and 1833, a perpetual struggle with the twenty-three separate Turnpike Trusts, among whom the 194 miles of road were divided. The Commissioners had no authority to supersede these Trusts. Each of them had to be separately argued with, and persuaded to allow Telford to execute the works necessary to improve its few miles of line. The seventeen English Trusts were left undisturbed in their nominal authority. In nearly all of them Telford managed to get a free hand for his alterations, and when

[1] *The Story of the King's Highway*, by S. and B. Webb, 1913, pp. 103, 182-183 ; 55 George III. c. 152, 1815.

[2] Sir Henry Parnell (1776–1842) deserves a biography, which, apart from the entry in the *Dictionary of National Biography*, does not appear to have been written. We give, in our *Story of the King's Highway*, 1913, pp. 184-187, a summary of his career, with a list of his works.

the work was completed the Trustees were required to add 50 per cent to their tolls, and to pay the amount of this surtax to the Commissioners. With the six little Welsh Trusts, controlling the most difficult 85 miles of the line, more drastic measures had to be taken. By one means or another Sir Henry Parnell, who devoted the spring of 1818 to attending their meetings, managed to induce them to allow their Trusts to be merged by Act of Parliament in a single new body of fifteen Commissioners, who were expressly required by their Act to employ a professional civil engineer as their surveyor.[1] Under Telford's superintendence an entirely new system of road management was introduced. The 85 miles of road were divided among three assistant surveyors, each having under him about half a dozen foremen, and each of these again being made definitely and permanently responsible for four or five miles of road, with a standing gang of hired labourers under him. All this work took both time and money. But so successful were its earlier stages that Parliament voted larger and larger annual grants and loans, and devolved greater and greater powers upon the Holyhead Road Commissioners, until, by 1830, more than three-quarters of a million had been thus allocated. In return for this large sum the Commissioners of the Holyhead Road, through Telford's engineering skill and Sir Henry Parnell's energy, had reconstructed a continuous line of 194 miles of road between London and Holyhead, which, under what was virtually the management of a Government department, could be claimed as a model of the most " perfect roadmaking that has ever been attempted in any country " ; and was, at any rate, the best piece of land travelling in the Britain of its time.[2]

[1] 59 George III. c. 30 (Shrewsbury and Bangor Turnpike Act, 1819).
[2] For the Commissioners of the Holyhead Road, see the account in our *Story of the King's Highway*, 1913, pp. 167-171, 182. The principal authorities are the various statutes, the numerous reports of Parliamentary Committees and the occasional discussions in Hansard between 1810 and 1833 ; the series of Reports by the Commissioners ; *Voyages dans la Grande Bretagne*, by Baron Charles Dupin, 1824, vol. v. " Voies Publiques," pp. 41-47 ; *A Treatise on Roads*, by Sir Henry Parnell, 1st edition, 1833, 2nd edition, 1838; *Life of Thomas Telford*, by himself, edited by John Rickman, 1838 ; *Lives of the Engineers*, by Samuel Smiles, 1861, vol. ii. ; *Roadmaking and Maintenance*, by Thomas Aitken, 1900, pp. 14-26 ; *The Holyhead Road*, by C. G. Harper, 1902. The Commission was merged in the Office of Woods and Forests by an Act of 3 & 4 William IV. (1833).

The Board of Agriculture and Macadam

Meanwhile another department of the National Government had been bestirring itself in the attempt to get a better administration of the roads. The Board of Agriculture, inspired by the practical genius of Sir John Sinclair, Bart. (1754–1835) and Arthur Young, had, from 1794 onwards, been incidentally reporting on the unsatisfactory condition of the English highways and constantly pressing for their improvement. Early in the Session of 1806 Sir John Sinclair, the Chairman of the Board, laid before the House of Commons a Bill for reforming highway administration generally, a step which produced, not an Act, but the first of the series of Parliamentary Committees on roads to which we have already referred. In the proceedings of the Committees of 1806, 1808, 1809, and 1811 we see Sir John Sinclair inviting communications from Justices of the Peace, Turnpike Trustees, County Surveyors and all sorts of cranks and enthusiasts ; and getting these, with other materials, sifted by the staff of the Board of Agriculture for presentation to the committees. Among the communications addressed to the Chairman of the Board of Agriculture there came, in 1810, a long memorandum from a fellow-Scotsman, one John Loudon Macadam, giving it as his opinion that the whole system of roadmaking was fundamentally erroneous, and begging to be allowed to bring under public notice a new plan which he " had been long endeavouring to get . . . fairly tried." " Sir John," we are told in his *Memoirs*, " being pleased with the suggestions in his letter, resolved to bring them under the notice of a Parliamentary Committee on Highways, which was then sitting, and of which Sir John Sinclair was Chairman. To give the new method a better chance of success (he) caused the information sent by Mr. Macadam to be arranged and condensed, and had it printed in the Appendix to the Report of the Committee." From this time onward, until his death in 1836, Macadam occupied, towards successive Parliamentary Committees on general road administration, much the same position of expert authority as did Thomas Telford in those concerned with the Scottish and Holyhead roads. And it is thus to Macadam, rather than to Telford, that we owe such modicum of reform as was

effected in the general law and administration of roads between
1810 and 1835.

We need not describe the system of roadmaking introduced
by Macadam, nor the extraordinary vogue that it gained between
1820 and 1840, which we have sufficiently dealt with in another
volume.[1] But besides the improvements in the administration
of many Turnpike Trusts that he and his son set going, under
the fostering influence of the Board of Agriculture, we have to
record the movement promoted at the same time for a general
consolidation of Turnpike Trusts, and an improvement in their
professional staffs. Successive House of Commons Committees
of 1819, 1820 and 1821, besides testifying to the genius of Macadam, strongly urged the appointment by Quarter Sessions of
one or more County Surveyors, who should superintend and

---

[1] *The Story of the King's Highway*, 1913, pp. 171-175. The distinctive
feature of Macadam's system was to abstain from the use of clay, dirt, or even
pebbles, but " to put broken stone on a road, which shall unite by its own
angles, so as to form a solid hard surface "—to substitute " small angular
stones, prepared from larger pieces, for the large rounded stones then generally
made use of in road construction "—and to dispense with " binding material "
or any " mixture of earth, clay, chalk or other matter that will imbibe water
and be affected by frost " (*Roadmaking and Maintenance*, by Thomas Aitken,
1907, p. 12 ; see also Cresy's *Encyclopædia of Civil Engineering*, 1847 ; also Report
of House of Commons Committee on the Highways of the Kingdom, 1819).
R. L. Edgeworth, on the contrary, " recommended that the interstices should
be filled up with small gravel or sharp sand," a practice which, though it was
condemned by Macadam, is now adopted by the best surveyors (*The Construction of Roads and Streets*, by Henry Law and D. Kinnear Clark, 1887, p. 9).
" Telford's name is associated with the system of handset stones as a pavement foundation on which the top metal or wearing surface is placed. . . .
Macadam was satisfied with laying the metalling directly on the surface of
the ground, after the irregularities had been levelled, and side ditches formed.
. . . A system of bottoming roads combining the methods practised by Telford
and Macadam has long been adopted," though the use of the steam-roller has
permitted the application of water, which was to Macadam anathema (*Roadmaking and Maintenance*, by T. Aitken, 1900, pp. 249, 251, 253 ; see also *The
Municipal and Sanitary Engineer's Handbook*, by H. Percy Boulnois, 1883);
and recently the use of tar, to both bind and render impervious the surface.
Not only Telford, but also, it is said, " Rennie had practised the same method
of making roads over his bridges long before " Macadam's publications (*Lives
of the Engineers*, by Samuel Smiles, 1861, vol. ii. p. 185). So, also, it is said,
did Abercromby, who constructed admirable roads in Scotland ; and various
French roadmakers, notably the great Pierre Trésaguet, whom Turgot employed
in 1764 (*The King's Highway, the Nature, Purpose and Development of Roads
and Road Systems*, by Reginald Ryves, 1911 ; *The Art of Roadmaking*, by Frost,
pp. 159, 160 ; *Highways and Horses*, by Athol Maudslay, 1888, p. 53). But
in 1830 the French Government officially adopted Macadam's system, which
received the highest praise in 1843 from Dumas, the engineer in chief of the
department of Ponts et Chaussées (*The King's Highway*, etc., by Reginald
Ryves, 1911, p. 65).

manage all the turnpike roads within each county, under the direction and for the benefit of the several Trusts. The Committees recommended also both the consolidation of the confused law about turnpikes and the combination of the Trusts themselves.

It must be said that the legislative results with regard to Turnpike Trusts were disappointingly small. It was not found possible even to remedy the more important defects of the general turnpike law. The various Public General Acts on the subject were, it is true, strung together in 1822 into mechanical unity by a consolidating Act, carried through Parliament by Sir Frankland Lewis ; but this left the real complications practically unchanged, and was itself promptly overlain by a new set of little amending Acts.[1] In spite of repeated recommendations Parliament failed, until 1831, to devise any remedy for the trouble and expense annually wasted over the periodical renewal of the Local Acts of the eleven hundred Turnpike Trusts ; or to protect their promoters from being mulcted in absurdly heavy fees by the officials of the two Houses of Parliament ; and even

[1] The general legislation about Turnpike Trusts between 1822 and 1834 comprised the 3 George IV. c. 126 (General Turnpike Act of 1822) ; amended by 4 George IV. c. 16 (1823) ; 5 George IV. c. 69 (1824) ; 7 & 8 George IV. c. 24 (1827) ; 9 George IV. c. 77 (1828) ; 1 & 2 William IV. c. 25 (1831) ; 3 & 4 William IV. c. 78 (1833) ; 4 & 5 William IV. c. 81 (1834). In 1824 a further consolidation was attempted by J. Cripps, M.P., himself a Justice of the Peace and Turnpike Trustee, who brought in a Bill to include in a single statute the entire law relating to highways, parochial as well as turnpike. This was deprecated by Sir Frankland Lewis as unwise, and was not pressed (Hansard, 25th March 1824).

On the vexed question of Parliamentary costs, it was pointed out in 1827 that Bills for the consolidation of Turnpike Trusts have " hitherto been visited . . . with the heaviest charges. Turnpike Bills generally have been always subjected to double House Fees, on some principle not sufficiently intelligible to your Committee ; but when Trusts are consolidated, or when roads are divided into two or more districts . . . the House Fee is again doubled or trebled, and so on, as the case may be ; the Committee Fees are also increased, though not in the same proportion." Yet, as was vainly urged, Turnpike Bills, being really measures for the public advantage, not for individual profit, might properly be relieved from all fees. The limitation of time inserted in them was " a precautionary provision of the Legislature, not at all requisite for the purposes of the Trust, but on the contrary, rather injurious to its interests, having been introduced for the sole benefit of the public, with a view to procure a periodical revision of the powers and proceedings of the Trust." All renewal Bills should therefore be exempt from the charges on Private Bills (Report of House of Commons Committee on Turnpike Trusts Renewal Bills, 1827 ; see also *A Second Supplement to the General Turnpike Road Acts for 1827*, by J. Bateman, 1827, p. 111 ; *Municipal Origins*, by F. H. Spencer, 1911, pp. 77-84).

Q

in 1831 could find no more efficient reform than the inclusion, each year, of all the expiring Acts in one annual renewal Bill.[1] No attempt was made by Parliament to effect any general reform in the administration of the existing Turnpike Trusts. It was all very well for Committee after Committee to urge the desirability of " consolidation of areas," but no Committee made any practical proposal for bringing it about. The great difference in financial position between the various Trusts, and the natural reluctance of every solvent body to take over the liabilities of a bankrupt concern, prevented anything of the kind taking place. The obvious, and perhaps the only possible, way of surmounting the financial entanglement of the thousands of separate mortgages of tolls remaining unpaid, of the great and growing arrears of interest owing by some of the Trusts, and of the pledging of particular tolls for separate debts, was compulsorily to amalgamate all the various Trusts, so as to give each of the mortgagees and other creditors a superior security, and so as to bring the total expenditure within the aggregate income. This meant, in effect, the merging of them all into a national department of toll-supported roads, a project frequently recommended by outside critics and irresponsible advisers. But under George the Fourth, as under George the Third, no Ministry was ever found willing to undertake such a reform, and no Parliament to sanction such an increase in the executive power and Government patronage. As an alternative to any scheme of consolidation under a national department, some substantial progress might have been made in compulsorily consolidating the Trusts of particular districts, a policy which had been strenuously recommended by the Committee of 1819, and its successors. A certain amount of this district consolidation presently got effected. We shall describe the successful combination in 1827 of the Metropolitan roads north of the Thames. But besides this great consolidation, others were made in different parts of the Kingdom to the great improvement of the administration. The 63 miles of the Surrey and Sussex Turnpike Trust—the aggregation second in importance in revenue (£19,000) to that of the Metropolitan roads—

[1] The first of the long series of annual Turnpike Trust Renewal Acts was 1 & 2 William IV. c. 6, 1831, entitled " An Act for continuing until the 30th day of June 1832 the several Acts for regulating the Turnpike Roads in Great Britain which will expire at the end of the present session of Parliament."

were steadily improved by the force of example. The same may be said of the Middlesex and Essex Trust (£11,000) with its 31 miles, and of the New Cross Trust (£14,000) with its 49 miles, both yielding exceptionally large toll receipts. " The whole of the south and south-western roads," as we learn incidentally from the historian of our taxes, " benefited by the impulse to locomotion in those parts, due to the patronage of Brighton " by George the Fourth. The much frequented roads about Bristol, where, already by 1799, the consolidation of small Trusts had put 172 miles under one management (revenue £15,000), were brought to a high state of excellence by the Macadams, and vied with those of the Bath Turnpike Trust (51 miles of very remunerative roads yielding £8000). Other extensive Trusts were those of Worcester (160 miles, £5000), Hereford (156 miles, £5000), Exeter (146 miles, £6000), and Alston in Cumberland (130 miles, £3000) ; whilst the Manchester and Buxton Trust, with only 45 miles of road, stood sixth in aggregate receipts (£8000). These eleven great Trusts managed, in the aggregate, 1165 miles of road (or about 6 per cent of the total mileage), but collected no less than £166,000 in revenue (or about 12 per cent of the whole turnpike receipts). Elsewhere, especially in the more remote and less frequented parts of the Kingdom, the thousand and odd little Trusts remained unconsolidated,[1] each administering its 10 or 20 miles of road, and its thousand or two pounds of revenue, by its miscellaneous fifty or a hundred Trustees ; gradually executing, it is true, the most elementary improvements, but for the most part squandering their tolls in extravagant administrative expenses, and piling up their debts until actual insolvency beset them, much as they had done for the previous couple of generations.

[1] The multiplicity of Trusts was, indeed, carried to an absurd extreme. Within the municipal boundaries of Leeds there were 46 miles of turnpike roads and 30 tollgates, belonging to no fewer than 18 different Trusts, and collecting, in 1842, £23,251 per annum (*Suggestions for consolidating the funds and management of turnpike roads within the Borough of Leeds*, by Richard Bayldon, 1843, p. 11). Within the boundaries of the Parliamentary Borough of Stroud (Gloucestershire) there were 13 different Trusts (*Rebecca at Stroud, or a few words about the Turnpike Trusts*, by David Ricardo, 1847). For an early advocacy of combination see the pamphlet, *A Letter to the Inhabitants of Hertford*, about 1771, in British Museum volume 8245, bb. 14. It was, more than anything else, this multiplicity of Trusts, and an excessive multiplication of tollgates that produced, in 1842–1843, the Rebecca riots in South Wales (*Rebecca and her Daughters*, by Henry Tobit Evans, 1910).

The Commissioners of Metropolitan Turnpike Roads

It was in London that the inefficiency of the Turnpike Trust became least endurable. The working constitution of the Turnpike Trust, like that of the Parish, the County [1] and the Court of Sewers, had completely broken down under the exceptional conditions of the Metropolitan area. The peculiar constitutional characteristic of the Turnpike Trust was, as we have indicated, its large and indiscriminate membership. When, as in the rural districts, this meant the inclusion within the Trust of practically every resident above the manual working and small shop-keeping classes, it provided, at any rate, a kind of popular control and popular assent absent from the more exclusive administration of the Close Vestry, the Municipal Corporation or the County. In the wilderness of the Metropolis, however, the large and indiscriminate membership of a Turnpike Trust secured neither popular assent nor popular control, whilst it served to accelerate the tendency, which marked nearly all the London governing bodies of the period, for the social status and personal character of the members steadily to sink to an ever lower level. The main roads in Middlesex, outside the City of London, were under the care of fourteen different Turnpike Trusts. Amid the many tens of thousands of residents of Marylebone and Paddington, Chelsea and Kensington, at the beginning of the nineteenth century, the few hundreds who sat on the Turnpike Trusts were but an unknown handful. As in the cases of the Metropolitan Close Vestries, the Middlesex Commission of the Peace or the Westminster Court of Sewers, the great people who figured in the list never deigned to attend the meetings, and the administration was, without publicity, without practical responsibility and even without audit, left in the hands of the smaller folk to whom the patronage, the perquisites and the opportunities for profit were an irresistible attraction. Already, in 1765, we see the Kensington Turnpike Trust squandering an almost incredible number of loads of gravel on Piccadilly, because one of the active Trustees himself supplied this material at a non-competitive price, whilst " all the carpenter's work," whatever this included, was secured at profitable

---

[1] *The Parish and the County*, by S. and B. Webb, 1907.

rates by the partner of another active Trustee.[1] With the enormous growth of the wheeled traffic and the revenue from tolls, the various Turnpike Trusts to which had been committed the roads radiating from Charing Cross and St. Paul's, evidently went from bad to worse. It was given in evidence by such competent witnesses as the Postmaster-General's Superintendent of Mail-Coaches and the leading coach proprietors, that the high roads just outside the centre of the city were far worse than those elsewhere ; that ten horses had to be used to do the work of eight ; that these horses lasted only three or four years, as compared with six years elsewhere ; and that the mail-coaches occasionally lost twenty minutes in labouring through a few score yards of soft road.[2] From 1819 onward Committee after Committee of the House of Commons insisted that something must be done to remedy the evils " of the numerous small Trusts . . . most inconveniently divided " ; the " frequency of turn-pike gates," and the consequent " great interruption of the traffic," under which the Metropolis suffered. An energetic attempt by a knot of private members, headed by Davies Gilbert and Sir Henry Parnell, to roll up into a single body all the various Trusts surrounding the capital—a reform to which the Committees of 1819 and 1821 had attached particular importance in the hope of rendering " the roads round the Metropolis," on which an " immense revenue " was " collected from the public," a " pattern for the kingdom," so that " the spirit of improvement radiating from this centre may . . . spread with rapidity throughout the country." This bill was an extensive proposal, which would have wiped out more than fifty separate Trusts in Essex, Middlesex, Surrey and Kent, comprising several thousands of Trustees, who were to be permitted to select a small body from amongst themselves as the new Trustees. Though the second reading was carried by a large majority, the measure naturally met with " a very great opposition by the several Trusts that were proposed to be consolidated, and there was no party possessing the means to forward the measure." Left entirely to the energy of a few private members, without Govern-ment support, it was obstructed, postponed and eventually

[1] Report of House of Commons Committee appointed to enquire into the application of money . . . for repairing any particular highway, 1765.
[2] See also the facts stated in an article on road-making in *London Magazine*, August 1828.

defeated in the House of Commons by 72 votes to 71. But the question was not allowed to drop. In 1825 Lord Lowther brought before the House of Commons an amazing indictment of the Trustees of all these Metropolitan Trusts, which collected, he said, over £200,000 a year in tolls, and were honeycombed by corruption on a large scale, the Trustees giving each other profitable contracts and appointments, and permitting each other to lend money to the Trusts at 10 per cent interest—an indictment, supported on the one hand by the speeches of Joseph Hume, and on the other by the writings of William Cobbett, who alleged also that excessive and illegal tolls were exacted.[1] These complaints led at last, in 1826, to the supersession of the fourteen Metropolitan Trusts North of the Thames—governing 131 miles of road from Uxbridge to the River Lea, and levying £75,000 a year in tolls—by a new body of Commissioners of eminence and distinction, carefully selected by the Ministry of the day, and presided over permanently by Lord Lowther, who, chosen by the Government, and working in constant communication with the Postmaster-General, applied himself assiduously for no less than thirty years to the management of this new department. Though the forms of a Turnpike Trust were retained, we gather that the " gentlemen of eminence and distinction " left the whole business to the Chairman and the salaried officers. James Macadam (1786–1852), the son and partner of the celebrated road-mender, was immediately appointed " Surveyor General of the Metropolitan Roads," an adequate official staff was engaged, the main thoroughfares of traffic were put into good order, the working expenses were greatly reduced, the inconvenient toll gates were removed to better sites and diminished in number, the tolls were gradually reduced in amount as the debt was paid off, and the whole service was run on lines of bureaucratic efficiency, rendering to Parliament the homage of the publication of an annual report and statement of accounts.[2]

[1] This was a subject of complaint by others. One writer of 1834 declared that " the gross oppression committed by Road Trusts in the mode and manner of imposing and levying the road tolls greatly surpasses their mismanagement " (*A Treatise on Internal Intercourse and Communication in Civilized States, and particularly in Great Britain*, by Thomas Grahame, 1834, p. 22).

[2] As to these Commissioners of Metropolitan Turnpike Roads, see our *Story of the King's Highway*, 1913, pp. 177-179, 190 ; the Reports of House of Commons Committees on Highways and Turnpike Roads, 1819, 1820, 1821 ; Hansard,

The Coming of the Railway

By 1827, therefore, in two most important cases, the Turnpike Trusts had been superseded by newly appointed bodies of Crown nominees, which were only slightly removed from being departments of the national government, working in close connection with the General Post Office. How far the example of the Metropolitan Roads Commission and the Holyhead Road Commission would have been followed, and the local Turnpike Trusts swallowed up in a national system, if we had continued to rely on the King's Highway as our only means of communication, affords material for interesting speculation. Already, by 1827, Telford had been set by the Postmaster-General to survey the whole line of the Great North Road from London to Edinburgh, and had prepared the plan of a new route, which would have saved twenty miles in distance, and substituted, for the existing windings, a hundred miles of road between York and Peterborough as straight as a French chaussée. A Committee of the House of Commons recommended the Government to appoint a Commission to make this road, on the precedent of that of Holyhead, and a Bill for the purpose was actually introduced in 1830. It had, however, to face a storm of opposition, and made no progress.[1] The reformers along this line would have had to

June and July 1820, February and April 1821, 5th May 1824, 17th February 1825, 31st March 1829, 12th March 1830 ; the statutes 7 George IV. c. 142 (1826) and 10 George IV. c. 59 (1829) ; *Morning Chronicle*, 6th April 1825 ; *Times*, 10th November 1826 and 12th June 1828 ; House of Commons Journals, 12th March 1830 ; evidence of Viscount Lowther and James Macadam in Report of House of Lords Committee on Turnpike Trusts, 1833 ; *Treatise on Road Legislation and Maintenance*, by Richard Bayldon, 1857, p. 23 ; and, above all, the 46 annual Reports to Parliament of the Commissioners themselves (1827–1872).

Notwithstanding the inroads made on their tolls by the competition of the new railways, the Commissioners managed to pay off all their debt by 1856, besides executing many road improvements. In 1864, at the instance of the Commissioners themselves, all their roads within the district of the Metropolitan Board of Works were freed from toll and transferred to the respective parishes (26 & 27 Vict. c. 78, Metropolitan Turnpikes Act, 1863). The Commission was terminated, and its remaining roads were freed, by a clause in the General Turnpike Acts Continuance Act, 1871. It thus came to an end in 1872, a few weeks after the death of its assiduous chairman, whose portrait was given in the *Illustrated London News* for 16th March 1872 (see also Bourke's *History of White's*, 1892, vol. ii. p. 116).

[1] Report of House of Commons Committee on the State of the Northern roads, 1830 ; House of Commons Journals, May and June 1830 ; Hansard, 3rd June 1830 ; *Lives of the Engineers*, by Samuel Smiles, 1861, vol. ii. pp. 433-434.

contend, not only with vested interests of all the local Trusts, but also with the current objections to any increase in Government expenditure, Government patronage, and Government control. On the other hand, short of the actual transfer of turnpike administration from the domain of local to that of central government, there seemed no possibility of effectually reforming the system. This was, in fact, a case in which the favourite panacea of the Whigs and Radicals appeared not to apply. So long as the road revenue continued to be raised by tolls, there was no constitutional argument in favour of substituting election by the local inhabitants for any other system of choosing Turnpike Trustees. The example of some Welsh and other rural Trusts had demonstrated that the pecuniary interests of the local residents were often quite opposed to those of the through travellers who paid most of the tolls. As the payers of tolls did not constitute a possible local constituency, the only way in which Taxation and Representation could be made to go hand in hand seemed the assumption of the entire service by the national government, representing the whole body of road users. For such a supersession of local government public opinion was in no way prepared. Even national superintendence was refused. In vain did Sir Henry Parnell propose, in 1833, that all Turnpike Trusts should be placed under the control of the Commissioners of Land Revenue, seeing that the latter were, under an Act of 1833, just taking over the duties of the Office of Works and the Commissioners of the Holyhead roads.[1] Another

---

[1] The alternative of a national department of roads, acting in conjunction with Local Authorities, had been suggested long before by two able writers, but seems to have been, in the seventeenth century as in the eighteenth and nineteenth, regarded as unworthy of serious consideration. Littleton, in 1692, had a complicated scheme based on finance. "It is therefore humbly proposed (1) that a constant yearly tax be laid upon land of 4d. in the £; (2) that the collectors of it in each parish pay the one moiety to the parish surveyor and the other moiety to the Surveyor of the Hundred; (3) that the Surveyor of the Hundred employ the one-half of his moiety upon the ways within his limit and pay over the other half to the Surveyor for the County; (4) that the County Surveyor remit one-quarter part of his money to the Surveyor-General of England; employing the residue upon the bridges and great roads of the county; (5) that the Surveyor-General employ his whole money in the London roads, the whole Kingdom being concerned in them " (*A Proposal for Maintaining and Repairing the Highways*, by E. Littleton, 1692, p. 2). A national department of roads was proposed by Daniel Defoe in 1697; an elaborate project for a complete system of road-making and maintenance for the whole kingdom, by a national commission of fifteen members, to be aided by ten others added by the county in which they were for the time being at work;

way out lay in a direction as yet unthought of. It did not occur to any one in 1820–1830 that the splendid Turnpike Roads along the main arteries of national traffic could ever be merged in the petty local administration of the miserable bye-lanes and minor highways through which they ran ;[1] or that the one and a half millions sterling of annual toll revenue could be abandoned and replaced by a more than equivalent addition to the local rates. Yet, as we now know, that was the solution destined within another generation to be adopted, the first unconscious step being taken in these very years, as we have shown in our *Story of the King's Highway*, in the General Highway Act of 1835. Meanwhile, however, the success of the new railways, and the astonishing results of the trial of the locomotive engines at Rainhill in 1829, diverted all public interest from the Turnpike Trusts ; producing even so strong a general impression that road traffic was about to become a thing of the past that all projects

---

the construction of new roads being done under Parliamentary powers, and executed, partly by pressed labour, partly by convict labour, partly out of the proceeds of surplus lands enclosed and sold, and partly by a general assessment (*An Essay upon Projects*, by D(aniel De) F(oe), 1697, pp. 68-112). It is interesting to see the turning towards nationalisation of some early Benthamite. In an article in the *Westminster Review*, then under the virtual editorship of John Stuart Mill, in commenting on Baron Dupin's praise of the turnpikes, the writer proceeds : " We doubt the whole system. In spite of our natural or acquired fears of government and jobs we still think that the whole system of roads ought to be one. . . . It is a national, not a private concern. There is no reason why one road should possess superfluous wealth, while another is starved. . . . There is no reason why enormous balances should remain in the hands of treasurers and attorneys for the purpose of jobbing with them in the funds. It is not a cheap administration ; it is not an effectual administration " (*Westminster Review*, October 1825, vol. iv. p. 344). The *Edinburgh Review*, on the other hand, economically more orthodox, was recommending, in 1819, giving to the Commissioners of Turnpike Trusts the stimulus of private profit. " Let the right of levying certain tolls be granted to the subscribers ; the surplus, after paying all outgoings, to be divided as profit " (*Edinburgh Review*, October 1819).

[1] It is remarkable how little attention was paid at this period to the four-fifths of highway mileage that was not under Turnpike Trusts. An able Berkshire Justice published an anonymous pamphlet in 1825, entitled *Highways Improved*. The Act of 1835 (5 & 6 William IV. c. 50) became the subject of many text-books, such as *The General Highway Act*, 1835, by Joseph Bateman, 1835 ; *The Present General Laws for Regulating Highways in England*, by W. F. A. Delane, 1835 ; *The General Highway Act of 5 & 6 William IV. c. 50*, by Leonard Shelford, 1835 ; *A Familiar Abridgement of the General Highways Act*, by F. A. Fry, 1836 ; *The Office of a Surveyor of the Highways*, by a Magistrate, 1836. Particulars of the history of these parish highways will be found in *The Story of the King's Highway*, 1913.

of reform were laid aside.[1] How the Turnpike Trusts lingered
on for another generation, many more of them becoming hopelessly insolvent : how the Government neglected to deal with
them, either in the Highways Act of 1835 or in the ensuing
decades; how, in 1842–1843, South Wales flared up in a genuine
little rebellion against the turnpike exactions, which compelled
the Government to take the South Wales roads virtually under
national control ; how the English Trusts were allowed to go
from bad to worse, to the ruin of innumerable investors ; how
the House of Commons, from about 1862 onwards, took the
matter into its own hands in the absence of a Ministerial policy ;
how a Select Committee in 1864 denounced the whole system of
tolls as " unequal in pressure, costly in collection, inconvenient
to the public, and injurious as causing a serious impediment to
intercourse and traffic," and advocated at least the union of the
Trusts into larger bodies ; how from that time forth the House
successively refused to renew the terms of many of the Trusts as
they expired ; how step by step the management of the highways
was transferred to new district and county authorities, until, in
1895, the last of the road functions of the Parish and the last of
the Turnpike Trusts alike came to an end, we have told in our
Story of the King's Highway.

---

[1] J. L. Macadam was not the only person who regarded the popular in-
fatuation for railways as a " calamity." Alexander Gordon, who published,
in 1832, *An Historical and Practical Treatise upon Elemental Locomotion by
Means of Steam Carriages on Common Roads,* continued to demonstrate *The
Fitness of Turnpike Roads and Highways for the Most Expeditious, Safe, Convenient and Economical Internal Communication* (1835) ; and in 1837 published
*Observations addressed to those interested in either Railways or Turnpike Roads,
showing the Comparative Expedition, Safety, Convenience and Public and Private
Economy of these two kinds of roads for Internal Communication.* Another pro-
jector advocated *The National Waggon-Post, to travel at the rate of twenty miles
per hour, carrying One Thousand Tons Weight, all over the Kingdom of England,
with Passengers, Goods and Stock,* by C. M. George, 1825.

CHAPTER IV

WE come to another, and in many respects a more interesting, series of Statutory Local Authorities in the bodies of Trustees or Commissioners for paving, lighting, cleansing, watching and otherwise improving the streets of the rapidly developing urban centres of the eighteenth century. Although they have never yet engaged the attention of the historian, these early Local Authorities for coping with the problems connected with the police and public health of towns were of greater contemporary interest than the Courts of Sewers or the Incorporated Guardians of the Poor, or even than the Turnpike Trustees. In the ordinary inhabitant the routine of administration of the sluices and embankments excited no attention, and whilst he might grumble at the state of the roads or the turnpike tolls, in only a minority of places was he occasionally called upon to pay either a sewers rate or a highway rate. To the average householder a change in the method of " governing the poor " made practically no difference, except in so far as it might work out in a reduction or increase in the poor-rate. But the bodies of Police, Paving, Street, Lamp or Improvement Trustees or Commissioners, which we have now to describe, dealt with matters of daily life which came home to every household ; they set going public services of an altogether novel kind ; they introduced a new regulation of individual enterprise and personal behaviour ; above all, they levied on every householder new and extra taxation constantly increasing in amount. The establishment, between 1748 and 1835, in nearly every urban centre, under one designation or another, of a new statutory body—which we shall term always Improvement Commissioners—was, in fact, the starting-point of the great modern development of town government. And it is these Improvement Commissioners, not the Mayor, Aldermen and Councillors of the old corporations, who were the progenitors of nearly all the activities of our present municipalities.

The State of the Towns

It is difficult for us at the present day to form any adequate idea of the state of a populous and rapidly growing town at a time when it was without anything in the nature of municipal government, as now understood. To begin with the houses—springing up on all sides with mushroom-like rapidity—there were absolutely no building regulations. Each man put up his house where and as he chose, without regard for building-line, width of street or access of light and air. Every householder encroached on the thoroughfare by overhanging windows, swinging signs, doors opening outwards, cellar-flaps habitually open, mounting blocks and flights of steps. " Streets of projecting houses nearly meeting at top ; rooms with small windows never meant to open ; and dirt in all its glory, excluded every possible access of fresh air." [1] Rain-water pipes were unknown, and projecting spouts from between the gutters of the roofs poured the rain in streams on the passers-by. The narrow ways left to foot and wheeled traffic were unpaved, uneven, and full of holes in which the water and garbage accumulated. Down the middle of the street ran a series of dirty puddles, which in times of rain became a stream of decomposing filth. Public provision for street cleansing or the removal of refuse there was none, so that garbage and horse dung accumulated, in places even a yard deep.[2] There were, of course, no sewers and no water-closets ; what is not commonly realised is that, except in the better parts of London and the wealthier residential cities, there were neither ashpits nor privies, nor any similar conveniences—with results that are indescribable. Pigs roamed about the streets—the only scavengers. Every yard and blind alley contained pigeons and poultry. Cowsheds and slaughterhouses occupied a large portion even of the main

---

[1] *A Philosophical Estimate of the causes, effects and cure of unwholesome air in large cities*, by A. Walker, 1777.

[2] Even in the middle of City of London, "in and about St. Paul's Church," we read, in 1647, that the " horsedung is a yard deep " (*The Familiar Letters of James Howell*, edited by Joseph Jacobs, 1892, vol. i. p. 542).

streets, down which the blood periodically ran in streams. At
night, when there was no moon, the streets were in pitch darkness, except for an occasional lantern swinging over the door of
an energetic shopkeeper or rich householder. With this obstruction, dirt and darkness, it was perhaps a minor matter that there
was no sort of police; outside the City of London, indeed, seldom
even a watchman dosing in his box or noisily calling the hour ; so
that, as the Islington Vestry complains in 1772, " the inhabitants
are exposed to frequent murders, robberies, burglaries and other
outrages." [1]
   Different parishes came, of course, at different dates into this
state, according to the period at which they felt the impulse of
the new industrial conditions, under which their populations
went forward with a bound. The City of London, for instance,
had put its streets into some sort of order after the Great Fire
of 1666, but Westminster remained, at the middle of the eighteenth century, practically as we have described. At this date,
when Jonas Hanway began his agitation for reform, " the
carriage ways were full of cavities which harboured water and
filth.[2] The signs, extending on both sides the way into the
streets at unequal distance from the houses that they might not
intercept each other, greatly obstructed the view, and, which is
of much more consequence in a crowded city, prevented the free
circulation of the air. . . . How comfortless must be the sensa-
tions of an unfortunate female, stopped in the street on a windy
day, under a large old sign, loaded with lead and iron, in full
swing over her head, and perhaps a torrent of dirty water falling
near her from a projecting spout ornamented with the mouth and
teeth of a dragon. . . . The footpaths were universally incom-
moded, even where they were so narrow as only to admit of one
person passing at a time, by a row of posts, set on the edge next
the carriage way. He whose urgent business would not admit of
his keeping pace with the gentleman of leisure before him, turned
out between the two posts before the door of some large house
into the carriage way. When he perceived danger moving

[1] Islington Local Act of 1772, preamble.
[2] Another writer describes the rough and broken pavements of the Westminster streets in 1756 as " so covered by filth as to make them scarcely visible
to the most cautious passenger by day. . . . The quantity of filth in our streets
is so great that man and beast in some places can hardly wade through it "
(*A Proposal or Plan for an Act of Parliament for the Better Paving, Cleansing
and Lighting, etc.*, by John Spranger, 1756).

towards him he wished to return within the protection of the row
of posts ; but there was commonly a rail continued from the top
of one post to that of another, sometimes for several houses
together, in which case he was obliged to run back to the first
inlet, or climb over, or creep under the railing, in attempting
which he might think himself fortunate if he escaped with no
other injury than what proceeded from dirt.   If, intimidated by
the danger he escaped, he afterwards kept within the boundary
of the posts and railing, he was obliged to put aside the travellers
before him, whose haste was less urgent than his, and these
resisting, made his journey truly a warfare." [1]   The cellar-flaps
long continued to be a source of serious danger.   " A considerable proportion of the London poor hid themselves at nightfall
in cellars.   These inhabitants of cellars were permitted to enjoy
and utilise the modicum of daylight that came to their darksome
rooms from the streets, and even to keep the flaps of their street
doors thrown back by day, for the more free admission of sun-
light during the day, provided they closed the flaps at nightfall
with proper care for the safety of pedestrians in the street.   Old
vestry books show that, from time to time, Vestries republished,
by the bellman, the old standing orders for closing cellarflaps
that opened into public ways, on the approach of nightfall.   But
the orders are never rigidly enforced for any considerable length
of time." [2]   At Birmingham, which between 1741 and 1791
trebled its population,[3] there was, prior to 1769, as Hutton
graphically tells us, no sort of regulation.   " When land is appropriated for a street, the builders are under no control ; every
lessee proceeds according to his interest or fancy ; there is no
man to preserve order or prescribe bounds : hence arise evils
without a cure, such as a narrowness which scarcely admits light,
cleanliness, pleasure, health or use ; unnecessary hills like that
in Bull Street ; sudden falls, owing to the floor of one house
being laid three feet lower than the next, as in Coleshill Street ;
one side of a street, like the deck of a ship, ' gunnel to,' several
feet higher than the other, as in Snow Hill. . . . Hence also that

[1] *Remarkable Occurrencies in the Life of Jonas Hanway*, by John Pugh,
1787, pp. 129-131.
[2] *Middlesex County Records*, edited by J. C. Jeaffreson, vol. iv. p. liv.
[3] Hutton gives the number of houses as follows : in 1700, 2504 ; in 1731,
3717 ; in 1741, 4114 ; in 1781, 8382 ; in 1791, 12,881 (*History of Birmingham*,
by William Hutton, 1781, p. 77).

crowd of enormous bulk sashes, steps projecting from the houses and the cellars ; buildings which, like men at a dogfight, seem rudely to crowd before each other ; penthouses, rails, palisades, etc., which have long called for redress." [1] The picture of Birmingham at this period may be completed by a quotation from its modern historian. "The streets . . . were narrow and irregular ; the pavements were wretchedly imperfect ; there was no drainage ; even the rainwater plashed off the house roofs and lay there, with the house refuse, until it dried up. The removal of refuse was unprovided for by any public organisation ; the streets and roads were unswept, except by volunteers, for there were no scavengers ; at night all was pitch dark, save for the light of the moon or the rays of a friendly lantern, for there were no lamps. Right in the centre of the town, New Street, one of the principal streets, was actually entered through a narrow gateway, and was used as a pig-market. The Bull Ring, the only open space, was blocked by shambles and slaughterhouses, and other offensive buildings." [2] Manchester, at the middle of the century, seems to have excelled in filthiness. "A general nastiness," declares a contemporary witness, "is become even a public scandal to our town. We cannot walk the streets without being annoyed with such filth as is a public nuisance. . . . We are grown infamous for a general want of good manners in our populace. . . . Our streets are no better than a common dunghill, and more sacred places are most shamefully polluted. Our very churchyards are profaned with such filth as was intended to create a detestation and abhorrence even of idol temples. I mean they are rendered no better than errant draught houses." [3]

The Commissioners of Scotland Yard

The extensive array of bodies of Improvement Commissioners may be said to begin with the public Act of 1662, which established

---

[1] *History of Birmingham*, by William Hutton, 1781, p. 91 ; *History of the Corporation of Birmingham*, by J. T. Bunce, 1878–1885, p. 46 ; *Old and New Birmingham*, by R. K. Dent, 1819–1881, p. 137.

[2] *History of the Corporation of Birmingham*, by J. T. Bunce, 1878–1885, p. 48.

[3] *Friendly advice to the Poor, written and published at the request of the late and present Officers of the Town of Manchester*, by John Clayton, M.A. (Manchester, 1755).

a new Local Authority in the Cities of London and Westminster.[1] Owing to the multitude of houses lately built, so the preamble declares, and the stopping and filling the ditches and sewers, through want of timely reparation, the common ways had become so miry and foul as to be noisome and dangerous. Powers were accordingly granted to a body of Commissioners, twenty-one in number, including the Dean, the High Steward, the Deputy Steward and two of the Chief Burgesses of Westminster. The Commissioners were empowered to make new sewers, to enlarge old ones and to remove nuisances. Householders were forbidden to throw dirt or refuse of any kind into sewers or watercourses. The Commissioners were authorised to appoint public rakers or scavengers, who were to make daily rounds with " carts, dungpots or other fitting carriages," heralded " by bell, horn, clapper or otherwise " making " distinct noise," so that the inhabitants might bring out their refuse. The Commissioners were also authorised to remove " encroachments by sheds, stalls, balks, shops, posts or walls " projecting into the streets, and to license the newly introduced hackney coaches. Householders were forbidden to throw their coal-ashes and filth into the streets ; they were to repair and maintain the surface in front of their premises ; and they were required to hang out lighted lanterns every night during the autumn and winter. These earliest Commissioners were, however, not given any general rating powers. Their duties related to regulation rather than construc-

[1] Unfortunately we know little about this body (historically interesting as being the only case in which the Cities of London and Westminster were given a common governing authority prior to 1855), except from the Acts from 1662 to 1697, by which it was established and regulated, namely, 13 & 14 Charles II. c. 2 ; 22 Charles II. c. 12 ; 2 William and Mary, sess. 2, c. 8 ; and 8 & 9 William III. c. 27. We have not discovered any of the archives. Evelyn notes in his *Diary* (edited by W. Bray, 1850–1852) that he was chosen one of the Commissioners for " reforming the buildings, ways, streets and incumbrances, and regulating the hackney coaches " ; and he mentions that he went to His Majesty's Surveyor's office in Scotland Yard. There are incidental references to these " Commissioners of Scotland Yard " in the extensive literature relating to Westminster Local Government, for which see *The Manor and the Borough*, 1908, pp. 212-231, especially p. 227 ; and *Local Government in Westminster*, being the Special Annual Report of the Vestry of St. Margaret and St. John on its supersession in 1889, pp. 114-115, 135-137. We do not know to what date these Commissioners for London and Westminster survived. The Act of 1691 extended the scope of the powers of regulation to all the parishes within the Bills of Mortality, but gave the authority to the Justices in Quarter Sessions. It is possible that the Commissioners then ceased to exist as a separate body.

tion. Their works were to be paid for by contributions levied on the particular properties benefited in proportion to their frontage, and the office of " chief raker " was, it incidentally appears, a source of considerable emolument, from the payments made to him by the more substantial householders for emptying their cesspools, and by certain Vestries.

The Improvement Commissioners

But the " Commissioners of Scotland Yard," as the new London and Westminster Local Authority was commonly called, afforded an exceptionally early example of statutory Improvement Commissioners, just as we have seen that the Corporation of the Poor of the City of London did of Incorporated Guardians. For another three-quarters of a century the example was not followed. We find, indeed, that, from 1696 onwards, certain towns on the sea-coast sought and obtained statutory powers to improve their harbours, and to levy port or shipping dues for this purpose. These harbour powers were sometimes granted to the Municipal Corporations, but in other cases special bodies of Harbour Commissioners were constituted, and in a few instances the Harbour Commissioners were authorised to deal with the cleansing, lighting and watching of the streets.[1] We have even one or two instances, such as those of Bristol in 1701 and Beverley in 1727, in which a Municipal Corporation was empowered to levy a regular rate for cleansing and lighting. But in 1736, when powers were obtained by the inhabitants of

[1] The principal bodies of Commissioners established for harbour purposes were, in the "first batch," those of Bridlington (1696), Dover and Rye (1699), Colchester (1699), Minehead (1700), Whitby (1702), Parton (1706) and Whitehaven (1709). Then we have a pause for a couple of decades, the march of improvement being resumed in Newhaven (1730), Scarborough (1731), Littlehampton (1732), Arundel (1733), Southwold (1746), Sunderland (1747), Ramsgate (1748), Great Yarmouth (1749), Lancaster (1749), New Shoreham (1760), Mevagissey (1775), Boston (1776), Aberystwith (1780), Margate (1787), Swansea (1791), Broadstairs (1792), Carnarvon (1793), Amlwch (1793), Barmouth (1797), Sheerness (1801), Bridport (1823), and Liverpool (1825).

These bodies were almost invariably formed on the type of the named list of persons, filling vacancies by co-option, with a certain ex-officio element. Only in Lancaster (1749), Swansea (1791), Liverpool (1825) and Rye (1830) do we find the elective element beginning in the form now commonly adopted for modern port authorities, the electors being shipowners and merchants, as payers of dock-dues (in Swansea, the burgesses elected but had to choose either colliery or ship owners). They were empowered to levy dues on ships and goods, but not to rate.

R

New Sarum (or Salisbury) for paving, lighting and watching the city, these were granted, not to the Municipal Corporation, but to a body of " Trustees," consisting of the Mayor, Recorder and Aldermen *ex officio*, and twelve other persons to be elected annually by the ratepayers of the three parishes of the city. This, too, was an exceptional instance, and it is not until 1748, in the case of Liverpool, that we find the real start of an almost continual stream of Local Acts establishing bodies of Improvement Commissioners, which steadily increases in volume. After the peace of 1763, there sets in everywhere a demand for improvements of one kind or another, among which the betterment of town conditions finds a place. " A general spirit prevails," we read in 1771, " for correcting ancient errors and establishing new improvements. . . . Every session of parliament is now marked by some bill for the inclosing of commons, cutting of canals, constructing of bridges, embanking of rivers, making, mending and watering of highways, and for the paving and lighting of streets." [1] The stream of Acts establishing new Local Authorities, or amending their constitution or powers, continued unabated right down to 1835, and even persisted, especially for unincorporated towns, down to the middle of the nineteenth century.

The new bodies of Improvement Commissioners created by these Acts are found in every part of England, from Truro to Berwick-on-Tweed, and, what is more surprising, in municipalities and unincorporated towns alike. Where a Municipal Corporation existed, it is rare to find the new powers of paving, cleansing, lighting, watching and regulating the town being given to the Mayor, Aldermen and Council, though these and other municipal officers would invariably be included in the new body as ex-officio members. In practically every municipal borough of any importance [2] there was created, between 1748 and 1835, a separate body of Improvement Commissioners, with its own funds and its own official staff, wielding its own distinct powers and levying its own rates. Between 1800 and 1835 these two hundred or more bodies of Improvement Com-

---

[1] *Critical Observations on the Buildings and Improvements of London*, 1771, p. 17.

[2] The only municipal boroughs, having in 1831 11,000 inhabitants, that had never any separate body of Improvement Commissioners seem to have been Leicester, Nottingham, Wenlock and Wigan.

missioners, in as many separate boroughs or urban parishes, together with nearly a hundred similar bodies in the Metropolitan parishes, far outweighed in importance, from the point of view of activity and expenditure in local government, the old Municipal Corporations that, in over a hundred cases, existed alongside them. And as these three hundred statutory police and sanitary authorities have never yet been described by the constitutional historian, we must devote a few pages to an account of their structure and working.[1]

To begin with the constitution of these bodies, we note at once how much more uniform they are in type than the statutory bodies of Incorporated Guardians that we have described. There is, it is true, the same endless diversity as regards the details of structure, and the same difficulty in finding any two precisely alike. A certain ex-officio element is frequent, though not universal ; in municipal boroughs, the Mayor and Aldermen ; sometimes the lord of the manor or occasionally the officers of the manorial courts ; [2] less frequently the members of Parliament, the clergymen or the resident Justices of the Peace.[3] With regard to the remainder of the membership, the whole of the three hundred distinct bodies established prior to 1835 for paving, cleansing, lighting and watching belong, if we ignore for the moment about a dozen anomalies,[4] to one or other of three types.

---

[1] For any study of these Improvement Commissioners there is even less printed material than in the case of the Incorporated Guardians. They are seldom described in town histories—often, indeed, they are not so much as mentioned. Besides the Acts themselves, and the MS. Minutes of the bodies established under them, we must refer the student to the fragmentary references scattered through the many volumes of reports of the Municipal Corporation Commission, 1835, the Commission on the Sanitary Condition of the Population, 1842, the Commission on the State of Large Towns, 1844–1845, and the Commissioners who investigated particular towns under the Public Health Act, 1848. Practically the only books dealing with the subject, and these chiefly from the standpoint of the Local Acts, are *The History of Private Bill Legislation*, by F. Clifford, 1885–1887—a confused medley of facts—and the systematic study of this legislation entitled *Municipal Origins*, by F. H. Spencer, 1911. See also the references given *supra*, pp. 5, 6, 8, and *The Manor and the Borough*, 1908, pp. 394–396.

[2] As at Manchester and Salford, by all the Acts from 1765 to 1830.

[3] At Nottingham, by the Act of 1762, the Improvement Commissioners included all the Commissioners for the Land Tax as ex-officio members.

[4] Among these anomalies we may mention the Hereford Acts of 1774 and 1816, by which the Commissioners were to consist of (*a*) all the local dignitaries from the Lord Lieutenant of the County and the Bishop of the diocese down to the Coroner and the Bailiff ; (*b*) two householders elected triennially by each of the several parish Vestries ; and (*c*) ten persons co-opted by the above at their

Of these, by far the most frequent and the most characteristic is that of the list of persons named in the Act, serving for life, and authorised to fill vacancies among their number by simple co-option. To this type belong nearly two hundred out of the total of three hundred separate bodies of Improvement Commissioners, and it is especially dominant among the Local Acts between 1760 and 1820.[1]

The type standing next in favour is that in which some, at any rate, of the Commissioners are elected. Of this there are a few instances in each decade from 1748 onwards, the number rising rapidly from 1820 to 1835, during which period some of the bodies originally formed in other ways adopted " the elective principle." About fifty bodies were originally established on this type, and about twenty more subsequently changed to it.[2] The election was, however, frequently little more than a pretence of democracy. The first Commissioners were often named in the Act, their " successors " only being furnished by election, at dates often undefined, and in a few instances only septennially. There was always not only a relatively high qualification for Commissioners, but almost invariably a substantial qualification for voters. Moreover, the elected representatives seldom form more than a small proportion of the whole body of Commissioners.

The third type is that in which the ex-officio element, and

---

first meeting, and renewed by co-option. The Charterhouse Square (London) Act of 1742 established a body of Commissioners consisting of the officers of the Charterhouse Charitable Foundation and ten persons chosen by the " proprietors " of the square. The Pembroke Dock Act of 1819 incorporated, as Commissioners, the chief naval officers at that station, and no one else. At Monmouth, in 1818, the Commissioners were to consist of the Municipal Corporation and eight persons selected by the Mayor and Common Council. The Foundling Hospital Estate (London) was, by Act of 1794, governed by twenty-one persons annually appointed by the Governors of the Hospital, and twenty-one elected by the freeholders. All these bodies had extensive taxing, spending and regulating powers.

[1] Among the two hundred bodies of this type may be mentioned the Improvement Commissioners of Birmingham, Bradford, Cardiff, Cheltenham, Coventry, Durham, Folkestone, Yarmouth, Huddersfield, Manchester and Salford (between 1765 and 1792), Northampton, Southampton, Winchester, Wolverhampton and three-fourths of those established in parishes or districts in the Metropolitan area.

[2] Among those originally established during the eighteenth century with some elective representation were Chester, Leeds, Liverpool, Lincoln, Oxford (for which see Oxford in the Eighteenth Century, by J. R. Green and G. Roberson, vol. xli. of Oxford Historical Society, 1901, pp. 333-337), Poole and Salisbury, whilst it was subsequently adopted by such places as Brighton, Carlisle, Dorchester, Dover, Gravesend, Hastings, Manchester, Sheerness and Sheffield.

frequently also the named list, are combined with all the individuals belonging to a specially defined class, such as all substantial freeholders and leaseholders, all residents owning a thousand pounds' worth of personalty, and all occupiers of premises rated at thirty pounds a year.[1] The bodies of this type vary from small oligarchies of the wealthy inhabitants to what are practically open Vestries with a definite voting qualification. We reckon that there were altogether about fifty bodies of this type, nearly all in provincial towns, and more than half of them established between 1820 and 1835.[2]

If, however, we go behind the formal constitution as defined by the Act of Parliament, and trace in the minutes the persons who actually attended the meetings of these bodies, we find, amid the diversity, an even greater identity. In town after town, the minutes reveal the fact that the local dignitaries, who were members *ex officio*, seldom or never attended. And even where the Acts provided for new members being elected, it is clear in many cases that no election took place, the vacancy being either left unfilled, or filled by simple co-option. Thus, in the vast majority of instances, the Improvement Commissioners were, to all intents and purposes, a self-elected and self-renewing little clique of " principal inhabitants." On the other hand, there are some cases, notably Leeds and Woolwich, in which the Commissioners were essentially an elected body, in active connection with a numerous and energetic constituency ; whilst in others again they were practically identical with an open Vestry, limited by a high voting qualification.

So much for the constitution of these three hundred bodies of Improvement Commissioners. To understand their practical importance in the sphere of local government, we must realise

[1] In Preston, by Act of 1815, all £50 leaseholders were Commissioners, except publicans, who were not admitted unless their premises were worth £100 a year. The Act of 1828, which reformed the Manchester Police Commissioners, also made the rating qualification for publicans twice that of other ratepayers.

[2] The most important instance of this type was the body which governed Manchester and Salford (between 1792 and 1828). Among others may be cited the Improvement Commissioners for Derby, Dudley, Godalming, Hanley, Lancaster, Lewes, Lichfield, Maidstone, Oldham, Preston, Rochdale, Ryde, Shrewsbury, Stockport and Worcester. Sometimes (as in the Bridgwater Act of 1779 and the Market Street, Manchester, Act of 1776), all persons subscribing £20 or more to the improvement are made Commissioners to execute it.

something of the range of their activities. It should be noted, in the first place, that their work, besides being specifically defined by the words of their Act, was practically always limited by their borrowing powers being confined to a fixed sum, and their rate being subject to a prescribed maximum. In the simplest examples these bodies were nothing more than little committees of the residents on a particular landlord's estate in London or Brighton, at first usually nominated by the freeholder, but recruiting their numbers by co-option ; charged with the paving, cleaning and lighting of the streets and squares in which they lived, and dividing the cost of the service among all the house-holders. More commonly the Improvement Commissioners, act-ing for some provincial town, begin in the dull routine business of paving, lighting and cleansing the streets, but gradually add new municipal services, such as providing a night watch, pre-venting encroachments, removing obstructions, regulating the traffic, licensing sedan chairs and hackney coaches, prohibiting the wandering of pigs in the thoroughfares, naming streets and numbering houses, putting down nuisances and making byelaws for the good order and government of the town. The minutes of these bodies are not exciting reading and furnish but few points of interest. Their services of paving, cleansing and lighting were almost invariably let out to contractors ; and the one or two officials who made up their staff were little better than work-ing foremen. But as the towns grew in population some enter-prising bodies of Improvement Commissioners launched out, under successive Local Acts, into municipal enterprises of first-rate importance. They constructed sewers to carry away flood water ; they levelled and widened the main streets of their town ; they bought the manorial rights, and erected markets and slaughter-houses ; they laid on a new water-supply and main-tained fire-engines, and in one case they even carried on a highly profitable manufacture and supply of gas.[1] This widened range of activities attracted popular interest, and gave scope for the discussion of general principles, the conflict of interests and all the excitement of political partisanship.

[1] Comparing even the most energetic of the Improvement Commissioners with a modern municipality, we notice the absence, from the list of services undertaken by them, of any provision of parks and open spaces, libraries and museums, picture galleries, baths and wash-houses, the means of transit and housing, and, above all, the various grades and kinds of education.

The Trustees of the Cubitt Estate

We begin with a specimen of the simplest type, which happens to come at rather a late date. At the opening of the nineteenth century, the well-known London builder Cubitt was laying out in streets and squares and covering with houses the Marquis of Westminster's fields at Belgravia and Pimlico. In 1826 the agents of the Marquis obtained a Local Act [1] creating a body of " Trustees for paving, lighting, watching, repairing and otherwise improving Grosvenor Place " and certain other streets in the neighbourhood. This body, consisting of some of the wealthier inhabitants, together with Cubitt and other builders, and renewing itself by co-option,was empowered to borrow £30,000 and to levy a rate not exceeding 2s. 9d. in the pound. The minute-book of this " paving board " reveals to us the fortnightly meetings of half-a-dozen persons, receiving complaints of " defective footways," cellars and basements flooded with liquid filth, lamps unlit, and all sorts of encroachments and nuisances. The Trustees order their one and only paid official to complain to the several contractors for paving, scavenging and lighting, of the non-fulfilment of their contracts. The ratepayers are always grumbling at the amount and inequality of the assessments, which are arbitrarily fixed by the Trustees. But the Trustees are evidently timid and afraid to act on their statutory powers. They give way to any clamorous ratepayer and satisfy him by reducing his assessment. We see them bargaining with a whole street as to extra services to be given for the increased rate.[2] They petition against being upset by Hobhouse's Bill. But when, in 1833, the great personages who dwell in Grosvenor Place insist on " the propriety and justice of adopting the representative system in the Board of Trustees, they meekly reply, that they have no power to change their constitution without Parliamentary leave, and request that if they have been open to censure," the great personages will " be good enough to point out their particular defects." [3] Finally, the democracy of

---

[1] 7 George IV. c. 58.

[2] " Mr. Edwards attended and stated that he thought that the inhabitants of houses in the Vauxhall Bridge Road would, if something was done for them, pay the rates ; and was informed by the Trustees that they will light and water the road if the rates are paid " (MS. Minutes of Trustees of the Cubitt Estate, London, 1st March 1830).

[3] *Ibid.* 8th July 1833.

Belgravia is too strong for them. A committee, headed by Lord Fitzwilliam, publishes an indignant criticism of their proceedings, exposing their apathy, their suspicious compositions with building speculators, their extravagance in paving and lighting contracts, and their neglect of the public interest in failing to charge the cost of new streets on the freeholders. Even the Marquis of Westminster " unequivocally declared himself in favour of the representative system." [1] A new Local Act in 1834 amends their constitution, requiring the existing Trustees to select by lot twenty-four of their members, to whom are added twelve persons elected by the ratepayers of the district. Through the annual retirement of one-third of the whole thirty-six members, and the annual election of their successors, the whole body (with the exception of three persons nominated by the freeholder and the builders) becomes representative of the ratepayers.[2]

Whole districts in the Metropolitan area were, for purposes of cleansing, lighting and paving, a mosaic of boards like the Cubitt Trustees. In the parish of St. Pancras alone there were no fewer than nineteen of them, whilst the total for the whole Metropolitan area approached one hundred.[3] About these bodies practically nothing is known, except that their results were thoroughly unsatisfactory. A contemporary London observer explains both their origin and their degeneration. " Nothing can be more proper than the origin of a modern Paving Act, which is always founded on the application of the parties interested, who propose to pave their own district at their own expense. From among the inhabitants are selected a large number of Commissioners whose names are inserted in the Act. The attorney who has been employed to solicit the bill in Parlia-

---

[1] *An Address to the Inhabitant Ratepayers from their Committee, Grosvenor Place District*, 1833, p. 4.

[2] 4 & 5 William IV. c. 58.

[3] " The number of independent boards for these objects in different parts of London, exclusive of the City and exclusive of those parishes in which the Vestries have power to regulate their own paving, lighting and cleansing, is nearly one hundred. As most of these boards are practically self-appointed and irresponsible, they of course publish no accounts of their receipts and expenditure " (*Local Government in the Metropolis*, 1836, p. 21). " Of paving boards alone, it is said that about the middle of the last century there were no less than eighty-four in the Metropolis—nineteen of them being in one parish. The lighting of the parish of Lambeth was under the charge of nine local Trusts. The affairs of St. Mary, Newington, were under the control of thirteen Boards or Trusts, in addition to two Turnpike Trusts " (*The Sanitary Evolution of London*, by Henry Jephson, 1907, p. 12).

ment usually becomes their clerk, and until the new pavement
is complete the attendance of the Commissioners is full and
frequent. By degrees zeal for the new undertaking seems
unnecessary, or according to the nature of the unresisted zeal
is gradually extinguished, and the care of maintaining the pavement cannot but devolve upon those whose duty binds them to
continue their attendance. These are usually the chairman of
the Commissioners and their clerk, assisted by the pavior employed, whose advice in subordinate details is indispensable." [1]
Notwithstanding all complaints these local paving boards were
in full vigour in 1835, and they continued, indeed, in the Metropolis until 1855, when they were at last merged in the reorganised
Vestries and District Boards, established by Sir Benjamin Hall's
Act, which sent representatives to form the Metropolitan Board
of Works (itself destined, in 1889, to be transformed into the
London County Council), whilst the Vestries and District Boards
became, under the London Government Act of 1901, the Metropolitan Boroughs of to-day.

The Plymouth Commissioners

The borough of Plymouth, incorporated by statute as early
as 1439, presents us with an example of the ordinary type of
Improvement Commissioners in a provincial town. The borough
was governed down to 1835, by a Mayor, Aldermen and Councillors
under a charter of 1697. This ancient Municipal Corporation
owned and exercised the manorial rights, administered a lucrative
water-supply and market, enjoyed valuable property and extensive patronage, and wielded, by its senior members, the sword
of justice in both civil and criminal cases. It remained right
down to the end of the eighteenth century an opulent and
dignified body, and in 1833 it earned the rare distinction by
being praised by the Municipal Corporation Commissioners as an
active and honest governing authority.[2] In the middle of the
eighteenth century the Mayor and Corporation were maintaining
a certain number of watchmen, hired out of the four shillings a
year which most householders paid as composition in lieu of

---

[1] *Eight Letters concerning the Pavement of the Metropolis and the adjoining
Turnpike Roads*, by X. Y., 1817.
[2] Municipal Corporations Commission Report (Appendix, part i. p. 595).

personal service. There were also a couple of town scavengers. The town had its own stone quarries, and the Corporation had made a beginning in the way of sewering and paving. It is therefore all the more interesting to find that when, after the conclusion of the Seven Years' War in 1763, there sprang up a demand for town improvements, these were not undertaken by the Corporation. In 1770, " a considerable movement having been set on foot in the town for the paving, lighting, and watching of Plymouth, an Act of Parliament was obtained, and a Board of Commissioners appointed for the purpose of carrying out its provisions." [1] This body consisted of the Mayor, Recorder, Town Clerk, Coroner, the twelve Aldermen and the twenty-four Common Councillors, *ex officio*, together with thirty named persons, who were to fill vacancies among their number by co-option of persons qualified by ownership of £40 a year freehold, or £1000 worth of personalty.[2]

The minutes of this body for the first twenty years of its existence have unfortunately not been preserved. It appears to have started off with some energy in the matter of street lighting, ordering 200 lamps, with wick and oil, " the same as that used in London," to be erected and lit by contract. With regard to the watch, it established a force of twenty men, " to be armed with halberds as usual," carrying bells, and calling out the hour and the weather. The householder's obligation to personal service of watch and ward was merged in the new rate levied by the Commissioners, but inhabitants who were not rated, including therefore all occupiers of small cottages, continued liable to serve, or to pay the composition.[3] The Commissioners were apparently least successful in the scavenging of the town. At first they were made the sole authority for this service, the

[1] See *History of Plymouth*, by Llewellyn Jewitt (Plymouth, 1873), pp. 343-347 ; *History of Plymouth*, by R. N. Worth, 1890, p. 223. Many references to the local government of Plymouth will be found in *The Manor and the Borough*, 1908 (see index). The well-kept archives are described in the *Calendar of the Plymouth Municipal Records*, by R. N. Worth (Plymouth, 1893).
[2] 10 George III. c. 14.
[3] " Ordered that the Clerk do call upon the several collectors to make out lists of the resiants in the present books, distinguishing such as are willing to pay their rates, from such as refuse to pay ; and that the constable and corporals of the watch do afterwards call out the resiants so refusing, to watch in rotation ; and on such condition they be excused from the payment of the said rates " (MS. Minutes, Improvement Commissioners, Plymouth, 27th November 1792).

Corporation having to contribute £40 a year to their funds. Amending Acts of 1772 and 1774 [1] restored the work to the Mayor and Corporation, who continued feebly to perform this function (often contracting with the Incorporated Guardians to employ paupers) right down to the reform of 1835. But the Commissioners were given powers to put down nuisances, and to require owners to pave and sewer streets—neither of which powers they appear to have exercised. [2]

From 1789, when the first existing minutes begin, down to 1824, when a new Act was obtained, the Commissioners were an apathetic and uninteresting body. They met nominally every week, but though the quorum was two only, many weeks in succession there would be no business for lack of one. [3] They had only two committees, one for examining accounts and one for general purposes, and we infer that only about a dozen out of the sixty or seventy members ever attended at all. The Commissioners, in fact, confined themselves to levying their maximum annual rate of sixpence in the pound on owners and sixpence on occupiers, making contracts for lamplighting, and for such small paving works as could be done out of their scanty resources ; and to paying the wages of the watchmen. When in 1820 their Surveyor of Pavement died, they decided (though he was their only executive officer other than the old-fashioned firm of solicitors who acted as their law clerks) not to appoint a successor. [4]

The Act of 1824 put new life into the Commissioners. [5] The attendance at meetings rises to about forty, special committees are appointed, the watch is increased, street improvements are

[1] 12 George III. c. 8 and 14 George III. c. 8.

[2] We may cite, as the sort of exception that proves the rule, the following resolution of 1821, which was probably not acted upon. "That the Clerks and Treasurers be directed to take the necessary measures for prosecuting any four persons for making obstructions and nuisances in the public streets, for the sake of public example—selecting such instances as may appear to be the fittest objects for such prosecutions" (MS. Minutes, Improvement Commissioners, Plymouth, 13th March 1821).

[3] In 1797–1798 there was no quorum for 48 successive weeks, in 1798–1799 for 36 successive weeks, and in 1799–1800, even for 50 successive weeks (*ibid.* 1797–1800).   [4] *Ibid.* 25th April 1820.

[5] *An Act for Better Paving, Cleansing, Watching and Improving the Town and Borough of Plymouth in the County of Devon, and for regulating the Police thereof, and for removing and preventing Nuisances and Annoyances therein* (Plymouth, 1824). This Act made no change in the composition of the Commissioners.

undertaken, and certain kinds of obstruction in the thoroughfares and nuisances are proceeded against. This spurt of
activity lasts only a few years, and the body soon sinks back to
its former level of scanty attendance and apathy. In 1830,
indeed, it is moved to protest against Hobhouse's bill, and the
solicitor is despatched to London in order to obtain the exclusion
of Plymouth from the scope of the measure.[1] In the following
year the fear of cholera, and the remonstrances of a local " Board
of Health " that had been formed, induced the Commissioners
to give notice " to the sub-surveyors that if they do not exert
themselves and cause the different nuisances to be removed
from all parts of the town in conformity with the provisions of
the Improvement Act, at the expiration of one month from this
time they will be dismissed from their appointments." [2]   But
nothing could galvanise the Plymouth Commissioners into
lasting activity or any sort of efficiency. Early in 1836, without
remonstrance or complaint, they ceded to the newly elected
Town Council the administration of the watch and the levying
of threepence out of their former rate. For another eighteen
years they lingered out a moribund existence, before being in
1854 finally merged in the Municipal Corporation on the application to the borough of the Public Health Act.[3]

The " Lamp Commissioners " of Birmingham

The Improvement Commissioners in some other places were
more successful than those of Plymouth. At Birmingham, for
instance, they made themselves, after thirty years of comparative
inactivity, into the principal governing authority of that important town.[4]   The " Borough and Manor of Byrmyngham," as

[1] MS. Minutes, 13th April and 8th June 1830.
[2] Ibid. 8th March, 1st November and 15th November 1831.
[3] Their minutes end 11th July 1854.
[4] For the local government history of Birmingham (with which we have
already dealt in The Parish and the County, 1907, pp. 117-118, 582-583, etc.,
and, more extensively, in The Manor and the Borough, 1908, vol. ii. pp. 157-160,
264-265, etc.) the most important sources are the MS. Minutes of the Improvement Commissioners from 1776 to 1851, and those of the Town Council from
1838 onward. The MS. Minutes of the Vestry of St. Martin's, and those of
the Incorporated Guardians are less fruitful, and the Court Leet records contain practically nothing of interest. On the other hand, the local histories are
exceptionally full and detailed, and much is to be gained from the various
editions of William Hutton's History of Birmingham (Birmingham, 1781 ; latest
edition, 1840) ; The History of the Corporation of Birmingham, by J. T. Bunce

it was called in the sixteenth century, was already in Tudor times a thriving industrial centre, which, although not legally incorporated, seems long to have enjoyed a certain measure of independent communal organisation.[1] The manorial courts dwindled, as we have elsewhere described, into little more than occasions for conviviality. The Vestry seems, for some reason, to have been an inert body, confining itself practically to church administration,[2] and when, about the middle of the eighteenth century, the population took to doubling itself in a generation, the need for some governing authority became imperative. An attempt to get a Local Act was made in 1765, but failed owing to the opposition to any new rate. Four years later a renewed effort was more successful, and a body of " Lamp," " Streets " or Improvement Commissioners was incorporated, renewing themselves by co-option, but with narrowly limited rating powers.[3] A subsequent Act of 1773 slightly enlarged the Commissioners' functions, but, as William Hutton remarks, " committed to the care of about seventy-six irresolute Commissioners . . . who wisely argue against the annihilation of one evil because another will remain," the new authority was for a long time not turned to any effective use. The well-kept but brief and formal minutes of the Commissioners, which exist from 1776, reveal only a scanty attendance, at very irregular meetings. The Commissioners engaged at first no salaried officers whatsoever. Dividing the

(Birmingham, 1878–1885), with a third volume by C. A. Vince (Birmingham, 1902) ; *A Century of Birmingham Life* (1868) and *Modern Birmingham and its Institutions* (1873–1877), both by J. A. Langford ; *Old and New Birmingham* (1879–1880) and *The Making of Birmingham* (1894), both by R. K. Dent ; and " Hints for a History of Birmingham," by James Jaffray, being a series of articles from the *Birmingham Journal* for 1855, collected into a volume in the Birmingham Public Library. Further references will be found in our book, *The Manor and the Borough*, 1908, pp. 157-160.

[1] In the *Survey of the Borough and Manor of Birmingham*, by Clement K. Throkmorton (Birmingham, 1891), dating from 1553, we find " the Bailiff and Commonalty of the Borough of Byrmyngham " holding stalls and standings in the market place, at a fixed rent, as tenants of the lord of the manor (pp. 60-61).

[2] The MS. Minutes of the Vestry of St. Martin's, Birmingham, the mother-parish, between 1795 and 1842, contain hardly any entries relating to local government.

[3] All houses under £6 a year value, all gardens and arable land, all stock-in-trade and personalty, and all empty premises were exempt ; on houses between £6 and £10 a year the rate was never to exceed twopence ; between £10 and £15, threepence ; between £15 and £20, fourpence ; and between £20 and £25, eightpence in the pound—an interesting example of " differential rating."

town into twelve districts, they appointed a committee for each, it being assumed that the Commissioners themselves would report all nuisances, and supervise the lamplighting for their own neighbourhoods.[1]   Their first work was a struggle, which lasted for a whole decade, against the " bulksashes," or bow windows, obstructing the narrow streets.[2]   Then the yawning cellars engage their attention, and these dangers to passengers are vigorously " closed down " or " filled up " or protected by iron gratings. The stone steps at front doors are declared nuisances and ordered to be removed.   Fireworks and squibs are forbidden ; barrels are not to be left about the streets, nor horses allowed to wander at large.   The washing of " brass dirt " and metals in the streets had been stopped.   The heaps of broken glass and crockery, casting-pots and brick-ends, slack, shop sweepings and other rubbish, had been carried away.   Dog-fighting and bull-baiting in the public streets had been suppressed.   But the Commissioners had, by the end of the century, not made much headway with the street improvements, which had been one of the primary objects of their establishment.   " The old fingerposts which had stood at every turning and had become shattered and crazy, they swept away.   The ravines . . . had been filled up.   The Shambles, the Round House and the Old Cross, which nearly filled the whole area of Bull Ring, they cleared away in 1784." [3] As at Plymouth, the narrow financial limits set to the Commissioners' powers soon stopped work in this direction.   Meanwhile a few lamps were erected, and their lighting was paid for by contract.   A feeble attempt was made about 1791 to pave the footways in one or two principal streets ; and a small sum was from time to time expended in clearing away the worst of the dirt that defiled the streets.[4]   Police there was none.   Prior to

[1] MS. Minutes, Improvement Commissioners, Birmingham, 10th December 1776.

[2] " That notice be given to the owner and builder of the houses in Newton Street that they will not be permitted to put out any bulk-sash, the streets not being 10 yards wide, and to take those down that are already built, or the penalty will be levied according to the Act " (*ibid.* 5th August 1777).

[3] " Hints for a History of Birmingham," by James Jaffray.

[4] " That Hill do immediately proceed to clean the several streets in rotation, agreeable to the printed list ; and that the gentlemen who are mentioned and appointed in the said list for overlooking the number of streets therein fixed be requested to superintend the scavengers during the time of cleaning such several streets and see that the same are properly done " (MS. Minutes, Improvement Commissioners, Birmingham, 11th November 1777).

1789, there were no night watchmen whatsoever, and, apart from the market, practically no constables. From 1789 to 1801 the provision of a nightly watch was left entirely to the private subscriptions of the wealthier quarters of the town.[1] Right down to the end of the eighteenth century, the Birmingham Commissioners seem fairly to have merited Hutton's reproach.[2]

With the opening of the nineteenth century comes a spurt of activity. A new Local Act is obtained in 1801, bringing into assessment all houses over one pound a year value, and giving additional borrowing powers. New byelaws are framed, greatly enlarging the list of practices forbidden as nuisances. The duty of maintaining a nightly watch, hitherto left to private subscription, is undertaken by the Commissioners, and a force of sixty men is, during the winter months, taken into public pay.[3] The market tolls, and with them the management of the market, are taken on lease from the lord of the manor.[4] In 1812 yet another Local Act is obtained, bringing all houses whatsoever into assessment, doubling the rate, and giving power to borrow £24,000. With this new authority, the Commissioners transform themselves into a regularly organised and fairly efficient municipal government. Their regular monthly meetings secure an attendance of between forty and sixty. All the executive work is now practically delegated to standing committees, of which there were eventually five, dealing respectively with finance,

[1] In 1789, we are told, " A meeting was held in the suburban district of St. Paul's, and a committee was appointed to establish a night patrol in that quarter. The example was contagious, so each of the districts of the town formed committees of their own and engaged watchmen on their own responsibility. The committee in their turn always accompanied the patrol in their nocturnal perambulations, in order to be assured that they did their duty. . . . It was considered excellent sport by the young bloods of Birmingham to have command of the patrol and many of their companions used to join them on duty, the result being a jolly night of it, and abundance of amusement " (" Hints for a History of Birmingham," by James Jaffray).

[2] Their total annual expenditure did not reach £1000 until their tenth year of existence ; and had not, after thirty years, attained £2000 (Hutton's *History of Birmingham*, pp. 224-225).

[3] *Ibid.* 5th October 1801. As late as 1829 the watchmen were employed officially only during the seven dark months of the year. They were allowed to " collect pay on their rounds during the summer months and this is universally practised " (MS. Report of Superintendent of Police, Manchester, of his Tour of Inspection to Glasgow, Edinburgh, Birmingham, etc., in 1829).

[4] For 21 years, at £60 a year ; *ibid.* 6th January 1806. These market rights (without the manor itself) were eventually acquired by the Corporation (*The Manor and the Borough*, by S. and B. Webb, 1908, p. 160).

markets, lamps and watching, sweeping and paving. The members of the Paving Committee were habitually appointed by the magistrates to be Surveyors of Highways for the parish, and as such levied their own distinct highway rate, and maintained their own separate offices and clerical establishment. Under this authority the streets were gradually paved. The Commissioners' annual revenue and expenditure in 1830, when the population had risen to 146,986 (1831 census), amounted to the respectable total of £17,000. They courted publicity, making their books and even the proceedings of their committee meetings " open to all ratepayers on paying a small sum to the clerk." [1] In 1828 a new Local Act was obtained, authorising the borrowing of no less than £100,000, including £25,000 for a Town Hall, and the levying of an additional rate of sixpence in the pound for this purpose, exclusively on premises valued at £15 a year and upwards. The markets, now become a profitable service, are enlarged, and the Commissioners take the management and toll-collecting into their own hands.[2] Their total rate rises to the considerable sum of half-a-crown in the pound. A Town Surveyor is appointed at a salary of £150 a year. The scavengering is no longer contracted for or left to amateur supervision, but is done in 1829 by a directly employed staff of 18 sweepers, 13 scrapers and 11 horses and carts, at a net cost of over £1000 a year. The lamps are lit by gas, and 106 watchmen patrol the town. Altogether, as we learn from a Manchester official in 1829, " the streets of Birmingham have an air of cleanliness and comfort to which Manchester is an entire stranger." [3] The Birmingham Improvement Commissioners continued in full activity, as a fairly efficient governing body, until they were, in 1851, by mutual consent, merged in the Municipal Corporation.

The " Police Commissioners " of Manchester

For the best example of a really energetic and successful body of Improvement Commissioners we must turn not to

---

[1] This is the only instance we know of in which a charge for inspection of the minutes has been formally authorised.

[2] *Birmingham New Market Place : a Letter addressed to one of the Commissioners of the Birmingham Street Act*, by Charles Fiddian (Birmingham, 1828) ; *Observations on a Letter . . .*, by *Mr. Charles Fiddian, etc.*, by William Haines (Birmingham, 1828).

[3] MS. Report of the Superintendent of Police, Manchester, of his Tour of Inspection to Glasgow, Edinburgh, Birmingham, etc., in 1829.

Birmingham, but to the greatest of the new manufacturing centres, in which the massing of population, the extension of enterprise and the growth of a wealthy class were, at the same time, creating the need for increased government and throwing up men capable of the task. The Vestry organisation of the great parish of Manchester had, as we have already described,[1] fallen towards the end of the eighteenth century into a state of indescribable disorder, owing to the impracticable relations between the Churchwardens and Overseers, the Justices of the Peace, the inhabitants in Vestry assembled and the officers of the Court Leet. But these separate and conflicting authorities, though they managed between them the poor, the highways and the primitive police force, had, fortunately for the town, in other matters been superseded by a statutory body of Commissioners. Perhaps, owing to the very disorganisation of the parish government, the Police Commissioners, as they were always called, had, from their inception in 1765 by the Act 5 George III. c. 81, down to their absorption in the Town Council in 1842, at no time any connection whatsoever with the Vestry or any of its officers. The first thirty years' records of the Manchester and Salford Police Commissioners have disappeared, but we learn that " soon after the passing " of the Act of 1792 (32 George III. c. 69), which repealed the 1765 Act, " the Commissioners thereby appointed divided and formed two distinct bodies," [2] one consisting of the Commissioners resident in Manchester, and the other of those resident in Salford. These two bodies, appointing separate establishments and levying separate rates, henceforth confined their activities to their respective towns. This voluntary (and, until 1828, entirely extra-legal) separation probably took place in 1797, from which date the records in the Manchester Town Hall begin.[3]

---

[1] *The Parish and the County*, by S. and B. Webb, 1907.

[2] Preamble to Manchester Local Act of 1828 (9 George IV. c. 117) which ratified this separation. Under the Act of 1792, " the Commissioners for better cleaning, lighting and regulating the towns of Manchester and Salford " consisted of the Warden and Fellows of the College of Christ in Manchester, the Boroughreeve and Constables and all owners and occupiers of premises of the yearly rent of £30, at the least, who took the prescribed oath (32 George III. c. 69). The legal establishment of the Salford Commissioners as a separate body was by the Act of 1828 (9 George IV. c. 17).

[3] For the Manchester Police Commissioners, the student may consult the MS. Minutes which exist from 1797 only ; the successive Acts, 32 George III. c. 69 ; 49 George III. c. 192 ; 53 George III. c. 20 ; 56 George III. c. 12 ; 1 & 2 George IV. c. 47 ; 1 & 2 George IV. c. 126 ; 4 George IV. c. 115 ; 5 George IV. c. 133 ; 9 George IV. c. 117 ; 11 George IV. c. 47 ; 1 William IV.

The Manchester Police Commissioners have for us a special interest. In their three-quarters of a century of existence they exemplify all the three representative types of statutory bodies of Commissioners ; beginning in 1765 as a limited number of named persons co-opting their successors ; then transformed in 1792 into a body consisting of the whole of a class ; and finally, in 1828, being reconstituted as a body of elected representatives. No less interesting is the fact that, especially between 1808 and 1835, these Commissioners included among their most active members most of the men who were then making Manchester famous for its commercial enterprise and aggressive political opinion—the Phillips, Potters, Taylors, Garnetts, Heywoods, Brookses, and, later on, Richard Cobden himself. During these years the Manchester Police Commissioners, as we shall presently describe, initiated in their municipal gas-works the most remarkable of all municipal experiments prior to 1835, and thus gave to the new Town Council an impetus which was not spent for a whole generation, and which secured to Manchester the premier place in English municipal development until the rise of Birmingham in the 'seventies. And it is in the records of these Commissioners that we discover the first instance of that marked cleavage in municipal policy—neither dependent on, nor exactly coinciding with, the contemporary cleavage in national politics—which has since accompanied all vigorous municipal life in this country.

The first volume of these minutes exhibits the new body of Commissioners struggling slowly and fitfully to establish their authority in the densely crowded streets and slums of the Manchester of that time. The meetings recorded from 1797 to 1807 were seldom attended by more than a dozen persons and often failed for lack of a quorum. The most pressing business was apparently the establishment of a Night Watch, beginning in 1797 with a force of 14 men. Then 1000 lamps were bought, which were frugally lit on " twenty dark nights per month from the 1st October to the 30 April." [1] Twenty-two firemen were

---

c. 16; 6 William IV. c. 16; 1 Vict. c. 37; 2 Vict. c. 2; 2 & 3 Vict. c. 87; 3 & 4 Vict. c. 30; 4 Vict. c. 8; 5 & 6 Vict. c. 117; 6 Vict. c. 17; the incidental references in the various forewords and footnotes in *The Manchester Municipal Code*, 6 vols. 1894–1901 ; the sources cited in *The Parish and the County* and *The Manor and the Borough* (see index) ; and such controversial pamphlets as those cited in the following pages, most of which are to be found in the Manchester Public Library.

[1] MS. Minutes, Police Commissioners, Manchester, 4th November 1797.

appointed to attend when required to work the public fire-engine.[1] In 1800 a special committee was directed to report what nuisances should first be taken in hand. In a vigorous report the Committee map out a scheme of work,[2] which occupied all the energy of the Commissioners for several years. The manifold encroachments on the streets by projecting steps and cellar entrances were to be removed ; war was declared against the stalls that obstructed the footways and the signboards that darkened the air ; the lines of posts that divided these footways from the road were to be cleared away ; dangerous places were to be fenced off from the highway ; the excessive smoke from factory chimneys was to be restrained ; and finally, wandering pigs were to be excluded from the streets.[3] This programme was not completely carried out for the next ten years, as the Commissioners found the mere management of the watching, lighting and scavenging of the city no light task, to say nothing of the trouble that it cost to assess and collect the rates. This is explained by the reluctance of the Commissioners to engage a salaried staff. The Commissioners resident in each ward were required personally to select the watchmen for that ward, to see that they were properly on duty, to give orders for the repair of their watch-boxes, to inspect the paving, to notice whether the contractor lit the lamps on the nights and at the hours stipulated for, to take care that the contractor cleaned the streets as agreed upon, and generally to act as amateur superintendents of police and inspectors of nuisances for their several neighbourhoods. It was not until after seven years' experience that the Commissioners could bring themselves (in 1804) to appoint an officer at £150 a year, to combine the command of the police with the superintendence of the scavenging and all the other manifold work of the town.[4] After 1807, when the accounts were for the first time " ordered to be printed for the information of the public," [5] we notice a steady development in organisation and growth in activity. The committees were more definitely organised ; and the ordinary work of lighting and scavenging,

[1] MS. Minutes, Police Commissioners, Manchester, 27th December 1799.
[2] *Ibid.* 5th September 1800.
[3] " That Mr. Braddock give notice to the shoemaker who has for some time been in the habit of permitting his pigs to remain and be fed in the street at the bottom of Hunt's Bank that unless he discontinues this practice he will be summoned and fined " (*ibid.* 7th May 1802).
[4] *Ibid.* 16th November 1804.   [5] *Ibid.* 13th November 1807.

together with the management of the watch, ran more smoothly. All the houses were numbered, and sometimes renumbered, at the public expense. Pigsties within the town were declared a common nuisance, and proceeded against at the Court Leet. The leading inhabitants were eager for further activity. A Town's Meeting called in the beginning of the year appointed an influential committee to consider the propriety of getting a new Local Act, giving greatly increased powers of self-government. This committee gave the necessary notices for a new Act. They recommended the purchase of the market and other manorial rights for a sum which they had provisionally agreed with the Lord of the Manor at £90,000 ; a large scheme of street improvement, including wiaening and repaving, with the purchase of adjoining land for recoupment ; the amalgamation of the Surveyors of Highways and the Commissioners for the Market Street Widening with the general body of Commissioners ; and many other reforms of various kinds.[1] But these reforming spirits were too bold for the citizens of their day. They had ventured to propose, not only " a moderate Sunday Toll to be collected from horses, cattle and carriages at the different avenues leading from the town "—those conveying persons to places of worship being exempted—but also a new fourpenny rate " charged upon and made payable by the owner," though " assessed with the Police Rate upon the occupier and collected from him." [2] This led to a storm of indignation, and a whole sheaf of pamphlets, under the influence of which these bold projects were dropped.[3]

[1] One of the authors takes a pleasure in recording that on this committee sat her great-uncle, Thomas (afterwards Sir T.) Potter, in 1838 first Mayor of Manchester.
[2] See the instructive *Reports of the several committees appointed in consequence of a Public Meeting of the inhabitants of Manchester for taking into consideration the following subjects, viz. The New Police Act, Paving, Flagging and Soughing, Sunday Toll, Local Administration of Justice, Purchase of the Manor of Manchester*, etc. (Manchester, 1808).
[3] Among them were the following : *An Address to the Inhabitants of Manchester on the impolicy of their purchasing the Manor*, by Charles M'Niven (Manchester, 1809) ; *A Reply to Mr. M'Niven's Address to the inhabitants of Manchester on the impolicy of their purchasing the Manor*, by one of the Addressed (Manchester, 1809) ; *Report of the committee appointed at a Public Town's Meeting of the Inhabitants of Manchester to treat conditionally with Sir Oswald Mosley for the purchase of the Manor* (Manchester, 1809); *The Murder is out, or Committeemen fingering Cash, being a sequel to New Taxes, Seventy Thousand Pounds, addressed to every householder in the Manor of Manchester*, by Francis Philips (Manchester, 1809) ; *A Letter to Francis Philips, Esq., on his pamphlet entitled " Murder is Out,"* etc., by a Native of the Parish of

Whilst they were still in controversy came a great struggle over the water question. In the session of 1809 two sets of promoters had rival schemes in Parliament for improving the water supply, both of them being vigorously opposed by the Commissioners on behalf of the citizens. Crowded town's meetings condemned the bills, and enthusiastically adopted the report of a committee which advocated the policy of municipalisation.[1] The Commissioners spent £1760 in this Parliamentary campaign, with little success. The "Stone Pipe Company" got its Act,[2] conceding only a few protective clauses; and its friends formally objected to the Commissioners' expenditure, which Quarter Sessions eventually disallowed. The Commissioners, it was held, "had no power to apply the police fund in a Parliamentary defence of the rights of the inhabitants, though such defence be directed and carried on by the inhabitants at large."[3] We hear little of the Commissioners for the next ten years, which were,

Manchester (Manchester, 1809); *Coke upon Lyttleton*; or *the Rejoinder*, by Francis Philips (Manchester, 1809); *The History of Johnny Shuttle and his cottage* (Manchester, 1809). Copies of these are rare, but they are described in *Manchester Court Leet Records*, vol. xii. preface, p. xvii. The Manor, which could have been acquired in 1808 for £90,000, was bought in 1846 for £200,000 (*The Manor and the Borough*, by S. and B. Webb, 1908, vol. i. p. 113 ; *Mediaeval Manchester and the Beginnings of Lancashire*, by James Tait, 1904, p. 37).

[1] "Your Committee are also of opinion that the supply of the town of Manchester with water ought to be under the direction of its own inhabitants and that it would be contrary to sound policy to entrust the furnishing and control of this important article of food and cleanliness on which the health and comfort of the inhabitants depend, to persons whose sole object will be the promotion of their own private interest, and who are induced to the undertaking from no other motive." It was therefore proposed that the town should have its own water supply, under the management of the Churchwardens and Overseers, acting in conjunction with the Commissioners and the Surveyors of Highways ; that the capital should be raised by the issue of Manchester Town notes transferable as currency but bearing interest ; and that the surplus profits should be devoted to the relief of the rates (*History of the Origin and Progress of the Water Supply of Manchester*, 1851, an excellent volume reprinted from the *Manchester Guardian*). Municipalisation did not come for another forty years. The company acquired the primitive waterworks owned by the Lord of the Manor at Holt Town, Beswick, and constructed additional works at Gorton. The whole undertaking was purchased by the Town Council in 1847, when extensive new works were constructed in the Longdendale Valley (*Manchester Municipal Code*, 1896, vol. iii. ; *History and Description of the Thirlmere Water Scheme*, by Sir J. J. Harwood, 1895).

[2] 49 George III. c. 192.

[3] *History of the Origin and Progress of the Water Supply in Manchester*, p. 28. See the MS. Minutes of the Commissioners, 4th May and 29th September 1809 ; and those of the Lancashire Quarter Sessions, Salford, 10th October 1810, where the total disallowed is stated as £2500. The active Commissioners presumably had personally to subscribe the sum disallowed, with costs.

in Manchester as elsewhere, " a time of transition from gloom to apparent prosperity." [1] It was, however, during this period of political repression and economic distress that the Commissioners started their boldest and most important experiment. Already in 1807 they had begun to make gas in a small way in order to light with it their office, and presently some of the street lamps. " As the use of gas thus spread, its superiority to all other light made the public anxious to obtain it for private consumption, and several public meetings were held for the purpose of urging the Commissioners of Police to extend the works so as to supply the general demand. In compliance with the feeling thus manifested, the Commissioners made a formal appeal to the ratepayers at large by calling a meeting specially for the purpose of obtaining an express sanction for that object. This meeting took place on the 30th April 1817, and resolved unanimously ' That it will be expedient to adopt the proposed mode of lighting the central parts of the town with gas, and for the purpose of effecting this object to raise the police rate from 15d. to 18d. in the pound.' " New gas-works were accordingly set up in 1817 to supply the public, and these were gradually extended year by year as the revenue came in.[2] That this " municipal trading " was entirely unauthorised by law did not apparently much trouble the Commissioners. For seven years they conducted their new enterprise without any specific Parliamentary powers, using the substantial annual profit to extend the works.[3] In

[1] *Reminiscences of Old Manchester and Salford*, by an Octogenarian (Manchester, 1887).

[2] No other public authority undertook the gas supply for many years. At Derby, for instance, when in 1819 the inhabitants held meetings to obtain a gas supply, it was taken for granted that the only way was to form a joint stock company (*Derby Mercury*, 27th May 1819).

[3] Baines (*History of the County Palatine of Lancaster*, vol. ii. p. 349) says that " the merit of originating these works on the present liberal plan is principally due to George William Wood," afterwards M.P. for South Lancashire. But their success was due in no small degree to Thomas Potter, another of the Commissioners, who, though at the head of a large business, devoted much time to their management. We have come across the statement as a current saying of the time, that " Tom Potter is always at the gasworks : he even goes there every Sunday after chapel, just to see how they were getting on." The great administrative ability of Thomas Wroe, appointed manager in 1834, definitely established their great financial success. For the history of the Manchester Gas Works, see (besides the MS. Minutes of the Commissioners) the able account given in the *Manchester Municipal Code* (Manchester, 1896), vol. iii. pp. 357-400 ; *Some Account of the Manchester Gas Works*, by John Shuttleworth (Manchester, 1861), a paper read at the British Association in

1823 a private enterprise—"The Manchester Imperial Joint Stock Oil Gas Company"—entered the field, and applied for an Act to enable it to supply gas in competition with the Commissioners, whose memorial in defence of municipal monopoly in gas supply is worth quoting as showing the spirit in which these Manchester merchants undertook their public work. They recite "that during the last seven years the Commissioners of Police acting on behalf and for the benefit of the public, have expended upwards of £30,000 in the erection of gas-works, which works they are preparing to extend as rapidly as circumstances will admit of; every inhabitant paying police rates is interested in these works in proportion to the amount of his rate, and when owning or occupying premises of the yearly value of £30 or upwards has a direct control in the appointment of a committee of management, in the choice of servants, and in every other matter connected therewith; the injury to the streets and the loss and annoyance to the inhabitants inevitable upon the laying down of gas pipes have already been incurred in the most public and important parts of the town; that every repetition of the process must produce a recurrence of its attendant evils, and the permanent inconveniences necessarily incident to works of this nature must be ever in proportion to the number of establishments formed. That in this great and rapidly increasing town there exists no permanent fund whatever for its general improvement, and the public, no less than the Commissioners of Police, have looked forward with great satisfaction to the acquisition of a fund applicable to that purpose; that the existing gas-works are productive of a profit which, instead of being applied to the private advantage of individuals, is available for general objects, and may be directed either to a reduction of the public rates, or to purposes of public improvement, according to the varying wants and circumstances of the times as may appear best to the inhabitants at large. That the consumers of gas are unquestionably entitled to an adequate supply of a quality as good as can be manufactured and at rates which, leaving only a fair and reasonable profit on the public capital invested, shall not exceed the prices paid in neighbouring towns; and that

1861 by the Chairman of the Gas Committee from 1843 to 1861; and a critical reply to this, entitled *Observations on the Paper read by John Shuttleworth, Esq., before the British Association on the Manchester Gas Works*, 1861.

these desirable objects are more likely to be obtained by a general establishment conducted under an effective public control than by any private association founded solely for immediate gain." [1] The Commissioners accordingly promoted a bill of their own, to ratify and authorise their municipal gas-works, which were to be managed by a committee of thirty Gas Directors, appointed by the Commissioners for three years, one-third retiring annually. Whether the Parliament of 1824 would deliberately have approved of this " municipal trading " seems doubtful, but the Manchester Commissioners were fortunate in their opponents. The promoters of the private company " resorted to gross frauds in getting up petitions in support of their bill, which proceeding excited great indignation, and produced a reactionary influence in favour of the project of the Commissioners," [2] which thus became law (5 George IV. c. 133)—the first legislative " recognition of the principle that gas establishments might be created by public funds and be conducted by public bodies for the public benefit."

This vigorous municipal policy of the Commissioners did not meet with universal approval. A numerous and pertinacious section—the owners of small cottage property, the shopkeepers and small masters, the beer sellers and publicans—regarded much of the activity of the Commissioners as both inimical to their pecuniary interests and contrary to their notions of political expediency. " It was forgotten," said a vigorous local critic, " that, whatever right the Commissioners might have to light the streets with gas . . . they had no more right to monopolise the manufacture of gas for the lighting of private establishments than they have to monopolise the spinning of cotton wicks because cotton wicks are spun and used by the Commissioners of Police in lighting the public streets. . . . It seems as manifestly unjust to excite public feeling and raise an outcry and contend with the public purse against an intended partnership in the sale of gas, as it would be were the same means used to oppose a set

---

[1] MS. Minutes, Manchester Police Commissioners, 5th November 1823.

[2] *Some Account of the Municipal Gas Works*, by John Shuttleworth, 1861; *Observations on the Paper read by John Shuttleworth, Esq., before the British Association on the Manchester Gas Works*, 1861, p. 4. The Parliamentary struggle is well described in *The Recorder of Birmingham, a Memoir of Matthew Davenport Hill*, 1878, pp. 93-95. Hill was counsel for the Commissioners, and had the courage to put forward an abstract case for municipalisation as a matter of principle.

of men about to establish a cotton factory. How loud would
have been the lamentations poured into the public ear had the
Commissioners resolved to appropriate the Police rate to the
erection of a factory to spin lamp wicks, a foundry to cast lamp
columns, or even a printing press to print their own placards and
rate-notes. But the exciters of public feeling who manage the
affairs of the town . . . did not sell gas. The spinners, the
iron merchants, the founders and the letterpress printers who
are their admiring auditors, did not perceive that they were led
to make a false step in police and political economy. . . . At
great expense we have converted the Commissioners of Police
into dealers and chapmen, and have secured to them the exclusive sale of their wares at such price as they shall deem
reasonable." [1] As the principal consumers of gas, the shopkeepers and publicans objected to the price of this article being
deliberately fixed far above its cost, in order to produce funds for
town improvements. As the occupiers of small workrooms, shops
and stalls, they disliked the growing stringency with which trade
signs, obstructions of the pavement and petty street nuisances
were being prosecuted. The whole class saw no advantage in
the increased expenditure on sewers, the night watch and paid
officials. Moreover, as Radical politicians of that day, they
objected on principle to any kind of monopoly, municipal or
otherwise ; to any authoritative interference with individual
action or personal behaviour ; and to the employment of salaried
and professional services in place of those rendered by unpaid
citizens. In our account of the parish organisation of Manchester we described how this party, followed by the Radical and
nonconformist factory operatives, were, between 1820 and 1833,
swarming into the open Vestry meetings at the Collegiate Church,
and contesting, with turbulent persistency, the expenditure of
the Constables and Churchwardens. About the same time the
attention of the leaders of this new democracy was attracted to
the proceedings of the Police Commissioners, and they inter-
vened in a manner, and with results, graphically described by
one of their prominent spokesmen. " Considerable dissatisfaction," writes Archibald Prentice, " had for several years been
manifested by a portion of the inhabitants of Manchester with

---

[1] *Impartial Remarks on the Necessity or Non-Necessity of an Immediate Change
in the Constitution of the Police Body* (Manchester, 1827).

the management of its municipal affairs.   There was no elective
authority in the town.   The Boroughreeve, who by ancient
custom rather than of right, exercised the functions of a mayor,
and the Constables who were at the head of the day police, were
elected at the Lord of the Manor's Court Leet, by a jury nominated
by the Lord of the Manor's steward.   The Police Commissioners,
whose duties were to superintend the night watch and the paving,
sewering and lighting of the town, consisted of such persons as,
being assessed on a £30 rental, chose to come forward and take
the oath of office.   The inhabitants had no control over the first
class of officers ; and they had long shewn themselves as anxious
to apprehend Radicals and put down reform principles, as to
detect thieves and prevent theft and robbery.   The Police Commissioners, abetted by the Court Leet Officers, were in like
manner apt to forget municipal duties in political, and there was
a suspicion that, provided their servants and the tradesmen
they employed were sufficiently ' loyal,' there would not be a
very sharp inspection of their accounts."   Prentice proceeds to
say that an additional source of dissatisfaction arose when gas
became a necessary to the shopkeepers.   " At that time the consumption of gas was confined almost to the shopkeepers and
publicans.   It was not used in warehouses, offices or dwelling-
houses or small factories, and the large spinning establishments
made their own.   Probably not one-fourth of the ratepayers
were gas consumers.   The small trader, whose shop, situated in
some dark and narrow street, required much artificial light,
complained that the enormous warehouses of the Bridgwater
Trust, and the great factories of the Birleys, the McConnells,
the Murrays. and the Houldsworths paid nothing towards the
supply of the town's lamps with gas, while the whole of that cost
was defrayed out of the profits derived from excessively high
prices.   A struggle was made by those who believed themselves to be unduly taxed to have a reduction of the burden.
Those who escaped from this fair share of contribution, and
thought that the gas consumers paid only a reasonable price for
their light, opposed themselves fiercely to any reduction of the
charge, which at that time was 14s. per 1000 cubic feet.   The
question became almost one of politics, and was discussed with
more than political rancour.   The taxed shopkeeper was the
Radical ; and the untaxed warehouseman was the Conserva-

tive.[1] The reformers, beaten on every division, began to ask questions as to their numbers, and as everybody who was assessed upon a rental of £30 a year was eligible, it was not difficult to persuade many to go and take the qualifying oath and gain the opportunity of putting a check to oppression. The same facility was presented to the other side, and great numbers qualified to protect the town's funds from 'spoilation.'[2] . . . Thus the meetings of Commissioners were constantly becoming more numerous and more stormy, till it was no uncommon thing to see 800 Commissioners present at a meeting and to witness proceedings as little deliberative and decorous as we sometimes see in the front of the hustings at a contested election." [3]

These stormy meetings, of which graphic descriptions exist,[4]

---

[1] This description is confirmed by other contemporary accounts, of which we append a specimen : " The gas is supplied by the Commissioners who executed the works out of public funds of the town—not by a company ; and the question at issue is whether the profits of the gas establishment shall be applied in aid of the general police fund for improving the town, or whether these profits shall go to reduce the price of gas to the consumers. There are two parties in the town, the ' high ' and the ' low.' The high party consists of the persons who are favourable to the gas profits being applied to the public improvements, and the low party to the price of gas being reduced to the consumers. The existing distinctions in general politics of Whig and Tory do not apply to this question . . . the higher classes generally favouring the proposal to apply the profits to public improvements, and the shopkeepers, or middle classes, who are great gas consumers, contending for a reduction of the price " (*Leeds Mercury*, 9th February 1827). The MS. Minutes and contemporary reports show that besides their running fight for the reduction of the price of gas, the new party constantly objected to the delegation of executive power to committees, and especially to " close committees," sitting in private ; they wanted the resolutions of the Commissioners to be voted on by secret ballot ; they disapproved of practically all prosecutions for nuisances ; they voted against any provision of sewers beyond what was necessary to carry off storm-water ; and they altogether protested against the maintenance of public fire-engines. " Let the fire-offices keep engines for the use of those who insured with them . . . if this town would keep none, the . . . fire-offices would keep engines for themselves, and such would be the competition that the town would be better served and at no expense " (*Report of the Proceedings of a Meeting of Police Commissioners*, by William Whitworth, Manchester, 1827).

[2] In the year 1826 the MS. Minutes show that more than a thousand new Commissioners took the oath of office, over six hundred at one meeting. In 1827 the total number qualified, and, acting for Manchester alone, is said to have exceeded 1800, and " the numbers attending the meetings have increased from about 50 to 900, thereby infinitely increasing the difficulties " (*Impartial Remarks on the Necessity or Non-Necessity of an Immediate Change in the Constitution of the Police Body*, Manchester, 1827).

[3] *Historical Sketches and Personal Recollections of Manchester*, by Archibald Prentice (Manchester, 1851), chap. xx.

[4] See, for instance, the *Report of the Proceedings at a meeting of Police Commissioners*, by William Whitworth (Manchester, 1827).

soon made government impossible. All parties were agreed as to the necessity for a change in the constitution. The Whigs and Tories coalesced in support of a bill, promoted by a majority of the Commissioners, to enable all £25 householders to elect 240 Commissioners having a qualification of £25, whilst leaving the price of gas unfettered. The Radicals furiously resisted this at every stage, demanding both a lower franchise and a lower qualification, the representation of wards in strict proportion to their population, and the limitation of gas profits to ten per cent on the capital outlay. Both parties sent deputations to London and spent money freely. Eventually the fight ended in a compromise, concluded at the very last moment, after the House of Lords Committee had begun to decide on the bill. The Commissioners conceded a £16 franchise for electors and a £28 qualification for candidates, these amounts being in both cases doubled as regards publicans. The price of gas was left unfettered. The representation of the several wards was made proportionate to population and assessment combined, seats being redistributed every fourteenth year.[1]

The new body, which carried on the municipal work of Manchester until 1842, was a well-organised and efficient representative council, including in its ranks most of the leading men of the town.[2] Its administrative procedure was definitely prescribed by the Act, so far as its two main committees were concerned, the Gas Directors and the Improvement Committee, which were each to consist of 30 members appointed for three years, of whom one - third retired annually. These two committees exercised a good deal of independent authority, merely reporting to the general body. The Commissioners appointed four other committees,[3] which sat weekly or fortnightly. But the Commissioners were not completely an elective body. The Boroughreeve and the two Constables, who were, as we have

---

[1] This little struggle cost the majority of the Commissioners £1162 and their opponents £1145. The former sum was naturally voted from the Police rate, and the Commissioners offered to do the same for their opponents' costs —an offer at first virtuously declined but eventually accepted.

[2] Among these we may name such commercial and manufacturing magnates as John Edward Taylor, J. E. Brotherton, W. Nield, Samuel Brooks, Mark Phillips, Thomas and Richard Potter, J. Garnett, Thomas Hopkins, H. H. Birley, R. H. Greg, G. W. Wood.

[3] Accounts, Finance, Watch (including Nuisances and Hackney Coaches) and " Lamp, Scavenging, Fire Engine and Main Sewers."

seen, merely the nominees of the Lord of the Manor's Court Leet, were Commissioners *ex officio*, and exercised great influence in the administration. The Boroughreeve always presided over the meetings, and was, moreover, both Treasurer and Chairman of the Accounts Committee, whilst one Constable was always Chairman of the Watch Committee and the other of the Lamp, Scavenging, Fire-Engine and Main Sewers Committee.

The Commissioners went energetically to work. They adopted formal standing orders of quite modern type, and directed that there should be a printed notice and agenda circulated before each meeting.[1] A public accountant was called in to audit the receipts and expenditure and prepare a statement of accounts, which was printed and published. A professional valuer was appointed to revise the assessment of the town, with instructions to include every kind of property. The collection of rates was systematised and regularly checked. The management of the little force of night police was overhauled, and the number of men increased by fifty per cent, their hours of duty being reduced and the old-fashioned watch boxes being discontinued, as " they hinder rather than promote service." [2] The paving of the town was taken seriously in hand, a separate committee being appointed for " Paving and Soughing." [3] The main sewers were extended ; two paid inspectors were appointed, and nuisances were sternly suppressed. A Town Hall was built, and certain minor street improvements were undertaken. The municipal trade in gas grew apace, and the abundant profits were the mainstay of the Commissioners' finances. Thus, they still continued to execute improvements out of current revenue, often having temporarily to borrow on the personal security of

[1] These standing orders were published ten years later in *Bye Laws made, ordained and constituted by the Commissioners for Cleansing, Lighting and Regulating the Town of Manchester for the regulation of their own proceedings* (Manchester, 1838).

[2] MS. Minutes, Police Commissioners, Manchester, 25th August 1830. The Commissioners were enterprising enough to send their principal officer to Birmingham, Edinburgh and Glasgow to enquire how these towns managed their watch, scavenging, fire brigade, lighting, hackney coaches, and assessment of rates. His report, a volume of 200 pages of closely written manuscript, preserved in the Manchester Town Hall, presents a unique and valuable picture of the technical details of municipal organisation in 1828–1829. This tour resulted in a new volume of *Regulations for the Government of the Watch Department of the Manchester Police* (Manchester, 1830).

[3] MS. Minutes, Police Commissioners, Manchester, 31st August 1831. " Soughing "=sewering.

the Commissioners themselves.[1] They soon found, however, that this primitive finance was inadequate for the expanding needs, and on this and other grounds, they successfully promoted new bills in 1830, 1831 and 1832, greatly extending their powers.[2] Throughout these years the policy of the majority of the Commissioners remained what would now be termed " Progressive," that is, in favour of increased municipal enterprise and extended municipal regulation. Thus in 1834, on a motion by the Radical minority that the gas-works should be sold to the highest bidder, the spokesman of the majority made an emphatic declaration in favour of municipalisation which might be to-day repeated by the leader of the Labour Party in the London County Council. " It was highly desirable," urged Thomas Hopkins in a remarkable speech, " that the inhabitants of a large town like Manchester should have the ownership of works like the gas-works, and amongst the many reasons why the works should be retained a

[1] It is worth recording that when they decided to build a Town Hall, 180 of the Commissioners pledged themselves personally to the bankers in a bond for £20,000 to secure the necessary advances. This bond was not returned and cancelled until 1829 (ibid. 4th November 1829). The Town Hall, until lately used as the Public Reference Library, was in these years a subject of great municipal fondness and pride. It was fearfully and wonderfully decorated inside, during 1831-1834, by an Italian named Aglio, who inveigled the leading Commissioners into granting him the job. These decorations, which cost £5000, were simply painted out by a subsequent generation having a different taste. (British Architect, 21st July 1876.)

[2] See report of Committee appointed to consider the amendments needed in the Police Acts, MS. Minutes, 16th December 1829. Among the new provisions in the 1830 Act may be mentioned the following. Coffee houses and cookshops are to close at 11 P.M. (on Saturdays, at midnight), and not to open before 4 A.M. in summer and 6 A.M. in winter. Publicans are to provide urinals. All doors and gates on the road are to be made to open inwards. No cranes are to be allowed above the first story. No new street or court is to be less than 24 feet in width. When half a street is built, the owners may be required to pave and drain it. The wandering of swine in the streets is prohibited under substantial penalty. Every householder is required to cleanse daily the footway in front of his house, and in times of frost to lay sand down before 9 A.M. The Commissioners are authorised to provide a public weighing-machine, and to set up a mounted police force.

In 1830 we find them, at the instance of J. E. Taylor and Thomas Hopkins, keenly alive to the danger of allowing the new " steam locomotive railway " the use of the streets. With reference to the proposals of the Stockport and Manchester Railway Company to cross a main road " at grade," they resolve " that the said company ought to be prohibited altogether from bringing locomotive engines into the town of Manchester, whether moved by steam aid or otherwise, and that their traffic should be carried on through the said town of Manchester by means of horses only, which should not in any case move through any of the streets at a greater speed than at the rate of three miles an hour " (MS. Minutes, Manchester Police Commissioners, 24th February 1830).

very important one was breaking up the streets. . . . He conceived also that water works and markets should always belong to the town, and some progress should be made to obtain the ownership of these. . . . It was of importance that the gas should be good, but what security would there be for its being good if the works went into the hands of a joint stock company ? Their interest would be to make as much money as they could. . . . For these reasons he considered that all public works should belong to the town or be under the control of the public, for they generally acted under the influence of more elevated feelings than those whose principal aim was profit. . . . The absence of a number of things of this kind in a town constituted its decline, but a number of advantages of this description gave it prosperity. . . . Instead of giving up what the town at present possessed, a plan of action should be laid down which would bring under the control of the town everything which ought to belong to it." [1]

But the change in the Commissioners' constitution, which transformed them into a democratically elected body, did not abate the opposition to their proceedings. The shopkeepers discovered that the compromise of 1828 had resulted in retaining in power the influential Whigs and Tories who had for many years dominated the counsels of the Commissioners. Against them there raged during the whole of this decade a noisy and persistent minority of Radicals and nonconformists, among whom we may name Archibald Prentice,[2] J. Wroe, John Hampson, P. T. Candelet,[2] Wm. Whitworth, Thos. Wheeler [2] and G. H. Winder,[2] who represented the shopkeepers and publicans. This party combined the advocacy of a crude and simple democracy with objection to all collective regulation or municipal enterprise, a demand for a reduction of the price of gas, and the defence of the small property owners. We see them demanding that no important step should be taken without a poll of the inhabitants, and that all property or rating qualification, either for voters or candidates, should be swept away. They objected to the compulsory purchase of houses for improvements, and they strongly denounced as confiscatory the levying of the cost of main sewers on the owners of the property benefited. They grumbled inces-

---

[1] *Manchester Times*, 25th January 1834.
[2] These were subsequently members of the Town Council.

santly at the increased activity in the way of regulation of the streets and prosecution of nuisances, protesting that the Commissioners " favoured the rich, whilst they enforced the utmost rigour of the law against shopkeepers and the poor, and the reason was that 18 of them were occupiers of warehouses." [1] They objected to any increase of the watchmen, and to the " excessive salaries " which, as they alleged, the Commissioners paid to their officers. They " saw no need of employing professional assessors at an expense of 5 to 10 guineas per day each. . . . Why should not the mode of making a new assessment be left open to the leypayers in general, who were well able to tell what sort of assessment they wanted. . . . He would engage to find men who would assess more equitably than any professional man, gratuitously, and upon rack rent. . . . By their exclusion a door was opened to the employment of any number of jobbing professional valuers." [2] It was considered " most infamous " that the Improvement Committee should hold " secret meetings," to decide which properties should be purchased, as " all public proceedings should be as public as the sun at noonday." [3] It was alleged " that the Improvement Committee and the Gas Directors consisted each of 30 members, and that 24 of these 30 were members, some of 4, some of 3, some of 2 committees. The Improvement Committee sat in a comfortable room at the Town Hall, determining what part of a man's property they would take, and then one of them said, ' Oh, how shall we get the money for these improvements ? ' another would say, ' We are eighteen of us also on the Gas Committee, we are sure to have a majority,' and they had just to step into another room, and then decide how much the consumers should pay for their gas in order to raise the money for carrying these cursed improvements into effect." [4]

---

[1] *Manchester Guardian*, 14th April 1832.
[2] Speeches by Prentice and Wroe at meeting of Commissioners, *Manchester Times*, 11th January 1834.
[3] *Wheeler's Manchester Chronicle*, 12th January 1833. The *Manchester Times*, 2nd April 1836, gives a good description of a deputation of these shopkeepers appearing before the House of Commons Committee and interviewing Lord Shaftesbury, as Chairman of Committees of the House of Lords, in opposition to the Police Commissioners' Bill of 1836. In addition to the above objections, they demanded compensation for " fixtures and goodwill " of tradesmen expropriated. Lord Shaftesbury allowed the insertion of a clause giving compensation " for all loss and damage, instead of good will." He said, " I do not like the words ' good will.' "
[4] Meeting of property owners, reported in *Manchester Guardian*, 1832.

But the most heinous crime of the Commissioners was their constant attempt to increase their statutory powers. In April 1830 a vigorous handbill was issued by the Radicals denouncing the Commissioners, not only for preparing a bill without consulting the inhabitants, but also for inserting clauses enabling them to borrow a capital sum of £25,000 for the extension of the gas works, and giving them powers of municipal regulation " too vexatious and oppressive to be safely entrusted to any body of men." [1]

The Radicals urged, moreover, that the election of the Commissioners should be annual; that all ratepayers should be entitled to vote ; and that the qualification for candidates should be reduced. They sent a deputation to London, which secured these concessions.[2]

We have described at some length the policy and proceedings of both the majority and the minority of the Manchester Police Commissioners, not only because it was, right down to its merger in the Town Council by the Act of 1842 (6 & 7 Vict. c. 17), in many ways the most important local governing body of the time, but also because their respective views are curiously typical of succeeding generations of municipal politicians. We now leave them to consider the general results of the whole three hundred bodies of Improvement Commissioners.

The Work of the Improvement Commissioners

We do not know how many of the three hundred bodies of Improvement Commissioners resembled, in their working, each of the four examples that we have described. We imagine that the ninety or a hundred bodies at work in the parishes which now make up the Administrative County of London did not differ very widely from the " Trustees of the Cubitt Estate," except, perhaps, in being usually less honest and even more inefficient. From our information as to the two hundred bodies in provincial towns, we infer that the great majority approximated much more nearly to the example of Plymouth than to those of Birmingham or Manchester. Judged from any modern standpoint, we imagine that their actual results in the way of town

---

[1] Copy in MS. Minutes of Police Commissioners, Manchester, 14th April 1830.
[2] *A Statement of Facts, being a History of the Opposition to the Police Bill*, by Thomas Walker, Manchester, 1832.

T

improvement were not great. In fact, the outstanding achievement of the Commissioners, alike in London and in the provincial towns, and certainly the most durable, was the new stone pavement which was provided for the main thoroughfares. This was not, as it would be to-day, regarded as a work of sanitation. Indeed, we shall fail to understand the efforts of the Improvement Commissioners unless we realise the limits of the contemporary conception of their functions. Nowadays the dominant idea of municipal government is the improvement of the public health. This, however, never occurred to any of the Improvement Commissioners of whom we are speaking. Right down to the cholera epidemic of 1831-1832, we find practically no suggestion that any work of town improvement should be undertaken on the ground that it would promote the public health. From 1748 to 1832 the long series of Local Acts were obtained, and all the expenditure on town improvement was incurred, not from any motives of sanitation, but in order to secure, incidentally, greater protection for life and property, and primarily and invariably greater comfort and convenience in passing along the streets. The Commissioners were, in fact, often called Street Commissioners, and it was principally in order that the thoroughfares of the towns might be better regulated that the Local Acts were passed. The statutory bodies arose simply because neither the Court Leet nor the Municipal Corporation, neither the Parish nor the Justices of the Peace, possessed the necessary coercive or regulative powers to deal with the town streets.

It is true that, as we have already explained, all public streets were, as they still are, legally parts of the King's Highway, and as such came within the network of obligation imposed upon the parish by the general law of highways to keep open a free passage for the King and his subjects. A street might, and frequently did, form part also of a turnpike road, and as such was subject to the general turnpike law and the particular turnpike Act. With all this we have dealt at length elsewhere. But a street was, in fact, if not in law, more than a parish highway or turnpike road.[1] When the public way came to be surrounded

---

[1] The word "street," said Lord Chelmsford in a judgment, "does not mean the roadway, but a thoroughfare with houses on each side" (Galloway v. Corporation of the City of London, 35 L.J. Ch. 493). But it need not necessarily be paved, nor continuously bordered by houses, nor even a thoroughfare. See *The Story of the King's Highway*, by S. and B. Webb, 1913.

by a mass of population, walled in by houses, made a place of resort as well as transit, incessantly traversed by men, beasts and vehicles, and used by night as well as by day, it required a higher degree and greater variety of collective action than was necessary on even the most frequented thoroughfare between one town and another. If the ordinary turnpike road needed to be straightened and widened, levelled and furnished with an artificial surface, the street required all this in a higher degree. But there were also new requisites peculiar to the street, and unprovided for in highway or turnpike law and administration. Channels along the thoroughfare itself to carry off the pent-in rain-water, special accommodation for foot passengers, systematic removal of the inevitable mud and filth which impeded free passage, were all requirements of the urban thoroughfares. Hence the need for fresh powers and, as it seemed, for new Local Authorities, to make passable the streets of the growing towns. We now seek to describe the way in which these statutory authorities provided the higher degree and new kind of service required for free passage along the town streets, as distinguished from the parish highway and the turnpike road. This superior service—apart from the regulation of personal conduct in the suppression of nuisances, and the beginnings of a police force, with both of which we hope to deal in subsequent volumes—consisted mainly in providing a pavement and in clearing away the dirt and refuse.

In the latter part of the seventeenth century we find the " high streets " and market-places of many of the ancient towns already paved with rounded stones, sloping to the middle, where there was a kennel or " denter stone " to carry off the water ; and provided in some cases with footways on each side, distinguished from the carriage-way by elevation, by lines of posts or, occasionally, by the shape of the stones.[1] These conveniences,

[1] The administrative history of street paving in England has engaged little attention, so that we can cite practically no authorities beyond the incidental references in contemporary newspapers and pamphlets, the MS. Minutes of Town Councils, Vestries and Improvement Commissioners, and the very casual mention of the subject in local histories, as given in our footnotes. We have unfortunately been unable to find any minutes or other archives of the " Commissioners of Scotland Yard," under the Act of 1662. *The History of London,* by William Maitland, 1756, embodies brief descriptions of the Metropolitan streets at different epochs. *The Paper read before the Institution of Civil Engineers on the Construction of Carriage Way Pavements,* by Bryan Donkin, 1824,

it is obvious, were beyond the resources of the Statute Labour and Team Duty required by the statute of 1555, even if supplemented by the limited Highway Rate which Quarter Sessions, at the very end of the seventeenth century, was empowered to authorise. Moreover, we know that, in the City of London and elsewhere, these street pavements, gutters and footways had existed long before any statutory obligation to repair the highways had been cast on the parish and its officers. To trace the origin of these ancient pavements, to discover how far they had been constructed by the effort and at the expense of the burgesses themselves or of the Municipal Corporation, the lord of the manor or a private benefactor, the parish or the frontagers, is outside our province. What is clear is that there was no general provision, at common law or by statute, either for their construction or for their maintenance. It is in the Local Acts, which we have described particular towns obtaining from Parliament, first in the fifteenth and sixteenth centuries, and then from the latter part of the seventeenth century onwards, that we find a new legal obligation imposed on the holder of a tenement abutting on a street, to pave and keep in repair the pavement in front of his tenement, down to the denter stone or channel which marked the middle of the thoroughfare. The history of street paving from the latter part of the seventeenth century down to the present day largely consists in the evolution of this personal obligation, and its gradual supersession by a specialised organ of collective administration acting by salaried officials and hired labour, and maintained by uniform poundage rates on all occupiers.

The London Pavements

We deal first with the Metropolitan area. The history of the construction of the London street pavements—the immemorial pavement of the ancient City ; the extension of this to the great thoroughfares leading eastward and westward, northward and

---

may be cited as perhaps the first of the long series of technological writings on the subject, which are mostly to be sought in the proceedings of the technical institutions. See, for the modern practice, *The Municipal and Sanitary Engineer's Handbook*, by H. Percy Boulnois, 1883 ; or (in America) *Treatise on Roads and Pavements*, by I. O. Baker (New York, 1914), and *Textbook of Highway Engineering*, by A. H. Blanchard and H. B. Downe (New York, 1913), 762 pp.

southward ; from thence to the " high streets " of the City of
Westminster ; the gradual paving during the eighteenth century
of such outlying parishes as St. George's, Hanover Square, St.
Marylebone and St. Pancras, and, in the early years of the nineteenth century, of some of the streets of Chelsea and Kensington
—affords an example of the origin and development of a colossal
public service, the very memory of which has now passed away.
For the purpose of our present work we do not need to probe the
antiquity of the pavements within the City walls, or to discuss
the statutes by which Tudor Parliaments compelled the frontagers between Strand Cross and Charing Cross,[1] between Holborn
Bridge and Holborn Bars, between Aldgate and Whitechapel
Church, and those in Chancery Lane and Gray's Inn Lane,
to pave these much-frequented highways.[2]   After a long interval
we find, immediately after the Restoration of Charles the Second,
the first of the modern Paving Acts, a temporary statute of 1662.
This Act set up, for London and Westminster, the so-called
" Commissioners of Scotland Yard " that we have described.
We do not find anything about the activities of these Commissioners after the close of the seventeenth century ; but the
Act of 1662, made permanent and extended to the whole Metropolis within the " Bills of Mortality " by an elaborate Act of
1691, governed for over seventy years the paving activities of
the inhabitants.[3]

[1] Already in 1320, after a petition to Parliament, two commissioners had
been appointed by the King to insist that the frontagers of the Strand should
repair the pavement in front of their houses (1 Rot. Parl. pp. 302-303).
[2] 24 Henry VIII. c. 11 (Strand Paving Act, 1532) ; 25 Henry VIII. c. 8
(Holborn Paving Act, 1533) ; 32 Henry VIII. c. 17 (Whitechapel Paving Act,
1541) ; see also 34 & 35 Henry VIII. c. 11 and 12 (1543) ; 13 Eliz. c. 23 (1571) ;
23 Eliz. c. 12 (1581) ; 3 James I. c. 22 (1606).
[3] 13 & 14 Car. II. c. 2 (1662) ; 2 William and Mary, sess. 2, c. 8 (1691).
A further Act of 1697 (8 & 9 William III. c. 37) enabled the justices to extend
their orders to pave the whole surface of streets lying partly in and partly
out of the limits of the Bills of Mortality.   The City of London had its own
Acts, 19 Car. II. c. 3 (1668) and 22 Car. II. c. 17 (1671).
  The reconstruction of the City after the Great Fire of 1666 does not appear
to have led to any important alteration of the carriageway pavement.   It was
in vain that Evelyn pleaded for a flat pavement, and wished "that the use of
sleds were introduced and as few heavy carts as might be countenanced. . . .
Why [should] not some of the distorted bricks to be found amongst the rubbish
be reserved for these purposes, especially the elevations destined for the foot
causeways before the fronts of the houses ?   Unless they will be at the charge
to lay it with Purbeck and flat stones, which indeed were to be preferred.
Yet their clinkers in Holland do well ; and, as I remember, the Roman streets
are so paved " (*London Restored, not to its pristine, but to a far greater Beauty,*

By the Act of 1691 every householder abutting on one of the streets already paved was once more [1] definitely required to maintain in repair the pavement in front of his tenement, down to the " denter-stone " or channel in the middle of the roadway. Moreover, the Middlesex or Surrey justices in Quarter Sessions were authorised, on the motion of any local magistrate, to require the householders of any unpaved street to pave it according to their directions. Unfortunately the law was, so far as concerned the majority of streets, neither obeyed nor enforced.[2] That even the primary obligation to repair existing pavements continued to be very imperfectly fulfilled we may infer from the

---

Commodiousness and Magnificence, by Sir John Evelyn (*circa* 1666) ; quoted in the *History of London*, by William Maitland, 1756, pp. 449-450). These suggestions were, as regards the carriage way, not adopted, and the City Commissioners of Sewers in 1671 directed the " high streets " to be " paved round, or causeway fashion." The provision of distinct foot pavements may have become somewhat more general in the rebuilt streets, together with the adoption for these of flat stones. The Commissioners, indeed, order that " the breadth of six feet, at the least, from the foundation of the houses, in such of the high streets which shall be allowed to be posted, shall be paved by the inhabitants or owners with flat or broad stone for a foot passage," under penalty of a fine of five shillings for every week that they remain unpaved after notice given (*ibid.* p. 454 ; see the *Rules, Orders and Directions published by the Commissioners of Sewers pursuant to the Act of the Common Council of 1st March 1671*). But it is plain that these orders were not generally obeyed. In 1684 the Grand Jury " take notice of the great defects of the pavements, and ill passage thereby, in and about this City, to the hindrance and danger of His Majesty's subjects passing in and about the several streets as well by night as by day." They present twelve householders to be prosecuted " for not repairing the same " (*Presentment by the Grand Jury . . . at the Old Bayley*, 1684).
    [1] Besides the Act of 1662, and those relating to the City of London exclusively, that of 1534 (25 Henry VIII. c. 8), whilst confining its injunctions for the making of a pavement to the frontagers of Holborn, had extended its penalties for failure to maintain pavement in repair to Southwark ; and the half-dozen other local paving Acts had already covered a wide extent of what was then the Metropolitan area.
    [2] The records of the Middlesex Quarter Sessions contain a certain number of these justices' orders to pave particular streets, and, after 1691, even to afford them such light as might be furnished by the lantern that each householder was directed to set up, from dark to midnight ; see *Calendar of the Sessions Books, 1689 to 1709*, by W. J. Hardy, 1905, pp. xxii, 27, 38-39, 40, 46, 48-50, 53, 56, 59-60, etc. (Further volumes have been prepared, down to 1747, and may be consulted in typescript, but have not yet been printed by Quarter Sessions. This should now be done.) In 1744-1746 we see the Middlesex Quarter Sessions in some cases ordering the inhabitants to perform their "Statute work" on specified highways; in others, sanctioning Highway Rates by particular parishes, the proceeds of which were spent by the parish authorities ; and in others, again, appointing committees of justices to " oversee the work " of paving by the "·paviour " (MS. Sessions Books, vols. 1020-30).

complaint of the Committee on Nuisances appointed by the
Middlesex Quarter Sessions in 1721, when the plague was raging
at Marseilles, on which occasion extracts from the Act of 1691,
reciting the penalties incurred by persons " not paving their
doors," were printed for general circulation.[1] But even where
some respect was paid to the law, this method of obtaining a
pavement proved very unsatisfactory. In an able pamphlet of
1745 this system of paving is described as one of the principal
public nuisances of the Metropolis : " By the statute of the
2nd and 3rd William and Mary the inhabitants are at their own
expense directed to pave with stone or gravel, or otherwise
amend all the ground in the front of their houses to the middle
of the street, as the justices shall order, with penalties in default
of paving or mending. This regards new pavements, but no
power is given by that statute to inspect or view the pavements
when made, so as to order amendments when and where wanted,
or the manner of paving when first or wholly paved; all which
is absolutely necessary to provide for, as also to preserve them
against inequality of paving. Now one housekeeper mends or
paves with small pebbles, another with great, a third with rag-
stones, a fourth with broken flint, a fifth is poor. a sixth is able,
but backward and unwilling. This last is worst of all, and nothing
but law can force them ; and yet for the sake of peace, or a more
sinister end, it is but rare that the law is put in execution. Neighbours will not complain of one another ; it may be their own
turn. Thus . . . there is no standard for paving, the subsisting
laws not sufficient and even those we have neglected to be carried
into any execution." [2] We may indeed affirm, on the authority
of Northouck, that right down to the accession of George III.,
" no considerable reformation had taken place in the pavement
since the Fire of London." In many of the City streets. and a
few others,[3] " they had indeed flat pavements on each side for

[1] MS. Minutes, Quarter Sessions, Middlesex, 12th October 1721.

[2] *Public Nuisances Considered*, 1745, an able and instructive anonymous
pamphlet. It was long before the idea of individual paving could be got rid
of. It was still to the fore in 1754, when John Spranger, the first advocate of
the improvements shortly afterwards carried out in London, made it the basis
of his project that notice be given to the inhabitants individually to put in
repair the pavement in front of their several houses, as far as the " denter
stone," or middle of the street.

[3] Strype, in 1720, describes " the fine freestone pavement secured from
carts and coaches by handsome posts set up " in St. Martin's Lane, then newly
improved (Stow's *Survey of London*, book vi. p. 18 of Strype's edition of 1720).

foot passengers, but these were very negligently repaired. . . .
The middle of the streets were paved with large pebbles of all
sizes and shapes, rough to the horse and uneasy to the rider,
which, continually worn by carriages into dangerous holes, the
mud lay in too great quantities to suffer the streets to be called
clean, except in extreme dry weather, when the dust was as
troublesome as the dirt while wet." [1] By the middle of the
eighteenth century the state of the Westminster streets in
particular had become an intolerable scandal. In 1754 two
remarkable pamphlets called attention to " the frequent and

But Maitland, in his *History of London* (1756) mentions a " freestone pavement "
for foot passengers as an exceptional advantage of particular thoroughfares.
And Nollekens gives an anecdote proving that hackney coaches could drive so
close to the houses as to enable a man to scramble from the roof of the coach
into a first-floor window (*Nollekens and his Times*, by John T. Smith, 1829 ;
quoted in Place MSS. 27826-123). Old prints (see the magnificent collection
in the London Library, supplementing that of the British Museum), for the
first half of the century, show the round pebble pavement to have usually
extended, at any rate outside the principal streets of the city, continuously
from house to house. The flagged footways did not, indeed, at once commend
themselves to everybody. When John Spranger proposed, in 1754, to pave
the carriage-ways of Westminster and Marylebone with broad Purbeck stone,
he suggested the paving of the footways with " good pebbles " (*A Proposal
or Plan for an Act for the Better Paving, etc.*, by John Spranger, 1754).

[1] *Reports on the Diseases of London and the State of the Weather from 1804
to 1816, etc.*, by Thomas Bateman, 1819, p. 15. Even Hanway, in 1754, assumed
that the concave form of the roadway, and the central channel, must be retained.
He describes the " great inconvenience . . . we labour under in respect to our
kennels. It is too well known that they are made with a sudden fall of four,
five and six inches, and some yet deeper, like a broad-cut cart rut. This seems
to be the remains of those days when these cities were about one-tenth part
so big, had not a twentieth part so much trade, nor a hundredth part so many
carriages for ease and luxury as at present. . . . But now in our miles of
streets, how often we must pass, and with what uneasiness and danger ! This
may be easily remedied when the streets are new paved. The kennel ought
to be constituted by the easy decline of the street, and terminated in the
division of two equal sides, by moderate-sized denter stones. . . . The passing
the kennels, or lowest part of the streets would then be hardly perceived by
the rider ; horses would tread true, whereas the kennel is now often concealed
with dirt ; they would consequently be in less danger of laming themselves, of
falling, or being otherwise injured. Carriages would no longer be subject to
overturn or to break their wheels by a sudden shock. Upon this principle the
collection of dirt would be a little more divided, yet if cleansed twice a week,
as proposed, the quantity would never be great " (*A Letter to Mr. John Spranger
on his Excellent Proposal for cleansing and lighting the Streets of Westminster*, by
Jonas Hanway, 1754, p. 13). As late as 1840 Capt. Vetch, R.E., in an able
memorandum on the structural arrangements of new buildings and protection
of the public health, proposed to reintroduce the central kennel instead of side
gutters, as likely to give greater cleanliness; see *General Report of the Poor
Law Commissioners on the Sanitary Condition of the Labouring Population*, 1842,
Appendix V. pp. 391-392.

melancholy distresses and disasters," the "fatal mischiefs"
and "dismal accidents" caused by the daily "struggle with
unequal, rough and broken pavements."[1] "All the pavements
of the streets," said a discontented citizen to Jonas Hanway,
"are made according to every man's humour; some are made
high and some low, some with kennels and some without, some
well done and some ill." "One can hardly find," adds Hanway
himself, "five yards square of true even pavement" in the whole
of Westminster. In the opinion of contemporaries the only
redeeming feature, besides the use of flat "flagstones" in a few
streets to mark off separate footways, was the erection of lines
of posts to protect the streams of pedestrians from the carriage
traffic. "The use of posts," said Hanway, "which I believe
is peculiar to us, is an excellent security to the foot passenger,
and the modern method of making them short and stout is a
great improvement."[2] That the carriage-way should be rough
and irregular, even to the point of dislocating wheels and breaking
axle-trees, was commonly accepted as inevitable. "Ever since
I was a boy of two feet and a half high," said one good citizen
to Hanway, "I have known people, gentlemen of long heads,
talk of paving streets; but it can't be done, Sir. . . . In the
first place, all the pavements of the streets are made according
to every man's humour, some are made high, and some low,
some with kennels and some without, some well done and some
ill. But this is not all, Sir; 'tis the waterworks which destroy
the pavements, and do you think that ever that will be mended?
Why, Sir, the owners of the waterworks are most of them Parliament men, Sir, all great men. Do you think that any one will
be able to oblige them to repair the pavements they break up. . . .

[1] *A Proposal or Plan for an Act . . . for the better Paving, Lighting and
Cleansing the Streets, Lanes, Courts, Alleys and other open passages, and for
Removing of Nuisances . . . within the several parishes of . . . Westminster
. . . Marylebone, etc.,* by John Spranger, 1754; *A Letter to Mr. John Spranger
on his Excellent Proposal for cleansing and lighting the Streets of Westminster, etc.,*
by Jonas Hanway, 1754.

[2] "It is true," he adds, "they occupy a considerable space"—they were,
it is clear, a constant cause of obstruction in the crowded streets—but their
utility was proved to Hanway by the experience of the French towns, where
there were no posts, and "the gentleman as well as the mechanic who walks
the streets of Paris is continually in danger of being run over" (*A Letter to
Mr. John Spranger, etc.,* by Jonas Hanway, 1754, p. 20). Foreign visitors
admired these footways, imperfect as they were, for being thus "defended by
posts from the coaches and wheel carriages" (Gonzales, *Voyage to Great Britain,*
1730; printed in Pinkerton's *Voyages,* vol. ii. of 1808 edition, p. 90).

I am sure it can't be done." [1] But Hanway persevered in his
practical way, until, in 1762, Sir Charles Whitworth brought the
subject before the House of Commons, and got a committee
appointed to enquire into the methods to be adopted for the better
paving of the streets of Westminster and the adjoining parishes—
a committee which reported, to use the summary of its chairman,
" That the streets in general were very ill paved and cleansed ;
that the method of taking care thereof by the Annoyance Jury
was ineffectual ; that the method of the inhabitants paving
before their own houses, without being limited either in time,
materials or method of doing it, is one cause of the bad pavement
of the streets ; that the squares, streets, lanes and allies were
not properly lighted ; that the paving, cleansing, repairing
and lighting, as well as removing nuisances, and making the
town more ornamental and commodious should be put under
the management of Commissioners ; that in most places a new
pavement was absolutely necessary instead of the old one ; but
that the expense would be too great to be borne wholly by the
inhabitants." The result was an Act of Parliament in 1762,
which, with the quickly following amending Acts, brought about
a complete change in the situation.[2]

The Westminster Paving Acts of 1762, 1763, 1764, 1765
and 1766 started a new era. Whilst retaining and emphasising
the obligation of the householder to maintain existing pavements
in repair, these Acts empowered an influential body of Commissioners themselves to undertake the paving of new streets
or the repaving of old ones, according to a systematic plan ;

---

[1] *A Letter to Mr. John Spranger, etc.*, by Jonas Hanway, 1754.
[2] Report of House of Commons Committee to consider proper methods for
the better paving, enlightening, etc., the streets . . . of Westminster, Marylebone, St. Giles, St. George-the-Martyr, St. George, Bloomsbury, St. Andrew's,
Holborn, Liberties of the Rolls, the Savoy and the Duchy of Lancaster, in
Journals, vol. xxix. p. 233, 15th March 1762 ; 2 George III. c. 21 (1762) ;
3 George III. c. 23 (1763) ; 4 George III. c. 39 (1764) ; 5 George III. c. 50
(1765) ; 5 George III. c. 13 (Sunday Toll Act, 1765) ; 6 George III. c. 54
(1766) ; 7 George III. c. 101 (1767) ; 11 George III. c. 50 (1771) ; *Observations
on the new Westminster Paving Act*, by Sir Charles Whitworth, 1771. These
Acts were amended and continued by 26 George III. c. 102 (1786) and 30
George III. c. 53 (1790).
    These Acts did not apply to the small areas already dealt with by their
own Local Acts, such as St. James's Square (under 12 George I. c. 25), Lincoln's Inn Fields (under 8 George II. c. 26), and Golden Square (under 24
George II. c. 27), nor yet to Dean's Yard and the adjacent area dealt with by
the Dean and Chapter of Westminster.

and to expend for this purpose, not only a special Parliamentary grant of £5000 and the proceeds of an extra Sunday toll to be collected at all the principal turnpike gates, but also a rate up to eighteenpence in the pound upon all the occupiers within the area benefited by the improvement. The rate could not be levied on the householders of any street or place until the new pavement had been completed there ; and its annual payment exonerated them from all further responsibility for the maintenance of the roadway.[1] Hence the old individual system of each householder repairing his own bit of pavement, at his own charges, and the new collectivist system of the service being undertaken by a public authority and paid for out of a common rate, went on side by side. The option between the two systems had been, by the original Act of 1762, made to rest exclusively with the Commissioners. By the amending Act of 1765 this option was extended to the owners and occupiers of any street or place, who could, by a three-fourths majority, require the Commissioners to begin operations, raising the necessary capital by a special loan on the security of the future paving rate to be levied on that particular street or place. This form of local option seems to have been extensively used by the inhabitants of the better streets in Westminster (especially as it was provided that, in computing the three-fourths majority those owners and occupiers who did not attend the meeting should be deemed to have consented to the proposition), and it appears to have greatly expedited the work of the Commissioners, by enabling the borrowing of the necessary funds.

The Westminster Paving Commissioners went energetically to work, and we find in contemporary writings abundant appreciation and criticism of " the new pavement." The old rounded pebbles, with " neither tail nor foot " so that " they roll about

---

[1] These reforms had been proposed a couple of decades before by the author of the able pamphlet from which we have already quoted. " If the care and management of the pavements was lodged in one Trust, with a sufficient power not attended with great expense, first to take a survey of the streets, lanes, etc., then to break up the present pavements, and to order a uniform pavement of all the streets afterwards, the whole to be paid for by an annual small levy upon the housekeepers in general . . . forbidding afterwards the breaking up any pavement, or laying any pavement anew, but by the order or consent of such trust only, or by those paviors who should have power under the Trust for this purpose, the streets would then be well laid with one equal pavement at first, and be afterwards kept in repair at a small charge, and all this done without complaint or punishment " (*Public Nuisances Considered*, 1745, pp. 5-6).

and hit one another incessantly upon a bottom which is nothing else but a heap of old dirt," [1] were replaced by squared blocks of " whin-quarry stone or rockstone . . . of a flat surface," [2] imported from Aberdeen, and set continuously in parallel lines from curb to curb, on a slightly convex surface. For the channel or denter stone, running down the middle of the old concave street, were substituted two gutters, one on each side of the carriage-way. The footways, now universally flagged, were made about four inches higher than the gutters, thus enabling the lines of protecting posts to be dispensed with.[3] " The new pavement . . . goes on with rapidity," reports a pamphleteer in 1771.[4] Foreign visitors to London waxed eloquent over the new conveniences, which became the wonder of the travelled world. Archenholtz, in 1787, in describing the transformation which had taken place within a generation, especially praises this " superb pavement . . . which cost £400,000." There " is a footpath," he adds with naïve admiration, " of hewn stone for those who walk, on which they are in no danger from carriages or horses. No coachman without incurring a penalty of twenty shillings dare encroach upon that footpath." [5] " L'on ne saurait

[1] *A Tour to London*, by M. Grosley, 1772, vol. i. p. 33. The translator notes that this observation of 1765 would not be accurate in 1772.

[2] *A Tour through the whole Island of Great Britain*, edition of 1769, vol. ii. p. 121 ; Birkbeck Hill's edition of Boswell's *Life of Johnson*, vol. vi. p. lxvii. Dr. Johnson noticed in 1773 that " New Aberdeen is built of that granite which is used for the new pavement in London " (*Piozzi Letters*, i. 116 ; Birkbeck Hill's edition of Boswell's *Life of Johnson*, vol. v. p. 85). A visitor in 1802 relates that " In the streets you admire that extraordinary neatness, which is to be met with nowhere else but in Holland. The ways for foot-passengers are paved with broad flagstones " (*A Foreigner's Opinion of England*, by C. A. G. Goede, translated by Thomas Horne, 1821, vol. i. p. 192). For other references to the new pavement, see *British Chronicle*, 13th-15th February 1765 ; *Gentleman's Magazine*, December 1773 ; *Metropolitan Guide and Book of Reference*, by Pigot & Co. (about 1820) ; *Travels in England*, by C. P. Moritz, 1797.

[3] The lines of posts protecting the footway from vehicles seem to have been mostly cleared away from the City and Westminster about 1762-1780. They remained in Lower Thames Street in 1804 (*Modern London*, by Richard Phillips, 1804, p. 107) ; and in 1834 it was said that " within the last twenty years there were posts and rails to divide the footway from the road on Croom's Hill," Greenwich (*Greenwich : its History, Antiquities, Improvements and Public Buildings*, by H. S. Richardson, 1834, p. 14).

[4] *Critical Observations on the Public Buildings and Improvements in London*, 1771, p. 23.

[5] *A Picture of England*, by Archenholtz, 1789, p. 130. Moritz in 1782 had remarked that " the footway paved with large stones on both sides of the street appears to a foreigner exceedingly convenient and pleasant, as one may there

inventer rien," writes a still more enthusiastic Frenchman, " de mieux pour circuler dans une ville que les trottoirs de Londres, trop rarement imités ailleurs, et toujours imparfaitement ; ils sont revêtus de grandes dalles . . . si unies que l'on y marche sans fatigue, ainsi que l'on retrouve avec une véritable peine les pavés raboteux et glissants du continent." [1] To slow-minded and penurious patriots, the " new pavement " seemed a fantastic extravagance, rendered more objectionable at that moment by the fact that the stone was brought from Scotland. " We shall not have a foot of English ground to walk upon," writes a satirical denouncer of " the new method of paving streets with Scotch pebbles." " In new modelling our streets," he con-tinues, " the Scotch, and their adherents, Scotified Englishmen, pretend that our advantage, and the improvement of the place, are their sole motives, and that they are entirely disinterested . . . whereas . . . I affirm . . . that the Scots are the only gainers by this Quixotic scheme." [2] " I had not been long landed," writes, in 1767, " An Old Englishman " lately returned from America, " but I beheld in every part of the town the streets unpaved." He was told that the object 'ᵗ was to pave them in a fashionable manner that our grandees and gentry may ride with greater ease over the stones ; but," continued he, " the poor feel little benefit from it, for they think, as well as myself, that the money that is expended about it could be put to better use, while every necessary of life bears such an exorbitant price as it does at present." [3] But in spite of these isolated complaints from " the meaner sort," public opinion agreed with Sir James Steuart, the most distinguished economist of the day, in regarding (already in 1767) " the new pavement of London "—by far the greatest municipal enterprise that had then been undertaken in

---

walk in perfect safety in no more danger from the prodigious crowd of carts and coaches than if one was in one's own room, for no wheel dares come a finger's breadth upon the curbstone " (*Travels in England*, by C. P. Moritz, 1797, p. 498).

[1] *L'Angleterre au commencement du dix-neuvième siècle*, par M. de Levis, 1814, p. 49.

[2] *A Seasonable Alarm to the City of London on the present Important Crisis, showing that the new method of paving the streets with Scotch pebbles, and the pulling down of the signs must be both equally pernicious to the health and morals of the People of England*, by Zachary Zeal, 1764 ; a rare pamphlet in the Bodleian Library.

[3] *British Chronicle*, 19th and 21st August 1767.

Great Britain—as a valuable example of wise public expenditure on improvements.[1]

The authority of the Westminster Paving Commissioners stopped at Temple Bar, the boundary of the old City ; but within its walls the pavement of the principal streets had become relatively good early in the eighteenth century. Already in the seventeenth century we find the householders compelled to employ the City paviors—men specially appointed for this work, who were sharply reprimanded by the Common Council when the repairs were executed in an unworkmanlike fashion, or in disregard of the convenience of passengers. Hence the City was distinguished for its flagged footways in the principal streets, as well as for its uniformly constructed carriage-ways, even at the opening of the century. But the improvement of the City pavements did not, after 1762, keep pace with that of Westminster. " While the inhabitants of the West End of the town," writes a discontented citizen in 1765, " are taking every expedient to make their streets commodious, it must give inhabitants of other parts no little concern to see the palpable inattention which is shown to theirs. Among a variety of other places which are to the last degree disagreeable and inconvenient, the pavement in Fetter Lane is in so wretched a condition that there is scarce a possibility of passing." [2] In the last decade of the century the *Times* more than once animadverts on the imperfections of the City pavements, which it attributes partly to quarrels about jurisdiction, and partly to the neglect and lack of supervision of the City paviors.[3] Somewhere about this time, however, the Commissioners of Sewers for the City, in whose hands the work lay, seem to have adopted a systematic plan for paving the carriage-ways with the same stone as that used in Westminster. From the interesting report of the Clerk

[1] *Inquiry into the Principles of Political Economy*, 1767, by Sir James Steuart, vol. iv. p. 317 of 1805 edition of his Works.

[2] *British Critic*, 13th-15th February 1765.

[3] *Times*, 4th April 1794 ; also, five years later, " A few days since the axle-tree of a carriage was broken in descending the slope of Blackfriars Bridge, in consequence of the very large hole at the bottom of it on the Surrey side, which is in the highest degree dangerous. We are not certain that an indictment would not lie against the Trustees of the Surrey Roads for the scandalous manner in which they are kept. They vie with the paviors in some parts of the City, and we know not which are the most inattentive, not to say worse of them. It is not to be conceived the number of horses that are foundered by holes in the streets and roads " (*ibid.* 5th October 1799).

of the Bristol Street Commissioners, who went to London in 1806 to see how the paving was managed, we learn that the City Commissioners insisted for the carriage-way on the use of Scotch granite from Aberdeen, and for the footways on Purbeck flags ; that they employed for each of the twenty-five wards, a single responsible pavior, whose labourers set the stone in screened gravel, according to a carefully drawn specification ; and that they appointed a salaried surveyor and no fewer than four salaried inspectors to supervise the work in their one square mile of streets.[1] From this time forward we hear no complaints of the City pavements.

Whilst the City of London was emulating the Westminster Paving Commissioners of 1762–1771, the pavement outside the walls was again giving rise to complaints. The Act of 1771 had set up, under the Commissioners, in Westminster and some adjoining parishes parochial committees, to which, by a retrograde step, the most important executive work was transferred. The householder's obligation to repair the pavement having been swept away, the state of the street now depended entirely on the public authority. The dozen separate parochial committees, each raising its own rate, making its own paving contracts and appointing its own inspector—composed, in fact, of cliques of the notorious " Select Vestrymen " of the time— proved to be more anxious to emancipate their parishes from the control of the Commissioners in contracts and works, and to diminish the local paving rate, than to keep their streets in such a state of repair as would serve the convenience of the whole Metropolis. One by one these Vestries secured from a heedless Parliament separate Local Acts withdrawing their parishes from the jurisdiction of the Westminster Paving Commissioners,[2] until that body, reduced to the supervision of only a few streets, ceased to function.

[1] MS. Minutes, Improvement Commissioners, Bristol, 17th June 1806.

[2] 22 George III. c. 44 (St. Margaret and St. John, Westminster, 1782); c. 84 (St. George's, Hanover Square, 1782) ; 23 George III. c. 42 (St. Paul, Covent Garden, 1783) ; c. 43 (St. Anne, Soho, etc.) ; c. 89 (St. Clement Danes, 1783) ; c. 90 (St. Martins in the Fields, 1783) ; 29 George III. c. 75 (St. George's, Hanover Square, 1789) ; 30 George III. c. 53 (optional streets in St. James's, St. Giles's, St. George's and St. Andrew's, 1790) ; 34 George III. c. 96 (Foundling Estate, in St. George the Martyr and St. George's, Bloomsbury, 1794). The Paving Committees of the parishes were apparently in 1798 still submitting their contracts for confirmation to the Westminster Paving Commissioners (see MS. Minutes, Paving Committee, St. Margaret and St. John, 4th September

Meanwhile there were springing up, outside the area both of the Corporation of the City of London and of the Westminster Paving Commissioners, miles of new streets and squares, extending continuously in all directions.[1] Some of these districts, like the extensive parish of St. Marylebone, were governed by powerful Select Vestries, which, under their own Local Acts, were compelling the householders to compound for their obligation to pave, and were themselves carrying on extensive paving operations partly by contractors and partly by squads of workmen in direct employment.[2] In the equally important parish of St. Pancras, on the other hand, each great landowner, or the knot of new householders on a particular estate, had obtained a separate Local Act, applicable only to a few streets and squares, leaving the intermediate parts of the parish without any kind of pavement or paving authority. Many of the main arteries of road traffic were in the hands of the different Turnpike Trusts, the paving powers of which varied according to their several Local Acts, and the actual extent and quality of the pavements according to their financial resources.[3] Such open Vestries as

---

1798). The Commissioners must, we assume, have obtained in 1807 a renewal of their Acts of 1765 and 1786 granting them the Sunday Toll (47 George III. c. 38), and must have continued to receive its proceeds, doubtless applying the same to the liquidation of their debt. But we hear no more of their paving activity. In 1817, on the passing of Michael Angelo Taylor's Act, the Commissioners, whose meetings had become very perfunctory, reduced their small establishment, and their proceedings became more formal and lifeless than before. Their minutes are among the archives of the City of Westminster.
  [1] " After the peace of 1763," we are told, " the North of the Metropolis, . . . extended with surprising rapidity, St. Marylebone and the parish of St. Pancras especially. The new mode of paving commenced about the same time, previous to which few of the streets had level footpaths for passengers, but were formed with small stones, and for the most part with a gutter down the middle " (Leigh's New Picture of London, p. 19 of ninth edition, 1839).
  [2] At the Marylebone Vestry in 1800 J. A. attended and prayed " the Board to order Nottingham Mews in this parish to be paved. Resolved that a Committee of Survey be requested to view the said Mews, and report their opinion thereon to this Board at some future meeting." Three weeks later, it is " Resolved that Nottingham Mews be paved according to the application of J. A. for that purpose, as soon as the composition money shall be paid for such paving " (MS. Vestry Minutes, Marylebone, 1st and 22nd February 1800).
  [3] When most of the Turnpike Trusts north of the Thames were consolidated in 1826, as we have described in a previous chapter, the new Metropolitan Turnpike Trustees received, by 7 George IV. c. 143, full power to pave, repair and repave all these roads, in whatever way they thought fit, as well as to license frontagers to put down such footways, etc., as the Trustees might approve. Under this authority we gather that macadamised surfaces largely replaced the squared stone " setts."

Chelsea and Kensington contented themselves, either with the road administration of particular Turnpike Trusts, or with the results they could obtain, under the ordinary parochial powers, by means of money compositions for Statute Labour and the limited Highway Rate. "Some of the parishes," it was said in the House of Commons, "were so poor that they could not defray the expense attending the proper pavement of their streets, and others were so divided among themselves on almost every occasion that they sat debating like a petty House of Commons, and neglected their most important duties."[1] With such a chaos of authorities, each pursuing its own policy, or lack of policy, the new pavement laid down between 1762 and 1780 by the Westminster Paving Commissioners rapidly deteriorated under the heavy traffic, whilst, especially in the newer quarters of the Metropolis, many streets, and even whole districts, remained mere muddy receptacles for water and filth.

The increased attention paid to road communication at the beginning of the nineteenth century was presently reflected in a growing discontent with the state of the streets of the Metropolis. "The pavement of London," contemptuously remarked a distinguished amateur road constructor, "is utterly unworthy of a great metropolis."[2] In 1811 the Chairman of the Grand Jury at the Middlesex Quarter Sessions called their special attention to the state of the highways. "I mean more particularly," he said, "the streets, squares, lanes and other thoroughfares of the Metropolis; that they are in many places in such a state of decay and want of repair as to be not only highly inconvenient, but absolutely unsafe and dangerous, and that, too, in many of the most populous parts." He proceeded to point out that even the most essentially urban thoroughfares "are highways and are indictable if not kept in repair "; whilst Local Acts for the better management of streets, etc., "will not indemnify any . . . parish against the general law, if highways are suffered to fall into a state of decay, unless some particular body of men or individuals are specially bound to repair them. A highway continued in a state of decay for a length of time is a public nuisance, whatever private jurisdiction it may be under."[3]

[1] *Hansard*, 7th March 1815, vol. xxxiii.
[2] *Essay on the Construction of Roads*, by R. L. Edgeworth, 1813, p. 7.
[3] *Address to the Grand Jury at the Middlesex Quarter Sessions*, 2nd December 1811, by William Mainwaring, Chairman, 1811, p. 4.

U

Acting on this direction, the Grand Jury formally presented Piccadilly, one of the streets that had been paved by the West-minster Commissioners, as being out of repair, and the wealthy and respectable parish of St. George's, Hanover Square, found itself indicted for the offence of failing to maintain this public highway. The Vestry's " Committee of Paving " could not deny the bad state of the roadway, and, after taking the opinion of the Attorney-General, the Vestry decided that it was incumbent on the Vestry " and not on any other body to answer to the said indictment." A committee of nine members was accordingly appointed to conduct the defence. The verdict was adverse, and the Paving Committee of this richest and best-governed parish in the London lying outside the City walls was driven reluctantly to put its most frequented thoroughfare into decent repair.[1] But the method of indictment was " found too dilatory and expensive to punish or to prevent "[2] the neglect of the London parishes ; and was, moreover, not strictly applicable to the new service of paving, as distinguished from ordinary road repair.[3] Nor did the parishes feel that they were entirely to blame. During these years the continuous tearing up of the streets for the new pipes of the gas and water companies was affording the Paving Committees an excellent excuse for procrastination, whilst rendering the nuisance of broken pavements and dangerous holes more intolerable than ever. At last, in 1814, a zealous and public-spirited Member of Parliament, Michael Angelo Taylor, began a vigorous agitation for reform. In an opening speech he drew the attention of Parliament to the wretched state of the streets, the depredations of the water and gas com-panies, and the continuous neglect of the Local Authorities.[4] In the following session he introduced a Bill to establish a Metro-politan Board of Paving Commissioners, to be appointed by the

[1] MS. Vestry Minutes, St. George's, Hanover Square, 14th December 1811 and 23rd May 1812.
[2] Report of House of Commons Committee on the State of the Pavement in the Metropolis, 1816, p. c.
[3] At Manchester, the Improvement Commissioners insisted on the parish doing its duty by the highways of the town, though these had become streets. But they were advised by counsel that they had no power " to compel the landowners or the Surveyors of the Highways to keep and maintain the paving and flagging in repair. The surveyors by the Highway Act are at liberty [either] to pave or gravel the streets and footpaths as they may judge neces-sary " (MS. Minutes, Improvement Commissioners, Manchester, 1808).
[4] Hansard, 28th June 1814.

Government, from among persons owning at least £300 a year in freehold property, or worth £10,000 in personalty, and to exercise a regulating, inspecting and compelling jurisdiction over all the various local bodies within a radius of five miles from the centre, throughout a district comprising, as was noted with alarm, no fewer than 867,933 inhabitants, living in 122,366 houses, of an aggregate annual rental of more than three millions sterling.[1] This Bill, which is interesting as affording the first known outline of anything like a municipal authority for the Metropolis as a whole, met with the determined opposition of all the hundreds of separate authorities within the proposed area, the powerful and exclusive Select Vestries of St. George's, Hanover Square, and St. Marylebone, being supported by such open and Radical Vestries as Chelsea and Kensington, and by the innumerable smaller bodies of Paving Trustees or Commissioners scattered throughout the Metropolis. Instigated by the Vestrymen of Marylebone, frequent conferences of " deputies " organised the " lobbying " of Members, and even set on foot a house-to-house agitation by the parish beadles, whilst petitions opposing the Bill poured into Parliament. Popular and local prejudices were excited against the proposed " new Commissioners and Police Magistrates, with discretional power, at the pleasure of their perambulating hired inspectors, to summon the former Commissioners and gentlemen, as well as clerks, like culprits to remote, and to police offices . . . and to compel the parishes and districts to defray the charges which

[1] *Hansard*, 21st February 1815 ; Report of a meeting of the Paving Trustees of St. Luke, Middlesex, in *Times*, 12th April 1815.

As an alternative to Michael Angelo Taylor's proposal of a superior Metropolitan authority, regulating and controlling all existing local bodies, an able correspondent of the *Times*—said to have been John Rickman—put forward in January 1816 a plan of dividing the Metropolitan area among about half-a-dozen separate Paving Boards, acting for the City, Southwark, Westminster, etc., superseding all existing bodies, and each independently appointing its own paid officers to execute the necessary works—an early suggestion of what was, eighty years later, termed the " tenification " of London instead of its unification (*Times*, 2nd January 1816, etc., republished as *Eight Letters concerning the Pavement of the Metropolis and the adjoining Turnpike Roads*, by X. Y., 1817). On the other hand, an influential witness in 1828 suggested, as the only effective reform, the transfer of all the paving and lighting of the Metropolitan parishes, together with the watching, to a central office under the Home Secretary—the system, that is, of the Metropolitan Police (Report of House of Commons Committee on the Police of the Metropolis, 1828, pp. 120-122).

they . . . impose, without any remedy against caprice, extortion or abuse, and even without appeal." [1] The Vestry of Marylebone declared that its pavements were both in excellent order, and efficiently administered, and threw itself with energy into the organisation of the opposition to any outside interference. [2] We find the Paving Trustees for St. Luke's Parish asserting that they " possess and exercise under the Local Act all the powers which are necessary to pave, repair and preserve the pavement of the streets " ; that but for " the temporary evil " of " the useful increase of water companies, and the establishments " for the " supply of gas," the pavement of their streets would be a model of " cleanliness, durability and comfort " ; and that " no causes exist within their jurisdiction for just complaint or for the introduction of any other interference and control." [3] The Chelsea Vestry vehemently urges that " it has no paved carriageways " within its whole area, and that a paving rate " would contribute greatly to the depopulation of this parish," [4] whilst St. George's, Hanover Square, haughtily resolves that the Bill is " very objectionable in most of its parts, and totally unnecessary for this parish." [5] Baffled by this united opposition, Michael Angelo Taylor had to withdraw his Bill, and content himself with a Select Committee to enquire into the State of the Pavement of the Metropolis. [6] This Committee proved to be time-serving and timid. Its meagre report threw the whole blame for the bad pavements on the then unpopular gas and water companies, and failed to grapple with, or even to set forth, the difficulties created by the multiplicity of separate paving authorities, and the absence, in many places, of adequate paving powers. Without attempting to remedy the constitutional chaos into which the government of the Metropolitan area had sunk, the Committee fell back, practically as their only proposal, on the intervention of the individual householder.

[1] *Times*, 12th April 1815.
[2] MS. Vestry Minutes, St. Marylebone, 4th April, 13th May, 11th November, 16th and 30th December, 1815, 12th March 1816.
[3] Report of meeting of the Paving Trustees of St. Luke's, *Times*, 12th April 1815.
[4] MS. Vestry Minutes, Chelsea, Middlesex, 17th April 1815.
[5] *Ibid.* St. George's, Hanover Square, 10th April 1815.
[6] *Hansard*, 25th April 1815, 7th March 1816. A slightly different account of these proceedings is given in an MS. note prefixed to the British Museum copy of the pamphlet (*Eight Letters*, etc.) mentioned above.

They did not, indeed, revert to the system of individual responsibility for the pavement, but they attempted to transform every aggrieved householder into a common informer. " The first remedy," they report, " should be afforded by the establishment of an universal power for every housekeeper to compel the speedy and effectual reparation of any pavements dangerous to persons traversing the streets of the Metropolis, without the trouble and changes of an indictment. And that for that purpose, Surveyors of Pavement should be appointed in every district by the different local Commissioners . . . to whom notices of any dangerous pavement may be immediately given, and who shall be compelled, by summary proceedings before magistrates, under heavy penalties, to repair, with all convenient expedition, every dangerous defect of which such notice may be given." [1] Michael Angelo Taylor made the best of the situation. Finding it impossible to overcome the opposition of the existing bodies to any central authority for the Metropolis as a whole, he adopted the futile proposal of the Committee as the ostensible basis of his Bill. But, as it passed into law in the session of 1817, his Act contained a great many valuable enactments. Its 147 clauses included provisions enabling minor street improvements to be effected with comparative cheapness —provisions which have, right down to the present day, continued to be used with advantage. It added cleansing, street-watering and house-numbering to the duties of paving authorities. It practically consolidated for the Metropolis the law relating to street nuisances, and by a series of drastic penal clauses curbed the depredations of the gas and water companies. And though the Act did nothing to compel the inefficient or apathetic Paving Authorities to do their duty, it gave, to all the more energetic and ambitious of them, wide scope for improvement. By sweeping general clauses most of the limitations and shortcomings of their respective Local Acts were removed ; they were authorised to extend their jurisdiction over neighbouring streets destitute of any paving authorities ; their powers of repaving were widened ; their potential paving rates were doubled or, in some cases, trebled, and the assessment and collection of these were facilitated ; whilst by various administrative clauses

[1] Report of House of Commons Committee on the State of the Pavement in the Metropolis, 1816.

each separate authority was enabled, if it chose, to put its internal organisation on an efficient basis.[1] Unfortunately, however, it was soon demonstrated that the failure to create a central body of Commissioners had, as regards paving, taken all the driving force out of Michael Angelo Taylor's reform. In how many districts the new Surveyors of Pavements were actually appointed we have been unable to ascertain. We have found absolutely no trace of their activity, and we imagine that the office was everywhere conferred upon the existing clerk or surveyor or superintendent of the Paving Authority, who gained thereby only one empty title the more. The aggrieved householder certainly did not become a common informer, and neither the Vestries nor the multifarious Paving Boards showed any disposition to use the permissive powers of widening their jurisdiction which the Act conferred on them. Some little improvement did, however, take place. The gas and water companies were gradually brought into the habit of making good their constant devastations as quickly as possible. One or two of the wealthier and more progressive of the Metropolitan Vestries, alarmed by the attack on their autonomy and stimulated by the series of Parliamentary enquiries between 1819 and 1833 on the means of communication, seem, during the next twenty years, to have made good use of their powers. We see, for instance, the energetic Select Vestry of Marylebone making extensive purchases of granite in Aberdeen, and permanently employing a staff of between fifty and a hundred paviors and labourers, divided into twenty companies, some of whom, dispersed among the nine districts, were " traversing each square and street to repair and fill in the holes in the carriageways of the parish," whilst others, under the Parish Surveyor and three salaried super-intendents, were kept at work paving the new streets that were

[1] " Michael Angelo Taylor's Act," as this 57 George III. c. 29 of 1817 has ever since been called, remained for nearly forty years the main basis of London street law, and is still in operation as regards some of its sections. Though applying to all the various parishes and districts in the Cities of London and Westminster, the Borough of Southwark, and the " Bills of Mortality," together with St. Marylebone and St. Pancras (which were thus for the first time made part of the Metropolitan area), it is classed and printed as a Local Act, and is thereby excluded from the ordinary editions of the Statutes. An edition, with notes, was published in 1839 under its full title, *An Act for Better Paving, Improving and Regulating the Streets of the Metropolis, and removing and preventing Nuisances and Obstructions therein*, 1839.

being continually opened on its northern and western sides.[1]
In 1828–1830 the Paving Committee was busily occupied in the
extensive task of tearing up the old squared stone pavement
of the carriage-ways—now regarded as intolerably noisy, dusty
and destructive to horses and carriages [2]—and replacing it by
a " macadamised " road, charging the householders along the
route one-third more rate, and executing the work whenever
requested by two-thirds of the rated occupiers. The Select
Vestry of St. George's, Hanover Square, was enlightened enough
in 1824 to engage the eminent road engineer, Thomas Telford,
to report upon the whole of the pavements of that parish, and
largely to govern itself by his professional experience.[3] But
this progressive policy was, we fear, characteristic of only a very
few of the Metropolitan Vestries. Over the greater part of the
rapidly extending range of streets, the pavement evidently continued in a disgraceful state. Complaints are rife of " sprained
ankles " and " shoes filled with mud," owing to " the wide,
gaping intersections or interstices between the paving stones " ;
of " falling horses " and smashed-up vehicles, due to the unevenness of the surface ; and of " deafening noise " and " blinding
dust " which passers-by and inhabitants had alike to endure.[4]
In the great Parish of Lambeth, on the south, as in that of
Christchurch, Spitalfields, immediately to the east, it is reported
by Francis Place in 1824, as the result of his own inspection,

[1] MS. Vestry Minutes, St. Marylebone, Middlesex, 30th December 1815,
12th March 1816, 10th February 1821, 11th July 1829, 13th November 1830.
[2] See, for instance, *Considerations on the Defective State of the Pavements of
the Metropolis*, by William Deykes, 1824, p. 8 ; *Practical Instructions for the
Improvement of the Carriage Pavements of London*, by J. C. Robertson, 1827 ;
Practical Treatise on Making and Repairing Roads, by Edmund Leahy, 1844,
pp. 66-72 ; the latter of whom tells us that pavements have been " generally
superseded by broken stones, which . . . may be said to be the general mode
of making and repairing roads " (p. 66).
[3] " Report respecting the Street Pavements, etc., of the Parish of St. George,
Hanover Square," by Thomas Telford, June 1824, printed as appendix to
A Treatise on Roads, by Sir John Parnell, 1833, pp. 348-361.
[4] See, for instance, *Considerations on the Defective State of the Pavement of
the Metropolis*, by William Deykes, 1824, pp. 8-10. In contrast with the
undoubted superiority of the whole of London paving in 1770, in 1827 it can
be claimed only that London excels Paris and other cities in its footways
(*Practical Instructions for the Improvement of the Carriage Pavements of London*,
by J. C. Robertson, 1827, p. 15). " At the time of our visit to Paris," writes
a traveller of 1826, " the Rue de la Paix was the only street which was provided
with a footpath " (*Frederic Hill: An Autobiography of Fifty Years in Times
of Reform*, edited by Constance Hill, 1894, p. 63).

that various streets, courts and alleys were " still paved [only] with pebbles and without any flagstone footpath . . . in a very dilapidated state." [1] Almost under the shadow of the Houses of Parliament, Horseferry Road was, in 1825, a slough of mud and filth, which the Vestry of St. Margaret's, Westminster, was then only beginning to survey,[2] whilst the outlying Parish of St. Paul, Deptford, was, in 1824, actually under indictment at Quarter Sessions for the non-repair of its streets as common highways.[3] But it was in the districts of the four or five score of independent Paving Boards, " self-appointed and irresponsible," and publishing " no accounts of their receipts and expenditure," [4] that " the evils of discontinuity, variety and inequality " [5] of pavement were most rampant. In the Parish of Bermondsey, for instance, which was, by 1831, becoming covered with a network of densely peopled courts and alleys, surrounding the wharves, tanneries and manufactories, the pavements provided by the five separate Paving Authorities varied from street to street, in every degree of unevenness, fracture and neglect.[6] Even in the new squares of Belgravia, as late as 1835–1836, innumerable complaints are brought before the Cubitt Estate Trustees—the sole Paving Authority for that area—of dangerous and dilapidated footways, pavements so much lower on one side than the other that kitchens were frequently flooded with liquid filth and storm water, posts so placed as to upset carriages, and unprotected cellar areas amounting to dangerous precipices.[7] The administration of the paving of the great Parish of St. Pancras, which in 1801 had still only 31,779, and by 1831 numbered over a hundred thousand inhabitants, remained for the whole

[1] Place MS. 27827-52/54.
[2] MS. Vestry Minutes, St. Margaret, Westminster, 7th March 1825.
[3] *Ibid.* St. Paul, Deptford, Kent, 11th March 1824.
[4] *Local Government in the Metropolis*, 1835, p. 21.
[5] Report of House of Commons Committee on the Police of the Metropolis, 1828, pp. 120-122.
[6] " Thus Bermondsey Street and several of the streets issuing out of it are parts of the East Division of Southwark as regards paving. . . . Long Lane forms a separate district, under another Act of Parliament for paving. . . . The waterside division of the parish has also a separate Act of Parliament for their purposes. The Grange Road and parts adjacent has also a separate Act. . . . And the Bermondsey New Road forms part of the Kent Road (Turnpike) Trust for these purposes " (*History and Antiquities of the Parish of Bermondsey*, by G. W. Phillips, 1841, pp. 110-111).
[7] MS. Minutes, Cubitt Estate Trustees (now among the archives of the Westminster City Council), 23rd October 1835 *et seq.*

of that generation a caricature of Local Government. For this area of little over four square miles, there were no fewer than nineteen separate paving authorities, the Parish Vestry being responsible only for about one-twentieth of the ground, and eighteen different Paving Boards governing as many scattered patches belonging to the several landowners. And yet, adds the Parish Surveyor in 1834, " some very closely inhabited streets and passages in the parish are left without any superintending care in regard to paving " ; including, as he explains, such populous districts " as the upper part of Grays Inn Lane . . . the back road from King's Cross to Bagnigge Wells Tavern . . . all the cross streets, courts and alleys between the two roads, the east side of the road from the Small Pox Hospital to St. Pancras Workhouse, and all the streets, alleys and passages branching therefrom." These densely crowded streets, courts and alleys, amounting to two miles in length, which no public body was authorised to pave, were entirely " without control, and the consequence is," he continues, " that the whole district is in a sad state of filth and dirt." Meanwhile, as the crowning absurdity, it must be mentioned that, as the local " Church Paths Rate," out of which the Vestry defrayed its paving expenses, was, by the terms of the Local Act, paid out of the Poor Rate, and as this was naturally levied equally on the whole parish, the occupiers of houses in the districts of the eighteen Paving Boards contributed their quota to the paving executed by the Vestry, in the one-twentieth of the parish for which alone it administered this service, in addition to paying separate local rates for their own paving ; whilst the unfortunate dwellers in " the uncontrolled district pay the same rate without any care being bestowed upon them "—contributing, in fact, to the cost of paving the rest of the parish whilst getting in their own streets absolutely no paving whatsoever.[1] In this chaotic condition the administration of the London pavements was destined to remain for another couple of decades—in fact, until the Metropolis Management Act of 1855 reorganised the whole local government of the Metropolis.

[1] Evidence of Surveyor of Highways of St. Pancras, in First Report of Poor Law Inquiry Commissioners, Appendix A, vol. i. (Codd's Report), 1834, pp. 54-55.

The Pavements of the Provincial Towns

Turning now to the hundreds of towns outside the Metropolitan area, we see, in some of the ancient provincial cities, street pavements as immemorial in their origin as those within the walls of the City of London, and chartered corporations resorting to Parliament for special paving powers even earlier than that of the capital city. The special privilege of levying a toll for " pavage," which the City of London enjoyed, was granted in the thirteenth and fourteenth centuries by charter or statute to various boroughs, notably Coventry, Warwick, Huntingdon, Bristol and Southampton, sometimes only for a limited term of years, apparently on the assumption that stone pavements could be laid down, as walls were built, once for all. But however the street pavement came into existence, there grew up a custom in these paved towns for the frontager wholly or partially to keep in repair the part in front of his tenement, down to the middle of the roadway. This obligation was embodied, as a matter of course, in the various paving Acts of the fifteenth and sixteenth centuries,[1] and was apparently enforced in many towns—often, we imagine, on the strength of mere manorial custom or municipal byelaw—by the Court Leet or other tribunal under local control.[2] Thus we are told in 1755 that, in the borough of Hull,

[1] In 1320 the University of Cambridge had induced the King to order that the householders should perform their customary obligation of repairing the pavement in front of their own premises (2 Rot. Parl. 48). See the Paving Acts for Northampton (1431), Gloucester (1473), Canterbury (1477), Taunton (1477), Cirencester (1477), Southampton (1477), Bristol (1487), Ipswich (1571) and Chichester (1576). The obligation to pave was usually restricted to the " high streets," or to specified main thoroughfares ; and the Acts were often limited in duration to a short term of years, though this limitation may not have affected the customary obligation to repair. The Municipal Corporation often co-operated with the inhabitants ; sometimes (as at Northampton and Chichester) undertaking the charge of the pavements in the market-place ; sometimes (as at Chichester) also the " ways of greatest resort " ; sometimes (as at Hull) supplying the stone ; and sometimes (as at Southampton in 1482) appointing a Town Pavior, provided with free lodging, who executed the paving work for the householders at customary charges (*History of Southampton*, by J. S. Davies, 1883, pp. 119-120). See *History of Private Bill Legislation*, by F. Clifford, 1887, vol. ii. pp. 255-268 ; and *Municipal Origins*, by F. H. Spencer, 1911, pp. 178-186.

[2] We see this at Ipswich, where it was (perhaps merely in pursuance of the Local Act, 13 Eliz. c. 24 of 1571), in 1737, " agreed and ordered " by the Town Council " that the Sergeants at Mace of this corporation be empowered to demand and receive the several amerciaments that shall be hereafter assessed by the Headboroughs of this borough for defaults in cleansing and paving the

" for the more regular and better paving and repairing of the streets, . . . it hath been customary for the Mayor and Aldermen . . . in common council assembled, from time to time as they saw occasion, to order . . . the said streets . . . to be new paved or repaired by such workmen as they, the said Mayor and Aldermen, thought fit; and the said Mayor and Aldermen have usually provided proper materials for the paving and repairing . . . and the occupiers of messuages . . . fronting to the said streets . . . have usually paid the said workmen for their labour . . . so much for every yard square . . . unto the middle thereof, as hath been from time to time agreed on and thought reasonable by and between the said Mayor and Aldermen and the said workmen." [1]   By the middle of the eighteenth century, however, the citizens of Hull demurred to this assumption of power, and the Corporation found it necessary in 1755 to obtain from Parliament a Local Act crystallising the ancient custom into statute law.   Similar statutory authority was sought at one time or another by nearly every town in the kingdom.

In the numerous Local Acts passed by Parliament during the last half of the eighteenth century for different towns, the Hull arrangement between the individual householder and the local authority was only one of a bewildering variety.   The limitation of the householder's obligation to the maintenance of the footway,[2] or to the mere repair of existing pavements ; [3] the new paving to be undertaken only at the request of a majority of the householders in each particular street,[4] or to be extended to any streets where such request is made ; [5] the extension of the frontager's obligation to new works and old, levelling and

---

streets within the town " (MS. Minutes, Town Council, Ipswich, 12th December 1737).   And at Gloucester, which had also an early Local Act (1473), and where the Court Leet continued to be held by the Municipal Corporation as lord of the manor, we find it, between 1784 and 1819, not infrequently amercing householders for allowing the pavement in front of their houses to be out of repair (MS. Minutes, Court Leet, Gloucester, vol. for 1784–1819).

[1] Preamble to 28 George II. c. 27 (Hull Paving, etc., Act, 1755).

[2] 26 George III. c. 119 (Newport, Isle of Wight, Streets Act, 1786) ; 26 George III. c. 116 (Cheltenham Streets Act, 1786). See, for this variety, *Municipal Origins*, by F. H. Spencer, 1911, pp. 178-186.

[3] 23 George II. c. 19 (Colchester Harbour and Streets Act, 1748).

[4] 11 George III. c. 9 (Winchester Streets Act, 1770).

[5] 31 George III. c. 80 (Lincoln Streets Act, 1791) ; 31 George III. c. 62 (Maidstone Streets Act, 1791).

guttering;[1] compulsion on him to execute his share of the work
by specified workmen,[2] or in a specified way,[3] or under the direction of a public officer;[4] compulsion on the local authority
itself to pave the market-place or certain "high streets"[5]
(all others being left to the householders); to contribute towards
the repair of specially wide streets; to pave in front of public
buildings or, where no individual can be made to pay,[6] to repair
its own streets in a definite order;[7] the grant of an option to
the local authority either to compel the householder to perform
the work or exact from him a money composition;[8] the further
option whether future repairs should be charged to the frontagers
or to a common rate; finally, the specific exemptions of poor
districts from both advantages and cost of pavement[9]—all
these represent different settlements between the individual
householder and the local authority embodied in the first Local
Acts obtained by different parishes and boroughs. But in spite
of the fact that eighteenth-century paving statutes, unlike
Turnpike Acts, were permanent in their operation, no town
contented itself with a single application to Parliament. In the
various amending Acts that each body of Improvement Commissioners secured, we find one uniform tendency—the gradual
supersession of the householder's obligation to pave or repair
the street by the evolution of municipal enterprise. By the
nineteenth century it was rare to find, whether in the first paving
Acts of new urban districts or in the amending Acts of older
communities, either the footway or the carriage-way left in the
hands of the householders. In one direction, however, the
obligation on the individual citizen became more specific and

[1] 20 George III. c. 21 (Worcester Paving, etc., Act, 1780); 41 George III.
c. 30 (Sculcoates Streets Act, 1801); 6 George IV. c. 196 (Macclesfield Streets
Act, 1825).
[2] 9 George III. c. 21 (Gainsborough Lighting and Paving Act, 1769).
[3] 31 George III. c. 64 (Deal Streets Act, 1791).
[4] 6 George III. c. 34 (Bristol Improvement Act, 1765).
[5] 13 George III. c. 15 (Gravesend and Milton Streets Act, 1772).
[6] 23 George II. c. 19 (Colchester Harbour and Streets Act, 1748), parish
to pay for having adjoining churches and churchyards, and for places "where
no sufficient distress can be made"; 26 George III. c. 119 (Newport, Isle of
Wight, Streets Act, 1786); 31 George III. c. 80 (Lincoln Streets Act, 1791).
[7] 16 George III. c. 57 (Weymouth Paving, etc., Act, 1775); 16 George III.
c. 27 (Dorchester Streets Act, 1775).
[8] Hove Paving Act, 1830.
[9] 12 George III. c. 18 (Chatham Paving, etc., Act, 1771); 19 George III.
c. 36 (Bridgwater Market and Streets Act, 1778).

more stringently enforced. Prior to 1800 there was seldom any distinction drawn, as regards paving law, between the most ancient thoroughfares and new streets in process of construction. With the rapid outgrowth of new suburbs, the Improvement Commissioners seem to have become tardily aware of the extravagance of permitting the owners of building estates to saddle the public with the cost of completing their new streets. Hence some specially enlightened Local Authorities began to insert clauses in their amending Acts, by which new streets or courts, " over which a dereliction of the way for the public shall have been made by the owner," were required to be properly levelled, paved, flagged and drained, at the expense of the proprietors, whenever the Local Authority thought such work necessary.[1] Moreover, it came to be provided that no such new streets should become repairable out of the common rate until they were certified to be properly paved and guttered.[2] With this exception, the responsibility of the private citizen for the state of the pavement gradually disappears ; its maintenance becomes a duty of the Local Authority ; and, in some Acts, the individual householder is even given the right summarily to compel the Local Authority promptly to put any particular bit of defective pavement into good repair.[3]

This generalised analysis of the paving clauses of the hundreds of Local Acts passed between 1700 and 1835 may be usefully supplemented and qualified by concrete examples of the paving history of particular towns. In many cases the inhabitants

[1] 50 George III. c. 41, sec. 55 (Hull Lighting, etc,. Act, 1810) ; 11 George IV. c. 15 (Liverpool Improvement Act, 1830). But this all-important power was, by 1835, very far from being general. Leeds, for instance, was seriously feeling the need of it ; we see the Improvement Commissioners resolving " that it is essentially necessary that the Commissioners should have power to compel the owners or occupiers of property adjoining the present and future streets and public passages in the Township of Leeds, and within one mile of the boundary of the town, to pave, drain and make all necessary levels opposite their respective premises " (MS. Minutes, Improvement Commissioners, Leeds, 1st November 1837). For the numerous complicated questions that arise in connection with this requirement, see *The Law and Practice as to Paving Private Streets*, by William Spinks, 1887 ; *The Law and Practice relating to Private Street Works*, by the same, 1904, 256 pp. ; *The Private Street Works Act*, 1902, by J. Scholefield and G. R. Hill, 1902, 161 pp. ; and *Notes on the Law of Private Street Works under the Public Health Acts*, by J. B. R. Conder, 1911, 114 pp.

[2] 41 George III. c. 30, sec. 23 (Sculcoates Improvement Act, 1801) ; 50 George III. c. 41, sec. 57 (Hull Lighting, etc., Act, 1810).

[3] 31 George III. c. 64 (Deal Streets Act, 1791).

paved their streets without obtaining any statutory power either to enforce an obligation to repair, or to levy extra taxation. Thus in 1708 the inhabitants of Maidenhead represent to the Berkshire Quarter Sessions "that the said town was about seven years since paved with stone at the great charge of the inhabitants and the voluntary contributions of the neighbouring gentry."[1] So, at Woolwich in 1717, the Vestry observes that " the inhabitants of this parish have been at very great expense in paving the town thereof, in doing of which the same is made more commodious, and of consequence much more healthful to the inhabitants," who are therefore enjoined to refrain from sullying the new pavement with refuse.[2] In the little borough of Peterborough, as late as 1790, the work of paving was accomplished by the voluntary subscription of £3000 by the ground landlords, the Parliamentary representatives, the trustees of the local charities and the local magistrates.[3] In 1822 we find the inhabitants of Leicester violently objecting to the grant of any new rating powers either for paving or for lighting and watching the borough, services which they thought " ought to be borne by the wealthier part of the inhabitants exclusively." The ancient Municipal Corporation, itself a large property owner, opposed the project for a rate, on the ground "that there is public spirit enough " to do the work " without subjecting the poorer inhabitants to any expense whatsoever."[4] The proposed

[1] MS. Minutes, Quarter Sessions, Berkshire, January 1708.
[2] MS. Vestry Minutes, Woolwich, 25th October 1717.
[3] " On Monday last a very respectable meeting was held at the Town Hall in the City of Peterborough to hear and determine on the different plans of the Committee for carrying into effect the paving and lighting this ancient and long neglected city. . . . Earl Fitzwilliam, with that well-known liberality which the inhabitants have on all occasions experienced . . . subscribed the sum of £1000, and . . . the worthy members £500 each, the Gentlemen Feoffees, with that generosity which will ever rebound to their honour, £500 ; with many more considerable sums by the respectable magistracy, gentlemen and others, amounting to the sum of £3000 " (Lincoln, Rutland and Stamford Mercury, 26th February 1790). Other instances might be cited. " Ashford (Kent) has been paved, substantially and satisfactorily, at not more than double the expense of what an Act of Parliament for this purpose usually costs. The inhabitants, fortunately, were unanimous ; and the sum necessary for the work, amounting to £300, was obtained, partly from the highway cess, and partly raised by subscription. . . . The cess for the highways has never been higher than ninepence in the pound ; it is now sixpence ; and the debt incurred in making the road has been paid off within £170 " (The State of the Poor, by Sir F. M. Eden, 1797, vol. ii. p. 278).
[4] MS. Minutes, Town Council, Leicester, 16th January 1822.

Local Act was therefore abandoned. But unfortunately neither the Municipal Corporation nor the wealthy inhabitants—not even the ground landlords of the new building estates, which were becoming rapidly covered with rows of workmen's cottages —actually carried out any paving works ; and the streets of this quickly developing manufacturing town remained in a terrible condition. In 1822, the parish of St. Mary, in the old part of the borough, found itself indicted at the Assizes, for neglect to maintain in good repair part of the pavement of its public highways. The Vestry, after seeking to find some other way out, decided that it was best not to make any defence, but immediately to put the streets in repair, at the expense of a rate. Similar action was taken in 1832 in the adjoining parish of St. Margaret, where the Surveyors of the Highways were directed to put the pavements in repair, by employing the necessary labourers out of the " composition rates," but lest their zeal should land the ratepayers in too much expense, they were reminded that " no street [is to] be repaired or repaved without the knowledge and sanction of the Vestry." [1] The opposition to the paving rate did not always come from the mob of smaller ratepayers, who crowded into the churches at Manchester,[2] Leeds or Leicester when a Vestry meeting took place. At Kingston-on-Thames, we read in 1770, " the tradesmen are stirring Heaven and earth to have their town new paved . . . but met with so

[1] MS. Vestry Minutes, St. Mary's, Leicester, 17th April 1822 ; *ibid.* St. Margaret's, Leicester, 2nd July and 13th August 1832.

[2] We know little of the history of paving at Manchester. As already stated, Improvement Commissioners were appointed, jointly with Salford, as early as 1765, but this Local Act remained, as we have already mentioned, for some unknown reason, a dead letter, and absolutely nothing seems to have been done until, as we have described elsewhere, the passing of a new Local Act in 1792, and the extra-legal separation of the Commissioners for the two towns sometime between 1792 and 1797, when the existing minutes for the Manchester body begin. Their first attention was paid to watching and lighting, but they presently began to deal with the pavement, using their powers of removing obstructions to get rid of the posts which divided the footway from the road. But though the Commissioners could put down nuisances, remove encroachments, and prohibit obstructions, they had, at first, no power to pave or compel the householders to pave. The repair of the roadways rested with the Surveyors of Highways of the township, subject to the liability of the whole extensive parish to be indicted. An influential committee, which reported in 1808, accordingly recommended the obtaining of further powers, the union of the office of Surveyor of Highways with that of the Commissioners, and the enactment of regulations as to the width and paving of new streets. This, however, as we have already described, led to violent opposition, and the project had to be abandoned.

much opposition from the gentry that the session of Parliament is over, and nothing is done."[1] At Greenwich, on the other hand, where the example of the new pavement of Westminster had its influence, it was " the gentry " who wanted " to new pave the town with regular shaped stones like the streets in London," but who, we read, were " violently opposed by the townsmen or tradesmen."[2]

It is only in two or three of the larger provincial towns that we have anything like a continuous record of the struggle between the Municipal Corporation, the Parish Vestry and the frontagers as to the fulfilment of the obligation and the provision of the cost of paving the town. Thus, at Liverpool, when in 1560 a vigorous effort was made to mend the streets, we are told that the Mayor " in his own proper person " laboured with the stones.[3] The Liverpool Corporation came to own a large part of the town, and it was commonly taken for granted that whatever works of paving were wanted should be executed at its expense. Little attention was, however, paid to this requirement during the eighteenth century. The footways were first complained of. " The streets," it was said in 1797, " are in general well, but not pleasantly paved, the footpaths, called here parapets, are disagreeable and offensive ; they are all laid with small sharp pebbles that render walking in the town very disagreeable, particularly to ladies. There is not one street in the town that is regularly flagged."[4] When the two rival water companies began, towards the end of the century, to lay their pipes all over

---

[1] *Middlesex Journal*, 22nd-24th May 1770.

[2] *Ibid.*

[3] *Selections from the Municipal Archives and Records from the 13th to the 17th century*, by (Sir) J. A. Picton, 1883, p. 92.

[4] *A General and Descriptive History of the Ancient and Present State of the Town of Liverpool*, 1797, p. 273, partly quoted in *Memorials of Liverpool*, by (Sir) J. A. Picton, vol. i. The writer continues as follows : " To avoid the sharpness and inconvenience of the pavement, that foot passenger for the most part walks on the curb, to which he is still further induced, as thereby he avoids the danger which might otherwise arise to him by reason of the projecting cellars. This comfortable relief to the feet of the passenger is, however, in time rendered less pleasing, by frequent use the friction is thereby so great as to wear them into deep cavities which in rainy weather become full of holes, at this season and during the greater part of the winter the footpaths are generally dirty, the pebbles gathering mud in their interstices, and as the custom is not general of daily sweeping before the houses, it soon becomes a clammy dirt, which adheres to the feet of the passenger " (*A General and Descriptive History of the Ancient and Present State of the Town of Liverpool*, 1797, p. 273, partly given in Picton, i. pp. 255-256).

the city, the pavement became everywhere intolerable. In 1799 the Corporation promoted a Bill to authorise extensive paving works, and the levy of a rate for the purpose. The Parish Vestry immediately opposed this Bill, on behalf of the inhabitants, declaring that " the parishioners are not bound by law, or under any obligation to pave or keep in repair the streets, lanes and public passages within the said town," and that this obligation legally devolved upon the Municipal Corporation. The latter body, however, persisted in its purpose, and drafted a new Bill, the contents of which were kept " a profound secret." On its introduction to Parliament in the session of 1801, it was found to contain clauses enabling the Corporation to carry on extensive paving and repairing operations, at the cost, so far as concerned the carriage-way, of a new rate, and so far as concerned the " parapets," or footways, at the expense of the frontagers. These proposals met with much opposition. " According to this clause," indignantly writes a local pamphleteer, " it should be actually supposed that the inhabitant adjoining to such footpath had the sole benefit of this improvement." [1] Meanwhile, the issue between the Corporation and the Parish Vestry was taken to Quarter Sessions, where it was decided, in August 1802, that the Corporation was, by prescription, bound to maintain and keep in repair the " ancient " streets of the town, but no others. The Parish Committee thereupon promptly got six of its members appointed as Surveyors of Highways, and took steps to restore the pavement of the other streets, which had got into a " dangerous and ruinous state . . . not by time or the want of repair, but by the laying down of waterpipes and the injudicious and imperfect manner of replacing the pavements by one or both of the companies of [waterworks] proprietors." This was to be effected at " the cost of a moderate rate to be applied to the repair of the streets," though it was hoped that some contribution might be got from the water companies.[2] The division of liability between the corporation and the parish, the absence of adequate control over the destructive operations of the water companies, and the lack of power to levy a special paving rate, seem to

---

[1] *Observations on a Bill introduced . . . by the Corporation of Liverpool for . . . enlarging the powers of . . . the Liverpool Improvement Act* (26 George III.), 1802, p. 18.
[2] MS. Vestry Minutes, Liverpool, 1st February 1799 and 12th April 1803.

X

have resulted in Liverpool being, in 1818, "one of the worst paved towns in the Kingdom." "The carriage-ways," we are told, "were pitched, with rough boulders. Many of the narrow streets had no footways, and were paved in the old continental fashion" (once universal in England, as we have seen), "with a channel along the middle. Where footways existed, they were paved with small angular pebbles, to which the natives had become hardened but which on strangers produced the most uncomfortable effect. A few cases in which flags had been laid down on the footways were exhibited to strangers as a curiosity. The Commissioners of the Highways at last took heart of grace and began to flag the footways and macadamize some of the principal streets. . . . A few years sufficed to render the town second to none in this department." [1]

At Bristol the story of the pavement is an even more complicated entanglement of personal obligation and public impost. How the ancient pavement in some of the streets had originally been formed, which Defoe at the opening of the eighteenth century found worn quite smooth and slippery,[2] we do not know. We read of a temporary Act of 1487, compelling the frontagers to put "the decayed broken, hollowed and pitted pavement" into repair ; and also of the permanent toll granted to the Municipal Corporation by its charters for the pavements of the town, as well as for its walls. The obligation of the frontager to keep the pavement in repair "unto the middle of the street" was definitely enacted in 1700,[3] but, as we gather, very imperfectly enforced. In 1748 the frontagers were let off some of their burden. Some of the streets—we suspect very few—were more than thirty feet wide ; and in these it was provided that the duty of repairing the pavement should be shared between the frontagers and the parishes, the borough justices in Quarter Sessions settling how far in each case the frontagers' obligation

---

[1] *Memorials of Liverpool*, by (Sir) J. A. Picton, 1875, vol. i. pp. 350-351.
[2] "They draw all their heavy goods here on sleds or sledges which they call geehoes, without wheels. This kills a multitude of horses, and the pavement is worn so smooth by them that in wet weather the streets are very slippery and in frosty weather, 'tis dangerous walking" (*A Tour through the whole Island of Great Britain*, by Daniel Defoe, vol. ii. p. 314 of 1748 edition). A diarist noted in the middle of the century, of the streets of Bristol, "that they there draw all their goods on sledges" (*Passages from the Diaries of Philip Lybbe Powys*, 1899, p. 49).
[3] 11 & 12 William III. c. 23.

was to extend.[1] This new division of responsibility, added to the already existing divisions between the frontagers, could not possibly produce a satisfactory pavement, and we are therefore not surprised to find, in 1766, the Act of 1748 simply repealed; and the whole obligation thrown once more on the frontagers. They are, however, now put under the direction of the Surveyors of Highways of the respective parishes, and it is enacted that " if any pavior, pitcher or other person . . . shall pave or pitch . . . in an uneven, irregular or unworkmanlike manner, or use any bad or improper materials," or otherwise act "contrary to the order and direction of such surveyors," he is to be liable to a fine of twenty shillings.[2] The pavement, it is hardly necessary to say, remained in a very bad state.[3] The advent of an energetic mayor in 1786, and the enactment of further powers for the suppression of nuisances in 1788,[4] seem to have wrought some temporary improvement, in the course of which separate footways appear to have been constructed. In 1794 we even read that " the streets are well paved with flat stones for foot passengers and smooth crossways from street to street executed very neatly." [5] But this improvement did not meet the growing requirements of the town. The Municipal Corporation was not disposed to incur any expenditure from its corporate funds, and in 1806 promoted a Bill to establish a separate body of Commissioners, elected by the different parishes and charged with repaving the whole city, and authorised to levy a rate for the purpose. As at Liverpool, the inhabitants protested against this transfer of the duty of paving and repairing from individual property owners or, as some contended, from the Municipal Corporation, to the ratepayers at large, but at Bristol their protest was ineffectual. The Town Council declared in reply that its Bill did but " render the usage of this city conformable to the general law of the land, to which it has hitherto been an exception ; that the powers which it gives to the (Corporation) magistrates are, in all material

---

[1] 22 George III. c. 20 (Bristol Paving, etc., Act, 1748).
[2] 6 George III. c. 34 (Bristol Improvement Act, 1766).
[3] " Viator," in *Bristol Gazette*, 26th October 1786, complains of "the wretched paving of the streets," which " no man will offer to deny, the hazard of limbs and life in riding through them is too evident. . . . But few streets will admit of a pavement of flat stones," for foot passengers, "from their narrowness." He promises that the new mayor intends to change all this.
[4] 28 George II. c. 32.
[5] *The New History, Survey and Description of* . . . *Bristol, 1794*, p. 50.

instances, the same as those exercised by the County magistrates, and that the mode of electing Commissioners . . . is the same as is directed for the election of Surveyors of Highways under the General Highway Act." [1] The Bill passed into law,[2] and the new Bristol Commissioners went vigorously to work, without stinting the cost. They sent their clerk to London and Bath to find out how the paving was done in those places ; they engaged a professional surveyor at a salary, and even imported an experienced Londoner for the post, against the importunities of Bristol freemen and other local residents ; and they entered into regular contracts for repairing the pavement of the whole City. But whilst, on the one hand, their plans included, from the outset, a universal renovation of the pavement from end to end, on the other, we see them summoning before them, street by street, the owners and occupiers of the houses in them, " to compound for the paving thereof agreeable to the directions contained in the 34th section." [3] Under this vigorous administration, the pavements were, in the course of the next few years, got into decent order. We hear no more complaints of their condition, though the inhabitants sometimes resented the Commissioners' rates. When, in 1830, the Town Dues levied by the Corporation on ships and wares became the subject of criticism, and the whole position of that body was the subject of Radical animadversion, " several of the merchants and citizens " drew the attention of the Commissioners to the fact that these Town Dues had been granted by charter, not for the general corporate income, but " in aid of the repairing and amending as well the walls of the Key (quay) as of other walls and pavements of the town of Bristol," and that such Town Dues were at that date yielding a large income which might properly be applied in relief of the heavy paving rate. The Commissioners were not unwilling to take the same view, and addressed a friendly memorial on the subject to the Town Council,[4] by whom the matter was shelved. The question of whether the Municipal Corporation was legally liable, in respect of its charter and its continued exaction of

[1] MS. Minutes, Town Council, Bristol, 30th April 1806.
[2] 46 George III. c. 26.
[3] MS. Minutes, Improvement Commissioners, Bristol, 10th, 17th and 24th June, 8th and 29th July, 5th and 26th August, 2nd and 23rd September, 7th and 14th October, 4th November 1806.
[4] MS. Minutes, Town Council, Bristol, 9th June 1830.

Town Dues, to maintain in repair the pavements of all the ancient streets seems to have never been formally decided.[1] The foregoing instances will suffice to give the student some notion of the variety, complexity and development of the arrangements made for the paving of the streets of provincial cities and boroughs. Right down to the Public Health Act of 1848 there was no general statute requiring the construction of pavements in English towns. Each town, and sometimes each parish or township within a borough, was, in this respect, a law unto itself. The surface of the streets might be left to be mended by the Surveyor of Highways out of Statute Labour, Team Duty and the limited Highway Rate ; they might be provided with a rude pavement by voluntary subscriptions, with or without a contribution from the Municipal Corporation ; [2] a Local Act might be obtained to compel frontagers to pave or repair the pavement ; finally, Parliament, at the request of the inhabitants, might set up a body of Improvement Commissioners, empowered to lay down new pavement, or repair old, at the expense of a general rate. By 1835, as we have described, all but four of the boroughs having more than 11,000 inhabitants had statutory paving authorities of the latter sort. The Commissioners sometimes

---

[1] The example of Bristol in the matter of paving seems, at the opening of the eighteenth century, to have greatly influenced the neighbouring town of Bath, of which, as the Municipal Corporation petitions in 1707, " the streets and lanes " had " become so ruinous by the great concourse of people, and horses and carriages," as to be very inconvenient, both to the inhabitants and to the rapidly increasing number of visitors to this fashionable resort (*House of Commons Journals*, 20th November 1707). An Act was thereupon passed (6 Anne, c.—) greatly increasing the powers of the Mayor and Aldermen, and compelling the frontagers to pave and repair. Under a subsequent Act (7 George I. c. 19) a body of Commissioners was appointed, with power to rate and pave. At the opening of the nineteenth century it was Bath which influenced Bristol. In 1806 the new Bristol Commissioners sent their clerk to Bath to learn how their paving work was done. He found them using the soft local oolitic stone for the carriage-ways, set side by side in squared blocks 8 inches deep, 12 inches long and 4 inches broad, forming a continuous pavement which needed repairing every other year. The footways were paved with Pennant flagstones. The whole work was done under a five years' contract, subject to specification and approval by a salaried surveyor (MS. Minutes, Improvement Commissioners, Bath, 24th June 1806).

[2] It was not unusual for the Municipal Corporation to make a voluntary contribution out of its corporate funds to particular works of paving executed either by the parish or the local Commissioners, or by individual inhabitants. Thus the Nottingham Town Council in 1803 voted £100 towards the cost of certain pavement near " the White Lion " (MS. Minutes, Town Council, Nottingham, 14th September 1803).

attempted to carry out their paving works by the direct employment of labour, either hired in the open market or borrowed from
the workhouse.[1] Sometimes, as at Exeter as late as 1834, they
engaged a surveyor, but allowed him also to undertake the work
he surveyed, executing it for a quoted price, and making whatever profit he could, under no other superintendence than his
own.[2] Sometimes, again, we find them buying their own stone,
engaging their own surveyor at a fixed salary, and putting the
work out to contract under his supervision—a method which, as
in the City of London and in Bristol, seems, at the beginning of
the nineteenth century, in the then state of administrative
machinery, to have proved the most successful of all.[3]

So little record is made of the day by day changes in the
common accessories of life that we do not find it easy to visualise
the pavements of the various provincial towns, and their gradual
transformation, during the eighteenth century and the first
thirty years of the nineteenth. In many of the smaller places
the streets evidently remained, from the beginning to the end of
the period, in the same intolerable condition. This by no means
implies an absence of stone pavements. "The art of sticking
the streets with the points of the stones upwards," says a diarist

[1] Thus, in 1824, we see the Plymouth Commissioners asking the Incorporated
Guardians of the Poor whether they would supply able-bodied paupers to
break stones for repairing the streets at the same rate as was being paid by the
neighbouring Turnpike Trusts for this work. This was actually done five years
later (MS. Minutes, Improvement Commissioners, Plymouth, 14th September
1824, 10th November 1829). At Leicester in 1832, on the other hand, the
Vestry directed the Surveyor of Highways to engage his own labourers for
paving (MS. Vestry Minutes, St. Margaret's, Leicester, 2nd July 1832).
[2] Exeter newspaper, 17th July 1834.
[3] To this arrangement, after various unsuccessful experiments, the Plymouth
Commissioners came in 1828, on the "report of a committee, which was convinced from the information it has collected from various quarters as to the
comparative advantage of having the town paved by the contract with the
present mode, that the advantages are decided by and greatly in favor of
paving and repaving the pavement by contract" (MS. Minutes, Plymouth Improvement Commissioners, 26th February 1828). So also did the Brighton
Commissioners, who found in 1825 that "under the present system of executing
works there is no possibility of checking the charges made by the persons
employed, neither have the Commissioners any means of knowing whether the
works charged for have been actually executed." They accordingly got rid of
their existing inferior officer, appointed a surveyor at a salary of £200 a
year, and decided to put all paving work out to contract (MS. Minutes, Improvement Commissioners, Brighton, 2nd and 6th September 1825). The
Paving Committee for the Vestry of St. Martin's-in-the-Fields advertise, in
1806, for tenders for a three years' contract for paving and repairing pavement
(*Morning Advertiser*, 24th April 1806).

of 1760, " greatly flourishes in every town almost." [1] " Our main streets," writes a Kendal historian of the period between 1763 and 1826, " were paved with large road cobbles, so very slippery that the inhabitants acquired a catch in their walk as if on ice. . . . The farmers positively refused to take their horses over the small sharp stones lest they might be lamed beyond recovery." [2] " During the whole of the time that Lancaster was in a state of prosperity " (notably during the first quarter of the nineteenth century), we are told that " no care appears to have been taken of the streets which were in a deplorable state. . . . They were roughly paved, with very deep channels running down the middle of each street to carry off the rainfall." [3] Even in so large a town as Birmingham the " petrified kidneys " remained the only paving, of foot- and carriage-ways alike, as late as 1830.[4]

> " The streets are pav'd, 'tis true, but all the stones
> Are set the wrong way up, in shapes of cones,
> And strangers limp along the best pav'd street,
> As if parch'd peas were strew'd beneath their feet,
> Whilst custom makes the natives scarcely feel
> Sharp-pointed pebbles press the toe or heel." [5]

These primitive pavements were, in fact, nothing more than an extension to the whole surface of the highway of the " cawsey," provided originally for the packhorses ; with " an open, rather deep gutter in the centre of the street for the reception of all the filth imaginable." [6] In the principal streets of such important centres of business or pleasure as Bristol and Bath, this mediaeval

---

[1] *Passages from the Diaries of Philip Lybbe Powys*, 1899, p. 61. The town immediately referred to was Arundel (Sussex).

[2] *Kirbie Kendall : fragments . . . relating to its ancient streets and yards*, by John F. Curwen, 1900, p. 15.

[3] *Lancaster Records, or Leaves from Local History, 1801–1850*, 1869, p. vi.

[4] *Going to Markets and Grammar Schools*, by Geo. Griffith, 1870, p. 13.

[5] *Birmingham : a Poem*, by J. Bisset, 1800 ; *A Century of Birmingham Life*, by J. A. Langford, 1868, vol. ii. pp. 119-122.

[6] *Records of ye Antient Borough of South Molton in ye County of Devon*, by John Cock, 1893, p. 65. The pavement of rounded cobble-stones, sometimes with the kennel in the middle, still characterises many North Country villages — we may instance Knutsford in Cheshire and Reeth in Yorkshire — contributing by its noisy clatter, uneasy jolting, and arid squalor to their inferiority in charm and comfort to those of the South of England. Similarly, the retention by Manchester of stone " setts "—an improvement on the cobbles in cleanliness though scarcely in noiselessness—instead of adopting, like London and South Country towns, the relatively quiet macadamised surface, contributed not a little to drive its wealthier residents to live outside its boundaries —to the manifold loss of the city, in municipal administration and much else.

type of pavement was, towards the end of the eighteenth or in the opening years of the nineteenth century, slowly exchanged for the type brought into vogue by the Westminster Paving Commissioners—a level or slightly concave carriage-way, laid with squared blocks of hard stone set closely side by side, with lateral gutters and elevated footways, marked off by curb stones.[1] This access of care in shaping and laying the paving stones was, however, even in the case of the Westminster Paving Commissioners and the most efficient provincial authorities, largely rendered nugatory by the fact, which we find first commented on in 1824, that "in most of our streets the pavement lies on a soft and yielding bed, . . . earth reducible to a semi-liquid mass by every shower of rain." It was an engineering novelty, reserved for such road constructors as Telford, to recommend "that a substratum be formed of more unyielding materials,"[2] without which, as we now know, the best laid pavements, either for carriages or pedestrians, wear quickly uneven, and into holes. This tendency to pave the carriage-way with "setts" of squared granite was interrupted by the advent of Macadam, and by the preference, especially of London and other towns of the south and west of England, for the relatively noiseless surface which he constructed for them.

How soon the "flagged footpaths" which, early in the eighteenth century, had excited the admiration of foreign visitors to the Metropolis, were introduced into provincial towns, we are unable to discover. We suspect that only in very few cases outside the Metropolis did there exist, at the end of the eighteenth century, any continuous lines of footway paved with broad flagstones ; and such as then existed had only lately been constructed. Among these exceptions were Bristol and Bath. It was, however, already noted, in 1799–1800, as somewhat disgraceful to Liverpool and Birmingham that they should be without flagged footways, and it seems that this improvement was introduced, during the first twenty years of the nineteenth

---

[1] Such a pavement existed, we gather, at the very beginning of the nineteenth century at Plymouth Dock, now Devonport, where we read " the streets . . . are paved with a species of marble which is very common in the quarries of Mount Wise and Stonehouse. In the more public streets where there is any descent the stones are extremely beautiful after heavy rains, with a variety of veins " (*The Plymouth Dock Guide*, about 1800).

[2] *A Paper read before the Institution of Civil Engineers on the Construction of Carriage-Way Pavements*, by Bryan Donkin, 1824.

century, by various large towns. But the great period for its
adoption was the decade between 1820 and 1830 when such
records as we have gathered show dozens of towns, great and
small, to have abandoned their pebbled ways. It was during
these years that the Liverpool authorities, we are told, " took
heart of grace and began to flag the footways and macadamise
some of the principal streets. Church Street was the first to
have the benefit of this improvement. A few years sufficed to
render the town second to none in this department." [1] At
Preston, the Improvement Commissioners began to flag the footways in 1821.[2] The ancient city of York was engaged in the
same work in 1829, still charging householders half the cost, as a
special luxury,[3] whereas the far less important borough of
Bewdley is reported to have completed its flagging by 1830.[4]
Birmingham seems during the same decade to have begun " the
gradual substitution of stone-flagging for the causeways, instead
of the sharp-pointed pebbles so long the opprobrium of the place." [5]
In the south of England, we learn that at Penzance " in 1825
nearly all the footpaths of the streets were pitchpaved ; the
flat paving was begun about 1826 or 1827." [6] At Devizes in
1825 " hardly a square yard of flagging was to be seen from
one end . . . to the other ; the occasional occurrence of posts
and pavements before some solitary door rather tending to trip
up 'the public, and render the long intervals of sharp pebbles
appear all the more toilsome." Within a few years from that
date, a new body of Improvement Commissioners had flagged
the town.[7] At the little town of South Molton in Devonshire,
" up to 1825 the principal streets appear to have been pitched
with large stones," and the " first flagging on the footpaths "
was put down in that year.[8] Even in the little town of Minchinhampton the Vestry called for tenders in 1824 as to " what rate

[1] *Memorials of Liverpool*, by (Sir) J. A. Picton, 1875, vol. i. pp. 350-351.
[2] *History of Preston*, by P. A. Whittle, 1837, vol. ii. p. 109.
[3] MS. Minutes, Improvement Commissioners, York, 2nd November 1829.
[4] *Going to Markets and Grammar Schools*, by George Griffith, 1870, p. 13.
[5] *The Picture of Birmingham*, by James Drake, 1825, p. 30.
[6] *Half a Century of Penzance, 1825-1875*, by J. S. Courtney, 1878, p. 43.
[7] *Chronicles of the Devizes*, by James Waylen, 1839, p. 167.
[8] *Records of ye Antient Borough of South Molton in ye County of Devon*, by
John Cock, 1893, p. 65. At Plymouth, in 1829, granite curb was laid down
free, wherever the frontager would consent to repave the footway " with the
best large slate stones (sawn, and not hewn with chisel) from Cann Quarry "
(MS. Minutes, Improvement Commissioners, Plymouth, 8th December 1829).

per yard the footpaths and the water course of the town can be pitched and paved," and appointed a committee to get the work done.[1] By 1835, though some places of importance still lagged behind, we infer that flagged footways had become the rule instead of the exception in the principal streets of nearly all the larger towns.[2]

All this praiseworthy enterprise in respect of street pavement had, from a modern standpoint, one disastrous limitation. "The pavement," it was observed in 1842, was "regarded as requisite solely for cart or carriage conveyance and not as a means of cleanliness."[3] The one and only thought of those who paved the town was, in fact, in 1830 as in 1762 and 1662, the safe, speedy and pleasant transit of vehicles and pedestrians— what John Spranger himself had described as "making the passage through our streets and lanes safe, easy and commodious."[4] It was to secure this end that obstructions had been prohibited, kennels had been filled in, side gutters had been constructed, footways had been flagged, and carriage-ways had been levelled, drained and provided with a hard surface. These paving improvements had been effected primarily in "the principal streets in which the carriage traffic is considerable," to which, in many towns, they were, in 1835, still confined.[5] They had been extended from thoroughfare to thoroughfare, not according to its population but according to the amount and importance of the traffic, poor and unfrequented localities being usually excluded from the advantages, and sometimes exempted from the cost, of the new pavement. It never occurred to the most reforming body of Improvement Commissioners in a crowded town that their task was incomplete so long as any

[1] MS. Vestry Minutes, Minchinhampton, Gloucestershire, 8th December 1824.
[2] In 1841, Sir Robert Peel alluded to "the man who found a piece of smooth pavement in some country town (Tamworth it might be), and walked to and fro for the purpose of enjoying the pleasure of contrast." Sir R. Peel to J. W. Croker, 8th November 1841, *The Croker Papers*, by L. J. Jennings, 1884, vol. ii. p. 410.
[3] *General Report of the Poor Law Commissioners on the Sanitary Condition of the Labouring Population of Great Britain*, 1842, p. 59.
[4] *A Proposal or Plan for an Act . . . for the better paving, lighting and cleansing the streets . . . of Westminster . . . Marylebone, etc.*, by John Spranger, 1754, preface.
[5] *General Report of the Poor Law Commissioners on the Sanitary Condition of the Lab uring Population of Great Britain*, 1842, p. 59.

square yard of surface lying between human habitations remained unprovided with an artificial covering, impervious to wet, and easily cleaned of filth. Hence, even in the best regulated towns, whole streets—sometimes whole districts—remained unpaved, whilst the thousands of densely populated courts and alleys, not to mention the backyards, were usually entirely outside the jurisdiction of any paving authority. These unpaved areas, left in a barbarous state of holes and heaps, became not only the receptacles for stagnant water, but also the dumping grounds of every kind of impurity, which spread, in poisonous dust or liquid filth, throughout the whole district. Thus it came about, in spite of all the work of the paving authorities, that when in 1831 the Asiatic cholera reached England, it found actually a larger superficial area of unpaved surface in the midst of crowded human habitations than had existed at any previous period.[1] Nor was this immediately, or even promptly, remedied. It was not until the cholera had, in 1831–1833, swept away thousands of lives, and in 1848 and 1854 thousands more, that town paving ceased to be regarded merely as a means of easy transit, and the necessity, on grounds of public health, of imperviously covering town surfaces became an axiom of municipal administration.

[1] As a specimen of the unpaved state of the manufacturing towns of Lancashire and Yorkshire we may append the following descriptions of Wigan, Manchester and Leeds in 1839. "Many of the streets are unpaved, and almost covered with stagnant water, which lodges in numerous large holes which exist upon their surface, and into which the inhabitants throw all kinds of rejected animal and vegetable matters, which there undergo decay and emit the most poisonous emanations. These matters are often allowed . . . to accumulate to an immense extent, and thus become prolific sources of malaria, rendering the atmosphere an active poison. . . . The waste land . . . is one complete pool of stagnant water, mixed with various descriptions of putrifying animal and vegetable matters " (*General Report of the Poor Law Commissioners on the Sanitary Condition of the Labouring Population of Great Britain*, 1842, p. 19). In Manchester, out " of 687 streets inspected by a voluntary association (in 1832) 248 were reported as undrained. Many . . . are so deep in mire or so full of hollows and heaps of refuse that the vehicle . . . cannot be driven along them. . . . Whole streets in these quarters are unpaved and . . . worn into deep ruts and holes, in which water constantly stagnates, and are so covered with refuse and excrementitious matter as to be almost impassable from depth of mud and intolerable from stench. In the narrow lanes, confined courts and alleys leading from these similar nuisances exist, if possible to a still greater extent " (*ibid*. p. 38). Leeds is in an equally bad condition. " Of the 586 streets of Leeds, 68 only are paved by the . . . local authorities, the remainder are either paved by owners, or are partly paved, or are totally unpaved, with the surfaces broken in every direction, and ashes and filth of every description accumulated upon many of them " (*ibid*. p. 40).

Street Cleansing

It would, however, be unfair not to describe, in this connection, a second service undertaken by practically all the bodies of Improvement Commissioners, namely, the organised cleansing of the principal thoroughfares from the mud and filth of all kinds by which they were constantly becoming encumbered. So far, we have been able to ascertain, the systematic cleansing of the streets always succeeded and never preceded their paving. In mediaeval times both services were initiated or enforced by the same authority, using the same customary or statutory sanctions, and practically the same administrative devices. Throughout the eighteenth and early nineteenth centuries the two services continued closely intertwined. The same series of Local Acts which established new bodies of Improvement Commissioners with power to pave or to enforce the maintenance of paving, gave these also the power to cleanse, and to enforce cleansing. Moreover, both in the law and in the administration of these common powers, we see the same transition from the enforcement on each householder of an ancient customary obligation, to the provision of an organised department of municipal enterprise, maintained out of the proceeds of a common rate. In its main lines the story of Street Cleansing from 1700 to 1835 is a mere duplication of that of Street Paving. But it has certain distinctive features of its own which a brief survey will bring to light. Municipal enterprise in street cleansing [1] is, even more than that of street paving, a development from the mediaeval conception of a common nuisance. Failure to fulfil the twin obligation of paving in front of a town tenement, and keeping this

---

[1] We know of no history of town cleansing in this country. *The Cleansing of Cities and Towns*, by A. May, 1911, 319 pp., seems to be almost the only general work upon the subject outside the essentially modern problem of sewage treatment. How complicated is now the organisation of street cleansing and the disposal of urban refuse may be seen in the American works, *Street Cleaning*, by Col. Waring ; *Modern Methods of Street Cleaning*, by G. A. Soper, 1909, 201 pp. ; and the New York Public Library *Bibliography of City Wastes and Street Hygiene*, 1912, 55 pp. In the period with which we deal the service was viewed as a simple one. Beyond contemporary pamphlets and newspapers, the minutes of local authorities, and the Local Acts, we have found most information in the *General Report of the Poor Law Commissioners on the Sanitary Condition of the Labouring Population of Great Britain*, 1842. But see also *The Sanitary Evolution of London*, by H. Jephson, 1907, 440 pp., and *The Health Agitation, 1833–1848*, by Miss B. L. Hutchins, 1909, 150 pp.

pavement clean, could be prosecuted as a passive nuisance, that is, as a neglect to do what the common good required. But the householders adjoining a filthy street, unlike those abutting on a ruinous pavement, were presumably guilty of an active as well as of a passive nuisance. A worn or broken pavement was in the main caused by the innocent activity of the whole body of citizens and strangers who used the thoroughfare : the heaps of soil, dung, dirt, ashes, garbage, etc., which disgraced the un-cleansed street were almost certainly due to the direct and intentional action of the inhabitants of the particular street, if not of some particular tenement. If streets were not to become impassable, some way of dealing with these active nuisances had to be found. The first move was to treat the heaps as ordinary obstructions of the King's Highway, and to prohibit all citizens from casting, laying or leaving dirt, refuse or ashes on the surface of the street, exactly as they were forbidden to stand their carts or trade implements, or to display their goods, to the detriment of the free passage. With this elaborate series of prohibitions we shall deal in another volume, concerned with the regulation of personal conduct and the Suppression of Nuisances. The massing of town population led, however, to one all-important exception to this prohibitory code. In the course of each day every household accumulated a certain quantity of filth and refuse which had, somehow or other, to be disposed of. So long as there existed, within easy reach of every family, some waste place or running river, some backyard or vault, where this refuse might be deposited, it was open to the local authority rigorously to enforce its prohibition of deposit in the street. The enlargement of the town area, the filling up of all available space by tenements, the diversion of watercourses from the streets, the culverting or arching over of their channels, the extinction of backyards and gardens, the growing disproportion between the number of privies, ashpits and middens on the one hand and that of the population on the other—all these common circum-stances of the seventeenth- and eighteenth-century English town rendered the simple expedient of prohibition a mere futility. It became inevitable that the household refuse should sooner or later be placed in the street. Spasmodically, when there was a special alarm of plague, the householder was even admonished and encouraged to oust the filth from his house. It is therefore not surprising to find the " great heaps and quantities of rubbish, dirt and other filth " [1] lying about the streets becoming noted as a characteristic feature of every large town of the seventeenth and eighteenth centuries.   The same problem was arising as to the disposal of the mud and dust created or brought into the street by the multitudinous traffic.   Each householder might conscientiously sweep in front of his tenement, but what was to happen to his sweepings ?   So long as there existed a running stream of water in the street, or so long as the deposits in the kennel were no more than could be washed away by every shower of rain, the problem hardly presented itself.   But with the growth of population and the accumulation of other kinds of filth, the street sweepings of the householder were merely added to the larger heaps of household refuse.   Confronted by these heaps, steadily growing in size and number, for which prohibition and injunction had proved vain, one authority after another adopted the device, not merely, as in paving, of enforcing by statute the householder's customary obligation, but of combining it in intimate partnership with an incipient form of municipal enterprise.

The administration of the City of London in the latter half of the seventeenth century affords the clearest example of this combination of administrative devices.   Each householder was under an ancient obligation to cleanse the pavement in front of his tenement, but (in a city in which, by exception, separate footways for pedestrians had long existed) this obligation was, at any rate in the seventeenth century, restricted in practice to keeping clean the part reserved for foot passengers, by posts or flagstones.   Certain places, " as far as may be, out of the City and common passages," [2] were set apart as " laystalls," where any one might deposit dirt and refuse of any kind.   The indiscriminate casting of filth or ashes into the streets was, like all other hindrances to free passage, peremptorily forbidden ; but the householder was permitted, and even enjoined to rid his house of its filth, " either by setting out the same overnight in tubs, boxes, baskets, or other vessels near and contiguous to

---

[1] *The Presentment of the Grand Jury at the Old Bayley*, 1684.

[2] *Orders formally conceived and agreed to be published by the Lord Mayor and Aldermen of the City of London . . . concerning the infection of the Plague, and now reprinted and published by order of the House of Commons*, 1646.

their houses, or by bringing out the same within convenient time," during the prescribed hours.[1] Each of the twenty-five wards had its " Scavenger," an unpaid officer chosen annually at the Ward-mote, whose duty it was to see that the law was obeyed. The actual work of sweeping the carriage-ways and carrying away all deposits was entrusted by the City authorities to specially appointed " Rakers," whom we should nowadays term dust contractors. In 1762 we find the Commissioners of Sewers of the City entering into an elaborate annual contract with the Fellowship of Carmen, which then exercised the monopoly of cartage within the City, owned by Christ's Hospital. This " Fellowship " undertook to send carmen with " tumbrils or carts " in the early hours of five days, and the afternoon of Saturday, in each week, to cleanse the streets, scour the sewers, and carry away " all the dung, soil, filth, seacoal, ashes and other dirt, as well from all the streets . . . as from all the houses." Every household, even the poorest and most ignorant, was to have the advantage of this service. " The said carmen, undertakers, their agents or servants," it is expressly provided, " shall give notice of their being in the streets with their tumbrils or carts, by loudly knocking a wooden clapper, especially in courts, alleys and other back passages, upon pain to forfeit 3s. 4d. upon every complaint duly proved." For this service the householders paid them " the customary rates by the Scavenger's Book " ; and those who had what we should now call " trade refuse " to dispose of (such as the " innkeeper, livery stable keeper, brewer, dyer, sugar baker, soap maker or other trader ") paid an extra quarterly allowance fixed by " the Assessors of each ward according to their best discretion, respect being had to the trade or other occasions in the making of more or less dung and soil

---

[1] An ancient order, reprinted as late as 1677, shows that, even in the City of London, a practice prevailed during the hours of night which was the opprobrium of the Edinburgh of the beginning of the nineteenth as it is that of Madrid at the beginning of the twentieth century. " No man shall cast any urine boles or ordure boles into the streets by day or night, afore the hour of nine in the night ; also he shall not cast it out, but bring it down, and lay it in the channel, under the pain of 3s. 4d., and if he do cast it upon any person's head, the party to have a law recompense if he have hurt thereby " (" The Statutes of the Streets of this City against Nuisances," in *The Laws of the Market*, printed by Andrew Clark, printer to the Honourable City of London, 1677 ; quoted in *Observations on Popular Antiquities*, by John Brand, vol. i. pp. 126, 132 of edition of 1841, and in the *General Report of the Poor Law Commissioners on the Sanitary Condition of the Labouring Population*, 1842).

by such traders." To inspect this elaborate organisation the Commissioners of Sewers nominated two civic dignitaries as honorary " supervisors," authorising them to appoint their own deputies " to see the same duly executed and performed." How long this particular agreement with the Fellowship of Carmen may have lasted, and how efficiently it was executed, we have not ascertained. In 1684 we have the Grand Jury at the Old Bailey complaining of the " great heaps and quantities of rubbish, dirt and other filth lying about the streets of this City, to the endangering of the inhabitants thereof in their healths, and breeding of manifold diseases, it being very inconvenient to passengers." " We therefore humbly offer and think it reasonable," proceeds the Jury, " that the several scavengers in and about the precincts and wards of this City be forthwith ordered to take some speedy course for the removing and carrying away the said soil so lying in the several streets ; and that such as they appoint do frequently call on the several inhabitants for the carrying away of such soil as shall be made in their several houses, to prevent distempers that may arise by reason of the stink thereof this hot weather, according to the duty of their several offices ; and that such persons as are neglecting therein be forthwith prosecuted for their several offences." [1]

Whatever may have been the efficiency of this organisation in the City of London—and on this point we have practically no evidence, and not even any complaints to quote—we infer that it went on, throughout the whole of the eighteenth century, and well into the nineteenth, with but one important change in the law and its administration, and with but few minor variations. Instead of the Raker collecting his payment from each individual householder, he became the paid servant or contractor of the Commissioners of Sewers. The " customary rates by the Scavenger's Book " were thus replaced by the even poundage rate levied by the Commissioners for their various purposes. By a statute of 1765, which strengthened the power of enforcement, the limitation of the City householder's cleansing obligation merely to the width of the footway was implicitly confirmed.[2] The laystalls, for which it grew more and more difficult to discover suitable sites, were replaced by " moveable or fixed

---

[1] *The Presentment of the Grand Jury at . . . the Old Bayley*, 1684.
[2] 6 George III. c. 26.

dust boxes, dust holes or conveyances wherein dust or other filth may be deposited for the scavengers or rakers." [1] Those who contracted to remove the filth and refuse were allowed under easy conditions the temporary use of vacant sites in the streets, as places of deposit. But the contractors had to take away all the " ashes, dirt and slop . . . twice in every week, in broad wheeled carts with flaps to cover them," before noon or after 3 P.M., with the obligation to dispose of this refuse elsewhere how they could. [2] At this point we leave the City of London, which was always praised by foreign visitors for the relative cleanliness of its crowded streets ; and we proceed to describe the gradual introduction of some kind of cleansing organisation into the other parts of the Metropolis.

The state even of the best thoroughfares in Westminster during the first half of the eighteenth century is a testimony to the low standard then existing among the wealthiest, most luxurious and most fastidious classes with regard to their own health and convenience in the use of the streets. Within this area lay the palaces of the King, the mansions of the great, the Houses of Parliament and the Courts of Justice, as well as the daily places of resort of the officers, lawyers and literary men. Yet we find practically no complaints from any of these governing classes about the incredible accumulations of horse dung in the carriage-ways, the heaps of dirt by which the footways were obstructed, the decaying animal and vegetable matter which blocked the kennels, and the pools of stagnant filth that lay amid the broken pavements. Mandeville was perhaps indulging in facetious humour when he demonstrated, in 1714, that " dirty streets are a necessary evil inseparable from the felicity of London. . . . There are, I believe," he said, " few people in London, of those that are at any times forced to go afoot, but what could wish the streets of it much cleaner than generally they are, whilst they regard nothing but their own clothes and private conveniency. But when once they come to consider that what offends them is the result of the plenty, great traffic and opulency of that mighty city, if they have any interest in its welfare, they will hardly ever wish to see the streets of it less

[1] 6 George III. c. 26.
[2] Advertisement of Commissioners of Sewers for the City of London in *The Diary*, 26th May 1790.

Y

dirty. For if we mind the materials of all sorts that must supply such an infinite number of trades and handicrafts as are always going forward . . . the multitudes of horses and other cattle that are always daubing the streets, the carts, coaches and more heavy carriages that are perpetually wearing and breaking the pavement of them, and above all the numberless swarm of people that are constantly harassing and trampling through every part of them—if, I say, we mind all these, we shall find that every moment must produce new filth, and considering how distant the great streets are from the river side, what cost and care soever be bestowed to remove the nastiness almost as fast as it is made, it is impossible London should be more cleanly before it is less flourishing." [1] But however we may discount as satirical Mandeville's defence of dirty streets, there can be no doubt of his facts. As late as 1756, on the unimpeachable authority of the sober John Spranger, we have it that " the rough and broken pavements were so covered by filth as to make them scarcely visible to the most cautious passenger by day." The " quantity of filth in our streets," he added, is " so great that man and beast in some places can hardly wade through it." [2]

Some effort had been made after the Restoration to mitigate this evil. Under the temporary Paving Act of 1662 a " Chief Raker " had been appointed for the Westminster parishes, who occupied towards the Commissioners on the one hand, and the individual householders on the other, practically the same position as did the Fellowship of Carmen in the City of London. At the end of the century, as we learn incidentally from an interesting lawsuit recorded in the archives of the Middlesex Quarter Sessions,[3] the business of this office was still being conducted by the widow of the original holder, with a considerable capital invested in horses, carts and laystalls. Besides this Chief Raker, or contractor, we gather that each parish appointed one of its inhabitants to the annual and unpaid office of Scavenger, whose duty it was to present householders neglecting their duty of cleansing the pavement in front of their tenements, and to see that the Chief Raker fulfilled his contract. But this Act of

---

[1] *The Fable of the Bees*, by Bernard de Mandeville, 1714, preface.
[2] *A Proposal or Plan for an Act of Parliament for the Better Paving, Cleansing and Lighting, etc. . . . of Westminster*, by John Spranger, 1756, preface.
[3] *Middlesex County Records*, by J. Cordy Jefferson, vol. iv. pp. xxxiv, 157-159.

1662, as we have already mentioned, was never generally enforced, and the " Commissioners of Scotland Yard," as they were
called, presently ceased to function, whereupon the parish organisation, at any rate in many places, promptly went to pieces.
" Many persons," we are told in 1691, " in the outparishes in
Middlesex and other parishes in the limits aforesaid, which have
been chosen to serve the office of Scavenger refuse to take the
execution of the said office upon them ; and others who have
been rated and assessed towards the cleansing and carrying away
the dirt and soil out of the streets, have refused to pay the rates
assessed upon them, there being no law in force to compel them
thereunto, so that no person can be employed to be Raker, to
carry the dirt out of the said streets, for want of some provision
for payment for doing that service : And the poorer sort of
people daily throw into the said streets all the dirt, filth and coal
ashes made in their houses : By reason thereof the said streets
are become extremely dirty and filthy, so that Their Majesties'
subjects cannot conveniently pass through the same about their
lawful occasions." [1] Hence, in the permanent Act of 1691,
which extended to all the places within the Bills of Mortality,
we find clauses re-enacted, specifically enforcing the obligation
of the householder, and providing for the offices of Scavenger and
Raker. In 1721, when London was in fear of the plague, the
committee appointed by the Middlesex Quarter Sessions distributed among householders printed copies of these clauses,
imposing penalties for " not . . . sweeping up the dirt, as well
as upon the Rakers and Scavengers for not taking it away, and
also for not cleaning and carrying away the filth and soil from
the several markets. Yet experience has shewed," conclude the
justices sadly, " that all these steps have not had the good effect
which might have been expected of them." [2] Householders continued to defile the streets and to neglect altogether to sweep
their pavements, whilst the Rakers not only left whole streets
unvisited, but, by their use of common carts without covers,
often made matters worse than before. This, declared Jonas
Hanway, in 1754, " is surely one of the greatest absurdities that
ever prevailed in the police of a civilised state ; for the Rakers

[1] 2 William and Mary, sess. 2, c. 8 (1691).
[2] Report of the Committee on Nuisances, MS. Minutes, Quarter Sessions,
Middlesex, 12th October 1721.

not only drop near a quarter part of their dirt, and render a whole street, perhaps already cleansed, in many spots very filthy, but it subjects every coach and every passenger, of what quality whatsoever, to be overwhelmed with whole cakes of dirt at every accidental jolt of the cart ; of which many have had a most filthy experience." [1] In despair of getting any improvement in cleanliness from the various parochial authorities, it was proposed, in 1752, " that the cleansing of " the entire Metropolitan area " should be put under one uniform public management, and all the filth be carried into lighters, and conveyed by the Thames to proper distances in the country." [2] This was, however, far too large a piece of construction for the amateur reformers in the House of Commons, to whom the Ministry afforded no assistance ; and nothing more was accomplished than the insertion of the word " cleansing " in the list of street functions entrusted, as we have described, in 1761 to the Westminster Paving Commissioners. These Commissioners were, however, during the brief period of their activity, wholly absorbed in the primary duty of equipping the Metropolis with the new pavement to which we have already referred ; and we hear nothing of any action by them for cleansing the streets. Within a few years, as we have already mentioned, the various Vestries obtained their own Local Acts, virtually excepting their several parishes from the executive jurisdiction of the Commissioners. It was therefore to the Vestries, and to the other bodies of Trustees or Commissioners under Local Acts for special areas, and to these alone, that the inhabitants of Westminster, as of the other parts of the Metropolitan area outside the City, could, right down to 1855, look for any cleansing of their streets.

The outlying parishes beyond the limits of the Bills of Mortality had even less organised provision for cleansing their streets than the City of London and the parishes of Westminster. In the first half of the eighteenth century such incipient urban districts as Kensington, Marylebone, and Bethnal Green had no other organisation for the management of their streets than that of a rural parish. Except where a road was under a Turnpike Trust, it was left to the direction of the unpaid Surveyor of High-

---

[1] A Letter to Mr. John Spranger, by Jonas Hanway, 1754, p. 37.
[2] Observations on the Past Growth and Present State of the City of London, by Corbyn Morris, 1752, p. 24.

ways, using the Statute Labour of the inhabitants. Occasionally, as we infer, there would arise a voluntary combination to get the household refuse removed. " Though there be no scavenging," we are told of Marylebone in 1756 (which had then about 5000 inhabitants in 577 houses), " yet the person that carries away the ashes receives by a voluntary contribution about £50 per annum." [1] Gradually, as we have already seen, the various districts of the Metropolis outside the City obtained Local Acts —sometimes applying to whole parishes, sometimes only to particular squares, or the streets on a particular landowner's estate—giving new powers of government, either to the Vestries or to special bodies of Trustees or Commissioners ; and in the matter of cleansing, in particular, extending to these areas practically the same legal machinery as that prevailing in the City of London—expressly enforcing, on the one hand, the obligation of the householder to cleanse the footway in front of his tenement ; [2] and in the other, enabling the Vestry or other body to appoint or contract with one or more "rakers or cleansers" to sweep the carriage-ways and remove both dirt and household refuse, by carts perambulating the streets, with " bell, horn or clapper, or otherwise by a loud noise or cry," giving notice to the householders " to bring forth to the doors of their respective houses their soil, ashes, rubbish, dirt, dust and filth." [3]

Under this system powerful Vestries like Marylebone managed to clear their streets of the heaps of dung and refuse, and to keep the footways in a tolerable state for pedestrians. But among the couple of hundred separate authorities [4] to whom the cleansing of the Metropolitan streets was entrusted, there existed, it is clear, every variety of neglect and incompetence. In the

[1] *History of London*, by W. Maitland, 1756, vol. ii. p. 1373.
[2] Thus, by one of the earliest of the parochial Local Acts in the Metropolitan area, the inhabitants of Bethnal Green were, in 1750, expressly required to sweep and cleanse the pavement in front of their tenements every Tuesday and Friday, between the hours of 7 and 10 in the morning or 2 and 5 in the afternoon, under penalty of five shillings fine (24 George I. c. 26 ; Bethnal Green Cleansing, Lighting and Watching Act, 1750). The inhabitants of New Gravel Lane and Shadwell were required to sweep and clean the footpaths every morning (15 George III. c. 54 ; New Gravel Lane and Shadwell Act, 1774).
[3] 15 George III. c. 15 ; St. George's in the East Poor, etc., Act, 1774.
[4] Including (a) the Commissioners of Sewers and the 25 Ward Motes and Ward Councils of the City of London, (b) the Open or Select Vestries of the three or four score parishes outside the City, (c) the four or five score of Paving Boards (already described by us as Improvement Commissioners) established by Local Acts, and (d) a score or two of separate Turnpike Trusts.

manuscript minutes of these Vestries or Commissioners during the ensuing three-quarters of a century, we watch their continual difficulties over this service—the inveterate neglect of the householders to perform their share of the duty of cleansing and the complete failure of the public authority to enforce this obligation, the careless and unscientific agreements made with the new race of contractors who came forward as Scavengers and Rakers, the constant failure of these to carry out their contracts with any strictness, and the perpetual conflict in the minds of the Vestrymen between the desirability of clean streets on the one hand and the pecuniary saving to the parish on the other, of accepting the very lowest tender at which they could get some one to agree to make any pretence at performance of the loosely defined service. The general standard of cleanliness remained scandalously low, even in the most important thoroughfares. Between 1798 and 1801, for instance, when the Paving Committee of St. Margaret and St. John, Westminster, insisted on retaining a certain Scavenger who took the contract cheaper than any other, the complaints of the inhabitants at his neglect to discharge his duties are loud and incessant, culminating, perhaps, in April 1799, in the following petition from the combined householders of Parliament Street, at the very entrance of the House of Commons. " The inhabitants of the said street would be obliged to the Committee to give orders to the Scavenger to immediately cleanse the said street, and in future to attend thereto, it having been most shamefully neglected, and was become one of the filthiest streets in London ; *that it had not been cleaned all over since 8 Nov. last*, except the kennels cleared, and the mud then left in such heaps as to be a greater nuisance than could be submitted to." Even the requirements of the local authorities were amazingly small. Thus, the Hans Town (Chelsea) Street Commissioners only required " the upper end of Sloane Street . . . to be cleansed at least eight times, Sloane Street and the several other streets and places . . . at least six times within the year " ; and to remove the dust and ashes of the householders only when specifically required to do so.[1] If this was the state of things in such thoroughfares as Parliament Street and Sloane Street, it may be imagined how utterly neglected and filthy remained the minor streets, lanes, courts and alleys in which

[1] See advertisement in *Morning Advertiser*, 25th February 1806.

the vast majority of Londoners resided. "The dust in dry weather," writes a very sober critic in 1824, " is greatly annoying and highly injurious to goods and furniture, to say nothing of personal feeling and annoyance in having the eyes blinded and the mouth choked therewith. And no sooner is there a wet day than the streets become ponds of mud. By the time the accumulation is almost intolerable, the Scavenger commences the annoyance of sweeping and scraping it into his carts, and splashing and bespattering every passer-by not prudent enough to cross out of his way, and content to be covered over the ankles with mud rather than over neck and ears." [1]

The story of street cleansing in the English provincial towns has been even less carefully recorded than that in the Metropolis, but such information as we possess indicates that the various towns went through much the same development as that we have described, marked by a diversity in the dates of the several stages at least equal to that shown by the different districts of the Metropolis, but exhibiting always the same gradual transformation of the householder's individual obligation into a collective service. Thus in the small Municipal Corporations of Louth and Rochester in the seventeenth century, as in that of Coventry in the fifteenth century, we find the individual householder expressly obliged by municipal byelaw, enforced by substantial fines, not merely to sweep the whole width of the street and clear out the kennels every week, but also " to carry the dirt away before twelve of the clock at night." [2]   A further stage had

---

[1] *Observations on the Defective State of the Pavement of the Metropolis*, by William Deykes, 1824, p. 8. Street cleansing was not omitted from Michael Angelo Taylor's Act of 1817, which contained clauses giving to all paving authorities within the Metropolis, irrespective of their Local Acts, power to cleanse the streets, to contract with " scavengers, rakers or cleansers," to appoint inspectors of street cleansing, and to dispose of the refuse. The contractors were required under penalty to take their carts through every street, and to give notice to the inhabitants in every narrow passage ; to accept and remove all soil, ashes, cinders, rubbish, dust, dirt and filth without charge to the inhabitants ; and to accept and remove at the householder's cost all building rubbish, and all earth, soil or rubbish produced by cleansing or repairing sewers or drains. But the Act made no change in the organisation.

[2] The Corporation of Coventry, in 1419 and 1423, ordered every householder, not only to repair but also to cleanse the pavement in front of his tenement (*History of Coventry*, by B. Poole, 1870, p. 343). The " Burrough Lawes " of 1640 of Louth in Lincolnshire include the following clause : " Item, it is ordered that every person or persons farming, using or occupying any houses or grounds adjoining to any street or common way within the said town shall weekly upon Saturday cause the cawsey or pavement of the said street or

been reached, already in mediaeval times, by such towns as Southampton, which had supplemented the exertions of the individual citizens in sweeping the streets, by the appointment of one or more public scavengers, paid either by the several householders or out of corporate funds, to carry away the ashes and refuse.[1] Outside the range of the byelaws of Municipal Corporations, we do not find that any provision was made for street cleansing prior to the eighteenth century. In 1716 one of the innumerable Highway Acts empowered Justices of the Peace in Quarter Sessions " in cities and market towns, not having already particular provision made for them therein by any former law," to appoint one or more scavengers for cleansing the streets, to give directions for their repair, and to authorise a sixpenny rate for these purposes.[2] Whether this Act was intended to apply to any but towns having their own Courts of Quarter Sessions is not clear ; but in the County records of West Kent and Suffolk we come across isolated instances of the power being exercised by the County Justices, for the benefit of such unincorporated market towns as East Greenwich, Hadleigh and Bungay,[3] and there may well have been others. It was probably

common way against his, her or their house, houses or ground to be well and sufficiently swept and made clean, and the filth and dung carried away, upon pain of every one offending for each offence sixpence " (*Louth Old Corporation Records*, by R. W. Goulding, 1891, p. 30). The Byelaws of Rochester, in Kent, as codified in 1673, require that " the inhabitants, as well within the high streets of the city as in the lanes and passages, shall every Saturday in the afternoon and at any other time when required by the Mayor or his Deputy, or by his order, clean the pavement before their houses, and the kennels thereunto adjoining, and carry the dirt away, before twelve of the clock at night. Twelve pence forfeit " (*An Authentic Copy of the Charter and Byelaws of the City of Rochester*, 1809, p. 35).

[1] By ancient custom at Southampton (Hampshire) every householder paid " scavage money," a fixed due collected in each ward by two persons chosen at the Court Leet, who also directed the Town Scavengers in their work (*History of Southampton*, by J. S. Davies, 1883, p. 124). There was also appointed in 1654 by the Court Leet a Town Chimney-sweep, bound and entitled to sweep all chimneys at fourpence each, but also paid a penny a year by each householder " as is used in many other cities and towns, called by the name of a Smoke Penny " (Court Leet Minutes of 1654 ; *ibid.*).

[2] 1 George I. c. 52. (The first session of George I. lasted from 1st August 1714 to 26th June 1716, and this was one of its latest statutes.) An error in drafting was corrected by 9 George II. c. 18 (1735). Exactly similar powers were granted to the justices of the municipal borough of Beverley " at their general Quarter Sessions," by the Local Act, 13 George I. c. 4 (the Beverley Beck Act, 1726).

[3] Thus we have found an order of the West Kent Quarter Sessions of 1738, reciting a petition from the inhabitants of East Greenwich ; appointing, ex-

in connection with an appointment under this Act that the energetic Vestry of Woolwich in 1717, having lately paved the streets at considerable expense, ordered " the present Scavenger and the Scavenger for the time being . . . twice every week throughout the whole year . . . (to) go through the said town and streets thereof with horse and cart," in order to receive " all the sand and ashes " " brought out of their houses by the inhabitants for this purpose." [1]

We suspect, however, that any collective organisation for cleansing the streets and disposing of household refuse remained quite exceptional, either in the ancient corporate towns or in the growing villages, until the passing, for one place after another, of those Local Acts to which we have so often had to refer, and which became so prominent a feature of the latter half of the eighteenth century. The cleansing clauses of these Acts obtained by provincial towns do not essentially differ from those granted to the Metropolitan authorities. They show the same three stages of development—the enforcement of the householder's obligation to " scrape, sweep and cleanse " the pavement and individually remove the dirt and refuse ; [2] the appointment of

pressly in pursuance of the statutes of 1716 and 1735, a local brewer and a local publican, " to be Scavengers for cleansing and repairing all the streets within the said town," for a year ; and making a rate of three half pence in the pound on all owners of houses, etc., to be collected by three named shopkeepers who are to account to any two Justices (MS. Order, 4th October 1738, in county archives, Kent Quarter Sessions). In the Minutes of the Suffolk Quarter Sessions we find other cases. In 1765 " this Court doth nominate and appoint R. F. and R. P. of Hadleigh to be Scavengers of the said Parish of Hadleigh for the year ensuing, and doth direct them from time to time to remove the dirt and filth out of the streets, and to sell or otherwise dispose of the same as to them shall seem meet " (MS. Minutes Quarter Sessions, Suffolk, 21st January 1765). So, in 1767, " this Court doth empower the Scavengers of the Divisions of Bungay, Boyscot and Bungay-Burgh, in the town of Bungay, to make a rate of 6d. in the pound for . . . repairing and cleansing the streets " (*ibid.* 27th April 1767).

[1] MS. Vestry Minutes, Woolwich, 25th October 1717.

[2] When, in the course of the eighteenth century, town after town obtained statutory powers of enforcing the householder's customary obligation to cleanse the pavement, this was (differing from the City of London) defined as extending to the middle of the street, and often also as to frequency. Thus at Beverley (East Riding of Yorkshire), where the need for keeping clear the creek or haven of the town had led, as early as 1726, to a Local Act, the obligation on the householders to " clean so much of the . . . streets, lanes and public places . . . as lie contiguous to and fronting their respective houses . . . between the same and the middle of the streets," had been, by that statute, still left resting only on " the ancient usage and custom of the said town," and it was found impossible to get the work satisfactorily done. Hence, in 1745, the

public " rakers, scavengers or cleansers " to carry away the dirt and refuse which had been " conveniently heaped " for them by the householders ; and the final limitation of the householder's obligation to sweep only the footway.[1] In the administration of these clauses by the provincial towns we find exactly the same features as in the Metropolis—the same practical inability to enforce the performance of his duty to the individual householder,[2] consequently the same unswept streets and uncleared

---

justices of the peace for the borough obtained power in a new Act (18 George II. c. 13) to require the inhabitants, by summons of the public bellman, to cleanse their streets down to the central denter stone, under penalty of having the work done at the defaulter's expense. When the neighbouring borough of Hull, ten years later, found it necessary to enforce by Act the householder's paving obligation, a similar clause to that of Beverley as to cleansing was also enacted (28 George II. c. 27, sec. 20, of Hull Paving Act, 1755). Subsequently Local Streets Acts for different towns enacted a similar obligation to cleanse the pavement with various degrees of particularity. At Nottingham in 1762, by a Lighting Act copied by Coventry, the obligation to cleanse down to the central gutter was definitely imposed, but the frequency left undefined (*History of Coventry*, by B. Poole, 1870, pp. 343-345). By the Manchester and Salford Act of 1765 every frontager was to sweep down to the middle of the street twice a week (5 George III. c. 81 ; see the contemporary print, *An Act for Cleansing and Lighting . . . Manchester and Salford, etc.*, 1765). Birmingham was content to make the duty a weekly one, to be performed every Friday (9 George III. c. 83, Birmingham Lighting, etc., Act, 1769 ; *History of Birmingham*, by William Hutton). At Plymouth, too, the duty was a weekly one, to be discharged every Friday, between six and two o'clock (10 George III. c. 14, Plymouth Paving, Lighting and Watching Act, 1770). At Wakefield the day appointed was Saturday, at any time between 6 A.M. and 6 P.M. (11 George III. c. 44, Wakefield Paving and Cleansing Act, 1771).

[1] 21 George III. c. 36, Devizes Streets Act, 1780, requires persons " to sweep, scrape and cleanse the footways before their respective houses . . . not less than eight feet from the same," on Wednesday and Saturday in every week. At Pontefract in 1810 the obligation was daily to sweep the foot pavements and also the gutter or channel of the carriage-way (50 George III. c. 40, Pontefract Streets Act, 1810). At Bishopwearmouth, Sunderland and many other places, the foot pavement only was mentioned, and the cleaning is to take place three times a week (50 George III. c. 25, Bishop Wearmouth Streets Act, 1810 ; *ibid.* c. 27, Sunderland Streets Act, 1810). Hastings, in 1820, required the occupier to sweep the footpath or pavement, and to collect together the soil and dirt therefrom, so as not to obstruct either the carriage- or footways, or the channels or water courses, in order that the same may be removed by the public scavenger (1 George IV. c. 12, Hastings Streets Act, 1820). The Leeds Commissioners in 1838 order the occupiers to sweep the causeways or foot pavements daily before 9 A.M. (MS. Minutes, Improvement Commissioners, Leeds, 5th December 1838).

[2] It is the rarest thing to find any mention of householders being actually proceeded against for neglect to sweep the pavement. " Last week at Manchester," says a Bristol journal of 1786, " seventy persons were fined, and paid the penalty of five shillings each, for neglecting to have the streets swept daily before their houses, agreeably to an Act of Parliament. As our magistrates (at Bristol) are about preparing a bill for regulating the police of this

kennels, the same interminable series of difficulties with the contracting rakers or cleansers, and the same resulting condition of disorder and neglect. The disastrous division of responsibility between the householder and the raker—the separation of the task of sweeping up from that of carrying away—led everywhere to the continuous presence of the " heaps of dirt " which seemed to contemporaries an inevitable incident of the street. Sometimes the rakers, who were now often known as public scavengers, had to collect twice a week, sometimes once a week, and sometimes only when required to do so by the local authority. But the heaps remained a constant feature of the street long after the duty of sweeping up the carriage-way had been united with that of carrying away the dirt and refuse.[1] Thus at Liverpool in 1797, where a contemporary critic admits that the carriage-ways were " generally well cleansed " by the Town Scavengers, " who are regular and diligent in their duty, but in the execution of their business while they remove one evil they never fail to create a greater ; the soil, instead of being immediately carried away as in London and other places, is raked into heaps about twelve feet by eight, and two feet deep. These cloacinian repositories are common in every part of the town, and remain eight or ten days, and sometimes longer, before they are carted away, whereby passengers in a dark night, and often in the day, tread in them to the midleg, and children are sometimes nearly suffocated by falling into them." [2] Thirty years later the same

---

city, a correspondent submits it to their consideration whether the insertion of a clause in it, for enforcing so wholesome and decent a practice, is not highly necessary " (*Bristol Gazette*, 9th November 1786). Three years later the same journal vainly calls on the Justices to enforce the new Local Act in this respect. " Were the magistrates to levy the fine a few times in the winter months, it would awaken the attention of some of the inhabitants " (*ibid.* 3rd December 1789). At Liverpool in 1797, in spite of repeated Local Acts, it was observed that " the footpaths are generally very dirty, the pebbles gathering mud in their interstices, and as the custom is not general of sweeping daily before the houses, it soon becomes a clammy dirt, which adheres to the feet of the passenger and is carried into the public shops " (*General Description of the History of Liverpool*, 1797, p. 274).

[1] At Plymouth power was given in 1772 to compound with the individual frontagers for their obligation to cleanse the pavements (12 George III. c. 8, Plymouth Paving Act, 1771). So at Wakefield it was provided in 1770 that the Street Commissioners might compound " for the sweeping and cleansing to be done by such inhabitants . . . provided such composition money be always paid down in advance " (11 George III. c. 44, Wakefield Streets Act, 1770).

[2] *General Description of the History of Liverpool*, 1797, p. 274 ; see *Memorials of Liverpool*, by Sir J. A. Picton, 1875, vol. i. pp. 275-276.

practice still prevailed. The Scavengers, complains a correspondent in 1828, rake up the mud " into the channels in great
quantities," where they leave it for several days, " whereby the
water courses are completely stopped up, and several respectable
persons have, during the last week, been almost up to their
knees, especially in the night time." [1] But Liverpool was, in
respect of cleansing its streets, not worse than other towns.
Here is a glimpse of Chester in 1825. " For weeks past not a
besom has been employed in this populous thoroughfare till
Friday last, and then, forsooth, an old invalided man and a
solitary female were employed on that long line of road. Nor
is this all. From Friday to yesterday the accumulated heaps of
mud . . . were suffered to remain without being carted away,
to the serious annoyance of neighbours and passengers." [2] We
conclude this vision of the heaps of dirt and filth by the following
satirical complaint to the *Manchester Times* of 1828. " I shall
be glad to be informed . . . what course I must pursue to find
a firkin of butter which my carter says fell off his cart between
Nos. 2 and 24 in Neverswept Street, Manchester. He says he
saw it drop on the sludge, but being obliged by the law to
attend to his team on the one hand, and being afraid that, if
he stopped, his cart would run a risk of sinking in the mire
on the other, he drove to the end of the street, and, on his
return, found to his great grief that the firkin had sunk to
rise no more ! " [3]

This account of practical failures in street cleansing must not,
however, be allowed to obscure the fact that, alike in the Metro-

---

[1] *Liverpool Mercury*, 15th February 1828. These contemporary records
bear out Picton's subsequent reminiscences of Liverpool during the first quarter
of the nineteenth century. "There were Scavengers to clean the streets. The
way in which they worked was to sweep the mud into long parallelograms here
and there, about a foot deep, which were left for days until carts could be got
to fetch it away. These heaps were called Corporation beds, from the notion
that they were sometimes used as places of repose by the guests returning
from the Corporation feasts " (*Sir J. A. Picton*, by J. Allanson Picton, 1891,
p. 19). Nor did things improve. In 1835 the local newspaper denounces " the
filthy state of the streets in almost every quarter of the town," which are
declared to be " in a far more filthy and dirty state this winter " than ever
within living memory. " Why," asks a correspondent, " are we charged for
Scavengers ? They do little or nothing, and have sinecures. Sometimes you
see a great number in one spot near the docks, in each other's way, idle and
staring about them " (*Liverpool Mercury*, 6th February 1835).

[2] *Chester Courant*, 15th March 1825.

[3] Quoted in *Liverpool Mercury*, 26th December 1828.

polis and in the larger provincial towns, the first thirty years of the nineteenth century witnessed a notable advance in the freedom from obstructive filth of the principal thoroughfares. This advance was due, in part, to the rise to power, in the representative Vestries and in the new bodies of Improvement Commissioners, of the well-to-do shopkeeping and manufacturing class, permanently residing in the towns, and constantly traversing the streets on foot. It was brought about largely by the elaboration of a detailed municipal code for the Suppression of Nuisances, which we shall describe in another volume. But part of the progress was the result of more extensive and more efficient municipal enterprise in the direction of scavenging. To this increased activity there contributed two adventitious contemporary circumstances—the growing demand for and increased value of ashes and manure between about 1790 and 1830, and the desire to find some employment for the multitude of paupers which the Old Poor Law in these years was producing.

Until the last quarter of the eighteenth century, both the practice of manuring land and the value of animal excreta for this purpose appear to have been practically unknown to many, and perhaps to the majority of English farmers. Arthur Young, in his tours, between 1767 and 1780, records his amazement at the neglect of farmers in all parts of the country to take advantage of opportunities already known to every agricultural expert. " There is no town in the kingdom of any size," he exclaims with eager enthusiasm, " but what yields a considerable quantity of manure annually—ashes of wood and coal, horse-dung, the cleaning of streets, the riddance of privies, poultry and hog dung, shambles offal, foot and a variety of other manures." [1] Yet this was nearly everywhere going to waste. At Lynn, in Norfolk, for instance, within easy reach of the Holkham experiments, he saw the town dung, in 1767, simply piled in a heap on the seashore.[2] Similar heaps were to be seen in the neighbourhood of the Metropolis and of other large towns. But at some

[1] *A Six Weeks' Tour through the Southern Counties*, by Arthur Young, 3rd edition, 1772, p. 293.

[2] " At one place, which is called the Fort, is a heap of exceeding rich manure "—the accumulated human excreta of the town—" which suffers no other decrease than what high spring tides occasion in washing part of it away ; and it is all brought here in carts at the expense of the inhabitants " (*ibid.* pp. 32, 292).

date between 1750 and 1780, according to local knowledge and local circumstances, the value of town manure began, in one place after another, rapidly to rise. Already in 1770, the facilities for water-carriage and the enterprise of a local innovator had made the excreta of Hull into a valuable property. " All sorts of manure," says Arthur Young, " are bought at high prices at Hull, and carried nine or ten miles round. . . . About fifty years ago the manuring from Hull was begun by a poor man who hired a close of grass ; he had four asses which he employed constantly in carrying away ashes and dung, and spreading them upon his pasture . . . whoever brought away manure, for many years were paid for taking it. Twenty-five years ago it was to be had for sixpence to a shilling a load ; by the country around by degrees all coming into the practice, the price has arose to its present height ; extraordinary good stuff will sell for five shillings a load." [1] " Formerly, not half a century ago," writes Marshall in 1799, of the Metropolis, " inns and livery stables paid the farmers, who brought them in hay and straw, for taking away their dung, or hired carts to carry it away to the outskirts of the town ; where large mounds of it remained but a few years ago. Twenty years ago the price in the stable yards was only a shilling to eighteen pence a load ; and even at this time, I understand no more than two shillings or half a crown is given for a full cart load of horse dung produced from hay and corn of the first quality." [2] At a somewhat later date other kinds of town refuse acquired an exchange value. Means were found to utilise the waste products of various manufacturing industries, and these soon ceased, accordingly, to augment the town's rubbish heaps. But the most important of these changes was the enormous extension of brickmaking, especially in the neighbourhood of London, and the discovery that coal-ashes, cinders, and generally town " dust " were valuable ingredients to mix with the clay. The huge " dust heaps " accumulated by the contractors all round the Metropolis became possessions of great value, for which, it is said, the demand was suddenly increased in 1814–1815 by their being eagerly bought up for shipment to

[1] *A Six Months' Tour through the North of England*, by Arthur Young, 2nd edition, 1770, vol. i. p. 163.
[2] *Minutes, Experiments, Observations and General Remarks on Agriculture in the Southern Counties*, by W. Marshall (edition of 1799, p. 31).

Russia, where the rebuilding of Moscow was calling for more bricks than that whole country could then supply. Thus it was that towards the end of the eighteenth century the pecuniary value of town refuse came to exceed the cost of its collection and removal, and it looked as if the service of scavenging, taken as a whole, was destined to become actually a source of municipal revenue. In 1798 and 1799, when the Paving Committee of St. Margaret and St. John, Westminster, advertised for tenders for cleansing the streets and removing the refuse of that parish, the lowest tenderers demanded £135 and £150 respectively for doing the work. But in 1800 one contractor agreed to pay the Committee £40 ; in 1801 another gave £150, and in 1808 another as much as £265 for the privilege.[1] It was held up in 1796 as an example to Bath, which still paid for the cleaning of its streets, that the well-administered parish of Marylebone was already drawing no less than £1050 a year from the scavenging contractors, who willingly paid this sum for the privilege of sweeping the streets and collecting the street sweepings and household ashes.[2] So keen, indeed, was the competition for household refuse in London that Marylebone in 1803 got as much as £2350 from its dust contractor, who undertook to send his carts round all the streets, either weekly, fortnightly, or monthly, according to specification, to keep clean all the footways and carriage-ways, and even to prevent snow or ice from blocking the drains.[3] In the little town of Bradford, in Yorkshire, which had got a body of Commissioners in 1803, the disposal of the privilege of gathering up the muck led at once to petty jobbery, the new Commissioners tumbling over each other in their eagerness to make a little profit out of the body to which they belonged. One, we are told, offered " to sweep . . . for the manure " ; only to be promptly outbid by two of his colleagues, " who agreed to sweep . . . twice a week . . . and pay the Commissioners thirty-six shillings per annum for the privilege." [4] In London the united parishes of St. Andrew, Holborn, and St. George the Martyr were

---

[1] MS. Minutes, Paving Committee, Vestry of St. Margaret and St. John, Westminster, 6th September 1798, 6th June 1799, 6th August 1800, 4th August 1801, 24th May 1808.

[2] Letter in *Gazetteer*, 4th March 1796.

[3] MS. Vestry Minutes, Marylebone, 1st March 1800, 19th February 1803.

[4] *Historical Notes on the Bradford Corporation*, by William Cudworth, 1881, p. 50.

getting £780 in 1808 ; whilst even the little Liberty of Saffron Hill made £250.[1] From the " street muck," it was natural to proceed to the household excreta ; and Local Authorities sought, by Local Acts, to vest in themselves the ownership of all the excreta and refuse of the town, in order that they might sell it for a high price. At Brighton, for instance, the Commissioners " let the town soil " to contractors, together with the ashes, for £350, and presently for £560 a year.[2]

We need not follow the fortunes of the Local Authorities in their several dealings with the new race of dust contractors. The greatest diversity, it is clear, prevailed in the terms obtained between place and place and even from year to year.[3] Presently, from economic changes which we cannot here investigate, the market value of town refuse fell as rapidly, and with as much diversity between place and place, as it had risen. The removal of human excreta first became unprofitable, then the sweeping up of the " street muck," and ultimately also the emptying of dust bins. Already before 1835 we see the tide turning. The Paving Committee of St. Margaret and St. John, Westminster, which had in 1825 received as much as £625 from its contractors, had, in 1831, to pay £150 for the same service.[4] The Vestry of Marylebone, which in 1803 was receiving £2350 a year out of its scavenging, taken as a whole, was in 1830 paying its contractors £2870 a year for " slopping "—that is, cleaning the streets— and only receiving from them £1170 for the privilege of collecting the " breeze," or household dust and ashes.[5] In 1842 the Poor

---

[1] MS. Minutes, Westminster Paving Commissioners, 24th May 1808.

[2] MS. Minutes, Improvement Commissioners, Brighton, 1820–1825. In 1798 we see the Town Council of Plymouth ordering " that the dung and soil of the town be advertised to be let from Ladyday next on the present tenant giving up his take in writing " (MS. Minutes, Town Council, Plymouth, 9th March 1799).

[3] Details are nearly always lacking, but the pecuniary value of the contracts must have varied enormously according to (a) the extent of the street sweeping and other laborious work that was stipulated for ; (b) the strictness with which the conditions were enforced ; (c) whether the contractor obtained " street muck," household ashes and " dust," or the emptyings of stables and privies, or only some of these classes of refuse, and in what proportions ; (d) the local facilities for water carriage or other circumstances affecting the cost of distribution ; (e) the local demand for the various kinds of refuse ; and, finally, (f) the administrative capacity of the Local Authority in obtaining the best possible terms and defeating the rings and " knock-outs."

[4] MS. Minutes, Paving Committee, St. Margaret and St. John, Westminster, 15th March 1825, December 1831.

[5] MS. Vestry Minutes, Marylebone, 27th February 1830.

Law Commissioners report, with regard to the Metropolis, that " with the exception of coal ashes (which are indispensable for making bricks), some descriptions of lees (from the soap-boilers), and a few other inconsiderable exceptions, no refuse in London pays half the expense of removal by cartage. . . . A considerable contractor for scavenging, etc., . . . states, with regard to the most productive manure, ' I have given away thousands of loads of night-soil; we knew not what to do with it.' " [1] The dust and ashes of the London households, though still retaining some exchange value, ceased about the same time to yield as much as would pay for the service of sweeping the streets and removing the street muck, with which the emptying of dustbins was usually combined.[2] From about 1840, therefore, the

[1] *General Report of the Poor Law Commissioners on the Sanitary Condition of the Labouring Population*, 1842, p. 46. " The great difficulty of the cleansing of the Metropolis arises from the want of proper receptacles for the filth. There is no filth in the Metropolis now that, as a general rule, will pay the expense of collection and removal by cart, except the ashes from the houses and the soaplees from the soap-boilers, and some of the night soil from the East End of the town where there happen to be in the immediate vicinity some market gardens where it can be used at once without distant or expensive carriage. The charge of removing night-soil from the poorest tenements may be about £1 per tenement—one house with another the expense may be said to be in London about 10s. per year, as the cesspools may be emptied once in two years. One house with another they will not produce more than a load of refuse from the cesspools. . . . I have given away thousands of loads of night-soil ; as we have no means of disposing of it. We know not what to do with it. . . . The sweepings from the macadamized roads consist of so much of granite that it is of very little use indeed " (Evidence of a great dust contractor ; in *General Report of the Poor Law Commissioners on the Sanitary Condition of the Labouring Population*, 1842, pp. 379-380).

[2] We place here an interesting account of the annual proceeds of the ashes, dust, breeze, etc., of Camberwell from 1815 to 1845, put up for sale by auction :

1815	.	. £68	1826	.	. £200	1837	.	. £127
1816	.	. 67	1827	.	. 245	1838	.	. 79
1817	.	. 62	1828	.	. 62	1839	.	. 217
1818	.	. 125	1829	.	. 83	1840	.	. 516
1819	.	. 180	1830	.	. 15	1841	.	. 137
1820	.	. 280	1831	.	. 15	1842	.	. 215
1821	.	. 148	1832	.	. No bidders	1843	.	. 275
1822	.	. 320	1833	.	. No sale	1844	.	. 378
1823	.	. 520	1834	.	. £70	1845	.	. 410
1824	.	. 471	1835	.	. 207			
1825	.	. 437	1836	.	. 90			

(*Ye History of Camberwell*, by W. H. Blanch, p. 164.) The effect of the depression in the building trade in South London, which followed on the panic of 1825, is very marked.

Z

service of scavenging gradually became once more a source of municipal expense, as it had been half a century before.[1]

This remarkable rise in the market value of town refuse, temporary though it proved to be, naturally reacted on the organisation for its removal from the houses and streets. The Rakers or contractors, we may believe, were more diligent in their collection, as the material became of pecuniary value. Vestrymen and Commissioners were more willing to see the service of scavenging expand—to make it co-extensive with the town, with more frequent collections—when this did not involve any additional burden on the rates. So far the economic revolution may be presumed to have promoted the greater cleanliness of the town. But there were, from the point of view of public health, grave drawbacks. When filth became of pecuniary value, householders were not so willing to have it removed, and preferred to let it accumulate, in order to dispose of it to greater advantage. Already in 1767 the inhabitants of Portsmouth had objected to a proposal of the new Local Act, which would have given the Commissioners the right to collect from them all their " cinders, ashes, dirt, soil or rubbish," and a proviso had been inserted allowing them to " keep or use " this valuable material within their own gardens or yards.[2] But those inhabitants who had not gardens or yards, where they could use their refuse, did not see why they should not make money out of it, so an amending Act of 1775 permitted any inhabitant of Portsmouth to sell or dispose of his refuse if he chose.[3] The householder's property in his refuse was further protected by its being made a punishable offence for any one, other than the parish officer or contractor, to take away the dust or ashes from any house, unless with the owner's consent.[4] In other places, where the Local Authorities made profitable contracts for the disposal of the dust and filth, it became necessary to protect

---

[1] We think the Poor Law Commissioners took too optimistic a view in 1842, when they reported that the receipts from dust equalled the cost of street cleaning : " At the rate of expense of one large parish, the present cost of cleansing in the Metropolis may be estimated at about £40,000 per annum. This expense, however, is generally repaid by the sale of the coal ashes, which are used in the manufacture of bricks " (*General Report of the Poor Law Commissioners on the Sanitary Condition of the Labouring Population*, 1842, p. 53).

[2] 8 George III. c. 59, Portsmouth Lighting and Watching Act of 1767.

[3] 16 George III. c. 59, Portsmouth Lighting and Watching Act of 1775.

[4] 13 George III. c. 48, Marylebone Watching, Paving and Lighting Act of 1772.

the contractor in his bargain by giving him a monopoly.[1] All this saving and storing of excreta, and the wholesale and retail dealing in it that went on, led, it is clear, to very unsavoury practices, which continued right down to the end of the period with which we are dealing. " In the parts of some towns," we read in 1840, " adjacent to the rural districts the cesspools are emptied gratuitously for the sake of the manure ; but they only do this when there is a considerable accumulation. . . . For the saving of cartage as well as the convenience of use, accumulations of refuse are frequently allowed to remain and decompose and dry amidst the habitations of the poorer classes." [2] At Witham, in Essex, we are told in 1842 that " a great number of the inhabitants accumulate filth and manure for the purpose of sale." [3] The most noisome accumulations continued in the towns, especially in the poorest and most crowded districts. At Leeds, for instance, it is difficult to say whether the contractor, or his neglects, created the greater sanitary nuisance. From one small court there was removed at the time of the cholera (1832) no less than 75 cart-loads of manure " which had been untouched for years." [4] Meanwhile " the contractor for the street sweepings . . . rented a plot of vacant land in the centre of the . . . largest ward in point of population . . . as a depot for the sweepings . . . both vegetable and general, for the purpose of exsiccation and accumulating till they could be sold as manure and carried away. . . . The inhabitants complained of . . . the insufferable stench." [5] It is, we think, impossible to avoid the

[1] Thus the Manchester Commissioners resolve in 1809, " That the practice of selling or otherwise disposing of any manure from the streets by the superintendent of the sweepers or any other person, except Samuel Foxcroft as the agent of the Commissioners, and except such as shall be expressly authorised by the Commissioners, is highly improper, and ought, if repeated, to be severely punished " (MS. Minutes, Improvement Commissioners, Manchester, 12th April 1809).
[2] *General Report of the Poor Law Commissioners on the Sanitary Condition of the Labouring Population of Great Britain*, 1842, p. 46.
[3] *Ibid.* p. 13. The fall in value led to still further evils : " The object of the nightmen is to get rid of the soil early, and return with the cart to complete the emptying in one night. Formerly, before the new police were so much about, the men would empty the cart in any bye-street or place where they could. . . . The site of the new London University (College) was a place in which the refuse was deposited, so was the site of the new row of grand houses in Hyde Park Gardens . . . the site of Belgrave Square was another place of deposit " (Evidence of a great dust contractor ; in *ibid.* p. 381).
[4] *Ibid.* p. 41.
[5] *Ibid.* p. 47. The climax of horrors was reached, we think, in some of the

conclusion that, whilst the temporary saleability of town refuse may have quickened the movement towards a complete scavenging system, the very notion of deriving profit from town refuse was, on the whole, inimical to sanitary progress. The organisation and methods for collection and disposal which yielded the greatest profit were not necessarily those most advantageous to the public health ; whilst the phantasm of getting a municipal revenue, or at any rate making the town refuse pay for its own removal, long prejudiced town administrators against incurring the expenditure necessary for this most efficient performance of this service.[1]

More useful to sanitation may have been the desire to find employment for the large numbers of able-bodied labourers who were, between 1795 and 1835, in receipt of Poor Law relief. This policy took two forms. In some parishes the local authority in charge of the streets itself directly employed the paupers, supervising their operations as it chose, and remunerating them as it thought fit. In others the Improvement Commissioners merely entered into contracts with the local Poor Law authority, under which the latter undertook to clean the streets for a lump sum. We shall deal elsewhere with the Poor Law aspect of this question, depending as it did upon such considerations as the amount of the pay given to the pauper and the conditions of his employment, whether the experiment served as a test of destitution or operated as a reformatory regimen. Regarded from the standpoint of street cleansing, the results are neither so conclusive nor so well recorded.

---

slums of the Scottish towns. "At Greenock in 1840," it is reported that "in one part of the street there is a dunghill—yet it is too large to be called a dunghill. I do not mistake its size when I say it contains a hundred cubic yards of impure filth collected from all parts of the town. It is never removed ; it is the stock-in-trade of a person who deals in dung ; he retails it by cartful. To please his customers, he always keeps a nucleus, as the older the filth is the higher the price." The Glasgow courts of 1840 contained spaces occupied entirely by dung-heaps. "There were," we are told, "no privies or drains there, and the dung-heaps received all filth which the swarm of wretched inhabitants could give." The reason was "that a considerable part of the rent of the houses was paid by the produce of the dung-heaps. . . . The dwellers of these courts had converted their shame into a kind of money by which their lodging was to be paid " (*General Report of the Poor Law Commissioners on the Sanitary Condition of the Labouring Population of Great Britain*, 1842, pp. 24, 47).

[1] The dust contractors were said in 1842 to be hostile to improved methods of removing refuse which would diminish its saleable value (*ibid.* p. 318).

In those cases in which the Commissioners merely put the cleansing of the streets out to contract with the local Poor Law authority, they seem to have made, if anything, a worse bargain than they did when they entrusted the work to a commercial contractor. Thus, the Bradford Commissioners, who entered into such a contract in 1805, quickly demurred to the charge made by the parish authorities, whilst the streets got into such a state that a local contemporary declared that they would " disgrace a Hottentot settlement." [1] The Brighton Commissioners, weary of the perpetual complaints of the neglect of the cleansing contractor, and alarmed at the rise in the Poor Rate, resolved in 1820 " to treat with the Directors and Guardians for the cleansing the streets by contract, as it would afford employment for the poor " ; and to pay them £300 a year.[2] Eighteen months later we see them, dissatisfied with the results, reverting to the ordinary contractor. And when in 1826 they again try the experiment of contracting with the Poor Law authority, paying £400 a year, a storm of complaints of the filthy state of the streets burst in upon the Commissioners. " No one street in the town," it was said, " has been properly cleansed for several months." [3] In 1832, when cholera was at hand, the Plymouth Town Council realised how badly the Incorporated Guardians were doing the work of removing the " town dung and soil," and the contract between the two bodies was promptly annulled.[4] The Leeds Commissioners, who were paying £500 a year for pauper labour, found in 1836 " that the present system of contracting with the Workhouse Board for the services of scavengers requires improvement ; and that the advantages resulting to the town under the existing arrangements are not in that respect such as ought reasonably to be expected from so large an expenditure out of the Improvement Rate." In 1838 they flatly refused a request for an increase in the charge which they were paying to the Workhouse Board for the men supplied for scavenging, " the men so sent being aged and infirm, and consequently

---

[1] *Historical Notes on the Bradford Corporation*, by William Cudworth, 1881, p. 50.

[2] MS. Minutes, Improvement Commissioners, Brighton, 28th April and 3rd May 1820.

[3] *Ibid.* 29th June, 8th September, 6th October 1824 ; 1st July 1825, 26th July 1826 ; *Brighton Herald*, 5th August 1826.

[4] MS. Minutes, Incorporated Guardians, Plymouth, 4th and 25th July 1832.

not able to do the work, and many others both lame and lazy, over whom the superintendent has no control." [1] The local newspaper gives us a vivid account of the " filthy state of the streets," the heaps of dirt " scraped to the side of the causeways in many of our streets and left there for days together," and the " large quantities of ashes and rubbish " suffered to remain on the pavements.[2]

When, however, the local authority in charge of the streets was either itself the Poor Law authority, or else itself employed the able-bodied paupers in street cleansing, the results seem to have been much more favourable. " We have found the system," says the Vestry Clerk of St. Paul, Covent Garden, in 1833, " of scavenging and watering the streets by means of pauper labour very useful ; it has kept many off our books. . . . Our parishioners say that the streets were never kept so clean as they have been since our new system prevailed ; the fact is that it is the interest of the contractor to employ as few labourers in the work as possible, to leave the streets until they are so dirty that large portions may be removed at once." [3] " The contractors," said another witness in 1833, " generally shuffle off cleansing the alleys as they cannot get the cart up them ; but we make our men take the wheelbarrow up the avenues. The paupers are by this system made spies to prevent any nuisance that may occasion them trouble. If they see any one throwing down filth they fetch the superintendent and the party is made to take it up again." [4] In the panic caused by the approach of cholera in 1831–1832, many local authorities all over the country found, in the temporary employment of paupers in removing nuisances of all kinds, a way of palliating, for the moment, the effect of the neglect of previous years. Thus, at Leeds, where a particular district of the town had been left utterly neglected, " when the cholera was prevalent (in 1832) the wretched state of this district occasioned great apprehension," and gangs of paupers were employed for two months " clearing away the

---

[1] MS. Minutes, Improvement Commissioners, Leeds, 6th April 1836, 19th February 1838.

[2] *Leeds Mercury*, 2nd March 1839.

[3] First Report of Poor Law Inquiry Commissioners, 1834, Appendix A, Part I. (Codd's Report) ; evidence of Vestry Clerk of St. Paul, Covent Garden.

[4] First Report of Poor Law Inquiry Commissioners, 1834, Appendix A, Part I.

immense mass of filth of every description which had accumulated." It was, in fact, as a primitive system of direct employment of labour, in substitution for contracting, that pauper
labour was most useful.[1] But the very lavishness with which
those street authorities, which were also Poor Law authorities,
could employ the incompetent and unsatisfactory labour of
paupers in street cleansing had a bad effect in deterring such
authorities from adopting mechanical or more highly organised
methods of accomplishing their task. " The parish officers,"
declared Chadwick in 1842, " frequently oppose improved modes
of paving and efficient cleansing (as they generally opposed the
new police on the ground that it diminished the means of subsistence of decrepit old men as watchmen) for the avowed reason
that it is expedient to keep the streets in their present state of
filth in order to keep up the means of employing indigent persons
as street sweepers and sweepers of crossings in removing it." [2]

What comes out most vividly from our survey is, however,
not this or that detail of the filthy condition of the town streets,
but the utter inability of the Local Authorities, even after the
cholera of 1832, to form any competent idea of the nature or
the magnitude of their task. It is not merely that the complicated modern problems of the harmless disposal of sewage
and the infinitely various methods of handling all the different
kinds of town garbage were as yet undreamt of. To a Local
Authority of 1835, urban cleansing was still closely bound up
with the mere convenience of passage along the streets. It was
for this that the streets were occasionally swept, and the heaps
of dirt removed. It was to prevent the otherwise inevitable
deposit in the thoroughfares that the dustbins or ashpits were

---

[1] That it was far less effective, and even more costly than would have been
the hiring of labour in the open market, we may well believe. But hardly any
town ventured, at this date, on such an extension of municipal enterprise as
would have been involved in the organisation of a street cleansing department.
At York, in 1825, we find the Commissioners timidly trying the experiment of
not " letting the sweeping " in the Micklegate Ward, and instructing their
Surveyor " to engage weekly such men as he may think necessary to sweep and
cleanse the streets . . . and to employ carts to convey the manure away as it
is collected by the sweepers ; also a yard or place to deposit it in, and to
report . . . the expenses incurred and the probable value of the manure
collected and to dispose of the same as opportunity offers " (MS. Minutes,
Improvement Commissioners, York, 28th August 1825).

[2] *General Report of the Poor Law Commissioners on the Sanitary Condition of
the Labouring Population*, 1842, p. 96.

emptied and the accumulations of excreta disposed of. Hence
it is that we find that whatever little improvement had been
brought about down to 1835 was confined almost entirely to
the main streets, in which the traffic was greatest, and to which
the principal inhabitants commonly resorted. It was for this
reason that, in every town, as in every district of the Metropolis,
the work of the public scavengers—inefficient at its best—was
restricted to sweeping the surface of the recognised public streets,
leaving wholly untouched all the " private streets," or those not
yet taken over by the Local Authority (which in towns like Manchester and Leeds included all the new workmen's quarters), and
all the narrow courts and alleys in which, alike in London and
the provincial towns, the majority of the poorer classes dwelt.[1]
The further extension of the municipal service of cleansing to
the backyards or inner courtyards of blocks of buildings was
unthought of—still less the enforcement of a healthy minimum
of cleanliness in the houses themselves. In short, it never
occurred, even to the most energetic and enlightened Local
Authority of 1835, that it had any responsibility for the freedom
from noxious filth of the town as a whole. Not for another
generation, and then not without the sharp lesson of repeated
visitations of Asiatic cholera, did even the beginnings of municipal sanitation permeate English local administration.

---

[1] The scavenging of Manchester in 1830 was "performed on those streets
which have been declared public highways, a necessary preliminary to which
is that they shall have been finished, with respect to sewering and paving, in a
manner satisfactory to the Surveyor. The number of private, unpaved and
consequently filthy streets is lamentably great in Manchester . . . the only
scavengers that enter them are dogs and swine, allowed to roam .at large ;
and they are useful in their way by consuming some of the offal which is indiscriminately cast in heaps before the doors . . . the offensive and disgraceful
exhibitions of accumulated filth which present themselves in every quarter "
(" Sketch of the Medical Topography and Statistics of Manchester," by Edmund
Lyon, M.D., in *North of England Medical and Surgical Journal*, August 1830,
p. 17).   In 1842 it was said that "The expense of cleansing the streets of the
township of Manchester is £5000 per annum.   For this sum the first class of
streets, namely the most opulent and the large thoroughfares, are cleansed
once a week, the second class once a fortnight and the third class once a month.
But this provision leaves untouched . . . the courts, alleys and places where
the poorest classes live, and where the cleansing should be daily " (*General
Report of the Poor Law Commissioners on the Sanitary Condition of the Labouring
Population*, 1842, p. 53).

The Passing of the Improvement Commissioners

It is remarkable that throughout the whole period with which we are dealing (1689–1835) we find, with respect to these Improvement Commissioners, practically no popular criticism or denunciation of their dominant type of constitution, the self-elected and self-renewing body, limited by substantial property qualifications. In the last decade of the period the " elective principle " was, as we have described, generally assumed to be desirable in any new constitution, but practically no accusation seems to have been made that the existing bodies of Improvement Commissioners were corrupt or inefficient. This popular acquiescence in the continuance of bodies largely controlled by ex-officio members—often, indeed, close bodies, in no way dependent on or responsible to the inhabitants at large—stands in contrast with the London outcry against the Select Vestries and the widespread provincial objection to the old Municipal Corporations. We attribute this acquiescence mainly to the fact that the Improvement Commissioners were comparatively new bodies, or at any rate bodies with constitutions recently reformed ; that they were composed of the principal inhabitants of the locality, generally without distinction of political party or religious denomination ; and that the rate which they levied was usually limited by the Act of Parliament, and was, in practice, uniform from year to year. To these reasons, for the lack of popular criticism, must be added the fact that, in most of the towns, the Improvement Commissioners refrained from obtruding themselves on the public attention by any great display of activity or any serious attempt to enforce even their own regulations. They lacked, in fact, not only the unlimited powers of the open Vestry, but also that administrative self-confidence which is enjoyed by a popularly elected body.

But although there was, even in 1820–1833, no general agitation against the Improvement Commissioners, there was, as we have seen, at Manchester and elsewhere, widespread criticism among Radicals and Reformers of the narrow basis of their constitution, the extent of their powers of regulation and expenditure and the absence of popular control. It was part of the intention of those who framed the Bill of 1835 for the reform of the Municipal Corporations that the newly formed Town Councils should take over all the powers and property of the various bodies established under Local Acts within the several boroughs. Unfortunately, in the haste with which the Bill was prepared, and under the influence of Lord Melbourne's desire to minimise the opposition to the measure which he had to get through both Houses of Parliament within a few weeks, the clause relating to the bodies of Commissioners were drafted in permissive terms. As enacted, it merely enabled the Commissioners voluntarily to merge themselves in the reformed Corporations. It was in vain that Francis Place pointed out that such a clause would inevitably prove quite inoperative. There was no time for a Parliamentary fight with three hundred bodies of Commissioners, which might all have claimed, like the Municipal Corporations, to be heard in defence of their statutory rights. The result was that the Municipal Corporations Act of 1835, like the General Highways Act of that year and the Poor Law Amendment Act of 1834, left untouched the Commissioners under Local Acts, whether for town improvements, turnpike roads or the administration of poor relief.

The position of the Improvement Commissioners in the Municipal Boroughs was, however, fatally undermined by the sweeping measure of 1835. When it was realised that the new Town Council, nominally charged with the " good government " of the whole borough, was elected for the same area as the Commissioners, on what was, in nearly all cases, a far more popular franchise, the movement in favour of the union of the two or more public authorities within the same borough came gradually to be irresistible. When the new Town Council set up its new police force, there was no longer any reason for the maintenance by the Commissioners of a separate Night Watch. There seemed no reason for making separate assessments and levying separate rates. Year by year, in one borough after another, the two bodies were induced to agree to an amalgamation, usually under the authority of the new Local Act which one or other consented to seek. The process was accelerated by the pressure of the Board of Health between 1848 and 1854. Whenever the Board made an order making the Public Health Act applicable to any town, it sought always to amalgamate the Improvement Commissioners with the Town Council. Whenever the Privy Council issued a charter of incorporation to a new borough the same merger was provided for. Within a quarter of a century of the passing of the Municipal Corporations Act, nearly all the bodies of Paving, Cleansing, Lighting, Watching, Street, Lamp, Police or Improvement Commissioners in the municipal boroughs to which the 1835 Act had applied, or in those newly incorporated under it, had merged in the Town Council,[1] to which they brought their own extensive statutory powers, in supplement of the meagre provisions of the Municipal Corporations Act. It was in this way, and not under the 1835 Act, that many provincial boroughs started their Public Health work ; that many more found themselves managing considerable departments of paving and cleansing the streets ; that the Manchester Town Council became (already in 1842) the greatest municipal purveyor of gas. It is, accordingly, the Improvement Commissioners, rather than the ancient chartered corporations, that we must regard as the immediate predecessors and lineal ancestors, not of the titles and dignities, but of most of the activities and statutory functions of the modern English municipality.

The hundred or so " Paving Boards " and other similar bodies in the Metropolitan Parishes outside the City of London, which we have included in the common designation of Improvement Commissioners, came to an end in a similar way. We find them all merged either in the reorganised Vestries or in the unions of parishes under District Boards, to which (in conjunction with the Metropolitan Board of Works) the municipal government of the area outside the City was confided by the Metropolis Management Act of 1855 ; to be transformed by the Local Government Act of 1888 and the London Government Act of 1899, respectively, into the London County Council and the Metropolitan Borough Councils.[2]

---

[1] Nevertheless, there were, in 1884, still 44 " Improvement Act districts," under bodies of Trustees or Commissioners ; and even in 1893, 31 such districts, outside municipal boroughs. (*An Outline of Local Government and Local Taxation*, by R. S. Wright and H. Hobhouse, second edition, 1884, p. 22, and third edition, 1906, p. 20.) They were then merged in the Urban District Councils created under the Public Health Acts and the Local Government Act, 1894.

[2] Leaving aside the analogous Harbour Commissioners, to which we have already referred, the most important body of the nature of what we have designated Improvement Commissioners that still existed in 1895 was the Commissioners of Sewers of the City of London, which was, from the outset, and has always continued to be, under Local Acts of 1667, 1671, 1691, 1708, 1737, 1744, 1761 and especially 1765, substantially nothing but a statutory

Viewed from the standpoint of to-day, we cannot rate very highly the actual achievements of the Improvement Commissioners themselves during the century or so of their operations. These three hundred or so separate authorities must, indeed, be criticised for the very reasons that shielded them from the denunciation of their contemporaries. The powers of municipal government which they sought from Parliament were inadequate to the task that lay before them ; and they usually came to the end of their borrowing powers, and found themselves levying their maximum rate, before they had done more than begin the " paving, cleansing, lighting, sewering, watching and generally improving " of their town, which was assumed to be their task. Of the magnitude and range of the work to be done no contemporary had any idea. Such criticism of the action of the Improvement Commissioners as we do find—notably that which we have described at Manchester after 1824—proceeded from a state of mind that we are to-day hardly able to imagine. The doctrinaire Radical shopkeepers and little property owners who objected on principle to street lighting, a salaried police force, and the suppression of nuisances, had even less conception of the gravity of the new problems of town life than the Improvement Commissioners or than Parliament itself. Their objections found no support among the mass of wage-earners who, paying no rates, remained stolidly indifferent to the whole business. The shopkeepers and publicans were

committee of the Corporation of the City of London, and which we have already referred to in *The Manor and the Borough*, 1908, vol. ii. pp. 577, 582, 610-612, 637, 640-641, 646.   See *ante*, p. 58 ; *A Practical Treatise on the Laws, Customs, Usages and Regulations of the City and Port of London*, by Alexander Pulling, 1842, 1844 and 1854, ch. xviii. ; the interesting Report of the Commissioners of Sewers of 15th November 1765 ; House of Commons Journals, 17th and 27th January 1766 and 23rd January 1771 ; the Reports of the Municipal Corporations Commission, 1837, the Royal Commission on the Corporation of London, 1854, and that upon London Government, 1899 ; and the *Modern History of the City of London*, by C. Welch, 1896, pp. 17-18. It was merged in the Corporation by the City of London Sewers Act, 61 and 62 Victoria c. 133 (1897).

It may be added that the Crown Estate Paving Commissioners, established by the Acts 5 George IV. c. 100 and 14 and 15 Victoria c. 95, still continue, and still levy on the Crown estate about Regent's Park a separate rate for paving, watering, etc.   The Conservators of Wimbledon and Putney Commons still levy a " Commons Rate " under their Act of 1871.   There are also more than 60 " Garden Rates " levied in London by bodies of Trustees or Commissioners, under old Acts or legally authoritative " schemes " under modern Acts, or under the Town Gardens Protection Act, 1863.

equally unsuccessful in appealing to the wealthy manufacturers or landowners, who saw the advantage of the Commissioners' reforms, and continued to support them to the last, even against the elected Town Councils. We must, in fact, conclude that such work as was done by the Improvement Commissioners was a clear gain to the community. Their sins were sins of omission. It passes human imagination to conceive the state into which the rapidly growing towns would have got if no such bodies had been established. But it is sad to think how much disease and premature death, how much human sorrow and demoralisation, or even how much unnecessary expense, has resulted, in every city of the land, from the extremely narrow range of the ideas of those who, from the middle of the eighteenth century onward, were responsible for providing the organisation by which alone the requirements of the rapidly increasing urban population could be met.

CHAPTER V

WITH the present volume we complete our survey of English Local Government from the Revolution to the Municipal Corporations Act—so far, at least, as constitutional structure is concerned. We now proceed to summarise in two concluding chapters the outstanding characteristics of this period, whether manifested in the decay of the old or in the evolution of new principles of government.

We may first explain the significance of these particular years. When we turned to the subject of Local Government, nearly a quarter of a century ago, our object was to describe the organisation and working of the existing local governing authorities, with a view to discovering how they could be improved. We realised from the outset that a merely statical investigation of what was going on around us would reveal little or nothing of the lasting conditions of disease and health in the social organisations that we were considering. We knew that, in order to find the causes of their imperfections and the directions in which they could be improved, we had to study, not only their present but also their past ; not merely what they were doing but also how they had come to be doing it. Somewhat naïvely, we accepted as our starting-point the beginning of the nineteenth century. But after a year's work on the records, it became apparent to us that the local institutions of the first quarter of that century were either in the last stages of decay or in the earliest years of infancy. We saw that it was impossible to appreciate the drastic innovations of 1834–1836, and their subsequent developments, without going much further back. After some reconnoitring of the seventeenth century, we decided that the Revolution of 1689 ranked, in the evolution of English Local Government, as the beginning of a distinct era which continued until the Reform Bill of 1832.

The best way of recalling to the reader the extensive and multifarious changes described in our volumes, will be first to discover and analyse the main principles—the ideas that governed men's minds, the traditional concepts still potent in constitutional organisation—inherited in 1689 from previous centuries and embodied in the local institutions of the eighteenth century. We shall therefore describe in this chapter (i.) the " Obligation to Serve," and to serve gratuitously in the discharge of local public duties ; (ii.) Vocational Organisation as the very basis of government ; (iii.) the principle of Self-Election or Co-option ; (iv.) the Freehold Tenure of profitable office ; (v.) the conception of property, and at the outset landed property, as an indispensable qualification for, if not actually a title to, the exercise of authority ; and, as explaining the absence of anything that could be called a system of Local Government, and the utter lack of uniformity or consistency, (vi.) the predominance of local customs and the Common Law as the very basis of the whole. In the next chapter we shall set forth the gradual evolution of a new set of principles arising out of the circumstances and thought of the new age : principles destined to become dominant in the Local Government of the nineteenth century.

A Policy of Non-Intervention by the Central Government

At the outset of our analysis appears, not any ancient principle, but a new policy, arising with dramatic suddenness out of the Revolution of 1689. A summary end to " arbitrary interference " with " local liberties " was one of the most important results of the dismissal of the Stuart dynasty. For more than a hundred years from that date, King and Parliament adopted a policy of indifference as to what the various local governing authorities did or abstained from doing. The interference of the Privy Council, and even that of the Courts of Law and the Assize Judges, sank to a minimum. In contrast alike with the centralised administration that was being built up, especially as regards poor relief, between 1590 and 1640, and with the

arbitrary " regulating " of Municipal Corporations of 1683–1688,
the King's Ministers after 1689, it is scarcely too much to say,
deliberately abstained from any consideration of the Local
Authorities ; and hardly ever found themselves driven to come
to any decision on the subject of their activities or their powers.
The Justices of the Peace, between the Revolution and the
Municipal Corporations Act, enjoyed, in their regulations, an
almost complete and unshackled autonomy. Unlike a modern
County Council making byelaws, Quarter Sessions was under no
obligation to submit its orders for confirmation to the Home
Secretary or to any other authority. Moreover, the Justices
were, in their own Counties, not only law-makers, but, either
collectively or individually, themselves also the tribunal to adjudicate on any breaches of their own regulations. Again, the Juries
of the Manor, of the Court of Sewers, of the Hundred and of
the County, were always " interpreting " the local customs, and
restricting or extending the conception of public nuisances, active
or passive, according to contemporary needs, or new forms of
the behaviour of individual citizens and corporate bodies ; whilst
the inhabitants in Vestry assembled, or the little oligarchy of
Parish Officers, were incurring (and meeting out of the ancient
Church Rate) expenditure on all sorts of services according to
local decision, without any one having any practical power of
disallowance. As for the Municipal Corporations, they regarded
their corporate property, their markets, their tolls, their fines
and fees, as well as their exemptions and privileges, as outside
any jurisdiction other than their own. When, in the course of
the eighteenth century, it became necessary or convenient to
invoke Parliamentary authority for the enforcement of new
regulations, or the levying of new imposts, this usually took the
form, not of a statute of general application, but (as we have
described in the present volume) of literally thousands of separate
Local Acts. These peculiar and little studied emanations of
national law were not devised by the Government or by its
central departments, but were spontaneously initiated and
contrived by little groups of the principal inhabitants of particular areas ; they were debated and amended in the House of
Commons, not by committees of impartial persons, but mainly
by the representatives of the Boroughs and Counties concerned ;
and as we have described in the Introduction to this volume, it

was not until the very end of the eighteenth century that the
" Lords' Chairman " began to insist on inserting clauses safe-
guarding what he considered to be the interests of the public at
large. Thus, the special epoch dealt with in our description
of the Parish and the County, the Manor and the Borough
and the Statutory Authorities for Special Purposes, is a
definitely bounded period, extending over more than a century
and a quarter, of something very like an anarchy of local
autonomy.

No System of Local Government

During the eighteenth century the anarchy of local autonomy
was heightened by the fact that there was nothing that could be
regarded, either in theory or practice, as a system of Local
Government. There was, as we have described in the foregoing
volumes, a confused network of local customs and the Common
Law, of canon law and royal decrees or charters, interspersed
with occasional and unsystematised Parliamentary statutes.
Out of this confused and largely unexplored network, there had
emerged four distinct organs of government : the Parish, the
County, the Manor and the Municipal Corporation—not to
mention the anomalous Commission of Sewers—to which was
added, in the course of the eighteenth century, a new type
described in the present volume—the Statutory Authority for
Special Purposes. These distinct organs of government are
found superimposed one on the top of the other, at different
periods of history, for different purposes, by different instruments
and with different sanctions. Alike in origins and in areas, in
structures and in powers, they are inextricably entangled one
with the other. What is common to them all is that not one of
them was, or claimed to be, a system of Local Government. If
any of the Dutch gentlemen who landed at Torbay with William
the Third had asked a Lord Lieutenant, a High Sheriff or a
Justice of the Peace to describe " the Local Government of
England," he would have met with a blank ignorance of any
such order of things. The Rulers of the County would have
thought of themselves not as Local Authorities at all, but as
the deputies of the King, with an obligation to provide what was
requisite for the King's soldiers, to hold the King's Courts, to
maintain the King's peace ; having a general commission to

2 A

govern their own County as they thought right, and especially to supervise all other citizens in fulfilling their respective obligations. The peers and country gentlemen who consented to spend some of their leisure, in and out of Parliament, in performing these tasks, would have been aware that the City of London was wholly exempt from their control; and that up and down the land there existed many Cities, Boroughs, Franchises and Liberties which successfully claimed to exclude this or that particular Court or official jurisdiction. But these were mere exceptions to the normal government exercised by the landed gentry of the Kingdom. The suggestion that there existed any kind of lawful autonomy in the fifteen thousand Parishes and Townships would have seemed to the country gentleman, at the end of the seventeenth century, an absurd and a dangerous contention. The two or three hundred Municipal Corporations would have accepted their status of exceptional privilege with complacency. They would have cited in proof their diverse Courts exercising jurisdiction over this or that area, entirely independent of the County; their infinitely varied constitutions, derived indifferently from charters, statutes or immemorial custom, and frequently amended by their own byelaws, without intervention on the part of Parliament or the Government. The Lord of the Manor, on the other hand, would have told the curious enquirer that, as a landowner, he had, by immemorial usage, Courts of his own; that in these Courts his tenants were compelled to appear; and that he himself, or his steward, was always anxious to agree with them on any matters of common concern. He might have added that there were such things as Juries of his tenants, with certain rights to give verdicts, to declare the local customs and even to present him before his own steward for failing to conform to these customs, or for permitting the continuance on his property of any public nuisance. The Parish Constable, Overseer or Surveyor of Highways, far from feeling himself a member of a Local Authority, would have complained that he was compelled to serve without payment in an unpopular office, exacting from him much time and labour, at the beck and call of any interfering Justice of the Peace. Finally, the Churchwarden would have been puzzled to know whether he belonged to a secular or to an ecclesiastical hierarchy; and how far he was compelled to obey, on the one hand the

archdeacon and " the Ordinary," or on the other, the little group
of " principal inhabitants " in Vestry assembled. But not one
of these personages would have regarded himself as forming
part of anything that could be called a system of Local Government. He could hardly have conceived even of the existence
of any such system. The very term, Local Government, was not
in use before the middle of the nineteenth century.[1] Throughout the seventeenth and eighteenth centuries and right into the
nineteenth century, the greatest county personage or the humblest
parishioner stood on his personal status, whether that status was,
in the main, one of authority over other men, as in the case of
the County Justices, the Municipal Magistrates or the Lords of
Manors ; or, in the main, one of graduated subservience to
superiors within an hierarchy, secular or ecclesiastical, as in the
case of the Parish Constables, Overseers, Churchwardens, the
citizens called out on the service of Watch and Ward in the town
streets or the labourers summoned to Statute Duty on the
country roads.

THE OBLIGATION TO SERVE

It was, indeed, this principle of obligation to render public
service, a principle coming down from time immemorial, that
was, and remained far into the eighteenth century, the axle
round which revolved all old-established local institutions,
whether manorial or parochial, of the Borough or of the County.
The particular obligations might rest on local custom or on the
Common Law ; they might be embodied in grant or charter, in
general statute or, in later times, in a Local Act ; they might
attach to individuals or corporations, or be appurtenant to the
ownership of particular estates. But however these obligations
arose, they included, not merely a duty to obey, but also a direct
charge on the will to act. They involved not only personal
responsibility to a superior, but also such power over other
persons as was incidental to the due performance of the public

[1] We find the phrase " local self-government " becoming current in the
second quarter of the nineteenth century, largely through its use by Von
Gneist and J. Toulmin Smith. From this, in the third quarter of the century,
seems to have sprung the phrase " local government." It is difficult to believe
that this cannot be found, here and there, at an earlier date ; but it was certainly
not until the middle of the nineteenth century that it came into common use.
We notice it in a leading article of the *Times* on 15th December 1856.

service. Thus, however men might differ in faculties and desires, or in status and fortune, they were all under obligation to serve in one way or another. It was, for instance, taken for granted that every respectable male resident was under legal obligation to undertake, without salary or other remuneration, one or other of the customary or statutory offices of Manor, Parish or County.[1] Though, as we have explained, the method of selection varied, both by statute and at Common Law, we find a widespread local custom that each office ought to be served in rotation by all parishioners, qualified according to certain traditional requirements. " In some places," said Chief Justice Holt in 1698, " people are to be Constables by house-row," or rotation among occupiers. " As it is an office of great burden," wrote Thomas Gilbert in 1786–1787, of the office of Overseer, " it generally goes by house-row in rotation through the parish." " In fact," summed up Dr. Burn in 1764, " the office goes by rotation from one householder to another "—in " indiscriminate rotation," records another observer, " among all those whose occupations render them liable to the office." It was, in fact, at the end of the seventeenth century, still no part of the conception of local administration that there should be anything of the nature of what we should now call official staffs ; that is to say, the voluntary and whole-time employment of persons at salaries and wages, to perform specified functions. Every service requisite for the simple life of the Manor or the Parish fell, in ancient times, within the duty imposed, as an incident of tenure or status, upon one or other inhabitant, either permanently or for a brief term in rotation with his neighbours. Nor was this universal obligation to render public service limited to individual residents or property owners. It was inherent in the very right to exist of corporate bodies of every kind. To the mediaeval statesman we may imagine that the Municipal Corporation, like the Manor itself, was primarily an organ of obligation, by means of which, in particular localities, the services required by the King might most conveniently be performed and could most easily be exacted. Similarly, in the eye of the law, neither Parish nor County was an organisation for local self-government. On one plane the Parish, on another the County, was essentially a unit of obligation. It was the Parish, in some cases in succession to

[1] *The Parish and the County*, p. 16.

the Manor, and not any of its officers, that was liable for the upkeep of the church fabric, as well as of the churchyard ; for compliance with this and that statutory obligation ; and for the maintenance of its own part of the King's Highway. The officers and Courts of the County were, on their own plane, merely devices by which the obligations of the County itself were performed, and through which they could be enforced, whether these obligations related to the furnishing of the *posse comitatus* to put down any resistance to the maintenance of the King's Peace, or in later times to the militia raised for national defence ; to the upkeep of the County Bridges without which there could be no free passage for the King and his men ; to the keeping of the common gaol which was the King's, or the accommodation of the King's Judges when they came to hold the Assizes. Far from constituting any system of local self-government, the Courts and Sessions of the County Justices, and the services of the County officials were, from the standpoint of constitutional law, only instruments within the County for the proper keeping of the King's Peace, for the due execution of the King's writs, for the enforcement of the decisions of the King's Judges, for the exact and punctual payment of the various revenues due to the King, for the keeping of the King's prisons and the King's Courts, and for the maintenance of the great bridges without which the King's Highway could afford no convenient passage through the Kingdom.

It is this principle of personal obligation, on which the whole of English Local Government was based, that affords the explanation of the great bulk of the administration being, even so late as the eighteenth century, cast in what to-day seems the strange form of presentment and indictment, traverse and trial, sentence and fine or estreat. In the Manor and the County we find innumerable varieties of presentment which particular officers, or particular Juries of various kinds, from Sewers and Leets to Franchises and Hundreds, and finally the Grand Inquest for the County as a whole, were always being charged to make. It was by means of these presentments, and the cumbrous legal proceedings which they initiated, that all derelictions were dealt with, whether the ordinary breaches of the law by private individuals, the shortcomings of parochial and manorial officers, the failure of Parishes to maintain their highways, their pounds and their stocks ; the neglect of Franchises and Hundreds to keep the peace, whereby damage had been done ; and equally the derelictions of duty of the County itself in failing to keep in repair the County Gaol or the County Bridges. What to-day emerges in the agendas and minutes of boards and councils as reports of committees and resolutions appeared, two or three centuries ago, as the proceedings of courts of justice, in the form of presentments, indictments, traverses, forfeitures and sentences.[1] It is, indeed, not too much to say that, at the close of the seventeenth century, in the Courts of the Manor or in the Court of Sewers, the inhabitants of every surviving Manor, and of nearly every area liable to be flooded, including all the landowners and frequently the Lord of the Manor himself ; and, at the Quarter Sessions and Assizes, all the Parishes and Hundreds, and at the Assizes all the Franchises, Liberties and Municipal Corporations, and even the County itself, represented by their unpaid and compulsorily serving officers, were, one or other of them, always in the dock, as defendants in nominally criminal proceedings, on which they were perpetually being amerced or fined. This, indeed, was the customary and regular procedure of the Local Government of the period.

The same notion of obligation elucidates what was understood by the conception of nuisance, which swelled into so large a part of the framework of law in which the ordinary citizen found himself. A nuisance implied a breach of obligation. If every person fulfilled his lawful duty, according to the customs of the Manor and the Common Law, no one would do or suffer anything to be done to the annoyance of his neighbours. Any breach of this fundamental obligation was therefore a nuisance, active or passive. Thus, the redress of nuisances came to include the remedying of every conceivable neglect or offence, from eavesdropping and disorderly drunkenness to the use of

[1] The local bodies, says Maitland, were not "the representatives of unorganised collections of men : they are the representatives, we might almost say, of corporations. . . . The same word (*comitatus*) serves to describe both the County, the geographical district, and the assembly. . . . The King's itinerant Justices from time to time visit the Counties ; the whole County (*totus comitatus*), *i.e.* the body of freeholders stands before them ; it declares what the County has been doing since the last visitation ; the County can give judgment ; the County can give testimony ; the County can be punished by fines and amercements when the County has done wrong ; if the County has given false judgment, the County can be summoned to Westminster" (*The Constitutional History of England*, by F. W. Maitland, 1919, p. 43).

false weights and measures or the sale of unwholesome food ; from filth and stench, and neglect to pave, up to riot, sedition and recusancy. " Cows, horses, sheep, pigs, dogs," we are told, " all required regulation, and had it." Pigs, as the most perverse of animals, required the firmest and most rigorous handling ; and hundreds of folio pages of Jury orders and presentments relate to swine alone, and their numerous misdeeds and nuisances, their " eating corn in the market," and their nameless desecrations of the churchyard. But the worst of all nuisances, because it cut at the root of common order, was the refusal to serve in any of the customary offices, a breach of obligation which was accordingly visited with exemplary fines.

The Inequality in the Incidence of the Obligation to Serve

The democratic conception of the equality of all men in the service of the community was, it is needless to say, entirely absent from the general obligation to undertake public office still embodied in the old-established local institutions of the eighteenth century. This was partly due to the intimate association of the obligation to serve with the traditionally vocational basis of English society, political as well as industrial—a point we shall presently elaborate. But apart from this intimate association of public duties with particular vocations, the various obligations fell only lightly on men of property, and much more heavily on the humbler ranks of society. The peer, by reason of his dignity ; the Member of Parliament, or the Justice of the Peace, on account of his office ; the practising attorneys and barristers ; the ministers of religion (originally of the one and only Church, and later also those of recognised nonconformist denominations), as well as the members of the three powerful corporations of physicians, of surgeons and of apothecaries, enjoyed a common, although not exactly uniform, exemption from service in such onerous and unpleasant offices as Parish Constable, Overseer of the Poor, or Surveyor of Highways.[1] And although it may have been theoretically doubtful whether any duly qualified person could lawfully refuse to be made a

---

[1] For the detailed qualifications of this summary statement see *The Justice of the Peace*, by Richard Burn (first edition, 1754), under the headings of the several officers.

peer, to be elected to the House of Commons, or to be included in the Commission of the Peace, there was practically no obligation of attendance in Parliament, whilst an unwilling Justice might always refrain from "taking out his dedimus," without which he could not act. It is an interesting sidelight that the only County office which was at once compulsory and expensive, that of the High Sheriff, was always imposed, unless occasionally a County personage deigned to accept it, on one of the minor gentry. Moreover, any well-to-do citizen, even if he could not claim exemption by status, might always buy exemption, either through the purchase of a " Tyburn Ticket," or by merely paying a fine.[1] Finally, however onerous and unprofitable may have been the office of Constable, Overseer, Churchwarden or Surveyor, it was accompanied by a little brief authority over fellow-citizens, a satisfaction denied to the still humbler inhabitants who had to carry out the orders of the Parish Officers in the town streets or on the country roads.

The Continually Increasing Inadequacy of the Principle of Obligation to Serve

Among the many reasons for the rapid acceleration of the decay of the Manor and the Municipal Corporation, for the distorted growth of Parish and County government, for the chaotic multiplication of Statutory Authorities for Special Purposes, and for the corruption and inefficiency characteristic of all these local institutions during the eighteenth and early nineteenth centuries, we know of no cause more universal and significant than the increasing inadequacy of the principle of obligation to serve as a method of local administration. We do not suggest that this principle of individual responsibility, and this obligation of personal service for the common good, is in itself objectionable. To many idealists it seems not only an attractive but also an ennobling social doctrine. As we shall indicate later on, it was a moral disaster that the public duties and obligations of citizens, as distinguished from their private interests and needs, should have been, by the Utilitarian reformers of 1832–1836, so entirely ignored. But however virtuous or wise may be a principle of public or private action, its survival

[1] *The Parish and the County*, pp. 19, 63.

as the ostensible method of achieving a desired result, *after that principle has ceased to be applicable or adequate to the circumstances of the time*, undermines the very foundations of personal conduct and social organisation.

We cannot estimate how far, in previous centuries, the principle of obligatory personal service, nearly always gratuitous, had ever proved sufficient for contemporary needs. What is clear from our researches into eighteenth-century Local Government is that, when certain conditions ceased to prevail, the principle became ineffective. In order to be fulfilled, the duties had to be accepted, as a matter of course, by the great majority of those on whom they were imposed; and supported by the public opinion of the community in which they lived. The services to be rendered had not only to be within the capacity of the ordinary citizen, but also consistent with his earning his livelihood and living his normal life. In short, the obligations had to be customary, limited in extent and unspecialised in character. In many a rural Manor and secluded Parish these conditions were maintained right down to the beginning of the nineteenth century. The little group of freeholders or copyholders, and " principal inhabitants," continued to fill, with integrity and sufficient skill, all the offices requisite for the life of the small and stationary community. Among these neighbours, each cultivating his agricultural holding or using the common land, or serving, like his forefathers, as village innkeeper or blacksmith, as indoor apprentice or farm-servant, the group-spirit was highly developed. The official relationships among the parties concerned were inextricably interwoven with the economic relationships among the same individuals in their private capacities. The Justice of the Peace was probably himself the Lord of the Manor; his tenants constituted the Leet Jury, presenting nuisances and declaring the customs of the Manor, and they individually served in rotation in all the Parish offices; they themselves were the employers of the labourers whose poverty they from time to time relieved out of the Poor Rate; and even the clergyman, who was in many respects the most independent person in the village, often owed his position to the squire, let his glebe to the Churchwarden, bargained with the Overseer as to the rates on his tithes, and drew these tithes from every occupier of land in the Parish. Hence, though there might be grumbling, there could be no effective resistance to the action of the governing group. On the other hand, though there were frequently no minutes, and certainly no printed accounts and no newspaper reporters, the persons who did the work and paid the exiguous rates themselves controlled every item of expenditure and knew everything that was going on. Flagrant acts of dishonesty were difficult, and the public approval or blame of the whole village was a real power. But with the increase of trade and population from the close of the seventeenth century, with the dislocation of economic ties, with the rapid transformation of rural districts into busy urban centres entailing new technical services, all the conditions that had made practicable the principle of obligatory, gratuitous and rotational service were swept away, to be replaced by conditions transforming the ancient functions of the old offices into so many opportunities for evasion, peculation and oppression. Round about the City of London, in the unincorporated mining and manufacturing districts of the Northern and Midland Counties, and even within the walls of some of the old-world Municipalities, the new industry and the unaccustomed development of trade were bringing great aggregations of population into ancient Parishes. Here the economic and social relations, which built up the Manor and the Parish, as organs of the " government by consent " of stable social and economic groups, either had never existed or were in process of rapid disintegration. The powerful tie of landlord and tenant or employer and wage-earner ; the strong but intangible link of family relationship or inherited social status, uniting the squire with the clergyman, the farmer with the handicraftsman and labourer, and all these with each other, no longer supplemented the bare legal relationships between the Lord of the Manor and his tenants, the Justice of the Peace and the Overseer, the Incumbent and the People's Churchwarden, the Parish Officers and the Parish ratepayers. The Manor Courts were ceasing to be held, their functions being more and more assumed by the Justices, the Parish Officers and the Vestries. The clergyman of the Parish, often assumed to be the proper chairman of the Vestry, was frequently an absentee, having no other secular or religious connection with his parishioners than the delegated exaction of his annual tithes and dues. The Justice of the Peace, whose co-operation was the

corner-stone of Parish government, without whose signature no
Overseer could be appointed, no accounts passed, nor any Poor
Rate collected, might be a County magnate, living far away
from the new industrial district ; or what was worse, a newly
enriched tradesman with merely commercial traditions, who had,
for personal ends, intrigued himself into the Commission of the
Peace. Nor was the failure of supervision of Parish government
by the upper classes compensated for, in the vast majority of
instances, by any increased watchfulness on the part of the
common citizens. The inhabitants of these new industrial
districts were unknown to each other ; many, as newcomers,
were uninterested in the local affairs and unacquainted with the
local customs. The time, place and method of appointment of
the Parish Officers, such as the Overseers, the Constable and the
Surveyor of Highways, together with their powers and functions,
were, as far as these uninstructed and indifferent citizens were
concerned, shrouded in mystery. Respectable householders
might find themselves compelled to undertake an onerous duty
against their will by the fact of their names coming next on some
list of which they had never heard, or merely because they had
been " presented " by the Vestry or by the previous occupant
of the office, either to the Justices or to a surviving Court Leet.
When such persons found themselves appointed to act as Constable or Surveyor, Overseer or Churchwarden, they usually did
their utmost to escape service. " The imposition of the office "
of Constable, writes Daniel Defoe in 1714, " is an insupportable
hardship ; it takes up so much of a man's time that his own
affairs are frequently totally neglected, too often to his ruin.
Yet there is neither profit nor pleasure therein." [1] " It is well
known," reports a Poor Law Commissioner in 1833, " that when
any person who has received a good education, and whose habits
are those of a gentleman, settles in a Parish, one of his first
objects is to endeavour to exempt himself from Parish office." [2]
When it is remembered that it was just in these new industrial
districts, or in the still denser aggregations of the Metropolitan
area, that the public business of the Parish was becoming every

[1] *Parochial Tyranny,* by Andrew Moreton (Daniel Defoe), p. 17 ; *The
Parish and the County,* p. 62.

[2] Communication from a J.P. in Codd's Report, p. 53 of Appendix A of
First Report of Poor Law Inquiry Commissioners, 1834 ; *The Parish and the
County,* p. 62.

day more complicated and difficult ; that the mere number of the paupers was becoming overwhelming ; that new buildings of diverse kinds were springing up on all sides ; that paving, cleansing, lighting and watching were alike wanting ; that the crowding together of tens of thousands of poverty-stricken persons was creating unspeakable nuisances ; and that the amount of the rates levied on the inhabitants was at the same time doubling and trebling, it will be easily understood why, in one district after another, the situation became intolerable.

It was not merely that, in these areas, a large part of the public revenue came to be levied in the invidious form of fines exacted from those who wished to buy exemption from the performance of public duties. The abandonment of the offices of the Parish and Manor by all the inhabitants of education, social position or independent means, left these offices to be filled by any one who sought them as opportunities for making illicit gains. There came to be an almost universal prevalence of perquisites, which might extend from frequent feasts and a total exemption from the payment of rates, up to the most extensive jobbery in supplying the Parish or the Borough with goods at exorbitant prices, and unlimited peculation at the expense either of terrified inhabitants or of the public funds. In our chapters on " The Uncontrolled Parish Officers " and " The Rule of the Boss," we have given detailed examples, typical of a large part of the new England that was growing up in the Northern and Midland Counties, in the ports and the great Metropolitan area, of peculation, extortion and corruption, carried to an extent, continued over terms of years and enjoying an impunity to-day almost incredible.[1]

But even if men of integrity and public spirit had continued to come forward to fill the old offices of the Manor and the Parish ; even if the average citizen had been exact and punctilious in the fulfilment of his accustomed obligations, in the avoidance of nuisances and in performance of Statute Duty, the very change in environment had rendered such personal services wholly un-equal to the tasks by which they were faced. Here it was the nature and extent of the obligation itself that was inadequate. The assumption on which universal and gratuitous personal service had always rested was that of a substantially unaltered

[1] *The Parish and the County*, pp. 61-90.

obligation year after year. The principle was devised for a stable and unchanging community. There was no provision for any new services that might be called for by altered circumstances. The common obligation of the landowners to maintain the sewers did not extend to making a new sewer ; that of the County to maintain a bridge carried with it neither duty nor power to construct a new bridge, however urgent might be the need. Whatever might be the growing throng or traffic on the highways, no Parish could lawfully make a new thoroughfare, or even raise a footway to a bridleway, or a bridleway to a cartway. It was no part of the obligation of the Parish or of the individual parishioners to transform a muddy country lane, along which a free passage was just possible, into the widened and straightened and artificially prepared road surface that the new traffic required ; and even if the new thoroughfare got constructed, nothing more technically skilled or scientifically expert could be required from the Parish in the way of maintenance than could be supplied by the untrained and unspecialised innkeeper or farmer who accepted a year's unpaid service as Surveyor of Highways, directing the temporarily conscripted labour of the crowd of farm-servants and other cottagers who were periodically called out to do Statute Duty on the roads. Even where the character of the required service remained unchanged, its very growth in magnitude took it outside the capacity of the temporarily serving unpaid Parish officer. It was one thing to make the assessment and collect the rates in a Parish of only a few dozen ratepayers, all of whom were personal acquaintances. It became quite another matter to make the assessment in a crowded Lancashire town, filled with mills and warehouses, shops and foundries of divers kinds ; and to collect the rates from thousands of occupiers, many of them merely transient residents.

VOCATIONAL ORGANISATION AS THE VERY BASIS OF GOVERNMENT

There was another principle behind the local institutions of the seventeenth and eighteenth centuries, one which had become, through senility, a factor of disorganisation and demoralisation, namely, the acceptance of vocational or occupational organisation as a basis of government. At the close of the seventeenth century governmental authority was frequently vested in a group, a company or a corporation associated for some production or supply of services or commodities. The Church, the Universities, the Inns of Court, the College of Physicians, the Company of Surgeons or the Society of Apothecaries could, it seemed, each exercise far-extending authority in connection with the service that its members rendered to the community as a means of livelihood. Such chartered incorporations as the East India Company, the New River Company, the Bank of England and the various national companies for colonial and foreign trade, or for mining or manufacture, could receive analogous powers.[1] A like association of authority over non-members with economic function and vocational organisation can be traced in some, at least, of the local institutions to which we have been referring. The Manorial Court, in its aspect of Court Baron (as distinguished from that of Court Leet, which was a King's Court) was essentially the organ, not of the citizens as such, or of the inhabitants as a whole, but of the particular group of owners or tenants of agricultural land within the Manor—that is to say, notwithstanding the feudal autocracy that formed its other side, it belonged, like the colleges and companies, to the genus of Associations of Producers. This explains why the typical officers of Local Government in the Manor were the Herdsman, the Common Driver, the Pigringer, the Hayward, and the Pinder or Pound Keeper. This it was that inspired the " customs " of the Manor, and dictated the elaborate regulation of the common field agriculture, which, as we have shown in the example of the Manor of Great Tew, occupied so much of the time of the Lord's Court. The same spirit is seen in the clinging of the Freemen of Alnwick or Berwick, Coventry or Newcastle-on-Tyne, to their chartered monopoly of the Town Moor, the Lammas Lands, or the " Meadows and Stints." The student of other species of vocational or occupational organisation will not be surprised to find the " Homage " resenting both the intrusion of " foreigners " into the Manor, and the invasion of the commons by " landless residents." The same spirit led, in many a Manor

---

[1] " In the earlier part of the seventeenth century," writes Dr. Cunningham, " it appeared to be assumed that the organisation of trade by persons who were concerned in it was essential " (*The Growth of English Industry and Commerce in Modern Times*, by Dr. W. Cunningham, 1900, p. 284).

or Manorial Borough, to the exaction of tolls and dues in the market and at the landing-stage exclusively from those who had not been admitted as tenants of the Manor ; and sometimes, even in unincorporated villages, induced the Reeve, as representative of the Homage, to charge a fee to such " foreigners " for the privilege of opening a shop. It was, we suggest, the fact that the Court Baron had the attributes that belong to an Association of Producers which caused it, as is apparent in our account of the Manorial Boroughs, to develop into a close body, renewing itself by co-option, from which the unprivileged inhabitant found himself automatically excluded. But although nearly every Borough retained, even as late as the seventeenth century, at least a remnant of interest in agriculture, most of these urban centres had become, by that time, predominantly communities of traders, whether master-craftsmen, retail shopkeepers or dealers of one sort or another, together with their journeymen, apprentices or other wage - earning assistants. Thus, the Association of Producers in agriculture had, in the Manorial Boroughs, become gradually transformed into an Association of Producers concerned rather with trade and manufacture. This transformation was reflected in the corporate officers and the corporate jurisdictions, involving the appointment of Ale-conners, Fish and Flesh Tasters, and Leather Searchers and Sealers. To the control of the common agriculture there was added a control of the common trading. When we pass from the Manorial Boroughs to the couple of hundred Municipal Corporations, creating their own Justices of the Peace, holding their own civil and criminal Courts, sometimes appointing their own Sheriffs, and in one case even having its own Lieutenancy, independent of the King's appointment, we find this independence frequently intertwined with (and, as some have suggested, usually rooted in, if not arising from) a varying assortment of Merchant or Craft Gilds or Companies, all of them originally Associations of Producers, and basing their membership, not, as in the Manor and the Manorial Borough, on their common interest as agriculturists, but on their common interest in some branch of trade or manufacture. We need not here consider such vexed questions as the exact relation of the Merchant Gild, so frequent in the thirteenth century, on the one hand to the Municipal Corporation itself, and on the other to the Craft

Gilds of the fifteenth century ; or the varying degrees of independent authority to be attributed, respectively, to the orders
and byelaws made by the Craft Gilds for their own trades, of the
regulations respecting artificers made by the Municipal Corporation itself, and of the provisions of the Elizabethan Statute of
Apprentices, under which, in fact, the eighteenth-century Town
Council usually preferred to take proceedings against non-
Freemen. What emerges from our analysis of these manorial
and municipal exceptions from the common rule of the government of the County by the King's Lieutenant and the King's
Justices, is the fact that practically all the regulative activities
of these organs of independent authority seem to be connected,
at least by traditional origin, not with the common interests of
all men as citizens and consumers, but with the particular
interests of the members as locally privileged groups of agriculturists, traders or manufacturers. It is to this primordial
conception of an organisation based on common interests as
producers, not wherever they resided but only within a
delimited area, that we trace the various forms of trade
monopoly which characterise alike the Craft Gild and Trade
Company, the Manorial Borough and the Municipal Corporation, from the prohibition of the letting of crofts, " stints,"
boats, market - stalls, shops or houses to " foreigners," up
to the restriction of trades to Freemen, or to the sons or
apprentices of Freemen, being also members of a particular
Gild or Company. We see the same principle in the habitual
secrecy of the proceedings of the Municipal Corporation as of
the Gild ; the same notion of its transactions being those of a
voluntary and private association ; the same abhorrence of any
external supervision or control ; the same inability to recognise
any justification for the demand for accounts, let alone an outside audit. We see the same idea in the exemption of Freemen
from the tolls and dues levied by the Municipal Corporation
(which was simply themselves), or if Freemen paid anything at
all, the mulcting of non-Freemen in higher charges. A Municipal Corporation, feeling itself merely a group of privileged
persons, inevitably considered its market or its port, like its
commons or its charitable endowments, as belonging morally as
well as legally to its members, and to its members exclusively.
And this Association of Producers retained, to the last, certain

characteristics of an essentially voluntary fellowship. Alike in the Municipal Corporation and in the Gild or Company, a new member could enter only by the consent of the existing corporate body, just as a new tenant of the Manor had to be formally admitted by the Homage at the Lord's Court. Any member could be, for sufficient reason and with due formalities, expelled from the Corporation at its discretion. The Municipal Corporation, like the Gild, was thus, in fact, not only an Association of Producers, but also an association voluntarily recruited at the option of the existing members, who felt that they had a privilege to bestow. It was therefore at all times an association falling far short of universality ; and in no way identified particularly with mere inhabitancy or residence, or, as would now be said, with local citizenship.[1]

The Undermining of the Vocational Basis of Local Institutions

At the close of the seventeenth century, when the National Government, as we have explained, ceased to give any attention to, or to take any interest in, the development of local institutions, the Manor, the Manorial Borough and the Municipal

---

[1] It would, we think, be far-fetched to emphasise traces of vocational organisation in the County or Parish government. But it is worth noting that the Justices belonged originally all to one class, that of owners of agricultural land, with which their connection was much more than that of receivers of rent. They were, in fact, the directors of agricultural enterprise. And though the Parish organisation, resting as it did, from at least the fourteenth century, on the meeting of the " principal inhabitants " in Vestry assembled, was distinctively communal in character, the members, in practice, were usually all agriculturists. It is perhaps for this reason that we find some of the statutory obligations of the Parish imposed upon groups of persons in their character as producers of a particular type. " Every person, for every plough-land in tillage or pasture " that he occupied in the Parish, and " also every person keeping a draught [of horses] or plough in the Parish," had to provide and send " one wain or cart furnished after the custom of the country, with oxen, horses, or other cattle, and all other necessaries meet to carry things convenient for that purpose, and also two able men with the same." Finally, " every other householder, cottager and labourer, able to labour, and being no hired servant by the year," was either to go himself to work or to send " one sufficient labourer in his stead." All these teams and labourers had annually to appear on the roads on the date and at the hour fixed by the Surveyor, there to work under his direction for eight hours on four, and afterwards on six consecutive days (2 and 3 Philip & Mary, c. 8). The drafting of this statute, it has been remarked, makes it appear as if it was the Manorial organisation that was thought of (*The Story of the King's Highway*, 1913, p. 15).

2 B

Corporation were already in an advanced stage of constitutional decay. Their functions in their character of Associations of Producers were already, for the most part, obsolescent, owing to the upgrowth of new and rival forms of organisation, alike in agriculture, in commerce and in manufacture, entailing a divorce continuously more complete and more universal, of the mass of the workers from all participation in the ownership and direction of the instruments of production. With the rapidly increasing statutory enclosures, and the still more revolutionary introduction of the factory, the machine-industry and the steam engine, and the universal improvement in the means of communication, this continuous retreat of the independent peasant cultivator and the master craftsman became, before the end of the eighteenth century, nearly everywhere a disastrous rout. The Manorial Courts, dependent on the continuance of groups of freeholders or copy-holders as agricultural producers, were one by one silently discontinued as organs of local administration. In such urban areas as Birmingham and Manchester, they lingered in distorted form as the framework of an attenuated Local Government, based on customary obligation, but divorced from all contact with the bulk of the residents, and becoming increasingly subordinated to the meeting of the inhabitants in Vestry assembled, or to the County Justices of the Peace. Much the same decay fell on the great majority of the Municipal Corporations, which found that their immemorial connection with the privileges of the Freemen, or with the Gilds or Companies, inevitably entailed an ever-increasing separation from the great body of the inhabitants. Only in a few cases, where the Freemen continued to be not so far behind the whole number of householders; and notably in the City of London, where the Livery Companies, though losing their connection with the vocations of which they bore the names, were wealthy property owners, their leading members continuing to be individually associated with commerce, do we see the members of the Corporation becoming, not indeed a vocational, but, in effect, a ratepayers' Democracy. And even in the City of London, the Companies themselves, like nearly all the Municipal Corporations elsewhere, shrank up into limited groups of privileged persons, recruiting themselves by co-option, and having an ever-dwindling community of interest with the inhabitants at large.

It was this progressive decay of the vocational basis of municipal structure that caused the vast majority of Municipal Corporations to become, from the standpoint of Local Government,
little more than an expedient for recruiting a local bench of
magistrates, who, within the privileged area, exercised much of
the authority of the County Justices.

THE PRINCIPLE OF " SELF-ELECTION " OR CO-OPTION

To the modern student, who might expect to find in the
eighteenth century the beginning of the political Democracy of
the nineteenth, it is a shock to discover that by far the most
widely approved constitution for local institutions, right down
to the early decades of the nineteenth century, was the distinctively oligarchical structure of a close body recruiting itself
by co-option. Among the Local Authorities of this period the
meeting of inhabitants in Vestry assembled was the only one in
which anything like a communal Democracy can be seen, or any
germ of a government of the people, by the people, and for the
people. And yet, even in Parish organisation, the Select Vestry
crops up sporadically over nearly all parts of England and
becomes actually the common form in the cities of London,
Westminster and Bristol, and in Northumberland and Durham.
Sometimes this Select Vestry, styled indifferently " the Gentlemen of the Four and Twenty," " the Company of the Twelve,"
" the Masters of the Parish," or " the Kirk Masters," claimed to
derive its authority from a custom " whereof the memory of man
runneth not to the contrary." But on examination of the
records we found this immemorial custom sometimes entangled in
the occupation or tenure of particular husbandries or farms,
probably inherited from some Manorial organisation ; in other
cases we found it originating in a resolution of the Open Vestry in
the sixteenth or seventeenth century, whereby " it is agreed by
the consent of the whole Parish, to elect and choose out of the
same, twelve men to order and define all common causes per-
taining to the church, as shall appertain to the profit and commodity of the same, without molestation or troubling of the rest
of the common people." [1] But for the most part these Select

[1] *Churchwardens' Accounts of Pittington and other Parishes in the Diocese
of Durham from 1580 to 1700* (Surtees Society, vol. lxxxiv., 1888), p. 12 ; *The
Parish and the County*, pp. 184-185.

Vestries were deliberately brought into being, expressly in order to exclude the common folk, not by local agreement, but by bishops' faculty ; or, in the course of the eighteenth or the first decades of the nineteenth century, by Local Act. Even as late as 1819 the redoubtable Thomas Rhodes succeeded in getting an Act completely extinguishing the turbulent Open Vestry of St. Pancras (which he had for twenty years been stripping of its powers), expressly forbidding any such body to meet for the future ; and transferring all the property and the powers, both of the Vestry and of the Directors of the Poor, to a Select Vestry of persons named in the Act, and entitled to fill up vacancies by co-option.

When we turn from Parish government to the Municipal Corporations, we find the great majority of these, amounting to three-quarters of the whole, governed each by a close body. This body, whether styled Court of Common Council, Court of Aldermen, or the Mayor and Commonalty, itself elected the Mayor or other head of the Corporation, and filled vacancies in its ranks by simple co-option. In these cases, even if there existed also a large body of members of the Corporation, styled Freemen, who were recruited by apprenticeship, patrimony or purchase, they found themselves excluded from the government of the Corporation, ranking merely as humble participants in some of its profitable privileges, such as freedom from toll, eligibility for charities, and right to " stint of common." [1] This kind of government it was that the Royal Commission of 1835 stigmatised as " the Corporation System," and assumed to be representative of all the Municipal Corporations. We need not here enquire whether the close body derived its authority from the original or from an amending charter ; or merely from the existence or presumption of a byelaw of the Corporation itself. " The Twenty-Four," recites one of these municipal byelaws, " shall be instead of the whole commonalty, and no other of the commonalty to intermeddle upon pain of five pounds." [2] It is

[1] The Law Courts seem willingly to have accepted mere usage as warranting this exclusion, and even to have been prepared to presume from usage within living memory the existence of a byelaw " restraining to a select body the right of election of the principal corporators, though vested by the ancient constitution in the popular assembly " (*The Law of Municipal Corporations*, by J. W. Willcock, 1828, p. 8 ; *The Manor and the Borough*, p. 274).

[2] MS. Minutes, Corporation of Romney Marsh (Kent), 1604 ; *The Manor*

significant of the state of public opinion, as late as 1808, that
we find " the public committee of Manchester citizens," which
then headed the reform movement in this unincorporated town,
expressing the desire that Manchester should be endowed with
municipal institutions similar to those of Leeds, " self-elect "
though these were. " We conceive," they declared, " that a
permanent body of guardians of the peace, clothed with the
authority of magistracy, would here, as in other places, be the
natural guardian of all interior public interests, able to conduct
them with uniformity and consistency, and ready at all times for
the immediate prevention or correction of abuses ; and might
represent the inhabitants in all their external relations with a
character and dignity becoming the largest provincial community
in the United Kingdom." [1]

Even among the County Justices, who gloried in being the
directly appointed officers of the King, we find the principle of
co-option coming in at the beginning of the nineteenth century,
if not earlier. As we have described, the scandalous breakdown
of the Middlesex Bench was attributed to the carelessness and
favouritism which permitted the appointment, in the name of
the Crown, of " men of low degree," who became the notorious
" Basket Justices " or " Trading Justices," shamelessly using
their office for corrupt, oppressive and even fraudulent purposes.
Many are the complaints, by the Justices themselves, to be
found not only in Quarter Sessions records, but also in the
" Magistrates' Book " in the Home Office archives, of " gross
misconduct and unfitness " and of " scandalous corruption and
extortion " among these unworthy nominees of the Crown.
With the upgrowth of the movement for " the reformation of
morals and manners," initiated by the Royal Proclamation
against vice and immorality, issued early in 1787 at the instance
of Wilberforce, the County Justices began to insist on nominating
their colleagues and successors. The reader will recall the case
of the Merionethshire County Magistrates who, in 1833, actually

---

and the Borough, p. 361. A lesser revolution might be effected by a byelaw
relating to the election or qualifications of the Common Council, the Aldermen,
or the Justices of the Peace ; usually of a restrictive tendency, either in transferring the right to appoint to a smaller body, or limiting the persons eligible
for appointment.

[1] *Report of Committee to obtain Reforms* (Manchester, 1808) ; *The Manor
and the Borough,* vol. ii. p. 422.

" went on strike " for a time, in their resentment of the appointment of a wealthy local landowner, because he had, within their
recollection, kept a retail shop, and still belonged to " the
Methodists." They objected to this individual, we are told,
not so much on account of religious differences, which might
possibly have been overlooked, but because his origin, his education, his connections, his early habits, occupations and station
were not such as could entitle him to be the familiar associate
of gentlemen. " The refusal of the County Magistrates," declared
an exceptionally Conservative member of the Municipal Corporations Commission, " to act with a man who has been a
grocer and is a Methodist is the dictate of genuine patriotism :
the spirit of aristocracy in the County magistracy is the salt
which alone saves the whole mass from inevitable corruption." [1]
Under the influence of this spirit of mingled reformation and
exclusiveness, the County benches came to be, at any rate from
the early part of the nineteenth century, normally recruited by
what practically amounted to co-option, the Lord Chancellor
habitually accepting the nominations of the Lord Lieutenant,
and the latter expressing the views and desires of the active
Justices. The result was, notwithstanding a rapid and continuous increase in the number of Justices during the first few
decades of the nineteenth century, a quickly developing homogeneity among them in social status and political opinions.

A conclusive demonstration of the common acceptance
during the eighteenth century of the oligarchical principle of
self-election or co-option is afforded by its deliberate adoption
for the great majority of Statutory Bodies for Special Purposes
described in the present volume. The most numerous of all
these bodies, the Turnpike Trusts, consisted, from first to last,
of persons named in the Act, who were always empowered to
continue the existence of the Trust by co-opting other persons to
fill vacancies. The more important, though far less numerous,
Improvement Commissions exhibited more variety in their constitutional structure. But throughout the eighteenth century,
the majority of these bodies were constituted as sets of named
persons, together with some ex-officio members, the body as a
whole always recruiting itself by co-option. It is only in the

---

[1] *Report on Certain Boroughs*, T. S. Hogg (H.C. No. 686 of 1838, p. 5) ; *The
Parish and the County*, p. 385.

early decades of the nineteenth century that we find the amending Acts tentatively introducing the element of election by the
ratepayers. And though in the Incorporated Guardians of the
Poor the principle of election was, even in the earliest examples,
usually introduced to some extent, amid ex-officio members and
others designated by status or named in the Act, vacancies were
usually filled by co-option.

To the political philosopher the principle of co-option or self-
election, as the method of recruiting a governing body, has
interesting affiliations to other oligarchical constitutions. By
their very nature, the non-elective Municipal Corporations were
assumed to belong to the same political category as the hereditary
monarchy, the House of Lords, the Established Church and the
freehold tenure of public office. Had not Edmund Burke himself declared that " Corporations, which have a perpetual succession and an hereditary *noblesse*, who themselves exist by succession, are the true guardians of monarchical succession " ? [1] Thus
it was not without reason that the " Corporation System "
found in the House of Lords of 1835 its last and most vehement
supporters. More interesting to the philosopher of to-day is the
historical connection of the principle of co-option with the two
other contemporary features that we have described—the
common obligation to hold public office and vocational organisation as the basis of government. Thus, we find in the records of
many Parishes that the officers for the time being, whether
Church-wardens, Overseers, Surveyors or Constables, habitually
nominated their successors. It was the serving officers who
were keenest to get other substantial inhabitants to take over
their onerous and troublesome duties. It was, in fact, the little
meeting of Parish Officers, with their empirical practice of
choosing their successors, that frequently constituted itself, by
one or other instrument, a Select Vestry for all purposes of Parish
organisation, to the exclusion of all the other inhabitants. The
same notion that those who do the work at any given time are
the best judges of those who should do it in the future, is deeply
rooted in all vocational organisation, both mediaeval and modern.
There is, however, one significant difference between mediaeval

---

[1] Burke to the Chevalier de Rivarol, in 1791, in *Correspondence of Edmund
Burke,* by Earl Fitzwilliam and Sir R. Bourke, 1844, vol. iii. p. 212 ; *The Manor
and the Borough,* p. 703.

and modern vocational organisation. Prior to the advent of the Trade Union Movement it was taken for granted that there must necessarily be, within each vocation, one or more superior grades —an inner oligarchy that would, whatever its own method of appointment, exercise some sort of jurisdiction over the humbler members. Bishops in the church, Benchers in the legal profession, Fellows in the Royal Colleges of Physicians and Surgeons, the master-craftsmen in the gilds, all alike claimed to hold the gateway through which were admitted into the vocation the junior or inferior grades of priests, barristers, licentiates or journeymen : in a word, the great body of practitioners of the profession or craft. Thus, if to the principle of vocational organisation be added the conception of graded status, there emerge in full view the " Corporation System " and the " Select Vestry System," which were swept away by the democratic reforms of 1830-1835.

The Virtues and Vices of the Oligarchical Principle of Co-option or Self-Election

Is it possible to summarise the effects, good and evil, which this oligarchical principle of renewal by co-option had on the administration and procedure of local institutions ? For it so happens that this very period of history gives us a unique opportunity of distinguishing the virtues and vices of this form of government in comparison with other and more democratic constitutions. Alike in Parish and Municipal government, and in the Statutory Authorities for Special Purposes, there is an opportunity of comparing Authorities recruited by co-option and Authorities established and renewed by popular election, either by the inhabitants at large, or by the ratepayers as such, or at least by large bodies of manual-working Freemen. In Parish government the oligarchical form was the exception, whilst the more democratic practice became increasingly the rule. In municipal government, on the other hand, democratic practice was exceptional and the oligarchical form was the rule ; whilst in the Statutory Authorities for Special Purposes we not infrequently see effected by Local Acts a sudden transformation of an oligarchical into an elective constitution.

The first conclusion to be deduced from this extensive and

varied material may seem paradoxical : it is that close bodies display not only the utmost variety among themselves ; but also even greater extremes than may be found among bodies of any other constitution. Some are more timid, others more audacious, in the use of their multifarious powers than democracies of inhabitants, democracies of ratepayers or democracies of Freemen. Some are seen to sink to the lowest depths of maladministration and venality, whilst a few reach a level of efficiency and honesty not attained during these hundred and fifty years by any other parochial or municipal authorities. Let us take first the Parish organisation. " These Select Vestries," said a blunt critic of 1828, " are a focus of jobbing ; the draper supplies the blankets and linen ; the carpenter finds the church pews constantly out of repair ; the painter's brushes are never dry ; the plumber is always busy with his solder ; and thus the public money is plundered and consumed." [1] " Select Vestries are select companies of rogues," [2] said another, seventy years before—a verdict undoubtedly true of the majority of these close bodies. But there were one or two exceptions. The Select Vestry of St. George's, Hanover Square, for instance, as it seems to us, attained a higher level of efficiency and integrity than any other contemporary Local Authority, and enjoyed a remarkable freedom from adverse criticism of either policy or administration. The minutes and other records of this Parish, from 1725 onward, reveal the Select Vestry as a little knot of public-spirited peers and gentry who governed their great and wealthy Parish with consistent honesty, and, relatively to the standards of the time, with exceptional efficiency. In later years this Select Vestry, strengthened by successive Local Acts, paved, watched and lighted the streets and squares ; carried out a certain amount of scavenging and suppressed nuisances ; systematised the assessment and collection of the rates, and put a stop to illegal exemptions ; and, in the administration of the Poor Law, voluntarily anticipated by several years some of the reforms of 1834. No evidence of maladministration was produced against these vestrymen before the House of Commons Select Committee of 1829 ; and when, in 1832, the inhabitants had the opportunity

[1] *Sunday Times*, 1828, quoted in *Considerations on Select Vestries*, 1828, p. 49 ; *The Parish and the County*, p. 233.
[2] *The Constitutional*, quoted in *The Select Vestry Justified*, 1754, p. 14 ; *The Parish and the County*, p. 233.

of electing a new Vestry, they contented themselves with unanimously choosing their old governors. Our own impression is that, during the eighteenth century and the first quarter of the nineteenth, St. George's, Hanover Square, was, under its Select Vestry, by far the best-governed Parish in the Metropolitan area.

Much the same may be said of the Municipal Corporations. No one who studies the records of such close corporations as those of Leicester and Coventry, together with case after case in a hundred other Boroughs, can doubt the substantial accuracy of the condemnation of many of these oligarchies by the Municipal Corporation Commissioners in 1835, as guilty of " mismanagement of the corporate property of the most glaring kind," the " alienation in fee of the corporate property to individual corporators," the " execution of long leases for nominal consideration," the " voting of salaries to sinecure, unnecessary or overpaid officers," the devotion of their income to " entertainments of the Common Council and their friends," the misappropriation of trust funds " to gain or reward votes both at the Municipal and Parliamentary elections " ; and, in short, of an almost unparalleled neglect of public duty and failure to promote the well-being of their respective Boroughs. On the other hand, there were a few Boroughs, no less oligarchical in their constitutions, such as Penzance at one end of the Kingdom and Wisbech at the other, which were reported as free from all the vices discovered among their neighbours—a verdict which our own closer investigation of the records has completely confirmed. Moreover, the greatest of all the provincial municipalities, that of Liverpool, whilst maintaining its rigidly exclusive oligarchy, showed itself, generation after generation, markedly superior in energy, dignity, integrity and public spirit to any other Municipal Corporation in the land, not excluding the " ratepayers' democracy " of the City of London itself. Its Bench of Aldermen discharged gratuitously the whole burdensome duty of magistracy for the town and docks ; governed the largest provincial police force of the Kingdom in a way to give satisfaction to the inhabitants ; and kept the five local prisons in a state of relatively high efficiency. The close body of the Mayor and two Bailiffs and thirty or forty Aldermen or Common Councilmen, recruiting itself exclusively by co-option, not only gave to the town its magistrates, but also acted itself as Lord of the Manor and owned in fee-simple a large portion of the land ; it governed the port ; it erected markets, warehouses and public baths ; it provided weigh-bridges and a chain-cable testing-machine for common use ; it spent large sums on widening the streets and generally improving the town ; it lavished money on the building and endowment of new churches, and latterly it established and maintained at its own expense extensive free schools. In any emergency the Corporation came forward to serve the interests of its important commercial community. More than once, during the eighteenth century, from 1715 down to 1803, it undertook the defence of the port, raising regiments, erecting batteries and equipping gunboats at its own expense. In the commercial crisis which occurred at the sudden declaration of war in 1793, when banks and business firms were failing on all sides, the Liverpool Corporation took the boldest financial step recorded in the annals of English Local Government. It first tried to borrow £100,000 from the Bank of England, with which to uphold the credit of the principal Liverpool houses ; and when the loan was not forthcoming, it promptly obtained power from Parliament to issue, up to a maximum of £300,000, its own promissory notes payable to bearer, which were accepted as currency. In this way it advanced no less than £140,000 to the local merchants, on the security of their temporarily unsaleable goods, to enable them to meet their engagements ; with the result that the panic was stayed, failures were prevented, and the whole sum, with interest, was within three years recovered without loss. It remains to be added that this self-elected Corporation made way for the representative body with unusual dignity. Unlike all the other wealthy Municipal Corporations, the Liverpool Town Council refused to oppose its own abolition. At a special meeting summoned to consider the Municipal Corporations Bill, we find it resolving " That this Council, conscious of having always discharged the important duties devolved upon it as the governing body of this Corporation with the utmost desire for the welfare and advantage of the Town of Liverpool, does not feel itself called upon to offer any opposition to the principle of the measure brought into the House of Commons, so far as relates to the removal of the members of this Council, and the substitution of another body by a different mode of election for the future management of the corporate estate, but that the same should be left to such determination as Parliament may think fit regarding it." [1]

The paradox of so extreme a divergence in administrative results among a group of Local Authorities practically identical in the form of their government is capable of explanation. The working of the principle of co-option depends in the main on two conditions : first the characteristics of the persons who are in office at the start, and secondly the existence, within the circle of eligibility, of persons of like character. The subsequent development of all these bodies is governed by the rule that " like attracts like." In the majority of urban Parishes in which a Select Vestry was started, this close body fell, from the outset, into the hands of the small shopkeepers, master-craftsmen and builders, to whom the opportunities for eating, drinking and making excursions at the public expense, and the larger gains of extending their little businesses by Parish work, offered an irresistible temptation. The Select Vestry came more and more to attract the less scrupulous and to repel the more refined members of this class, whilst the filling of vacancies by co-option tended inevitably to make the whole body homogeneous in its low standard of public morality. " As the old ones drop off," Defoe had remarked in 1714, " they are sure to choose none in their room but those whom they have marked for their purpose beforehand ; so rogue succeeds rogue, and the same scene of villainy is still carried on, to the terror of the poor parishioners." [2] On the other hand, in St. George's, Hanover Square, the Select Vestry was composed, from the start, exclusively of persons unconnected with trade, and moving in a different sphere. The " noblemen and gentlemen " of the West End squares were, as a class, quite as unscrupulous as the shopkeepers of Spitalfields, in obtaining pay without work, at the public expense. But the opportunities of this class for plunder and jobbery—for the most scandalous public sinecures and pensions, and bribes from the secret-service money dispensed at the Treasury—lay in another direction. Feeding and driving in carriages at the Parish expense

---

[1] MS. Minutes, Corporation of Liverpool, at special meeting to consider the Municipal Corporations Bill, 17th June 1835 ; *The Manor and the Borough*, pp. 490-491.

[2] *Parochial Tyranny, or the Housekeeper's Complaint against the Insupportable Exactions and Partial Assessments of Select Vestries, etc.*, by Andrew Moreton (*i.e.* Daniel Defoe), 1714 (?), p. 10 ; *The Parish and the County*, p. 245.

was no temptation to them. The supply of groceries to the workhouse, or the repainting of the Parish church, offered them no chance of profit. Hence this Select Vestry attracted to itself, not the unscrupulous and avaricious members of its class, but those who took an interest as owners, occupiers, or philanthropists, in the good government of their parish. And here, equally, the practice of co-option tended constantly to a homogeneity of motives and manners and morals.

It is needless to trace the same principle of "like attracting like" in the degeneration of the majority of the Municipal Corporations. In those few municipalities in which, for some reason, the Corporation business continued in the hands of a close body of old-established and reputable resident families (in the case of Liverpool, substantial merchants and shopkeepers ; in the cases of Penzance and Wisbech, hereditary fishermen, master-craftsmen and yeomen cultivators), the municipal business was carried on by successive generations of honourable and public-spirited administrators in the interests of the whole community. But with the surging of new populations in some Boroughs, and with the progressive exclusion or withdrawal of the principal inhabitants or more respectable citizens from the close bodies of other Corporations, we see these oligarchies more and more recruiting themselves from inferior strata. When once the deterioration began the disease grew rapidly worse, without possibility of recovery. The close body made up of venal corrupt and incompetent men continued to recruit itself from men of like character, and became a source of infection to all who came in contact with it. Such being the tendencies at work, it is not surprising that, whilst one or two close bodies remained superior alike in initiative and honourable conduct to any of their contemporaries, the vast majority fell even below the mediocre standard of administrative efficiency and pecuniary honesty that prevailed in the open Vestries and democratically controlled municipalities of the eighteenth and early nineteenth centuries.

The Vice of Exclusiveness

There was one vice which even the best of the close bodies manifested, a vice which, as a matter of fact, was eventually more responsible for their undoing than any lapse in administrative capacity or pecuniary honesty. The same law of " like attracts like," inherent in the device of co-option, caused " the Gentlemen of the Four-and-Twenty," or " the Company of the Twelve " of the Select Vestry, and the little oligarchy called the Court of Aldermen, or the Common Council, or the Mayor and the Bailiffs and Commonalty of the Municipal Corporation, vehemently to object to inviting any person to participate in the work of government who did not share their own political and religious views. Already, in 1635, we find it reported to the Star Chamber that the Parish of St. Andrew's, Holborn, had " a Selected Vestry of twelve persons, grave and ancient inhabitants, men of approved, honest and good discretion, and (which is ever regarded in their choice) men that are known to be well addicted to the rites and ceremonies of the Church of England, and no way prone to faction." [1] In Bristol the gross political partisanship of the close Vestries, century after century, was notorious. It was the support which the Metropolitan Close Vestries gave to the Tory and High Church party that, more than anything else, earned for them, during the eighteenth century, the repeated hostile criticism of the Whigs in the House of Commons ; the not unbiassed accusations of such contemporaries as Oldmixon and Calamy, and the satirical abuse of Daniel Defoe. After the French Revolution these same Close Vestries everywhere formed a wall of resistance to Radicalism against which those who strove for reforms of any kind long beat in vain. In the Municipal Corporations the vice of exclusiveness had even more sensational results. These oligarchies often controlled large incomes and an indefinite amount of patronage. They provided the bench of magistrates which administered justice, and they controlled such police forces as existed. More important than all, they frequently elected the Members of Parliament. For the most part, this political and religious partisanship, gross and unashamed, was inextricably entangled (as at Coventry and Leicester) with favouritism and bribery, and even oppression of fellow-citizens. The Leicester corporators, it is to be noted, gloried in their religious and political exclusiveness. " Holding with fervour," they resolved in 1790, " that conscientious men have the strongest of all possible motives to support and extend their own party,

---

[1] MS. Chartae Miscellaneae, vol. vii. p. 57, in Lambeth Palace Library ; The Parish and the County, p. 242.

namely, the supposition that they alone are in possession of the truth," they avowedly never " scrupled to use their whole influence and authority, whether as magistrates, as landlords, as trustees of charities or as municipal administrators to put their own party into power." [1] But even without corruption or misappropriation of funds, the very zeal and public spirit of an oligarchical Municipal Corporation might make its exclusiveness more offensive. The Mayor, Bailiffs, and Burgesses of Liverpool would probably have aroused less hostility among the powerful groups of dissenters rising to wealth in this flourishing port if they had merely wasted the corporate funds on feasting and jaunts, in corrupt leases and contracts, instead of spending the income, not only on docks and street improvements but also in repairing and redecorating old churches, in building new ones, in endowing clergymen, and most obnoxious of all, in maintaining free schools in which the catechism of the Established Church was made the basis of religious instruction. It was true that bribery, licentiousness and corruption disgraced the municipal elections of the so-called municipal democracies of Norwich and Ipswich. But in this pandemonium Whigs and Tories were alike involved ; though the majority of citizens, the non-Freemen, found themselves excluded from the chance of sharing in the spoils. What was at the time the most powerful and the most complete municipal democracy in the world, the City of London, scandalously neglected its port, its prisons and its police, and spent little or nothing out of its huge income on religion, education, science or art.[2] Yet it was exempted from the iconoclastic Municipal Corporations Act of 1835—an exemption due, not to any purity of administration or freedom from jobbery, but primarily to the fact that it was not a close body, which made it inconvenient for the City to be included in the main Report of the Commissioners. It had, as we have seen, become virtually a ratepayers' democracy, with a long tradition of defiant independence, in the name of the people, of either King or Government. This development into a ratepayers' Democracy gave the City of London, notwithstanding the scandalous corruption and extravagance that continued for at least another generation,

---

[1] MS. Minutes, Corporation of Leicester, 23rd February 1790 ; *The Manor and the Borough*, vol. ii. pp. 477-479.

[2] *The Manor and the Borough*, vol. ii. pp. 690-692.

sufficient political influence to save it from the reform that hardly any " close " body escaped. Thus, it was not the administrative inefficiency or the failure in honesty that brought down the local oligarchies, but above all their exclusiveness. Without the prodding of hatred caused by their political and religious partisanship it is doubtful whether there could have arisen in 1830–1836 any popular movement for their radical reform.

FREEHOLD OFFICE

Another characteristic feature of the ancient order continued into the eighteenth century ; and may, indeed, be found lingering down to our day. This was the permanent, or as it was often expressed, freehold tenure of the older offices. In the Parish, not only the incumbent of the living, whether rector or vicar, but also the immemorial Parish Clerk, once usually in minor orders, held office for life ; and were legally entitled to enforce payment of their customary dues and fees of office, irrespective of any particular service rendered. In the County a like tenure was enjoyed by an officer of far greater importance in the local administration, namely, the Clerk of the Peace, who was, in fact, under no control at all. The appointment, on the occurrence of a vacancy, was in the hands, not of the Justices in Quarter Sessions, but of the Lord-Lieutenant ; who had, however, no power of dismissal from office, and no right to give any instructions as to the performance of the customary duties, for which fees could be exacted. The Clerk of the Peace had an exclusive legal right to perform these duties, and to receive the fees ; and these rights he was by statute [1] authorised to devolve upon a deputy, whom he could appoint at his discretion. The office was, in certain cases, almost openly bought and sold ; but more usually, whilst the Clerkship of the Peace was held as a sinecure, the Deputy Clerkship was held, practically as an hereditary possession, by the principal firm of solicitors in the County town, which took the multitudinous fees as part of its profits. Under these circumstances it was natural that the Justices should find it almost impossible to get done any work for which a fee could not be charged. " For a considerable time past," reports a

[1] 37 Henry VIII. c. 1, sec. 3 ; 1 William and Mary, c. 21, sec. 4.

Committee of the Middlesex Quarter Sessions, " great inconvenience has been felt for want of due attention in certain departments of the office of the Clerk of the Peace. Public business is
often impeded and the time of the magistrates unnecessarily
consumed by the irregular attendance of the proper officer, and
by the delays occasioned in searching for books and papers which,
if found at all, are with much difficulty procured." [1]   When Sir
James Graham, then newly elected to Parliament for Carlisle,
alarmed at the rapid rise of the County rate, began to overhaul
the accounts of the Clerk of the Peace (who ran up his fees by
charging, for instance, £7 or £10 for his attendance at each meeting), and demanded a regular checking of the quarterly bills by
one or two Justices before they were formally presented to the
Court to be passed for payment, he was met by an indignant
protest. " It is a very unpleasant thing," complained the
offended official, " to have one's bill handed round for every one's
inspection." [2]   The remuneration of public officers by allowing
them to charge fees on all the business that they transacted,
went along with the right of property in offices. But it was
especially characteristic, as we have mentioned,[3] " of the system
which aimed at making the administration of justice self-supporting." The scandal of the system was that unscrupulous officers,
not excluding Justices of the Peace, made the fees yield an income
by a perpetual flow of business, which it thus became their interest
to promote.

Another ancient office of the County held practically by life-
tenure was that of the Coroner, who was, apart from numerous
exceptions in particular Liberties or Franchises, elected by the
freeholders of the County, had a legal right to perform the
customary duties, and could enforce payment of the customary
fees. The Coroner was under no one's orders ; and although he
was nominally subjected to dismissal from office by the Crown by
special writ, he was in practice irremovable. For the rest, it
must be said that the Lord-Lieutenant and the Justices of the
Peace, like almost all nominees of the Crown, were normally
appointed for life ; and only in the rarest cases, usually connected

[1] Report of Committee on the Records, MS. Minutes, Quarter Sessions,
Middlesex, 9th December 1824 ; *The Parish and the County*, p. 505.
[2] Lonsdale's *Worthies of Cumberland*, 1868, vol. ii. p. 81 ; *The Parish and
the County*, p. 507.
[3] *The Parish and the County*, p. 326.

2 c

with political partisanship, were they dismissed. In the Manorial Boroughs and Municipal Corporations, as in the Select Vestries and in nearly all the various Statutory Authorities for Special Purposes, life-office was the rule ; and though here and there the Crown might, in theory, have a more or less nominal right of removal, the tenure was, in normal times, rightly looked upon as equivalent to freehold.

Now, what was open to objection in this life-tenure in public office, which had once been a matter of course, when public office was so frequently, to use the words of Blackstone, an incorporeal hereditament, was not the security of tenure itself, enjoyed to-day by all persons exercising judicial functions, and even by the bulk of our Civil Servants, but (in administrative offices) the absence of any control and power of direction ; (in all offices) the lack of any practical means of even requiring the due performance of the duties of the position ; and, what was specially characteristic of the eighteenth century, the assumption that all those who were selected to fill offices of honour or authority should be owners of property, and, originally, even owners of a particular kind of property, namely, land.

The Property Qualification

Running like a red thread through all the local institutions of the eighteenth century was the assumption that the ownership of property, more particularly landed property, carried with it, not only a necessary qualification for, but even a positive right to carry on, the work of government. " We may describe feudal-ism," writes F. W. Maitland, " as a state of society in which all or a great part of public rights and duties are inextricably inter-woven with the tenure of land, in which the whole governmental system—financial, military, judicial—is part of the law of private property. . . . It is utterly impossible to speak of our mediaeval constitution except in terms of our mediaeval land law." [1] It must be admitted that, if we accept this definition, the feudal system was far from being extinct in the England of the eighteenth and early nineteenth centuries. It is needless to recall to the reader the intimate connection between the ownership of land and the still surviving Courts and officers of the Manor and the

---

[1] *The Constitutional History of England*, 1919, pp. 23-24.

Manorial Borough ; and the intermingling of the occupation of
land with the ecclesiastical and secular constitution of Parish
government. In the foregoing chapters of this volume we have
shown how this red thread of property qualification (and, wherever possible, landed property) is an almost universal feature in
the constitution of the Statutory Authority for Special Purposes. Far more significant was the fact that the most powerful
of all the local institutions of this period, the Commission of the
Peace, was based on the landed interest. " In this Kingdom,"
writes an indignant pamphleteer of 1748, " any booby is invested
with the ensigns of magistracy, provided he has as many acres of
land as are necessary to qualify him under the Act. . . . Thus,
they are nominated by dint of estate, or ministerial influence,
without any regard to their knowledge, virtue, or integrity. . . .
After this manner in every County we have ignorant petty tyrants
constituted to lord it over us, instead of honourable, ingenuous,
upright, conscientious, learned and judicious magistrates." [1]
Nor can it be said that the practice into which the Crown, during
the eighteenth century, sometimes fell, of appointing men as
magistrates without the qualification of good estate, was justified
by its results. " In places inhabited by the scum and dregs of
the people and the most profligate class of life, gentlemen of any
great figure or fortune," writes a contemporary journalist, " will
not take such drudgery upon them." [2] Successive Lord Chancellors found themselves, especially in Middlesex, driven to fill
the Commission with small professionals and tradesmen who,
as it was said, " had picked up a little knowledge by attending
on Special Juries, and thought themselves lawyers." [3] " The
Justices of Middlesex," said Burke without contradiction in
1780, " were generally the scum of the earth—carpenters, brick-
makers and shoemakers ; some of whom were notoriously men
of such infamous characters that they were unworthy of any
employ whatever, and others so ignorant that they could scarcely
write their own names." [4] Thus we find, up and down the

[1] Pamphlet of 1748 quoted in *Morning Chronicle*, 3rd December 1824 ;
The Parish and the County, p. 346.
[2] *Applebee's Journal*, 19th August 1732, quoted in *Gentleman's Magazine*,
August 1732, p. 910 ; *The Parish and the County*, p. 324.
[3] *Memoirs, etc., of Laetitia Matilda Hawkins*, 1824, vol. i. p. 18 : *The Parish
and the County*, p. 324.
[4] *Parliamentary History*, 8th May 1780, vol. xxi. p. 592 ; *The Parish and
the County*, p 325.

country, but especially in Middlesex (including Westminster and the Tower Hamlets) and the Metropolitan parts of Surrey, a particular type of Justice who, as we have seen, gained, in the documents and literature of the eighteenth century, an infamous notoriety under the appellation of a " Basket " or " Trading Justice." With the improvement in the choice of Justices, and the slowly rising standard of manners and morals, the " Justice of Mean Degree " had, at the end of the first quarter of the nineteenth century, been gradually eliminated. Meanwhile the tacit adoption by the Lords-Lieutenant of the principle of co-option, coupled with the real social apprehension and fierce political cleavages that marked the era of the French Revolution, had caused the Rulers of the County to be chosen, more than ever, exclusively from one social class—the landed gentry, who, it must be added, belonged, for the most part, also to one political party and one religious denomination. The philanthropists, lawyers and statesmen who busied themselves in the course of the eighteenth century with such matters as prisons and pauperism, highways and bridges, all alike proposed, in their various schemes of reform, to extend the powers of the County Justices, either as direct administrators of their own institutions and services, or as local legislators dictating a policy to subordinate authorities. This unhesitating acceptance of the landed gentry as an autonomous County oligarchy is to be seen reflected in parliamentary procedure as well as in legislation. So far as the internal local administration of the rural districts was concerned the House of Commons felt itself to be scarcely more than a legislative " clearing house " of the several Courts of Quarter Sessions. The Knights of the Shire who sat at Westminster habitually regarded themselves as the spokesmen of these Courts, from which they received instructions as to Bills to be promoted, supported, amended or opposed. To give an instance among many : when Whitbread brought in his comprehensive Poor Law Bill in 1807 it was taken for granted that it would be circulated to the Justices. Rose, latterly Pitt's ablest subordinate, thought that " it might go to Quarter Sessions in its present shape." Another Tory member objected that " the opinion of the Justices could not be collected at the next Quarter Sessions " on so extensive a Bill, and urged that it should " be divided into parts for their consideration," a course which Whitbread thought it prudent to adopt.[1] The student will now realise what we meant by the assertion that, in spite of the apparently centralised legal constitution of English Local Government, and of the complete dependence in law of the Commission of the Peace on the will of the monarch and his ministers, at no period did the landed gentry enjoy so large a measure of local autonomy and irresponsible power as between the accession of the House of Hanover and the close of the Napoleonic wars. It was this "local self-government" of each County by a Commission of the Peace made up of voluntarily serving territorial magnates and landed gentry, that seemed, to Rudolf von Gneist, the greatest foreign student of English Local Government, the most unique, distinctive and admirable feature of the British constitution.

LOCAL CUSTOMS AND THE COMMON LAW AS THE FOUNDATION OF LOCAL INSTITUTIONS

We pass now from the principles embodied in the structure and function of the old-established local institutions of the eighteenth century to the subsoil of local customs and the Common Law [2] in which these institutions were deeply rooted.

[1] *The Parish and the County*, pp. 554-555.

[2] F. W. Maitland thus defines Common Law : " . . . This term common law, which we have been using, needs some explanation. I think that it comes into use in or shortly after the reign of Edward the First. The word 'common' of course is not opposed to ' uncommon ' : rather it means ' general,' and the contrast to common law is special law. Common law is in the first place unenacted law ; thus it is distinguished from statutes and ordinances. In the second place, it is common to the whole land ; thus it is distinguished from local customs. In the third place, it is the law of the temporal courts ; thus it is distinguished from ecclesiastical law, the law of the Courts Christian, courts which throughout the Middle Ages take cognisance of many matters which we should consider temporal matters — in particular marriages and testaments. Common law is in theory traditional law—that which has always been law and still is law, in so far as it has not been overridden by statute or ordinance. In older ages, while the local courts were still powerful, law was really preserved by oral tradition among the free men who sat as judges in these courts. In the twelfth and thirteenth century, as the king's court throws open its doors wider and wider for more and more business, the knowledge of the law becomes more and more the possession of a learned class of professional lawyers, in particular of the king's justices. Already in John's reign they claim to be *juris periti*. More and more common law is gradually evolved as ever new cases arise ; but the judges are not conceived as making new law— they have no right or power to do that—rather they are but declaring what has always been law " (*The Constitutional History of England*, by F. W. Maitland, 1919, pp. 22-23).

We can imagine no more unpleasant nightmare for the meticulous-minded solicitor of to-day, acting as clerk to a Town or County Council, or a Rural or Urban District Council, than to find himself suddenly in the eighteenth century, and called upon to act as steward of the Manor, clerk of the Vestry, chamberlain to some Municipal Corporation or Clerk of the Peace to Quarter Sessions. Listening with bewilderment to what was taking place around him, his first instinct would be to call for the Act of Parliament determining the constitution, the procedure and the activities of the body that he was called upon to advise and serve. To the little group of tenants who appeared before him as steward of the Manor in the guise of manorial officers or members of the Leet Jury, the question would have been meaningless : they would have told him that their right to declare the customs of the Manor, to make presentments and to give verdicts, as well as their obligation to serve, came down from " time out of mind," and that there were no Acts of Parliament which affected them. The little knot of Parish Officers and principal inhabitants, who formed the Vestry to which he acted as clerk, would have been puzzled at his question. The chairman, who was also the incumbent of the Parish and probably himself a Justice of the Peace, would assert that the Parish Officers took their orders from the Justices ; and that with regard to these orders he had better look up the noted work of the Rev. Richard Burn, a contemporary clerical Justice ; but that he doubted whether there would be anything in it about the constitution of the Vestry. If this clerical Justice happened also to be a man of learning he might proceed to tell the ignorant clerk that neither the King by charter, nor the High Court of Parliament by statute, had ever endowed the Parish with a precise constitution, or even with any constitution at all. With respect to some of the most important of its features—such, for instance, as its area and boundaries,[1] the number and method of appoint-

---

[1] " The settling parochial rights or the bounds of parishes," says Archbishop Stillingfleet, " depends upon an ancient and immemorial custom. For they were not limited by any Act of Parliament, nor set forth by special commissioners, but as the circumstances of times and places and persons did happen to make them greater or lesser " (*Ecclesiastical Cases Relative to Duties and Rights of Parochial Clergy*, etc., by Edward Stillingfleet, 1698, Part I. p. 348 ; *The Parish and the County*, p. 9). Thus, the Vestries of Tooting and Streatham, in 1808, in connection with " beating the bounds " of their respective parishes, formally agreed by resolutions to exchange certain strips of land and groups

ment of its most characteristic officers, and their powers of
taxation—the Parish had no better warrant than ancient tradition, handed down from generation to generation, seldom embodied in any document, and admittedly differing from place to
place according to local usage, of which no one outside the locality
concerned had any exact knowledge. A modern solicitor would
find himself even more distressed by the constitution of a Municipal Corporation of the eighteenth century. As Chamberlain
to the City of London, for instance, he would have been told that
the Corporation consisted of an agglomeration of distinct Courts,[1]
originating at different periods and for different purposes, deriving
their authority indifferently from immemorial prescription and
royal charter. Rigid constitution there was none, seeing that
the Corporation claimed and exercised the right of altering its
own constitution without the interference of Parliament. The
Clerk of the Peace of to-day might hope to find himself more at
home attending a Court of Quarter Sessions in the eighteenth
century. Of Acts of Parliament, indeed, there was no lack,
dealing with the poor, the vagrants, the highways and so on.
But he would be disheartened to discover that there was no
statute establishing or even describing his own office ; that his
fees were regulated only by local custom, and it was long uncertain
whether or not the Justices of the Peace could lawfully dispute
his charges. Moreover, the whole procedure of presentment by
Juries of the defective highways and bridges left it uncertain
what works could be ordered by the Justices, and whether they
could assess the inhabitants for the widening of a road or the

---

of houses, with apparently no thought that this matter concerned any one
but themselves (*The Parish and the County*, 1907, p. 53).

[1] In our chapter on " The Municipal Corporation " we show that a Municipal
Corporation, like the Manor and unlike the Parish and the County, was, in fact,
not primarily a territorial expression. " It was a bundle of jurisdictions
relating to persons, and only incidentally to the place in which those persons
happened to be. But beyond this simple form, every additional jurisdiction,
it is scarcely too much to say, involved, for its operation, a separate and different
geographical area. There was one at least of the Municipal Franchises that
had no geographical limits whatever, though it is precisely the one which to-day
we associate most directly with definite boundaries, namely, the right to return
Burgesses to sit in Parliament. . . . Thus the geographical extension of a
Municipal Corporation can be represented only by an indefinite number of
circles, differing among themselves from jurisdiction to jurisdiction. One
of these—as we think the most important—was the area over which the Corporate Justices exercised their magisterial powers " (*The Manor and the Borough*,
p. 289).

making of a new bridge.[1] And when the Clerk of the Peace followed the Justices into the parlour of the tavern where, over their walnuts and wine, they issued general instructions to keep and cause to be kept the King's peace, he would be startled to find that the Justices considered themselves (as Ritson complained in 1791) " a sort of legislative body," having power to determine the behaviour of their fellow-citizens ; to forbid fairs, wakes, revels and any meetings they objected to ; to shut up public houses, and even to give to the principal inhabitants of the townships the option of closing any public houses which they or a majority of them might consider to be ill-conducted or unnecessary.[2] Or the Justices might require every Petty Constable within the County to report to them " what number of men and women servants each inhabitant within his constabulary hath, and what quality and what wages every master gives to every particular servant " ; in order that the Justices might settle what wages should be paid in future.   The Justices would even take upon themselves to alter Local Government areas, to dictate the basis of assessment to the local rates and even to divide the County into two or more entirely autonomous districts, with separate finances, separate County properties and separate rates ; whilst, as Cobbett indignantly pointed out in 1822, enactments vitally affecting the right of the destitute person to poor relief could be made in the name of the Hampshire Court of Quarter Sessions by " two squires " and " five parsons " from behind the closed doors of the " Grand Jury Room." [3] Even the Justices themselves would occasionally complain of the informality and legislative assumptions of their so-called " deliberative assemblies."   " I observed a paragraph and advertise-

---

[1] In 1710, relates a lively writer in the *Gentleman's Magazine*, " I remember a gentleman went to the Quarter Sessions, holden at Easter in a Northern County, to oppose " certain expenditure on a bridge, " for which £130, as an introductory sum, had been paid by the Petty Constables to the Chief.   The lawyer he retained addressing himself to the Court, said, Gentlemen, you must maintain the ancient bridges, but have no authority to build new ones where there never were any, without an Act of Parliament.   Then moved for a discharge of the order granted before, and for repayment of the money, which were agreed to without objection, every Petty Constable soon after receiving his respective share " (*The Story of the King's Highway*, by S. and B. Webb, 1913, pp. 95-96).

[2] *The Parish and the County*, p. 536.

[3] Cobbett's *Political Register*, 21st September 1822 ; *The Parish and the County*, p. 551.   See the " Berkshire Bread Act " or " Speenhamland Act of Parliament " (*ibid.* pp. 544-550).

ment," deprecatingly writes an eminent Suffolk magistrate in 1793, who objected to the device of a legally prescribed non-competitive wage, " in your paper of yesterday, reporting a resolution passed at the Quarter Sessions held at Bury. I assuredly did not concur in it ; but, as far as I understood it to be before the company as a matter of conversation (for I did not contemplate it as a question before the Sessions), I opposed it, and the resolve must have passed in my absence." [1] The Clerk of the Peace, in fact, was as powerless to control the Justices as the Justices were to control him. All the authority of the Justices was in its nature judicial ; it was concerned with the enforcement of the obligations of individuals or of corporations, or of pseudo-corporate bodies, under the law of the land. Once the Justices abandoned judicial procedure and retired from the " Open Court " into their private room, for mingled deliberation and conviviality, it became exceedingly doubtful whether all their proceedings were not extra-legal in character, and without formal authority.

The dependence of local administration on local customs and the Common Law had curiously conflicting results. It meant that from one end of England to the other, each of the Local Authorities enjoyed, in practice, an almost unchecked autonomy, unless and until any of its actions or decisions happened to be brought into a Court of Law. The autonomy of the Parish was checked by the subordination of its officers to the local Justices of the Peace, but the autonomy of the Manor, of the Manorial Borough and of the Municipal Corporation could only be questioned by suit in the Courts at Westminster, a very expensive and uncertain method of redress. As for the Justices of the Peace, they were judges to enforce their own decisions, and any individual Justices or local bench of Justices could do practically anything they liked so long as they had Quarter Sessions on their side. The Court of Quarter Sessions itself was subject to no formal appellate jurisdiction, and equally to no external audit or systematic scrutiny of its proceedings, the legality of which could be challenged only by action in the Courts of King's Bench, Common Pleas or Exchequer. Notwithstanding the expense and trouble of such an action, it was through the public spirit

---

[1] Capel Lofft to the editor of the *Bury Post*, 15th October 1795 ; *The Parish and the County*, p. 551.

or obstinacy of aggrieved or recalcitrant individuals that, once or twice, in every generation, led to authoritative judicial decisions, which determined, until the next time that the issue was tried, what were the qualifications and obligations, the powers and the duties, of the several officers of the Parish and County ; within what limits the Manorial Court could, by creating new nuisances, active or passive, prescribe the conduct of the local residents or mulct them in fines ; in what sense the frequently conflicting charters of a Manorial Borough or a Municipal Corporation were to be understood, and how far their decaying authority could be stretched to meet new circumstances ; what the Courts of Sewers could command in the way of assessments to make new sewers, and how the Sewers Juries were to be summoned ; and how the obligation of the Parish to keep up its highways and those of the County to maintain its bridges could be construed to include the new methods of roadmaking, and the upkeep of bridges of the very existence of which the County had had no official cognisance. It must be remembered that, in every such action, the Courts of Law decided, in terms, no more than the liability of a particular defendant in a particular issue. There was no general promulgation, and not even any official report of the decisions. The enterprise of publishers and unofficial law-reporters provided an ever-growing number of volumes of " Reports of Cases," which were hard to read and still harder to construe. The decisions were not always consistent with each other ; and it remained in all cases uncertain in what sense future judges would apply them to the differing circumstances of future actions. What was supposed to be the law might at any moment be completely changed—as we have shown to have happened, for instance, with regard to the legality of Select Vestries, and with regard to the liability of the County to maintain privately constructed bridges—if a new case was brought before a different judge, presented with additional knowledge of former precedents and existing facts, and argued by more learned or more ingenious counsel. The popular manuals of Local Government law from " Burn " to " Stone " strove in vain to condense this voluminous mass of " case law " into a systematic code to be relied upon as legally authoritative and at the same time understandable by the country gentleman or sorely perplexed Overseer.

But though, in the absence of general statutes prescribing the constitution and powers of the various Local Authorities, there existed a local autonomy amounting almost to anarchy, there was grave difficulty in enforcing, against any recalcitrant offender, any judgment or decision whatsoever. The Court of the Manor could " amerce " but not imprison ; and it was popularly supposed that no amercement could exceed forty shillings. Wealthy sinners preferred to pay the fine and continue the offence. The Justices of the Peace might, in practice, be as autocratic as they chose ; but they were sometimes checked by Lords of Manors who threatened to take a prohibition of fairs or markets into the Courts at Westminster, as an infringement of their property rights. Moreover, against the judgments of a " Single " or a " Double " Justice, there was an appeal to Quarter Sessions ; and always the possibility of the case being carried to Westminster on a point of law. What was more serious was that serious breaches of the law could only be dealt with by the dilatory and expensive process of indictment, just as civil actions for debts or damages involved, in the usual absence of any petty debt-court in the locality itself, a costly and long-delayed action in the King's Courts. Thus, the great mass of common people could be, in practice, autocratically governed, and even harried and oppressed by arbitrary taxation ; whilst the wealthy person could, by threatening to take the case to Westminster, or fight the matter at the Assizes, go far to reduce authority to a nullity. It was, more than anything else, this uncertainty of the law and of the powers of the various Local Government Courts and officers, coupled with the growing need for summary jurisdiction in dealing with offenders or recal-citrants, that gradually led to the establishment of new Statutory Authorities for Special Purposes, the steady increase in the kinds of cases which the magistrates could deal with summarily, and (in the early part of the nineteenth century) the enactment of general statutes seeking to systematise, and to codify for universal application, the laws relating to the various functions of Local Government. To the dismay and regret of those who, like Toulmin Smith,[1] upheld the ancient autonomy of the Parish

[1] In a remarkable series of volumes between 1848 and 1870, the erudite and conservative-minded J. Toulmin Smith idealises under the term " Local Self-Government " the autonomy arising out of the Common Law of England

and the Manor, and the supremacy of immemorial local customs and the Common Law, the whole field of Local Government came gradually to be dominated by Acts of Parliament. The active control of the structure and function of local governing bodies by the National Legislature was one of the new principles gradually evolved in the course of the eighteenth century.

and local customs interpreted by Juries of inhabitants. " To attempt," wrote Toulmin Smith in 1851, " in any one age, to tie down institutions of Local Self-Government to certain definitive and peculiar tasks—still more, to attempt to tie them down to the fulfilment of any of these in a particular way—does but betray the grossest ignorance of human nature and of the foundations of social and political union. It is what the Common Law and the Constitution of England never have attempted to do, though empirical pretenders in modern legislation have oftentimes done their best in this direction—with the necessary result of leading to mischief instead of good " (*Local Self-Government and Centralisation*, by J. Toulmin Smith, 1851, p. 35). " The institution of Trial by Jury," he states, " forms one, but a highly important, practical application of the system of Local Self-Government—that by which law is *administered by the people*. Hence, like every other form of manifestation of Local Self-Government, it has become, in our time, the object of the insidious attacks of the strivers after centralisation " (*Ibid.* p. 22. See also *Government by Commissions Illegal and Pernicious*, 1849 ; *The Laws of England Relating to Public Health*, 1848 ; *Centralisation or Representation*, 1848 ; *The Parish*, 1854, second edition, 1857 ; *The Metropolis Local Management Act*, 1855 ; *Practical Proceedings for the Removal of Nuisances*, 1857 ; *The Local Government Act*, 1858 ; *The People and the Parish : the Common Law and its Makers*, 1853 ; *Local Self-Government Unmystified*, 1857 ; *The Metropolis and its Municipal Administration, showing the essentials of a sound system of municipal self-government, as applicable to all town populations, etc.*, 1852 ; *What is the Corporation of London ; and Who are the Freemen ?* 1850 ; *The Right Holding of the Coroner's Court*, 1859 ; *Practical Directions for the Formation of Sewerage Districts*, 1854 ; *National Defence in Practice*, 1859 ; *On Church Property : showing that the Church of England was not endowed by the State*, 1870 ; *English Gilds* (Early English Text Society, 1870)—all by Joshua Toulmin Smith.

CHAPTER VI

THE EMERGENCE OF THE NEW PRINCIPLES

WE have now to consider what were the new ideas of social organisation, or the new principles of government, by which the old-established local institutions of the Manor and the Borough, the Parish and the County were gradually transformed. These new principles of government were not introduced deliberately, suddenly or universally : they gradually emerged in different decades in different places, with varying degrees of awareness on the part of their promoters and opponents. It is, in fact, only " by being wise after the event " that we can isolate each principle, and trace its evolution as a process of continual action and reaction between the new physical and mental environment, on the one hand, and the waxing and waning activities of the various organs of Local Government on the other. " It is not only from the point of view of logical distinctions," declares Professor Vinagradoff, " that analogies and contrasts in law have to be considered. It is clear that there is a background of social conditions which account to a great extent for the stages of the doctrinal evolution." [1]

To enable this revolution in the principles of Local Government to be understood, we open this chapter with a brief survey of the changes that were occurring, in the course of the eighteenth and the first quarter of the nineteenth century, in the life and labour of the English people. We proceed to discuss some of the novel concepts and new methods of thought that partly arose from, and partly gave birth to the changes in the material environment. But our main task in this concluding chapter will be to disentangle and to analyse the distinctive principles

[1] *Essays in Legal History*, edited by Professor Paul Vinagradoff, 1913, p. 7,

resulting from the new physical and mental circumstances in which the various local institutions had to operate : circumstances effecting so momentous a transformation in both parish and county administration, and stimulating the establishment of so many new Statutory Authorities, as eventually to render almost inevitable the revolutionary reconstructions of the Municipal Corporations Act and the Poor Law Amendment Act.

The main forces transforming the environment of English local institutions between the Revolution and the Municipal Corporations Act were, first, the Industrial Revolution (in its largest sense, including agriculture and commerce) doubling the numbers, altering the geographical distribution and transforming the status and the circumstances of the English people ; and, secondly, the new conceptions of political liberty and personal freedom, arising, possibly, in connection with religious nonconformity, subsequently manifested in and advertised by the American and French Revolutions, and incorporated in Great Britain in the administrative and legislative projects of the Utilitarian school of social philosophy.

The Industrial Revolution in Relation to Local Institutions

We are not here concerned with the two outstanding and dramatic results of the Industrial Revolution : on the one hand, the enormous increase in wealth and power of the British Empire through its dominance of the world markets ; and, on the other, the transformation of the great bulk of the inhabitants of England from independent producers, owning the instruments and the product of their labour, into a vast wage-earning proletariate, in large part subsisting always on the brink of destitution and chronic pauperism. The student who concentrates on one or other of these aspects may regard this period either as the most glorious or the most infamous in English history. The investigator into the contemporary developments of English local institutions finds the resulting transformations alike more complicated and less easy to value one against the other.

The Massing of Men

The most obvious of the changes made by the Industrial Revolution in the circumstances of the Parish and the County, the Manor and the Borough, was the vast increase in population, and the new massing of men, women and children in particular areas, a process steadily intensified from the close of the eighteenth century onward. When William of Orange landed at Tor Bay his future English subjects numbered fewer than six millions ; and these, apart from the exceptional aggregation of the Metropolis, were scattered, more or less evenly, throughout all the Counties of England, from Cornwall to Berwick, from Harwich to Holyhead. They lived, for the most part, in tiny hamlets and small villages, surrounded by wastes and common fields, with here and there a market town or cathedral city, enclosing within its ancient boundaries a hundred or two, or, at most, a thousand old-established households of traders and master craftsmen. Omitting for the moment the anomalous City of London, with its outlying villages, and the ancient cities of Bristol and Norwich, which counted each thirty thousand inhabitants, there were, in 1689, no towns of even twenty thousand —a figure not reached at that date by either York or Exeter— whilst only half-a-dozen others exceeded five thousand. The unique aggregation in the Metropolitan area alone could boast of half a million people. A hundred years afterwards the total population had reached nine millions, and when England emerged triumphant from the Napoleonic wars it had increased to nearly twelve millions, having doubled its population within a century and a quarter. But even more important than the growth in total numbers was the ever-increasing concentration of these new masses in densely crowded industrial centres. By 1835 the bulk of the English people were no longer country folk engaged in agriculture and domestic handicrafts ; an actual majority of them had become denizens of the mean streets springing up in irregular agglomerations, for the most part outside the jurisdiction of any Municipal Corporation. Over large parts of Middlesex, Surrey, Lancashire, and the West Riding of Yorkshire, in Durham and Nottinghamshire, in Birmingham and the Midlands, the Juries of the Lord's Court or the Church-wardens and Overseers and principal inhabitants in Vestry assembled, found themselves dealing, not with a little group of neighbours centring round church and manor-house, but with uncounted hordes of unknown men, women and children, crowded together in hastily built tenements ; with the ancient King's highway, which had

become encumbered with wagons and travelling beasts, transformed into streets lined with warehouses, with here and there
a factory, forge or mine, each employing hundreds, and even
thousands of " hands," and contaminating the ground, the
streams and the air with its output of filthy refuse—a neighbourhood from which the country gentleman and the incumbent,
who alone were Justices of the Peace, had usually withdrawn to
more agreeable places of residence. Exactly where the local
institutions were of the weakest type, the population became
the greatest. Some of the old Municipal Corporations, with
their own magistrates and corporate officers, often with their
own representatives in the House of Commons, had shrunk into
rural hamlets, whilst elsewhere the Manorial and Parish Officers
often found themselves the only Local Authorities in densely
peopled and rapidly increasing mining or manufacturing areas.

The Devastating Torrent of Public Nuisances

Without citing illustrative cases, as described by contemporaries, it is not easy to make the student understand the
extent and the disastrous character of the changes in the physical
environment of the common people wrought by the Industrial
Revolution, notably in the latter part of the period under review.
The successful warehousemen or millowners in and around
Manchester, for instance, who were between 1763 and 1832
growing rich beyond the dreams of avarice, failed entirely to
realise the inroads which their profit-making enterprise was
making upon the common conditions of healthy existence. Even
as late as 1795 Manchester, as pictured in Aikin's classic work,[1]
lay in the midst of smiling meadows and well-growing planta-
tions, interspersed with ponds stocked with perch and pike, and
clear streams yielding abundantly both of trout and salmon.
But in the town itself, as we have indicated, the worst nuisances
were already rife. In the last decade of the eighteenth century,
it could be said by a medical man that, " in some parts of the
town, cellars are so damp as to be unfit for habitations " ; that
there is one street in which " is a range of cellars let out to
lodgers which threaten to become a nursery of diseases " ; that
" near the extremities of the town . . . the lodging-houses . . .

---

[1] *A Description of the Country from Thirty to Forty Miles round Manchester*,
by Dr. John Aikin, 1795.

produce many fevers . . . by want of cleanliness and air."[1]
Thirty years later, all these kinds of nuisances were found
in undiminished intensity with the important difference that,
instead of one such street or group of underground dwellings or
lodging-houses there were, in 1830, literally thousands in the
same awful state. This meant that the wretched inhabitants
of these cellars and tenement houses had become, not only
more densely crowded together, but also increasingly hemmed
in, so that their whole lives were passed in the slums. The
growth of Manchester, together with the corresponding transformation of Salford, Stockport, Stalybridge, Hyde, Ashton,
and other townships, had, for miles in every direction, defiled
the atmosphere, polluted the streams and destroyed the vegeta-
tion. Whilst the Manchester Police Commissioners had been
widening one or two main thoroughfares for their own lorries and
carriages ; or imperfectly paving, lighting, cleansing and watching the principal streets in which their own mansions and warehouses were situated, unregulated private enterprise had been
covering the green fields with mile upon mile of squalid " back
to back " cottages, crammed close together in narrow courts
and blind alleys ; with underground cellars occupied indifferently
by human beings, animals and stores of cinders and filth ; with
dunghills, middens and open cesspools in which every conceivable
refuse lay putrefying. The enormous multiplication of steam-
engines, and the growth of every kind of industry had, in spite
of the half-hearted admonitions of the Authorities, both deepened
and broadened the pall of black smoke, which ever overhung the
houses, and from which every fall of rain brought down showers
of soot. Inside the town the continued increase of population
had augmented every evil. The few private slaughter-houses,
which had in old days supplemented the shambles of the market-
place, had grown to nearly fourscore, stowed away in back
yards, closed courts or even underground cellars, which they
infected with putrefying blood, offal and filth. When in 1832
the outbreak of cholera led to " an inspection of the town, conducted under the orders of a well-organised Board of Health,"
there were " disclosed in the quarters of the poor . . . scenes of
filth and crowding and dilapidation," which could, we think,

[1] Dr. Ferrier's Report to a Committee, quoted in *A Description of the
Country . . . round Manchester*, by J. Aikin, 1795, p. 193.

2 D

hardly have been paralleled in character, and certainly not in extent, in any city, at any previous period whatsoever. Out of no more than 687 streets inspected, there were 248 wholly unpaved, " 53 paved partially, 112 ill-ventilated (closed-in courts, etc.), 352 which have heaps of refuse and stagnant pools at the doors " ; whilst, out of 6951 houses inspected, 2221, or nearly a third, were found to be destitute of any kind of sanitary accommodation whatsoever. Throughout one whole quarter of the town, reports the Board of Health, " the privies are in a most disgraceful state, inaccessible from filth, and too few for the accommodation of the number of people, the average number being two to 250 people. The upper rooms are, with a few exceptions, very dirty, and the cellars much worse ; all damp, and some occasionally overflowed. The cellars consist of two rooms on a floor, each nine to ten feet square, some inhabited by ten persons, others by more ; in many the people have no beds and keep each other warm by close stowage, on shavings, straw, etc. A change of linen or clothes is an exception to the general practice. Many of the back rooms where they sleep have no other means of ventilation than from the front rooms." [1] The deplorable result of free " and unregulated private enterprise " in the development of building estates was, indeed, apparent in every growing town, not excluding the Metropolis itself. " The principle of speculation," reports a Marylebone resident in 1814, " is to take large tracts of ground by the acre, and to crowd as many streets and lanes into it as they can, in order to create so many feet lineal [of frontage] to underlet for building ; and the fruit of the speculation is the sale of the increased ground rents. These houses are therefore of the meanest sort ; are built of the worst and slightest materials, and but for their dependence on each other for support, would, many of them, not stand the term of their leases. . . . A very few years will exhibit cracked walls, sagged floors, bulged fronts, crooked roofs, leaky gutters, inadequate drains and other ills of an originally bad construction." [2]   An observer of 1768 reports

[1] MS. Minutes, Local Board of Health, Manchester, 21st December 1832. (Report of Special Sub-Committee on " Little Ireland " district.)   Part of this is printed in the *General Report on the Sanitary Condition of the Labouring Population of Great Britain*, 1842, p. 39.
[2] *Some Account of the Proposed Improvements of the Western Part of London*, 1814, pp. xxv, xxviii.

that, "in one morning's walk which we took along the Strand last week, we counted no less than seventy odd houses made up of nothing but laths and plaster—a frightful number this in a street the most frequented of the whole town ; and no wonder that so many fires are continually alarming the Metropolis while such edifices as those are suffered to stand in various parts of it." [1]   But it was not only the jerry builder who was at work. Between 1806 and 1816 the Paving Committee of the Joint Vestries of St. Margaret and St. John, Westminster, carried on a prolonged wrangle with the new joint stock gas and water companies, whom they denounced for " so frequently disturbing the pavement," and thereby heedlessly increasing by their works and omissions the dangerous obstruction of the streets. The "dilapidation of the pavements," which had, in 1816, attracted the attention of the House of Commons, was ascribed by the Select Committee to " the frequency with which the numerous water and gas companies, as well as the Commissioners of Sewers, disturb the pavements, to the great inconvenience of the public, and to the severe loss and expense of the districts which they pervade." [2]   " All the competition or rivalry which they produced," declared in 1819 a spokesman of the Vestries in the House of Commons, " was the rivalry of who should pull the pavement most violently to pieces." [3]   " It is highly desirable," concluded a leading Manchester citizen in 1834, " that the inhabitants . . . should have the ownership of works " for gas and water, on account of the " breaking up of the streets." [4]

To any Englishman of the present day, who found himself suddenly transported to the London or Birmingham, the Liverpool or Sheffield of a century ago, the most striking feature would probably be the " general nastiness " of the ground he trod upon, defiled by an almost incredible accumulation of every kind of filth.   He might next notice the noisome and all-pervading stench, which was so customary and continuous as to be scarcely ever commented upon.   A specially disgusting instance is given by an anonymous writer early in the eighteenth century. The Parish Authorities, he writes, " dig in the churchyards

[1] *The Occasionalist*, No. XIV., 1769.
[2] *Report of the Select Committee on the Present State of the Pavement of the Metropolis*, 1816, p. 3.
[3] *Hansard*, 17th May 1819.
[4] Speech of Thomas Hopkins, *Manchester Times*, 25th January 1834.

or other annexed burial-places large holes or pits in which they
put many of the bodies of those whose friends are not able to
pay for better graves ; and then those pits or holes (called the
Poor's Holes) once opened are not covered till filled with such
dead bodies. Thus it is in St. Martin's, St. James's, St. Giles
in the Fields and other places. . . . How noisome the stench is
that arises from these holes so stow'd with dead bodies, especially
in sultry seasons and after rain one may appeal to all who
approach them." [1]   A hundred years later, there was, at Bristol,
in 1822, " generally two or three times a week, a most sickening
and offensive vapour," supposed, we are told, to arise from the
gas works or salt refinery, " which hangs over the whole city
for about two hours, whose noxious effluvia is capable of awaken-
ing the soundest sleeper, and interrupting the respiration of all
who have not very strong lungs." [2]   Another way in which the
air was habitually polluted by poisonous stench was the result
of the much-valued practice of keeping pigs in back yards,
front areas, cellars and even inside rooms.   This prevailed to an
incredible extent in every town, not excluding the Metropolis
itself.   At Rochester in 1673, the Municipal Corporation, whilst
objecting to pigs roaming at large, expressly sanctioned their
being kept in the citizens' houses.[3]   In 1768 Sir John Fielding
declared that this particular " evil . . . is increased to an enormous degree ; and a number of sows for breeding, and other
hogs are kept in cellars and other confined places in the City and
Liberty of Westminster, which are very offensive and unwholesome." [4]   In the notorious district of Kensington, known as
" the Potteries," nearly every family kept pigs, which " usually
outnumbered the people three to one, and had their styes
mixed up with the dwelling houses." [5]   The almost universal
pollution of the water supply in every aggregation of people,
which inevitably resulted from the dirt and filth of the thoroughfares, and the absence of any means of disposing of excreta,
was, as we now realise, a constant cause of disease.   The dense

---

[1] *Some Customs considered, whether prejudicial to the Health of this City*
(n.d. ? 1721), pp. 7, 10.
[2] *Bristol Journal*, 10th August 1822.
[3] *An Authentic Copy of the Charter and Bye-Laws of the City of Rochester*,
1809, p. 35.
[4] *Extracts*, etc., by Sir John Fielding, pp. 100-103.
[5] *The Observance of the Sanitary Laws Divinely Appointed*, by the Rev.
Charles Richson, with notes by Dr. John Sutherland, 1854, p. 12.

swarms of pallid, undersized and wretchedly clothed wage-earners, who constituted all but a tiny minority of the population, might have been noticed, by a twentieth-century observer, to be perpetually suffering from ill-health, and to be, in fact, practically all either sickening for or recovering from attacks of what we should now term either enteric or typhus. Whilst the number of births everywhere increased by leaps and bounds—coincidently with the common abandonment of the practice of the " living in " of farm labourers and town apprentices and journeymen—the death rate was, at all ages, enormous. There are, in fact, indications that, during the eighteenth as doubtless during the fourteenth century, in the worst areas in the slums of the great towns—continually recruited by immigration from the rural districts—the mortality actually exceeded the births.[1]

The Growth of Pauperism

The catastrophic transformation in the physical environment of large sections of the inhabitants of England, in the homes they lived in, in the ground they trod, in the water they drank and in the air they breathed, was accompanied by an equally drastic change in the circumstances, the amount and the security of their livelihood. We do not need to repeat the eloquent description by Mr. and Mrs. Hammond of the effect, on the one hand, of the enclosures on the agricultural worker, and on the other, of the novel capitalist industry on the new class of wage-operatives. " How much," they exclaim, " the working classes lost in happiness, in physical energy, in moral power, in the inherited stamina of mind and body, during the years when these overwhelming forces were pressing them down, it is impossible to estimate." [2] What seemed more relevant to the Church-wardens and Overseers, and to the little meeting of principal inhabitants in Vestry assembled, as well as to the County Justices, was the continuous growth of pauperism, which dates, in many parts of England, from the very beginning of the

---

[1] We do not suggest that sanitary conditions may not have been quite as bad in the crowded towns of the fifteenth century as in those of the eighteenth century. But prior to the eighteenth century the town population was small.

[2] *The Town Labourer*, by J. L. and Barbara Hammond, 1917, p. 141. See also *The Village Labourer*, 1912, and *The Skilled Labourer*, 1919, by the same authors.

eighteenth century.   Instead of merely having to succour
by doles a few dozen or a few score of aged or sick
neighbours, individually known and complacently tolerated in
their indigence, the Church-wardens and Overseers of Parish
after Parish found themselves confronted with the administrative difficulties attendant on maintaining hundreds and
sometimes even thousands, of men, women and children, often
immigrants from other Parishes, whose circumstances were
unknown to the Officers, and whose requirements seemed to
threaten a serious inroad on the incomes of the minority of
solvent ratepayers.   We have described in our chapter on the
Incorporated Guardians of the Poor how this problem led to
the establishment of new Local Authorities, which erected workhouses and experimented, with uniform but constantly repeated
ill-success, in " setting the poor to work " to produce their own
maintenance.   In our description of the activities of the Justices
of the Peace, in legislating for the County, we have seen them
reverting to the simpler device of Outdoor Relief, which they
elaborated by " the Allowance System," into a comprehensive
scheme of making up everybody's earnings to a prescribed
minimum, varying with the price of bread.   The peace of 1815
brought with it social conditions even worse than those of the
couple of decades of war.   " From the beginning of 1816, England
was visited by an-unexampled stagnation of trade.   The poor,"
said Brand in the House of Commons on March 28th, 1816, " in
many cases have abandoned their own residences.   Whole
Parishes have been deserted, and the crowd of paupers increasing
in numbers as they go from Parish to Parish, spread wider and
wider this awful desolation." [1]

All this new destitution, complicated by the Law of Settlement and the Allowance System, confronted the unpaid Parish
Officers with intricate administrative and financial problems
which they were wholly unable to solve.   At the beginning of
the eighteenth century the total Poor Rate levied throughout
England scarcely reached one million pounds.   During the
ensuing three-quarters of a century it rose slowly to a million
and three-quarters.   Between 1776 and 1785 it suddenly bounded
up by 25 per cent.   At the beginning of the nineteenth century

---

[1] *Hansard*, vol. xxxiii. p. 671 ; *The Life of Francis Place, 1771–1854*, by
Graham Wallas, 1898, p. 114.

it had risen to over four million pounds, by 1813 to nearly seven millions, and by 1818 to nearly eight millions. Meanwhile the rates levied by the new Improvement Commissioners, who were feebly grappling with the outburst of public nuisances, together with the rising County Rate for bridges and prisons, added substantially to the local burden. Moreover, the task of assessing and collecting the rates had been completely altered from the informal agreement among a group of neighbours, as to the contributions in respect of their old-established homes or holdings, into a series of elaborate calculations without the data by which alone such assessments could be made on any equitable basis. The bewildered Church-wardens and Overseers were confronted, not only with streets on streets of dwellings of every sort and description, but also with the multitudes of newly erected forges and factories, blast-furnaces and warehouses, not to mention the newly opened collieries and canals. How was it possible for the Parish Officers to estimate the rental value of premises which had never been in the market, and the size of which, measured in three dimensions, still more the cost, was wholly beyond the capacity of their imaginations ? The mere collection of the greatly swollen rates from thousands of shifting occupiers, to say nothing of the control of an expenditure which had risen to unexampled sums, involved, in itself, a transformation of the machinery of Local Government.

The Increase in Crime

To the noblemen and gentlemen to whom, as Justices, was committed the keeping of the King's peace, there was a consequence even more sinister than the rise in the Poor Rate. The transformation of the bulk of the English nation from a settled population of yeomen cultivators, peasant copyholders, domestic handicraftsmen and " small masters," owning the instruments and the product of their labour, and accepting without question the existing order of society, into a migratory swarm of propertyless wage-earners, crowded together in the labyrinths of houses characteristic of the Metropolis, the great ports and the new urban centres, inevitably meant an enormous increase of disorder, licentiousness and crime. There is, we think, reason to agree with contemporary writers, that the overgrown and unorganised conglomeration of houses of the Metropolitan area was, from the beginning to the end of the eighteenth century, pre-eminent in criminality. We despair of conveying any adequate picture of the lawless violence, the barbarous licentiousness, and the almost unlimited opportunities for pilfering and robbery offered by the unpoliced London streets of that century. Down to 1697 the whole districts of Whitefriars and the Savoy were, by immemorial custom, sanctuaries, into the precincts of which no officer of justice ventured ; and though these privileges were taken away by statute in that year, the crowded streets and alleys of " the Mint," in Southwark, maintained a similar immunity until 1723. But even without legal privileges, the very size of the Metropolis, with its bewildering mass of narrow thoroughfares, served as one vast sanctuary, from which thieves could sally out in practical safety. " Whoever, indeed, considers," said Henry Fielding, " the cities of London and Westminster, with the late vast addition of their suburbs, the great irregularity of their buildings, the immense number of lanes, alleys, courts and byeplaces, must think that, had they been intended for the very purpose of concealment, they could scarce have been better contrived. Upon such a view, the whole appears as a vast wood or forest, in which a thief may harbour with as great security as wild beasts do in the deserts of Africa or Arabia ; for by wandering from one part to another and often shifting his quarters, he may almost avoid the possibility of being discovered." Innumerable references occur, from 1700 onward, to " the frequency of street robberies of late years." [1] " London," writes Shenstone in 1743, " is really dangerous at this time ; the pickpockets, formerly content with mere filching, make no scruple to knock people down with bludgeons in Fleet Street and the Strand, and that at no later hour than eight o'clock at night ; but in the Piazzas, Covent Garden, they come in large bodies armed with *couteaus* and attack whole parties, so that the danger of coming out of the playhouses is of some weight in the opposite scale when I am disposed to go to them oftener than I should." [2] Shenstone's account is borne out by official documents. " Divers confederacies of great numbers of evil-disposed persons," declared the Common Council

[1] *London Journal*, 19th March 1726.
[2] Letter by Shenstone in 1743 (*Works*, 3rd edition, vol. iii. p. 73).

of the City of London in 1744, " armed with bludgeons, pistols, cutlasses and other dangerous weapons, infest not only the private lanes and passages but likewise the public streets and places of usual concourse, and commit most daring outrages upon the persons of your Majesty's good subjects whose affairs oblige them to pass through the streets, by robbing and wounding them ; and these acts are frequently perpetrated at such times as were heretofore deemed hours of security." [1] " One is forced to travel," wrote Horace Walpole in 1752, " even at noon, as if one were going to battle." So great was the " increase of robberies within these few years," wrote Fielding in 1753, " that the streets of this town, and the roads leading to it, will shortly be impassable without the utmost hazard ; nor are we threatened with seeing less dangerous gangs of rogues among us than those which the Italians call the Banditti." [2] From London these gangs of robbers, and individual pilferers, radiated into the country on all sides. We have the high authority of Sir John Fielding for the statement that " There are more highway robberies committed . . . within twenty miles of London than . . . in the whole kingdom besides." [3] " The robberies," says a newspaper of 1754, " are chiefly in and about London ; and even when they happen in the country, they are generally committed by rogues, who make excursions out of London at fairs, horse races and other public meetings ; which clearly and evidently points out the true cause of them to be the overgrown size of London, affording infinite receptacles to sharpers, thieves and villains of all kinds. In the villages adjacent to the Metropolis, scarce any one resident therein, be his condition ever so low, can call anything his own." Right down to the end of the eighteenth century the neighbourhood of the great Metropolis continued to present the same scene of disorder and rapine. " The fields near London," wrote Middleton in 1798, " are never

[1] MS. Minutes, Court of Aldermen, City of London, 1744 ; given in *Eighteenth Century*, by J. Andrews, p. 230.
[2] *An Enquiry into the Causes of the late Increase of Robbers*, etc., by H. Fielding, 1751.
[3] *A Plan for Preventing Robberies within 20 Miles of London*, by Sir John Fielding, 1755, p. 7 ; see also his *Extracts from such of the Penal Laws as particularly relate to the Peace and Good Order of the Metropolis*, 1768. " Housebreaking in London," records the *Annual Register* for 1770, " was never known to be so frequent; seldom a night passing but some house or other was entered and robbed " (p. 78).

free from men strolling about, in pilfering pursuits by day, and committing greater crimes by night." [1] No one, said Colquhoun in 1800, could be approaching the Capital in any direction after dark, without risk of being assaulted and robbed, and perhaps wounded or murdered. We cannot lay down to rest in our habitations without the dread of a burglary being committed, our property invaded, and our lives exposed to imminent danger before the approach of morning." [2]

For the first half of the eighteenth century, all the evidence leads to the impression that crime and disorder were much less prevalent in the rural districts and the provincial towns than in the Metropolis. The records of convictions at Quarter Sessions are relatively few and light. Such provincial newspapers as can still be consulted reveal no serious grievances in the way of the prevalence of robbery or assault. The impression of the country districts that we derive from many contemporary sources is that of a stolid, home-keeping and reasonably contented population ; gross and sensual in its habits, but not incited to plunder or riot by extreme want ; inclined occasionally to riot in resentment of this or that grievance, but saved by generous poor relief from destitution, and intellectually submissive to the justices of the peace. After the middle of the century the picture gradually changes for the worse. With the increase in vagrancy, coupled with the growth of passenger traffic and mails, there appears, on all the great roads, the professional highwayman. With the new and rapid growth of the Northern and Midland industrial centres, we find developing whole classes of local professional pickpockets and pilferers, swindlers, cheats, sharpers and " scuffle-hunters " of every kind. The very growth of crowded slums in Liverpool and Manchester led to a reproduction on a smaller scale, of all the disorderly life of the Metropolis. " Bodies of miscreants," we read of Chester in 1787, " infest the streets and rows early in the evenings, and insult with impunity, and lay under contribution whomsoever they meet. There are no watchmen, or others who can be applied to for redress." [3] Towards the latter part of the century, the insidious but unmistakable

---

[1] *General View of the Agriculture of Middlesex*, by John Middleton, 1798, p. 460.
[2] *A Treatise on the Police of the Metropolis*, by Patrick Colquhoun, 1800, p. 2.
[3] *Gentleman's Magazine*, October 1787.

worsening of the economic condition of the agricultural population, brought about by the enclosure of the commons and the rise in the cost of living, coupled with a spasmodic stringency in poor relief, is reflected in a general increase of rural delinquency. In 1786, we read of the West of England, " Such depredations are committed in the different parts of the country by the horse and sheep stealers that the farmers are afraid to turn out their flocks into the fields. Within this week or two five horses have been carried off from the neighbourhood of Pendock in Worcestershire, and at different times within two years a gentleman farmer not far from thence has lost three score sheep." [1] What seems to have been a sort of epidemic of rural crime is reported in 1788 at Pyrland, a village near Taunton (Somerset), on the estate of Sir William Yeo. " Innumerable are the depredators and stealers of deer, sheep and fowls that have been already discovered. . . . Men, women and children have all been conspirators, and the whole country is in an uproar. We have strong evidence of twenty deer, and as many sheep, having been slaughtered and devoured in an old farmhouse belonging to Sir William Yeo. The chambers of this house are a perfect Golgotha, and horse-loads of deer skins have been sold at a time from hence. Three or four years' wool was stolen out of the lofts over his stables, packed up in the open court, and carried off without interruption during his absence. The deer were killed early in the morning, if the baronet was at home, or shot openly in the middle of the day if absent. The sheep were mostly eaten by his out of door workmen and dependents, and five or six at a time have been driven away and sold, by persons of this description. . . . These thieves used to play at cards on their nights of feasting, and the stake to be played for was always declared, perhaps three or four turkeys, geese or ducks, etc., and the loser was to go forth and steal them against the next entertainment, or undergo punishment." [2]

From the middle of the eighteenth century desperate mobs of destitute persons appear on the scene, enraged at one or other result of the Industrial Revolution. There were food-riots at Manchester in 1762, and others in Derbyshire in 1767.[3] We

[1] *Bristol Gazette*, 13th July 1786.
[2] *Bristol Journal*, 8th March 1788.
[3] *The Early English Cotton Industry*, by G. W. Daniels, 1920, p. 84.

THE NEW PRINCIPLES

have already mentioned the spasm of insurrection of the Suffolk labourers in 1765, against the erection of Houses of Industry and the withdrawal of Outdoor Relief : an insurrection which caused the destruction of thousands of pounds worth of property, and was only put down, after more than a week's unrestrained licence, by a charge of dragoons. There were riots in Lancashire in 1779 " owing to the erection of certain mills and engines . . . for the manufacturing of cotton, which . . . tend to depreciate the price of labour." [1] Sheffield broke into revolt in 1791, in resentment of the enclosure of a large common. " Hundreds of people assembled and [were] busily employed in pulling down the town gaol, after having given all the prisoners their liberty. From thence they went to Justice Wilkinson's house and set fire to his valuable library, but happily the fire was got under. They then set fire to seven large haystacks belonging to him, which are now in flames. . . . When the soldiers arrived they were obliged to fire several times. . . . The mob then dispersed. . . . The workmen are all in an uproar, and business of every kind is at a standstill." [2] At Birmingham and other places, amid the terribly high prices of 1800, there were bread riots, against which the Yeomanry had to be called out, and a force of dragoons sent for. Between 1800 and 1810, when the press-gang was at work obtaining soldiers and sailors for the Napoleonic war, and County Benches were suppressing liquor licenses and otherwise reforming the morals and manners of the lower orders,[3] there seems to have been a temporary diminution of riots and disorder. When again these break out, in 1811–1812, and still more after the distressful year 1816, they show signs of being changed in character. The riots of the eighteenth century had been, almost exclusively, the mere impulses of an untamed people, born of their impatience of suffering or restraint, the habitual licentious disorder of the individuals gathering itself up from time to time into mob outrages on a large scale, excited by some local and temporary grievance—it might be the erection of a turnpike or the enclosure of a common, the introduction of a new machine or the establishment of a House of Industry, the

[1] MS. Minutes, Quarter Sessions, Lancashire, 11th November 1779 ; *Manchester Mercury*, 16th November 1779.
[2] *Public Advertiser*, 1st August 1791.
[3] *History of Liquor Licensing*, by S. and B. Webb, 1903, chap. iii., and the Appendix on the Movement for the Reformation of Manners.

scarcity of corn or the high prices of the butchers. There was, to put it briefly, in these eighteenth-century riots, no intermixture of sedition. From 1812 to 1832 a new spirit may be detected in the riots. They are still often wild protests against high prices or angry attacks on machinery. But instead of the eighteenth-century feeling of loyalty to the King and the Constitution, and the conviction that the grievances are innovations, there appears, practically for the first time, an unmistakable consciousness among the rioters, demonstrators, machine destroyers and rick burners, that what they are in rebellion against is the established order of society, laid down by Parliament, upheld by the Courts and enforced by the standing army.

Laying the Foundations of Democracy

These four main evils wrought by the Industrial Revolution in the environment of local institutions—the massing of men in urban districts, the devastating torrent of public nuisances, the catastrophic increase in destitution and pauperism, and the consequent prevalence of crime and sedition—had, as we indicated in the last chapter, completely undermined the old principles of government inherited from time immemorial and embodied in local custom, the Common Law and the Tudor and Stuart legislation. But the results of the Industrial Revolution were not exclusively iconoclastic. The pioneers of the new Capitalism were unwittingly laying the foundations of modern Democracy. One of the barriers to reform, whether of national or of Local Government, was the Municipal Corporation, with its decaying groundwork of vocational organisation, its oligarchical constitution, its trade privileges and monopolies, not to mention its representation in the House of Commons, its inveterate policy of excluding from citizenship, and frequently from employment, all those who did not belong to one or other of its original trade groups. It was exactly against the static exclusiveness of the old vocational basis of society that the new capitalists were waging a persistent, relentless and eventually successful war. Throughout the Northern and Midland Counties, the cotton manufacturers and the machine makers, the canal constructors and the colliery owners, were building up new communities, for the most part outside the area of any Municipal Corporation.

If they were multiplying public nuisances, they were also defying the Lords of Manors ; if they were massing men, women and children in mean streets and keeping them day and night in the works, they were also nullifying the Law of Settlement and enabling the poor to escape from the jurisdiction of the incumbent and the squire as Justices of the Peace. Above all, they were successfully posing as the only representatives of the consumers' desire for cheap and plentiful commodities. Moreover, it must not be forgotten that not all the displaced copyholders and independent handicraftsmen were pressed down into the sweated industrial proletariat. A not insignificant proportion of the more vigorous, self-controlled and acquisitive among them utilised their new economic freedom to make themselves foremen and managers, and even to become themselves millowners and capitalist *entrepreneurs.*

The universal freedom of competition and freedom of contract preached by Adam Smith and practised by the new capitalist industry were, in fact, liberating not only industrial, but also political energy. The very diversity of origin of the employers combined with their rise in economic power to make them reformers. It was from the class of the " new rich," the manufacturers and warehousemen of Manchester, the shipowners and merchants of Liverpool, who found themselves excluded alike from the County Commission of the Peace and the Municipal Corporation, that emerged the most powerful recruits to the first stages of a movement towards political Democracy. Few of them, it is true, had, like Robert Owen and Francis Place, any sympathy with the industrial or political aspirations of the wage-earners. What they demanded was, in the phrase of the Liverpool reformers of 1830, " equal privileges for all of equal station." But it was from this essentially " caste " struggle between the Tory squires and the Radical manufacturers that sprang, not only " free trade in corn," the Factory Acts and an ever-widening Parliamentary franchise, but also, at successive removes, the general adoption throughout the whole Local Government of the Kingdom, of the modern Consumers' Democracy of universal suffrage.

But the Industrial Revolution unwittingly made an even greater contribution to the cause of industrial and political Democracy. The power-driven, machine-worked and ruthlessly managed establishments of the new industries produced, not only the sinews of war and the dominance of British enterprise in foreign markets, but also the British Trade Union Movement. " Whilst industrial oppression belongs to all ages, it is not until the changing conditions of industry had reduced to an infinitesimal chance the journeyman's prospect of becoming himself a master, that we find the passage of ephemeral combinations into permanent trade societies." [1] So long as all classes of the English people were divided up vertically into occupational groups, the majority of the families owning alike the instruments and the products of their labour, whether as agriculturists, as domestic manufacturers, or as town handicraftsmen, their economic aspirations and personal loyalties were attached to the leading members of the same occupational groups, even if these were their social superiors or economic exploiters. Hence we find, throughout the seventeenth century, the master craftsmen and the journeymen in each trade frequently supporting, by their petitions, the applications for privilege and monopoly made by the promoters of the national manufacturing and trading companies ; whilst the copyholders and yeomen were always on the side of the rural landowners as against other sections of the community. This vocational bias was heightened by the instinctive Conservativism of the lower orders of the English people. The "mob" of the eighteenth century, made up of the rabble from village and town, was invariably Tory in sympathy ; and its violence was constantly directed against the reformers of the British constitution and the dissenters from the Established Church. It is therefore not surprising that the early trade clubs of town artisans, and even the ephemeral combinations of factory operatives, instinctively turned first to the House of Commons and the Justices of the Peace for protection against the inroads made by the new Capitalism on the sufficiency and security of their livelihood. For some time, as we have described elsewhere,[2] the country gentleman of the House of Commons supported this appeal for the maintenance of the mediaeval and Tudor order ; but towards the end of the eighteenth century, and especially during the financial strain of the Napoleonic war, the new industrial policy of unrestricted

---

[1] *History of Trade Unionism*, by S. and B. Webb, edition of 1920, p. 6.
[2] *Ibid.* pp. 48-51.

freedom of enterprise became almost universally accepted by the governing class. The abandonment of the operatives to the operation of free competition was even carried out with unflinching determination as a matter of principle. The Select Committee of the House of Commons in 1808 reported that the ancient legal protection of the workers' Standard of Life and security of employment was " wholly inadmissible in principle, incapable of being reduced to practice by any means which can possibly be devised, and, if practicable, would be productive of the most fatal consequences " ; and " that the proposition relative to the limiting the number of apprentices is also entirely inadmissible, and would, if adopted by the House, be attended with the greatest injustice to the manufacturer as well as to the labourer." [1] Needless to say, the governing class was by no means impartial in the application of the new doctrines. Mediaeval regulation acted in restriction of free competition in the labour market not only to the pecuniary loss of the employers, but also to that of the employees, who, as the economists now see, could obtain the best terms for their labour only by collective instead of individual bargaining. Any such combination of the wage-earners, however, was in 1800 made more definitely than ever a criminal offence, which it took the organised workers the greater part of the nineteenth century wholly to abolish. We have traced elsewhere the gradual evolution of the Trade Union Movement during the past two hundred years, and its emergence into politics in the twentieth century, developing into the wider Labour Party of workers by hand or by brain, which is striving persistently to secure, for the community that "lives by working," as contrasted with the still dominant section that "lives by owning," such a Parliamentary majority as would enable it to constitute the government of the country. This brings us a long way from the slow and gradual rise of the new capitalist industry, from the latter part of the seventeenth century onward. But it is not too much to say that it was the sweeping away by the Industrial Revolution of the peasant copyholder, the domestic manufacturer and the independent craftsman, that made possible the transformation of the bulk of English people into a horizontally

---

[1] *Reports on Petitions of Cotton Weavers, 1809 and 1811*; quoted in *The History of Trade Unionism*, new edition, 1920, p. 56.

stratified democracy of workers, claiming alike industrial and political control for those who constitute the great majority of the community.

The New Conceptions of Political Liberty and Personal Freedom

It will always be a matter of dispute how far the Industrial Revolution, with its novel ideas of free competition and free contract, was itself the result of the new conceptions of personal freedom and political liberty that may be traced in the rise of religious Nonconformity, and that were so dramatically manifested in, and so widely advertised by the American Declaration of Independence and the French Revolution. Whilst some eminent thinkers, like Burke, combined an almost fanatical adhesion to the existing political order with a naïve credulity in the beneficence of free competition, there were many disciples of Adam Smith who welcomed alike the success of the American Rebellion and the sweeping political changes inaugurated by the French Revolution. At the end of the eighteenth century there seemed to be no incompatibility between complete political Democracy and the unrestrained exercise of property rights in everything that could possibly be made subject to private ownership. In the seventeenth century there had been, we think, a clearer vision. In those illuminating debates in the Council of War at Reading in 1647, we watch Cromwell and Ireton spending day after day in trying to persuade their officers and men " That which is most radicall and fundamentall, and which if you take away there is noe man hath any land, any goods, [or] any civill interest, that is this : that those that chuse the Representors for the making of Lawes by which this State and Kingedome are to bee govern'd, are the persons who, taken together, doe comprehend the locall interest of this Kingedome; that is, the persons in whome all land lies, and those in Corporations in whome all trading lies. . . . If wee shall goe to take away this fundamentall parte of the civill constitution, wee shall plainly goe to take away all property and interest that any man hath, either in land by inheritance, or in estate by possession, or any thinge else." [1]

---

[1] *The Clarke Papers : Selections from the Papers of William Clarke,* edited by C. H. Firth, for the Camden Society, 1891, vol. i. pp. 302-303. And see *English Democratic Ideas in the Seventeenth Century,* by G. P. Gooch, pp. 202-226.

And they defended their proposal of excluding from the
Parliamentary suffrage all men without landed property or
corporate privileges, by comparing them to foreigners who come
to live in the Kingdom, having no permanent interest in it. It
was useless for the protagonist of the other party, Colonel Rainborow, to assert " I doe nott finde anythinge in the law of God,
that a Lord shall chuse twenty Burgesses, and a Gentleman butt
two, or a poore man shall chuse none. I finde noe such thinge
in the law of nature, nor in the law of nations. Butt I doe finde,
that all Englishmen must bee subject to English lawes, and I
doe verily beleive, that there is noe man butt will say, that the
foundation of all law lies in the people. . . . Therefore I doe
[think] and am still of the same opinion ; that every man born
in England cannot, ought nott, neither by the law of God nor
the law of nature, to bee exempted from the choice of those who
are to make lawes, for him to live under, and for him, for ought
I know, to loose his life under." [1]   Again and again Cromwell
and Ireton reiterate that if "one man hath an equall right
with another to the chusing of him that shall governe him—by
the same right of nature, hee hath an equal right in any goods
hee sees : meate, drinke, cloathes, to take and use them for his
sustenance. . . . If the Master and servant shall bee equall Electors,
then clearlie those that have noe interest in the Kingedome will
make itt their interest to chuse those that have noe interest.
Itt may happen, that the majority may, by law, nott in a confusion, destroy propertie ; there may bee a law enacted, that
there shall bee an equality of goods and estate." [2]   At last
Colonel Rainborow ironically retorts : " Sir I see, that itt is
impossible to have liberty butt all propertie must be taken
away. If itt be laid downe for a rule, and if you will say itt,
itt must bee soe." [3]

No such foreboding of the economic implications of Political
Democracy hampered the leaders of either the American or the
French Revolution. In the Continental Congress of 1776 the
founders of the United States saw no contradiction in terms
between the institution of slavery and the declaration " that all

---

[1] *The Clarke Papers : Selections from the Papers of William Clarke*, edited
by C. H. Firth, for the Camden Society, 1891, vol. i. pp. 304-305.
[2] *Ibid.* p. 307.
[3] *Ibid.* p. 315.

men are created equal ; that they are endowed by their Creator
with certain inalienable rights, and among these are life, liberty
and the pursuit of happiness." It is accordingly not surprising
to find Hamilton and Jefferson alike without any inkling of a
possible incompatibility between a universal equality of individual liberty and the tacit inclusion of land and other instruments of production among the things in which private property
was to be maintained and ensured.[1] A few years later the
French revolutionists could unhesitatingly assume that an absolute right of private property, without limits or qualifications,
was actually implicit in the " Rights of Man," and in political
citizenship. " The end of all political association," declared the
French National Assembly in 1789, " is the preservation of the
natural and imprescriptible rights of man ; and these rights are
Liberty, Property, Security and Resistance of Oppression."[2]
The explanation of this common lack of appreciation of the
American and the French revolutionaries, as of the economic
optimism of the Adam Smith of 1776, is to be found in the fact
that the full results of the Industrial Revolution on the practical
freedom of the individual wage-earner had not then revealed
themselves. In the United States, where land was still to be
had for the asking, and any but the smallest capitals were non-
existent, the fullest " Individualism " was as practicable in the
production of subsistence as in political association. The French
cultivator was conscious of political oppression, but not yet of
Capitalism as itself depriving him of freedom. The taxation
and personal servitude to which he was subjected came, not
from his being ousted from his fragment of a communal ownership of the land, but from the arbitrary exactions of his *seigneur*,
together with the *gabelle* and other direct imposts of the Govern-

---

[1] For Hamilton's special sense of the importance of giving influence to
property, see *The Federalist*, No. 54 (p. 364 of Ford's edition). John Adams
lays it down that " the moment the idea is admitted into society that property is not as sacred as the laws of God, and that there is not a force of law
and public justice to protect it, anarchy and tyranny commence " (*Works* of
John Adams, edited by C. F. Adams, 1851, vol. vi. p. 9).

[2] *Declaration of the Rights of Man and of Citizens, by the National Assembly
of France*, translated in *Rights of Man*, 1791, by Thomas Paine, included in
vol. i. p. 79 of his *Political Works*, 1819. In the later amplifications of this
declaration it is explained that " The right to property being an inviolable and
sacred right, no person may be deprived of it, unless for reason of public necessity, legally certified, and with the condition of an equitable compensation "
(*Histoire de la France contemporaine*, by Ernest Lavisse, 1921, vol. i. p. 81).

ment. The labourers, who had swelled the population of the little market towns, as of Paris itself, saw their enemies not in the capitalist employer, but in the restrictions of the obsolescent *jurandes* or of the antiquated Municipal Authorities, by which the newcomers, or the unapprenticed man, or indeed any one outside the privileged circles, was prevented from obtaining remunerative employment.[1] In the contemporary England, too, " the country," Thomas Paine could declare, " is cut up into monopolies. Every chartered town is an aristocratical monopoly in itself, and the qualification of electors proceeds out of those chartered monopolies. Is this what Mr. Burke means by a constitution ? In these chartered monopolies, a man coming from another part of the country is hunted from them as if he were a foreign enemy. An Englishman is not free of his own country : every one of those places presents a barrier in his way, and tells him he is not a freeman, that he has no rights. Within these monopolies are other monopolies. In a city, such for instance

---

[1] The story of the suppression of mediaeval craft, professional and trading, corporations in France is well worth further investigation. In 1776 the great Minister, Turgot, passed an Act abolishing all corporations, which applied in theory throughout all France, but specifically to Paris. Every person, even foreigners, were to be free to exercise any profession whatsoever, and no combinations or meetings, either of masters or men, were to be permitted. This Act was repealed on the fall of Turgot in the same year. In the famous Declaration on the Rights of Man made by the revolutionary National Assembly in August 1789, it was laid down that all men are born and remain free and equal in rights, an abstract proposition which was elaborated in the constitution of September 1791, that all citizens are free to enter any employment without any distinction other than of virtue and talent. Meanwhile an Act had been passed in March 1791 in connection with a tax on the licence to exercise a profession, abolishing all the ancient mediaeval corporations connected with crafts, arts and commerce, and suppressing all professional privileges whatsoever. A more comprehensive Act arising out of the innumerable strikes in Paris and other French towns during the Spring of that year, and drafted by Chapelier, passed in June 1791, abolishing and forbidding all corporations of citizens or combinations, or even meetings of citizens belonging to particular professions, as wholly inconsistent with the fundamental basis of the French constitution. It was on the occasion of the passage of this Act that Marat wrote his famous letter to the Assembly, laying down that though it was necessary that liberty of meeting should be guaranteed to citizens, no meeting or assembly of citizens of particular professions having economic interests in common should be allowed. " Il n'y a plus de corporations dans l'État ; il n'y a plus que l'intérêt particulier de chaque individu, et l'intérêt général." Marat went on to explain that even Friendly Societies were objectionable because they led to conspiracies. Full particulars are given in *Histoire des classes ouvrières et de l'industrie en France de 1789-1870*, E. Lavasseur, 2 vols., 1903. See also *Histoire des Corporations de Métiers*, 1897, pp. 474-510, by Étienne Martin Saint-Léon.

as Bath, which contains between twenty and thirty thousand inhabitants, the right of electing representatives to Parliament is monopolised into about thirty-one persons. And within these monopolies are still others. A man, even of the same town, whose parents were not in circumstances to give him an occupation, is debarred, in many cases, from the natural right of acquiring one, be his genius or industry what it may." [1]

It was therefore inevitable that, with all these personal oppressions, these municipal and vocational monopolies, these hampering restrictions on men earning a livelihood as they best could, that the whole strength of the reform movement should have been directed to the removal of what were obviously "artificial" restraints on individual freedom. The twin movements for political and industrial freedom seemed to be but parts of a common bursting of bonds. Thus, the constant aspiration of the revolutionaries of the close of the eighteenth century, alike in England and in France, was to get back to the individual, the common citizen, the undifferentiated man. Parcelled out into equal electoral districts so that each man should count as one, and for no more than any other man, this mass of identical citizens were to elect their representatives and thereby control their agents, in the indispensable work of government. Thus, the undifferentiated citizen, whose needs the government was to serve, and whose freedom in disposing of his income was to be absolute, was visualised, not as a producer, whether lawyer or land cultivator, cleric or craftsman, physician or farrier, but entirely as a consumer of commodities and services. It was this particular conception of political liberty and personal freedom that was one of the ferments that in England determined the new principles of Local Government presently to be described.

At this point in our analysis of the new mental environment of English Local Government between the Revolution and the Municipal Corporations Act we are brought against religious Nonconformity and its rapid spread, especially among the industrial workers of the North and Midlands, during the latter part of this period. With the theological and emotional aspects of this revolutionary movement of thought we are not here

---

[1] *Rights of Man*, by Thomas Paine, 1791 ; included in his *Political Works*, 1819, vol. i. p. 46. See also Godwin's *Political Justice*.

concerned. For our present purpose it counts merely as one among many expressions of the new conceptions of political liberty and personal freedom. Perhaps the most bitterly resented manifestation of the oligarchical principle was the exclusion of Dissenters from all offices of power and dignity, alike in the Counties and in the Municipal Corporations : an exclusion actually sanctioned by statute law. On the other hand, the humbler and more onerous offices of Overseer, Constable and Surveyor of Highways, and, oddly enough, also that of Churchwarden, were, as we have shown, obligatory on all inhabitants not expressly granted a privileged exemption. Moreover, it was always in the power of a select body recruited by co-option to exclude Nonconformists even from membership, as well as from all offices whatsoever, and, this as we have shown, was the invariable practice of the Select Vestries of Bristol and London. Hence, even the wealthy shipowners and merchants of Liverpool and the millowners and warehousemen of Manchester, the shopkeepers of St. James's and St. Marylebone, if, as was frequently the case, they did not belong to the Anglican Church, found themselves, like the Roman Catholics, not only excluded from public office, but actually taxed and governed by trade rivals who happened to adhere to the established creed. It was, more than anything else, this ostracism because of their religion that made these opulent reformers so persistent in their demand, as expressed in the Liverpool petition, that " all in equal station should enjoy equal privileges." [1] In the new manufacturing districts in which the Nonconformists were in the majority they sometimes took their revenge. We have described in our account of the open Vestry [2] the turbulent public meetings in the ancient Parish churches of Leeds and Manchester, when Nonconformist Churchwardens, even occasionally with their hats on, whilst smoking their pipes, sitting on the Communion table, objected to such items in the Parish accounts as payment for the sacramental wine and the washing of surplices ; and refused resolutely, amid the applause of a disorderly mob, to make any Church Rate. Beneath the rivalry of religious creeds we see emerging the contemporary struggle between government by the minority who performed the service,

[1] *The Manor and the Borough*, p. 701.
[2] *The Parish and the County*, pp. 91-103.

and government by the mass of undifferentiated citizens who were assumed to enjoy it.[1]

The Utilitarians

The impulse to change supplied by the common faith in political liberty and personal freedom, and the emphasis laid on satisfying the desires of the average citizen-consumer, were greatly strengthened, from the end of the eighteenth century, by the persuasive force of a new social philosophy. The Utilitarians, as Professor Graham Wallas remarks in his admirable *Life of Francis Place*, " though they broke with the French revolutionary thinkers and the whole doctrine of Natural Rights, nevertheless retained many of the characteristic habits of eighteenth-century thought. They believed themselves to have found a common-sense philosophy, by which ordinary selfish men could be convinced that the interests of each invariably coincided with the interests, if not of all, at any rate, of the majority." [2] What was needed to complete this all-embracing principle of individual self-interest was knowledge, by which term Jeremy Bentham and James Mill meant, not the observation and analysis of facts, but a series of logically accurate deductions from a single law of human nature, namely that every man will follow his own interests as he understands them : a law as certain and as uniform in its operation in human society as the law of gravitation in the physical universe. " So complete was my father's reliance on the influence of reason over the mind of mankind," we are told by John Stuart Mill in his *Autobiography*, " whenever it is allowed to reach them, that he felt as if all would be gained if the whole population were taught to read, if all sorts of opinions were allowed to be addressed to them, by word and in writing, and if, by the means of the suffrage, they could nominate a legislature to give effect to the opinions they adopted." [3]

It was plain that this choice by every man of the pursuit of

---

[1] The three rival conceptions of government, by the vocation concerned, by political democracy, and by consumers' democracy, can be followed in the history of the Christian churches. Whilst the Roman Catholic Church is a purely vocational government, most of the English nonconformist denominations are unmixed consumers' democracies. The Church of England presents a mixed government of vocational and political control, to which has been added by recent legislation, a certain degree of congregational or consumers' participation.   [2] *Life of Francis Place*, by Graham Wallas, 1898, p. 89.

[3] John Stuart Mill's *Autobiography*, p. 106 ; *The Life of Francis Place*, by Graham Wallas, 1898, p. 93.

his own interests was, in the England of George the Third, hampered and prevented by all sorts of obsolete and ill-contrived laws, as well as by institutions devised for the purpose of giving exceptional advantages to favoured classes and individuals. Accordingly, Bentham [1] and his disciples, here following Jefferson and Priestley, were perpetually emphasising the fact that any social institution, even the British Constitution itself, ought to be swept away if it ceased to be useful ; that is, if it could be shown not to conduce to the greatest good of the greatest number. Hence all laws ought to be periodically reviewed and suitably amended, or even replaced by entirely new laws according to the circumstances of the time. The old plea in favour of local customs, " that they had existed from time immemorial," or the claim that the Common Law of England must be maintained because it embodied the wisdom of past generations, appeared to Jeremy Bentham and James Mill as a pernicious superstition. It was at this point that the Utilitarians found themselves in practical agreement with those who believed, with fanatical fervour, in the " Rights of Man." The most vital of the three fundamental Rights of Man, Dr. Price had explained in his famous sermon on the fourth of November, 1789, were to choose our own governors, to cashier them for misconduct, and to frame a government for ourselves.[2] These rights, it is clear, involved a

[1] We need not refer the student to Bentham's *Works*, in Sir John Bowring's edition in 11 volumes. Much suggestive analysis of the influence and significance of the Utilitarians will be found in Sir Leslie Stephen's *The English Utilitarians* as in the *Life of Francis Place* and other works by Professor Graham Wallas. But we have found most illuminating, in connection with Local Government, the three brilliant volumes, by M. Elie Halévy, on *La Formation du Radicalisme économique* (*La Jeunesse de Bentham*, 1901 ; *L'Evolution du doctrine utilitaire*, 1901 ; and *Le Radicalisme philosophique*, 1904).

An interesting confirmation of the influence of the Benthamites on the legislation of 1832–1836 is supplied by the works of Toulmin Smith, who, in his successive pamphlets and books, attributed the contemporary movement towards centralisation and bureaucracy and the commercialisation of local administration, to the pedantic doctrinairism and materialist ends of the followers of Bentham, especially Edwin Chadwick and his colleagues at the Board of Health.

[2] The three fundamental rights of man were, according to Dr. Price, " The right to liberty of conscience in religious matters ; the right to resist power when abused ; and the right to choose our own governors, to cashier them for misconduct and to frame a government for ourselves " (*A Discourse on the Love of our Country*, delivered on November 4th before the Society for Commemorating the Revolution in Great Britain, 1789, by Robert Price, D.D., LL.D., F.R.S., London, 1789).

freedom of perpetual innovation on the part of each succeeding generation. " The reasonableness and propriety of things," declared Thomas Paine in 1792, " must be examined abstractedly from custom and usage ; and in this point of view, the right which grows into practice to-day is as much a right, and as old in principle and theory, as if it had the customary sanction of a thousand ages. . . It is, however, certain," he continued, " that the opinions of men, with respect to systems and principles of government, are changing fast in all countries. The alteration in England, within the space of little more than a year, is far greater than could then have been believed, and it is daily and hourly increasing. It moves along the country with the silence of thought." [1]

The effect of the Utilitarian social philosophers was thus not only to discredit local custom and the Common Law, and to lead to the enactment of brand new statutes, and their constant revision and codification, but also to suggest new principles of administration. For, although the Utilitarians firmly believed that each person always acted in such a way as he believed would increase his own pleasures or diminish his own pains, Bentham never had as much faith as Adam Smith in the assurance that this free play of individual self-interest would automatically, without social contrivances of one sort or another, produce the greatest happiness of the greatest number. Accordingly, unlike Adam Smith, Bentham was constantly devising new laws and new social institutions to replace the old ones. Never has there been, at any time or in any country, such a stream of projects for deliberate and often compulsory social improvement, as issued from the little house near Birdcage Walk, whether in the way of amendments of the Poor Law, the institution of reformatory prisons, the collective organisation of " Schools for All," the reorganisation of the magistracy and the Courts of Justice, the codification of the law, so that it might be brought within the knowledge of every citizen, and the most ingenious social devices for systematically preventing error, fraud, misunderstanding or deceit. All these separate projects had in common the idea of artificially combining the pecuniary self-interest of the individual citizen with the greatest happiness

---

[1] *Letter Addressed to the Addressers, on the late Proclamation*, by Thomas Paine, 1792, included in his *Political Works*, 1819, vol. ii. p. 34.

of the greatest number. Far from dispensing with law and public administration, what Bentham desired was that his uncouth formula, "the duty-and-interest-junction-principle," should dominate the whole field of government, which he always recognised as indispensable. This explains his obsession in favour of "farming," or "putting out to contract, at the lowest price yielded by competitive tender, every function in which this plan was conceivable, whether the execution of public works, the conduct of a prison, the setting to work of the unemployed, or even the maintenance of orphan children. But he could not ignore the fact that the contractor would himself seek his own pecuniary advantage ; and to prevent this militating against the public interest, Bentham devised an equally bewildering array of checks, from the " central inspection chamber," perpetually surveying the radiating corridors and workshops of the Panopticon, to the " life-warranting principle," by which the prison or Poor Law " farmer " had to pay a forfeit, at a progressive rate, for every death above the previous average that took place among those committed to his charge. All this, as subsequently elaborated by Edwin Chadwick, involved a hierarchy of centrally appointed inspectors, to whose pecuniary advantage it would be to "catch out " the army of contractors. In short, Bentham sought, as would now be said by the business man, to introduce into government departments the motives and methods of profit-making enterprise. His influence, exercised through his disciples, and notably in the couple of decades of Edwin Chadwick's official life, was to " commercialise " public administration.

There was another implication of the Benthamite philosophy which had a special bearing on English Local Government. As what had to be secured was the interest of the majority of the whole community, it seemed to follow that no geographical section of the community, and therefore no Local Authority, could be trusted or permitted to enjoy complete autonomy in the interests of its own constituents. We forget to-day how novel a hundred years ago was the inference that, not only general laws applicable to the whole nation, but also central government departments able to secure the interests of the community as a whole, even against the desires of any one locality, were imperatively required. The Benthamites foresaw that these central departments at Whitehall would have, for their function, by their ubiquitous inspection and continuous instruction, to overcome the "froward retention of custom," the bucolic ignorance, the secretiveness, the bias, and the possible corruption characterising remote districts, small areas of administration, and any "localised" or "sectional" group. Hence a commercialised municipal administration was to be incessantly stimulated, guided and checked, under the control of the national Representative Assembly, by an authoritative expert bureaucracy. It is easy, after a century of experience, to see defects and limitations in the elaborate official reconstruction that formed an indispensable part of the Benthamite scheme. It was characteristic of the extreme intellectualism of the Benthamites that they vastly exaggerated the superiority in width of information, extent of experience, and knowledge of principles, which a central government might be expected to possess as compared with any Local Authority ; just as they enormously over-estimated the certainty with which the able investigators and distinguished administrators of the central departments could be trusted to decide what were the interests of the community as a whole ; or the persuasiveness with which they could induce a recalcitrant Local Authority to believe in the superiority of Whitehall. We may to-day recognise how much there is to be said for a more highly organised and more delicately adjusted relation, and for a more balanced estimate of the claims and wills of local and central authorities respectively, than Bentham ever visualised or than Chadwick would admit. But no one who realises the state of things in 1833, when under the Reformed Parliament, the Benthamites, for a few brief years, came into their own, can doubt the great public benefit, even with all their shortcomings and defects, effected by the Commissioners who enquired into the Poor Law, the Municipal Corporations, and the sanitary condition of the population ; or the imperative necessity of some such central departments as they wished to see established to inspect, guide and control the local administration of poor relief, public health and municipal government generally.

The New Principles in Local Government

We have now to trace the emergence, amid the revolutionary changes both in the industrial environment and in thought, between the Revolution and the Great Reform Bill, of new principles in Local Government. These new principles are found embodied, not only in the succession of Parliamentary statutes culminating in the Poor Law Amendment Act, the Municipal Corporations Act and the Acts for registering Births, Deaths and Marriages, but also in the administrative expedients spontaneously adopted by the Parish and the County, the Municipal Corporations and the new Statutory Authorities for Special Purposes.

The more important of these new conceptions were in direct contradiction of the old principles that they superseded. The use of the contractor, employing labour at competitive wages, gradually ousted the citizen's obligation to serve gratuitously in public office, and introduced the ratepayer as the predominant economic interest in Local Government. Government by citizen-consumers superseded the decaying remnants of the vocational organisation that underlay the constitution of the Manor and the Borough. Representative Democracy gradually gained ground on, though it never entirely eliminated, the oligarchical principle of Co-option. The advent of the salaried expert, bringing the technique required for the new services, threatened the authority, if not the very existence, of the inheritor or pur-chaser of freehold office, endowed with the right to rule or to tax his fellow-citizens. Equally important with these changes, in the very structure and function of the local institutions, was the increasing intervention of Parliament, prescribing the con-stitution and powers of local governing bodies, with the resulting substitution of innovating statutes for immemorial local custom and the Common Law. Finally, in the supervising, inspecting and sanctioning authority vested in central government depart-ments, there is the beginning of a new kind of national executive control of local affairs. The only conception that was, down to the very end of the period, retained almost intact, was that which made property, if possible landed property, a necessary qualifica-tion for important public office, thereby maintaining the landed gentry as the Rulers of the County ; though their activities were increasingly encroached upon by new forms of Ratepayers' Democracies.[1]

The Contractor and his Staff of Wage Labourers

When the task of Local Government became too onerous for the unpaid and compulsorily serving officer of the Parish or Manor, Borough or County ; when the work to be done involved the continuous labour, day after day, not of one but of a number of pairs of hands ; when even the planning and direction of the operation transcended both the time and the skill of the farmer or tradesman conscripted for his turn of service as Overseer, or that of the country gentleman called upon to act as Bridge-master, recourse was had to the paid service of the contractor, with his staff of men at wages. At the outset, this new expedient was far removed from the nineteenth century professional profit-maker wielding armies of workmen of different kinds and grades. The first innovation was no more considerable than to permit the Churchwarden or Surveyor of Highways, the Town Clerk or Bridgemaster to make payments to one or more workmen, who

---

[1] It is significant of the slow and gradual evolution of English institutions that, in 1922, after nearly another century of extensive changes, we find still in existence many isolated survivals of all the old principles that characterised the institutions of the close of the seventeenth century. Thus the citizen's obligation to serve gratuitously in public office continues in the Jury and the High Sheriff. Under the Act of 1872, residents may still be appointed to serve as Parish Constables if the Justices in Quarter Sessions think this neces-sary (sec. 92). The liverymen of the City Companies fictitiously representing old-established trades, still elect the Lord Mayor and Sheriffs of the City of London, whilst in some other ancient Municipal Corporations the Freemen still enjoy privileges. The principle of co-option not only survives in the Alder-men, but has been introduced at various points in the municipal organisation of the new public services of Education and Health. Freehold office is still the characteristic form in the Anglican Church, whilst no sacrilegious hand has been laid on the office by tenure of the immemorial Lords of the Level of Romney Marsh. Local customs are still successfully pleaded in the Courts of Justice, and the actual domain of the Common Law is probably no less extensive, notwithstanding the vast development of statutory enactment and various attempts at systematic codification, than it was in 1689. Even the possession of landed·property lingers as a necessary qualification for appointment as High Sheriff or as Commissioner of Sewers ; and, by Act of 1917, any owner of real property, by freehold or any other tenure, is qualified to be elected a member of any Local Government Authority for the area in which the pro-perty is situated, without being a resident, a ratepayer or a registered elector (7 and 8 George V. c. 64, §§ 3-10). Except for this, no one can be a member of the Metropolitan Asylums Board whose name is not on the ratebook of some London Parish for property rated at £40 a year.

could carry out the necessary repairs or works at the customary rates. Presently the whole service was entrusted to a master-craftsman or local trader, who might or might not assume the title of Town Carpenter or Pavior, but who was habitually employed, either by the Local Authority itself, or successively by individual citizens, to do what was required in building or paving. As the business grew, in variety as well as in magnitude, and especially when the needs to be met were those of a new and .rapidly growing urban district, there came to be a whole set of tradesmen employed on various kinds of building and sewer work, on the multitudinous repairs of the increasing public property of one kind or another, and on the furnishing or decorating of the different institutions. Meanwhile, the habit of contracting for public services had been growing along another line. Up and down the country, in every conceivable service, the easiest way of getting done any continuous duty, seemed to be to " farm " it, or put it out to contract to the man who offered the most advantageous terms. It is the almost universal prevalence of this contract system in the eighteenth century that explains the exiguity of the executive staff. The stretch of highway could be repaired and kept in order by a contractor. The troublesome accumulation of garbage could be kept down by getting some one to contract for its removal, with no more demand on the time or labour of the unpaid public officers than the periodical payment of the " farmer's " account. The rows on rows of street lamps, which took the place of the swinging lantern of the individual householder, could be made and fixed by contract, cleaned by contract and lit by contract. The collection of the public revenue could equally be " farmed " ; and tolls and dues, from parish pounds and manorial cornmills up to municipal markets and turnpike roads, could be made the basis of contractual payments, leaving the contractor to incur all the labour and risk which would otherwise have fallen on the Local Authority or its gratuitously serving officers. It was early discovered that the poor could be " farmed," and their main-tenance secured, either for so much per head, or even for a fixed lump sum per annum, the " farmer " making what profit he could out of " setting the poor to work." Having got under his control the contingent of pauper labour, the contractor could then profitably tender for the service of cleaning the streets at a fixed sum. But the most scandalous of all these forms of contract, because of the opportunity and the temptation that it gave for the worst oppressions, was the farming of the prisons. These, like the workhouses, could be let by contract to the gaolers, keepers, masters or governors ; the wretched inmates, if fed and clothed at all, could be fed and clothed by contract, and even physicked by contract. The vagrants were conveyed by contract, fed by contract and also whipped by contract ; and when the felons were sent beyond seas, they were habitually transported by contract, and sold by auction on arrival to those who contracted at the highest rate to employ them.

Now, this substitution, as the motive and reward for the execution of the function of the Local Authority, of profitmaking and the earning of wages for public work—inevitable as it may have been—had all sorts of far-reaching results, upon which it is unnecessary here to dwell. But one of its accompaniments, in the very rudimentary stage at which government organisation had then arrived, was an unchecked, and, indeed, an entirely unashamed prevalence of what is now stigmatised as favouritism and corruption. When the holder of a public office was allowed to make its exercise an opportunity for private profit, it became almost inevitable that his interests as a profit-maker should come into conflict with his duty as a vigilant steward of the public funds. When the jobs to be paid for by the Parish or the Borough were given, as a matter of course, to the uncontrolled Parish Officers or to the various members of the Select Vestry or of the Town Council, or even when they were shared among a relatively small body of Freemen, without competition and without any impertinent scrutiny of their bills, the way was clear for the orgy of corruption which characterised, in varying degrees, nearly all the Local Government of the eighteenth and early nineteenth centuries. The very exclusiveness inherent in the dominant principle of Co-option, as a method of recruiting the governing group, accelerated the downward drift into favouritism and corruption. " Every Parish Officer," wrote a shrewd London observer in 1796, " thinks he has a right to make a round bill on the Parish during his year of power. An apothecary physics the poor ; a glazier, first in cleaning, breaks the church windows, and afterwards mends them, or at least charges for it ; a painter repairs the Commandments, puts new coats on Moses and Aaron, gilds the organ-pipes, and dresses the little Cherubim about the loft as fine as vermilion, Prussian blue, and Dutch gold can make them. The late Churchwardens [of the writer's own London Parish] were a silversmith and a woollen draper ; the silversmith new-fashioned the communion plate, and the draper new-clothed the pulpit and put fresh curtains to the windows." [1] It would, however, be unfair to suggest that predominantly Tory membership of the Close Bodies was any worse at this game than the predominantly Radical and popularly elected Common Councillors of the City of London. The most common form of plunder, in which nearly all the members of that Corporation participated, was the execution of work or the provision of goods for the Corporation, in their respective trades, without competition, often at the most extravagant prices. " Here the sacred office of a Common Councilman," we are told by a contemporary writer, " is prostituted to the lowest and basest ends." [2] The multiplication of standing or permanent master craftsmen undertaking work as profit-making contractors for the Corporation was carried on, we are told by a contemporary writer, " to an incorrigible extent." There was the " Land Carpenter of the Bridge House, the Water Carpenter, the Bridge House Mason, the Bridge House Bricklayer, the City Plasterer, the City Plumber, the Bridge House Plumber, the City and Bridge House Painter, the City Printer, the City and Bridge House Glazier, the City Stationer, the City Smith, the Bridge House Smith, the City Founder, the City and Bridge House Purveyor," and so on, *ad infinitum*.[3] Spasmodic attempts were made by the more honourable members of the Court to prevent the grossest of the favouritism by Standing Orders, which it cost a whole half-century of effort to get adopted, designed to stop the habitual practice of the shopkeeper members giving each other orders for supplies or work, or actually appointing each other to the salaried offices in their gift. Unfortunately the Standing Orders could always be suspended ; and we are told by a newspaper critic in 1826 that this course was habitually taken.

[1] *The Olio*, by Francis Grose, 1796, pp. 217-218 ; *The Parish and the County*, p. 79.
[2] *City Corruption and Maladministration Displayed*, by a Citizen, 1738, p 4 ; *The Manor and the Borough*, p. 650.
[3] *Ibid.*

" Whenever a case arises in which they ought to be strictly enforced, some Honourable Member rises in his place and moves that they be suspended, and, as a matter of course, they are suspended accordingly. . . . Whenever any snug situation . . . is declared vacant . . . any member of the Court . . . per-suades some kind friend . . . to move that in his particular case the Standing Orders may be suspended. . . . The Court finds it impossible to resist an appeal of this kind, as it is made on the principle, ' Do this for me to-day, and I will do as much for you another time.' " [1]

To the modern administrator it must seem strange that not for something like a century is there any systematic attempt to prevent this naïve combination of profit-making with public office. The eighteenth century does not seem to have been able to bring itself to give up the plan of gratuitously serving public officers, constrained to undertake onerous duties. Even in the nineteenth century the engagement of a salaried official staff was commonly denounced—as it still occasionally is in the twentieth century—as " bureaucracy." The first remedy for corruption was an attempt to restrain the unpaid representative, whose duty it was to protect the common purse, from himself contract-ing for public work. Not until the last decades of the eighteenth century do Parish Vestries decide, in one form or another, " that none of the gentlemen hereafter chosen and appointed to the offices of Churchwardens and Overseers of the Poor of this Parish shall, under any pretence whatever, be permitted to serve the workhouse with provisions, or any other article or commodity whatsoever, or send any materials, or do any work either in or about the workhouse, or otherwise on the Parish account while in office.' " [2] It occurred to some one to embody such a self-denying ordinance in statute law, and this was effected in some of the Local Acts.[3] Not until 1782 was it made a penal offence

---

[1] No. 629 of " Sketches of Aldermen, etc." (MSS. Guildhall Library) ; *The Manor and the Borough*, p. 651.

[2] *The Parish and the County*, p. 120.

[3] It seems that in one of the Local Acts obtained by the City of London in the first half of the eighteenth century, the House of Commons insisted, against the wishes of the representatives of the Common Council, on inserting a clause excluding members of the Common Council from participating in any of the contracts under it (*The Manor and the Borough*, p. 650). Exactly when similar clauses became the rule in Local Acts we have not been able to discover. But in 1773 we find the following clause in an Act for the building

2 F

for Churchwardens or Overseers, or other persons responsible for
the maintenance or management of the poor, themselves to
contract for, or supply, goods to be paid for out of the public
funds for which they' were themselves responsible.[1] In 1824 a
similar prohibition was applied to members of Turnpike Trusts.[2]
Even then no general statute forbade a member of a Municipal
Corporation, or, indeed, a member of any Local Authority not
being a Turnpike Trust, and not concerned with poor relief, to
supply goods to, or do work for, or enter into profitable contracts with the corporate body of which he formed part. Not
until the Municipal Corporations Act of 1835, and then only
with regard to the Boroughs to which that Act applied, was this
even made a cause of disqualification for office.[3]

At the beginning of the nineteenth century, the Philosophic
Radicals and Political Economists thought they had found an
additional or an alternative remedy in the universal insistence on
competitive tendering, and the automatic acceptance of the
lowest tender.[4] This unredeemed competitive tendering, when it

---

of a bridge : " No person shall be capable of acting as a Commissioner in any
case in which he shall be interested, or in any manner whilst he shall hold any
office, or in his private capacity be concerned in any contract or agreement
relative to the execution of this Act ; and if any person shall act as a Commissioner, not having the requisite qualification of estate, or being otherwise
hereby disqualified from acting, he shall, for every offence, forfeit the sum of
£50 " (13 George III. c. 83 ; An Act for building a Bridge across the River
Thames from Richmond in the County of Surrey to the opposite Shore, in the
County of Middlesex, etc.).

[1] In the so-called Gilbert Act of 1782 (22 George III. c. 83, sec. 42) we find
the following clause : " If any visitor, guardian or governor, shall sell or furnish
any materials, goods, clothes, victuals, or provisions, or do any work in his
trade for the use of any workhouse, poor house, or poor persons, within any
parish, township, or place, for which he shall be so appointed to act, or be
concerned in trade or interest with any person or persons who shall sell, provide,
do, or furnish the same, he shall for every such offence, forfeit a sum not
exceeding twenty pounds, nor less than five pounds, on being duly convicted
thereof by a justice of the peace " (The Laws relating to the Poor, by Francis
Const, 1807, vol. i. para. 1007).

[2] 3 George IV. c. 126, c. 65 (General Turnpike Act, 1824).

[3] 5 & 6 William IV. c. 76, sec. 28 (Municipal Corporations Act, 1835) ;
extended to contracts for the borough gaol by 7 William IV. and 1 Victoria,
c. 78, sec. 39.

[4] It is remarkable that not until 1819 was any power given generally to
Parishes to appoint a salaried officer to perform the duties of Overseer (59
George III. c. 12). By 1834 this power had been acted upon chiefly in the
urban districts of the North of England, there being then 267 Assistant Overseers in Lancashire and 205 in Yorkshire (Third Annual Report of Poor Law
Commissioners, 1837, p. 21). The Poor Law Commissioners, in their early
years, prided themselves on putting out, by competitive tendering, even the

was not defeated by " rings " and " knock-outs," such as those
constantly resorted to by the farmers of turnpike tolls, when these
were put up to auction, led to a steady degradation, alike in the
quality of the workmanship or the efficiency of the service, and
in the rates of wages paid to the unorganised crowds of labourers
by whom the manual work was done.   Whatever may have been
the immediate pecuniary saving to the ratepayer, the moral
results were disastrous.   It is not too much to say that the
ubiquitous introduction of the profit-making contractor, intent,
on the one hand, upon buying labour in the cheapest market,
even in the workhouse or the prison, and on the other, upon
extracting from the public authority, by fair means or foul, the
highest possible price—evoking, as the system did, among the
sweated workers, a like desire to do as little labour as possible,
without regard to the efficiency of the service—has left, even
to-day, an evil tradition of inefficiency and greed in the lower
branches of municipal work.

The Coming of the Ratepayer

The abandonment of the obligatory and gratuitous service of
the ordinary citizen in public office involved the establishment
of the " cash nexus " as the basis of all the transactions of the
Local Authority.   For it is clear that the payment of an ever-
growing volume of salaries and wages, if not also of contractor's
profits, meant the raising of a corresponding money revenue,
which took the form of a periodical levy of leys, cesses, scots or
rates on all the occupiers of land or buildings.   We cannot here
explore the innumerable ramifications, in the course of the past
hundred years, of this substitution of taxation upon every house-

---

medical attendance on the sick poor ; in some cases even prescribing a maximum sum which could not be exceeded, however numerous might be the poor
on whom the Medical Officer was required to attend.   " We have considered,"
said the Commissioners in their First Annual Report, 1835 (p. 53), " that the
interests of the public and the profession itself were the best served by keeping
the situations of Medical Officers in the new Unions open to the competition
of the whole body of medical practitioners.   Instead of attempting to fix the
price of the services of the medical practitioners for the Union, we deemed it
the most advantageous that each practitioner should fix the price of his own
services under competition. . . . In some Unions . . . it has been provided
that the terms of the contract should be a remuneration, at a given sum per
head on the number who receive medical relief ; but with the proviso that the
gross sum should not exceed a given amount "

holder all the time for personal service by a minority of citizens in rotation. From it have sprung all the intricate problems of the economic incidence of local taxation upon different classes of citizens, different kinds of property and different forms of industry. To the same root may be traced the financial expedients of loans for short periods and long, the subsidising of some municipal services out of the profits made in others, and the necessity of "equalising" the burdens of the various Local Authorities by subventions from the National Exchequer. Another result of far-reaching importance, and one which was already beginning to be manifested at the opening of the nineteenth century, was the new cleavage of interest between those citizens who felt themselves directly benefited by this or that municipal service, and those who were conscious only of paying for it in new and onerous taxation. This cleavage already appears in the objections of the turbulent Democracy, which swarmed into the open Vestries, to the expenditure on the new safeguards and amenities of urban life desired by the more substantial citizens. The mass of wage-earning labourers of Plymouth Dock [now Devonport] vehemently protested in 1813 against being saddled with the payment of new rates for "lamping, lighting and watching the town of Dock, the enormous expense of which they deprecate and see no necessity for. . . . The population of this Parish will consist principally of persons employed in His Majesty's Dockyard. . . . Mechanics and the labouring classes . . . will amount to about seven or eight in ten of the inhabitants, whose employments are of that nature as to call them early to bed and early to rise ; and consequently partaking in no one degree of the benefits of a measure towards which they will be called upon materially to contribute ; with respect to their property it may be said in a general way that it does not consist of more than they themselves are able to protect." [1] It is not necessary to comment on the analogous cleavage, a hundred years later, which leads to the constant struggle, in the Local Government of to-day, of the class that resents having to pay rates for schools which its own children do not use, for maternity and child welfare institutions which its own families do not require, and for the healthy maintenance of the unemployed workmen and their

---

[1] MS. Minutes, Stoke Damarel Vestry [now Devonport], 10th October and 14th November 1813 ; *Municipal Origins*, by F. H. Spencer, 1911, p. 33-34.

dependents, in whom the upper and middle class have no interest.

There were, however, two immediate consequences of the steady increase of Local Government based on local taxation, which began, even in the eighteenth century, to perplex the local administrators. The fact that every householder had to contribute towards the cost of every step taken by the Parish or the County, the Improvement Commissioners or the Borough, and that the benefits of such action were enjoyed in common, emphasised the position of the Local Authority as being, virtually, an Association of Consumers, in which membership was obligatory and universal. It seemed to follow, as a necessary corollary— at least to those who believed that Representation and Taxation should always be united—that the ratepayers were entitled to elect and to control all those who spent the ratepayers' money.

Government as an Association of Consumers

We pause here to consider what seems to us one of the most interesting questions in the natural history of institutions, namely at what stage and at what date did government begin to appear as predominantly an Association of Consumers. There is much to be said for the contention that all the governmental institutions in olden time were rooted in the assumption that the persons concerned had a common vocation, or at least a common right to exercise a particular function, to render a particular service or to produce a particular product. And, broadly speaking, it was to the vocation itself, whatever its constitution, that was committed the direction of its activities. That is to say, the Manor and the Municipal Corporation, and even the landowners who as Justices of the Peace ruled the Counties— like the King and his warriors, the Church and its priesthood, such nascent professions as the lawyers and the medical men, the chartered National Companies for overseas trade or for mining or other monopolies at home, and, last but not least, the Merchant and Craft Gilds—were all of the nature of Associations of Producers. It is scarcely too much to say that, in connection with anything like the exercise of governmental functions, so far as our limited researches have gone, we do not come upon the conception of an Association of Consumers until the close of the seventeenth century. Even in that century, as we have shown, and for long afterwards, it was upon the decaying remnants of vocational organisation that continued to rest the constitutional structure and the authority of the Manorial Courts, the Municipal Corporations and, we may almost say, Quarter Sessions itself. There remains to be considered the Parish, upon the nature and antiquity of which there has been much controversy, based, as we think, upon inadequate historical knowledge. Whether it is at all true, as Toulmin Smith vehemently asserted, that the Parish was an essentially secular Authority, of immemorial antiquity, connected with, or identical with, the Township or the Manor, we cannot pretend to decide. There is more evidence for Maitland's view that the Parish Vestry, at any rate, as an organ of secular government, was a relatively modern institution, which can hardly be carried back further than the fourteenth or fifteenth century, and that its functions as a Local Authority may have grown chiefly by the imposition upon it, by royal decree, of specific obligations and duties. However this may be, the Vestry, as the governing body of the Parish, was certainly essentially the congregation of heads of households joined together by the universal and obligatory participation in the religious services of the Church. As such, it necessarily had a communal character, irrespective of vocation; and even in its earliest historically demonstrated functions of managing "the Parish stock," whether of money or of sheep; maintaining the fabric of the church and seeing to the upkeep of the churchyard and its wall; and providing the sacramental wine, it can be regarded only as an Association of Consumers. In the course of the next three centuries the Parish took on successively, not only the various duties placed upon it by statute, but also the provision and management of all sorts of services, which the inhabitants " in Vestry assembled " decided that they required, and preferred to have provided at the common expense. The Church Rate, levied only on the basis of immemorial custom, became, in fact, a secular public revenue, applicable to such diverse purposes as the payment of any expenses necessarily incurred by the Parish Officers, the destruction of vermin, the repair of any parochial property and, at a later date, occasionally even the purchase of substitutes for any parishioners unfortunate enough to be drawn for service in the militia. The Parish, under the government of the inhabitants " in Vestry assembled " (though always remaining entangled in the ecclesiastical organisation, dominated by the Incumbent and the Incumbent's Churchwarden, and subject to interference by the Archdeacon and the Ordinary, not to mention also the Justices of the Peace), undoubtedly took on the character, if only gradually, and so to speak unself-consciously, of an Association of Consumers.

But the Parish Vestry, with its infinite variety of constitution and activity, is an equivocal example. At the end of the seventeenth century there emerged, in one or other form, the deliberately constructed and specifically designed Association of Consumers, for the purpose of getting carried out something recognised as a governmental function. It is significant that our earliest instance is that of a voluntary association ; and that its object was the performance of the most primitive of all governmental functions, namely the protection of life and property. Thus, when in 1698 the inhabitants of the Tower Hamlets were " much perplexed by pilfering people, picklocks, housebreakers and such ill persons," and annoyed by scenes of open profligacy, which the Justices of the Peace did nothing to repress, the inhabitants themselves set to work, as members of the local Society for the Reformation of Manners ; and they were soon able to report that, " by means of this society alone, about 2000 persons have been legally prosecuted and convicted, either as keepers of houses of bawdry and disorder, or as whores, nightwalkers and the like. . . . They have also been instrumental to put down several music houses, which had degenerated into notorious nurseries of lewdness and debauchery." [1] In the latter half of the eighteenth century, with the increase of crime and disorder due to the massing of the population in industrial districts, associations formed specifically for the prosecution of felons became widely prevalent all over England. There was, it must be remembered, no public prosecutor. It was left to any aggrieved person to incur the trouble of getting a thief arrested and committed to prison, and then the expense and labour of preferring an indictment, producing witnesses and engaging counsel. The result was that thefts and assaults were com-

[1] *An Account of the Rise and Progress of the Religious Societies in the City of London, etc., and of the Endeavours for Reformation of Manners which have been made therein,* by Josiah Woodward, 1698, pp. 74, 78, 79.

mitted with impunity. The society for the prosecution of felons
undertook the task for any of its members, and sometimes maintained its own paid officials, who were sworn in as Constables
to apprehend offenders. Thus, the farmers of the village of
Diss, in Norfolk, formed, in 1777, their own association for
apprehending and prosecuting horse-stealers. The manufacturers
in the Northern industrial centres resorted to the same device,
sometimes against robbers of their bleaching grounds, sometimes against the weavers to whom they gave out work, but
always including in their aim the receivers of the stolen goods.
Even " the qualified sportsmen of England," we read, " associate
in clubs for the better detection of those who are prohibited from
killing, or having game in their possession, many of whom, it
must be confessed, have been prosecuted with a resentful warmth
which the nature of the offence did not seem fully to justify." [1]
The most usual of these police associations was, however, that
of the property owners of a given Parish or district. The Manchester newspaper of 1772 repeatedly advertises the existence
of a society " for the more effectual security of this town, the
neighbouring towns and the country adjacent, against housebreaking, thieves, and receivers of stolen goods," by means of
the prompt prosecution of depredators on the property of the
subscribers. In 1784 " several robberies and burglaries having
been lately committed in the Parish and village of Twickenham,
the nobility, gentry and other inhabitants have entered into a
subscription for the apprehending and prosecuting to the utmost
any person who shall be guilty of any robbery or felony in the
said Parish." [2] As late as 1811–1812 there is a renewed outburst of these associations, largely connected, we imagine, with
the Luddite outrages ; and in 1819 they again abound, perhaps
even to a greater extent than at any previous period. In 1827
it is reported that " associations against thieves have been
formed in all the districts of the country." [3] They continue
throughout the first half of the nineteenth century, principally
in the rural districts ; and they do not entirely disappear until
the universal establishment of the County Constabulary after
1856.

[1] *Hints respecting the Public Police*, by Rev. H. Zouch, J.P., 1786, p. 3.
[2] *Gazetteer*, 19th January 1784.
[3] *The Subordinate Magistracy and Parish System considered*, by Rev. C. D.
Brereton (Norwich, 1827), p. 9.

It was, however, naturally in connection with the new con-
structive services rendered necessary by the Industrial Revolution that witnessed the greatest development of these Associations of Consumers for the performance of governmental functions.
We have mentioned in the present volume the organisation of
Local Authorities for the construction and improvement of
harbours.[1] Others, like that of the Manchester traders in 1776,
dealt with the erection of market buildings, and the daily
administration of the markets in the growing trading centres.
The Turnpike Trusts, which eventually reconstructed, at the
instance, and largely at the cost of the principal local users, all
the main roads, constituted the most numerous class ; and they
drew their considerable revenue from the very persons who
enjoyed the conveniences that they supplied. But the greatest
development, as we have described in detail, was in the organisation of the services required by the multiplication of houses and
the ever-increasing traffic of the town streets. The watching,
lighting, paving, cleansing and otherwise improving the rapidly
increasing urban aggregations became the most imperative of
the tasks of Local Government. In nearly all cases these urban
services began in voluntary associations of the principal inhabitants. Sometimes the association was transient only, and
merely voluntary, as when the leading parishioners of the little
town of Ashford in Kent subscribed, once for all, the necessary
sum to pave the principal streets. More frequently, the association was that of the owners and occupiers of a district—in some
cases those of a particular " square " in a Metropolitan Parish—
who joined together to provide the lamps or the watchmen, the
pavement or the sweeping necessary for their own comfort. In
such cases what invariably happened was that the voluntary
basis was presently found to be inadequate or inconvenient ;
and the association obtained a Local Act compelling all the
inhabitants to pay their shares of the annual expenses. We
have sufficiently described in this volume the great development
of Local Authorities established under their own Local Acts,
which, between 1748 and 1836, gradually came to be, so far as
specifically " municipal " administration was concerned, the most
important form of English Local Government. What impresses
the student of their records is the complete contrast, alike in

[1] *Ante*, p. 24.

conception and in constitutional structure, between these char-
acteristic Local Authorities of 1748–1836, and the earlier Manorial
Courts and Municipal Corporations that they succeeded. The
Paving, Lighting, Police or Improvement Trustees or Commis-
sioners were, in fact, the representatives of Associations of
Consumers, in which membership was locally obligatory.

It was characteristic of this new form of governmental organisation that it had absolutely no connection with, and, indeed,
practically no consciousness of, the producers of the commodities
and services which it supplied. When each inhabitant was under
obligation to supply and light the lantern at his door, to pave
and sweep the street in front of his own house or workshop ; to
supply his own horses or his own labour for the mending of the
roads he used ; to maintain at his cost the bit of primitive
embankment that protected his holding from the flood, or even
to perform in his turn the duties of the various Parish offices,
it was of his own pains and costs, his own efforts and sacrifices
in the process of production that he was most vividly conscious.
But the minutes of the Manchester Police Commissioners or the
Westminster Paving Commissioners exhibit these representatives
of the consumers organising their growing services, and giving
out their extensive contracts, on the basis of buying labour as
a commodity, just like lamp irons or paving-stone ; quite unconscious, indeed, that it is sentient beings whom they are
enlisting, and the conditions of human lives that they are determining. All that they were concerned with—and this, in their
inexperience of public administration, they lamentably failed to
secure—was " buying in the cheapest market," and getting the
work done at the lowest possible monetary cost to the constituency that they taxed. Among the crowds of nondescript
unskilled workers who were concerned in work of this character
there was, at that time, no Trade Unionism, or protective combination of any kind. Taken in conjunction with the rapidly
spreading Benthamite philosophy the result was the rooting of
the growing municipal services, so far as concerned the great
bulk of the manual labourers by whom these services were performed, in a morass of " sweating," out of which it did not
emerge until the last decades of the nineteenth century.

But whilst the organisation of public services by the representatives of the Associations of Consumers that we have

described took on, so far as the conditions of the wage-earners were concerned, all the characteristics of the capitalist employment that it quite frankly imitated, the fact must not be ignored that this collective or communal organisation contained within it the germ of an actual supersession of capitalist enterprise— a supersession not in the interest of the producers of the services but in that of the whole body of consumers. For the most part the services organised by the new Local Authorities were not those in which the private capitalist had hitherto found a source of profit. The maintenance of the highways, the paving of the town streets, the watching, cleansing and lighting of the thoroughfares, and the provision of sewers by the new Local Authorities deprived no private capitalist of his business ; and even increased his opportunities for profit-making as a contractor for the necessary works. And though here and there a Lord of the Manor or a fortunate landowner found himself in possession of a profitable market or bridge, a ferry or even a harbour as part of his estate, the provision of similar conveniences elsewhere did not seem to threaten any encroachment on private enterprise. In the nineteenth century, however, there arose, among some of the new Local Authorities claims and aspirations to serve the public of consumers in ways which purported to dispense with the toll of private profit. We have described how the Manchester Police Commissioners in 1809 fought unsuccessfully in favour of a public provision of the water supply, in opposition to a capitalist company, avowedly on the ground that " it would be contrary to sound policy to entrust the furnishing and control of this important article of food and cleanliness, on which the health and comfort of the inhabitants depend, to persons whose sole object will be the promotion of their own private interest, and who are induced to the undertaking from no other motive." [1] Parliament, on that occasion, gave the victory to the capitalist company ; but the Association of Consumers, which the Manchester citizens had secured in their statutory Police Commissioners, was already beginning a more significant enterprise. Whilst capitalist promoters in other towns were projecting profit-making gas companies, the Manchester Police Commissioners, from 1807 onwards, were making gas by a municipal staff, in

---

[1] *Ante,* p. 261 ; *History of the Origin and Progress of the Water-Supply in Manchester,* 1851.

municipal retorts, for municipal use, and supplying this new means of lighting to all the inhabitants who desired it. For no less than seventeen years this municipal enterprise was conducted without statutory authority, this being obtained only in 1824 ; and then less from any deliberate act of policy by Parliament than by a happy accident. This incipient Municipal Socialism, as we have related, did not fail to be denounced by those who objected to interference with capitalist enterprise ; [1] but it proved to be the beginning, in all parts of the country, of an ever-increasing volume and range of " municipal trading," often in actual supersession of capitalist profit-making, the whole scope of which it is impossible, at the present day, even to forecast.[2]

The reader will now appreciate how this new form of Local Government by Associations of Consumers, empirically evolved in the course of the eighteenth century, acted and reacted on the contemporary movement towards Political Democracy. In every act of their administration, all these various bodies representing the mass of undifferentiated citizens of particular areas, necessarily had forced on their attention the fact that the producers of each commodity or service constituted only a tiny minority, whilst the consumers, for whom the commodity was produced or the service performed, were the whole of the inhabitants. When the Westminster Paving Commissioners hired gangs of labourers to put down the Aberdeen granite and York sandstone on which the surging traffic walked or drove in comfort, it was obvious that the few score labourers were serving hundreds of thousands of citizens, rich and poor, men, women and children. The dozen or two of workmen whom the Manchester Police Commissioners hired to make gas to light the whole town were plainly serving the whole of the inhabitants. The Benthamite formula of seeking the greatest good of the greatest number seemed to imply a complete subordination of the interests of the municipal employees to those of the ratepaying citizens. At the same time, the current Radical conception of the " Rights of Man," and the necessary union of taxation with representation, irresistibly led towards a consumers' or ratepayers' Democracy.

---

[1] Ante, pp. 262-265.
[2] See the authors' Constitution for the Socialist Commonwealth of Great Britain, 1920.

For nearly the whole of the nineteenth century the only question agitating the successive generations of " reformers " seemed to be how exactly this exclusively territorial Democracy was to be organised.

Government by Elected Representatives

The conception of government by representatives of the whole community was, as we have shown, not embodied in the local institutions of the eighteenth century. The distinctly oligarchical expedient of a Close Body recruiting itself by co-option was the dominant, if not the universal, device of all the constitutions resting on the decaying remnants of vocational organisation. The right of the persons charged with carrying out any service to nominate their colleagues and successors, was taken for granted in the essentially vocational organisations of the seventeenth and eighteenth centuries. The new Statutory Authorities for Special Purposes frequently adopted a similar oligarchical principle in their various forms of Co-option. Among the Local Authorities of this period the meeting of inhabitants in Vestry assembled was the only one in which can be discerned a communal Democracy. But this nascent Democracy had not then developed a representative system. It was, indeed, not without reluctance and many complaints,[1] that Englishmen

---

[1] " One of the great books that remain to be written," we are told by F. W. Maitland, " is the History of the Majority. Our habit of treating the voice of a majority as equivalent to the voice of an all is so deeply engrained that we hardly think that it has a history. But a history it has, and there is fiction there : not fiction if that term implies falsehood or caprice, but a slow extension of old words and old thoughts beyond the old facts. In the earlier middle ages it is unanimity that is wanted ; it is unanimity that is chronicled ; it is unanimity that is after a sort obtained. A shout is the test, and in form it is the primary test to-day in the House of Commons " (*Township and Borough*, by F. W. Maitland, 1898, pp. 34-35). The erudite but reactionary Toulmin Smith, in his embittered criticism of the new principles of Local Government, was always objecting to government by representative bodies : " Unless constant attention be fixed on this," he states, " Parliaments and Common Councils become but other names for oligarchies. They become but a mask and a juggle ; a means to fasten the machinery of real despotism on a people, and to rob them of their liberties under the disguise of names " (*Local Self-Government and Centralisation*, 1851, p. 73). In his view the preferable alternative was " that other part of the Local Institutions which . . . the long practice of the Common Law and Constitution of England require, namely, the Folk and People, themselves meeting in frequent, fixed, regular, and accessible assemblies, as matter of individual right and duty ; and discussing and hearing discussed, the matters which the local body, entrusted to administer in their behalf, has done or is doing " (*ibid.* p. 32).

abandoned the simpler expedient of government by the common consent of all those concerned. At the end of the eighteenth century it was this common agreement of the inhabitants, by tradition and practice *the principal inhabitants*, rather than decision by a numerical majority, whether of representatives or ratepayers, for which, particularly in matters of Local Government, men yearned. And down to the end of the eighteenth century, this note of common agreement, as the end of discussion and debate, remained strong. " It is most convenient," says a widely read eighteenth-century law-book, " that every Parish Act," done at a Vestry " be entered in the Parish book of accounts,"—not, be it noted, as having been carried by a majority vote, but with " every man's hand consenting to it . . . set thereto ; for then it will be a certain rule for the Churchwardens to go by." [1] " Agreed and consented to by us whose names . . . are hereunto subscribed " is, in fact a phrase constantly found preceding the lists of signatures by which the inhabitants in Vestry were accustomed to authenticate their minutes.[2]

What broke down this old conception of government by consent of all the persons concerned was the surging into the Vestry meetings of such populous Parishes as Manchester or Leeds, Woolwich or St. Pancras, of large numbers of parishioners, who were naturally, for the most part, not the " principal inhabitants " to whom the government had habitually been left, and whose turbulent proceedings led to the withdrawal from attendance of the quieter and " more respectable " inhabitants. In a few Parishes the practical impossibility of " government by public meeting " of this sort led to the establishment, quite extra-legally, of a Parish Committee, elected at a Vestry meeting, which took upon itself the whole functions of Parish government, merely reporting to and seeking covering sanction from Open

---

[1] Shaw's *Parish Law*, p. 55 ; *The Parish and the County*, p. 52.

[2] *Ibid.* p. 52. As late as the middle of the nineteenth century, Toulmin Smith sought to argue that this principle of common consent was necessary to any alteration of the law, whatever a mere majority might decide. He quoted Bracton as authoritative for the dictum that " the laws of England having been approved by the consent of those who use them (utentium), and guaranteed by the oath of the King, cannot be changed nor set aside within the common consent and counsel of all those by whose counsel and consent they were first put forth " (Bracton, *De Legibus*, lib. i. chap. ii. par. 7 ; *Local Self-Government and Centralisation*, by J. Toulmin Smith, 1851, p. 27).

Vestry meetings held at periodical intervals. We have described the highly organised and remarkably efficient government of the great Parish of Liverpool by such an extra-legal committee.[1]

But such a Parish Committee had in it the weakness of possessing no legal authority. The Parish Officers could, at any moment, decline to act upon its resolutions. Any recalcitrant ratepayer might invoke the interference of the Justices of the Peace or the Courts of Law against its action. Such Parish Committees were, in fact, upset in various Parishes.[2] An alternative expedient, and one that could be employed also to strengthen a Parish Committee, was to take a poll, in order to ascertain the real opinion of the whole mass of parishioners, who (contrary to the opinion of some legal authorities) were allowed to vote whether or not they had been present at the meeting at which the poll was demanded. In adopting the device of a poll of all the parishioners, the Vestry, it will be seen, was abandoning the conception of government by common consent, in favour of government by the decision of the majority for the time being. In 1819, the well-known Sturges Bourne Act enabled any Parish to appoint annually in Open Vestry a Committee empowered to carry out, not, indeed, all the work of the Parish, but all matters relating to the relief of the poor, and reporting to meetings of the Open Vestry at least twice a year. So far the Act was "adoptive" only. But the statute also provided that, in all Parishes outside the City of London and Southwark, and not governed by Local Acts of their own, the ratepayers should each have from one to six votes, in proportion to the rateable value of their premises. It was not foreseen that the recording of these various votes necessarily involved taking separately the decision of each voter, and thus a poll which could not, in practice, be confined to those persons who had been present at the previous Vestry meeting. Thus Sturges Bourne's Act introduced, in effect, into English Local Government, at the option of any one ratepayer in attendance at the meeting, a popular Referendum upon any decision whatsoever. We have described how this limitation of the work of the Parish Committee to the one function of poor relief, coupled with the

---

[1] *The Parish and the County*, pp. 134-145.

[2] In St. Giles, Cripplegate, 1731 ; and in St. Mary Abbots, Kensington, in 1776 ; see *The Parish and the County*, p. 143.

introduction of an obligatory Referendum, heavily weighted in
favour of the larger ratepayers, created confusion and disorder
in the Vestries of the larger Parishes. Any section outvoted at
the meeting immediately claimed a poll of the Parish ; and this
had to be granted as a matter of legal right. As the wealthier
classes abstained from the public meeting, and, moreover, had
most to gain by the strict counting of the plural votes, it was
usually the Tories who demanded this Referendum, and the
Radicals who objected to it. This unpremeditated experiment
in the use of the Referendum—handicapped as it was by every
unfavourable circumstance—practically introduced a fatal element of discord into the most smoothly working constitutions
of populous parishes. Even at Liverpool, where Toryism and
the Church of England dominated the working men as well as
the upper classes, we see, from 1828 onward, a constantly increasing number of appeals from the Vestry meeting to the poll.
In one year (1832) no fewer than eight of these polls were taken,
on such questions as the amount of salary to be paid to an
official, the election of Churchwardens and Sidesmen, the assessment of the owners of cottage property, and whether the Churchwardens' account should or should not be passed. The active
spirits who, in the heated years of the Reform controversy,
carried the Open Vestry meetings, were habitually defeated at
the poll. They revenged themselves on the Tory party by
turning the half-yearly meeting at the old Parish Church into a
pandemonium. At Leeds, if the Nonconformist Radicals carried
the election of Churchwardens at one of the large and turbulent
Vestry meetings that we have described, the Tories insisted on
a poll of the Parish. From 1833 onwards this becomes a regular
practice. When a poll was refused, they obtained a mandamus
ordering it to be conceded. The Tory newspaper, in April 1835,
candidly avowed, that " the only method now left to the friends
of law and order is to appeal from such packed Vestries to the
Parish at large. Nor will the appeal be in vain. . . . Rated
females are entitled to vote as well as males. We do not wish for
a gynocracy ; but we are sufficiently gallant to perceive that too
many of the wayward lords of creation are disposed to make a bad
world of it ; therefore the sooner the ladies interfere the better." [1]

[1] *Leeds Intelligencer*, 25th April 1835 ; *The Parish and the County*, pp.
168-169.

The first embodiment in legislation of this change of opinion was " An Act for the Better Regulation of Vestries and for the Appointment of Auditors of Accounts in Certain Parishes of England and Wales." [1]   Whilst Sturges Bourne in 1818–1819 had merely sought to regularise and supplement the decision and control of the open Vestry Meeting, another aristocratic reformer, John Cam Hobhouse, more under the Benthamite influence, a dozen years later, gave to every Parish the opportunity of superseding the Vestry altogether by a body of elected representatives in whom the whole government of the Parish was vested.   Based on ratepayers' suffrage, equal voting, the ballot and annual elections, with provisions for publicity and an independent audit, " Hobhouse's Act," as it was universally called, was " the first legislative attempt to apply the principle of municipal self-government to the inorganic masses of population and property forming the modern additions to London."   But the Act applied only to those Parishes in which the ratepayers chose to adopt it on a poll ; and its operation was, in fact, confined to a relatively few large Parishes, principally those having Select Vestries in the Metropolitan area.

Government by bodies of elected representatives was, however, by this time definitely accepted as the necessary form for new constitutions.   For some years it had been becoming steadily more usual in Improvement Commissions.   The Manchester Police Commissioners, at that time perhaps the most important Local Authority—apart from the exceptionally busy Municipal Corporations of Liverpool and Bristol—outside the City of London, were changed, by the 1828 Act, from being a class of all the substantial householders, thousands in number, to an elected assembly of 240 members.[2]   When the time came for the urgently needed reform of the Poor Law, in the first flush of triumph of the Reformed Parliament, though much was said against the new principles on which relief was to be given, and against both the Union area and the workhouse, not a voice was raised in opposition to the work being entrusted, not to the ratepayers at large, but to a representative body.[3]

[1] 1 & 2 William IV. c. 60.
[2] *Ante*, p. 268.
[3] So strong was the tendency towards entrusting Local Government to representative bodies that the very existence of another alternative was ignored.   It is usually forgotten that the report of the Poor Law Inquiry

2 G

The seal was set upon the principle of government by a representative body by the agitation for the reform of the Municipal Corporations, which culminated in the Municipal Corporations Act of 1835. The public resentment of the Close Bodies which had continued to govern the property and privileges of the Boroughs was doubtless mainly political in its origin. So far as Local Government was concerned, the complaint was not so much that the Corporations performed the Municipal functions badly, as that they did not, in the great majority of cases, perform them at all. The Reformed Parliament of 1833 willingly saw the appointment of a Royal Commission to enquire into the Municipal Corporations ; and the habit of the time of manning all such Commissions by eager young intellectuals of Whig opinions determined, as we have shown, the tenor of the verdict.[1] There was, in fact, at the moment, no rival, among those with reforming instincts, to the Benthamite political philosophy which had erected representative Democracy, based on universal suffrage and ballot voting, into a panacea. The Municipal Corporation Commissioners (with a dissenting minority of two only) made their recommendations with no uncertain voice. Lord Melbourne's Cabinet, pressed for time, found no other policy. Public

Commissioners of 1832 was as adverse to the administration of elected Parish Committees, Select Vestries under Sturges Bourne's Act, and Local Act Incorporations of Guardians of the Poor as it was to that of Open Vestries and the compulsorily serving Parish Officers. "[Nassau] Senior's principal suggestion," we are told, "is to take away the controlling power of the magistracy, and to vest it, together with the duty of revising and auditing the accounts, in paid local authorities, who might also be employed for other purposes" (*Letters of the Rt. Hon. Sir George Cornewall Lewis, Bart.*, 1870, p. 13). What Chadwick wanted, and what was strongly recommended was, to use his own words, at a later date, "that the administration of the Poor Laws should be entrusted, as to their general superintendence, to one Central Authority with extensive powers ; and as to their details, to *paid officers*, acting under the consciousness of constant superintendence and strict responsibility. . . . The functions assigned to the unpaid Guardians were not executive but solely supervisory ; they were analogous to those of the Visiting Justices to the prisons. I failed, however, in getting the administrative principle, as set forth, acted upon, or in preventing the rules and orders being so couched ; I failed also to take from the unpaid officers [Boards of Guardians] the responsibility of the executive details, these being left to be disposed of by the unpaid Guardians at their weekly meetings—often in crowds of cases in large towns—perfunctorily and most objectionably. . . . Among other evils there has been that of generally putting the paid officers under the necessity of having to work down to ignorance instead of up to science" (Chadwick's statement, quoted in the third volume of Nicholls' *History of the Poor Law*, by Thomas Mackay, 1899, pp. 93-94).

[1] *The Manor and the Borough*, pp. 740-751.

opinion throughout the country gave the reform overwhelming support. The House of Commons put up practically no opposition ; and even Sir Robert Peel could see no alternative. Only in the House of Lords was the principle of representative Democracy seriously contested ; and here, as we have described, the opposition was eventually driven to give way, owing to the refusal of the Tory leaders in the House of Commons to support the Upper House. The passing of the Municipal Corporations Act in 1835, even subject to the concessions that were, by way of compromise, made to the House of Lords, meant, for English Local Government, much more than the substitution, in 178 towns, of an elected Town Council for the former Close Body. Coupled with the unopposed adoption in the Poor Law Amendment Act of 1834 of a representative body for the administration of the Poor Law, it meant, as the subsequent history has demonstrated, the definite acceptance of representative Democracy throughout the whole sphere of Local Government. Francis Place was right in 1836 when he foresaw, as the outcome of Lord Melbourne's Act, " the whole country " becoming eventually " Municipalised " ; by which he meant, " an incorporation of the whole country which will be the basis of a purely representative government." [1]

It is worth notice how sweeping, in many respects, was the revolution thus made, and how little public attention its universality attracted at the time. With the one significant exception of the red thread of Property Qualification running through all forms of authority, which was retained intact, and in some ways even strengthened by the Reformed House of Commons, the barriers which had divided the English people into mutually exclusive groups were, in 1834–1836, so far as Local Government was concerned, almost wholly broken down. In the government of his Parish, his Poor Law Union and his Borough, the undifferentiated citizen-consumer, electing whatever representatives he chose, became, in effect, supreme. The vocational qualification, once the very basis of Manor and Borough, finds no place in the reorganised municipality.[2] Less complete, but scarcely

[1] Place to Parkes, 3rd January 1836, Add. MSS. 35,150, p. 102 ; *The Manor and the Borough*, p. 751.

[2] The reservation (by the Municipal Corporations Act, 1835, sec. 2) to the existing Freemen, their wives, children and apprentices, of all rights of property and beneficial exemptions that they enjoyed in 1835, including the right

less significant, was the tacit abandonment, so far as concerned the government of the Parish, the new Poor Law Union and the urban area under Improvement Commissioners, of the barrier of sex. Women occupiers had never been declared to be ineligible for the onerous Parish offices, any more than for those of the ancient organisations for maintaining the embankments and sluices of districts within the jurisdiction of Courts of Sewers ; and they had never been excluded from attendance and voting at the Open Vestries. Now, under both Sturges Bourne's and Hobhouse's Acts, the rights of occupiers in the government of the Parish were definitely made independent of sex ; and this precedent was followed in the Poor Law Amendment Act of 1834, as well as in the General Highways Act of 1835, not merely in respect of the right to elect the members of the Board of Guardians and Highway Boards, but also, as it seems, in respect of eligibility for election.[1] But the Municipal Corporations Act, 1835, failed to go so far. Though the status of Burgess was extended to inhabitant "occupiers,"[2] they were, until 1869, definitely required to be males.

The most important enfranchisement, however, was that gained by the sweeping away of religious exclusiveness. Owing to the curious heedlessness which Parliament and the Government displayed about the Parish, neither Nonconformists nor, as it seems, Roman Catholics, were ever legally disqualified, either for membership of the Open Vestry, or from service in the Parish offices, any more than from membership of the Juries of the

---

to vote for Members of Parliament, was but a transient exception. It may be added that the Municipal Corporations omitted from the Act retained their old constitutions, to be swept away (with the exception of that of the City of London) only in 1883. The nominally vocational basis of the Liverymen of the City of London, with their equally nominal participation in the election of the Lord Mayor and a few other officers, remains, we believe, in 1922, the only survival of the old vocational organisation in English Local Government.

[1] It remained uncertain, however, whether a married woman could either vote or be elected ; not because of any disability by sex, but because it was doubtful whether a woman "under coverture," being (until the Married Women's Property Act of 1870) unable legally to own property, could legally, in her own person, be an "occupier." The point can hardly be said to have been definitely and generally decided in her favour until the passing of the Sex Disqualification Removal Act of 1920.

[2] Having been occupiers within the Borough for two whole years, inhabitant householders therein or within seven miles, British subjects, not defaulters in payment of rates, and not receiving parochial relief or corporate charities within twelve months past.

Manor or of the Court of Sewers, or of the offices connected
therewith. They were, however, normally excluded from all
Close Bodies, whether Select Vestries or Municipal Corporations,
as they were from the Commission of the Peace, and from the
County shrievalty. The Statutory Authorities for Special
Purposes, growing up in the course of the eighteenth century, had
entirely ignored differences of religion ; and the reorganisation
of Parish government by Sturges Bourne's and Hobhouse's Acts,
together with the Poor Law Amendment Act itself, tacitly
adopted the same policy. Most potent of all, however, was the
like sweeping away of religious disabilities in the reformed
Boroughs by the Municipal Corporations Act, which brought to
a summary end a much-prized monopoly of the Established
Church. This part of " Corporation reform " it was that its
author, Lord Melbourne, regarded as the most revolutionary.
" You may not," he felt, " see all the consequences of this to-
morrow ; but you have given by law a permanent power in all
the centres of industry and intelligence to the Dissenters which
they never had before, and which they never could have had
otherwise. They are the classes who will really gain by the
change, not the mob or the theorists ; every year their strength
will be felt more and more at elections and their influence in
legislation. Depend upon it, it is the Established Church, not
the hereditary peerage, that has need to set its house in order." [1]

The Salaried Officer

The student will have realised how universally prevalent,
down to the latter part of the seventeenth century, was the conception of the performance of all the work of Local Government
by unpaid, compulsorily serving and constantly changing average
citizens. For many offices, however, notably those which could
be made remunerative to the holder by the exaction of sufficient
fees, the alternative principle of freehold tenure was adopted.
Both these conceptions yielded during the eighteenth century,
but only slowly and incompletely, to a fundamentally different
principle of administration. The change was threefold. In
place of the constantly changing service of ordinary citizens,

[1] *Memoirs of Lord Melbourne*, by W. T. McCullagh Torrens, 1878, vol. ii.
p. 156 ; *The Manor and the Borough*, p. 750.

there is the continuous employment of the same person, who necessarily developed a certain professional expertness. Instead of the independent authority enjoyed by the unpaid citizen who was appointed to exercise as he thought best the customary or statutory powers of the Churchwarden, the Overseer, the Constable or the Surveyor of Highways, or the absolute autonomy of the holders of such freehold offices as Clerk of the Peace or Coroner, there is the employment of a salaried agent to carry out, as he was bid, the orders of the superior Authority. Finally there emerges, at the very end of the period, in contradistinction to the notion that any man of honesty and zeal is equal to the duties of any office whatsoever, the modern conception of specialist qualifications, without which even the most virtuous candidate could not be deemed fit for appointment.

It is needless to enumerate all the instances of this change of principle. One of the earliest examples was the gradual and silent passing away of the immemorial freehold office of Parish Clerk. From the latter part of the seventeenth century onward, we find, especially in the South of England, vacancies being filled, here and there, by the appointment of a Vestry Clerk, whose office was regulated neither by custom nor by statute ; who was paid such salary as the Vestry chose, and who could be required to act in any way the Vestry desired.[1] An even greater innovation, and one long characteristic chiefly of Northern and Midland Parishes, was the appointment of a " standing," " perpetual " or " hireling " Overseer, to whom a salary was assigned, and on whom the whole onerous duty of the Overseer was cast, to be carried out under the direction of the Churchwardens, the Parish Committee, or the inhabitants in Vestry Assembled. In 1819 this institution of a salaried Overseer was legalised by Sturges Bourne's Act, when it was very widely adopted.[2] When the Parish established a workhouse, it frequently, as we have seen, put the management out to contract. But otherwise it had to appoint a paid " master " or " governor " of the institution, frequéntly other servants, and occasionally even a surgeon and

---

[1] A humbler servant of the Vestry, scarcely earlier in origin than the Vestry Clerk, was the Parish Beadle, who could be used for any service whatsoever, and whose duties during the eighteenth century became steadily more multifarious.

[2] In some urban Parishes paid watchmen supplemented the efforts of the unpaid Constable, or replaced him.

a chaplain. Only in a few cases do we find a salaried Surveyor of Highways. But at the beginning of the nineteenth century, some of the principal roads were coming to be reconstructed by the promoted stone mason, Telford, one of the founders of the Institute of Civil Engineers, the premier professional organisation of the most scientific of modern professions.[1] Owing to his influence a clause was inserted in the Act of 1818 (merging into one five Turnpike Trusts concerned with a portion of the Holyhead road) compelling the new body to employ a professional civil engineer as their surveyor for the whole of their mileage of road. In other parts of the country the management of the Turnpike Trusts came, more and more, as we have already described, to be undertaken by Macadam and his son. " Gratuitous services," Macadam urged, " are ever temporary and local ; they are dependent on the residence and life of the party ; and have always disappointed expectation. Skill and executive labour must be adequately paid for, if expected to be constantly and usefully exerted ; and, if so exerted, the price is no consideration when compared with the advantage to the public." [2] Equally scientific was Macadam's organisation of his constantly increasing

---

[1] The professional organisation of the civil engineers began at the end of the eighteenth century, but did not take shape until 1818. In the latter half of the eighteenth century the land surveyors and master craftsmen employed by landed proprietors, speculators, or Municipal Corporations in the construction of docks, harbours, canals, bridges, roads, land drainage, or embankments, began to call themselves " civil engineers." In 1771 the most prominent among those in London, John Smeaton, started a dining club in order that " the sharp edges of their minds might be rubbed off . . . by a closer communication of ideas " ; that they might " promote the true end of the public business upon which they should happen to meet in the course of their employment." It seems that the main purpose of this club was to prevent the promoters and lawyers, in passing private Bills through Committees of Lords and Commons, from using one expert engineer to contradict the facts and theories of another. The civil engineers desired, in fact, to form a profession, having its own technique, its own code of manners and its own solidarity against other professions and the public. In 1818 a more business-like organisation was called for ; and six young engineers established a society " for promoting regular intercourse between persons engaged in the profession, to the end that such persons might mutually benefit by the interchange of individual observation and experience." This society was, in 1828, by the potent aid of the great road-maker and bridge-builder, Thomas Telford, incorporated as the Institution of Civil Engineers—the type of professional organisation which has not only spread in this country to other brainworkers, but has also been adopted by the engineering profession in the United States of America and on the Continent. See *The New Statesman, Supplement on Professional Associations*, by S. and B. Webb, 21st April 1917.

[2] *The Story of the King's Highway*, p. 173.

staff of subordinate road engineers, representing the coming in of
the definite professional qualifications.   The same tendency is to
be seen in the whole experience of the Improvement Commissioners.   For the new duties and new services, in so far as these
were not put out to contract, salaried officers were employed.
These gradually became professionally expert gas engineers or
gas managers, police superintendents, managers of markets,
harbourmasters, or what we now call Municipal Surveyors
or Municipal Engineers.   And although the County Justices
continued, right down to our own day, to be advised by such
independent freeholders as the Clerk of the Peace and the Coroner,
in one County after another they appointed salaried officers to
manage the repairs and rebuilding of the bridges (for which the
Shropshire Justices were wise enough to engage Telford), and,
eventually, in the nineteenth century, even salaried governors
of the new prisons in substitution for the old-time gaoler who
lived by his fees and other exactions.   Not the least important
of these substitutions, though one long confined to the Metropolis
and only extended to a few provincial towns, was that of stipendiary magistrates for the unpaid Justices, who had too often
proved themselves to be " Trading Justices."   These Metropolitan stipendiaries, at first secretly developing from what we
have called the Court Justice, and statutorily authorised only in
1792, were, in the nineteenth century, always appointed from the
Bar, and were thus always professionally qualified for the office.[1]

[1] It is interesting to find the notorious younger Mainwaring in 1821, a few
months before his discreditable career as unpaid Justice of the Peace and
Treasurer of the County of Middlesex was brought to an end, unctuously
expounding the superiority of the " Great Unpaid," " a national, independent,
gratuitous magistracy, giving their time, their learning, and their efforts, to
the preservation of the peace and good order of society, and the due administration of the laws throughout the country reconciles all even to their severest
exercise, inasmuch as it proves that general good, and no sinister motive or
interest, can actuate those who so engage in the public service. . . . Can such
a feeling prevail with respect to a stipendiary body ? . . . Will not the feeling
be . . . that the members of such a body are the servants of the Government,
instead of the independent guardians of the public interest ? " For these
reasons this bankrupt peculator supplicates, from the King, " the gracious boon
of an independent magistracy for the Metropolis " (*Observations on the Police
of the Metropolis*, by G. B. Mainwaring, 1821, pp. 128-129, 133 ; *The Parish and
the County*, pp. 565, 579-580).

" ' To lay down the principle that men are to serve for nothing,' said
Cobbett, in criticising the system of unpaid magistrates, ' puts me in mind of
the servant who went on hire, who, being asked what wages he demanded, said
he wanted no wages : for that he always found about the house little things to
pick up ' " (*The Village Labourer*, by J. L. and B. Hammond, 1911).

Finally, the Poor Law Amendment Act of 1834 and the Municipal Corporations Act of 1835 definitely adopted the principle of the execution of the work of Local Government by salaried officers, appointed by the Local Authority, subject to its orders, and holding office only at its will. What was absolutely unknown as an instrument of Local Government in the seventeenth century—a hierarchical bureaucracy working under a body of elected representatives—became, in the nineteenth century, not only the successor of the holders of freehold offices and the unpaid, compulsorily serving citizens, but also, in one service after another, a practicable alternative to the profit-making contractor or capitalist entrepreneur.[1]

The Innovations of Statute Law

It is difficult to realise, in the twentieth century, how dominant in the whole range of Local Government was still, in the seventeenth century, the Local Custom and the Common Law. At the beginning of that century no less an authority than Chief Justice Coke could be quoted in support of the inviolable supremacy of the Common Law, and in depreciation of the innovating statutes by which Parliament was beginning spasmodically to interfere with it.[2] A couple of centuries later, Toulmin Smith

---

[1] It was this introduction of the salaried official as the alternative to the unpaid, compulsorily serving citizen, taking his turn in public office, that Toulmin Smith denounced as " one of the most alarming symptoms of the successful attempts that have, of late years, been made—under cover, at the best, of a pedantic doctrinairism—to overlay the free Institutions of England, their working and their spirit alike, by the system of Bureaucracy and Functionarism " (*The Parish, its Powers and Obligations at Law*, 1857, by Toulmin Smith, p. 211). Here as elsewhere with him the old principle was the alternative to the new. " The best of all practical education—namely, the taking actual part in the working of institutions—will be shared equally among all men, and be thus felt as a burthen by none. . . . *One day a year* would certainly be more than the average call on the time of each man. . . . Empirical remedies, and cant cries of Law Reform, will never do anything but help the growth of Functionarism " (*ibid.* pp. 220-221).

[2] " It is not almost credible to foresee, when any maxim or fundamental law of this realm is altered, what dangerous inconveniencies do follow. . . . New things which have fair pretences are most commonly hurtful to the Commonwealth ; for commonly they tend to the hurt and oppression of the subject, and not to that glorious end that at first was pretended " (Coke, 4 Inst. 41). Throughout the seventeenth and eighteenth centuries there was a continuous controversy in the law books concerning the relative supremacy of Parliament on the one hand, and on the other the " fundamental law of the land " as handed down in the Common Law. Toulmin Smith, the nineteenth-century

passionately clung to the idea that English " Local Self-Government," a glorious heritage from " time out of mind," was independent of Parliament, inviolable by innovating statutes, and inherently superior in moral, if not also in legal authority, to Parliament itself.[1] Prior to 1689, indeed, the innovations of Parliament in Local Government had been few and far between, and more by way of prescribing new functions than in materially altering either the constitution of Manor or Parish, Borough or County, or their ancient authority. But at the close of the seventeenth and throughout the eighteenth century we find, as we have described, ever-increasing crowds of innovating statutes. To the hundreds of brand-new Local Authorities that they set up, we have had to devote a whole volume. As the century wore to its close, Act after Act, of a character once unusual, imposed general rules and wide-reaching prohibitions upon all the Parishes in respect of their relief of the poor, upon all the Turnpike Trusts in their maintenance of the roads, upon all the Courts of Quarter Sessions in their upkeep of the bridges and their management of the Houses of Correction and County gaols.

---

protagonist of the Common Law, quotes the following dictum in a legal treatise of 1771 : " ' Our Legislative Authority is, by its own nature, confined to act within the line of the Constitution and not break through it ; because the House of Commons is only vested with a trust by the people, to the end they may protect and defend them in their rights and privileges. And therefore it is a contradiction in terms to say they have a right to consent to a law that may restrain or destroy them. I think it is as plain as any proposition in Euclid, that the House of Commons could not consent to such a law, without a notorious violation of the trust reposed in them ' " (*An Historical Essay on the English Constitution*, 1771, pp. 141, 146 ; quoted in *Government by Commissions Illegal and Pernicious . . . and the Rights, Duties and Importance of Local Self-Government*, by J. Toulmin Smith, 1849, p. 44). On the other hand, Maitland quotes an uncompromising assertion of the sovereignty of Parliament from an older and weightier authority : " The Parliament abrogateth old laws ; maketh new ; giveth orders for things past and for things hereafter to be followed ; changeth rights and possessions of private men ; legitimateth bastards ; establisheth forms of religion ; altereth weights and measures ; giveth forms of succession to the Crown. . . . And to be short, all that ever the people of Rome might do either in *centuriatis comitiis* or *tributis* the same may be done by the Parliament of England, which representeth and hath the power of the whole realm, both the head and body. For every Englishman is intended to be there present, either in person or by procuration and attorneys, of what pre-eminence, state, dignity or quality soever he be, from the prince, be he king or queen, to the lowest person of England. And the consent of the Parliament is taken to be every man's consent ' " (Sir Thomas Smith, *De Republica Anglorum*, ed. L. Alston, 1906, Bk. II. c. 1 ; quoted in *The Constitutional History of England*, by F. W. Maitland, 1919, p. 255).

[1] See, for instance, *Local Self-Government and Centralisation*, by J. Toulmin Smith, 1851, p. 23.

But it was in the nineteenth century, and particularly in its second, third and fourth decades, that this tendency for Parliament to prescribe, by statute, general rules in supersession of Local Custom and the Common Law for all the Local Authorities from one end of England to the other, became a regular habit. Sir Samuel Romilly induced the House of Commons summarily to cut down the oppressive powers of all the bodies of Incorporated Guardians under Local Acts ; by Sturges Bourne's Act and Hobhouse's Act, all the Parishes were reformed ; nearly every year saw a new General Turnpike Act ; the lunatic asylums, the prisons, the roads, the relief of the poor, were made the subject of statutes which applied to every Local Authority dealing with these functions of Local Government. What had empirically become the practice of the House of Commons was raised by the Benthamite philosophy almost to a dogma. Parliament became increasingly careless of local peculiarities and local customs, and more and more disposed empirically to supersede them by a national uniformity based on the current social philosophy. To those who were directly or indirectly inspired by Bentham and James Mill, this national uniformity in what was judged rationally to be the utilitarian course seemed, in the new statecraft, merely obvious wisdom. Thus, the way was open for the Reformed Parliament in a couple of sessions to smooth out of existence, by two all-embracing statutes, the infinite variety of Local Customs and particular Charters or Byelaws that had continued to characterise the Municipal Corporation, and all the casual habits and peculiarities which had marked the separate administration, by more than a hundred incorporated bodies of Guardians and over ten thousand autonomous Parishes and Townships, of the Elizabethan Poor Law.

The Rise of Specialised Central Departments

The gradual development of general statute law, introducing a measure of uniformity in the several branches of Local Government, was accompanied by a still more gradual and tentative development of the authority of the National Executive, with regard to one function after another ; taking eventually the form of the establishment of specialised Government Departments of supervision and control.

We may begin with the service of the prevention and punishment of crime and disorder, in which the intervention of the
Government long manifested itself, not so much in a regulation
and control of Local Authorities, as in a direct utilisation of
the Lord-Lieutenant and the Justices of the Peace as agents
of a centralised National Executive. During the whole of the
eighteenth century, down to the French Revolution at any rate,
this intervention came to little more than the issue of periodical
proclamations, sometimes merely on the accession of a new
sovereign, sometimes on the occurrence of some riot or tumult,
commanding " all our Judges, Mayors, Sheriffs, Justices of the
Peace, and all other of our officers and ministers, both ecclesiastical and civil, to be very vigilant and strict in the discovery
and effectual prosecution and punishment of all offenders."
But although these proclamations were solemnly read at the
Assizes, circulated to the Lord-Lieutenants and printed in the
London Gazette, no one, in ordinary times, took much notice of
them, and no attempt was made by the Government, either by
calling for specific reports or by further investigation, to make the
solemn formality effective. Nor were the other Privy Council
proclamations of the eighteenth century of much more interest
to the student of Local Government. From time to time some
particularly heinous murder or street robbery, some exceptional
deer stealing or forest depredations, would provoke a verbose
proclamation, of which the only operative part would be the offer
of a large reward, often £100, for the discovery and conviction
of the culprits.[1]

After the outbreak of the French Revolution—still more after
the Peace of 1815—the attitude of the National Executive
changes. There is no more effective action than before against
mere licentiousness or ordinary crime. But, at any rate from
1815 onward, the Ministers strove with might and main to put
down the popular tumults and mob disorders, which, with some
justification, they now associated with incipient rebellion. This
methodical repression is revealed in the reports and doings of

---

[1] See, for instance, the proclamations against street robberies and murders
of 21st January 1720, 29th February 1727, 9th July 1735, 7th November 1744,
11th January 1749 and 20th December 1750 ; those of 2nd February and 8th
October 1723 against deer stealers ; and that of 12th June 1728 against the
" great destruction . . . in the Forest of Needwood " (MS. Acts of Privy
Council, George I. and George II.).

the Government spies and informers, which so much impressed
the members of the Privy Council and of the various Secret
Committees of both Houses of Parliament ; in the constant
instructions which were given to the Justices of the Peace acting
in the disturbed districts, and in the activities of the " Bow
Street runners," in co-operation with such willing agents as
Nadin, the permanent police officer of the Boroughreeve and
Constables of Manchester. Even more repressive and alarming
to the ordinary citizen was the readiness with which, in 1795–
1800, in 1811–1812, between 1816 and 1819, and in the rural
counties of the South of England in 1830–1831, the Government
made use of the military forces, horse, foot and artillery, in disorders often connected only with industrial disputes, which, at
the present day, would be quite successfully dealt with by the
constabulary of the Local Authorities.[1]
Out of this spasmodic and so to speak revolutionary extension
into the provinces of the authority of the National Executive,
there developed, to some extent under Lord Sidmouth between
1816 and 1822, and more systematically under Sir Robert Peel
between 1822 and 1830, a more continuous supervision by the
Home Office than had ever before been customary, of the County
Justices and the Corporate magistracies in their capacity of
Police and Prison Authorities. The Home Office in 1815 got
passed an Act requiring all Prison Authorities to furnish statistical
reports of their gaols and Houses of Correction ; and on the basis
of these reports, supported by the recommendations of House of
Commons Committees of 1820 and 1822, Peel was able to induce
Parliament to enact the Prisons Act of 1823, " the first measure
of general prison reform to be framed and enacted on the responsibility of the National Executive." [2] This Act, besides
consolidating the whole statute law relating to prisons, for the
first time made it the duty of the Local Authorities for prisons
to organise their administration uniformly upon a prescribed
plan, which became a statutory obligation ; and peremptorily
required these Local Authorities to furnish quarterly to the

---

[1] See for all this, the Home Office archives, 1795–1832, now accessible in
the Public Record Office ; and the able and interesting books of Mr. and Mrs.
Hammond (*The Village Labourer, 1760–1832* ; *The Town Labourer, 1760–1832* ;
and *The Skilled Labourer, 1760–1832*).
[2] 4 George IV. c. 64; *English Prisons under Local Government*, 1922
p. 73.

Home Secretary detailed reports of every branch of their prison administration. This Act, applying to all the Courts of Quarter Sessions of the Counties, to the Cities of London and Westminster, and to seventeen of the principal Municipal Corporations, was the first that dictated to Local Authorities the detailed plan on which they were to exercise a branch of their own local administration ; the first that made it obligatory on them to report, quarter by quarter, how their administration was actually being conducted ; and the first that definitely asserted the duty of a Central Department to maintain a continuous supervision of the action of the Local Authorities in their current administration. In 1835 a second great Prisons Act, passed on the reports which the Home Office got adopted by an exceptionally authoritative Select Committee of the House of Lords,[1] prescribed a still " greater uniformity of practice in the government " of all the prisons in England and Wales ; authorised the Home Secretary to make binding regulations from time to time on all the details of administration, and subjected all the Local Authorities, for the first time, to constant inspection of their work in this branch of Local Government, by a staff of salaried professional experts, by whose outspoken critical reports, regularly submitted to Parliament and thereby published to the world, both the National Government and public opinion were kept informed of every seeming imperfection.

In another service of the Local Authorities, that of the maintenance of the highways, the new intervention of the National Executive was almost entirely concentrated within the second and third decades of the nineteenth century ; and a sudden change of circumstances prevented the development of a specialised Government Department. We have told elsewhere how, at the very beginning of the nineteenth century, the Post Office became greatly troubled at the bad state of the Holyhead road ; how in 1815 the Treasury summoned up courage to ask the House of Commons to vote £20,000 for the improvement of this main artery of communication with Ireland ; how the work was undertaken by a new body of ten Commissioners, three of whom

---

[1] See the voluminous five successive reports of the House of Lords Committee on the State of the Gaols and Houses of Correction, 1835 ; the Act 2 & 3 William IV. c. 38 ; and our *English Prisons under Local Government*, 1922, pp. 111-112.

were Ministers of the Crown ; and how, in the course of the next fifteen years, these Commissioners of the Holyhead Road, virtually a central Government Department, spent three-quarters of a million pounds, without actually superseding the Turnpike Trusts, in order to enable Telford to construct what was deemed in 1830 the "most perfect roadmaking that has ever been attempted in any country." Meanwhile, what was, in effect, another central Government Department, although based on an unpaid advisory board, began to press the Local Authorities to improve their roads. The Board of Agriculture, under Sir John Sinclair, from 1810 onward brought forward J. L. Macadam, with his plan for constructing a road surface both better and cheaper than any previously in use. For a couple of decades we watch the influence of the Government, and the diligence of Macadam effecting, through the Turnpike Trustees, an almost continuous and almost universal improvement in the roads—until in 1829, the amazing success of Stephenson's locomotive engine turned everybody's attention to the coming railways ; and the National Executive ceased, with dramatic suddenness, to trouble itself about a service seemingly doomed to rapid obsolescence.

A greater measure of permanence was gained by the inter-vention of the National Executive in another branch of Local Government, that which was then thought of as the Suppression of Nuisances and is now styled Public Health. Here it was the Privy Council that suddenly brought its influence to bear on the Local Authorities. In the spring of 1831 England began to be alarmed by reports that a new and frightful epidemic disease, afterwards known as Asiatic Cholera, was advancing steadily westwards through Europe. The Privy Council, after sending two doctors to St. Petersburg to report on the disease, not only put in force all the precautionary measures of quarantine, which had been used against the Levantine plague, but also, following precedents of 1721 and 1805, established a Central Board of Health of medical and other dignitaries, which issued solemn proclamations of advice to all and sundry how to keep them-selves from disease. But the Asiatic Cholera paid no attention to the futilities of the Central Board of Health ; and in the autumn of 1831 it broke out in Sunderland and spread rapidly, during the ensuing twelve months, to nearly all parts of the country. In this emergency the central Board of Health was reconstituted, and by Orders in Council Local Boards of Health were appointed in a large number of towns and populous places, on which were placed the local magistrates, clergy, doctors and other " principal inhabitants " ; and which were charged to suppress nuisances, and to take any elementary measures of public sanitation that commended themselves. For all this the Parish Officers were directed to pay, and the Parish Vestry was asked to provide for by rate. When some of them demurred, an Act of Parliament was hastily passed in 1832 making this financial provision obligatory on all the Parishes for which Local Boards of Health had been set up.

These Local Boards of Health, which were eventually established in nearly all towns and populous districts of any magnitude, are interesting to the student of Local Government as affording a simple instance of an *ad hoc* body ; established wherever desired, independently of Municipal Corporation or Parish Vestry ; nominally by appointment from above, but practically by the self-election of some zealous citizens who volunteered their services at a public meeting or otherwise, and the co-option of others ; and making what was virtually a precept on the Parish Overseers for the amount of their expenditure. These Local Boards of Health all came to an end when the cholera died away, not to be revived again until there was a renewed alarm in 1848. What is more significant is the fact that the central Government Department concerned, in this case the Privy Council, continued its interest in the health work of the Local Authorities, and thus established a claim to be the Central Health Authority, which—temporarily entrusted to its creature, the much-resented Central Board of Health in 1848–1854—issued in 1871 in the Local Government Board, to be still further specialised in 1919 (at least in name) by its conversion into the Ministry of Health.[1]

For the rest of the services specially characteristic of town government—in 1835 mostly in the hands of Improvement Commissioners—no specialised Government Department was set up. By the Municipal Corporations Act, 1835, it was intended and hoped that these bodies would be led voluntarily to merge themselves and their services in the reformed Municipal Corpora-

---

[1] Bentham deserves credit for his sketch of a Ministry of Health a century before such a Ministry was established ; see *Works*, vol. ix. p. 443.

tions ; and this in fact occurred, though not without much further legislation ; and it took another half century for all these separate Commissions to be absorbed. But not even Lord Melbourne dared to subject the reformed Municipal Corporations in all their work to the same systematic inspection and control as he was able to enact, for them as well as for the County Justices, in respect of their administration of prisons. The only approach to central control in the Municipal Corporations Act of 1835, is the section making it necessary for a Corporation desiring to alienate any of the Corporate real estate first to obtain the consent of the Lords Commissioners of the Treasury—a control transferred in 1871 to the Local Government Board.

A more significant example of Benthamite centralisation was the establishment, by two Acts of 1836, of the Registrar-General, who was placed in control of the new machinery for the official registration of births, deaths and marriages throughout the whole of England and Wales.

The most impressive instance of the development of the influence and authority of Parliament and the National Executive into the establishment of a specialised Government Department is afforded by the history of poor relief. Throughout the eighteenth century there had been occasional statutes enlarging or amending the powers and duties of the Local Authorities. These Authorities had been permitted from time to time to unite in larger areas, to erect and maintain workhouses ; and even to exercise great authority over vagrants and other persons neglecting to earn their living. They had been, by one or other Act, alternately encouraged and restrained, in this direction or that. They had, on two occasions, even been statutorily required to render statistical returns of their proceedings, which were presented to Parliament. But throughout the whole period, their action was regarded as of strictly local concern. What the Parish Officers chose to do, the Parish Vestry to acquiesce in and the Local Justices of the Peace not to prohibit was not made the subject of any official criticism from London. In the relief of the poor the Local Authorities were, right down to 1834, left unsupervised and uncontrolled by any Government Department. The innovation of 1834 was not preceded and led up to by any tentative interference of the National Executive. Save for occasional enquiries by Committees of the House of Commons,

2 H

466 THE NEW PRINCIPLES

out of which came such constitutional reforms promoted by private members of Parliament as Sturges Bourne's Act and Hobhouse's Act, there seem to have been no official preparations for the revolutionary change of 1834. What brought it about was, of course, the enormous and continued rise in the Poor Rate, which went from one million pounds in 1700 to three millions in 1800, to seven millions in 1820, and remained for fifteen years near that figure. Coupled with this drain on the rental of the land and buildings, on the ownership of which the authority of the governing class rested, was the realisation by a large proportion of the educated classes of the widespread demoralisation that was being caused by the methods of pauperisation that were employed. The prevalent opinion of the Reform Parliament was in favour of drastic reform, and the celebrated Poor Law Commission was promptly appointed. But although there had been no official preparation for an administrative revolution, the permeation of "enlightened public opinion" by the necessary political theory had been effective. Nor was the Whig Ministry averse. In the all-important Commission, the members, the secretary and the Assistant Commissioners were alike chosen from among those who had been influenced by the Benthamite philosophy. Their investigations, their discoveries and their recommendations were all dominated by the potent contemporary doctrines of Philosophic Radicalism. They were all based on the conception of local administration, not by compulsorily serving amateurs, but by salaried officials ; not as each district might choose, but according to a uniform and centrally prescribed plan ; yet without complete autonomy for the executive officers, who were to be supervised by an elected body, representing the ratepayers on whom the cost was to fall ; and these local representative bodies were to be controlled by a central Government Department which—continuously informed by a staff of salaried, peripatetic, expert inspectors —alone would be competent to devise and enforce a policy that would be for the greatest good of the greatest number. Eagerly accepted by the Whig Ministry and the House of Commons, this drastic reform of the Poor Law was embodied in the Poor Law Amendment Act of 1834, which established, in what were called " the three Bashaws of Somerset House," the first Government Department deliberately created exclusively for the purpose of controlling and directing Local Authorities in the execution of their work. The reader will not need to be reminded how the Poor Law Commissioners, denounced and derided, nevertheless held their own, and were continued in 1848 as the Poor Law Board; and how in 1871 this body was combined with the Public Health Department of the Privy Council and the Local Act Branch of the Home Office to become, in the Local Government Board, more explicitly than ever, the central Government Department to the authority of which all local governing bodies were subjected; and how, in 1919, the Local Government Board, following the tendency towards the specialisation of Government Departments according to function, was united with the National Health Insurance Commission to constitute the Ministry of Health.

The Property Qualification

Of all the old principles of English Local Government that we described in the last chapter as dominant at the close of the seventeenth century one only was destined to survive the changes of the century and a half, and even the iconoclastic years, 1832–1836, which, throughout nearly the whole range of Local Government, set the seal on the new principles by which the old ones were replaced. The fortunate survivor was the principle—in some respects actually strengthened by the Reformed Parliament—of the ownership of property, or at any rate the evidence of more than average fortune, as a necessary qualification for the exercise of governmental authority.

The dominance of this Property Qualification is seen most strikingly in the continued rule, in the Counties, of the Justices of the Peace. Apart from Middlesex and Surrey, in which the unregulated spread of the Metropolis had led, as we have described, to the degradation of the County Bench, the Commission of the Peace had everywhere remained restricted, with few exceptions, to the landowning class, to the exclusion of even wealthy ironmasters or merchants; the squires being reinforced only by the leading rectors or vicars of the County, as owners of freehold benefices. In the early decades of the nineteenth century, in the struggle of the landed gentry to maintain a position of dominance in the nation, their class-exclusiveness

became even more rigid.[1] Moreover, the clerical Justices of the
type of the Rev. Henry Zouch, zealous for the "reformation of
manners" of the "lower orders," incurred widespread unpopularity, not only among those with whose pleasures they interfered, but also among the "friends of freedom" in all classes.[2]
Even in the honest administration of their office, the Justices of
the Peace made themselves, throughout the whole country,
thoroughly disliked. Their attempts to regulate and limit the
number of the inns and alehouses were objected to, both as
interfering with legitimate amusement and as violating the
natural right of every man to invest his capital in any profit-
making enterprise that he thought advantageous to himself. In
their control of the local administration of the Poor Law, the
Justices were objected to when they sought to limit the reckless
generosity of the Vestry or the Overseer; and equally when, in
the Allowance System, they strove to get the relief made adequate
to the needs of each family. When they sought to obey the
injunctions of Parliament, and to provide the County with
decent prisons and lunatic asylums, not to say also to build the
enlarged bridges that the growing traffic on the highroad required,
they were denounced by all the ratepayers, and by most of the
Radical reformers, for the rise of the rates that their "extravagance" necessitated. But what more than anything else made
the authority of the Justices unpopular among the masses of the
people was the arbitrariness and severity with which they
habitually administered the Game Laws, especially against any

[1] Thus, in 1827, there was a great lack of magistrates in the mining districts
of Monmouthshire; but the Lord - Lieutenant refused to recommend, for
appointment to the County Bench, the younger son of an ironmaster who had
become a landed proprietor. The heir apparent, it was explained, might be
recommended, but not a younger son, even if he possessed the legal qualification (Duke of Beaufort to the Lord Chancellor, 16th November 1827; in MS.
Home Office archives in Public Record Office). The scandalous "Trading
Justices," never common, we believe, outside the Metropolitan area, had, by
the nineteenth century, been eliminated from the County Benches. Even in
the Metropolitan area the disreputable "Justices of mean degree" were largely
superseded in 1792 by the establishment of "public offices"—now the Metropolitan Police Courts—at which twenty-four salaried magistrates performed
all the police and judicial duties (*The Parish and the County*, pp. 577-578).

[2] "Most of the magistrates distinguished for over-activity are . . . clergymen" (Hansard, 1828, vol. xviii. N.S. p. 161). Windham was reported to
have said "that he did not know a more noxious species of vermin than an
active Justice of the Peace" (*A Letter to the Rt. Hon. Lord Brougham and
Vaux on the Magistracy of England*, 1832, p. 24; *The Parish and the County*,
pp. 358-359).

labourer suspected of poaching; and the reckless selfishness with which, particularly in the North of England after 1815, they abused their legal powers of stopping up the public footpaths that had from time immemorial crossed their estates. Meanwhile the wild panic which spread through the country houses of England, from the outbreak of the French Revolution onward—a panic maintained between 1816 and 1830 by the industrial and political unrest of the suffering wage-earning population—led to an administration of the Vagrancy Laws that can only be described as scandalously tyrannous. Any Justice of the Peace committed to prison any man or woman of the wage-earning class whom he chose to suspect of being of a seditious or even of a disturbing character. To the perpetual denunciations of the County Justices by the Philosophic Radicals and the rural rate-payers, there was thus added a furious underground hatred of these oppressors by the mass of factory operatives and farm labourers.[1]

Notwithstanding this widespread unpopularity of the Justices; notwithstanding the violation of all the cherished principles of Radicalism in the government and taxation of the County by the unrepresentative Court of Quarter Sessions ; notwithstanding the very real shortcomings and limitations of these Rulers of the County, nothing was done to amend the constitution of the County Bench, and there was practically no proposal even for a removal of the Property Qualification.[2] What happened was the beginning of a process of erosion of the Justices' powers and functions, particularly as exercised by any single Justice, or pair

[1] We believe that the state of feeling of the nation is accurately represented by the works of Mr. and Mrs. Hammond (*The Village Labourer, The Town Labourer* and *The Skilled Labourer*).

[2] By the Acts 13 Richard II. c. 7 and 2 Henry V. stat. 2, c. 1, Justices had to be made, within the County, of the most sufficient knights, esquires and gentlemen of the land. The qualification (for other than judges, peers and their heirs-apparent, or the heirs-apparent of landowners of at least £600 a year) was, by 5 George II. c. 18 and 18 George II. c. 20, fixed at the ownership of real estate producing at least £100 a year. Not until 1875 was the alternative qualification introduced of occupation within the County, for the preceding two years, of a dwelling-house rated at not less than £100 a year, County Court Judges, Metropolitan Police Magistrates and Vice-Wardens of the Stannaries in Devon and Cornwall being exempt (38 & 39 Vict. c. 54). This was removed by statute in 1901, when the qualification for a County Justice was made the same as that for a Borough Justice, namely the mere occupation of any rated premises, coupled with residence in or within seven miles ; whilst all qualification except that of residence was removed in 1906 (6 Edward VII. c. 16).

of Justices. They were practically ousted in the decade following
the Act of 1834 from the Poor Law administration; by the
General Highways Act of 1835 they lost the right of formally
appointing the Surveyor of Highways and their practical power
of directing the highway administration; they found themselves
virtually excluded from the growing territory placed under the
reformed Municipal Corporations, whilst, so far as civil administration was concerned, the Parishes in which Vestries were
established under Hobhouse's Act were entirely abstracted from
their control. The Prisons Act of 1835 made the magistrates
definitely subordinate to the Home Office and its outspoken
peripatetic inspectors. The Acts of 1836 and 1837 instituting
a centralised system of registration of births, deaths and
marriages, entirely ignored the Justices. With regard to their
judicial functions, even within the territory left to them, their
powers were successively restricted by the increasing transfer
of their authority from the "justice rooms" of their own
mansions to the formal sittings of Petty Sessions "in open
Court," and by the greater opportunities of appeal to Quarter
Sessions.[1] Nevertheless, in spite of this steady erosion of the
structure of the Justices' power, it was still possible in the
middle of the nineteenth century, for Rudolf von Gneist, in
the successive editions of his account of English Local Government,[2] to regard the whole class of country gentlemen, protected
in their exclusive occupancy of the County Benches by the high
property qualification, as the effective rulers of rural England.

In the other Local Authorities the prescribed qualification for
office underwent, in the course of the eighteenth century, a
gradual change, which became generalised during the first third
of the nineteenth century. This change, whilst it significantly
transformed the character of what we have called the Property
Qualification, left it nevertheless effective as an instrument for
the retention of authority by the relatively small minority of the

[1] This is not the place in which to describe the successive limitations of the
Justices' functions during the remainder of the nineteenth century, culminating
in 1888 in their practical supersession as administrators by the elective County
Councils. What is here significant is that it was not until the twentieth
century that the restrictive qualification for appointment to the Commission
of the Peace was quite removed.

[2] *Adel und Ritterschaft in England*, 1853; *Geschichte und heutige Gestalt
der Aemter in England*, 1857; *Die englische Communal-verfassung, oder das
System des Self-Government*, 1860, 1863, 1871.

population who constituted the propertied class. The first step was to admit, as an alternative qualification for certain offices, the ownership of a substantial amount not of property in land only, but of wealth of any kind. Alongside of this qualification by ownership of personal property was presently admitted, for some, and eventually for most offices, a qualification by mere occupancy, for a specified term, of a dwelling-house or other premises of a rateable value fixed at a figure so high as to exclude the vast majority of the inhabitants.

This introduction of a high rating qualification, or, indeed, any qualification at all beyond local inhabitancy, into the Local Government of the Parish was an innovation on behalf of the propertied class. No law had ever excluded any adult inhabitant from the Vestry meeting; and if, in all Parishes, the women abstained from attendance, and, in the rural Parishes, few if any labourers presumed to put in an appearance, this was merely a matter of use and wont. The open Vestry meetings of Manchester and Leeds, Liverpool and Woolwich, which themselves decided the important issues of Parish administration, were attended by all classes of the inhabitants, rich or poor, and were even frequently dominated by " the rabble." Moreover, until the passing of Sturges Bourne's Act in 1819, each person in attendance, or voting in the poll taken as an adjournment of the Vestry meeting, had one vote, and one vote only. Similarly, no law had prescribed any qualification (apart from special exemptions which were privileges), beyond that of residency, for the ancient office of Churchwarden, for which persons of the smallest fortune and of the humblest station, even Roman Catholics or Dissenters, were both eligible and liable to compulsory service. The case was the same for the statutory office of Overseer of the Poor, for which mere cottagers and day-labourers were held to be eligible and liable to serve, even if only resident part of the year, and women equally with men, at least if no more " substantial householders " were available.[1] There was just a beginning of a qualification for Parish office in 1691, when the Parish Officers and the inhabitants in Vestry assembled were required to present to the Justices a list of parishioners owning property, or at least occupiers of land or premises worth £30 a year, " if such there be," and if not, " of the most sufficient

[1] R. v. Stubbs, 2 T.R. 395, 406, etc.

inhabitants," out of which the Justices were to appoint one or more as Surveyors of Highways.[1] Even in the Municipal Corporations, where power had, for the most part, fallen into the hands of small and usually close bodies, there continued, in some Boroughs, a relatively considerable class of Freemen, often consisting, to the extent of a majority, of manual-working wage-earners or otherwise indigent folk, who enjoyed, irrespective of whether or not they were occupying ratepayers, or whether they were rich or poor, the franchise for such elections as were held. In these Corporations, which included such extensive towns as Liverpool, Bristol, Norwich and Coventry, once a man had been admitted as a Freeman, whether by patrimony, apprenticeship, purchase or gift, he needed no other qualification, whatever his occupation, station or fortune, for appointment to any corporate office or dignity, not excluding that of membership of the close governing body, or the mayoralty itself. On the other hand, a non-Freeman remained in these Boroughs, right down to 1835, not only absolutely ineligible for any corporate office, however wealthy he might be, however extensive his business in the Borough, or however high the rateable value of the premises that he occupied ; but also excluded from the valuable exemptions from tolls and dues, and the profitable right of sharing in the " commons and stints " or other common property, enjoyed by his business rivals who were " free " of the Corporation.

With regard to membership of a public body, it was naturally in the new Statutory Authorities for Special Purposes, to which we have devoted the present volume, that the novel form of qualification came in. The Court of Sewers continued in this as in other respects closely to resemble the Court of Quarter Sessions.[2] For the membership of the Turnpike Trusts, however, we invariably find a statutory qualification, in which the ownership of £1000 of personal property, or some other amount, was admitted as an alternative to the possession of an estate in land. In the Incorporated Guardians of the Poor, as we have seen, the

---

[1] 3 William III. c. 12 ; re-enacted in 13 George III. c. 78, where it is further expressly specified that the Justices may, if the list contains none whom they think " qualified," appoint any " substantial inhabitants " living within the County and within three miles of the Parish.

[2] The qualification for a Commissioner of Sewers, originally stated as land worth " 40 marks " annually, and by 13 Elizabeth c. 9 (1571) as forty pounds sterling, was actually raised in 1833 to £100 a year freehold, or £200 a year leasehold, within the County (3 & 4 William IV. c. 22).

qualification varied ; but usually the County Justices and the Incumbents of benefices were reinforced not only by the owners of freehold estates, but also by the leaseholders (in which we think were included the farmers under any agreement of tenancy) of land worth at least £60 per annum. It is, however, in the more multifarious and diverse bodies of Commissioners for Paving, Lighting, Watching, Cleansing and otherwise Improving the various urban centres that we find both the greatest variety of qualification for office and the most obvious transition from the old forms of qualification to the new. Among the thousand Local Acts, by which, during the eighteenth century, the three hundred or so bodies of Commissioners were established or amended, there was introduced first the qualification of owner- ship of real estate ; then the alternative of possession of £1000 or other specified amount of any form of wealth ; and in the later constitutions, first as a new alternative and latterly, in a few cases, as the only permissible form of qualification, the occu- pation within the town of premises of what was at the time a high annual value [1]—sometimes (as in Manchester in 1828) £28 per annum, sometimes twice that sum, which, in the early part of the century, indicated the shop or warehouse of a very sub- stantial trader or the mansion of a man of wealth.

With regard to the qualification for the franchise, it was a characteristic feature of the Local Government reforms of the first third of the nineteenth century that, along with the privileges of the Freemen in the Municipal Corporations, the remaining laxity as to qualification in Parish administration was brought to an end.[2] It became the general rule that no one should exercise any right to vote, and in most cases, that no one should be eligible for any elective office, unless his name was actually entered in the ratebook as that of a ratepayer, whether as occupier or as owner, of premises within the area concerned. Alike for the Parish Committees under Sturges Bourne's Act, for the elective Vestries under Hobhouse's Act, for the Boards of

---

[1] It is curious to find the requirement that publicans, to be eligible, needed a rating qualification twice as great as other inhabitants ; *ante*, p. 245.

[2] The strenuous fight of the House of Lords against the Municipal Cor- porations Bill in its original form maintained the vote, for the new Town Councils, of the possibly non-occupying, indigent and even pauper Freemen of Liverpool, Coventry and other ancient Boroughs, so far as the existing holders of privileges were concerned, though the Act abolished the privilege as regards future generations.

Guardians under the regulations made upon the authority of the Poor Law Amendment Act, for the Town Councils under the Municipal Corporations Act, and even for the Highway Committees under the General Highways Act, it was taken for granted, when not expressly laid down by regulation or statute, that the franchise was confined to independent occupiers of dwelling-houses or other premises, whose names were on the ratebook as direct payers of the local rates, and whose rates during the prescribed period had been actually paid. The prescribed period of occupancy and ratepaying was, in some cases (as by the Municipal Corporations Act) fixed at two years next previous to the making of the last rate. And when to this was added the disfranchisement, not merely of those householders who were aliens, but also (for Boards of Guardians) of all persons who (or any member of whose family) had received during the prescribed period any kind of parochial relief, and (for the new Town Councils) of all occupiers of the female sex—when it is realised that it became an almost universal practice of the landlord of small cottage property or tenement dwellings himself to pay the rates, and thus keep all his tenants off the ratebook—it will be seen how very far was the franchise for the elective Local Authorities, even after the reforms of 1832–1836, from that of a universal Democracy of Consumers. Exact statistics do not exist, but it is probable that the aggregate electorate of all the elective Local Authorities of England and Wales did not, in 1836, for a population then amounting to over 14 millions, or some three million families, exceed the total number of Parliamentary electors, which is commonly estimated at 800,000. Speaking generally, it may be said that, whereas at the end of the seventeenth century every householder, male or female, could legally attend and vote at the Parish Vestry, and in the Municipal Corporations even the poorest Freeman was a member of the Corporation; after the Local Government revolution of 1818–1836 only one householder out of four could cast a vote.[1]

But the restriction of the Local Government franchise to those who had been, over a prescribed period, directly assessed to, and had actually paid the local rates, with the further dis-

[1] It is something more than a coincidence that the proportion of weekly wage-earners and their families to the whole population certainly amounted to three-fourths.

franchisement of aliens, paupers, married women and (for the Town Councils) even independent women ratepayers, was not the whole of the establishment of what amounted virtually to a new Property Qualification. By Sturges Bourne's Act of 1819, followed by the much more important Poor Law Amendment Act of 1834, as amended by that of 1844, the device of Plural Voting was introduced in such a way as to place the dominant power even more certainly in the hands of the richer inhabitants. Each registered owner (who might be only a leaseholder of a mortgagee), and each rated occupier of the premises in the rate-book, was accorded, in the election of the Poor Law Authority, from one up to six votes, according to the annual value of the premises, with the further aggravation that where (as became usual with all cottage property or tenement dwellings) the land-lord's name appeared on the ratebook as owner and also as paying the rátes for his tenants, he enjoyed double votes, thus being given as much as twelve times the weight of such occupants of the smaller dwellings as had votes at all. At the same time statutory provision was made in 1844 to enable joint stock companies or other corporate bodies to vote as persons, and individual owners were even enabled to send an agent to cast their votes for their property, with the singular proviso that "except a tenant, bailiff, steward, land-agent or collector of rents," no such agent was allowed to cast votes on behalf of more than four owners ![1]   Here, perhaps, is found the most ingenious application of the principle of Property Qualification for the exercise of authority, seeing that it secured the predominance of the propertied class in the State without necessarily involving the exclusion of even the poorest resident. The most straight-forward defence of this device of plural voting, because it shows how the commercialised political philosophy of the time had spread even to the oldest English aristocracy, is that made by Lord Salisbury in resisting the coming of Household Suffrage. His daughter, Lady Gwendolen Cecil, describing and quoting from his article on the subject in 1864, thus summarises his argu-ment : " A democratic extension of the franchise would not only give a share to every man in the government of the country, but would give to every man an equal share. *Yet with regard to the chief subject-matter of Parliamentary action* [the italics are ours],

---

[1] 7 & 8 Vict. c. 101, sec. 15 (1844).

there is, and always will be, a ubiquitous inequality of interest in the decisions taken. He suggests an analogy in the management of joint stock companies. The best test of natural right is that right which mankind, left to themselves to regulate their own concerns, most naturally admit. Joint stock companies, like States, finding themselves too numerous to undertake directly the management of their affairs, have adopted a representative system. How do they settle this thorny question of the suffrage ? The system under which, by universal agreement, such bodies are universally managed is that the voting power should be strictly proportioned to the stake which each man holds in the company. It is a system whose justice has never been disputed. The question has never even been a matter of controversy. The wildest dreamer never suggested that all the shareholders should each have a single vote, without reference to the number of shares they might hold." [1]

If it is significant to find the Cecil of 1864 unhesitatingly assuming that the " chief subject-matter of Parliamentary action " is the maintenance of private property (for it is in this only that there can be said to be " a ubiquitous inequality of interest in the decisions taken "), it is interesting to see how mistaken he proved to be in supposing that " mankind left to themselves " invariably adopted the joint stock principle of voting according to the amount of wealth at stake. The consumers' Co-operative Movement, which was, in 1864, in its infancy, now (1922) includes in its membership in the United Kingdom some four million households, or more than a third of the total. These men and women, far more numerous than the entire aggregate of shareholders in joint stock companies, and owning among them over £100,000,000 worth of capital in their Co-operative Movement—have always, spontaneously and unquestioningly, adopted in the constitution of the Co-operative world, the principle of " One Member one Vote," irrespective, not only of age and sex, station or fortune, but also of the amount of share or loan capital possessed by each.[2]

The qualification for public office was, in certain cases, even

---

[1] *Life of the Marquis of Salisbury*, by Lady Gwendolen Cecil, 1921, vol. i. p. 152. It may be recalled that Burke had declared that " Property . . . never can be safe from the invasion of ability unless it be, out of all proportion, dominant in the representation " (*Reflections on the French Revolution*).

[2] *The Consumers' Co-operative Movement*, by S. and B. Webb, 1921.

more restrictive in its effects than that for the franchise. Thus the Poor Law Commissioners, in framing their regulations for the new Boards of Guardians under the Poor Law Amendment Act, which had empowered the fixing of a rating qualification not exceeding £40 a year, willingly adopted this statutory maximum for all the Unions in the Metropolitan area, and for some of those elsewhere, whilst in all Unions whatever such a rating qualification was fixed as to exclude not only the whole wage-earning class, and all the smaller shopkeepers, but also, incidentally, most of the independent women occupiers.[1]

We may point out that there was the less need, in the nineteenth as in the twentieth century, for any such rigid exclusion from office of the four-fifths or seven-eighths of the adult population who could not prove either their ownership of landed or other property, or even their occupancy of a dwelling-house rated at £40 a year, in that service in the elected offices was almost invariably unpaid. The whole aggregate of persons in industrial or commercial employment at wages or salaries, together with all those in the service of public bodies, and all the more necessitous shopkeepers and other employers or professional men, were (as they still are) normally excluded from the elective Local Authorities by their inability to give the necessary time. The refusal to provide either salary or fees for the members of local governing bodies, even such merely as would pay for the time actually spent on the public service, amounts in itself practically to the maintenance of a Property Qualification, which, without any further restriction, necessarily confines membership to the small minority who are able and willing to afford such a sacrifice of their time. The actual result has been, in the nineteenth century, to throw the Town Councils and Boards of Guardians almost entirely into the hands, not of the largest and wealthiest merchants and traders, any more than of the landowners or of the mass of wage-earners, but of the substantial resident shopkeepers, builders and publicans in the towns, and farmers in the country, with a small intermixture of auctioneers, petty contractors, and here and there a few solicitors, doctors or

---

[1] The rating qualification for Guardians was not reduced until 1893, when it was fixed at £5 only. It needed another statute to abolish the qualification altogether; see Local Government Act, 1894, sec. 20 (5). Even then, the qualification of £40 remained (and still remains) for membership of the Metropolitan Asylums Board for any one not possessing real estate within the area.

persons retired from business. Apart from the Courts of Quarter Sessions and the Courts of Sewers, English Local Government was, by the series of reforms that culminated in 1836, in effect handed over, almost exclusively, to a particular stratum of the middle class.

But still no System of Local Government

We end our analysis of the new principles that emerged in English Local Government between the Revolution and the Municipal Corporations Act, on the same note as we struck in opening our previous chapter. In 1836, as in 1689, there was still nothing in Local Government that could be called a system. The separate forms of social organisation, the Manor and the Borough, the Parish and the County, originating indifferently in prescription and local custom, charter and Royal Commission, Common Law and Parliamentary statute, superimposed one on top of another·according to the needs and circumstances of each century, and inextricably entangled in each other's growth and decay, had been made even more complicated and confused by the establishment, during the eighteenth and early nineteenth centuries, of the eighteen hundred new Statutory Authorities for Special Purposes, only partially connected with the constitution and activities of the other local institutions, that we have described in the present volume. By Sturges Bourne's Act and Hobhouse's Act, the Poor Law Amendment Act and the Municipal Corporations Act, the General Highways Act and the Births and Deaths Registration Acts, this heterogeneous complex of overlapping Local Authorities was not straightened out into any systematic organisation. Not one of the fifteen thousand or more separate local governing bodies found itself actually abolished, even by the most iconoclastic of these statutes. What these Acts accomplished was finally to dispossess the old principles—save for certain surviving remnants —and to set the seal upon the adoption, in the reorganised bodies to which all authority was gradually transferred, of the new principles that we have described. But no organic system of Local Government as a whole could at that time be recognised. The Metropolitan Vestries, the Parish Committees of provincial Vestries, the Municipal Corporations, the new Boards of

THE CHAOS OF AREAS

Guardians, not to mention such survivals as the Courts of Sewers, the Turnpike Trusts and the Improvement Commissioners, the still existing City of London and other unreformed Corporations, and such ephemeral Authorities as the Local Boards of Health and the Highway Boards, had, without reference to each other, all been created or reformed by separate statutes, to meet particular circumstances. Their methods of election were unlike. The qualifications for the franchise and for office differed materially and irrationally from one to the other. The areas over which the several Authorities exercised their diverse jurisdictions overlapped each other; their several powers and functions were sometimes inconsistent and frequently duplicated; they levied on the same ratepayers a multitude of different imposts, assessed under different rules, and payable at different dates. The position of these multifarious Local Authorities to each other was undefined; whilst their relations to the National Executive were as diverse as their constitutions or their functions. Thus, whilst the Municipal Corporations, like the rural Parish Vestries, had the very minimum of contact with any Government Department, and were subject to practically no control, the new Boards of Guardians were bound hand and foot to the autocratic Poor Law Commissioners; in their administration of the Births, Marriages and Deaths Registration Acts the new Local Authorities had to obey the commands of the Registrar-General; and even the Courts of Quarter Sessions were, in respect of their prison administration, brought under the peremptory injunctions of the Home Office.

What was effected in 1832–1836, so far as English Local Government was concerned, was definitely to cut it off from Vocational Organisation, with its exclusiveness, industrial, political or religious; its methods of Co-option and of universal rotational tenure of public office, and above all its assumption that the direction of any service should be vested in those who performed it—and to base the new bodies on election by a rate-payers' or consumers' Democracy, in which those who enjoyed the benefit of the public services, and paid for them by local taxation, were themselves assumed to exercise all authority through their elected representatives, who ordered and directed the work of contractors or paid servants. It was, as we can now

see, this form of government that was destined, in the course of
the nineteenth century, to become universal. It is on the basis
of this Ratepayers' Democracy of 1832–1836, completed as a
Consumers' Democracy by the franchise or rating reforms of
1867, 1869, 1888, 1894, 1900, 1917 and 1918, that English Local
Government, after a further three-quarters of a century of effort,
has ceased to be the chaos of areas, chaos of Authorities and
chaos of rates, which it was left in 1836 ; and has at last, in
the twentieth century, become, as Francis Place predicted, fairly
well systematised in the municipal form.

Unfortunately, as we have seen, the reforms of 1832–1836
failed not only to systematise Local Government, but also—
mainly by the froward retention of the old principle of Property
Qualification in its new guise—failed to make the Ratepayers'
Democracy coextensive with the consumers of the public services
which it had collectively to provide. By the ratepaying qualification, nearly always fixed at a high figure, coupled with the refusal
of any payment for public work, the framers of the legislation of
1818–1836 not only excluded from the reformed Councils, as
they intended, the manual-working class, and, indeed, the great
mass of folk of all occupations absorbed in earning a livelihood,
but also, as was probably not foreseen, practically the men of
wider education, the brain-working professions, the heads of the
more important businesses, and all others who did not actually
reside within the particular ward or local district for which
representatives had to be elected. Incidentally all women,
whether married or unmarried, were long debarred, either by law
or by the practice of the rating Authorities, from serving on any
public bodies. The result was that nearly the whole of Local
Government, outside the restricted scope of the Courts of Quarter
Sessions and the Courts of Sewers, was handed over to the class
of retail shopkeepers and farmers, whose virtues, whose shortcomings and whose general outlook on life became everywhere
dominant, alike in the Town Council, in the Parish Vestry and
in the Board of Guardians. We cannot express it better than in
the carefully weighed judgment—already quoted by us in connection with the relatively democratic Corporation of the City
of London, and full of significance to students of political science
—which De Tocqueville passed upon the government of France
between 1830 and 1848. The dominating spirit of that govern-

ment, he said, was the spirit characteristic of the trading Middle Class ; a spirit active and assiduous ; always narrow ; often corrupt ; occasionally, through vanity or egotism, insolent, but by temperament timid ; mediocre and moderate in all things except in the enjoyment of physical indulgence ; a spirit which, when combined with the spirit of the manual-working wage-earners and the spirit of the aristocracy, may achieve marvels, but which, taken alone, inevitably produces a government without elevation and without quality.[1] We may add a significant comment on the Local Government of the generation that followed immediately on the reforms of 1832–1836 by a well-instructed official. " Too often," said Tom Taylor, who had been Secretary to the Central Board of Health, " ' local self-government ' is another name for the unchecked rule of the least informed, noisiest and narrowest, or, as often, of the most self-seeking, who can achieve seats in a Town Council or at a Local Improvement Board. . . . But, in the whirl of complicated affairs, among the incessant demands of private interests stimulated by the closest competition, the bewildering action and counter action of class wants and claims, and the self-consciousness bred of too exclusive a pursuit of material advancement, it is no wonder if the most public-spirited, the most anxious to do their best for the interests of the community of which they are a part, who often find themselves more and more perplexed and baffled, and discover, to their dismay, that active participation in local affairs too often resolves itself into an unsuccessful struggle with the grossest ignorance, the most offensive mob oratory, and the most sordid self-seeking. Only very stout hearts indeed can long maintain the struggle. The temptation is too often irresistible to withdraw from the Town Council or Local Board, and to seek in the exercise of more secluded benevolence for a satisfaction of those inward urgings to unselfish duty which can find no useful employment in the public arena without." [2]

[1] *Souvenirs d'Alexis de Tocqueville*, 1893, p. 6 (freely translated); *The Manor and the Borough*, p. 692.

[2] " On Central and Local Action in Relation to Town Improvement," by Tom Taylor, M.A., in *Transactions of the National Association for the Promotion of Social Science*, 1857, p. 475. Tom Taylor proceeds to suggest the importance of central control. " Are local powers," he says, " a trust for the public advantage, or a means of enforcing the supremacy of local cliques, and a machinery for rewarding local partisanship with power, patronage and place ?

2 I

Such is the pessimistic verdict of a competent observer of
1857. But no judicial estimate of the nature and results of the
revolutionary transformation of the machinery of Local Government effected in 1832–1836 could be made in that generation.
It would be misleading and unfair to leave off on Tom Taylor's
depressing note. A popular dramatist turned bureaucrat, grappling with the " Early Victorian " stupidities of local officials,
and the prejudices of the average sensual man, could hardly be
expected to take an optimistic view of Local Government. It
is more instructive to consider the exceptional difficulties with
which the new elective bodies had to cope. For it must be
remembered that all the disastrous changes in the environment
of the common people, due to the Industrial Revolution described in the opening pages of this chapter, continued in operation, in some cases with accelerating speed, during the whole of
the first half of the nineteenth century, and even later. The
population, in spite of (and perhaps because of) widespread
destitution and servitude, went on increasing, and more and
more crowding into the urban slums. The devastating torrent of
nuisances, characteristic of unrestricted profit-making enterprise,

---

If, as I contend, such powers are a public trust, then their exercise ought to be
watched and recorded on behalf of the public, the lessons which the
experience of each place supplies ought to be deduced and made known
for the benefit of all ; glaring instances of neglected duty and their
consequence should be stigmatised ; conspicuous examples of activity and
well-directed efforts, and their results should be held up for imitation.
This duty, to be performed not for a single town or district, but for the
whole Kingdom, turns local facts to general use, whether by way of warning
or example. Some would add to these central duties that of acting as a court
of appeal against local oppression, and as a court of mandamus in cases of
default. . . . Reviewing what had been said, it will be found that the necessity
of central action on matters of local improvement is maintained :

" (1) To accord the conferred powers for such improvement cheaply and
effectually ; to invest with the local character of ' towns ' areas of dense
population not having yet acquired a known and defined boundary ; and to
fuse, into a consistent whole, existing Local Acts, and a general measure of
town improvements.

" (2) When such powers are conferred, to forward generally the wise and
efficient exercise of them by diffusing the light of a general experience, and by
communicating the results of such special enquiries as the Central Department
may be charged to make, by advising in cases of doubt or difficulty, and generally by assisting but never superseding, local efforts.

" (3) To protect posterity, by examining and deciding upon application for
leave to mortgage roads ;

" (4) To report to Parliament on the exercise of local powers.

" (5) To act as a court of appeal against local oppression in certain specified
cases, and a court of mandamus in cases of local default " (*ibid.* pp. 478-479).

went on spreading over the land, maintaining the sickness-rate, the accident-rate and the death-rate at appallingly high figures, whilst the insanitary factories and workshops, and the unregulated mines and smelting works were insidiously lowering the vitality of men, women and children. To guide the new Local Authorities there was no administrative science. There was no fully organised National Executive charged with protecting the race from the worst results of the capitalist system. Not until the last quarter of the nineteenth century, and then only imperfectly, can even the educated public be said to have realised the necessity for the legal limitation and regulation of capitalist enterprise ; or can our Factory and Workshop Acts, Mines Regulation Acts and Merchant Shipping Acts be said to have more than begun to ensure to the whole population that fundamental National Minimum of the conditions of civilised life without which Local Government can be no more than a botch. And the instruments were as lacking as the science and the law. To replace the ordinary citizen temporarily conscripted to unpaid public service, there was, in 1835, no body of trustworthy, trained, professional officials. The specially characteristic modern vocations, whether of engineers, architects, surveyors, accountants, and auditors ; or of teachers, nurses, sanitary inspectors and medical officers of health ; or even of draughtsmen, bookkeepers, clerks and policemen, were as yet only beginning to be developed. Without effective vocational organisation they were still without either tradition or training, and wholly unprovided with the code of professional ethics on which, as we now know, the highest administrative efficiency so much depends. The obsolescent and obstructive mediaeval vocational organisation had been cleared out of the way ; and the new and virile type of vocational organisation, of which the germs lay in the then persecuted and prescribed Trade Union Movement and the beginnings of modern Professional Association, had not yet been created.

No less important was the nature of the functions to which the nascent Local Government of the nineteenth century was still confined. By far the most extensive service was, for several decades after 1836, that of the relief of the poor. Now, necessary as may have been the Poor Law revolution of 1834, and devoted as were the services of many of those who worked at its administration, it proved impossible to enlist either administrative genius or public support for a purely deterrent and repressive treatment of destitution and vagrancy. Scarcely more inspiring seemed municipal government, so long as this was confined, in the main, to the suppression of those nuisances which threatened the health or lessened the amenity of the life of the Middle Class. It took, we may usefully remember, all the rest of the nineteenth century to generalise and extend to the whole field of Local Government, even the structural reforms of 1832–1836. It was at least as long before the new Local Government got into its stride as the obligatory Association of Consumers for the collective provision of those services and commodities for which profit-making enterprise seemed less well adapted than communal organisation. With the gradual assumption, as communal ser-vices, of the whole range of education from the nursery school to the university ; of the organisation in parks and open spaces, in libraries and museums, in music rooms and picture galleries, of recreation and amusement ; of a general provision, not merely for the treatment of the sick, but also actually for the promotion of health of future generations as well as of the present ; of town planning, local transport and housing not merely as the correctives of slums but as the creators of the city of to-morrow ; and, last but by no means least, of the supply of water, gas, electricity, power, and local transportation as necessary adjuncts of muni-cipal life, the whole scope and spirit of Local Government has been transformed. Merely in magnitude and range of affairs the Local Government of 1922 is much further removed from that of 1836, than that of 1836 was from its predecessor of 1689. The ten or twelve millions sterling of annual revenue of all the English Local Authorities on the accession of Queen Victoria have become the three hundred million pounds of gross receipts of the Local Authorities of to-day ; the few thousand persons whom they employed, for the most part contractors and low-paid labour, have grown into an average staff, at salaries or wages, of something like a million on the pay roll of 1922, com-prising as many as one in fifteen of the entire working population ; whilst the capital administered by the various Local Authorities of England and Wales, formerly infinitesimal, now exceeds in value 1500 millions sterling. With this growth of Local Government in magnitude and variety ; and especially with its

expansion from essentially repressive or eleemosynary functions
into the communal organisation of the city life, new classes
have reinforced the municipal service, both as elected representatives and as officials. The wage-earning class has, in the
twentieth century, not only supplied from its educated children
the great bulk of the new hierarchy of Local Government staffs ;
but has also, by electing to the Councils its Trade Union officials,
and sometimes by providing for its representatives a modest
salary, increasingly managed to overcome the barrier presented
by Property Qualification and the Non-Payment of Councillors.
And Local Government in its modern guise, with its new and
larger aims and vaster problems, has come to attract, both as
elected representatives and as officials, ever more and more of
the ablest and best trained intellects, who find, in its service,
whether paid or unpaid, an inspiration and a scope actually
superior, in their own estimation, to that offered by the pursuit
of pecuniary profit. In short, English Local Government, in
1832–1836 handed over, in effect, to a particular stratum of the
Middle Class, has gradually become representative of all the best
sections of English life.

But this story is not for us to tell. How from the unsystematised and, as we have indicated, " commercialised "
chaos of separate Authorities of 1836, English Local Government has, in the course of three-quarters of a century, become
generally organised as a Consumers' Democracy ; how the
invidious and, as we think, calamitous exclusion of the great
mass of the consumers has been, by a whole series of minor
reforms of franchise and rating, largely remedied ; how the
merely eleemosynary and largely deterrent " relief of destitution " has been, in one department after another, replaced by
the institution of communal services, and the demoralising
Poor Law Authority increasingly superseded by municipal
activities ; how new vocational organisation has arisen to
redeem an untempered consumers' government, and the necessary provision—absolutely ignored in 1836—for the participation
in the administration of those who are actually engaged in the
service is, in the twentieth century, at least beginning to be
made ; how the still unsolved problems of areas, of the equalisa-
tion of burdens, and of the relation between local and central
Authorities are being tentatively explored ; how with this

greater inclusiveness and with the elaboration of an administrative science the outlook and purpose of Local Government
has been gradually defined, widened and ennobled—all this
fascinating evolution of Parish and Borough and County into
the Local Government of to-day we must regretfully leave to
be described by younger students.[1]

---

[1] We may be permitted to refer to some incomplete studies that subsequent
enquirers may find useful. With regard to the provision of roads, and the
maintenance of prisons, we have sought to bring the Local Government history
down to the twentieth century in our books, *The Story of the King's Highway*,
1913, and *English Prisons under Local Government*, 1922. A corresponding
volume on The Evolution of Poor Relief and the Repression of Vagrancy is
in preparation. With regard to the manifold functions of the Poor Law
Authorities, we may refer to the Minority Report of the Poor Law Commission,
1909, separately published in two volumes, with lengthy introductions, as
The Break-up of the Poor Law, 1909, and *The Public Organisation of the Labour
Market*, 1909 ; to *The State and the Doctor*, 1910 ; and (for the evolution of
policy since 1834) to *English Poor Law Policy*, 1910 ; together with the
systematic survey entitled *The Prevention of Destitution*, 1911, reissued with
new preface, 1920. Only a brief sketch of the period after 1835 is given in
The History of Liquor Licensing in England, 1903. On the other hand, *Grants
in Aid, a Criticism and a Proposal*, 1911 ; second edition, 1920, deals exclusively
with that period.

For a general view of the evolution of Local Government during the nineteenth century, the summary outline entitled *Towards Social Democracy ?
A Study of Social Evolution during the Past Three-quarters of a Century*, 1916,
may be consulted. For a survey of the position in 1920, and a speculative
forecast, we may cite *A Constitution for the Socialist Commonwealth of Great
Britain*, 1920 ; some parts of this being amplified in the final chapter of *The
Consumers' Co-operative Movement*, 1921.

INDEX OF PERSONS

INDEX OF PLACES

Blackfriars Bridge, 286
Blackwall, Commissioners of Sewers for, 85 ; Dyke at, 48
Bloomsbury, Guardians of Poor for, 146 ; paving of, 282, 287 ; and Westminster Commission of Sewers, 80
Blything Hundred, Commissioners of Sewers for, 38 ; Poor Law administration at, 131, 136-37
Bolingbroke, Soke of, 20, 55
Bosmere Hundred, House of Industry of, 125
Boston, Harbour Commissioners of, 241 ; Court of Sewers at, 52, 56
Boughton, highways of, 166
Bradford, Improvement Commissioners for, 244 ; street cleansing at, 335, 341
Braintree (Essex), Gentlemen of the Four and Twenty of, 25
Brentford, Sewer Commissioners for, 77 ; Turnpike Trustees for, 195
Bridgewater, Act of, 245 ; Court of Sewers for, 41-45, 53 ; Market and Streets Act for, 300 ; Turnpike Trust, 266. See also *Somerset*
Bridport, Harbour Commissioners of, 241
Brighton, Improvement Commissioners for, 244 ; contract with Poor Law Authority for street cleansing, 341 ; paving contracts, 310 ; revenue from sale of street refuse, 336
—— Road, 227 ; Turnpike Trust of, 195
Bristol, Corporation of the Poor of, 111, 114, 148-49 ; Close Vestries of, and political partisanship, 382 ; Freemen of, 472 ; Harbour Commissioners of, 241 ; Hospital of St. Peter at, 143 ; Improvement Act of, 300, 307-309 ; Incorporated Guardians of, 116 ; Municipal Corporation of, 307, 449 ; paving at, 298, 306-10, 312 ; pollution of air at, 404 ; Select Vestry of, 371, 422 ; street cleansing at, 287, 330-31 ; Turnpike Trust of, 204, 220, 227 ; turnpike riots at, 174-75 ; toll bridges at, 182
Brixton, drainage of, 100
Broadstairs, Harbour Commissioners of, 241
Brue (Somerset), drainage of, 41, 45
Buckinghamshire, Turnpike Trustees of, 159
Bulcamp, House of Industry at, 125, 140
Bungay, street cleansing in, 328-29
Bury St. Edmund's, union of Parishes at, 116 ; Quarter Sessions at, 393

Buxton, Incorporated Guardians of Poor of, 125
Byrmyngham. See *Birmingham*

Cainscross (Gloucester), turnpike riots at, 174
Camberwell, sale of refuse in, 337
Cambridge, University of, and paving regulations, 298
Cambridgeshire, Commissioners of Sewers of, 39 ; drainage of fens of, 28, 53 ; roads of, 157-58, 161-62
Canterbury, 33 ; Commissioners of Sewers for, 46, 49 ; Jury of Sewers at, 50 ; Paving Act for, 298 ; Sheriff of, 50 ; union of Parishes at, 116
Cardiff, Improvement Commissioners for, 244
Carlford. See *Colneis and Carlford*
Carlisle, fees of Clerk of Peace in, 385 ; Improvement Commissioners of, 244
Carnarvon, Harbour Commissioners for, 241
Carsdyke, 29
Caxton, turnpike toll at, 158
Chatham, Paving Act for, 300 ; and Canterbury Turnpike Act, 188
Chedzoy (Somerset), Sewers, Jury of, 42
Chelmsford, petition of, to Essex Quarter Sessions, 188-89
Cheltenham, Improvement Commissioners for, 244
Cheshire, turnpikes of, 158
Cheshunt, Turnpike Trust of, 212
Chester, crime at, 410-11 ; Improvement Commissioners of, 244 ; street cleansing at, 332 ; union of Parishes at, 116
Chichester, Paving Act of, 298 ; union of Parishes of, 116
Christchurch, Guardians of the Poor of, 145
Cinque Ports, liberty of the, 18, 46 ; Lord Warden of the, 50, 106
Cirencester, Paving Act of, 298
Clayton Hundred, House of Industry of, 125
Clobsdon, sewers of, 38
Colchester, Guardians of the Poor of, 115 ; Harbour Commissioners of, 241 ; Harbour and Streets Act for, 299-300
Coley House, 164
Colneis and Carlford Hundred, Guardians of Poor of, 124-26, 127, 130, 132-33 ; Acts relating to, 121-23, 127, 137 ; House of Industry of, 140
Congresbury (Somerset), drainage awards for, 41

2 K*

Longdendale Valley, Water Supply from, 261
Longport (Kent), highways of, 166
Lothingland, Hundred of, Commissioners of Sewers for, 38
Loughborough and Derby, Turnpike Act for, 163
Louth (Lincolnshire), drainage of, 15; street cleansing in, 327-28
Ludlow, Turnpike Act for, 192
Lymne, 33
Lynn (Norfolk), street cleansing at, 333. See also *King's Lynn*

Macclesfield, Streets Act for, 300; and Buxton Turnpike Trust, 181
Maidenhead, pavement at, 302; and Reading turnpike, 181; toll bridge at, 183
Maidstone, Improvement Commissioners for, 245; Streets Act for, 299; union of Parishes at, 116
Manchester, administration of markets at, 441; and Buxton Trust, 227; Court Leet of, 266; crime in, 410; desire for "select" corporation, 373; food riots at, 411; gas works of, 262-63; highways rate of, 168; Imperial Joint Stock Oil Gas Company at, 263; Manorial Court administration in, 370; Manufacturers of, 414; Market Street Act of, 245; Market Street Widening, Commissioners for, 260; municipal water supply for, 261; Nonconformist Churchwarden of, 422; and Oldham Turnpike Trust, 210, 217; open Vestry meetings at, 471; paving at, 303; Police Officer Nadin of, 461; Poor Law administration in, 144; public nuisances at, 400, 401, 402; Public Reference Library at, 270; streets of, 239, 256, 315, 403; street cleansing in, 332, 344; Street Commissioners for, 105; street regulations in, 270; Surveyor of Highways for, 168; Town Council of, 273, 347; turnpike tolls, 195; Vestry of, 257, 446; voluntary associations for crime suppression in, 440
—— Improvement Commissioners, 268, 290, 339. See also *Police Commissioners of*
—— Local Government, exclusion of Nonconformists and R.C.'s from, 422; improvement in, 269
—— Police Commissioners, 245, 256-273, 401, 442; Bill of 1836, 272-73; constitution, 258, 259, 264-66, 268-269; an elected assembly, 449; finance of, 260-63, 273; gas supply,

municipal administration of, 262, 264-65, 266, 270, 272; gas and water supply, 261, 443-44; Police rate, 261-63, 266-67; statutory powers of, 273; taxes levied by, 260; and Town Improvement, 259-60
Manchester and Salford Act of 1765 (Street Cleansing), 330
—— and Salford Improvement Commissioners for, 244-45; constitution of, 243-44; functions of, 303; Local Act regarding, 303
Manners, movement for reformation of, 412, 439
Margate, Harbour Commissioners for, 241
Marseilles, plague at, 279
Marshland (Norfolk), Embankment of, 54
Medway, River, drainage of, 58
Melton, House of Industry at, 123-25, 141; meetings of Directors and Acting Guardians of, 133-34; maladministrating at, 143
Merionethshire, County Magistrates of, 373-74
Metropolis, the, Courts of Sewers in, 57; growth of, 11; Improvement Commissioners in, 244, 248-49; Incorporated Guardians for, 151; opposition to municipal authority for, 291; overcrowding in, 407, 408; Poor Law Administration in, 145-47; population in, 399; public nuisance in, 404; result of private building enterprise in, 402. See also *London, names of places in the Metropolitan area*; also under *Metropolitan* in *Index of Subjects*
Mevagissey, Harbour Commissioners for, 241
Middlesex, breakdown of magistracy of, 373; Committee on Nuisances for, 323; Commission of the Peace for, 82-83, 91, 228, 373, 385, 387, 388, 467; Commission of Sewers for, 23, 72-73, 104; sewers of, 27, 80; Sheriff of, 73; street cleansing in, 322-23; turnpike roads in, 181; Turnpike Trusts of, 208, 228-230
—— Quarter Sessions, 385; Indictment of Paving Commissioners in, 289-90; Justices' paving regulations for, 278-79, 322-23; personnel of, 82-83, 91
—— and Essex, Turnpike Trust for, 227
Milne, Incorporated Guardians of the Poor of, 125
Minchinhampton, Paving Committee at, 313-14

Welland Canal, presentment by Jury of, 56
Wells, Court of Sewers at, 43, 45
Wenlock, Improvement Commissioners for, 242
Westfirle, Guardians of the Poor for, 139
Westmoreland, turnpike roads of, 204
Weston Zoyland (Somerset), sewage rate of, 42
Weymouth, Paving Act for, 300
Whetstone, Turnpike Trust of, 153, 195
Whitby, Harbour Commissioners for, 241
Whitchurch, employment of poor at, 118
Whitehaven, Harbour Commissioners for, 241
Whitstable, Commissioners of Sewers for, 46
Wickham Market, meetings of Guardians at, 133
Wigan, Improvement Commissioners for, 242 ; state of streets of, 315
Wilton, turnpike riots at, 175
Wiltshire, turnpikes of, 158
Winchester, Improvement Commissioners for, 244 ; Streets Act for, 299
Windsor, employment of poor at, 111 ; toll bridge at, 182-83

Wisbech, 38, 378, 381
Witham (Essex), sale of refuse at, 339
Wolverhampton, Improvement Commissioners for, 244
Woodbridge (Suffolk), turnpike weighing machine at, 198
Woodford Road (Essex), the, 158, 215
Worcester, Improvement Commissioners for, 245 ; Paving Act for, 300 ; Turnpike Trust for, 227 ; Guardians of Poor of, 115
Worcestershire, crime in, 411
Wye, Commissioners of Sewers for, 46
Wymendham and Attleborough Road, the, 158

Yarm, petition of, against toll-gate, 180
Yarmouth, Harbour Commissioners for, 241 ; Improvement Commissioners for, 244
Yeovil Improvement Commissioners for, 161
York, Improvement Commissioners for, 313 ; street cleansing at, 343-344 ; population of, 399 ; Turnpike Trust for, 160
—— Road, the, 231
Yorkshire, Assistant Overseer of Poor in, 434 ; Turnpike Trustees in, 180

INDEX OF SUBJECTS

2 L

THE END

.

For Product Safety Concerns and Information please contact our EU
representative GPSR@taylorandfrancis.com
Taylor & Francis Verlag GmbH, Kaufingerstraße 24, 80331 München, Germany